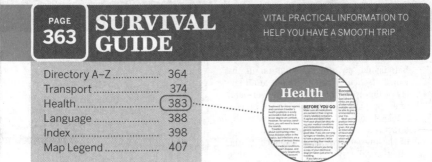

THIS EDITION WRITTEN AND RESEARCHED BY

Ryan Ver Berkmoes,

Adam Skolnick

welcome to
Bali & Lombok

A Place Like No Other

Bali is like no other destination in the world. Its rich culture plays out at all levels of life, from the exquisite flower-petal offerings placed everywhere to the processions of joyfully garbed locals, shutting down major roads as they march to one of the myriad temple ceremonies, to the other-worldly traditional music and dance performed island-wide.

Bali's Essence

Yes, Bali has beaches, surfing, diving, and resorts great and small, but it's the essence of Bali – and the Balinese – that makes it so much more than just a fun-in-the-sun retreat. It is possible to take the cliché of

the smiling Balinese too far, but in reality, the inhabitants of this small island are indeed a generous, genuinely warm people. There's also a fun, sly sense of humour behind the smiles. Upon seeing a bald tourist, many locals exclaim *'bung ujan,'* which means today's rain is cancelled – it's their way of saying that the hairless head is like a clear sky.

One Island, Many Destinations

On Bali you can lose yourself in the chaos of Kuta or the sybaritic pleasures of Seminyak and Kerobokan, surf wild beaches in the south or just hang out on Nusa Lembongan. You can go family friendly in

The mere mention of Bali evokes thoughts of a paradise. It's more than a place; it's a mood, an aspiration, a tropical state of mind.

(left) Sunset at Champlung (p82), Seminyak Beach
(below) Walking in rice terraces, Ubud (p145)

Sanur or savour a lavish getaway on the Bukit Peninsula. Ubud is the heart of Bali, a place where the spirit and culture of the island are most accessible. It shares the island's most beautiful rice fields and ancient monuments with east and west Bali. The middle of Bali is dominated by the dramatic volcanoes of the central mountains and hillside temples such as Pura Luhur Batukau (one of the island's 20,000). North and west Bali are thinly populated but have diving and surfing that make any journey worthwhile.

Lombok & the Gilis, Too

Almost as big as Bali, Lombok is the undiscovered place next door. From its volcanic centre to untrodden idyllic beaches like Mawun, it rewards travellers who want to explore. Many are drawn to mighty Gunung Rinjani, Indonesia's second-highest volcano. Rivers and waterfalls gush down its fissured slopes, while its summit – complete with hot springs and a dazzling crater lake – is the ultimate trekker prize. The fabled Gili Islands – three exquisite droplets of white sand sprinkled with coconut palms and surrounded by coral reefs teeming with marine life and, on Gili Trawangan, legendary nightlife.

⟩Bali & Lombok

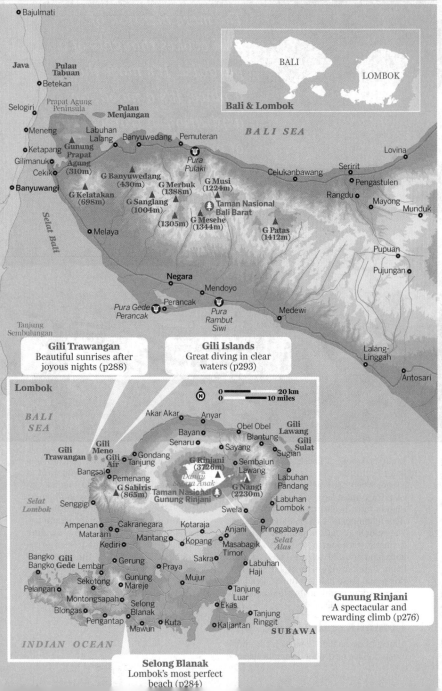

BALI

LOMBOK

Bali & Lombok

Bajulmati

Java

Pulau
Tabuan

Betekan

Selogiri

Prapat Agung
Peninsula

Meneng

Labuhan
Lalang

Pulau
Menjangan

Banyuwedang

Pemuteran

BALI SEA

Ketapang

Gunung
Prapat
Agung
(310m)

Gilimanuk

Cekik

Banyuwangi

G Banyuwedang
(430m)

Pura
Pulaki

G Musi
(1224m)

Lovina

Celukanbawang

Seririt

Pengastulen

Rangdu

Mayong

Munduk

G Merbuk
(1388m)

G Kelatakan
(698m)

G Sanglang
(1004m)

Taman Nasional
Bali Barat

Selat Bali

Melaya

(1305m)

G Mesehe
(1344m)

G Patas
(1412m)

Pupuan

Pujungan

Negara

Mendoyo

Tanjung
Sembulungan

Pura Gede
Perancak

Perancak

Pura
Rambut
Siwi

Medewi

Lalang-
Linggah

Gili Trawangan
Beautiful sunrises after
joyous nights (p288)

Gili Islands
Great diving in clear
waters (p293)

Antosari

Lombok

BALI
SEA

Akar Akar

Anyar

N

0   20 km
0   10 miles

Gili
Trawangan

Gili
Meno

Gili
Air

Bayan

Senaru

Obel Obel

Blantung

Gili
Lawang

Sayang

Gili
Sulat

Suglan

Gondang

Tanjung

G Rinjani
(3726m)

Sembulun
Lawang

Bangsal

Pemenang

G Sabiris
(865m)

Danau
Segara Anak

Labuhan
Pandang

Selat
Lombok

Senggigi

Taman Nasional
Gunung Rinjani

G Nangi
(2230m)

Labuhan
Lombok

Swela

Ampenan

Cakranegara

Kotaraja

Mataram

Mantang

Anjani

Pringgabaya

Selat
Alas

Kediri

Kopang

Masabagik
Timur

Bangko
Bangko

Gili
Gede

Lembar

Gerung

Sakra

Labuhan
Haji

Pelangan

Sekotong

Praya

Mujur

Gunung
Mareje

Montongsapah

Selong
Blanak

Tanjung
Luar

Blongas

Pengantap

Mawun

Kuta

Ekas

Kaliantan

Tanjung
Ringgit

SUBAWA

INDIAN OCEAN

Gunung Rinjani
A spectacular and
rewarding climb (p276)

Selong Blanak
Lombok's most perfect
beach (p284)

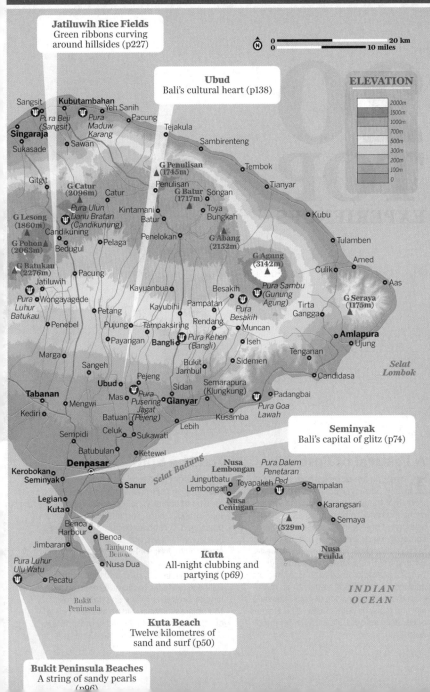

Jatiluwih Rice Fields
Green ribbons curving
around hillsides (p227)

Ubud
Bali's cultural heart (p138)

ELEVATION

2000m
1500m
1000m
700m
500m
300m
200m
100m
0

0   20 km
0   10 miles

Sangsit
Kubutambahan
Pura Beji   Yeh Sanih
(Sangsit)   Pura   Pacung
Singaraja Maduw   Tejakula
           Karang
Sukasade   Sawan
           Sambirenteng
Gitgit
G Catur   Catur   **G Penulisan**
(2096m)   ▲(1745m)
Pura Ulun Penulisan
G Lesong Danu Bratan **G Batur** Songan
(1860m) (Candikunung) ▲(1717m)   Tembok
Candikuning Kintamani   Tianyar
G Pohon▲ Batur Toya
(2063m) Pelaga Bungkah
Bedugul Penelokan   Kubu
G Batukau▲   **G Abang**
(2276m) Pacung   ▲(2152m)   Tulamben
Jatiluwih   **G Agung**   Amed
Pura Wongayagede Kayuanbua ▲(3142m)   Culik   Aas
Luhur   Besakih Pura Sambu
Batukau Petang Kayubihi Pampatan (Gunung   **G Seraya**
   Penebel Pujung Rendang Agung) Tirta ▲(1175m)
           Tampaksiring Pura Muncan Gangga
Marga Payangan **Bangli** Besakih   **Amlapura**
   Sangeh   Pura Kehen Iseh Ujung
      Pejeng Bukit (Bangli) Sidemen
Tabanan **Ubud** Jambul   Tenganan *Selat
   Mas Pura   Semarapura   Candidasa Lombok*
Kediri Mengwi Pusering Sidan (Klungkung)
      Jagat **Gianyar**   Padangbai
   Batuan (Pejeng) Lebih Kusamba Pura Goa
   Celuk Sukawati   Lawah
Sempidi Ketewel   **Seminyak**
Batubulan   Bali's capital of glitz (p74)
Denpasar   *Selat Badung* Nusa   Pura Dalem
Kerobokan   Lembongan Penetaran
Seminyak   Sanur Jungutbatu Toyapakeh *Ped* Sampalan
      Lembongan
Legian   Nusa   Karangsari
Kuta   Ceningan
Benoa   ▲   Semaya
Harbour Benoa   (529m)
Jimbaran Tanjung   Nusa
Pura Luhur Benoa   Penida
Ulu Watu Nusa Dua **Kuta**
   Pecatu All-night clubbing and
      partying (p69)
*Bukit
Peninsula*   *INDIAN
            OCEAN*

Kuta Beach
Twelve kilometres of
sand and surf (p50)

Bukit Peninsula Beaches
A string of sandy pearls
(p96)

20 TOP
EXPERIENCES

A Festival of Festivals

1 There you are sipping a coffee at a cafe in, say, Seminyak or Ubud, when there's a crash of the gamelan (traditional Balinese orchestra) and traffic screeches to a halt as a crowd of elegantly dressed people comes flying by, bearing pyramids of fruit, tasselled parasols and a furred, masked Barong (mythical lion-dog creature) or two. It's a temple procession disappearing as suddenly as it appeared, with no more than the fleeting sparkle of gold and white silk and hibiscus petals in its wake. Dozens occur daily across Bali. Balinese ceremony, Kuta, Bali

Aaah, a Spa

2 Whether it's a total fix for the mind, body and spirit, or simply the desire for a bit of serenity, visitors to Bali spend many happy hours (sometimes days) being massaged, scrubbed, perfumed, pampered, bathed and blissed out. Sometimes all this attention to your well-being happens on the beach or in a garden; other times it's in stylish, even lavish, surroundings. As the Balinese massage techniques of stretching, long strokes, skin rolling and palm-and-thumb pressure result in an all-over feeling of calm, it's the perfect holiday prescription. Spa with banana-leaf wrapping, Ubud (p144)

Sybaritic Stays

3 On an island that honours art and serenity, is it any wonder you'll find some of the world's finest hotels and resorts? From blissful retreats on south Bali's beautiful beach in Kerobokan or Seminyak to perches on cliffs above the dazzling white sands that dot the Bukit Peninsula, these stylish hotels are as lovely outside as they are luxurious inside. Further resorts by vaunted architects can be found in Ubud's river valleys and in remote idyllic coastal locations. Hotel resort, Nusa Lembongan (p127)

Bali's Food

4 'Oh goody!' It's virtually impossible not to say this when you step into a classic warung (food stall) for lunch to find dozens of freshly made dishes on the counter awaiting you. It shouldn't surprise that this fertile island provides a profusion of ingredients that combine to create fresh and aromatic dishes. Local specialities such as *babi guling* (roast suckling pig that's been marinated for hours in spices) will have you lining up again and again. Try lunch at one of the excellent Balinese cafes in Denpasar (p123). Bowls of traditional Indonesian food in Ubud

3

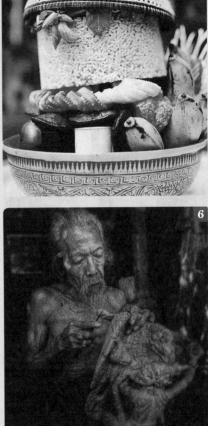

Offerings

5 A wisp of smoke rises from an incense stick perched in an exquisite array of orange flower petals on a banana leaf no bigger than a deck of cards. You'll quickly realise these Balinese offerings are everywhere – outside your hotel room door, a tiny shrine on the beach, even at the end of the bar. They come in all shapes and sizes and are made throughout the day and night. Some are grand assemblages of fruit and food but most are tiny, appearing as if by magic.

Crafts of the Islands

6 Using a simple knife others might use to cut an apple, a Balinese craftsman sits in the shade of his family compound's frangipani tree and carves a masterpiece. Yes, schlock is sold here in profusion, as it is everywhere, but true local crafts draw on experience handed down for generations. Wood carvings are used for temple ceremonies and traditional performances such as the Barong, where colourful, animated wooden masks are integral to the story, while in Batubulan (p174) stone carvers create art from rocks. Woodcarver, Ubud

JOHN W BANAGAN/GETTY IMAGES ©

JOHN W BANAGAN/GETTY IMAGES ©

IMAGEBROKER/ALAMY ©/GETTY IMAGES ©

Ubud

7 Famous in books and movies, the artistic heart of Bali exudes a compelling spiritual appeal. The streets are lined with galleries where artists, both humble and great, create. Beautiful performances showcasing the island's rich culture grace a dozen stages nightly. Museums honour the works of those inspired here over the years, while people walk the rice fields to find the perfect spot to sit in lotus position and ponder life's endless possibilities. Ubud (p138) is a state of mind and a beautiful state of being. Women carrying temple offerings, Ubud

Balinese Dance

8 The antithesis of Balinese mellow is Balinese dance (p337). It's amazing how people who relish lounging in *bales* (open-sided pavilions) can also produce art that demands complete methodical precision. A performer of the Legong, the most beautiful dance, spends years learning minutely choreographed movements from her eyeballs to her toes. Each movement has a meaning and the language flows with a grace that is hypnotic. Clad in silk and ikat, the dancers tell stories rich with the very essence of Balinese Hindu beliefs and lore. Legong dancers, Ubud

Kuta's Never-Ending Night

9 It starts with stylish cafes and bars in Seminyak, open-air places where everything seems just that bit more beautiful amid the twinkling of candles and enrapturing house beats. Later the world-class clubs of Kuta (p69), Bali, draw you in, with famous international DJs spinning their legendary sets in a glam scene that hints at immediate celebrity. Some time before dawn, Kuta's harder, rawer clubs suck you in like black holes, spitting you out hours later into an unsteady daylight, shattered but happy. Beach bar at night

Jatiluwih Rice Fields

10 Ribbons of green sinuously curve around hillsides crested by coconut palms: the ancient rice terraces of Jatiluwih (p227) are as artful as they are elegant, and a timeless testimony to the Balinese rice farmers' love and respect for the land. You'll run out of words for green as you walk, bike or drive the little road that wanders through this fertile bowl of the island's sacred grain. The entire area was recognised in 2012 by Unesco when they added Bali's rice-growing traditions to the World Heritage List.

Underwater Gilis

11 Taking the plunge? There are few better places than the Gilis, encircled by coral reefs teeming with life and visited by pelagics such as cruising manta rays. Scuba diving is a huge draw – there are several professional schools and all kinds of courses taught (from absolute beginner to nitrox specialist). With easy access from beach to reef, snorkelling is also superb, and you're very likely to see turtles. Want to take snorkelling to the next level? Try freediving – Trawangan has one of Asia's only breath-hold diving centres (p292).
View of Gili Trawangan (p288)

PETE ATKINSON/GETTY IMAGES ©

KIMBERLEY COOLE/GETTY IMAGES ©

Diving Bali

12 Feel small as a manta ray blocks out the sun's glow overhead, its fluid movement causing barely a disturbance in the surrounding waters as it glides past. And there's another, and another. Just when you think your dive can't get more dramatic, you turn to find a 2.5m sunfish hovering motionlessly, checking you out. Nusa Penida (p131) is but one of the many dive sites ringing Bali. The legendary 30m wall at Pulau Menjangan (p256) thrills, one dive after another. Inside the wreck of the Liberty (p212)

Selong Blanak

13 Southern Lombok's coastline has a wild savage beauty and few visitors, generating lots of talk about the vast tourism potential of the region. When you set eyes on pristine Selong Blanak beach (p283), it's easy to appreciate the hype. Cross over a rickety bridge from the village to a perfect swath of sand where the swimming in clear, turquoise-tinged water is superb. At the rear of the bay is a crescent of powdery white sand. Most days this dream of a beach is all but empty. Boats on Selong Blanak beach

Bukit Peninsula Beaches

14 A little plume of white sand rises out of the blue Indian Ocean and fills a cove below limestone cliffs clad in deep green tropical beauty. It sounds idyllic, and it is. The west coast of the Bukit Peninsula (p96) in south Bali is dotted with beaches like that, such as Balangan Beach, Bingin and Padang Padang. Families run funky surfer bars built on bamboo stilts over the tide, where the only views are the breaks metres away. Grab a lounger and be lulled by the waves. Clifftop cafe, Ulu Watu Beach, Bukit Peninsula

14

Surfing Bali

15 If it's a month containing the letter 'r', go east; during the other months, go west. Simplicity itself. And on Bali you have dozens of great breaks in each direction. This was the first place in Asia where surfing took off, and like the perfect set, it shows no signs of calming down. Surfers buzz around the island on motorbikes with board racks, looking for the next great break. Waves blown out? Another spot is just five minutes' away. The scene at classic surfer hang-outs such as Balian Beach (p250) is pure funk. Sunset, Kuta Beach, Bali

15

Kuta Beach

16 Tourism on Bali began here (p50) and is there any question why? The sweeping arc of sand curves from Kuta into the misty horizon northwest to Echo Beach. Surf that started far out in the Indian Ocean crashes to shore in long symmetrical breaks. You can stroll the 12km of sand, enjoying a foot massage and cold beer with thousands of your new best friends in the south, or revel in utter solitude up north. Kuta Beach was and always will be Bali's best beach. Sunset, Kuta Beach, Bali

Seminyak

17 People wander around Seminyak (p74) and ask themselves if they are even in Bali. Of course! On an island that values creativity like few other places, the capital of glitz is where you'll find inventive boutiques run by local designers, the most eclectic and interesting collection of restaurants, and little boutique hotels that break with the island clichés. Expats, locals and visitors alike idle away the hours in its cafes, at ease with the world and secure in their enjoyment of life's pleasures. Ku De Ta (p83), Seminyak

16

17

MATTHEW MICAH WRIGHT/GETTY IMAGES ©

TRAVELSTOCK44/ALAMY ©

MICHELE FALZONE/GETTY IMAGES ©

ANDREY ARTYKOV/GETTY IMAGES ©

TJETJEP RUSTANDI/GETTY IMAGES ©

Hiking Rinjani

18 Glance at a map of Lombok and virtually the entire northern half of the island is dominated by the brooding, magnificent presence of Gunung Rinjani (3726m; p276), Indonesia's second-highest volcano. Hiking Rinjani is no picnic, and involves planning, hiring a guide and porters, stamina and sweat. The route winds up the sides of the great peak until you reach the rim of a vast caldera, where there's a jaw-dropping view of Rinjani's sacred crater lake (an important pilgrim site) and the smoking, highly active mini-cone of Gunung Baru below. Danau Segara Anak with Gunung Baru, inside Gunung Rinjani

Surfing Lombok

19 From Lombok to the Antarctic is virtually half the globe – that's some distance for the azure rollers of the Indian Ocean to build up speed and momentum, so it's no surprise that the island's coastline has some truly spectacular waves. Tanjung Desert (Desert Point) is the most famous of these, an incredibly long ride that tubes over a sharp, shallow reef. If that sounds a little too hard core, head to the town of Kuta, where you'll find dozens of challenging surf breaks a short distance away.

Sunrise Over Trawangan

20 If you think Gili Trawangan (p288) is a stunner by daylight, you should see it at dawn after a night of dancing to some of the hottest electro, trance, reggae and house music in the region. You won't find slick decor, flashy visuals, door staff and stiff entrance prices in Trawangan, where the parties started as raves on the beach and still have a raw, unorganised spirit. Local DJs normally spin hypnotic tribal sounds and superstar DJs have been known to turn up and play unannounced sets. Quiet sunrise on Gili Trawangan

need to know

Currency
» Rupiah (Rp)

Language
» Bahasa Indonesia and Balinese

When to Go

North Bali
GO year-round

Ubud
• GO year-round

South Bali
GO year-round

Gili Islands
GO year-round

Lombok
GO year-round

Tropical climate, wet & dry seasons
Tropical climate, rain year-round

High Season
(Jul & Aug)

» Rates zip up by 50% or more.

» Many hotels are booked far ahead; the best restaurants need to be booked in advance.

» Christmas and New Year are equally expensive and crowded.

Shoulder
(May, Jun & Sep)

» Coincides with the best weather (drier, less humid).

» You may find a room deal, and last-minute bookings are possible.

» Best time for many activities such as diving.

Low Season
(Jan–Apr, Oct & Nov)

» Deals everywhere, good airfares.

» Rainy season; however, rainfall is never excessive.

» Can do most activities except volcano treks.

Your Daily Budget

Budget less than

US$100

» Room at guesthouse/homestay: less than US$50

» Cheap food and drink, especially at places with local foods

» Can survive on US$40 per day

Midrange

US$100 –220

» Room at midrange hotel: US$50–US$150

» Can eat and drink almost anywhere

» Spa treatments and other luxuries

Top End over

US$220

» Room at top-end hotel/resort: over US$150

» Major expenses will be lavish spas

Money

» ATMs in all but rural areas on Bali and tourist areas of Lombok. Credit cards accepted at midrange and top-end hotels and restaurants.

Visas

» Usually a renewable 30 days granted on arrival.

Mobile Phones

» Cheap local SIM cards work with any unlocked GSM phone.

Driving

» Drive on the left; steering wheel is on the right-hand side of the car.

Websites

» **Bali Advertiser** (www.baliadvertiser. biz) Bali's expat journal with insider tips and good columnists.

» **Bali Discovery** (www.balidiscovery. com) Excellent weekly summary of news and features; hotel deals.

» **Bali Paradise** (www. bali-paradise.com) Compendium site of info and links.

» **Lombok Guide** (www.thelombokguide. com) Comprehensive site covering main areas of interest.

» **Lonely Planet** (www. lonelyplanet.com/ indonesia) Destination information, hotel bookings, traveller forum and more.

Exchange Rates

Australia	A$1	8760Rp
Canada	C$1	8880Rp
Japan	¥100	10,720Rp
New Zealand	NZ$1	6830Rp
UK	UK£1	14,170Rp
US	US$1	8970Rp
Euro zone	€1	12505Rp

For current exchange rates, see www.xe.com.

Important Numbers

Bali has six telephone area codes and Lombok has two. Numbers that begin with 08 are mobiles. Drop the 0 in phone numbers when calling from abroad.

Indonesia country code	✆62
International call prefix	✆001/017
International operator	✆102
Directory assistance	✆108

Arriving in Bali

» **Ngurah Rai Airport (DPS; aka Denpasar or Bali) on Bali**

Taxi to Kuta – 50,000Rp

Taxi to Seminyak – 80,000Rp

Taxi to Ubud – 210,000Rp

» **Lombok International Airport (LOP) near Praya**

Taxi to Kuta – 60,000Rp

Taxi to Mataram – 100,000Rp

Taxi to Senggigi – 150,000Rp

Bali is Easy

Forgot something at home? You can get it on Bali. Don't speak the language? They probably speak yours. Afraid to get sick? You don't need shots, and clean drinking water and healthy food are readily available. Not sure how you'll get around? Friendly drivers will take care of that. Where to stay? Anywhere, from the world's most luxurious hotels to welcoming family-run guesthouses. Is it safe? Probably safer than your home town. But aren't there touts and scammers? Easily avoided on 98% of the island. How will I stay in touch? Fast wi-fi and mobile service in tourist areas mean friends at home will see pics of every wave you ride. Is the food too hot? The cheeseburgers are always served right off the grill. My biggest concern? Not wanting to leave.

what's new

For this new edition of Bali & Lombok, our authors have hunted down the fresh, the revamped, the transformed, the hot and the happening. Here are a few of our favourites. For up-to-the-minute reviews and recommendations, see lonelyplanet.com/indonesia/bali and lonelyplanet.com/indonesia/lombok.

Unesco Recognition

1 After years of waiting, Bali rejoiced when Unesco added its traditional rice-growing culture to the World Heritage List. Included: the Jatiluwih rice terraces and Pura Taman Ayun. (p248)

Popular Canggu

2 Shops, restaurants and inns are giving vitality to the villas and rice fields of the Canggu area. The long, wave-pounded beaches are ever-more popular. (p89)

Kerobokan's Beach

3 Glossy new resorts and clubs are appearing along the beach north of Kerobokan. The W Resort and the Mozaic and Potato Head beach clubs are but three examples. (p85)

Bukit Excitement

4 The cute little beaches of the Bukit Peninsula from Jimbaran south to Ulu Watu are gaining yet more offbeat and often creative boutique lodgings and beach cafes. (p96)

New Airport

5 Bali's Ngurah Rai Airport will get a huge new terminal, replacing its over-crowded old facility by 2014. The big question: will they actually staff the many dozens of immigration stations? (p374)

New Toll Road

6 By 2014 you'll be able to zip over the coastal mangroves in the south on an elevated toll road that will link Sanur, Nusa Dua and the airport. (p377)

Traffic Schemes

7 Visitors and residents alike are fed up with south Bali's ceaseless traffic jams. A complex new intersection of the Jl Ngurah Rai Bypass and Sunset Rd east of Kuta is one scheme meant to fix this. (p168)

Lombok International

8 The long-completed, rather gleaming new Lombok International Airport near Praya is finally open for business, with more international and domestic flights. (p375)

Dive Schools Galore

9 Several new dive schools have sprouted on the Gilis. Hence, formation of the Gili Island Diving Association in 2012, an effort by the best of the bunch to safeguard local reefs and their guests. (p33)

The Anti-Gilis

10 Okay, technically they're Gilis too, but Gili Gede and Gili Asahan have a far more removed, untrammeled and tranquil feel than their famed counterparts. (p264)

Way Out Lombok's West

11 The spectacular white-sand beach of Selong Blanak and secluded bay at Blongas have high-end villas, an elegant cafe, and schooling hammerheads and rays. (p283)

Low-Rent Trawangan

12 It's no longer a backpacker kingdom, but with the opening of the island's first dedicated hostel, a bohemian crash pad (Woodstock), and an exile outpost (the Exile), Gili T value lives on. (p288)

if you like...

Beaches

Beaches ring the islands, but iconic ones with white sand are not as common as you'd think – most are some variation of tan or grey. Surf conditions range from limp to torrid, depending on whether there's an offshore reef.

Seminyak Beach This wide stretch of sand boasts great surf that both swimmers and surfers can frolic in. It's a place enjoyed by locals and visitors alike – especially at sunset (p74)

Balangan Beach This curving white-sand beach on the Bukit Peninsula, backed by an impromptu resort, is ramshackle in an endearing way and perfect for a snooze or booze (p99)

Gili Island beaches The beaches on these three islands are uniformly gorgeous, with circles of white sand, great snorkelling and a timeless traveller vibe (p286)

Selong Blanak An idyllic Lombok wonder that astounds first-time visitors (p283)

Temples

With over 20,000 temples, Bali has such a variety that you can't even categorise them. The best evoke the great traditions of the island's unique form of Buddhism that has been shaped by priests and prophets for centuries.

Pura Luhur Batukau One of Bali's most important temples is found far up its namesake volcano. It's a misty, remote place that is steeped in ancient spirituality (p228)

Pura Taman Ayu A beautiful moated temple that has a royal past; part of Unesco's recognition of Bali's rice traditions (p248)

Pura Pusering Jagat One of the famous temples at Pejeng, which date to the 14th-century empire that once flourished here (p172)

Pura Luhur Ulu Watu As important as it is popular, the temple has sweeping Indian Ocean views, sunset dance performances and monkeys (p103)

Nightlife

Nightclubs on Bali and the Gilis draw acolytes from across Southeast Asia. The large numbers of relatively well-heeled tourists and nonexistent licensing laws have spawned an ever-changing line up of clubs that book celebrity DJs spinning mixes that are soon heard worldwide. Bouncing from one club to another all night long is a Bali tradition, guaranteeing overheating from the exertion, the mixes, the booze, the companionship or all of the above.

Seminyak Start the evening in hipster/scenester hang-outs where the glow of candles makes everyone beautiful (p82)

Kuta All raw energy and a mad mix of party-goers, from Marg from Melbourne having her first big night out to Made from Munduk enjoying every aspect of modern Balinese life (p69)

Gili Trawangan The place for pounding beats and searing mixes three times weekly (p296)

ANDREW BROWNBILL/GETTY IMAGES ©

» Gamelan musicians (p339) perform during the Bali Arts Festival

Culture

The island's creative heritage is everywhere you look and there's nothing manufactured about what you see. Dance and musical performances are the result of an ever-evolving culture with a legacy of centuries. Villages save their highest honours for the artists who live there. The culture is vibrant and accessible, and one of the aspects of a trip to Bali that make it like no other.

Dance Rigid choreography and high levels of discipline are hallmarks of beautiful, melodic Balinese dance. No visit is complete without enjoying this purely Balinese art form (p337)

Gamelan The ensemble orchestra makes its unforgettable music on bamboo and bronze instruments, and can be heard at every dance performance and temple celebration (p339)

Painting Balinese and Western styles merged in the 20th century and the results are often extraordinary. See some of the best in Ubud's museums (p341)

Great Food

Balinese food is pungent and lively; there is nothing shy about this cuisine. You'll find shades of South Indian, Malaysian and Chinese flavours in the island's food. It has evolved from years of cross-cultural cook-ups and trading with sea-faring pioneers, and perhaps even pirates, across the seas of Asia. And your dining won't be limited to local fare either: excellent cuisine drawn from around the globe is on offer.

Seminyak Hands down the place with the greatest variety of top restaurants; on a 10-minute stroll you can wander the world of food (p79)

Kerobokan The go-to area for the hottest and best restaurants, plus some superb simple Balinese warung (food stalls; p86)

Denpasar Truly local cafes serve exceptional Balinese and Indonesian food in simple surrounds (p123)

Ubud A profusion of restaurants and cafes, many organic (p159)

Shopping

For some people Bali is a destination for shopping; for others it becomes their destiny. You'll find a plethora of shops and stalls across the island – everything from cheap T-shirt vendors to exquisite boutiques with alluring housewares and fashion by local designers with worldwide followings.

Seminyak It seems you can't run into someone in Seminyak and *not* have them claim to be a designer; the reality is that many actually are. The shopping scene here is constantly changing: new boutiques appear, old ones vanish, some change into something else while others move up the food chain. The odds that you'll stumble upon a star of tomorrow are good (p83)

Kerobokan The next Seminyak in every sense. Starting to match its tiny neighbour to the south for energy and creativity (p88)

Ubud Excellent for handicrafts and art (p167)

month by month

Top Events

1 **Nyepi**, March or April

2 **Galungan & Kuningan**, varies

3 **Ubud Writers & Readers Festival**, October

4 **Bali Arts Festival**, June to July

5 **Perang Topat**, November or December

February

The rainy season pours on and the islands take a breather after the Christmas and New Year's high season.

Nyale Festival

The ritual harvesting of *nyale* (wormlike sea fish) takes place on Seger beach near Lombok's Kuta. The evening begins with poetry readings, continues with gamelan performances and carries on until the dawn when the nyale start appearing. Usually February but also in March.

March

The rainy season is ending and there is a lull in the crowds as this is low season for tourism.

Nyepi (Day of Silence)

Bali's major Hindu festival, Nyepi (p326) celebrates the end of the old year and the start of the next. It's marked by inactivity – to convince evil spirits that Bali is uninhabited, so they'll leave the island alone for another year. The night before Nyepi sees community celebrations with *ogoh-ogoh*, huge papier-mâché monsters that go up in flames. Held in March or early April.

April

The islands dry out after the rainy season, but things remain quiet on the visitor front.

Bali Spirit Festival

A fast-growing yoga, dance and music festival (www.balispiritfestival.com) from the people behind the Yoga Barn in Ubud. There are over 100 workshops and concerts, plus a market and more. It's usually held in early April but may begin in late March.

Malean Sampi

Buffalo race over waterlogged earth in Narmada, near Mataram on Lombok. Jockeys tear down the track, clinging onto a couple of stampeding yoked buffalo. It's as dangerous, muddy and fun as it sounds. Early in the month.

May

A great month for visiting. It's not high season but the annual rains have stopped (although you'll still get downpours at any time). Trails are drying out for hiking yet the rivers are still high for rafting.

Bali Art Festival of Buleleng

Every year Singaraja hosts this large arts festival in north Bali. Over one week, dancers and musicians from some of the region's most renowned village troupes, such as those of Jagaraga, perform.

June

The airport is getting busier, but much of what makes May a good month also applies in June.

Bali Arts Festival

Denpasar's arts festival (p122) is the premier event on Bali's cultural calendar. Based at the Taman Wedhi Budaya arts centre, the festival is a great way to see traditional Balinese dance and music. Village-based dance and musical groups compete fiercely for local pride. Held mid-June to mid-July.

July

Along with August, July is the busiest month for visitors on Bali and the Gilis (Lombok is always rather quiet). Don't expect to have your pick of places to stay, but do plan to enjoy the energy of big happy crowds.

⭐ Bali Kite Festival

In south Bali scores of kites soar overhead much of the year. Often huge (10m plus), they fly at altitudes that worry pilots. There's a spiritual connection: the kites urge the gods to provide abundant harvests. During this festival (p115) the skies fill with these huge creations controlled by dozens of villagers.

October

The skies darken more often with seasonal rains, but mostly the weather is pleasant and the islands go about their normal business.

⭐ Ubud Writers & Readers Festival

This Ubud festival (www.ubudwritersfestival.com) hosts scores of writers and readers from around the world in a celebration of writing – especially that which touches on Bali.

PAUL KENNEDY/GETTY IMAGES ©

(Above) Kites aloft at the Bali Kite Festival (p115)
(Below) Carved and painted demon masks (p348) at a festival in southern Bali

GREGORY ADAMS/GETTY IMAGES ©

GALUNGAN & KUNINGAN

One of Bali's major festivals, Galungan celebrates the death of a legendary tyrant called Mayadenawa. During this 10-day period, all the gods come down to earth for the festivities. Barong (mythical lion-dog) prance from temple to temple and village to village, and locals rejoice with feasts and visits to families. The celebrations culminate with the Kuningan festival, when the Balinese say thanks and goodbye to the gods.

Every village in Bali will celebrate Galungan and Kuningan in grand style, and visitors are welcome to join in.

The 210-day *wuku* (or Pawukon) calendar is used to determine festival dates. The calendar uses 10 different types of weeks between one and 10 days long, which all run simultaneously, and the intersection of the various weeks determines auspicious days. Dates for future Galungan and Kuningan celebrations are as follows:

YEAR	GALUNGAN	KUNINGAN
2013	27 Mar & 23 Oct	6 Apr & 2 Nov
2014	21 May & 17 Dec	31 May & 27 Dec
2015	15 Jul	25 Jul

Kuta Karnival

A big beach party on the big beach in Kuta (www.kutakarnival.com); games, art, competitions, surfing and much more on the first October weekend and the days right before.

November

It's getting wetter, but not really so wet that you can't enjoy the islands to the fullest. Usually a quiet month crowd-wise.

Perang Topat

This 'rice war' on Lombok is fun. It takes place at Pura Lingsar just outside Mataram and involves a costumed parade, and Hindus and Wektu Telu pelting balls of *ketupat* (sticky rice) at each other. Usually November but also December.

December

Visitors rain down on Bali and the Gilis ahead of the Christmas and New Year holidays. Hotels and restaurants are booked out and everybody is busy.

Peresean

Martial arts, Lombok-style. Competitors, stripped to the waist, spar with sticks and cowhide shields. The winner is the first to draw blood. It's held annually in Mataram. Late in the month.

itineraries

Whether you've got three days or 30, these itineraries provide a starting point for the trip of a lifetime. Want more inspiration? Head online to lonelyplanet. com/thorntree to chat with other travellers.

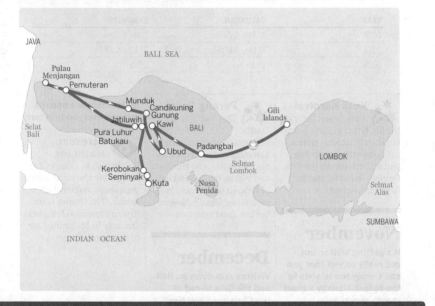

Two Weeks
Bali & the Gilis

Start your trip in **Seminyak**, which has the best places to go out for a meal, a drink or even a new frock. Allow at least three days to experience the refined charms of **Kerobokan** and the wild nights of **Kuta**. Once you're sated, head west, driving through the rice terraces of **Jatiluwih** and on to **Pura Luhur Batukau**, a holy temple up in the clouds. Head northwest to the crescent of mellow beach resorts at **Pemuteran**. From here, you can snorkel or scuba Bali's best dive site at **Palau Menjangan**. Driving east, stop in **Munduk** for some hiking to remote waterfalls.

Carry on via **Candikuning** to **Ubud**, the cultural centre of Bali. Nights of dance and culture are offset by days of walking through the serene countryside. Do a day trip to the ancient monuments at **Gunung Kawi**. Head down to the cute little beach and port town of **Padangbai** and catch a fast boat to the **Gili Islands**. Wander the islands, enjoy Gili T's surprising nightlife and go snorkelling to spot a turtle.

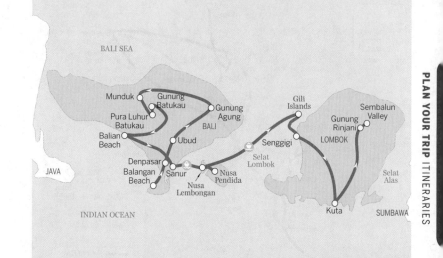

Three Weeks
Total Bali & Lombok

> Begin your trip at **Balangan Beach**. Settle back in the sand and let the jet lag vanish. Stop in **Denpasar** for a purely Balinese lunch and then head up the hill to **Ubud** to get a full taste of Balinese culture. Next, tackle **Gunung Agung**, the spiritual centre of the island. Start early to reach the top and take in the views before the daily on-slaught of clouds and mist.

Having climbed Bali's most legendary peak, head west to the village of **Munduk**, which looks down to the north coast and the sea beyond. Go for a walk in the area and enjoy water-falls, truly tiny villages, wild fruit trees and the sinuous bands of rice paddies lining the hills like ribbons. Then head south to the wonderful temple of **Pura Luhur Batukau**, and con-sider a trek up Bali's second-highest mountain, **Gunung Batukau**. Head down to the newly popular **Balian Beach** on the west coast for some chilled-out time in a funky surfer scene.

Next, bounce across the waves from **Sanur** to **Nusa Lembongan**, the island hiding in the shadow of **Nusa Penida**. The latter is visible from much of the south and east – it's lush, arid and almost unpopulated and makes a good day trip. Take in the amazing vistas from its cliffs and dive under the waves to check out the marine life.

Head to the **Gilis** via the direct boat from Nusa Lembongan for more tranquil time cir-cumnavigating the three islands and diving offshore. Take a boat to **Senggigi**, but ignore the resorts and head south. Well off the beaten path, the south coast near Lombok's **Kuta** has stunning beaches and surfing to reward the intrepid. The seldom-driven back roads of the interior will thrill the adventurous and curious, with tiny villages where you can learn about the amazing local handicrafts. Many of these roads lead up the flanks of **Gunung Rinjani**, the volcanic peak that shelters the lush and remote **Sembalun Valley**. Trekking from one village to the next on the rim can take days but is one of the great walks.

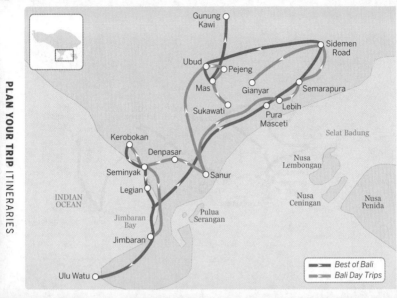

One Week
Bali Day Trips

This is for the traveller who wants to unpack only once, seeing what's possible on Bali during a series of relaxed day trips. Start with a beachside hotel in **Sanur**, such as Hotel La Taverna or Tandjung Sari, both of which have a refined yet relaxed charm.

Day trip one starts with the short drive to the markets and museums of **Denpasar**, followed by a visit to the shops of **Seminyak** and **Kerobokan**. Finish up with a sunset seafood grill at **Jimbaran**.

Day trip two heads to **Ubud** for a half-day strolling the streets, looking at the shops, galleries and museums. Take different routes there and back so you can enjoy sights such as the temples of **Pejeng**, the carvers of **Mas** and the village market at **Sukawati**.

Day trip three follows the wave-tossed volcanic beaches along the coast road to the northeast. Stop at **Lebih**, which has a temple and mica-infused glittering sand. Go inland to the temple ruins and market at **Semarapura**, then head north along the beautiful **Sidemen Road**. Next, loop west and head back down through the tidy regional centre of **Gianyar**, where you can check out large traditional fabric showrooms.

One Week
Best of Bali

Start at a beachside hotel in **Seminyak** or **Kerobokan**; shop the streets of either and spend time at the beach.

Enjoy a seafood dinner on **Jimbaran Bay** as part of a day trip to the monkey-filled temple at **Ulu Watu**.

In the east, take the coast road to wild beaches like the one near **Pura Masceti**, followed by the well-mannered royal town of **Semarapura** with its ruins. Head north up the breathtaking **Sidemen Road**, which combines rice terraces with lush river valleys and cloud-shrouded mountains. Then go west to **Ubud**, the crowning stop on any itinerary.

To spoil yourself, stay in one of Ubud's many hotels with views across rice fields and rivers. Sample the offerings at a spa before you try one of the myriad great restaurants. Bali's rich culture is most celebrated and most accessible in Ubud and you'll be captivated by nightly dance performances. Check out local craft studios, including the woodcarvers of **Mas**. Hike through the surrounding rice fields to river valleys, taking a break in museums bursting with paintings. Finish by heading north to the imposing 1000-year-old rock monoliths at **Gunung Kawi**.

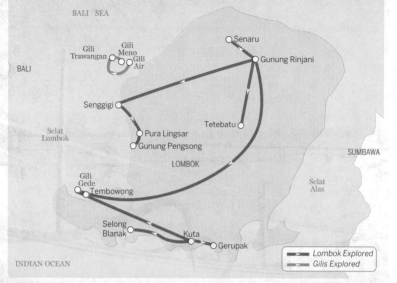

BALI SEA

Gili Trawangan · Gili Meno · Gili Air

Senaru

Gunung Rinjani

BALI

Senggigi

Tetebatu

Selat Lombok

Pura Lingsar
Gunung Pengsong

SUMBAWA

LOMBOK

Selat Alas

Gili Gede · Tembowong

Selong Blanak

Kuta

Gerupak

INDIAN OCEAN

Lombok Explored
Gilis Explored

Two Weeks
Lombok Explored

Kick off in gorgeous **Kuta** and spend a day or two finding the perfect beach. East or west of town there are a dozen or so bays to choose from: magnificent **Selong Blanak** is just one. While you're here, it would be rude not to sample the fabled south Lombok surf – tiny **Gerupak** is an excellent place to either take a lesson or hitch a boat ride to an epic break. Tranquil southwest Lombok is not far away for more aqua action; swim in sheltered transparent water or explore the dozen or so islands here by boat. Tiny **Gili Gede** makes a perfect base; you can reach it by boat from **Tembowong**.

Sacred **Gunung Rinjani** is next up; get here via roads from Tembowong. Either explore its foothills from the rustic base of **Tetebatu**, or go the whole hog and trek from **Senaru** to the crater rim, the sublime crater lake or the summit itself (depending on your time, energy and commitment level). After Rinjani your body will need some serious pampering, and the spas of **Senggigi** are the ideal place to recuperate, with massages and treatments for all budgets. Finish off with a trip or two to the sights around Mataram, such as the intriguing temple of **Pura Lingsar** or the hilltop shrine **Gunung Pengsong**.

One Week
Gilis Explored

The ideal place to get to grips with island life is **Gili Air**, where the main beachfront strip is perfect tropical lounging territory. Here you can wile away a day or two doing nothing but chilling with a book, taking a dip when you need to cool off, snorkelling the offshore coral (maybe you'll spot a turtle) and feasting on inexpensive fresh seafood. OK, now you've acclimatised.

Next up is **Trawangan**, where there's much more action. Here the perfect day could start with a morning dive at a site such as **Shark Point**, followed by a healthy lunch and an afternoon snooze. Then take a gentle cycle round the sandy lanes of the island, slipping in a sunset cocktail on the west coast. After dinner it's time to feel the beat and strut your stuff at one of Trawangan's parties, or catch a reggae band at Sama Sama.

The final stop is idyllic **Gili Meno**, where, once you've secured the perfect place to stay, there's little to do except wonder at the sheer drop-dead beauty of the island and the clarity of the sea. If you can drag yourself away from the beach, you could pop by the turtle hatchery.

» (above) Boats at Mushroom Bay, Nusa Lembongan (p127)
» (left) Munduk Waterfall (p226)

Bali & Lombok Outdoors

When to Go

The dry season, April to September, is best for long cycling trips, treks up volcanoes and diving (as there's less silt in the water). But the rest of the year is not that much rainier and people hike, bike and otherwise enjoy themselves. The local bromide for surfing is go east during months containing the letter 'r' and west at other times.

Best Surfing

Ulu Watu World famous. (p103)
Tanjung Desert (Desert Point) Legendary and elusive in Lombok. (p266)
Batu Bolong All-round great. (p89)

Best Diving & Snorkelling

Pulau Menjangan Spectacular 30m wall. (p256)
Tulamben Sunken WWII freighter; snorkelling and diving from shore. (p212)
Gili Islands All types of diving and snorkelling in beautiful waters. (p286)

Best Hiking

Munduk Lush, spice-scented, waterfall-riven landscape. (p225)
Ubud Beautiful walks from one hour to one day. (p145)
Tirta Gangga Rice terraces, gorgeous views and temples. (p204)

Bali offers so much more than a beach holiday with an overlay of amazing culture – it is an incredible place to get outside and play. Sure, you may have to get up off your beach towel, but the rewards are many.

In waters around the island you'll find world-class diving that ranges from reefs to shipwrecks to huge, rare sea life. When that water hits shore, it creates some of the world's best surfing. No matter what time of year you visit, you'll find legendary surf spots.

On land, hikes abound through the luxuriant green of the rice fields, deep into the river valleys and up the sides of the three main volcanoes. Or you can just whiz through the beautiful scenery on a bike.

Lombok doesn't have the same level of organisation but it has fine diving, surfing (often in remote locations) and hiking, including a famous volcano trek.

Surfing

Surfing kick-started Bali tourism in the 1960s. It's never looked back. Many Balinese have taken to surfing, and the grace of traditional dancing is said to influence their style.

Where to Surf: Bali

Swells come from the Indian Ocean, so the surf is on the southern side of the island and, strangely, on the northwest coast of Nusa

Bali & Lombok Surf Breaks

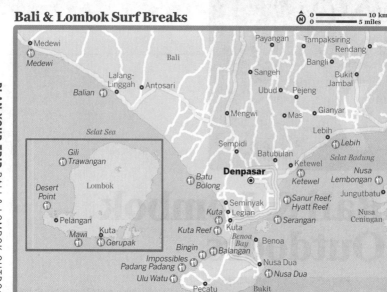

Lembongan, where the swell funnels into the strait between there and the Bali coast.

In the dry season (around April to September), the west coast has the best breaks, with the trade winds coming in from the southeast; this is also when Nusa Lembongan works best. In the wet season, surf the eastern side of the island, from Nusa Dua around to Padangbai. If there's a north wind – or no wind at all – there are also a couple of breaks on the south coast of the Bukit Peninsula.

Note that breaks listed below almost always have good beaches of the same name at the surf's edge.

Balangan

Go through the growing Pecatu Indah resort and follow the road around to the right past Dreamland to reach the Balangan warung. Balangan is a fast left over a shallow reef, unsurfable at low tide, but good at mid-tide with anything over a 4ft swell; with an 8ft swell, this can be one of the classic waves.

Balian

There are a few peaks near the mouth of Sungai Balian (Balian River) in western Bali. The best break here is an enjoyable and consistent left-hander that works well at mid- to high tide if there's no wind. Lots of inns are springing up here.

Batu Bolong

North of Kerobokan, on the northern extremity of the bay, Batu Bolong (often called Canggu) has a nice light beach and many surfers. An optimum size for Batu Bolong is 5ft to 6ft. There's a good right-hander that you can really hook into, which works at high tide.

Bingin

North of Padang Padang and accessible by road, this spot can get crowded. It's best at mid-tide with a 6ft swell, when it manufactures short but perfect left-hand barrels. The cliffs backing the beach are lined with funky accommodation.

Impossibles

Just north of Padang Padang, this outside reef break has three shifting peaks with fast left-hand tube sections that can join up if the conditions are perfect.

Ketewel & Lebih

These two beaches are northeast of Sanur. They're both right-hand beach breaks, and are dodgy at low tide and close out over 6ft.

Kuta Area

For your first plunge into the warm Indian Ocean, try the breaks at Kuta's beach. At full tide, go out near the life-saving club at the southern end of the beach road. At low tide, try the tubes around **Halfway Kuta**, probably the best place in Bali for beginners to practise. Start at the beach breaks if you are a bit rusty, but treat even these breaks with respect.

Further north, the breaks at **Legian Beach** can be pretty powerful, with lefts and rights on the sandbars off Jl Melasti and Jl Padma.

For more serious stuff, go to the reefs south of the beach breaks, about a kilometre out to sea. **Kuta Reef**, a vast stretch of coral, provides a variety of waves. You can paddle out in around 20 minutes, but the easiest way is by boat, for a fee. The main break is a classic left-hander, best at mid- to high tide, with a 5ft to 6ft swell, when it peels across the reef and has a beautiful inside tube section.

As elsewhere, when in doubt here, ask the locals.

Medewi

Further along the south coast of western Bali is a softer left called Medewi. It's a point break that can give a long ride right into the river mouth. This wave has a big drop, which fills up then runs into a workable inside section. There's accommodation nearby.

Nusa Dua

During the wet season, you should surf on the east side of the island, where there are some very fine reef breaks. The reef off Nusa Dua has very consistent swells. The main break is 1km off the beach to the south of Nusa Dua – go past the golf course and look for the row of warung (food stalls), and some boats to take you out. There are lefts and rights that work well on a small swell at low- to mid-tide. Further north, in front of the Club Med, there is a fast, barrelling right reef break called **Sri Lanka**, which works best at mid-tide.

Nusa Lembongan

In the Nusa Penida group, this island is separated from the southeast coast of Bali by Selat Badung (Badung Strait).

The strait is very deep and generates huge swells that break over the reefs off the northwest coast of Lembongan. **Shipwreck**, clearly visible from the beach, is the most popular break, a longish right that gets a good barrel at mid-tide with a 5ft swell.

A bit to the south, **Lacerations** is a very fast, hollow right breaking over a very shallow reef – hence the name. Still further south is a smaller, more user-friendly left-hander called **Playground**. Remember that Lembongan is best with an easterly wind, so it's dry-season surfing.

Padang Padang

Just Padang for short, this super-shallow, left-hand reef break is just north of Ulu Watu towards Kuta. Check this place carefully before venturing out. It's a very demanding break that only works over about 6ft from mid- to high tide. It's a great place to watch from the clifftop.

If you can't surf tubes, backhand or forehand, don't go out: Padang is a tube. After a ledgy take-off, you power along the bottom before pulling up into the barrel. Not a wave for the faint-hearted and definitely not a wave to surf when there's a crowd.

Sanur

Sanur Reef has a hollow wave with excellent barrels. It's fickle, and doesn't even start until you get a 6ft swell, but anything over 8ft will be world-class, and anything over 10ft will be brown-boardshorts material. There are other reefs further offshore and most of them are surfable.

Hyatt Reef, over 2km from shore, has a shifty right peak that can give a great ride at full tide. The classic right is off the Grand Bali Beach Hotel.

Serangan

The development at Pulau Serangan (Turtle Island) has caused huge disruption on the southern and eastern sides of the island; paradoxically, these changes to the shape of the shore have made the surf here much more consistent. In addition, the causeway has made the island more accessible, and several warung face the water, where waves break right and left in anything over a 3ft swell.

South Coast

The extreme south coast, around the end of the Bukit Peninsula, can be surfed any time of the year provided there is a northerly wind, or no wind at all – get there very early to avoid onshore winds. The peninsula is fringed with reefs, and big swells are produced, but access is a problem; the shoreline is all cliff. Try the steps down to the beach at Pura Mas Suka or charter a boat on a day with no wind and a small swell.

Ulu Watu

When Kuta Reef is 5ft to 6ft, Ulu Watu, the most famous surfing break in Bali, will be 6ft to 8ft with bigger sets. It's way out on the southern extremity of the bay and consequently picks up more swell than Kuta.

Teluk Ulu Watu (Ulu Watu Bay) is a great set-up for surfers – local boys will wax your board, get drinks for you and carry the board down into the cave, which is the usual access to the waves. There are warung and there's accommodation for every budget.

Ulu Watu has about seven different breaks. The **Corner** is straight in front of you to the right. It's a fast-breaking, hollow left that holds about 6ft. The reef shelf under this break is extremely shallow, so try to avoid falling head first. At high tide, the **Peak** starts to work. This is good from 5ft to 8ft, with bigger waves occasionally right on the Peak itself. You can take off from this inside part or further down the line. It's a great wave.

Another left runs off the cliff that forms the southern flank of the bay. It breaks outside this in bigger swells, and once it's 7ft, a left-hander pitches right out in front of a temple on the southern extremity. Out behind the Peak, when it's big, is a *bombora* (submerged reef) appropriately called the **Bommie**. This is another big left-hander and it doesn't start operating until the swell is about 10ft. On a normal 5ft to 8ft day, there are also breaks south of the Peak.

Observe where other surfers paddle out and follow them. If you are in doubt, ask someone. It is better having some knowledge than none at all. Climb down into the cave and paddle out from there. When the swell is bigger you will be swept to your right. Don't panic – it is an easy matter to paddle around the white water from down along the cliff. Coming back in you have to aim for the cave. When the swell is bigger, come from the southern side of the cave as the current runs to the north.

Where to Surf: Lombok

Lombok has some good surfing and the dearth of tourists means that breaks are uncrowded.

Desert Point

Located in an extremely remote part of Lombok, Desert Point is a legendary if elusive wave that was voted the 'best wave in the world' by *Tracks* magazine. Only suitable for very experienced surfers, it's a fickle beast, in a region known for long, flat spells.

On its day this left-handed tube can offer a 300m ride, growing in size from take-off to close-out (which is over razor-sharp coral). Desert Point only really performs when there's a serious ground swell – May to September offers the best chance. Wear a helmet and boots at low tide. The nearest accommodation is about 12km away in Pelangan, so many surfers either camp next to the shoreline, or cruise in on surf safaris from Bali.

Gerupak

This giant bay 6km east of Kuta boasts four surf breaks, so there's always some wave action no matter what the weather or tide. **Bumbang** is extremely dependable: best on an incoming tide, this right-hander over a flat reef is good for all levels and can be surfed year-round. **Gili Golong** excels at mid- to high-tide between October and April. **Don-Don** needs a bigger swell to break but can be great at any time of year. Finally **Kid's Point** (or Pelawangan) only breaks with big swells, but when it does it's barrels all the way. You need to hitch a boat ride (around 70,000Rp) to each wave.

Gili Trawangan

Much better known as a diving mecca, Trawangan also boasts a little-known surf spot off the island's southwestern tip, offshore from the Vila Ombak hotel. It's a quick right-hander that breaks in two sections, one offering a steeper profile, over rounded coral. It can be surfed all year long but is best at high tide.

Mawi

About 18km west of Kuta, the stunning bay of Mawi has a fine barrelling left with a late take-off and a final tube. It's best in the dry season from May to October with easterly offshore winds and a southwest swell. As there are sharp rocks and coral underwater, and the riptide is very fierce, take great care. Unfortunately, thefts have been reported from the beach, so leave nothing of value behind and tip the locals to look after your vehicle.

Equipment: Pack or Rent?

A small board is usually adequate for the smaller breaks, but a few extra inches on your usual board length won't go astray. For the bigger waves – 8ft and upwards – you'll need a 'gun.' For a surfer of average height and build, a board around the 7ft mark is perfect.

If you try to bring more than two or three boards into the country, you may have problems with customs officials, who might think you're going to try and sell them.

There are surf shops in Kuta and elsewhere in south Bali. You can rent boards of varying quality (from 30,000Rp to 50,000Rp per day) and get supplies at most popular surf breaks. If you need repairs, ask around: there are lots of places that can help.

Other recommended equipment you might bring:

» Solid luggage for airline travel

» Board-strap for carrying

» Tough shoes for walking down rocky cliffs

» Your favourite wax if you're picky

» Wetsuit or reef booties

» Wetsuit vest or other protective cover from the sun, reefs and rocks

» Surfing helmet for rugged conditions (and riding a motorbike)

Surf Operators

Surf schools operate right off Kuta Beach in Kuta and Legian.

Wave Hunter (p51) Rents stand-up paddle boards, gives lessons and arranges great-value transport to and from whatever beaches have good conditions on a particular day.

Surf Goddess (☑0858 997 0808; www .surfgoddessretreats.com) Surf holidays for women that include lessons and lodging in a posh guesthouse in Seminyak.

Diving & Snorkelling

With its warm water, extensive coral reefs and abundant marine life, Bali offers excellent diving and snorkelling adventures. Reliable dive schools and operators all around Bali's coast can train complete beginners or arrange challenging trips that will satisfy the most experienced divers. The Gilis provide equally excellent opportunities, while Lombok is close behind with good sites, especially around its northwest coast.

Snorkelling gear is available near all the most accessible spots, but if you're keen, it's definitely worthwhile bringing your own and checking out some of the less-visited parts of the coasts. The Gilis now have a professional freediving school (p292) if you want to take snorkelling to the next level. They also have Gili Islands Dive Association (GIDA), which sets professional and environmental standards.

Equipment: Pack or Rent?

If you are not picky, you'll find all the equipment you need in Bali, the Gilis and Lombok (the quality, size and age of the equipment can vary). If you provide your own, you can usually get a discount on your dive. Some small, easy-to-carry things to bring from home include protective gloves, spare straps, silicone lubricant and extra globes/ bulbs for your torch/flashlight. Other equipment to consider bringing:

» **Mask, snorkel & fins** Many people bring these as they are not too big to pack and you can be sure they will fit you. Snorkelling gear rents from about 30,000Rp per day and is often shabby.

» **Tanks & weight belt** Usually included with the cost of a dive.

» **Thin, full-length wetsuit** For protection against stinging animals and possible coral abrasions. Bring your own if you are worried about size. If diving off Nusa Penida, be sure you'll be able to use a wetsuit thicker than 3mm, as up-swells bring up deep water that's 18°C.

» **Regulators & BCVs** Most dive shops have decent ones. (BCVs are also known as BCDs or buoyancy control devices.)

Dive Operators

Major dive operators in tourist areas can arrange trips to the main dive sites all around the islands. Distances can be long though, so it's better to stay relatively close to your destination.

For a local trip, count on US$50 to US$90 per person for two dives, which includes all equipment. Note that it is becoming common to price in euros.

Wherever there is decent local diving on Bali and Lombok there are dive shops. Usually you can count on some reefs in fair condition reachable by boat. Recommended sites with shops include the following:

» Amed

» Candidasa

FELIX HUG/GETTY IMAGES ©

JOHN BORTHWICK/GETTY IMAGES ©

» (above) Snorkelling in the clear waters of Gili Meno (p298)
» (left) Horse riding along the beach (p280)

» Lovina

» Nusa Lembongan

» Padangbai

» Pemuteran

» Sanur

» Gili Air

» Gili Meno

» Gili Trawangan

» Kuta (Lombok)

» Senggigi

Choosing a Dive Operator

In general, diving in Bali and Lombok is safe, with a good standard of staff training and equipment maintenance. Here are a few tips to help you select a well set up and safety-conscious dive shop.

» Are its staff fully trained and qualified? Ask to see certificates or certification cards – no reputable shop will be offended by this request. Guides must reach 'full instructor' level to teach. To guide certified divers on a reef dive, guides must hold at least 'rescue diver' or preferably 'dive master' qualifications.

» Do they have safety equipment on the boat? At a minimum, a dive boat should carry oxygen and a first-aid kit. A radio or mobile phone is also important.

» Is the boat's equipment OK and its air clean? This is often the hardest thing for a new diver to judge. As a guide, smell the air: open a tank valve a small

way and breathe in. Smelling dry or slightly rubbery air is OK. If it smells of oil or car exhaust, that tells you the operator doesn't filter the air correctly.

» When the equipment is put together, are there any big air leaks? All dive centres get some small leaks at some time; however, if you get a *big* hiss of air coming out of any piece of equipment, ask to have it replaced.

» Is it conservation-oriented? Good dive shops explain that you should not touch corals or take shells from the reef, as well as work with local fishers to ensure that certain areas are protected. Some even clean beaches.

Responsible Diving

Bear in mind the following tips when diving and help preserve the ecology and beauty of reefs:

» Never use anchors on reefs, and take care not to run boats aground on coral.

» Avoid touching or standing on living marine organisms or dragging equipment across the reef.

» Be careful with your fins. Even without contact, the surge from fin strokes near the reef can damage delicate organisms. Don't kick up clouds of sand, which can smother organisms.

» Practise and maintain proper buoyancy control. Major damage can occur from reef collisions.

» Do not collect or buy corals or shells or loot marine archaeological sites (mainly shipwrecks).

BEST DIVING & SNORKELLING SITES

The following are Bali and Lombok's most spectacular diving and snorkelling locations, drawing people from near and far.

LOCATION	DETAILS	WHO SHOULD GO?
Nusa Penida	Serious diving that includes schools of manta rays and 2.5m sunfish	Skilled divers will enjoy the challenges, but novices and snorkellers will be in over their heads
Pulau Menjangan	Spectacular 30m wall off a small island, good for diving and snorkelling	Divers and snokellers of all skills and ages
Tulamben	Sunken WWII freighter; snorkelling and diving from shore	Divers and snorkellers with good swimming skills
Gili Islands	All types of diving and snorkelling in beautiful waters	Divers and snokellers of all skills and ages, although some sites may require advanced skills
Southwest Lombok	Good reefs	Divers and snorkellers with good swimming skills

» Ensure that you take home all your rubbish and any other litter you may find as well. Plastics are a serious threat to marine life.

» Do not feed the fish.

» Minimise your involvement with marine animals. *Never* ride on the backs of turtles.

Learning to Dive

If you're not a qualified diver and you want to try some scuba diving in Bali, you have several options, including packages that include lessons and cheap accommodation in a pretty place.

Introductory/orientation courses (US$60 to US$100) are perfect for novices who want to see if diving is for them, or you can learn the basics on a three- to four-day limited course (US$300) – these are popular at resorts. A PADI open-water certification, which is recognised everywhere, costs between US$350 and US$400.

Hiking & Trekking

You could wander Bali and Lombok for a year and still not see all the islands have to offer, but their small size means that you can nibble off a bit at a time, especially as day hikes and treks are easily arranged. Guides can help you surmount volcanoes, while tour companies will take you to remote regions and emerald-green valleys of rice terraces. In terms of what to pack, you'll need good boots for mountain treks and solid hiking sandals for walks.

Where to Hike: Bali

Bali is very walkable. No matter where you're staying, ask for recommendations and set off for discoveries and adventures. Ubud, the Sideman area and Munduk are obvious choices.

Even from busy Kuta or Seminyak, you can just head to the beach, turn right and walk north as far as you wish alongside the amazing surf while civilisation seems to evaporate.

Bali does not offer remote wilderness treks beyond the climbs of the volcanoes and day trips within Taman Nasional Bali Barat. For the most part, you'll make day trips from the closest village, often leaving before dawn to avoid the clouds and mist that usually blanket the peaks by mid-morning. No treks require camping gear.

Where to Hike: Lombok

Gunung Rinjani draws trekkers from around the world. Besides being Indonesia's second tallest volcano, it holds cultural and spiritual significance for the various people of the region. And then there is its stunning beauty: a 6km-wide cobalt blue lake some 600m below the rim of the vast caldera.

Expert advice is crucial on the mountain as people die on its slopes every year. You can organise explorations of Gunung Rinjani at Sembalun Valley, Senaru and Senggigi.

Equipment: Pack or Rent?

Any gear you'll need for your hike, you'll need to provide. Guides may have a few bits of gear but don't count on it. Consider bringing depending on the hike:

» Torch

» Warm clothes for higher altitudes

» Waterproof clothes as rain can happen at any time and most of the mountains are misty at the least

» Good hiking sandals, shows or boots – definitely items you won't find locally

Hiking Tour Operators

Guides and agencies are available in various areas such as Ubud, Gunung Agung and Tirta Gangga on Bali and the Sembalun Valley on Lombok. In addition to these, Bali-wide agencies include the following:

Bali Nature Walk (☑0817 973 5914; dade putra@hotmail.com) Walks in isolated areas in the Ubud region. Routes are customisable depending on your desires.

Bali Sunrise Trekking & Tours (☑0818 552 669; www.balisunrisetours.com) Leads treks throughout the central mountains.

Safety Guidelines for Trekking

Before embarking on a trekking trip, consider the following points to ensure a safe and enjoyable experience:

» Pay any fees and carry any permits required by local authorities; often these fees will be rolled into the guide's fee, meaning that it's all negotiable.

» Be sure you are healthy and feel comfortable walking for a sustained period.

» Obtain reliable information about environmental conditions along your intended route, eg the weather can get quite wet and cold in the upper reaches of the volcanoes.

» Confirm with your guide that you will only go on walks/treks within your realm of experience.

» Carry the proper equipment. Depending on the trek and time of year this can mean rain gear or extra water. Carry a torch; don't assume the guide will have one.

Cycling

Cyclists are discovering Bali in a big way. The back roads of the island more than make up for the traffic-clogged streets of the south. The main advantage of touring Bali by bike is the quality of the experience – you can be totally immersed in the environment, hearing the wind rustling in the rice paddies or the sound of a gamelan practising or catching the scent of flowers.

Lombok is also good for touring by bicycle. In the populated areas the roads are flat, and the traffic across the island is less chaotic than on Bali.

Some people are put off cycling by the tropical heat, but when you're riding on level ground or downhill, the breeze really moderates the heat.

Where to Cycle: Bali

It's really easier to tell you where *not* to ride in Bali. Denpasar south through Sanur in the east, and Kerobokan to Kuta in the west suffer from lots of traffic and narrow roads.

HIKING HIGHLIGHTS

Bali

One of Bali's great joys is hiking. You can have good experiences across the island, often starting right outside your hotel. Hikes can last from an hour to a day.

LOCATION	DETAILS
Danau Buyan & Danau Tamblingan	Natural mountain lakes, few people
Gunung Agung	Sunrises and isolated temples
Gunung Batukau	Misty climbs amid the clouds, with few people
Gunung Batur	Hassles but other-worldly scenery
Munduk	Lush, spice-scented waterfall-riven landscape
Sidemen Road area	Rice terraces, lush hills and lonely temples; comfy lodging for walkers
Taman Nasional Bali Barat	Remote, wild scenery, wildlife
Tirta Gangga	Rice terraces, gorgeous views, remote mountain temples
Ubud	Beautiful walks from one hour to one day; rice fields and terraces, river-valley jungles and ancient monuments

Lombok

Like the island itself, Lombok has walks and hikes that are often remote, challenging or both.

LOCATION	DETAILS
Air Terjun Sindang Gila	One of many waterfalls
Gilis	Beach-bum circumnavigations
Gunung Rinjani	Superb for trekking; climb the 3726m summit then drop down into a crater with a sacred lake and hot springs
Sembalun Valley	Garlic-scented hikes on the slopes of Rinjani

CYCLING SUGGESTIONS

You can't get too lost on an island as small as Bali. The following are areas good for exploring on two wheels:

LOCATION	DETAILS
Bukit Peninsula	Explore cliffs, coves and beaches along the west and south coasts; beach promenade at Nusa Dua; avoid the area by the airport
Central mountains	Ambitious; explore Danau Bratan, Danau Buyan and Danau Tamblingan; downhill to the north coast via Munduk and to the south via small roads from Candikuning
East Bali	Coast road lined with beaches; north of the coast is uncrowded with serene rice terraces; Sidemen Road has lodges good for cyclists
North Bali	Lovina is a good base for day trips to remote waterfalls and temples; the northeast coast has resorts popular with cyclists circumnavigating Bali
Nusa Lembongan	Small; easily done in half a day; nice remote beaches
Nusa Penida	For serious cyclists who bring bikes; nearly traffic-free, with remote vistas of the sea, sheer cliffs, white beaches and lush jungle
Ubud	Many tour companies are based here; narrow mountain roads lead to ancient monuments and jaw-dropping rice-terrace views
West Bali	Rice fields and dense jungle rides in and around Tabanan, Kerambitan and Bajera; further west, small roads off the main road lead to mountain streams, deserted beaches and hidden temples

Where to Cycle: Lombok

East of Mataram are several attractions that would make a good day trip: south to Banyumulek via Gunung Pengsong and then back to Mataram, for example. Some coastal roads have hills and curves like a roller coaster. Try going north from Senggigi to Pemenang along a spectacular, recently improved, paved road, and then (if you feel energetic) return via the steep climb over the Pusuk Pass. The Gilis are good for riding only as a means to get around – literally.

Equipment: Pack or Rent?

Serious cyclists will want to pack personal gear they consider essential. For top-end gear, there's **Planet Bike Bali** (☑0361-746 2858; Jl Gunung Agung 148, Denpasar). It stocks Giant, Trek, Shimano and other brands. Otherwise casual riders can rent bikes and helmets.

Cycling Tour Operators

Popular tours start high up in the central mountains at places such as Kintamani or Bedugul. The tour company takes you to the top and then you ride down relatively quiet mountain roads soaking up the lush scenery, village culture and tropical scents. The cost including bicycle, gear and lunch is US$35 to US$70. Transport to/from south Bali and Ubud hotels is usually included.

The following are companies to consider:

Archipelago Adventure (☑0361-808 1769; www.archipelago-adventure.com) Offers a range of tours, including ones on Java. In Bali, there are rides around Jatiluwih and Danau Buyan, and mountain biking on trails from Kintamani.

Bali Bike-Baik Tours (☑0813 3867 3852, 0361-978 052; www.balibike.com) Tours run downhill from Kintamani. The emphasis is on cultural immersion and there are frequent stops in tiny villages and at rice farms.

Bali Eco Cycling (☑0361-975 557; www .baliecocycling.com) Tours start at Kintamani and take small roads through lush scenery south to Ubud; other options focus on rural culture.

Banyan Tree Cycling Tours (p148) Enjoy day-long tours of remote villages in the hills above Ubud. It's locally owned by Bagi; the tours (from 450,000Rp) emphasise interaction with villagers. Very popular.

C.Bali (☑0813 5342 0541; www.c-bali.com) Offers excellent bike tours in and around Gunung Batur.

Rafting

Rafting is popular, usually as a day trip from either south Bali or Ubud. Operators pick you up, take you to the put-in point, provide all the equipment and guides, and return you to your hotel at the end of the day. The best time is during the wet season (November to March), or just after; by the middle of the dry season (April to September), the best river rapids may be better described as 'dribbles.'

Some operators use the Sungai Ayung (Ayung River), near Ubud, where there are between 19 and 25 Class II to III rapids (ie potentially exciting but not perilous). The Sungai Telagawaja (Telagawaja River) near Muncan in east Bali is also popular. It's more rugged than the Ayung and the scenery is more wild.

Advertised prices run from US$55 to US$80; discounts are common. Consider the following:

Bali Adventure Tours (☑0361-721 480; www.baliadventuretours.com; rafting trips adult/child from $79/52) Sungai Ayung; also has kayak trips.

Mega Rafting (☑0361-246 724; www.mega raftingbali.com) Sungai Ayung.

Sobek (☑0361-768 050; www.balisobek .com) Trips on both the Sungai Ayung and Sungai Telagawaja.

Travel with Children

Beaches
Surf schools at Kuta Beach or flying kites at Sanur Beach – for kids of all ages.

Water
Play in the ocean at Nusa Lembongan, or dive or snorkel at Pulau Menjangan or in the Gilis. For something different, walk across rice fields – who could resist the promise of muddy water filled with ducks, frogs and other fun critters?

Frolicking
Kids can make like monkeys at Bali Treetop Adventure Park in Candikuning, hit the aquatic playground of Waterbom Park just south of Kuta, splash about on a river rafting trip or pedal along on a bike tour.

Animals
It's a jungle out there: Ubud's Sacred Monkey Forest Sanctuary; the Bali Bird Park and Rimba Reptile Park south of Ubud; the Elephant Safari Park north of Ubud; and the Bali Safari & Marine Park, in East Bali.

Cool Old Things
Kids will love the Indiana Jones–like pools at Tirta Empul, the ancient water palace and park at Tirta Gangga northeast of Ubud, and Pura Luhur Ulu Watu, a beautiful temple with monkeys.

Travelling anywhere with *anak-anak* (children) requires energy and organisation, but in Bali these problems are lessened by the Balinese affection for children. They believe that children come straight from God, and the younger they are, the closer they are to God. To the Balinese, children are considered part of the community, and everyone, not just the parents, has a responsibility towards them. If a child cries, the Balinese get most upset and insist on finding a parent and handing the child over with a reproachful look. Sometimes they despair of uncaring Western parents, and the child will be whisked off to a place where it can be cuddled, cosseted and fed. In tourist areas this is less likely, but it's still common in traditional environments.

Bali & Lombok for Kids
Children are a social asset when you travel in Bali, and people will display great interest in any Western child they meet. You will have to learn your child's age and sex in Bahasa Indonesia – *bulau* (month), *tahun* (year), *laki-laki* (boy) and *perempuan* (girl). You should also make polite enquiries about the other person's children, present or absent.

Lombok is generally quieter than Bali and the traffic is less dangerous. People are fond of kids, but less demonstrative about

STAYING SAFE

The main danger to kids – and adults for that matter – is traffic and bad pavement and footpaths in busy areas.

The sorts of facilities, safeguards and services that Western parents regard as basic may not be present. Not many restaurants provide highchairs, places with great views might have nothing to stop your kids falling over the edge, and shops often have breakable things down low. Given the ongoing rabies crisis in Bali, be sure to keep children away from stray dogs.

them than the Balinese. The main difference on Lombok is that services for children are much less developed.

The obvious drawcards for kids are the loads of outdoor adventures available. But there are also many cultural treats that kids will love.

» **Dance** A guaranteed snooze right? Wrong. Check out an evening Barong dance at the Ubud Palace or Pura Dalem Ubud, two venues that look like sets from *Tomb Raider* right down to the flaming torches. Sure, the Legong style of Balinese might be tough going for fidgety types, but the Barong has monkeys, monsters, a witch and more.

» **Markets** If young explorers are going to temples, they will need sarongs. Give them 100,000Rp at a traditional market and let 'em loose. Vendors will be truly charmed as the kids try to bargain and assemble the most colourful combo (and nothing is too loud for a Balinese temple).

» **Temples** Pick the fun ones. Goa Gajah (Elephant Cave) in Bedulu has a deep cavern where hermits lived and you enter through the mouth of a monster. Pura Luhur Batukau is in dense jungle in the Gunung Batukau area with a cool lake and a rushing stream.

Planning

The critical decision is deciding where to base yourselves for the holiday.

Where to Stay

A hotel with a swimming pool, air-con and a beachfront location is fun for kids and very convenient, and still provides a good break for parents. Fortunately there are plenty of choices.

Many hotels and guesthouses, at whatever price level, have a 'family plan', which means that children up to about 12 years old can share a room with their parents free of charge. The catch is that hotels may charge

for extra beds, although many offer family rooms.

Large international resorts often offer special programs or supervised activities for kids; where this isn't the case, most hotels can arrange a babysitter.

Hotel staff are usually very willing to help and improvise, so always ask if you need something for your children.

What to Pack

Huge supermarkets and stores in south Bali such as Carrefour stock almost everything you'd find at similar stores at home, including many Western foods; nappies, Western baby food, packaged UHT milk, infant formula and other supplies are easily purchased. Suggested items to bring by age:

Babies & Toddlers

» A front or back sling or other baby carrier: Bali's barely walkable streets and paths are not suited to prams and pushchairs.

» A portable changing mat, hand-wash gel et al (baby changing facilities are a rarity).

» Kids' car seats: cars, whether rented or chartered with a driver, are unlikely to come with these.

Six to 12 Years

» Binoculars for young explorers to zoom in on wildlife, rice terraces, temples, dancers and so on.

» A camera or phone that shoots video to inject newfound fun into 'boring' grown-up sights and walks.

Teens

» Wi-fi device or mobile (check rates) so young travellers can tell those at home about *everything* they're missing.

BEST REGIONS FOR KIDS

Although Bali and Lombok are generally quite kid-friendly, some areas are more accommodating than others.

LOCATION	PROS	CONS
Gili Air	Small island so kids won't get lost, gentle surf, many tourist amenities and activities such as snorkelling	Can feel cramped and still maybe too close to Gili T debauchery
Legian	Much the same as Kuta with beachfront resorts on the sand	Much the same as Kuta without the busy beach road (but there's traffic elsewhere); strong surf
Lovina	Modest, quiet hotels near the beach, limited traffic, reef-protected beach with gentle waves	Far from the rest of Bali, boring for teens and adults, limited diversions
Nusa Dua	Huge beachside resorts, reef-protected beach with gentle waves, modest traffic, quiet	Can be dull for teens and adults; insulated from the rest of Bali
Sanur	Beachside resorts, reef-protected beach with gentle waves, close to many kid-friendly activities, modest traffic	Can be dull, especially for teens and adults
Seminyak	Appealing mix for all ages; large hotels on beach	Traffic, strong surf
Senggigi	Modest, quiet hotels on the beach; limited traffic; reef-protected beach with gentle waves	Somewhat isolated, boring for teens and adults, Lombok offers limited kid-specific diversions
Tanjung Benoa	Beachside resorts, reef-protected beach with gentle waves, close to many kid-friendly activities	Far from the rest of Bali, boring for teens and adults
Ubud	Quiet in parts; many things to see and do; walks, markets and shops	No beach, evenings may require greater creativity to keep kids amused, adults like it
Kuta	Teens will love it; kids will be able to buy all manner of cheap souvenirs and fake tattoos and get their hair braided; surf lessons	Teens will love it too much; busy road between beach and hotels; crowded, crazy, strong surf

» Cool shades and other gear to effect the right look from the minute the plane lands.

Eating with Kids

Eating out as a family is one of the joys of visiting Bali and Lombok. Kids are treated like deities by doting staff who will clamour to grab yours (especially young babies) while mum and dad enjoy some quiet time together.

Bali especially is so relaxed that kids can just be kids. There are plenty of top-end eateries in Seminyak and elsewhere where kids romp nearby while their parents enjoy a fine meal.

What to Eat

For older babies, bananas, eggs, peelable fruit and *bubur* (rice cooked to a mush in chicken stock) are all generally available.

Obviously, if your children don't like spicy food, show caution in offering them the local cuisine. Many warung (food stalls) will serve food without sauces upon request, such as plain white rice, fried tempeh or tofu, chicken, boiled vegetables and boiled egg.

Otherwise, kid-pleasers like burgers, chicken fingers, pizza and pasta are widespread as are fast-food chains in south Bali.

regions at a glance

Kuta and Seminyak are the main towns in the most touristed part of Bali, the part of the south that follows the magnificent stretch of sand from the airport northwest to Echo Beach. The Bukit Peninsula combines remote surf breaks with vast resorts. Ubud occupies the heart of Bali in many respects and shares some of the island's most beautiful rice fields with east Bali. The latter has no major centre but does have popular areas such as Padangbai and the Amed Coast.

Bali's centre is dominated by dramatic volcanoes. North and west Bali are thinly populated but have fine diving.

Lombok is largely mountainous, volcanic and rural, while the Gili Islands are tiny coral islands fringed with white sand.

Kuta & Seminyak

Beaches ✓✓✓
Nightlife ✓✓✓
Shopping ✓✓✓

Beaches
Kuta's famous sweep of wave-pounded sand extends for 12km past Legian, Seminyak, Kerobokan and Canggu, before finally ending up on the rocks near Echo Beach. At Kuta there are beach bars (chairs in the sand) and vendors; these dwindle as you go northwest.

Nightlife
Restaurants and cafes in Seminyak and Kerobokan are some of the best on Bali. Some have gorgeous sunset views, while the bars and clubs have a vaguely sophisticated air. Nightlife becomes manic in Kuta, where the party goes all night.

Shopping
Shopping in Seminyak is reason enough to visit Bali; the choice is extraordinary.

p48

South Bali & the Islands

Beaches ✓✓✓
Surfing ✓✓✓
Diving ✓✓

Beaches
Beaches can be found right around south Bali: little coves of white sand such as Balangan are idyllic, while those in Nusa Dua, Tanjung Benoa and Sanur are family friendly. The beaches out on Nusa Lembongan offer a funky escape.

Surfing
You can't say enough about the surf breaks on the west coast of the Bukit Peninsula; the multitude of breaks around Ulu Watu are world-renowned. Surfer guesthouses let you stay near the action.

Diving
The best diving is at the islands. Nusa Lembongan has coral and mangroves; Nusa Penida has challenging conditions and deep-water cliffs.

p94

Ubud & Around

Culture ✓✓✓
Indulgence ✓✓
Walks ✓✓✓

Culture

Ubud is the nexus of Balinese culture. Each night there are a dozen performances of traditional Balinese dance, music, puppets and more. Also here are talented artists, including superb woodcarvers who make the masks for the shows.

Indulgence

Spas, traditional medicine sessions and yoga classes are just some of the ways you can indulge yourself in Ubud. International practitioners join local healers to offer services for mind and body.

Walks

Rice fields surround Ubud and they are some of Bali's most picturesque. You can walk for an hour or an entire day, enjoying river valleys, villages and enveloping natural beauty.

p137

East Bali

Beaches ✓✓
History ✓✓
Hikes ✓✓

Beaches

Beaches are found along much of the east Bali coast. The coast road has wave-tossed beaches of dark volcanic sand, many with important temples. Pasir Putih always charms, as do the small beach coves of Amed.

History

Taman Kertha Gosa has the moving remains of a palace lost when the royalty committed ritual suicide rather than surrender to the Dutch in 1908.

Hikes

Some of Bali's most alluring rice fields and landscapes are found in the east. You're spoiled for choice along Sidemen Road, or try Tirta Gangga, which excels at remote temple walks. Gunung Agung awaits the ambitious.

p179

Central Mountains

Hikes ✓✓
Culture ✓✓
Solitude ✓✓

Hikes

The centre of the island is all about hiking. The alien landscape of Gunung Batur, an active volcano, thrills many. Around Munduk there are misty walks through spice plantations and jungle to waterfalls.

Culture

Pura Luhur Batukau never fails to touch the spirit of those who find this important temple on the slopes of Gunung Batukau. The perfectly realised rice fields of Jatiluwih embody the deep significance rice has to the Balinese psyche.

Solitude

Cooler than the rest of Bali, the mountains feel lonely. A solitary visit to Pura Luhur Batukau can be followed by retreats to nearby remote lodges.

p215

North Bali

Resorts ✓✓
Beaches ✓
Diving ✓

Resorts

The crescent of beach hotels at Pemuteran is the real star of north Bali. Beautifully built, the hotels form a fine human-scaled resort area, and they're close to Pulau Menjangan. Lovina is good for those looking for a low-cost, quiet getaway.

Beaches

There's a lot of tan and grey sand along Bali's north coast. Much of the coast is protected by reefs and the waves are small.

Diving

The real draw underwater is the night diving around Lovina. Dive shops run well-managed trips, on which you're likely to see huge amounts of marine life not visible by day.

p230

West Bali

Diving ✓✓✓
Surfing ✓✓
Beaches ✓

Diving
Pulau Menjangan lives up to its many superlatives. A 30m coral wall close to shore delights both divers and snorkellers with a cast of fish and creatures that varies from sardines to whales. The island is part of a national park and is undeveloped.

Surfing
Breaks at Balian Beach and Medewi have a following, and at the former a small surfer community has sprung up with idiosyncratic guesthouses and a stylish hotel.

Beaches
Balian Beach is the main strand in the west and makes a good place to hang even if you're not surfing.

p245

Lombok

Hiking ✓✓
Coastline ✓✓✓
Tropical Chic ✓✓

Hiking
A majestic volcano, Gunung Rinjani's very presence overshadows all of northern Lombok. Hiking trails sneak up Rinjani's astonishing caldera, where you'll find a shimmering crater lake, hot springs and a smoking minicone.

Coastline
Lombok's southern coastline is nature in the raw. There's nothing genteel about the magnificent shoreline, which is pounded by oceanic waves that make it a surfer's mecca. Empty beaches allow exceptional swimming.

Tropical Chic
Lombok excels at the tropical-chic thing. For total immersion, the Sire area offers uberluxury. Delve into Senggigi's hip hotels and sleek restaurants.

p258

Gili Islands

Diving ✓✓✓
Adventure ✓✓
Chilling ✓✓✓

Diving
Forming one of Indonesia's most species-rich environments, the Gilis' coral reefs teem with fascinating sea life. The islands are perfect for divers (including free divers) and snorkellers, and you're almost guaranteed to see turtles.

Adventure
They may be miniscule, but the Gilis are loaded with intriguing possibilities. Try kayaking, ride a horse, learn to free dive or surf.

Chilling
We've all dreamed of finding the ultimate beach: a vision of palms trees, blinding white sands and a turquoise sea, perhaps with a seashell or two and a bamboo shack selling cool drinks and fresh fish. Find yours here.

p286

Every listing is recommended by our authors, and their favourite places are listed first

Look out for these icons:

 TOP CHOICE Our author's top recommendation

 A green or sustainable option

FREE No payment required

On the Road

Kuta & Seminyak

Best Places to Eat

» Sardine (p86)

» Biku (p86)

» Warung Sulawesi (p87)

» Mama San (p80)

Best Places to Stay

» Hotel Tugu Bali (p89)

» Oberoi (p78)

» Un's Hotel (p55)

» Samaya (p78)

Why Go?

Crowded and frenetic, the swath of south Bali hugging the amazing wide ribbon of beach that begins in Kuta is the place many travellers begin and end their visit to the island. Not a bad choice.

In Seminyak and Kerobokan there is a bounty of restaurants, cafes, designer boutiques, spas and the like that rivals anywhere in the world, while Kuta and Legian are still the choice for rollicking all-night clubbing, cheap singlets and hair-plaiting and carefree family holidays.

Renowned shopping, all-night clubs, fabulous dining, cheap beer, sunsets that dazzle and relentless hustle and bustle are all part of the experience. But just when you wonder what any of this has to do with Bali – the island supposedly all about spirituality and serenity – a religious procession appears and shuts everything down. And then you know the answer.

When to Go

Bali's ever-increasing popularity means that the best time to visit Kuta, Seminyak and their neighbours is outside of the high season, which is July, August and the weeks around Christmas and New Year. Holidays elsewhere mean that visitor numbers spike and it can require actual effort to organise tables in the best restaurants, navigate trendy shops and get a room with a view. Many prefer April to June and September, when the weather is drier and slightly cooler, and the crowds manageable.

Kuta & Legian

♫ 0361

Loud, frenetic and brash are just some of the adjectives commonly used to describe Kuta and Legian, the centre of mass tourism in Bali. Only a couple of decades ago, local hotels tacked their signs up to palm trees. Amid the wall-to-wall cacophony today, such an image seems as foreign as the thought that the area was once rice fields. Worse, parts are just plain ugly, like the unsightly strips that wend their way inland from the beach.

Although this is often the first place many visitors hit in Bali, the region is not for everyone. Kuta has narrow lanes jammed with cheap cafes, surf shops, incessant motorbikes and an uncountable number of T-shirt vendors. However, newly opened flashy shopping malls and chain hotels suggest a more mainstream future.

Kuta has Bali's most raucous clubs, and you can still find a simple room for US$15 in dozens of hotels. Legian appeals to a slightly older crowd (wags say it's where fans of Kuta go after they're married). It is equally commercial and has a long row of family-friendly hotels close to the beach. Tuban differs little in feel from Kuta and Legian, but does have a higher percentage of visitors on package holidays.

As for the waves, they break on the beach that put Kuta on the map. The strand of sand stretching for kilometres from Tuban north to Kuta, Legian and beyond to Seminyak and Echo Beach is always a scene of surfing, playing, massaging, chilling, imbibing and more.

Navigating the region will drive you to a cold one even earlier than you had planned. Busy Jl Legian runs roughly parallel to the beach from Kuta north into Seminyak.

◎ Sights

The real sight here is, of course, the beach. You can immerse yourself in local life without even getting wet. A pleasant walkway runs south from where Jl Pantai Kuta meets the beach. Stretching almost to the airport, it has fine views of the ocean and the efforts to preserve some of Tuban's nearly vanished beach.

Wanderers, browsers and gawkers will find much to fascinate, delight and irritate amid the streets, alleys and constant hubbub. You can even discover the odd non-touristy site, such as an old **Chinese Temple** (Map p52).

Memorial Wall   MONUMENT
(Map p52; Jl Legian; ⊙24hr) Reflecting the international scope of the 2002 bombings is the memorial wall (p316), where people from many countries pay their respects. Listing the names of the 202 known victims, including 88 Australians and 35 Indonesians, it is starting to look just a touch faded. Across the street, a parking lot is all that is left of the **Sari Club site** (Map p52).

🏃 Activities

From Kuta you can easily go surfing, sailing, diving, fishing or rafting anywhere in the southern part of Bali and still be back for the start of happy hour at sunset.

Many of your activities in Kuta centre on the superb **beach**. Hawkers will sell you sodas and beer, snacks and other treats, and you can hire lounge chairs and umbrellas (negotiable at 10,000Rp to 20,000Rp) or just crash on the sand. You'll see everyone from bronzed international youths strutting their stuff, to local families trying to figure out how to get wet *and* preserve their modesty. When the tide is out, the beach seems to stretch forever and you could be tempted for a long stroll. Sunsets are a time of gathering for just about everyone in south Bali. When conditions are right, you can enjoy an iridescent magenta spectacle better than fireworks.

Except for the traffic, the Kuta area is a pretty good place for kids: they can cavort on the beach for hours. Almost all the hotels and resorts above the surfer-dude category have pools, and the better ones offer kids' programs. **Amazone** (Map p56; Jl Kartika Plaza, Discovery Shopping Mall; ⊙10am-10pm) has hundreds of screeching arcade games on the top floor of the mall.

The very popular **Double Six Beach** (Jl Arjuna), at the north end of Legian, is alive with pick-up games of football and volleyball all day long. It's a fine place to meet locals.

LEGIAN'S BEST BEACH

The beach in front of the Sari Beach Inn (p65) is far from any road, is backed by shady trees, is never crowded and has somnolent vendors, and isn't crossed by a stream with dubious water. You'll have a huge stretch of sand to yourself and you'll hear something rarely heard further south in Kuta: the surf.

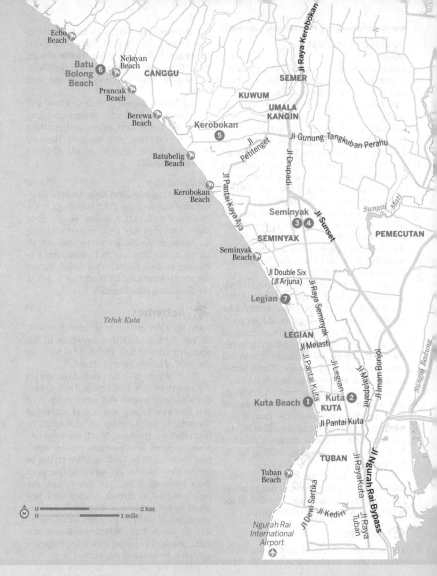

Kuta & Seminyak Highlights

1 Lolling away your day on **Kuta Beach** (p50), Bali's original tourist magnet

2 Raving through the night in the teaming, manic clubs and legendary nightlife swirl of **Kuta** (p69)

3 Ignoring your resolve shopping in the myriad boutiques of **Seminyak** (p83)

4 Letting your tension melt away at a spa in **Seminyak** (p75)

5 Savouring a meal at one of the growing number of fabulous restaurants in **Kerobokan** (p86)

6 Losing the crowds at **Batu Bolong Beach** (p92), a mellow swath of sand near Canggu

7 Soaking in the sunset while sipping a cheap beer from a beach vendor in **Legian** (p50)

KUTA COWBOYS UNSADDLED

You see them all around Bali's southern beaches: young men who are buff, tattooed, long-haired and gregariously courtly. Long known as 'Kuta cowboys', they turn the Asian cliché of a younger local woman with an older Western man on its ear. For decades women from Japan, Australia and other nations have found companionship on Bali's beaches that meets a need, be it romantic, adventurous or otherwise.

The dynamic between these foreign women and Balinese men is more complex than a simple exchange of money for sexual services (which is illegal in Bali): although the Kuta cowboys do not receive money directly for sex, their female companions tend to pay for their meals, buy gifts, and may even pay other expenses such as rent.

This well-known Bali phenomenon was thrust into the headlines in 2010 with the release of the lighthearted documentary *Cowboys in Paradise* (www.cowboysinparadise.com). Director Amit Virmani says he got the idea for the film after he talked to a Balinese boy who said he wanted 'to sex-service Japanese girls' when he grew up. The result looks at the lives of the Kuta cowboys and explores the economics and emotional costs of having fleeting dalliances with female tourists on a schedule.

After news of the film went viral, local authorities became concerned that spotlighting the island's romance trade would hurt Bali's image, and local police arrested 28 men on Kuta beach on suspicion of selling sex. In addition to these 'image' issues, health authorities warn that HIV is a risk: the HIV rate in Bali is, for example, 84 times that of Australia.

Surfing

The beach break called **Halfway Kuta**, offshore near the Hotel Istana Rama, is popular with novices. More challenging breaks can be found on the shifting sandbars off Legian, around the end of Jl Padma, and at Kuta Reef, 1km out to sea off Tuban Beach.

Shops large and small sell big-brand surf gear and boards. Stalls on the side streets hire out surfboards (for a negotiable 30,000Rp per day) and boogie boards, repair dings and sell new and used boards. Some can also arrange transport to nearby surfing spots. Used boards in good shape average US$200. For more on surfing, see p29.

Surf schools and shops include the following:

Wave Hunter SURFING
(Map p52; www.supwavehunter.com; Jl Sunset 18X at Jl Imam Bonjol; rental per day 250,000Rp) Rents stand-up paddle boards, gives lessons and arranges great-value transport to and from whatever beaches have good conditions on a particular day.

Pro Surf School SURFING
(Map p52; www.prosurfschool.com; Jl Pantai Kuta; lessons from €45) Right along the classic stretch of Kuta Beach, this well-regarded school has been getting beginners standing for years. It has a fun cafe.

Rip Curl School of Surf SURFING
(Map p52; ☎735 858; www.ripcurlschoolofsurf.com; Jl Arjana; lessons from 650,000Rp) Usually universities sell shirts with their logos; here it's the other way round: the beachwear company sponsors a school. You can learn to surf at popular Double Six Beach; there are special courses for kids.

Naruki Surf Shop SURFING
(Map p52; ☎765 772; off Poppies Gang II; ⊙10am-8pm) One of dozens of surf shops lining the gang of Kuta, the friendly guys here will rent you a board, fix your ding, offer advice or give you lessons.

Water Park

Waterbom Park AMUSEMENT PARK
(Map p56; ☎755 676; www.waterbom.com; Jl Kartika Plaza; adult/child US$31/19; ⊙9am-6pm) Just south of Kuta, this watery amusement park covers 3.5 hectares of landscaped tropical gardens. It has assorted water slides, swimming pools and play areas, a supervised park for children under five years old, and a 'lazy river' ride. Other indulgences include the 'pleasure pool', a food court and bar, and a spa.

Massages & Spas

Spas have proliferated, especially in hotels, and offers are numerous. Check out a few before choosing.

Kuta & Legian

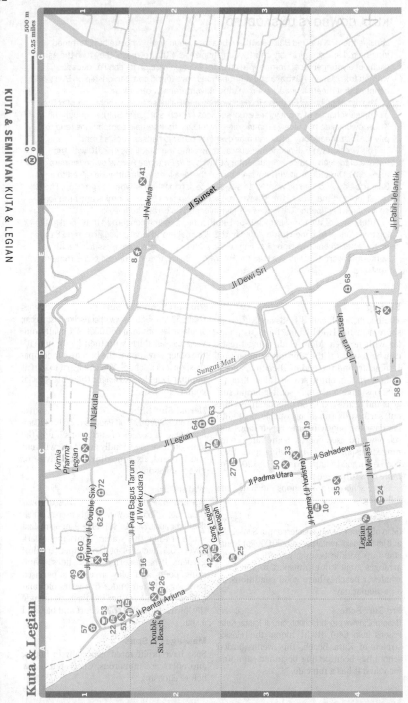

500 m
0.25 miles

Jl Sunset

Jl Nakula

Jl Patih Jelantik

Jl Dewi Sri

Sungai Mati

Jl Pura Puseh

Kimia
Pharma
Legian

Jl Nakula

Jl Legian

Jl Pura Bagus Taruna
(Jl Werkudara)

Jl Arjuna (Jl Double Six)

Jl Sahadewa

Jl Padma Utara

Jl Padma (Jl Yudistira)

Jl Melasti

Gang Legian
Tewogah

Legian
Beach

Jl Pantai Arjuna

Double
Six Beach

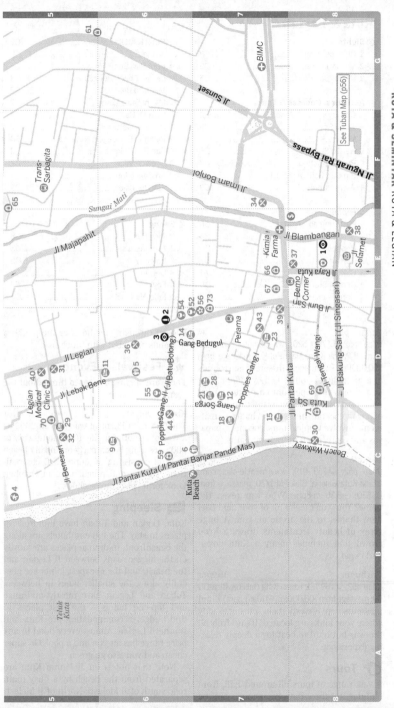

Kuta & Legian

◎ Sights
1	Chinese Temple	E8
2	Memorial Wall	D6
3	Site of Sari Club	D6

✪ Activities, Courses & Tours
	Garbugar	(see 65)
4	Jamu Spa	C5
	Miracle	(see 65)
5	Naruki Surf Shop	D6
6	Pro Surf School	C7
7	Rip Curl School of Surf	A1
8	Wave Hunter	E2

⏾ Sleeping
9	Bali Bungalo	C6
10	Bali Mandira Hotel	B4
11	Bendesa	D6
12	Berlian Inn	D7
13	Blue Ocean	A1
14	Gemini Star Hotel	D6
15	Hard Rock Hotel	C7
16	Hotel Kumala Pantai	B2
17	Island	C2
18	Kuta Puri Bungalows	C7
19	Legian Beach Bungalow	C3
20	Maharta Beach Resort	B2
21	Mimpi Bungalows	D7
22	O-CE-N Bali	A1
23	Poppies Cottages	D7
24	Pullman Bali Legian Nirwana	B4
25	Sari Beach Inn	B3
26	Seaside Villas	B2
27	Sri Beach Inn	C3
28	Suji Bungalow	D7
29	Un's Hotel	C5

◎ Eating
30	Ajeg Bali	C8
31	Aroma's Cafe	D5
32	Balcony	C5
33	Delicioso	C3
34	Feyloon	F7
35	Indo-National	C4

Jamu Spa SPA
(Map p52; ☑752 520; www.jamutraditionalspa.com; Jl Pantai Kuta, Alam Kul Kul; massage from 550,000Rp; ⏰9am-9pm) In serene surrounds at a resort hotel, you can enjoy indoor massage rooms that open onto a pretty garden courtyard. If you've ever wanted to be part of a fruit cocktail, here's your chance – treatments involve tropical nuts, coconuts, papayas and more, often in fragrant baths.

Miracle SPA
(Map p52; ☑769 019; www.miracle-clinic.com; Istana Kuta Galeria, Blok PM 1/20; massage from US$30; ⏰8.30am-8pm) Who can resist the name? You won't feel a bit of your acid peel here thanks to the arctic air-con. A huge array of beauty treatments draws a loyal crowd that includes many a Kuta doyen and expat.

Garbugar MASSAGE
(Map p52; ☑769 121; Istana Kuta Galleria, Blok OG 09; massage from 100,000Rp; ⏰10am-8pm) Blind masseurs here are experts in sensing exactly where your kinks are located. It's no-frills all the way but hard to beat for a deeply relaxing experience.

☞ Tours

A vast range of tours all around Bali, from half-day to three-day excursions, can be booked through your hotel or the plethora of stands plastered with brochures.

⚝ Festivals & Events

There are **surfing contests** throughout the year.

Kuta Karnival FESTIVAL
The first Kuta Karnival was held in 2003 as a way of celebrating life after the tragedy of 2002. It's a big beach party on the big beach in Kuta consisting of games, art, competitions, surfing and much more in October. Look for its page on Facebook.

⏾ Sleeping

Kuta, Legian and Tuban have hundreds of places to stay. The top-end hotels are along the beachfront, midrange places are mostly on the bigger roads between Jl Legian and the beach, and the cheapest joints are generally along the smaller lanes in between. Tuban and Legian have mostly midrange and top-end hotels – the best places to find budget accommodation are Kuta and southern Legian. Almost every hotel in any price range has air-con and a pool. Go super cheap and you also go green.

Note that hotels on Jl Pantai Kuta are separated from the beach by a busy main road south of Jl Melasti. North of Jl Melasti in Legian, though, part of the beach road is protected by gates that exclude almost all vehicle traffic. Hotels here have what is in effect a quiet, paved beachfront promenade.

Any place west of Jl Legian won't be more than a 10-minute walk to the beach.

TUBAN
There is a string of large hotels along the sometimes-not-existent Tuban Beach. They are popular with groups.

Discovery Kartika Plaza Hotel RESORT HOTEL **$$$**
(Map p56; ☑751 067; www.discoverykartikaplaza.com; Jl Kartika Plaza; r US$160–300; ❄@🌐☂) The 312 spacious rooms in four-storey blocks at this large resort front expansive gardens and a gigantic swimming pool. For a real splurge, rent one of the private villas on the water (units two to seven are best).

KUTA
Wandering the gang looking for a cheap room is a rite of passage for many. Small and family-run options are still numerous even as chains crowd in. Some of the hotels along Jl Legian are of the type that assume men booking a single actually aspire to a double.

ON THE BEACH
Hard Rock Hotel RESORT HOTEL **$$$**
(Map p52; ☑761 869; www.hardrockhotels.com; Jl Pantai Kuta; r from US$300; ❄@🌐☂) Nothing is understated about this hotel's ostentatious 418 rooms, which, despite various themes, all feel like a retail opportunity. The enormous pool is more fantasyland than amenity. The staff are skilful and you need never wait long to buy a T-shirt in the megastore. It's on the beach.

CENTRAL KUTA
TOP CHOICE Un's Hotel HOTEL **$$**
(Map p52; ☑757 409; www.unshotel.com; Jl Benesari; r US$35–80; ❄🌐☂) A hidden entrance sets the tone for the secluded feel of Un's. It's a two-storey place with bougainvillea spilling over the pool-facing balconies. The 30 spacious rooms in a pair of blocks (the southern one is quieter) feature antiques, comfy cane loungers and open-air bathrooms. Cheaper rooms are fan-only.

Poppies Cottages HOTEL **$$**
(Map p52; ☑751 059; www.poppiesbali.com; Poppies Gang I; r US$95–120; ❄@🌐☂) This Kuta institution has a lush, green setting for its 20 thatch-roofed cottages with outdoor sunken baths. Bed choices include kings and twins. The pool is surrounded by stone sculptures

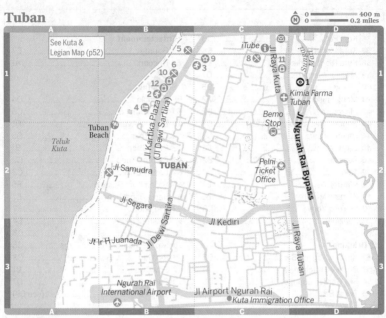

Tuban

and water fountains in a garden that almost makes you forget you are in the heart of Kuta.

Kuta Puri Bungalows HOTEL $$
(Map p52; ☎751 903; www.kutapuri.com; Poppies Gang I; r US$60-130; ❄🅿🛜🏊) The 47 bungalow-style rooms here are well maintained and nestled in verdant tropical grounds. The pool has a shallow kids' area. Enjoy the splish-splash of a fountain. Some rooms are fan only.

Bali Bungalo HOTEL $$
(Map p52; ☎755 109; www.bali-bungalo.com; off Jl Pantai Kuta; r 500,000-600,000Rp; ❄🛜🏊)

Large rooms close to the beach yet away from irritations are a big part of the appeal of this older, 44-room hotel. It's well maintained and there are statues of prancing horses to inspire horseplay in the pool. Rooms are in two-storey buildings and have patios/porches; not all have wi-fi.

Suji Bungalow HOTEL $
(Map p52; ☎765 804; www.sujibglw.com; off Poppies Gang I; r US$38-50; ❄@🛜🏊) This cheery place offers a choice of 47 bungalows and rooms in two-storey blocks set in a spacious, quiet garden around a pool (which has a slide into

Bali's Best Beaches

Beaches »
Surfing »
Diving & Snorkelling »
Marine Life »

View of Gili Meno and its crystal clear waters

Beaches

Bali and Lombok are ringed by beaches, with sand from white to black and surf from wild to tame. They draw visitors by the score for surfing, playing and sunbathing.

Going to the beach is one of the top reasons people come to the islands. With such a huge diversity of options, you are sure to find one – or several – that suit you. And it's likely you'll spend a lot of your time on the sand. Locals and visitors alike pause on west-facing beaches at sunset and the Balinese hold fascinating purification and other ceremonies at the shore.

You can enjoy a wild party scene or revel in utter solitude, the choices are yours.

1. Parasailing, Nusa Dua (p105) 2. Ulu Watu (p103)
3. Beach restaurant, Legian (p66) 4. Sunset beach view,
Legian (p50)

JOHN W BANAGAN/GETTY IMAGES ©

1. Iconic Kuta Beach (p50) **2.** Surfboards on a Bali beach
3. Cliffs of Ulu Watu (p103)

GLOWIMAGES/GETTY IMAGES ©

Surfing

Kuta Beach

1 Kuta Beach, Bali's original surf beach, is still a winner. First, the entire place just exudes surf culture, starting with the famous surf shops on shore. Second, you can easily learn to surf here. Schools abound and there are classes all day long. Third, the breaks are uber-reliable.

Echo Beach

2 Echo Beach has wild waves and plenty of spectators. It's really an extension of Batu Bolong but where that break fronts an often-quiet swath of sand, Echo Beach has a line of cafes that are always brimming with fans. It's always a good mix of locals and visitors here.

Ulu Watu

3 Ulu Watu is where you'll find Bali's most legendary surfing. It's really the climax of a string of breaks that march down the west coast of the Bukit Peninsula. The conditions are challenging and you can spend days just sussing out the scene. The cliffs are lined with classic surfer cafes.

JOHN SEATON CALLAHAN/GETTY IMAGES ©

Nusa Lembongan

4 Nusa Lembongan off Bali is an excellent place for days of riding. Breaks are immediately offshore past the reefs. Better, there are cheap places to stay with good views of the action so you can pick your moment to plunge in.

Desert Point

5 Desert Point on Lombok wins plaudits, and that's just not from surfers congratulating themselves for trekking out to this remote spot. Fickle – its season is a short one: May to September – this break is tough for even the most experienced and a reward for all.

Diving

Tulamben

1 Tulamben seems like a wide spot in the coast road of east Bali until you notice all the dive shops. The big attraction here lies right offshore: an old ship, the *Liberty,* sunk during WWII. You can dive and snorkel the wreck from right offshore and arrange lessons and excursions with the scores of operators.

Gili Trawangan

2 Gili Trawangan is a fabulous centre for diving and snorkelling. World-class dive shops abound on Gili T. Great places to explore the depths abound in the waters around all three Gilis. Freediving is popular here, you can snorkel right off the beaches and there are reefs in all directions.

Nusa Penida

3 Seldom-visited Nusa Penida is surrounded by what could be an underwater theme park. Conditions can be challenging – the services of an excellent dive shop are essential – but depending on the time of year you can see enormous (3m fin-to-fin) mola mola sunfish and whole schools of manta rays.

Nusa Lembongan

4 Nusa Lembongan is a good base for exploring dozens of sites here and at the two neighbouring islands, Nusa Penida and Nusa Ceningan. With the guidance of a good operator, you can drift dive between the latter and Lembongan. The mangroves are good for hours of snorkelling and diving.

Pulau Menjangan

5 Pulau Menjangan is Bali's best-known dive and snorkel area and has a dozen superb dive sites. The diving is excellent – iconic tropical fish, soft corals, great visibility (usually), caves and a spectacular drop-off. It's best visited as part of an overnight jaunt to Pemuteran, which has resorts.

MICHAEL AW/GETTY IMAGES ©

1. Sea fan and feather star, Tulamben (p212)
2. Biorock structure (p289), Gili Trawangan 3. Manta Ray, Nusa Penida (p133)

Marine Life

There is a rich variety of coral, seaweed, fish and other marine life in the coastal waters off the islands. Much of it can be appreciated by snorkellers, but you're only likely to see the larger marine animals while diving.

Some of the most dramatic sightings are found seasonally in the waters around Nusa Penida: huge, placid sunfish and manta rays lure divers from around the world.

Dolphins can be found right around the islands and have been made into an attraction off Lovina. But you're just as likely to see schools of dolphins if you take a fast boat between Bali and the Gilis.

Sharks are always dramatic and there are very occasional reports of large ones including great whites throughout the region, although unlike, say, the east coast of Australia, they are not considered a massive threat. In the Gilis, reef sharks are easily spotted at Shark Point.

Sea turtles are also common although greatly endangered. Long considered a delicacy by the Balinese it is a constant struggle by environmentalists to protect them from poachers. Still, you can find them, especially on snorkelling and diving trips in the Gilis.

Smaller fish and corals can be found at a plethora of spots around the islands. Everybody's favourite first stop is Bali's Menjangan. Fish as large as whale sharks have been reported but what thrills scores daily are the coloured beauty of an array of corals, sponges, lacy sea fans and much more. Starfish abound and you'll easily spot clownfish and other polychromatic characters.

Below
Butterflyfish and diver

the kiddie area). The verandas and terraces are good for relaxing. Not all rooms have wi-fi.

Berlian Inn
HOTEL $

(Map p52; ☑751 501; off Poppies Gang I; r 120,000-250,000Rp; ✳) A stylish cut above other budget places, the 24 rooms in two-storey buildings here are pleasingly quiet and have ikat bedspreads and an unusual open-air bathroom design. Pricier rooms have air-con and hot water.

Mimpi Bungalows
HOTEL $

(Map p52; ☑751 848; kumimpi@yahoo.com.sg; r 200,000-500,000Rp; ✳🖥🏊) The cheapest of the 10 bungalow-style rooms here are the best value (and are fan-only). Private gardens boast orchids and shade, and the pool is a good size. Mimpi's owner, Made Supatra, is a tireless promoter of Kuta. There are many more choices nearby.

Gemini Star Hotel
HOTEL $

(Map p52; ☑750 558; aquariushotel@yahoo.com; Poppies Gang II; r 140,000-300,000Rp; ✳🏊) Only the monosyllabic mutterings of lounging surfers interrupt the peace at this 12-room hotel on a narrow alley. A pair of two-storey blocks shelter the large and sunny pool area. Cheap rooms have fans and hot water; more money adds air-con and fridges.

Bendesa
HOTEL $

(Map p52; ☑754 366; www.bendesaaccommodation.com; off Poppies Gang II; r US$15-45; ✳🖥🏊) The 42 rooms here are in a three-storey block overlooking a pleasant-enough pool area. The location manages to be quiet amid the greater hubbub. The cheapest rooms – all clean – have cold water (some with bathtubs) and fan. Not all rooms have wi-fi.

LEGIAN

ON THE BEACH

There is a building boom going on along Legian's beachfront.

Bali Mandira Hotel
HOTEL $$$

(Map p52; ☑751 381; www.balimandira.com; Jl Pantai Kuta; r US$140-250; ✳🖥🏊) Gardens filled with bird-of-paradise flowers set the tone at this 191-room, full-service resort. Cottages have modern interiors, and the bathrooms are partly open air. A dramatic pool at the peak of a stone ziggurat (which houses a spa) offers sweeping ocean views, as does the cafe.

Maharta Beach Resort
HOTEL $$

(Map p52; ☑751 654; www.mahartabeach.com; Jl Padma Utara; r US$90-140; ✳🖥🏊) Tucked into a tiny beachfront pocket, the pretension-free Maharta is vintage but solidly maintained. Its real allure is its (admittedly narrow) beach frontage. The 34 rooms, with patios/balconies, have typical Balinese wood furnishings, and some come with bathtubs and tile floors (although none have views). Some beds boast an oddly angled overhead mirror that invites contortions by narcissists.

Sari Beach Inn
HOTEL $$

(Map p52; ☑751 635; www.saribeachinn.com; off Jl Padma Utara; r US$70-100; ✳🖥🏊) Follow your ears down a long gang to the roar of the surf at this good-value beachside hotel that defines mellow. The 21 rooms have patios and the best have big soaking tubs. Grassy grounds boast many little statues and water features.

Seaside Villas
VILLA $$$

(Map p52; ☑737 138; www.seasidebali.com; 18 Jl Pantai Arjuna; villas US$140-400; ✳🖥🏊) Tucked into a popular stretch of sand just south of ever-so-happening Double Six Beach, there are three villas set in lush gardens. There's a vague Santa Fe motif to the one- to three-bedroom units and the overall atmosphere is surprisingly intimate given the location. Pass through a double-doorway, pass a fountain and parked cars and you're on the beach.

Pullman Bali Legian Nirwana
RESORT HOTEL $$$

(Map p52; ☑762 500; www.accorhotels.com; Jl Melasti 1; r US$140-300; ✳@🖥🏊) This huge resort is composed of 387 condo units. Most units are simply one-room hotel-standard with rich wood furnishings. The resort is shaped like a club on a deck of cards and many rooms offer the full *Rear Window* peer-at-your-neighbour experience. The beach is across the busy street. Other megaresorts nearby include the new 'The Stones'.

CENTRAL LEGIAN

Island
HOTEL $$

(Map p52; ☑762 722; www.theislandhotelbali.com; Gang Abdi; dm US$25, r 550,000-700,000Rp; ✳@🖥🏊) A real find, literally. Hidden in the attractive maze of tiny lanes west of Jl Legian, this hotel lies at the confluence of gang 19, 21 and Abdi. In a rarity for Bali, it has a very deluxe dorm room with eight beds. Regular rooms are stylish and surround a nice pool.

KUTA: WHERE BALI TOURISM BEGAN

Mads Lange, a Danish copra trader and 19th-century adventurer, set up a successful trading enterprise near modern-day Kuta in 1839. He mediated profitably between local rajahs (lords or princes) and the Dutch, who were encroaching from the north. His business soured in the 1850s and he died suddenly, just as he was about to return to Denmark. It's thought that his death may have been the result of poisoning by locals jealous of his wealth. His restored **tomb** (Map p56; Jl Tuan Langa) is at the site where he used to live in a quiet, tree-shaded area by the river. Lange bred Dalmatians and today locals assume that any dog with a hint of black and white has some of this blood.

Beach tourism got its start in Bali when Bob and Louise Koke – a globetrotting couple from the US – opened a small guesthouse on virtually deserted Kuta Beach in the 1930s. The guests, mostly from Europe and the US, were housed in thatched bungalows built in an idealised Balinese style. In a prescient move, Bob taught the locals to surf, something he'd learned in Hawaii.

Kuta really began to change in the late 1960s when it became a stop on the hippie trail between Australia and Europe. By the early 1970s it had relaxed *losmen* (small Balinese hotels) in pretty gardens, friendly places to eat, vendors peddling magic mushrooms and a delightfully laid-back atmosphere. Enterprising Balinese seized the opportunity to profit from the tourists and surfers, often in partnership with foreigners seeking a pretext to stay longer.

Legian, the village to the north, sprang up as an alternative to Kuta in the mid-1970s. At first it was a totally separate development, but these days you can't tell where one ends and the other begins.

Sri Beach Inn
GUESTHOUSE $

(Map p52; ☑755 897; Gang Legian Tewngah; r 150,000-300,000Rp; ❄️🛜) Follow a series of paths into the heart of old Legian; when you hear the rustle of palms overhead, you're close to this homestay with five rooms. More money gets you hot water, air-con and a fridge. The gardens get lovelier by the year; agree to a monthly rate and watch them grow.

Legian Beach Bungalow
HOTEL $

(Map p52; ☑751 087; legianbeachbungalow@ yahoo.co.id; Jl Padma; r 150,000-250,000Rp; ❄️🏊) The entrance here is perfectly suited to the neighbourhood: it's ugly. But inside is a fine, simple budget hotel. The cheapest of the 22 rooms only have cold water but all have air-con; some have bathtubs. The single- and two-storey blocks hem in the pool.

DOUBLE SIX BEACH

Hotel Kumala Pantai
HOTEL $$

(Map p52; ☑755 500; www.kumalapantai.com; Jl Werkudara; r 700,000-1,000,000Rp; ❄️@🛜🏊) One of the better deals in Legian. The 108 rooms are large, with marble bathrooms featuring separate shower and tub. The three-storey blocks are set in very lush grounds across from popular Double Six Beach. Wi-fi charges can be high.

O-CE-N Bali
HOTEL $$$

(Map p52; ☑737 400; www.outrigger.com; Jl Arjuna 88X; r US$160-300; ❄️@🛜🏊) This flashy resort affiliated with the Outrigger chain looms over a popular stretch of Double Six Beach. The 112 rooms scattered about the concrete complex range from hotel-simple to apartment-deluxe.

Blue Ocean
HOTEL $

(Map p52; ☑730 289; off Jl Pantai Arjuna; r 200,000-400,000Rp; ❄️🏊) Almost on the beach, the Blue Ocean is a clean and basic place with hot water and pleasant outdoor bathrooms. Many of the 24 rooms have kitchens and there's action nearby day and night.

🍴 Eating

There's a profusion of places to eat around Kuta and Legian. Tourist cafes with their cheap menus of Indonesian standards, sandwiches and pizza are ubiquitous. Look closely and you'll find genuine Balinese warung tucked in amid it all.

If you're looking for the laid-back scene of a classic travellers' cafe, wander the gang and look for the crowds. For quick snacks and 4am beers, Circle K convenience stores are everywhere and are open 24 hours.

Beware of the big-box restaurants out on Jl Sunset. Heavily promoted, they suffer

from traffic noise and are aimed squarely at groups who go where the bus goes.

TUBAN
The beachfront hotels all have restaurants or cafes, which are often good for nonguests to enjoy a snack or a sunset drink.

B Couple Bar n' Grill
SEAFOOD $$

(Map p56; ☑761 414; Jl Kartika Plaza; meals 60,000-200,000Rp; ⊘24hr) A vibrant mix of upscale local families and tourists (menus are even in Russian) tuck into Jimbaran-style grilled seafood at this slick operation. Pool tables and live music add to the din while flames flare in the open kitchens.

Warung Nikmat
INDONESIAN $

(Map p56; ☑764 678; Jl Banjar Sari; meals 15,000-25,000Rp; ⊘10am-3pm) This Javanese favourite is known for its array of authentic halal dishes, including beef rendang, *perkedel* (fried corn cakes), prawn cakes, *sop buntut* (oxtail soup) and various curries and vegetable dishes. Get there before 2pm or you'll be left with the scraps.

Pantai
SEAFOOD $$

(Map p56; ☑753 196; Jl Wana Segara; meals 50,000-150,000Rp) It's location, location, location here at this dead-simple beachside bar and grill. The food is purely stock tourist (seafood, Indo classics, pasta etc) but the setting overlooking the ocean is idyllic. There's none of the pretence (or prices) of the hotel cafes common down here. Follow the beach path south past the big Ramada Bintang Bali resort.

Kafe Batan Waru
INDONESIAN $$

(Map p56; ☑766 303; Jl Kartika Plaza; meals 50,000-150,000Rp) The Tuban branch of one of Ubud's best eateries is a slicked-up version of a warung, albeit with excellent and creative Asian and local fare. There's also good coffee, baked goods and kid-friendly items such as pasta and chicken fingers.

Discovery Mall
FOOD COURT $

(Map p56; Jl Kartika Plaza; ❄) This mall is home to many places to eat, including a top-floor food court (meals 15,000Rp to 30,000Rp) with scores of vendors selling cheap, fresh Asian food. You can eat outside on a terrace overlooking Kuta Beach. Elsewhere the mall has several chain cafes and bakeries.

KUTA
Busy Jl Pantai Kuta boasts one huge beachside mall with chain restaurants, with more to come. Beach vendors are pretty much limited to drinks.

CENTRAL KUTA

TOP CHOICE Ajeg Bali
BALINESE $

(Map p52; Kuta Beach; meals 15,000Rp; ⊘8am-3pm) A simple stand right on Kuta Beach dishes up some of the freshest local fare you'll find. Tops is a bowl of spicy *garang asem*, a tamarind-based soup with free-range chicken or pork and many traditional seasonings. Come early as it's often sold out by 10am. Enter the beach where Jl Pantai Kuta turns north and walk south 100m along the beach path.

Poppies Restaurant
WESTERN, INDONESIAN $$

(Map p52; ☑751 059; Poppies Gang I; meals from 90,000Rp) Poppies was one of the first restaurants to be established in Kuta (Poppies Gang I is even named after it). It is popular for its lush garden setting: there are little pebbles underfoot and it feels slightly

---

ℹ HOTELS TOO FAR

When booking a south Bali hotel room, be careful where you book.

As tourist numbers on Bali have exploded, so have the number of chain hotels. The boom in building large hotels with room counts in the three figures in the traditional tourist areas of Kuta and Legian will ultimately change the area's character in fundamental ways, especially as the many family-run, cheap and cheerful small inns are pushed out.

However, demand for scarce development sites means that large hotels are now also cropping up in areas far from the beach. Once you get more than a few hundred metres east of Jl Legian and its northern extension Jl Seminyak, the beach will at best be a long slog. Get east of Jl Sunset and you'll be needing a scarce cab to get to the most interesting areas of the Kuta-Seminyak conurbation. Get east of Jl Ngurah Rai Bypass and you'll be on the wrong side of a traffic-choked road unsafe to cross as a pedestrian and with nothing nearby worth a walk.

mysterious in a romantic way. The delicious food is upmarket Western and Balinese.

Made's Warung INDONESIAN $$
(Map p52; Jl Pantai Kuta; meals from 40,000Rp) Made's was the original tourist warung in Kuta. Through the years, the Westernised Indonesian menu has been much copied. Classic dishes such as *nasi campur* (rice served with side dishes) are served in an open-fronted setting that harkens back to when Kuta's tourist hot spots were lit by gas lantern.

Kuta Night Market INDONESIAN $
(Map p52; Jl Blambangan; meals 15,000-25,000Rp; ⊙6pm-midnight) This enclave of stalls and plastic chairs bustles with locals and tourism workers chowing down on hot-off-the-wok treats, grilled goods and other fresh foods.

Kuta Market MARKET $
(Map p52; Jl Raya Kuta; ⊙6am-4pm) Not big but its popularity ensures constant turnover. Look for some of Bali's unusual fruits here, such as the mangosteen.

ALONG JALAN LEGIAN

The eating choices along Jl Legian seem endless; worthy choices are not.

Kopi Pot CAFE $$
(Map p52; ☑752 614; Jl Legian; meals 60,000-150,000Rp; 🛜) Shaded by trees, Kopi Pot is a favourite, popular for its coffees, milkshakes and myriad desserts. The multilevel, open-air dining area sits back from noxious Jl Legian.

Mama's GERMAN $$
(Map p52; ☑761 151; Jl Legian; meals 80,000-270,000Rp; ⊙24hr; 🛜) This German classic serves up schnitzel and other pork-heavy dishes around the clock. The menu is so authentic that you'll find dishes such as *Königsberger klopse* (pork meatballs in white sauce). Bintang comes by the litre and the open-air bar is a merry place for enjoying various other imported beers and the excellent local Storm microbrew.

ON & AROUND POPPIES GANG II

Balcony INTERNATIONAL $$
(Map p52; ☑757 409; Jl Benesari 16; meals 50,000-150,000Rp; ⊙from 5am) The Balcony has a breezy tropical design and sits above the din of Jl Benesari below. Get ready for the day with a long breakfast menu. At night it's sort of upscale surfer: pasta, grilled meats and a few Indo classics. It's all nicely done and the perfect place for an impromptu date-night.

Rainbow Cafe INTERNATIONAL $
(Map p52; ☑765 730; Poppies Gang II; meals from 50,000Rp) Join generations of Kuta denizens quaffing the afternoon away. The vibe at this deeply shaded spot has changed little since people said things like 'I grok that, man'. Many current customers are the offspring of backpackers who met at adjoining tables.

EAST OF JALAN LEGIAN

Feyloon CHINESE $$
(Map p52; ☑766 308; www.feyloonrestaurant.com; Jl Raya Kuta 98; meals 80,000-250,000Rp; 🌐) A glossy Hong Kong seafood palace where all manner of creatures swim in an aquarium's worth of tanks at the entrance, unaware that they will soon become part of your dinner. Presentation is artful and the selection vast. You can vary your eating with a number of good duck dishes. Lunch dim sum is a never-ending array of treats.

Take JAPANESE $$
(Map p52; ☑759 745; Jl Patih Jelantik; meals 70,000-300,000Rp) Flee Bali for a relaxed version of Tokyo just by ducking under the traditional fabric shield over the doorway here. Hyper-fresh sushi, sashimi and more are prepared under the fanatical eyes of a team of chefs behind a long counter. Dine at low tables or hang out in a booth.

LEGIAN

Along the streets of Legian, the ho-hum mix with the good, so browse a bit before choosing.

Indo-National WESTERN, SEAFOOD $$
(Map p52; Jl Padma 17; meals from 50,000Rp) This popular restaurant is home away from home for legions of happy fans. Grab a cold one with the rest of the crew at the bar while you take in the sweeping view of Legian's action, such as deciding which hair-plaiting style you like best. Then order the heaped-up grilled seafood platter.

Mang Engking INDONESIAN $$
(Map p52; ☑882 2000; Jl Nakula 88; meals 100,000-200,000Rp) Serving the food of Indonesia, this large restaurant is a metaphor for the islands themselves, with various thatched dining pavilions set amid ponds and water features. Hugely popular with Bali's fast-growing middle class, the long menu focuses on fresh seafood. Service is snappy like the jaws of a shark, but far more friendly.

Warung Murah

INDONESIAN $

(Map p52; Jl Arjuna; meals from 30,000Rp) Lunch goes swimmingly at this authentic warung specialising in seafood. An array of grilled fish awaits; if you prefer fowl over fin, the *satay ayam* is succulent *and* a bargain. Hugely popular at lunch; try to arrive right before noon.

Warung Asia

ASIAN, CAFE $

(Map p52; off Jl Arjuna & Jl Pura Bagus Taruna; meals from 30,000Rp; 🛜) Look down a little gang for this gem: traditional Thai and Indonesian dishes served in a stylish open-air cafe, an authentic Italian espresso machine and lots of newspapers to peruse.

Aroma's Cafe

INTERNATIONAL $$

(Map p52; ☑751 003; Jl Legian; meals 60,000-100,000Rp; 🛜) A gentle garden setting encircled by water fountains is a perfect place to start the day over great juices, breakfasts and coffee. A very pleasant place for a time out from Jl Legian.

Delicioso

GELATO $

(Map p52; Jl Padma) This small stand offers up real Italian gelato that's big on flavour and even bigger on refreshment on a hot south Bali day. A combo of creamy mango and green mint will have you cooing 'aaah'.

Warung Yogya

INDONESIAN $

(Map p52; ☑750 835; Jl Padma Utara; meals from 30,000Rp) Hidden in the heart of Legian, this simple warung is spotless and has had a mod makeover. It serves up hearty portions of local food for prices that would almost tempt a local. The gado gado comes with a huge bowl of peanut sauce.

Saleko

INDONESIAN $

(Map p52; Jl Nakula 4; meals from 15,000Rp) Just off the madness of Jl Legian, this modest open-front place draws the discerning for its simple Sumatran fare. Spicy grilled chicken and fish dare you to ladle on the volcanic sambal. Saleko is a perfect spot to start trying Indonesian fare that has not been utterly rethought for timid tourist palates. Everything is cooked halal.

ON THE BEACH

Various restaurants and cafes face the water along Jl Pantai Arjuna, and there are more along Jl Padma Utara. All are good come sunset.

TOP CHOICE Mozarella

ITALIAN, SEAFOOD $$

(Map p52; www.mozzarella-resto.com; Maharta Bali Hotel, Jl Padma Utara; meals from 60,000Rp) The best of the beachfront restaurants on Legian's car-free strip, Mozarella serves Italian fare more complex and authentic than that of its south Bali competition. Fresh fish also features; service is rather polished and you have various open-air areas for star-highlighted dining plus a more sheltered dining room.

Seaside

INTERNATIONAL $$

(Map p52; ☑737 140; Jl Double Six; meals 60,000-180,000Rp) The curving sweep of seating at this sleek place provides beach views for one and all. Upstairs, there's a vast patio with oodles of tables for counting stars after the sun goes down. Seafood and meat dishes come with a touch of style.

Zanzibar

WESTERN $$

(Map p52; ☑733 529; Jl Arjuna; meals from 50,000Rp) Always buzzing, this popular patio fronts a busy strip at Double Six Beach. Sunset is prime time; the best views are from the tables on a 2nd-floor terrace. Dishes include the *nasi* family and the burger bunch. If it's crowded, the many nearby competitors will also do just fine.

🍷 Drinking & Entertainment

Around 6pm every day, sunset on the beach is the big attraction, perhaps while enjoying a drink at a cafe with a sea view or with a beer vendor on the beach. Later on, the legendary nightlife action heats up. Many ragers spend their early evening at one of the hipster joints in Seminyak before working their way south to oblivion.

It won't take you long to find out what the venues of the moment are. The stylish clubs of Seminyak are popular with gay and straight crowds, but in general you'll find a mixed crowd anywhere in Kuta and Legian.

Check out the free mag *The Beat* (www.beatmag.com) for good club listings and other 'what's on' news.

TUBAN

DeeJay Cafe

CLUB

(Map p56; ☑758 880; Jl Kartika Plaza 8X, Kuta Station Hotel; ⏲midnight-9am) The choice for closing out the night (or starting out the day). House DJs play tribal, underground, progressive, trance, electro and more. Beware of posers who set their alarms for 5am and arrive all fresh.

KUTA

Jl Legian is lined with interchangeable bars with bar stools moulded to the butts of hard-drinking regulars.

GETTING AWAY FROM IT ALL

Dodging cars, motorcycles, touts, dogs and dodgy footpaths can make walking through Tuban, Kuta and Legian seem like anything but a holiday. It's intense and can be stressful. You may soon be longing for uncrowded places where you hear little more than the rustling of palm fronds and the call of birds.

Think you need to book a trip out of town? Well, think again. You can escape to the country without leaving the area. Swaths of undeveloped land and simple residential areas where locals live often hide behind the commercial strips.

In Legian, take any of the narrow gang into the area bounded by Jl Legian, Jl Padma, Jl Padma Utara and Jl Pura Bagus Taruna and soon you'll be on narrow paths that go past local houses and the occasional simple warung or shop. Wander at random and enjoy the silence accented by, yes, the sound of palm fronds and birds.

TOP CHOICE Sky Garden Lounge BAR, CLUB

(Map p52; www.61legian.com; Jl Legian 61; ⊗24hr) This multilevel palace of flash flirts with height restrictions from its rooftop bar where all of Kuta twinkles around you. Look for top DJs, a ground-level cafe and paparazzi-wannabes. Munchers can enjoy a long menu of bar snacks and meals, which most people pour with shots. Roam from floor to floor of this vertical playpen, where everybody seems to end up at some point.

Apache Reggae Bar BAR

(Map p52; Jl Legian 146; ⊗11pm-4am) One of the rowdier spots in Kuta, Apache jams in locals and visitors, many of whom are on the make. The music is loud, but that pounding you feel the next day is from the free-flowing *arak* (distilled palm and cane alcohol) served in huge plastic jugs. Stumbling between here and Bounty is a Kuta tradition.

Twice Bar BAR

(Map p52; Poppies Gang II; ⊗5pm-late) From the small opening, walking into this long, narrow bar feels like entering an old carnival funhouse, the kind with black walls and the potential for a surprise a step or two away. In back, however, you'll find Kuta's best effort at an indie rock club, with all the grungy – and sweaty – feel you could hope for.

Bounty CLUB

(Map p52; Jl Legian; ⊗10pm-6am) Set on a faux sailing boat amid a minimall of food and drink, the Bounty is a vast open-air disco that humps, thumps and pumps all night. Climb the blue-lit staircase and get down on the poop deck to hip hop, techno, house and anything else the DJs come up with. Foam parties, a loose sexual vibe and lots of cheap shots add to the rowdiness.

LEGIAN & DOUBLE SIX BEACH

Most of Legian's bars are smaller and appeal to a more sedate crowd than those in Kuta. The very notable exception is the area at the end of Jl Arjuna/Jl Double Six where there are cafes and clubs. A string of beach bars runs north from here on the Seminyak beachwalk.

De Ja Vu Kitchen CAFE

(Map p52; www.dejavukitchen.com; Jl Pantai Arjuna; ⊗11am-late) This former late-night club has morphed into the kind of sleek tune-filled beach cafe that is a cliché in Byron Bay, Australia. There's still plenty of house music, but now the emphasis is on drinking cocktails with improbable names while gazing at the view from the rooftop bar.

Cocoon CLUB

(Map p52; www.cocoon-beach.com; Jl Arjuna; ⊗10am-late) A huge pool with a view of Double Six Beach anchors this sort of high-concept club (alcohol-branded singlets not allowed!) which has parties and events around the clock. Beds, loungers and VIP areas surround the pool; at night some of Bali's best DJs spin theme nights.

🔒 Shopping

Kuta has a vast concentration of cheap tawdry shops, as well as huge, flashy surf-gear emporiums. As you head north along Jl Legian, the quality of the shops improves and you start finding cute little boutiques, especially past Jl Melasti. Jl Arjuna has wholesale fabric, clothing and craft stores, giving it a bazaar feel. Continue into Seminyak for absolutely fabulous shopping.

Large malls are also making inroads. In Tuban, the Discovery Mall is popular but has been literally massively overshadowed by

the flash new Beachwalk complex on Jl Pantai Kuta. Kuta Sq stumbles along, in need of new energy.

Simple stalls with T-shirts, souvenirs and beachwear are everywhere (especially along the Poppies). Many of these stalls are crowded together in 'art markets' such as the Kuta Square Art Market or the Jl Melasti Art Market, where the 'art' consists of Bintang logo reproductions.

Bali's top-selling souvenir for those left at home are penis-shaped bottle openers in a range of colours and sizes. Bargain hard to avoid paying a stiff price.

Accessories

Earthy Collection ACCESSORIES
(Map p52; ☑748 8400; Jl Legian 456) Handbags in every shape, size and colour imaginable, mostly made from materials woven right on Bali. The staff will be happy to help you realise your fantasy with a custom order.

Djeremi Shop ACCESSORIES
(Map p52; ☑0815 578 8169; Jl Legian) Woven goods for yourself and your home. If the idea of a romantic mosquito net draped over your bed gets you all itchy, come here.

Arts & Crafts

Schlocky stuff is the norm but you can find some interesting items that go beyond a gag gift at a stag or hen party.

Kiki Shop MUSIC
(Map p52; ☑0819 1612 4351; Jl Pantai Kuta) Custom-made musical instruments. Get a bongo drum and drive people mad in hostels worldwide.

Makmur Helmet HELMETS
(Map p52; ☑486 451; Jl Pura Puseh) Helmets are mandatory for riding motorbikes (a lack thereof is a good way to attract unwanted and potentially costly police interest) and this shop will kit you out in style – even if the helmets may not meet every international standard for safety. Mohawk, Viking and more.

Beachwear & Surf Shops

A huge range of surf shops sells big-name surf gear – including Mambo, Rip Curl and Billabong – although goods may be only marginally cheaper than overseas. Local names include Surfer Girl and Quiksilver. Most have numerous locations in south Bali.

Surfer Girl SURF WEAR
(Map p52; Jl Legian 138) A local legend, the winsome logo says it all about this vast store

for girls of all ages. Clothes, gear, bikinis and plenty of other stuff in every shade of bubblegum ever made.

Rip Curl SURF GEAR
(Map p52; Kuta Sq) Cast that mopey black stuff aside and make a bit of a splash! This mothership of the surfwear giant has a huge range of beach clothes, waterwear and surfboards.

Next Generation Board Bags SURF GEAR
(Map p52; ☑0813 3700 0523; Jl Benesari) Choose from myriad patterns and colours and then watch your bag (from 250,000Rp) get made on the shop floor in two days or less. There are lots of other family-run surfer shops nearby.

Bookshops

Small used-book exchanges can be found scattered along the gang and roads, especially the Poppies.

Kerta Bookshop BOOKS
(Map p52; ☑758 047; Jl Pantai Kuta 6B) A book exchange with a better-than-average selection; many break the Patterson-Brown-Cornwall mould.

Periplus Bookshop BOOKS
(Map p56; ☑769 757; Jl Kartika Plaza, Discovery Mall) Large selection of new books.

ℹ️ **FOLLOW THE PARTY**

Bali's trendiest clubs cluster in about a 300m radius of the top-rated Sky Garden Lounge. The distinction between drinking and clubbing is blurry at best, with one morphing into another as the night wears on (or the morning comes up). Most bars are free to enter, and often have special drink promotions and 'happy hours' that run at various intervals until after midnight. Savvy partiers follow the specials from venue to venue and enjoy a massively discounted night out (club owners count on the drink specials to lure in punters who then can't be bothered to leave). Look for cut-price-drinks coupon fliers.

Bali club ambience ranges from the laid-back vibe of the surfer dives to high-concept nightclubs with long drink menus and hordes of prowling servers. Prostitutes have proliferated at some Kuta clubs.

DON'T MISS

SUNSET DRINKS IN LEGIAN

Bali sunsets regularly explode in stunning displays of reds, oranges and purples. Sipping a cold one while watching this free show to the beat of the surf is the top activity at 6pm. In Legian, the best place for this is the strip of beach that starts north of Jl Padma and runs to the south end of Jl Pantai Arjuna. Along this car-free stretch of sand you'll find genial young local guys with simple chairs and cheap, cold beer (15,000Rp).

Times Bookstore BOOKS
(Map p52; ☑767 198; Kuta Sq) In Matahari Department Store, this bookshop has a good range of fiction.

Clothing
The local clothing industry has diversified from beach gear to sportswear and fashion clothing. From the intersection with Jl Padma, go north on Jl Legian to Seminyak for the most interesting clothing shops.

Animale CLOTHING
(Map p52; ☑754 093; Jl Legian 361) One of Bali's top-end international brands, Animale has the full range of its collection at this location (one of many).

Desy Shop SHOES
(Map p52; ☑733 595; Jl Arjuna 61) Zillions of sandals, all made right here. Show some interest and the owner will offer to make you 100, wholesale.

Malls & Department Stores
Beachwalk MALL
(Map p52; www.beachwalkbali.com; Jl Pantai Kuta; ◎10am-midnight) This vast open-air mall and condo development across from Kuta Beach is filled with international chains: from Gap to Starbuck's. Cooling mists pour from the ceilings and water features course amid the generic retail glitz. Other developments planned nearby will vastly overshadow quaint and tawdry Poppies Gang II and continue Kuta's transformation into a glitzy international beach resort.

Discovery Mall MALL
(Map p56; ☑755 522; www.discoveryshoppingmall. com; Jl Kartika Plaza; ◎9am-9pm) Swallowing up a significant section of the shoreline, this huge, hulking and popular enclosed Tuban mall is built on the water and filled with stores of every kind, including the large **Centro** and trendy **Sogo** department stores.

Istana Kuta Galleria MALL
(Map p52; Jl Patih Jelantik) An enormous open-air mall that seems like a dud until you find an interesting shop amid the canyon of glass. There is a hardware store in the rear if your needs run towards rope and duct tape.

Carrefour MALL
(Map p52; ☑847 7222; Jl Sunset; ◎9am-10pm) This vast outlet of the French discount chain combines lots of small shops (books, computers, bikinis etc) with one huge hypermarket. It's the place to stock up on staples and there's a large ready-to-eat section and a food court as well. The downside, however, is inescapable: it's a mall.

Matahari DEPARTMENT STORE
(Map p52; ☑757 588; Kuta Sq; ◎9.30am-10pm) This store has the basics – fairly staid clothing, a floor full of souvenirs, jewellery and a supermarket. Get some decent-quality luggage here should you need extra bags to haul your wretched excess home.

Fabric
Stroll Jl Arjuna in Legian for open-air wholesalers selling fabric, clothes and housewares. Some recommendations include the following.

Busana Agung TEXTILES
(Map p52; ☑733 442; Jl Arjuna) Here you'll find stacks of vibrant batiks and other fabrics that scream 'sew me!'.

Sriwijaya FABRIC
(Map p52; ☑733 581; Jl Arjuna 35) Makes batik and other fabrics to order in myriad colours.

Furniture
On Jl Patih Jelantik, between Jl Legian and Jl Pura Puseh, there are scores of furniture shops manufacturing everything from instant 'antiques' to wooden statues. However, a few of the stores make and sell teak outdoor furniture of very high quality at very low prices. A luxurious deckchair goes for about 200,000Rp to 300,000Rp; most of the stores work with freight agencies.

ⓘ Information
Dangers & Annoyances
The streets and gang are usually safe but there are annoyances. Scooter-borne prostitutes (who

hassle single men late at night) cruise after dark. Walking along you may hear 'massage' followed by 'young girl' and the ubiquitous 'transport' followed by 'blow'. But your biggest irritation will likely be the sclerotic traffic.

ALCOHOL POISONING There are ongoing reports of injuries and deaths among tourists and locals due to arak being adulterated with methanol, a poisonous form of alcohol. Avoid free cocktails and any offers of arak.

HAWKERS Crackdowns mean that it's rare to find carts in the Kuta tourist area, but street selling is common, especially on hassle street, Jl Legian, where selling and begging can be aggressive. The beach isn't unbearable, but the upper part has souvenir sellers and masseurs (who may grab hold of you and not let go).

SURF The surf can be dangerous, with a strong current on some tides, especially up north in Legian. Lifeguards patrol swimming areas of the beaches at Kuta and Legian, indicated by red-and-yellow flags. If they say the water is too rough or unsafe to swim in, they mean it. Red flags with skull and crossbones mean no swimming allowed. The lifeguards are very dedicated, as anyone who saw the Bali series of the show Bondi Rescue can attest.

THEFT Visitors lose things from unlocked (and some locked) hotel rooms and from the beach. Going into the water and leaving valuables on the beach is simply asking for trouble. Snatch thefts from crooks on motorbikes are more common, but valuable items can be left at your hotel reception.

WATER POLLUTION The seawater around Kuta is commonly contaminated by run-off from both built-up areas and surrounding farmland, especially after heavy rain. Swim far away from streams, including the often foul and smelly one at Double Six Beach.

Emergency
Police station (☏751 598; Jl Raya Kuta; ☺24hr) Ask to speak to the tourist police.

Tourist Police Post (☏784 5988; Jl Pantai Kuta; ☺24hr) This is a branch of the main police station in Denpasar. Right across from the beach, the officers have a gig that is sort of like a Balinese Baywatch.

Internet Access
There are scores of places to connect to the internet. Most have poky connections and charge about 300Rp a minute.

Medical Services
See p384 for medical clinics serving all of Bali.
Kimia Farma Legian (Jl Legian; ☺24hr) Kuta (☏755 622; Jl Pantai Kuta; ☺24hr) Tuban (☏757 483; Jl Raya Kuta 15; ☺24hr) Outlets of the local chain of well-stocked pharmacies.

Carries hard-to-find items, like that antidote for irksome partiers in the morning: earplugs.
Legian Medical Clinic (☏758 503; Jl Benesari; ☺on call 24hr) Has an ambulance and dental service. It's 600,000Rp for a consultation with an English-speaking Balinese doctor. Hotel room visits can be arranged.

Money
ATMs abound and can be found everywhere, including in the ubiquitous Circle K and Mini Mart convenience stores.
Central Kuta Money Exchange (☏762 970; Jl Raya Kuta) Trustworthy; deals in myriad currencies.

Post
Postal agencies that can send but not receive mail are common.
Main post office (Jl Selamet; ☺7am-2pm Mon-Thu, to 11am Fri, to 1pm Sat) On a little road east of Jl Raya Kuta, this small and efficient post office has an easy, sort-it-yourself poste restante service. It's well practised in shipping large packages.

Tourist Information
Places that advertise themselves as 'tourist information centres' are usually commercial travel agents, or worse: time-share condo sales operations.
Hanafi (☏0818 568 364; www.hanafi.net; Jl Pantai Kuta 1E) This gay- and family-friendly tour operator and guide operates in Kuta from

---

KUTA'S FAVOURITE STORE

The mobs out the front look like they're making a run on a bank. Inside it's simply pandemonium. Welcome to **Joger** (Map p56; Jl Raya Kuta; ☺11am-6pm), a Bali retail legend that is the most popular store in the south. No visitor from elsewhere in Indonesia would think of leaving the island without a doe-eyed plastic puppy (4000Rp) or one of the thousands of T-shirts bearing a wry, funny or simply inexplicable phrase (almost all are limited edition). In fact the sign out the front says 'Pabrik Kata-Kata', which means 'factory of words'. When we were there the big seller said 'I love you' in a haiku of English, Chinese and Indonesian. Warning: conditions inside the cramped store are simply insane.

a small veterinary clinic he shares with his sister. He's a valuable source of information.

ℹ Getting There & Away

Bemo

Bemos (minibuses) regularly travel between Kuta and the Tegal terminal in Denpasar – the fare should be 8000Rp. The route goes from Jl Raya Kuta near Jl Pantai Kuta, looping past the beach, then on Jl Melasti and back past Bemo Corner for the trip back to Denpasar.

Bus

For public buses to anywhere in Bali, you'll have to go to the appropriate terminal in Denpasar first.

Perama (☏751 551; www.peramatour.com; Jl Legian 39; ⊙7am-10pm) is the main shuttle-bus operation in town, and may do hotel pick-ups and drop-offs for an extra 10,000Rp (confirm this with the staff when making arrangements). It usually has at least one bus a day to its destinations, which are as follows:

Destination	Fare (Rp)	Duration
Candidasa	60,000	3½hr
Lovina	100,000	4½hr
Padangbai	60,000	3hr
Sanur	25,000	30min
Ubud	50,000	1½hr

ℹ Getting Around

The hardest part about getting around south Bali is the traffic. Besides using taxis, you can hire a motorbike, often with a surfboard rack, or a bike – just ask where you're staying. One of the nicest ways to get around the area is by foot along the beach.

To/From the Airport

An official taxi from the airport costs 35,000Rp to Tuban, 50,000Rp to Kuta and 60,000Rp to Legian. When travelling to the airport, get a metered taxi for savings.

Taxi

Bluebird Taxi (☏701 111) are the best. In traffic, a ride into Seminyak can top 50,000Rp and take more than 30 minutes; walking the beach will be quicker.

Seminyak

☏0361

Seminyak is flash, brash, phoney and filled with bony models. It's also the centre of life for hordes of the island's expats, many of whom own boutiques or design clothes, surf, or seem to do nothing at all. It may be immediately north of Kuta and Legian, but in many respects Seminyak feels almost like it's on another island.

It's also a very dynamic place, home to dozens of restaurants and clubs and a wealth of creative shops and galleries. World-class hotels line the beach – and what a beach it is, as deep and sandy as Kuta's but less crowded.

Seminyak seamlessly merges with Kerobokan, which is immediately north – in fact the exact border between the two is as fuzzy as most other geographic details on Bali. Note that despite the hype not every beachfront hotel here is world-class or charges world-class prices. All those restaurants and clubs combine to give travellers the greatest choice of style and budget in Bali. Sure there are exclusive boutiques, but there are also workshops where everything is wholesale. And when it all becomes too much, just head to a quiet corner of the beach and chill.

◉ Sights

Pura Petitenget TEMPLE
(Map p76; Jl Pantai Kaya Aya) North of the string of hotels on Jl Pantai Kaya Aya and across from the beach, this is an important temple and the scene of many ceremonies. It is one of a string of sea temples that stretches from Pura Luhur Ulu Watu on the Bukit Peninsula north to Tanah Lot in western Bali. Petitenget loosely translates as 'magic box', a treasured belonging of the legendary 16th-century priest Nirartha, who refined the Balinese religion and visited this site often.

Also in the compound, look for **Pura Masceti** (Map p76), an agricultural temple where farmers pray for relief from rat infestations, and savvy builders make offerings of forgiveness before planting yet another villa in the rice fields.

Beaches

Seminyak continues the long swath of Kuta Beach. A good stretch is found near Pura Petitenget. It is usually uncrowded and has plenty of parking (2000Rp). It is often the scene of both religious ceremonies and surfing. For the latter, hire a board at **Deluta Surf** (Map p76; Jl Petitenget 40x) right near the temple.

Another good stretch of beach runs south from the end of Jl Abimanyu to Jl Arjuna in Legian. The vendors here are mellow and a sunset lounger and ice-cold Bintang cost about 15,000Rp. A walkway makes wandering

PICK A NAME, ANY NAME

A small lane or alley is known as a gang, and most of them in Bali lack signs or even names. Some are referred to by the name of a connecting street, eg Jl Padma Utara is the gang going north of Jl Padma.

Meanwhile, some streets in Kuta, Legian and Seminyak have more than one name. Many streets are unofficially named after a well-known temple and/or business place, or according to the direction they head. In recent years there has been an attempt to impose official – and usually more Balinese – names on the streets. But the old, unofficial names are still common.

Following are the old (unofficial) and new (official) names, from north to south:

Old (unofficial)	Current (official)
Jl Oberoi	Jl Laksmana
Jl Raya Seminyak	northern stretch: Jl Basangkasa
Jl Dhyana Pura/Jl Gado Gado	Jl Abimanyu
Jl Double Six	Jl Arjuna
Jl Pura Bagus Taruna/Rum Jungle Rd	Jl Werkudara
Jl Padma	Jl Yudistra
Poppies Gang II	Jl Batu Bolong
Jl Pantai Kuta	Jl Pantai Banjar Pande Mas
Jl Kartika Plaza	Jl Dewi Sartika
Jl Segara	Jl Jenggala
Jl Satria	Jl Kediri

this stretch a breeze and you can choose from various beach bars. Come here for sunsets.

Because of the limited road access, the beaches in Seminyak tend to be less crowded than further south in Kuta. This also means that they're less patrolled and the water conditions are less monitored. The odds of encountering dangerous rip tides and other hazards are ever-present, especially as you head north.

🏃 Activities

Massages & Spas

Seminyak's spas (and those of Kerobokan) are among the best on Bali and offer a huge range of treatments, therapies and pleasures.

TOP
CHOICE **Jari Menari**   SPA
(Map p76; ☎736 740; Jl Raya Seminyak 47; sessions from 300,000Rp; ⏰10am-9pm) Jari Menari is true to its name, which means 'dancing fingers': your body will be one happy dance floor. The all-male staff use massage techniques that emphasise rhythm. Many say this is the best place for a massage in Bali, a claim backed up by numerous awards.

Prana   SPA
(Map p76; ☎730 840; www.thevillas.net; Jl Kunti; massage from 450,000Rp; ⏰10am-10pm) A palatial Moorish fantasy that is easily the most lavishly decorated spa in Bali, Prana offers everything from basic hour-long massages to facials and all manner of beauty treatments. Feel cleansed after Ayurvedic treatments.

Mana Holistics   HEALING
(Map p76; ☎318 5634; www.manaholistics.com; Jl Petitenget; treatments average 500,000Rp; ⏰9am-8pm) Rolfing, shiatsu and homeopathy are just some of the healing techniques employed at this spalike health centre that emphasises natural methods. Body cleansing – inside and out – along with detox programs are designed to give you a fresh physical palette.

Bodyworks   SPA
(Map p76; ☎733 317; www.bodyworksbali.com; Jl Kayu Jati 2; massage from 222,000Rp; ⏰9am-10pm) Get waxed, get your hair done, get the kinks rubbed out of your joints – all this and more is on the menu at this uber-popular spa in the heart of Seminyak. The rooms are airy and everything is stress-free casual.

Seminyak & Kerobokan

Cooking Schools

TOP CHOICE Sate Bali COOKING COURSE

(Map p76; ☑736 734; Jl Laksmana 22; course from 400,000Rp; ☺9.30am-1.30pm) Sate Bali runs an excellent Balinese cooking course taught by noted chef Nyoman Sudiyasa. Students learn to prepare Balinese spices and sambals, which are then used to flavour duck, fish and pork dishes. Not up to attending school? The restaurant is delicious.

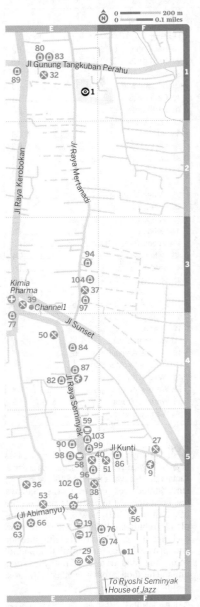

Sleeping

Seminyak has a wide range of places to stay, from world-class resorts such as the Oberoi to more humble hotels hidden away on backstreets. This is also the start of villa-land, which runs north from here through the vanishing rice fields. Booking a private villa is possible.

Many of Seminyak's most pleasant hotels are located on small lanes off major roads such as Jl Abimanyu and Jl Laksmana. They are both quiet and close to the action.

JALAN ABIMANYU & AROUND

Raja Gardens GUESTHOUSE $$
(Map p76; ✆730 494; jdw@eksadata.com; Jl Abimanyu; r 500,000-700,000Rp; ❀ 🛜 ≋) Enjoy spacious, grassy grounds in this quiet inn almost on the beach. The nine rooms are fairly bare-bones but there are open-air bathrooms and plenty of potted plants. The basic rate gets you a fan; more money buys air-con and a fridge.

Green Room GUESTHOUSE $
(Map p76; ✆731 412; www.thegreenroombali.com; Jl Abimanyu 63B; r US$40-70; ❀ 🛜 ≋) A new-age cheapie, the Green Room evokes *Robinson Crusoe* from its hammocks to its banana-tree motif. Lounge around the small, ink-blot-shaped pool or chill in the open *bale* (pavilion) with its media centre. Some of the 14 rooms (the cheapest are fan-only) in a two-storey block feature jungle themes.

Sarinande Beach Inn HOTEL $$
(Map p76; ✆730 383; www.sarinandehotel.com; Jl Sarinande 15; r 450,000-600,000Rp; ❀ 🛜 ≋) Excellent value. The 26 rooms are in older two-storey blocks around a small pool; the decor is a bit dated but everything is well maintained. Amenities include fridges, satellite TV and a cafe. The beach is three minutes by foot.

Bali Agung Village HOTEL $$
(Map p76; ✆730 367; www.bali-agung.com; off Jl Abimanyu; r/villas from US$85/150; ❀ ≋) Off a hidden backstreet, this attractive place has 42 rooms in bungalow-style units that are popular with budget-conscious groups. The grounds are lush and there's a profusion of Balinese wood and stone carvings. Look for the statue of a giraffe as you navigate along the alleys.

Ned's Hide-Away GUESTHOUSE $
(Map p76; ✆731 270; nedshide@dps.centrim.net.id; Gang Bima 3; r from 120,000Rp; ❀) There are 18 good-value basic rooms behind Bintang Supermarket. A new expansion includes some extracheap rooms.

Inada Losmen GUESTHOUSE $
(Map p76; ✆732 269; putuinada@hotmail.com; Gang Bima 9; r from 150,000Rp) Buried in a gang

Seminyak & Kerobokan

behind Bintang Supermarket, this budget champ is a short walk from clubs, beach and other Seminyak joy. The 12 rooms are small and somewhat dark.

JALAN LAKSMANA & AROUND

TOP CHOICE Oberoi
HOTEL **$$$**

(Map p76; ☎730 361; www.oberoihotels.com; Jl Laksmana; r/villas from US$260/500; ❋@🛜☀) One of the world's top hotels, the beautifully understated Oberoi has been a refined Balinese-style beachside retreat since 1971. All accommodations have private verandas, and as you move up the food chain, additional features include private villas, ocean views and private walled pools. From the cafe, overlooking the almost-private sweep of beach, to the numerous luxuries, this is a place to spoil yourself.

TOP CHOICE Samaya
VILLA **$$$**

(Map p76; ☎731 149; www.thesamayabali.com; Jl Pantai Kaya Aya; villas from US$400; ❋@🛜☀) Understated yet cultured, the Samaya has been one of the best bets right on the beach in south Bali. Now it has been completely rebuilt and the 30 villas are new, each featuring a highly tasteful interior and private pool. The 'Royal Compound' across the road trades location for larger units. The food, from breakfast onwards, is superb.

Bali Baik Villa
VILLA **$$$**

(Map p76; ☎847 8192; www.balibaikvilla.com; Jl Telaga Waja 18; r from US$200; ❋@☀) About a 10-minute walk from the beach, Bali Baik is in the heart of Seminyak's villa land. Here the units are very large and have even larger pools (no mere plunge dip here). Common areas outside are spacious and you can have no end of fun behind the privacy – ensuring walls. Staff will appear in a flash to prepare a fresh breakfast or other services.

Casa Artista GUESTHOUSE **$$$**
(Map p76; ☑736 749; www.casaartistabali.com; Jl Sari Dewi; r from US$150; ❋❈❄❆) You'll literally dance for joy at this cultured guesthouse where the owner, a professional tango dancer, offers lessons. Ten compact rooms in an elegant two-storey house surround a pool. Go for a 2nd-floor room and relax amid flamboyant bling.

Mutiara Bali HOTEL **$$**
(Map p76; ☑734 966; www.mutiarabali.com; Jl Braban 77; r US$100-140, villas from US$250; ❋@❄❆) Although hidden on a small road behind Jl Laksmana, the Mutiara is close to fine dining (two minutes) and the beach (five minutes). There are 29 good-sized and nicely furnished rooms in two-storey

blocks around a frangipani-draped pool area. Seventeen large private villas occupy one half of the compound. Wi-fi can be pricey.

Eating

Jl Laksmana is the focus of Seminyak eating but there are great choices for every budget virtually everywhere. Note that some restaurants morph into clubs as the night wears on. Conversely, some bars and clubs also have good food.

JALAN ABIMANYU

Warung Mimpi INDONESIAN **$**
(Map p76; ☑732 738; Jl Abimanyu; meals from 40,000Rp) A sweet little open-air shopfront warung in the midst of cacophonous nightlife. A dear husband-and-wife team cook Indo classics simply and well. It's all fresh and tasty.

SEMINYAK'S CURVING SPINE

The thriving heart of Seminyak lines meandering Jl Laksmana (aka Jl Oberoi). It heads towards the beach from bustling Jl Raya Seminyak and then turns north through a part of Seminyak that some people call Petitenget (and where the proper road name is the little-used Jl Pantai Kaya Aya). The road is lined with a profusion of restaurants, upscale boutiques and hotels as it curves through Seminyak and into Kerobokan. Most agree that the name changes to Jl Raya Petitenget when it eventually veers east and intersects Jl Raya Kerobokan. Like so much of Bali, it would be the perfect road for a window-shopping or cafe-hopping stroll if not for the lack of decent footpaths for pedestrians. As you dodge taxis and gaping potholes in front of an exclusive boutique, think of it as an adventure.

La Sal SPANISH $$
(Map p76; ☏738 321; www.lasalbali.com; Jl Drupadi; meals from US$15; ⊘5-11pm) The Manchego cheese comes direct from the Iberian Peninsula at this tapas place, which also has more substantial meals of steaks and paella. Dine in the twinkly garden or in the open-sided room with Moorish hints. A good selection of reds washes it all down.

JALAN RAYA SEMINYAK

TOP CHOICE **Mama San** FUSION $$
(Map p76; ☏730 436; www.mamasanbali.com; Jl Raya Kerobokan 135; meals 60,000-120,000Rp) All the action is on the 2nd floor of this buzzy warehouse-sized restaurant right on the edge of Seminyak and Sunset roads. A long cocktail list provides liquid balm for the mojito set and has lots of tropical-flavoured pours. The menu emphasises small dishes from across Southeast Asia.

Warung Taman Bambu BALINESE $
(Map p76; Jl Plawa 10; meals from 20,000Rp; ☏) You'll be diverted from reaching the pretty garden out back by the array of lovely food out front. This classic warung may look simple from the street but the comfy tables are – like the many fresh and spicy dishes on offer – a cut above the norm. There's a small stand for *babi guling* (suckling pig) right next door.

Made's Warung II INDONESIAN $$
(Map p76; ☏732 130; www.madeswarung.com; Jl Raya Seminyak; meals 40,000-160,000Rp) Freshly expanded, the northern branch of Made's has a buzz many thought unlikely for such a long-running veteran. But the well-prepared Indonesian food is as visitor-friendly as ever and the presentation artful. The little bags of Balinese snack crackers are a delight. You'll need to book (or wait) in high season.

Warung Italia ITALIAN $$
(Map p76; ☏737 437; Jl Kunti 2; meals 40,000-100,000Rp; ⊘8am-7pm; ✳) The climax in any classic warung happens at lunch, when happy diners walk along in front of the display cases and have their plates filled with a wide selection of treats. Here, warung-style meets Italian, as diners select from a range of pastas, salads and more. Next to the open-air warung area, a restaurant section with a wood-burning pizza oven features a long menu.

Mannekepis BELGIAN $$
(Map p76; ☏847 5784; www.mannekepis-bistro.com; Jl Raya Seminyak 2; meals 60,000-200,000Rp; ☏) That little icon of Brussels is permanently peeing out front at this surprisingly good Belgian bistro. Tear your eyes away from the fish swimming in the ceiling tank to peruse a selection of excellent steaks, all served with top-notch *frites*. There is live jazz and blues many nights. Sit on the upper-floor terrace away from the bedlam of the street.

Warung Ibu Made INDONESIAN $
(Map p76; Jl Raya Seminyak; meals 15,000Rp; ⊘7am-7pm) The woks roar almost from dawn to dusk amid the constant hubbub on this busy corner of Jl Raya Seminyak where several stalls cook food fresh under the shade of a huge banyan.

Bali Deli SUPERMARKET $$
(Map p76; Jl Kunti 117X) Almost at Jl Sunset, the lavish deli counter at this market is loaded with imported cheeses, meats and baked goods. This is the place to come for above-average wines for the villa or to prepare a killer picnic.

Bintang Supermarket SUPERMARKET $
(Map p76; ☏730 552; Jl Raya Seminyak 17) Always busy, this large supermarket is the grocery favourite among expats (although Carrefour is tough competition). Affordable sunscreen, bug spray and other sundries as well.

JALAN LAKSMANA

Saddled by some with the unimaginative name 'Eat Street', this restaurant row rewards the indecisive as you can stroll the strip and see what sparks a craving. Prices are uniformly popular.

TOP CHOICE Ultimo
ITALIAN $$

(Map p76; www.balinesia.co.id; Jl Laksmana 104; meals 60,000-220,000Rp) It's simple to count your way to dining joy at this vast and always popular restaurant in a part of Seminyak as thick with eateries as a good risotto. Choose a table overlooking the street action, out back in one of the gardens or inside. Ponder the surprisingly authentic menu and then let the army of servers take charge.

Sate Bali
INDONESIAN $$

(Map p76; Jl Laksmana; meals from 90,000Rp; ☺11am-10pm) Ignoring the strip-mall location, enjoy traditional Balinese dishes at this small cafe run by chef Nyoman Sudiyasa (who also has a cooking school here). The multicourse *rijsttafel* is a symphony of tastes, including the addictive *babi kecap* (pork in a sweet soy sauce) and *tum bebek* (minced duck in banana leaf).

La Lucciola
FUSION $$$

(Map p76; ☎730 838; Jl Pantai Kaya Aya; meals from 120,000Rp) A sleek beachside restaurant with good views from the 2nd-floor tables across a lovely lawn and sand to the surf. The bar is big with sunset-watchers, although most then move onto dinner. The menu is a creative melange of international fare with an Italian flair.

Hu'u
FUSION $$$

(Map p76; ☎736 443; www.huubali.com; Jl Petitenget; ☺11am-2am) Oodles of little tea candles provide a romantic glow at night for tables under the stars. There's steak, seafood and a good selection of vegetarian dishes plus interesting takes on local dishes. Service is polished; late in the evening Hu'u takes on a nightclub vibe.

Tuesday Night Pizza Club
PIZZERIA $$

(Map p76; ☎730 614, 876 6600; Jl Laksmana; pizzas 25,000-200,000Rp; ☺6pm-midnight) Tasty pizzas come in five sizes (If you're hungry? get a medium) at this joint with a postindustrial vibe. Pizzas have a range of pop-culture names like Hawaii Five-O (ham and pineapple). There are tables but fast and efficient delivery to hotels and villas is hugely popular.

Mykonos
GREEK $$

(Map p76; ☎733 253; Jl Laksmana; meals US$10-20) This long-time Greek place honours the land of Apollo with a classic menu of Hellenic standards. The excellent 'Mykonos shrimp' is fragrant with garlic and lemon.

Earth Cafe
CAFE $

(Map p76; Jl Laksmana; meals from 40,000Rp; ☑) The good vibes are organic at this vegetarian cafe and store amid the upmarket retail ghetto of Seminyak. Choose from creative salads, sandwiches or wholegrain vegan goodies. A retail section sells healthful potions and lotions. While perusing the bookshelves, don't get ahead of yourself in the colonic irrigation section.

Warung Aneka Rasa
INDONESIAN $

(Map p76; Jl Laksmana; meals from 15,000Rp) Decision time: you can get some bland, salty snack from the ubiquiutous Cirkle K or you can dive into this local gem and try some Indonesian snacks. Suggestion: do the latter. Nutty, spicy and fiery treats are sold here as well as all manner of local classics in the simplest surrounds imaginable.

Ibu Mangku
BALINESE

(Map p76; Jl Kayu Jati; meals from 20,000Rp) Where your driver takes lunch. Look for the cabs in front of this bamboo place with a serene garden out the back. The must-have is the minced-chicken satay, redolent with lemongrass and other spices. The *nasi campur* is great value.

🍷 Drinking

Seminyak has developed a full-on cafe culture. The idle masses can while away hours on terraces or overlooking the beach.

JL RAYA SEMINYAK

TOP CHOICE Buzz Cafe
CAFE

(Map p76; Jl Raya Seminyak 99; 🛜) The name is eponymous at this busy cafe located behind some rare Seminyak trees right where Jl Kunti T-bones Jl Seminyak. The open front lets you wave in fellow glitteratti as they santer past. The fresh drink of choice is the Green Hornet – a combo of lemon, lime and mint. The food is fresh and simple (meals from 30,000Rp).

Café Seminyak
CAFE

(Map p76; ☎736 967; Jl Raya Seminyak 17) Right in front of the busy Bintang Supermarket, this cute and casual place has excellent smoothies, and sandwiches made with freshly baked bread.

SEMINYAK BEACH SUNSETS

At the beach end of Jl Abimanyu in Seminyak you have a choice: turn right for trendy beach clubs, or turn left for a much more frolicsome experience. You'll discover mock-Moorish affairs with oodles of huge pillows for lounging, and all manner of simple bars lining the path along the sand. It's all more flash than the local guys selling beers from coolers in Legian but just as much fun. Often there's even live music as the light fades.

One of our favorites is Champlung, which has plush pillows and chairs clustered on the sand and traditional frilly Balinese ceremonial umbrellas providing more colour than actual shade.

Café Moka CAFE
(Map p76; ☎731 424; Jl Raya Seminyak) Enjoy French-style baked goods (fresh baguettes!) at this popular bakery and cafe. Many escape the heat and linger here for hours over little French treats. The bulletin board spills over with notices for villa rentals.

JALAN LAKSMANA

Grocer & Grind CAFE
(Map p76; Jl Kayu Jati 3X; meals from 40,000Rp; wi-fi) Keep your vistas limited and you might think you're just at a sleek Sydney cafe, but look around and you're unmistakeably in Bali, albeit one of the trendiest bits. Classic sandwiches, salads and big breakfasts issue forth from the kitchen. Eat in the open air or choose air-con tables in the deli area.

Bali Bakery CAFE
(Map p76; Jl Laksmana; wi-fi) The best features of the fashionable Seminyak Sq open-air mall in the heart of Seminyak are this bakery's shady tables and long menu of baked goods, salads, sandwiches and other fine fare. A good place to linger before heading back out to shop.

Café Zucchini CAFE
(Map p76; ☎736 633; Jl Laksmana 49) Hidden behind trees, shrubs and a vivid yellow-striped canopy, this Italian cafe is an ideal refuge from the surrounding retail pressures. Juices and various coffee drinks are the stars. There are a few substantial Italian mains if you need real sustenance.

Mano CAFE
(Map p76; Petitenget Beach) Tucked away behind Pura Petitenget, this basic beachside cafe overlooks a lovely and uncrowded stretch of sand in otherwise busy Seminyak. Escape the crowds and fake glam elsewhere for a cold one here: the sunset is just as spectacular.

☆ Entertainment

Like your vision at 2am, the division between restaurant, bar and club blurs in Seminyak. Although it lacks any real hard-core clubs where you can greet the dawn (or vice versa), stalwarts can head south to the rough edges of Kuta and Legian in the wee hours.

Numerous bars popular with gay and straight crowds line Jl Abimanyu, though noise-sensitive locals complain if things get too raucous.

JALAN ABIMANYU

Ryoshi Seminyak House of Jazz JAZZ
(Jl Raya Seminyak 17; ⊙from 8pm Mon, Wed & Fri) The Seminyak branch of the local chain of Japanese restaurants has live jazz three nights a week on an intimate stage under a traditionally thatched roof. Expect some of the best local and visiting talent.

Bali Jo LIVE MUSIC
(Map p76; Jl Abimanyu; ⊙8pm-3am) Simply fun – albeit with falsies. Drag queens rock the house, the crowd lining the street and the entire neighbourhood with songs amped to 11 nightly. Surprisingly intimate, it's a good place to lounge about for a few.

Obsession MUSIC
(Map p76; Jl Abimanyu; ⊙6pm-2am) It's rather plush and lush at this rather intimate venue. Latin, blues, soul and more add to the pink glow through the night.

JP's CAFE, BAR
(Map p76; www.jps-warungclub.com; Jl Abimanyu) From a modest open front to the street, JP's unfolds in a series of rooms that add up to a quite large U-shaped lounge with a variety of areas, from dining to dancing to chilling, which can suit most moods. Live music can be Cuban, local rock or even a well-known jazz flautist.

JALAN LAKSMANA

Red Carpet Champagne Bar BAR
(Map p76; Jl Laksmana 42) The closest most will come to posing for paparazzi is at this over-the-top glam bar on Seminyak's couture strip. Waltz the red carpet and toss back a

few namesake flutes while contemplating a raw oyster and displays of frilly frocks. It's open to the street (but elevated dahling) so you can observe the rabble.

Ku De Ta
CLUB

(Map p76; Jl Laksmana; ☉7am-1am) Ku De Ta teems with Bali's beautiful people (including those whose status is purely aspirational). Scenesters perfect their 'bored' look over drinks during the day, gazing at the fine stretch of surf right out the back. Sunset brings out crowds, who snatch a cigar at the bar or dine on eclectic fare at tables. The music throbs with increasing intensity through the night.

Zappaz
MUSIC

(Map p76; ☑742 5534; Jl Laksmana; ☉11am-midnight) Brit Norman Findlay tickles the ivories nightly at this cheerful piano bar, where he's been not-quite-perfecting his enthusiastic playing for years and years. Why suffer abuse trying to croon your way to idol-dom on TV when you can simply sing at your own bar?

🛍 Shopping

Seminyak shops could occupy days of your holiday. Designer boutiques (Bali has a thriving fashion industry), funky stores, slick galleries, wholesale emporiums and family-run workshops are just some of the choices.

The best shopping starts on Jl Raya Seminyak (aka Jl Basangkasa) at about Bintang Supermarket. The retail strip branches off into the prime real estate of Jl Laksmana and upstart Jl Kayu Jati while continuing north on Jl Raya Kerobokan into Kerobokan itself. Of course, this being Bali, try not to get too overwhelmed by the glitz or you'll step into one of the yawning pavement caverns (although Jl Raya Seminyak has been given excellent new footpaths, which make strolling a pleasure).

If you need help navigating this retail paradise, check out the 'Retail Therapy' column in the *Bali Advertiser* (www.baliadvertiser.biz). It's written by the singularly named **Marilyn** (retailtherapym@yahoo.com.au), who brings a veteran retailer's keen eye to the local scene. For advanced studies, she's available for consultations.

Accessories

Street Dogs
ACCESSORIES

(Map p76; Jl Laksmana 60) Bracelets made with shells and resin as well as recycled brass demand immediate wearing.

Vivacqua
ACCESSORIES

(Map p76; Jl Raya Seminyak 8) Bags of all shapes and sizes, from stylish ones you'll take to a top Kerobokan restaurant so you can filch a breadstick to large ones ready for all manner of beach paraphernalia.

Luna Collection
JEWELLERY

(Map p76; ☑0811 398 909; Jl Raya Seminyak) Handmade sterling-silver jewellery in a range of designs. The local craftspeople are quite creative and the mother-of-pearl works are museum quality.

Sabbatha
ACCESSORIES

(Map p76; ☑731 756; Jl Raya Seminyak 97) Megabling! The glitter, glam and gold here are almost blinding and that's just what customers want. Opulent handbags and other sun-reflecting accessories are displayed like so much king's ransom.

Beachwear

Blue Glue
WOMEN'S CLOTHING

(Map p76; Jl Raya Kerobokan) How best to show off your form on the see-and-be-seen stretches of Bali beach, especially in uberhip Seminyak? Try one of these trendy Bali-designed bathing suits at this flash new boutique.

Drifter
BEACH GEAR

(Map p76; ☑733 274; Jl Laksmana 50) High-end surf fashion, gear, books and brands such as Obey and Rhythm.

Bookshops

Periplus Bookshop
BOOKS

(Map p76; Seminyak Sq) A large outlet of the islandwide chain of lavishly fitted bookshops. Besides enough design books to have you fitting out even your garage with 'Bali Style', there's bestsellers, magazines and newspapers.

Clothing

🔺 **Dinda Rella**
WOMEN'S CLOTHING

(Map p76; ☑734 228; www.dindarella.com; Jl Raya Seminyak) Upscale frocks for women are designed and made on Bali by this much-honoured brand. The place to get that sexy little cocktail dress. There's another location on Jl Laksmana.

Milo's
CLOTHING

(Map p76; www.milos-bali.com; Jl Laksmana) The legendary local designer of silk finery has a lavish shop in the heart of designer row. Look for batik-bearing, eye-popping orchid patterns.

Lily Jean WOMEN'S CLOTHING
(Map p76; Jl Laksmana) Saucy knickers underpin sexy women's clothing that both dares and flirts; most is Bali-made. This popular shop has flash digs in fashion's ground zero.

Divine Diva WOMEN'S CLOTHING
(Map p76; Jl Laksmana 1A) It's like a Dove soap commercial for real women in this shop, filled with Bali-made breezy styles for larger figures. One customer told us: 'It's the essence of agelessness.'

Paul Ropp CLOTHING
(Map p76; www.paulropp.com; Jl Laksmana) The elegant main shop for one of Bali's premier high-end fashion designers. Most goods are made just a few kilometres away in the hills above Denpasar. And what goods they are – rich silks and cottons, vivid to the point of gaudy, with hints of Ropp's roots in the tie-dyed 1960s.

Nico Perez MENSWEAR
(Map p76; Jl Laksmana) The shop of a French designer based on Bali; look for fine linen menswear in neutrals and colours.

Samsara CLOTHING
(Map p76; Jl Raya Seminyak) True Balinese-made textiles are increasingly rare as production moves to Java and other places with cheaper labour. But the local family behind this tidy shop still sources hand-painted batik for a range of exquisite casualwear.

Biasa CLOTHING
(Map p76; www.biasabali.com; Jl Raya Seminyak 36) This is Bali-based designer Susanna Perini's

---

premier shop. Her line of tropicalwear for men and women combines cottons, silks and embroidery. The results are elegant and would pass for resortwear any place posh.

Allegra WOMEN'S CLOTHING
(Map p76; Jl Kayu Jati) Clothes that are very feminine yet also girly and quirky. The owner/designer is from Australia and this is a top spot on the booming strip of Jl Kayu Jati.

Lilla Lane SHOES
(Map p76; Jl Raya Seminyak) High-end sandals in myriad forms; suitable for local use or when you are weekending in the Hamptons or Cannes.

Le Toko CLOTHING
(Map p76; Jl Kunti) Stylish tropicalwear that will fill in for all the things you couldn't buy before you left your frozen homeland.

Coco Rose CLOTHING
(Map p76; Jl Kayu Jati) On an up-and-coming strip of shops, this boutique has ultracasual resortwear; think the sorts of sundresses you yank on over your bikini so you can go parading through the lobby.

Inti WOMEN'S CLOTHING
(Map p76; Jl Raya Seminyak 11) Shoppers tired of pawing through racks of size-2 clothes will sigh with relief at this shop filled with resortwear aimed at mature women.

Bamboo Blonde WOMEN'S CLOTHING
(Map p76; ☑780 5919; Jl Laksmana 61) Frilly, sporty or sexy frocks and more formal wear tempt from this cheery designer boutique.

Galleries

Theater Art Gallery PUPPETS
(Map p76; Jl Raya Seminyak) Specialises in vintage and reproduction puppets used in traditional Balinese theatre. Just browsing the animated faces peering back at you is a delight.

Biasa Art Space ART
(Map p76; ☑744 2902; www.biasaart.com; Jl Raya Seminyak 34) This large, airy and chilly gallery is owned by Biasa designer Susanna Perini. Changing exhibits highlight bold works.

Kody & Ko ART
(Map p76; Jl Kayu Cendana) The polychromatic Buddhas in the window set the tone for this vibrant shop of art and decorator items.

WRONG NUMBER?

Bali's landline phone numbers (those with area codes that include ☑0361, across the south and Ubud) are being changed on an ongoing basis through ☑2014. To accommodate increased demand for lines, a digit is being added to the start of the existing six- or seven-digit phone number. So ☑0361-761 xxxx might become ☑0361-4761 xxxx. The schedule and plans for the new numbers change regularly, but usually you'll hear a recording first in Bahasa Indonesian and then in English telling you what digit to add to the changed number.

There's a large attached gallery with regular exhibitions.

Kemarin Hari Ini　　　　　　GALLERY
(Map p76; ☑735 262; Jl Raya Seminyak) Glass objects created with laminated Japanese paper sparkle in the light at this airy gallery. Primitive works mix with the starkly modern.

Housewares

TOP CHOICE **Ashitaba**　　　　　　HANDICRAFTS
(Map p76; Jl Raya Seminyak 6) Tenganan, the Aga village of east Bali, produces the intricate and beautiful rattan items sold here. Containers, bowls, purses and more (from US$5) display the very fine weaving.

Folk Art Gallery　　　　　　HOMEWARES
(Map p76; ☑738 113; Jl Laksmana) Tribal and folk art from across Asia are arrayed attractively in this cute little boutique.

Les Enfants du Paradis　　　GIFTS, BEAUTY
(Map p76; www.enfants-paradis.com; Jl Raya Seminyak) A beautiful shop filled with interesting gift and personal items. The Japanese-influenced stationery may encourage you to actually write something that doesn't have an @ in the address, and the organic cosmetics are dreamy.

St Isador　　　　　　TEXTILES
(Map p76; ☑738 836; Jl Laksmana 44) The workshops upstairs spew forth lovely bed linens, pillows and other items made of fabrics imported from across Asia.

❶ Information

Seminyak shares many services with Kuta and Legian.

Dangers & Annoyances
Seminyak is generally more hassle-free than Kuta and Legian. But it's worth reading up on the warnings, especially those regarding surf and water pollution .

Medical Services
Kimia Pharma (☑916 6509; Jl Raya Kerobokan 140; ☺24hr) At a major crossroads, this pharmacy, part of Bali's best chain of pharmacies, has a full range of prescription medications.

Money
ATMs can be found along all the main roads.

Post
Postal agency (☑761 592; Jl Raya Seminyak 17, Bintang Supermarket)

❶ Getting There & Around

Metered taxis are easily hailed. A trip from the airport in an official airport taxi costs about 80,000Rp; to the airport, about half that. You can beat the traffic, save the ozone and have a good stroll by walking south down the beach; Legian is only about 15 minutes away.

Kerobokan

☑0361
Continuing seamlessly north from Seminyak, Kerobokan combines some of Bali's best restaurants, lavish lifestyles and still more beach. Hotels are upstaged by villas, which sprout from the ground like a bad rash. At times the mix of commerce and rice fields can be jarring.

❂ Sights

Unless you are eating, drinking, shopping or sleeping, there is little reason to visit Kerobokan, with one exception: **Batubelig Beach**, which continues the sweep of sand from Kuta in the south. Wave-tossed, it is still often uncrowded; a collection of rustic beach cafes was bulldozed in 2012 and the area is ripe for development.

One notable landmark is the notorious **Kerobokan jail** (Map p76), home to prisoners both infamous and unknown.

🏃 Activities

Amo Beauty Spa　　　　　　SPA
(Map p76; ☑275 3337; www.amospa.com; 100 Jl Petitenget; massage from 180,000Rp; ☺9am-9pm) With some of Asia's top models lounging about it feels like you've stepped into the studios of *Vogue*. Besides massages, other services range from hair care to pedicures and unisex waxing.

Spa Bonita　　　　　　SPA
(Map p76; ☑731 918; www.bonitabali.com; Jl Petitenget 2000X; massage from 100,000Rp; ☺9am-9pm) Part of the delightful Waroeng Bonita, this male-oriented spa has a range of services in a simple, elegant setting.

Umalas Stables　　　　　HORSE RIDING
(Map p90; ☑731 402; www.balionhorse.com; Jl Lestari 9X; beach rides from US$72) Pick your pony in this elegant compound set among the paddies. It has a stable of 30 horses and ponies, and offers 30-minute rice-field tours and two- and three-hour beach rides (a trip highlight for many tourists). Lessons in beginner to advanced equestrian events such

as dressage and show jumping can also be arranged.

🛏 Sleeping

Kerobokan is villa country, with walled developments simmering away amid rice fields. See p365 for considerations in renting a villa.

Taman Ayu Cottage
HOTEL $$

(Map p76; ☎730 111; www.tamanayucottage.com; Jl Petitenget; r US$50-100; ❋@🛜🏊) In a fast-growing part of Kerobokan sits this great-value hotel. The cottage in the name here is a bit of a misnomer, as most of the rooms are in two-storey blocks around a pool shaded by mature trees. Everything is a bit frayed around the edges, but all is forgotten when one of the hotel's pet rabbits romps over to say hello.

Grand Balisani Suites
HOTEL $$

(Map p90; ☎730 550; www.balisani.com; Jl Batubelig; r US$100-160; ❋@🛜🏊) Straddling the border between midrange and top end, this elaborately carved complex is right on ever-more-popular Batubelig Beach. The 96 rooms are large and have standard teak furniture plus terraces.

W Retreat & Spa
Bali – Seminyak
RESORT $$$

(Map p76; ☎473 8106; www.starwoodhotels.com; Jl Petitenget; r from US$300; ❋@🛜🏊) The big flash on Kerobokan's beach is this huge new resort under the guise of the trendy W brand. The usual too-cute-for-comfort vibe is at work (how 'bout an Extreme Wow Suite?) but the location on a wild stretch of sand and the views are hard to quibble with. Stylish and hip bars and restaurants abound.

The rooms all have balconies, but not all have ocean views. Amble down the long entrance lane and have a gander, noting that this is the best way to the beach in the vicinity.

🍴 Eating

Kerobokan boasts some of Bali's best restaurants, whether top end or budget.

JALAN PETITENGET

TOP
CHOICE **Sardine**
SEAFOOD $$$

(Map p76; ☎738 202; www.sardinebali.com; Jl Petitenget 21; meals US$20-50) Seafood fresh from the famous Jimbaran market is the star at this elegant yet intimate, casual yet stylish restaurant in a beautiful bamboo pavilion that is ably presided over by Pascal and Pika Chevillot. Open-air tables overlook a private rice field that is patrolled by Sardine's own flock of ducks. The inventive bar is a must and open to 1am. The menu changes to reflect what's fresh. Booking is vital.

TOP
CHOICE **Biku**
FUSION $$

(Map p76; ☎857 0888; www.bikubali.com; Jl Petitenget; meals 40,000-120,000Rp) Housed in an old shop that used to sell antiques, Biku retains the timeless vibe of its predecessor. The menu combines Indonesian, other Asian and Western influences; book for lunch or dinner. Dishes, from the exquisite breakfasts and the elegant local choices to Bali's best burger, are artful and delicious. There's a long list of teas and myriad refreshing cocktails. Many swoon at the sight of the cake table.

Waroeng Bonita
INDONESIAN $$

(Map p76; www.bonitabali.com; Jl Petitenget 2000X; meals 70,000-200,000Rp) Balinese dishes such as *ikan rica-rica* (fresh fish in a spicy greenchilli sauce) are the specialities at this cute little place with tables set out under the trees. There's a breezy style that attracts people every night but on certain nights Bonita positively heaves because of the drag shows starring everyone from visiting queens to the busboy.

Cafe Degan
ASIAN $$

(Map p76; Jl Petitenget 9; meals 90,000-160,000Rp) The young couple running this cultured little warung have created a winner. The menu veers towards Indonesian but overall features dishes from the region you don't often find, such as *daging sambal hijau* (spicy beef with green chillies). A small aircon bakery has an array of delectables for dessert.

Warung Kolega
INDONESIAN $

(Map p76; Jl Petitenget; meals 25,000Rp; ⏱11am-3pm) A Javanese halal classic. Choose your rice (we prefer the fragrant yellow), then pick from a delectable array that includes tempeh in sweet chilli sauce, *sambal terung* (spicy eggplant), *ikan sambal* (spicy grilled fish) and other daily specials. Most of the labels are in English.

Tulip
TURKISH $$

(Map p76; ☎785 8585; www.tulipbali.com; Jl Petitenget 69; meals 60,000-200,000Rp) From a long meze menu of small plates with Mediterranean flair to a more complex dinner menu of grilled meats and seafood, Tulip has a wide range of fresh and appealing choices. The open-air dining area is stylish and looks over a rice paddy. There's live music and DJs many nights and the bar menu includes shishas.

Sarong
FUSION $$

(Map p76; ☑737 809; www.sarongbali.com; Jl Petitenget 19X; meals US$10-30; ☺noon-10pm) The food is almost as magical as the setting at this top-end, high-concept restaurant. Largely open to the evening breezes, the dining room has plush furniture and gleaming place settings that twinkle in the candlelight. But opt for tables out the back where you can let the stars do the twinkling. The food spans the globe; small plates are popular with those wishing to pace an evening enjoying the commodious bar.

Bali Catering Co
BAKERY $

(Map p76; ☑732 115; Jl Petitenget 45; snacks from 30,000Rp; ❄) Like a gem store of treats, this upscale deli-bakery serves an array of fanciful little delights. Many spend all day battling the temptation of the mango ice cream; others succumb to the croissants.

Métis
FUSION $$$

(Map p76; ☑737 888; www.metisbali.com; Jl Petitenget 6; meals US$15-40) High-profile – and not just because of the huge building – Métis aims to be one of Bali's finest restaurants. It certainly has the provenance, with roots in the vaunted old Cafe Warisan (the current incarnation under that name bears no resemblance). Set ostentatiously in a surviving rice field, the restaurant and its carefully prepared cuisine work best when filled with buzzing crowds – think high season.

ELSEWHERE IN KEROBOKAN

TOP CHOICE **Warung Sobat**
SEAFOOD $

(Map p76; ☑738 922; Jl Batubelig 11; meals 50,000-150,000Rp) Set in a sort of bungalow-style brick courtyard, this old-fashioned restaurant (with bargain prices) excels at fresh Balinese seafood with an Italian accent (lots of garlic!). First-time visitors feel like they've made a discovery, and if you have the sensational lobster platter (a bargain at 350,000Rp for two; order in advance), you will too. Book.

Mozaic Beach Club
FUSION $$$

(Map p76; ☑473 5796; www.mozaic-beachclub. com; Jl Pantai Batubelig; meals 300,000-

DON'T MISS

KEROBOKAN'S FAVOURITE WARUNG

Although seemingly upscale, Kerobokan is blessed with many a fine place for a local meal. One of the very favourites is **Warung Sulawesi** (Map p76; Jl Petitenget; meals from 25,000Rp; ☺10am-6pm). Here you'll find a table in a quiet family compound and enjoy fresh Balinese and Indonesian food served in classic warung style. Choose a rice, then pick from a captivating array of dishes that are always at their peak at noon. The long beans – yum!

1,000,000Rp) The original Mozaic restaurant in Ubud is renowned for its fanatical attention to detail and that tradition continues at this beautiful beachside restaurant. No expense is spared (certainly not the customer's) in a wide-ranging menu that focuses on seasonal ingredients and fresh seafood. A casual lounge set around a pool has a long and pricey drinks and tapas menu (which includes a 'foie gras corner').

L'Assiette
FRENCH $$

(Map p76; Jl Raya Mertanadi 29; meals 50,000-100,000Rp; ☎) The huge quiet garden behind this airy cafe is the perfect place to enjoy a salad nicoise or any of the many other fresh and tasty classic French-cafe fare here. Perhaps a steak frites or a terrine will strike your fancy. If not, there are Asian-accented dishes as well.

Naughty Nuri's
INDONESIAN $$

(Map p90; Jl Batubelig 41; meals from 50,000Rp) This large Kerobokan cafe avoids the overhype of the Ubud original by delivering solid fare and the trademark kickass martinis. As you'd expect, ribs are grilling on open coals up front but whereas the main location often runs short of tables, this commodious outpost nearly always has room for you to enjoy a cold Bintang or something more fun.

Fruit Market
MARKET $

(Map p76; cnr Jl Raya Kerobokan & Jl Gunung Tangkuban Perahu; ☺7am-7pm) Bali's numerous climate zones (hot and humid near the ocean, cool and dry up the volcano slopes) mean that pretty much any fruit or vegetable can be grown within the island's small confines. Look for the full range at the many vendor tables

SHOPPING SAFARI

East of Seminyak and Kerobokan, a series of streets is lined with all manner of interesting shops selling and manufacturing housewares, baubles, fabric and other intriguing items. Head east of Kerobokan jail for about 2km on Jl Gunung Tangkuban Perahu and then turn south on – get this – a street with the same name (this is Bali, after all).

This particular Jl Gunung Tangkuban Perahu has been called 'the street of amazement' by a shopaholic friend. It meanders south, ending at Jl Gunung Soputan, which has shops in both directions, and then heads east where it ends at the intersection with Jl Sunset and Jl Kunti.

Steven's (⌨733 435; Jl Gunung Tangkuban Perahu 199) Dusty treasures from across Indonesia.

Heider (⌨0819 1644 7400; Jl Gunung Tangkuban Perahu 100) Vintage bags from Lombok; huge collection of primitive-ish carvings.

IQI (⌨733 181; Jl Gunung Tangkuban Perahu 274) Placemats, runners and other woven items made here; outfit your table for about US$5.

Wijaya Kusuma Brass (⌨0813 3870 4597; Jl Gunung Soputan) Brass accessories for furniture and your home. Who doesn't want to grab a frog pull to access their undies?

Matrái Shop (⌨729 813; Jl Gunung Atena) Smart little shop where intricate containers are made out of wire and beads. Exquisite.

---

here, including oddball fruits you'll have never seen before (try a nubby mangosteen).

☆ Entertainment

Some of Kerobokan's trendier restaurants, such as Sardine and Tulip, have stylish bar areas that stay open late.

TOP CHOICE Potato Head CLUB
(Map p76; Jl Petitenget; 🛜) Kerobokan's popular beach club is south Bali's grooviest. Wander up off the sand or follow a long drive off the main road and you'll discover a truly captivating creation on a grand scale. The clever design is striking and you'll find much to amuse, from an enticing pool to a cafe and a swanky restaurant.

🔒 Shopping

Look for boutiques interspersed with the trendy restaurants on Jl Petitenget. Jl Raya Kerobokan, extending north from Seminyak, has interesting shops primarily selling decorator items and housewares. Wander Jl Raya Mertanadi for an ever-changing line-up of homewares shops, many of them more factory than showroom.

TOP CHOICE JJ Bali Button ARTS & CRAFTS
(Map p76; Jl Gunung Tangkuban Perahu) Zillions of beads and buttons made from shells, plastic, metal and more are displayed in what

at first looks like a candy store. Elaborately carved wooden buttons are 700Rp. Kids may have to be bribed to leave.

Bathe BEAUTY, HOMEWARES
(Map p76; Jl Petitenget 100X) Double-down on your villa's romance with the handmade candles and bath salts at this shop that evokes the feel of a 19th-century French dispensary. You can't help but smile at the tub filled with rubber ducks.

Namu CLOTHING
(Map p76; Jl Petitenget) Designer Paola Zancanaro creates comfy and casual resortwear for men and women that doesn't take a holiday from style. The fabrics are lusciously tactile; many hand-painted silk.

Horn VINTAGE
(Map p76; Jl Petitenget) Vintage clothing for all ages is curated with a kooky sensibility in this large and engaging shop. The classic silks are irresistible and the accessories fun.

Ganesha Bookshop BOOKS
(Map p76; Jl Petitenget) In a corner of the fabulous Biku restaurant, this tiny branch of Bali's best bookshop up in Ubud has all manner of local and literary treats.

2nd Skin CLOTHING
(Map p76; www.2ndskinonline.com; Jl Petitenget) Handbags, jackets, miniskirts, sandals and

much more fill this rich-smelling leather boutique. But the real forte here is the custom design and tailoring. Let your imagination for all things leather run wild.

Hobo HOMEWARES

(Map p76; Jl Raya Kerobokan) Elegance mixes with quirky at this enticing shop filled with gifts and housewares, most of which can slip right into your carry-on bag. This part of Jl Raya Kerobokan abounds in shops worth browsing.

Pourquoi Pas ANTIQUES

(Map p76; Jl Raya Mertanadi) Owned by the French family behind L'Assiette, this adjoining antique store is filled with treasures from across the archipelago and Southeast Asia.

Lio HOMEWARES

(Map p76; Jl Raya Kerobokan) A minor empire with shops all along this stretch of road. Housewares, rattan antiques, reproductions and more.

Nôblis DECOR

(Map p76; ☎0815 5800 2815; Jl Raya Mertanadi 54) Feel like royalty here with regal bits of decor from around the globe.

You Like Lamp HOMEWARES

(Map p76; ☎733 755; Jl Raya Mertanadi) Why yes, we do. All manner of endearing little paper lamps – many good for tea lights – are sold here cheap by the bagful. Don't see what you want? The staff working away on the floor will rustle it up immediately.

ℹ Getting There & Around

Taxis from the airport will cost at least 100,000Rp. In either direction at rush hour the trip may verge on an hour. Note also that Jl Raya Kerobokan can come to a fume-filled stop for extended periods.

The plethora of villas can stymie even the saviest of cab drivers so it's helpful to have some sort of map or directions when you first arrive and for forays out and about during your stay. Taxis can be hailed along the main roads.

Although the beach may seem tanalisingly close, few roads or gang actually reach the sand from the east.

North of Kerobokan

☎0361

Growth is marching north and west along the coast, much of it anchored by the endless swath of beach, which, despite rampant

development, remains fairly uncrowded. Kerobokan morphs into Canggu, while neighbouring Echo Beach is a big construction site. Cloistered villas lure the well-heeled who whisk past stooped rice farmers in air-con comfort. Traffic may be the ultimate commoner's revenge: road building is a decade or two behind settlement. See the boxed text, p92 for details of the area's sandy pleasures.

CANGGU

More a state of mind than a place, Canggu is the catch-all name given to the villa-filled stretch of land between Kerobokan and Echo Beach. It is getting ever-more trendy cafes, restaurants and places to stay. It includes many beaches such as Berewa and Batu Bolong (and which are referred to by some generically as 'Canggu Beach').

If you need time away from the sand, some of Bali's best artists show at **Sukyf Arch & Art** (Map p90; www.sukyf.com; Jl Subak Sari 4; ⏰10am-6pm), an attractive gallery in the middle of ever-expanding Canggu, not far from the Canggu Club.

🏃 Activities

Very popular for surfing, the Canggu area beaches draw a lot of locals and expat residents on weekends. Access to parking areas usually costs 2000Rp and there are cafes and warung for those who work up an appetite in the water or watching others in the water.

Desa Seni YOGA

(Map p90; ☎844 6392; www.desaseni.com; Jl Kayu Putih 13; classes from 120,000Rp; ⏰varies) Desa Seni comprises classic wooden homes that have been transformed into a luxurious hotel. It is also renowned for its wide variety of yoga classes, which are offered daily and have a large following among local expats and nonguests.

Canggu Club SPORTING CLUB

(Map p90; ☎844 6385; www.cangguclub.com; Jl Pantai Berawa; day pass adult/family US$60/85; 🛜) Bali's moneyed elite shuttlecock themselves silly at the Canggu Club, a new-age version of something you'd expect to find during the Raj. The vast, perfectly virescent lawn is manicured for croquet. Get sweaty with tennis, squash, polo, cricket, the spa or the 25m pool. Many villa rentals include guest passes here.

🛏 Sleeping

TOP CHOICE **Hotel Tugu Bali** HOTEL $$$

(Map p90; ☎731 701; www.tuguhotels.com; Jl Pantai Batu Bolong; r US$200-500; ✳@🛜🏊) Right at

Canggu & Echo Beach

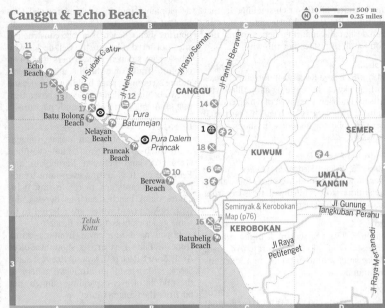

Canggu & Echo Beach

Batu Bolong Beach, this is an exquisite hotel surrounded by rice fields and beach. It blurs the boundaries between a museum and a gallery, especially the Walter Spies and Le Mayeur Pavilions, where memorabilia from the artists' lives decorates the rooms. There's a spa and customised dining options.

The stunning collection of antiques and artwork begins in the lobby and extends throughout the hotel. Even by day, candles twinkle amid the flowing fabrics in the breezy public areas. The cooking classes (from US$100) are quite luxe.

Desa Seni   HOTEL $$$
(Map p90; ☎844 6392; www.desaseni.com; Jl Kayu Putih 13; r US$150-400; ❄@🛜⛱) One person described this place as like a hippie Four Seasons, and that's not far from the truth. Desa Seni bills itself as a 'village resort', and what a village it is. Ten classic wooden homes up to 220 years old have been brought to the site from across Indonesia and turned into luxurious quarters. Guests enjoy a menu of organic and healthy cuisine plus yoga courses.

Villa Serenity — GUESTHOUSE $

(Map p90; www.balivillaserenity.com; Jl Nelayan; r 150,000-500,000Rp; ❄️🎧🏊) Funky in the best way, this hotel is an oasis among the sterility of walled villas. Rooms range from shared-bath singles to quite nice doubles with air-con and bathrooms. The grounds are appealingly eccentric; the beach a five-minute walk. There is a cafe as well as a huge DVD library. There is yoga and you can hire surfboards, bikes, cars and more.

Legong Keraton — HOTEL $$

(Map p90; ☎730 280; www.legongkeratonhotel.com; r US$100-210; ❄️@🏊) Right on the quiet sands of Berewa Beach, the well-run 40-room Legong Keraton is the perfect place for a corporate retreat. The grounds are shaded by palms and the pool borders the beach. The best rooms are in bungalow units facing the surf.

Green Room — HOTEL $$

(Map p90; ☎923 2215; www.thegreenroombali.com; Jl Subak Catur; r US$60-140; 🎧🏊) Popular with surfers, the Green Room exudes hippie chic. Lounge on the 2nd-floor veranda and check out the waves (and villa construction) in the distance. The 14 rooms are comfy and breezy with a bit of a flashpacker vibe.

✕ Eating

TOP CHOICE Green Ginger — ASIAN $

(Map p90; Jl Pantai Berawa; meals from 30,000Rp; 🌿) Art, a profusion of flowering plants and eccentric bits of furniture mark this cool little boho cafe on fast-changing strip in Canggu. The menu has fresh and tasty vegetarian dishes from across Asia.

Trattoria — ITALIAN $$

(Map p90; Jl Pantai Berawa; meals 90,000-160,000Rp) The latest outlet of this Seminyak original anchors a collection of restaurants surrounding a pleasant courtyard at the Canggu Sq complex in the centre of Canggu. Trattoria has a large menu of classic Italian fare and pizzas; other adjoining venues include sushi and a fine coffee house.

Om Cafe — INTERNATIONAL $

(Map p90; Jl Pantai Batu Bolong; mains from 30,000Rp; 🎧) Everything seems to be made of bamboo here – except the food. While the surf booms right in front of you, you can choose from a sprightly selection of fresh dishes with Asian accents. It's a fine spot to while away an afternoon and a cut above your typical beach warung.

ℹ️ Getting There & Around

You can reach the Canggu area by road from the south by taking Jl Batubelig west in Kerobokan almost to the beach and then veering north past various huge villas and expat shops along a curvaceous road. It's much longer to go up and around via the traffic-clogged Tanah Lot road. An ever-growing number of tiny lanes thread haphazardly through the rice fields and villas, allowing you to link up with the beaches.

Getting to the Canggu area can cost 70,000Rp or more by taxi from Kuta or Seminyak. Don't expect to find taxis cruising anywhere, although any business can call you one.

ECHO BEACH

One of Bali's most popular surf breaks, Echo Beach has reached critical mass in popularity and is quite the scene with tourists, expats and locals, who come down to wet their feet at the often spectacular sunsets. Meanwhile huge villa developments are filling the area. If it seems a mite crowded right at the cafes, walk 200m along the beach in either direction for solitude.

A local taxi cooperative has taxis waiting to shuttle you back to Seminyak and the south for about 70,000Rp.

🛏️ Sleeping & Eating

Cafes from basic to vaunted front some of Bali's most reliable surf breaks. Enjoy a beverage while critiquing the board-riders, or take the plunge yourself.

Canggu Mart — GUESTHOUSE $

(Map p90; ☎824 7183; Jl P Batu Mejan 88; r 150,000-350,000Rp) About 300m from Echo Beach, this basic place has four simple yet very comfy rooms (with terraces) behind a convenience store, a key resource for cheap, cold beer.

Mandira Cafe — CAFE $

(Map p90; Jl Pura Batu Mejan; meals 25,000-50,000Rp; 🎧) Although Echo Beach is rapidly going upscale, this classic surfers' dive has battered picnic tables with front-row seats for surfing action. Quaff a cheap Bintang while you Instagram the best action out on the breaks. The timeless menu includes jaffles, banana pancakes, club sandwiches and smoothies.

Beach House — CAFE $$

(Map p90; Jl Pura Batu Mejan; dishes 30,000-100,000Rp; 🎧) Face the Echo Beach waves

CANGGU

Teluk Kuta

Jl Pantai Batu Bolong

Jl Nelayan

Jl Pamelisan Agung

Jl Raya Semat

Walking Tour
Canggu Beach Walk

› Walking the sands of the Canggu area beaches you'll cover stretches of empty sand and ford a few streams with only the roar of the surf for company. A few villages, temples, expat villas and cafes provide interest away from the water. Be aware you'll get wet on this walk; have waterproof bags for everything.

Start this walk at ❶ **Batubelig Beach**. Look northwest along the beach and you can see the developments at Echo Beach in the distance. The biggest obstacle on this entire walk is only about 500m from the start.

The ❷ **river** and lagoon here flow into the ocean, often at a depth of 1m but at times not at all. However, after rains it may be much deeper. In this case, take the fun little footbridge over the lagoon to Warung Agung Kayu Putih, which has a basic menu and a phone for a taxi.

Greyish ❸ **Berewa Beach** has a couple of surfer cafes by the pounding sea; the grey volcanic sand here slopes steeply into foaming water.

Almost 1km further on you'll come to another (shallow) water crossing at ❹ **Prancak Beach** that also marks the large temple complex of Pura Dalem Prancak. A beach vendor or two may offer drinks.

A collection of fishing boats and huts marks the very mellow stretch of sand at ❺ **Nelayan Beach** that fronts villa-land just inland.

The beach at ❻ **Batu Bolong** boasts the large Pura Batumejan complex with a striking pagoda-like temple. There is surfboard hire (100,000Rp per day), impromptu lessons, some groovy cafes and a vendor 200m further on with comfy loungers.

Construction along the shore means you've reached ❼ **Echo Beach**, where cafes offer relaxation after your adventurous walk. A growing flock of stores means you can replace any clothes that are drenched beyond repair, otherwise retrieve your camera from its waterproof bag and nab shots of the popular surf break.

from stylish loungers or chill on a variety of couches and picnic tables. Enjoy the menu of breakfasts, salads, grilled fare and tasty dishes such as calamari with aioli. On Sunday nights it offers a hugely popular outdoor barbecue.

PERERENAN BEACH

Yet to be found by the right developer, Pererenan Beach is for you if you want your sand windswept and your waves unridden. It's an easy 300m further on from Echo Beach across sand and rock formations (or over 1km by road). This also marks the end of any walk that followed the vast sweep of sand that begins near the airport.

Once you've found it, why leave? The friendly guys at **Pondok Wisata Nyoman** (Map p90; ☑0812 390 6900; pondoknyoman@ yahoo.com; Jl Raya Pantai Pererenan; r 200,000-500,000Rp) have four simple rooms (although the bathrooms have a certain colourful flair) just behind the beach. There are also a couple of good cafes here that don't have the mobs of Echo Beach but still enjoy sweeping surf views.

South Bali & the Islands

Best Places to Eat

» Bumbu Bali (p109)
» Cak Asm (p123)
» Teba Mega Cafe (p98)
» Manik Organik (p116)

Best Places to Stay

» Hotel La Taverna (p113)
» Indiana Kenanga (p129)
» Temple Lodge (p101)
» Alila Villas Ulu Watu (p104)

Why Go?

You won't have seen Bali if you haven't fully explored south Bali. The island's capital, Denpasar, sprawls in all directions from the centre and is a vibrant place, offering traditional markets, glitzy malls, great eating and plenty of Balinese history and culture, even as it threatens to absorb the tourist hubs of Seminyak, Kuta and Sanur.

The Bukit Peninsula (the southern part of south Bali) has multiple personalities. In the east, Tanjung Benoa is a beach-fronted playground of modest resorts while Nusa Dua attempts to bring order out of chaos with an insulated pasture of five-star hotels. On the west side, however, is where the real action is. Small coves and beaches are dotted with edgy little guesthouses and five-star eco-resorts. The vibe, derived from the fab surfing around Ulu Watu, is funky and free.

To the east, the haunted island of Nusa Penida dominates the horizon, but in its lee you'll find Nusa Lembongan, the ultimate island escape from the island of Bali.

When to Go

The best time to visit south Bali is outside the high season, which is July, August and the weeks around Christmas and New Year's Day. Visitor numbers spike and rooms from Bingin to Tanjung Benoa and Sanur to Nusa Lembongan may be filled. Many prefer April to June and September when the crowds are manageable. Surfing is best at the world-class breaks along the west coast of the Bukit Peninsula from February to November, with May to August being especially good.

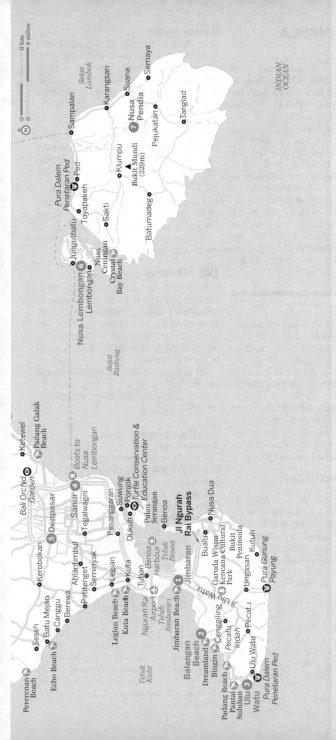

South Bali & the Islands Highlights

1 Picking a lobster for the grill at one of the many beachfront seafood joints in **Jimbaran** (p97)

2 Perching precariously on a bamboo stilt bar at **Balangan Beach** (p99)

3 Surfing **Ulu Watu** (p103), where boards break on the world-class breaks

4 Watching from **Sanur** (p110) as a full moon climbs over Nusa Penida, casting a mysterious glow over everything

5 Savouring the best US$2 meal you've ever had in **Denpasar** (p123)

6 Escaping a small island (Bali) for a funkier, smaller one: **Nusa Lembongan** (p127)

7 Diving from **Nusa Penida** (p133), where you can swim with manta rays and other large fish

BUKIT PENINSULA

📞0361

Hot and arid, the southern peninsula is known as Bukit (meaning 'hill' in Bahasa Indonesia). It's popular with visitors, from the cloistered climes of Nusa Dua to the sybaritic retreats along the south coast.

The booming west coast with its string-of-pearls beaches is a real hot spot. Accommodation sits precariously on the sand at Balangan Beach while the cliffs are dotted with idiosyncratic lodges at Bingin and elsewhere. New places sprout up daily and most have views of the turbulent waters here, which have world-famous surf breaks all the way south to the important temple of Ulu Watu. For full details of the famous and infamous surf breaks along the Bukit Peninsula and around Ulu Watu, see p29.

Jimbaran

Located just south of Kuta and the airport, Teluk Jimbaran (Jimbaran Bay) is an alluring crescent of white-sand beach and blue sea, fronted by a long string of seafood warung and ending at the southern end in a bushy headland, home to the Four Seasons Jimbaran Bay.

Jimbaran remains a relaxed alternative to Kuta and Seminyak to the north (and you can't beat the airport access!). Its markets are fun to visit and even with some new resorts appearing it should still be a good escape.

◎ Sights & Activities

TOP CHOICE Fish Market   MARKET

(Jimbaran Beach; ⊙6am-3pm) A popular morning stop on Bukit Peninsula ambles is this smelly, lively and frenetic fish market – just watch where you step. Brightly painted boats bob along the shore while huge cases of everything from small sardines to fearsome langoustines are hawked. The action is fast and furious.

Jimbaran Beach   BEACH

One of Bali's very best beaches, Jimbaran's 4km-long arc of sand fronts its namesake bay. The sand is mostly very clean and there is no shortage of places to get a snack, a drink, a seafood dinner or to rent a sun lounger. The bay keeps the surf mellower than at Kuta, although you can still get breaks that are fun for body surfing.

Morning Market   MARKET

(Jl Ulu Watu; ⊙6am-noon) This is one of the best markets in Bali for a visit because: a) it's compact so you can see a lot without wandering forever; b) local chefs swear by the quality of the fruits and vegetables (ever seen a cabbage that big?); and c) they're used to tourists tromping about.

Pura Ulun Siwi   TEMPLE

(Jl Ulu Watu) Across from the morning market, this ebony-hued temple from the 18th century is a snoozy place until it explodes with life, offerings, incense and more on a holy day.

Ganeesha Gallery   GALLERY

(📞701 010; www.fourseasons.com; Four Seasons Jimbaran Bay) Ganeesha has exhibitions by international artists and is worth a visit – walk south along the beach.

🛏 Sleeping

Some of south Bali's most luxurious large resorts are found in and around Jimbaran, as well as a few midrange places off the beach. Most offer some form of shuttle through the day to Kuta and beyond. A new Meridien Resort near the southern seafood warung will be a stylish addition.

Being a much more 'real' place (ie it's not an artificially planned resort), Jimbaran makes a good resort alternative to the monoliths of Nusa Dua.

TOP CHOICE Four Seasons
Jimbaran Bay   RESORT HOTEL $$$

(📞701 010; www.fourseasons.com; villas from US$800; ✳@🛜🏊) Each of the 147 villas here is designed in a traditional Balinese manner, complete with a carved entrance way, which opens onto an open-air dining pavilion overlooking a plunge pool. The spa is guests-only, which maintains the very exclusive air. The site is a hillside overlooking Jimbaran Beach, which is a very short walk away; most villas have good views across the bay.

Keraton Jimbaran   HOTEL $$$

(📞701 991; www.keratonjimbaranresort.com; Jl Mrajapati; r US$160-300; ✳@🛜🏊) Sharing the same idyllic Jimbaran Beach as the neighbouring pricier resorts, the low-key Keraton is a good find. Its 102 rooms are scattered about one- and two-storey bungalow-style units. The grounds are spacious and typically Bali-lush. Turn right as you hit the beach and you're almost immediately at the Middle Seafood Warung.

Jimbaran

0 — 400 m
0 — 0.2 miles

Udayana Kingfisher Eco Lodge
LODGE **$$**

(☎747 4204; www.ecolodgesindonesia.com; r US$70-85; ✱@🕏🏊) Feel like a bird perched in a green canopy from the 2nd-floor common areas of this lodge, which is a bit of a Bukit oasis. There are grand views over south Bali from its perch on a knoll in 70 hectares of bushland. The 10 rooms are comfortable and there is an inviting common area with an excellent library. Much effort has been made to preserve and reuse water. The lodge is inland near Udayana University, off a road that runs uphill from the McDonald's on the bypass.

Jimbaran Puri Bali
HOTEL **$$$**

(☎701 605; www.jimbaranpuribali.com; Jl Yoga Perkanti; cottages from US$300; ✱@🕏🏊) Under the umbrella of luxe Orient-Express Resorts, this beachside retreat is set in nice grounds complete with a mazelike pool that looks onto open ocean. The 41 cottages have private gardens, large terraces and a stylish room design with sunken tubs. It's a lavish yet low-key escape.

Hotel Puri Bambu
HOTEL **$$**

(☎701 377; www.hotelpuribambu.com; Jl Pengeracikan; r US$75-105; ✱@🕏🏊) A mere 200m from the beach, the flash-free Puri Bambu is an older but well-run place – and the best-value option in Jimbaran. The 48 standard rooms (some with tubs) are in three-storey blocks around a large pool.

✗ Eating

Jimbaran's three groups of seafood warung cook fresh barbecued seafood every evening, drawing tourists from across the south. The open-sided affairs are right by the beach and perfect for enjoying sea breezes and sunsets. Tables and chairs are set up on the sand almost to the water's edge.

Fixed prices for seafood platters in a plethora of varieties have become common and allow you to avoid the sport of choosing your fish and then paying for it by weight on scales that cause locals to break out in laughter. However, should you go this route, be sure to agree on costs first. Generally, you can enjoy plenty of grilled seafood, sides and a couple of beers for under US$20 per person. Lobster will goose that figure up considerably.

The best kitchens marinate the fish in garlic and lime, then douse it with chilli and oil while grilling over coconut husks. Thick clouds of smoke from the coals are part of the atmosphere, as are roaming bands, who perform cheery, dated tunes from the 'Macarena' playlist. Almost all take credit cards.

PASCAL CHEVILLOT: SEAFOOD CHEF

Owner of the very popular Sardine restaurant in Kerobokan, Chevillot is a fixture at the Jimbaran fish market up to six mornings a week – so he knows what's been brought in fresh.

Best Market

The Jimbaran fish market. New seafood arrives constantly as boats pull up to the beach. You know you'll find certain things like excellent shellfish all the time, but it's also an adventure as you are constantly surprised.

Best Fish for Sale Here

Sea bream, mahi mahi, skate, snapper and more.

Best Way to Visit

Get there as early as possible and then stay out of the way. Wander around the dark interior; it's like a warren and you'll be surprised at what Bali's waters yield. The vendors are actually happy to see you there, figuring you'll eat more seafood.

Also right on the beaches, the luxury hotels' cafes and restaurants afford beautiful views of the surf, sea and sunset.

NORTHERN SEAFOOD WARUNG

The longest row of warung is the northern seafood warung, south of the fish market. This is the area you will likely be taken to by a taxi if you don't specify otherwise. Most of these places are restaurant-like, with tables inside and out on the immaculate raked sand. Call for free transport to/from much of the south. Note that this is the area with the hardest sell from legions of guys flagging down your driver.

Blue Marlin SEAFOOD $$
(Jl Pantai Kedonganan; meals 80,000-200,000Rp) Most of the northern places are like this brick-clad establishment.

MIDDLE SEAFOOD WARUNG

The middle seafood warung are in a compact group just south of Jl Pantai Jimbaran and Jl Pemelisan Agung. These are the simplest affairs, with old-fashioned thatched roofs and wide-open sides. The beach is a little less manicured, with the fishing boats resting up on the sand. Huge piles of coconut husks await their turn on the fires.

Roman Café SEAFOOD $$
(☑703 124; Jl Pantai Kedonganan; meals 80,000-200,000Rp) Always seems just a slight cut above the cheek-to-jowl competition.

Warung Bamboo SEAFOOD $$
(off Jl Pantai Jimbaran; meals 80,000-200,000Rp) Warung Bamboo is slightly more appealing than its neighbours, all of which have a certain raffish charm.

SOUTHERN SEAFOOD WARUNG

The southern seafood warung (also called the Muaya group) are a compact collection at the very south end of the beach. There's a parking area off Jl Bukit Permai, and the beach here is well groomed with nice trees. Call for transport.

Teba Mega Cafe SEAFOOD $$
(off Jl Bukit Permai; meals 80,000-200,000Rp) Teba is the favourite of many long-term Bali expats. Its seafood platters are just a smidge better than the rest.

Lei Lei Seaside Barbeque SEAFOOD $$
(off Jl Bukit Permai; meals 80,000-200,000Rp) An especially cheery outpost, with sparkling tanks filled with future taste-treats.

🔒 Shopping

Jenggala Keramik Bali Ceramics CERAMICS
(Jl Ulu Watu II; ⊘9am-6pm) This modern warehouse showcases beautiful ceramic homewares that are a favourite Balinese purchase. There's a viewing area where you can watch production as well as a cafe. Ceramic courses are available for adults and children.

❶ Getting There & Away

Plenty of taxis wait around the beachfront warung in the evening to take diners home (about 60,000Rp to Kuta). Some of the seafood warung provide free transport if you call first. Expect to pay 2000Rp per vehicle to use the beach access roads.

Around Jimbaran

Folding around limestone bluffs, sightly **Tegalwangi Beach**, 4.5km southwest of Jimbaran, is the first of cove after cove holding patches of lovely sand all down the west coast of the peninsula. A small parking area lies in front of **Pura Segara Tegalwangi** temple, a popular place for addressing the ocean gods. There's usually a lone drinks vendor offering refreshment before – or after – you make the short but challenging trip over the bad paths down to the beach. Immediately south, the vast Ayana resort sprawls over the cliffs.

From Jimbaran, follow Jl Bukit Permai past the Four Seasons Jimbaran Bay for 3km until the gates of the Ayana, when it veers west 1.5km to the temple.

Central Bukit

Jl Ulu Watu goes south of Jimbaran, climbing 200m up the peninsula's namesake hill, affording views over southern Bali.

Garuda Wisnu Kencana Cultural Park (GWK; Map p100; ☑703 603; admission 15,000Rp, parking 5000Rp; ☺8am-6pm; ⓘ) is the yet-to-be-completed, potentially huge cultural park that is meant to be home to a 66m-high statue of Garuda. This Brobdingnagian dream is supposed to be erected on top of a shopping and gallery complex, for a total height of 146m.

So far the only completed part of the statue is the large bronze head. The buildings that do exist are mostly empty. However, besides the perverse fascination with big things gone bad, there's another good reason to visit the site: the **views**. From a small cafe off the parking lot there are sweeping vistas across all of south Bali. And if it's clear enough to see the volcanoes, then GWK is a must-stop off the main Ulu Watu road.

About 2km south off GWK is a vital crossroads with a useful landmark, the **Nirmala Supermarket** (Map p100). There are ATMs and a few cafes here.

Balangan Beach

Balangan Beach is a real find. A long, low strand at the base of the cliffs is covered with palm trees and fronted by a ribbon of near-white sand, picturesquely dotted with white sun umbrellas. Surfer bars, cafes in shacks and even slightly more permanent guesthouses precariously line the shore where buffed First World bods soak up rays amid Third World sanitation. Think of it as a bit of the Wild West not far from Bali's glitz.

At the northern end of the beach is a small temple, **Pura Dalem Balangan** (Map p100). Bamboo beach shacks line the southern end, visitors laze away with one eye cast on the action at the fast left surf break here.

🛏 Sleeping & Eating

You have two choices for spending the night at Balangan Beach. Firstly, you can stay up on the bluff at some fairly simple yet quite nice guesthouses that have pools and an air of permanency. The beach is a mere five-minute walk away. Or you can find a room in one of the beach shacks where many of the bars have small, windowless thatched rooms next to cases of Bintang. Be sure to negotiate and you should be able to pass out to the sounds of alcohol-fuelled hilarity backed by the roar of the surf for under 100,000Rp.

Flower Bud Bungalows GUESTHOUSE $$ (Map p100; ☑0828 367 2772; www.flowerbudbalangan.com; r 350,000-600,000Rp; ❀❄) On the knoll. Eight bamboo bungalows are set on spacious grounds near a classic kidney-shaped pool. There's a certain Crusoe-esque motif, and fans and sprightly pillows are among the 'luxuries.'

PILLAGING BUKIT PENINSULA

Many environmentalists consider the always-arid Bukit Peninsula a harbinger for the challenges that face the rest of Bali as land use far outpaces the water supply. The small guesthouses that once perched above and on the string of pearls that are the beaches on the west side had a modest impact on the environment. But with the area's exploding popularity have come large developments, which in unregulated Bali are having a huge impact. Besides the vast Pecatu Indah development, a growing number of projects are carving away the beautiful limestone cliffs to make way for huge concrete structures housing condos such as the **Anantara** (www.balianantarauluwatu.com), a lavish resort built into the side and above a previously unspoiled stretch of coast.

Now, however, a nascent protest movement has formed and environmental groups are questioning unfettered development. How it plays out will have effects on Bali's future beyond the peninsula.

Balangan Beach & Ulu Watu

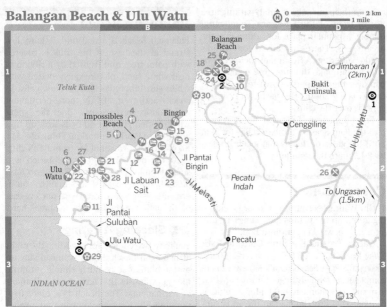

Balangan Beach & Ulu Watu

Balangan Sea View Bungalows GUESTHOUSE **$$**
(Map p100; ☑0812 376 1954; robbyandrosita@hotmail.com; r 375,000-650,000Rp; ☞❄) A cluster of thatched bungalows with 25 rooms surrounds a small pool all located in an attractive compound. The small cafe has wi-fi. It is situated directly across from Flower Bud Bungalows.

Point
GUESTHOUSE **$**

(Map p100; ☑0857 3951 8317; r 200,000-300,000Rp) Built on actual rocks on the beach using cement blocks, the Point sits slightly apart from its bamboo-stilted neighbours. The five rooms have fans and windows; a couple look out to the surf, some 10m distant. The porch cafe is shady.

Nasa Café
CAFE **$**

(Map p100; meals from 30,000Rp) A vibrant azure ribbon of crashing surf is the wraparound view through the drooping thatched roof of the bamboo bar builton stilts above the sand. Simple Indo meals set the tone for the bare-bones rooms off the bar (about 100,000Rp), which are little more than a mattress on the floor. It's one of about a dozen similar choices.

Man Sis Cafe
CAFE **$**

(Map p100; 0819 1653 8049; meals from 30,000Rp) A bamboo place on the sand that could star in any post-apocalyptic beach fantasy, Man Sis has a sign on a broken surfboard, grandma slicing vegetables up front, US$10 beds upstairs and cold Bintang around the clock.

ℹ️ Getting There & Away

Balangan Beach is 6.2km off the main Ulu Watu road via Cenggiling. Turn west at the crossroads at Nirmala Supermarket, which is a good place to stock up on necessities like water. The road to the beach takes many twists and turns, but it is paved and there are a few signs. When you near the bluff, the road ends at a large parking area at the north end of the beach with good steps down (although then it is a 300m slog through soft sand to the action).

Taxis from the Kuta area cost at least 50,000Rp per hour for the round trip and waiting time.

Pecatu Indah

This 400-hectare **resort complex** (www .balipecatu.com) rises between central Bukit Peninsula and the coast. The land is arid but that hasn't stopped developers from building a huge hotel, condos, houses and a water-sucking 18-hole golf course. Follow the grand boulevards and you can see a lot of tank trucks hauling water in all the way from Denpasar.

Less obvious is the gradual destruction of a sweet little beach community named Dreamland for the construction of **Klapa** (Map p100; ☑848 4581; Pecatu Indah; admission

100,000Rp; ⊙10am-11pm), a brash and heavily promoted beach club where disco lights flash as you enter. There's no arguing with the views, however, which you can enjoy along with a pool and the privatised beach. Note that parking is a stiff 5000Rp. The area is being marketed under the moniker 'New Kuta Beach.'

Bingin

An ever-evolving scene, Bingin comprises several funky lodgings scattered across cliffs and on the strip of white-sand beach below. A rough 1km road turns off the paved main road (look for the thicket of accommodation signs).

An elderly resident collects 5000Rp at a T-junction (and will offer you a bootleg DVD) near parking for the trail down to the beach. The surf here is often savage but the sands are calm and the roaring breakers mesmerising.

The scenery here is simply superb, with sylvan cliffs dropping down to a row of surfer cafes and the foaming edge of the azure sea. The beach is a five-minute walk down a fairly steep path.

🛏️ Sleeping & Eating

More than two dozen places to stay are scattered along and near the cliffs. All have at least simple cafes, although for nightlife – like the rest of this coast – you'll be heading north to Kuta (unless your idea of nightlife is more intimate).

The following places are all fairly small and are noninvasive to the overall clifftop Bingin atmosphere.

TOP CHOICE Temple Lodge
BOUTIQUE HOTEL **$$**

(Map p100; ☑0857 3901 1572; www.thetemplelodge. com; r US$60-230; 🛜🏊) Funky and artsy just begin to describe this beautiful collection of huts and cottages made from thatch, driftwood and other natural materials. Sitting on a jutting shelf on the cliffs above the surf breaks there are superb views from the infinity pool and some of the seven units. At night you can arrange for suitably exquisite meals.

Mick's Place
GUESTHOUSE **$$**

(Map p100; ☑0812 391 3337; www.micksplacebali. com; r/villa from US$100/300; ✳️🛜🏊) The turquoise water in the postage-stamp infinity pool matches the turquoise sea below. Something of a hippie-chic playground, this highly personable place with six artful round huts is set in lush grounds. Candles

DAMN MONKEYS

Pura Luhur Ulu Watu is home to scores of grey monkeys. Greedy little buggers, when they're not energetically fornicating, they snatch sunglasses, handbags, hats and anything else within reach.

If you want to start a riot, peel them a banana...

provide the flickering ambience at night and by day there's the 180-degree view. Don't expect luxe amenities, this is all about roughing it in style.

Mu
GUESTHOUSE $$

(Map p100; ☏847 0976; www.mu-bali.com; r €60-270; ✳@☎☒) Turn left after the toll gate for the most stylish option in Bingin. Eleven very individual bungalows with round, pointed thatched roofs are scattered about a compound dominated by a cliffside infinity pool. All have open-air living spaces; some have air-con bedrooms and hot tubs with a view.

Bingin Garden
GUESTHOUSE $

(Map p100; ☏0816 472 2002; tommybarrell76@yahoo.com; r from 250,000Rp) Six basic rooms in bungalows are set around tidy grounds back from the cliffs and 300m north of the toll gate. Each unit sleeps two and has cold water and a fan.

Merta Sari Bungalows
GUESTHOUSE $

(Map p100; ☏0815 5805 8724; Jl Pantai Bingin; r 150,000-300,000Rp) Just before the toll gate, there are eight simple rooms here set in lush grounds. It's very quiet and you can expect good service from the affable manager, Ryan (a name to trust!). The more expensive rooms have hot water and air-con.

Jiwa Juice
CAFE $

(Map p100; ☏742 4196; Jl Melasti; mains 20,000-30,000Rp; ✳) Jiwa means 'soul', and the juices and fresh, light food here are good for the same. This popular roadside stop has internet access.

Impossibles Beach

About 100m west of Jl Pantai Bingin on Jl Melasti you'll see another turn towards the ocean. Follow this paved road for 700m and look for a scrawled sign on a wall reading Impossibles Beach. Follow the treacherous path and you'll soon understand the name.

It's a tortuous trek but you'll be rewarded with an empty cove with splotches of creamy sand between boulders.

Padang Padang

Small in size but not in perfection, Padang Padang Beach is a cute little cove. It is near Jl Melasti where a small river flows into the sea. Parking is easy and it is a short walk through a temple and down a well-paved trail.

If you are feeling adventurous, you can beat the crowds here and enjoy a much longer stretch of deserted white sand that begins on the west side of the river. Ask locals how to get there.

A metered taxi from Kuta will cost about 150,000Rp and take an hour, depending on traffic.

🛏 Sleeping & Eating

The main road near Padang Padang is becoming dotted with good places to eat and sleep.

Pink Coco Bali
HOTEL $$

(Map p100; ☏824 3366; www.pinkcocobali.com; Jl Melasti; r US$60-150; ✳☎☒) One of the pools at this romantic hotel is suitably tiled pink. The 21 rooms have terraces and balconies plus artistic touches. There is a lush Mexican motif throughout. Surfers are catered to and you can hire bikes and other gear.

Thomas Homestay
GUESTHOUSE $

(Map p100; ☏0813 3803 4354; r from 200,000Rp) Enjoy stunning views up and down this spectacular coast. Seven very simple rooms lie at the end of a very rough 400m track off the main road. You can take a long walk down stairs to the mostly deserted swath of Padang Padang Beach west of the river.

Guna Mandala Inn
HOTEL $

(Map p100; ☏0815 5891 6575; Jl Melasti; r 150,000-250,000; ☎) Two-storey blocks surround the courtyard of this very well-run hotel just across the road from the entrance to Padang Padang Beach. The 20 cold-water rooms are basic but comfy, with chairs for sitting outside.

Trattoria
ITALIAN $$

(Map p100; Jl Melasti; meals from 60,000Rp; ☎) The entire Ulu Watu area had an upgrade in cuisine when Bali's home-grown chain of Italian eateries opened an outlet here. Enjoy pasta classics and great pizza in an open-air dining room in front of the Pink Coco Bali hotel.

Ulu Watu & Around

Ulu Watu has become the generic name for the southwestern tip of the Bukit Peninsula. It includes the much-revered temple and the fabled namesake surf breaks.

About 2km north of the temple there is a dramatic cliff which has steps that lead to the legendary Ulu Watu surf breaks. All manner of cafes and surf shops spill down the nearly sheer face to the water below. Views are stellar and it is quite the scene.

◉ Sights & Activities

Pura Luhur Ulu Watu　　　　TEMPLE
(Map p100; admission incl sarong & sash hire 20,000Rp; ☺8am-7pm) This important temple is perched precipitously on the southwestern tip of the peninsula, atop sheer cliffs that drop straight into the ceaseless surf. You enter through an unusual arched gateway flanked by statues of Ganesha. Inside, the walls of coral bricks are covered with intricate carvings of Bali's mythological menagerie. Only Hindu worshippers can enter the small inner temple that is built onto the jutting tip of land. However, the views of the endless swells of the Indian Ocean from the cliffs are almost spiritual. At sunset, walk around the clifftop to the left (south) of the temple to lose some of the crowd.

Ulu Watu is one of several important temples to the spirits of the sea along the south coast of Bali. In the 11th century the Javanese priest Empu Kuturan first established a temple here. The complex was added to by Nirartha, another Javanese priest who is known for the seafront temples at Tanah Lot, Rambut Siwi and Pura Sakenan. Nirartha retreated to Ulu Watu for his final days when he attained *moksa* (freedom from earthly desires).

An enchanting and popular Kecak dance is held in the temple grounds at sunset.

Surf Breaks　　　　SURFING
Ulu Watu (Ulu's) is a storied surf spot – the stuff of dreams and nightmares. Its legend is matched closely by nearby **Pantai Suluban**. Since the early 1970s these breaks have drawn surfers from around the world. The left breaks seem to go on forever. The area boasts numerous small inns and warung that sell and rent out surfboards, and provide food, drink, ding repairs or a massage – whatever you need most.

🛌 Sleeping & Eating

The cliffs above the main Ulu Watu breaks are lined with cafes and bars. There are also plenty of cheap and midrange places to stay; your best bet is to wander around and check out a few.

Gong　　　　GUESTHOUSE $
(Map p100; ☎769 976; thegongacc@yahoo.com; Jl Pantai Suluban; r from 200,000Rp; @☀) Few stay away long from the Gong. Twelve tidy rooms with good ventilation and hot water face a small compound with a lovely pool; some have distant ocean views. It is about 1km south of the Ulu Watu cliffside cafes.

Sriyana　　　　GUESTHOUSE $
(Map p100; ☎0878 6149 6402; Jl Pantai Suluban; r 300,000-400,000Rp; ☀☀) It seems like another new budget place aimed at surfers opens every week in Ulu Watu. It was a good week when the Sriyana opened as the 10 bungalow-style units here are basic but clean and modern with terraces and views of the large pool. The Ulu Watu cliffside is a short walk west.

Delpi Rock Lounge　　　　CAFE $
(Map p100; meals from 50,000Rp) At one branch of the Delpi empire, you can nab a sunbed on a platform atop a rock nearly surrounded by surf. Further up the cliff there is a cafe which has three simple rooms for rent (room from 300,000Rp).

Single Fin　　　　CAFE $
(Map p100; meals from 50,000Rp) Right near the east parking area above the Ulu Watu surf break and cliffs, this is a top spot for those who don't want to clamber down the steep concrete steps to the cafes close to the action. The views are panoramic and you can choose from a classic beach menu of sandwiches, seafood and Indo fare. The cocktail list reflects the splash of style at the bar.

Yeye's Warung　　　　CAFE $
(Map p100; Jl Labuan Sait; meals from 30,000Rp) A gathering point away from the cliffs at a spot between Padang Padang and Ulu Watu, Yeye's has an easygoing ambience, cheapish beers and tasty Indonesian, Western and vegetarian food. Many gather at night for the pizza.

☆ Entertainment

Kecak Dance　　　　TRADITIONAL DANCE
(Map p100; Pura Luhur Ulu Watu; admission 80,000Rp; ☺sunset) Although the performance

WORTH A TRIP

PANDAWA BEACH

An old quarry on Bali's remote southern coast of the Bukit Peninsula is being transformed into a fascinating detour and day trip. Four 23m statues of Hindu gods are being carved into huge niches in the side of the limestone cliffs above the seaside village of **Kutuh**. As if this wasn't reason enough to visit, there is a long swath of sand known as Pandawa Beach, which is all but deserted most of the time except for a few village seaweed farmers.

A couple of warung provide refreshments and sun-lounger hire and the reef-protected waters are good for swimming. Look for signs reading 'Kantor Perbekel Desa Kutuh' on the main road between Ungasan and Nusa Dua. It's then 2km down to the village where you can park by the sand.

obviously caters for tourists, the gorgeous setting at Pura Luhur Ulu Watu in a small amphitheatre in a leafy part of the grounds makes it one of the more evocative on the island. The views out to sea are as inspiring as the dance.

ℹ Getting There & Away

The best way to see the Ulu Watu region is with your own wheels. Note that the cops often set up checkpoints near Pecatu Indah for checks on motorcycle-riding Westerners. Be aware you may pay a fine for details such as a 'loose' chin strap.

Coming to the Ulu Watu cliffside cafes from the east on Jl Melasti you will first encounter a gated parking area (car/motorcycle 5000/3000Rp), which is right at the cliffs. Continuing over a bridge, there is a side road that leads to another parking area (car/motorcycle 2000/1000Rp), from where it is a pretty 200m walk north to the cliffside cafes.

A taxi ride out here will cost at least 160,000Rp, which makes getting a car and driver for the day a better bet given the flexibility you'll have to explore.

Ungasan & Around

If Ulu Watu is all about celebrating the surfer vibe, Ungasan is all about celebrating yourself. From crossroads near this otherwise nondescript village, roads radiate to the south coast where some of Bali's most exclusive oceanside resorts can be found. With the infinite turquoise waters of the Indian Ocean rolling hypnotically in the distance it's hard not to think you've reached the end of the world, albeit a very comfortable one.

◉ Sights

Bali's southernmost **beach** can be found at the end of a 3km-long road from Ungasan

village. Here you can see **Pura Gunung Payung**, a temple that sits on the seaside. Newish concrete steps lead down the 200m cliff to a sweet swath of sand on the pounding ocean. Bring a picnic and a good book to enjoy the atmosphere.

Diminutive **Pura Mas Suka** (Map p100) is reached by a twisting narrow road through a mostly barren red-rock landscape that changes dramatically when you reach the Karma Resort, which surrounds the temple. A perfect example of a Balinese seaside temple, it is often closed so consider that before setting off on the rough track from the good resort road to the temple.

🛏 Sleeping & Eating

TOP CHOICE **Alila Villas Ulu Watu**   RESORT $$$
(Map p100; ☎848 2166; www.alilahotels.com; r from US$685; ❇@☎☲) Visually stunning, this vast new destination resort has the full seal of eco-approval from Green Globe (something others in the area might emulate...). Designed in an artful contemporary style that is at once light and airy while still conveying a sense of wealth, the 85-unit Alila offers gracious service in a setting where the blue of the ocean contrasts with the green of the surrounding (hotel-tended) rice fields. It's 2km off the main Ulu Watu road, about 1km south of Pecatu Indah.

Karma Kandara   RESORT HOTEL $$$
(Map p100; ☎848 2200; www.karmaresorts.com; Ungasan; villas from US$600; ❇@☎☲) More Mediterranean than Balinese, this beautiful resort clings to the side of hills that roll down to the sea. Stone paths lead between walled villas draped in bougainvillea and punctuated by painted doors, creating the mood of a tropical hill town. Units come with one to four bedrooms. The restaurant,

Di Mare (meals US$15-30), is linked to the bifurcated property by a little bridge, and is a popular lunch stop for day trippers. The beach cove below is reached via a little elevator. Bear left at the fork in the main Ulu Watu road, about 1km south of the junction with the roads to Balangan Beach and Ungasan, and continue 4km to the Karma.

Nusa Dua

Nusa Dua translates literally as Two Islands – although they are actually small raised headlands, each with a small temple, including Pura Bias Tugal. But Nusa Dua is much better known as Bali's gated compound of resort hotels. It's a vast and manicured place where you leave the rest of the island behind as you pass the guards. Gone are the street vendors, hustle, bustle and engaging chaos of the rest of the island. Here you even talk more quietly.

Built in the 1970s, Nusa Dua was designed to compete with international beach resorts the world over. Balinese 'culture,' in the form of attenuated dances and other performances, is literally trucked in for the masses nightly.

With thousands of hotel rooms, Nusa Dua can live up to some of its promise when full, but during slack times it's rather desolate. Certainly, it is closer in atmosphere to a generic beach resort than to anything Balinese – although some of the hotels try to apply a patina of Bali style.

◉ Sights & Activities

TOP CHOICE **Pasifika Museum** MUSEUM
(☏774 559; Bali Collection Shopping Centre, Block P; admission 70,000Rp; ◷10am-6pm) When groups from the nearby resorts aren't around, you'll probably have this large museum to yourself. Several centuries of art from cultures around the Pacific Ocean are displayed (the tikis are cool). The influential wave of European artists who thrived in Bali in the early 20th century is well represented. Look for works by Arie Smit, Adrien Jean Le Mayeur de Merpes and Theo Meier.

Pura Gegar TEMPLE
Just south of Gegar Beach is a bluff with a good cafe and a path that leads up to Pura Gegar, a compact temple shaded by gnarled old trees. Views are great and you can spy on swimmers who've come south in the shallow, placid waters around the bluff for a little frolic.

Beach Promenade WALKING
One of the nicest features of Nusa Dua is the 5km-long beach promenade that stretches the length of the resort and continues north along much of the beach in Tanjung Benoa. Not only is it a good stroll at any time but it also makes it easy to sample the pleasures of the other beachside resorts. The beaches along the walk are all clean; offshore reefs mean that surf sounds are almost nil.

Spas SPA
All the resort hotels have pricey spas that provide a broad range of therapies, treatments and just plain, simple relaxation. The most lauded of the spas are at the Amanusa, Westin and St Regis hotels in Nusa Dua and at the Conrad in Tanjung Benoa. All are open to nonguests; expect fees for a massage to start at US$100.

Fly Bali PARAGLIDING
(☏0812 391 6918; www.flybali.info; rides from US$80; ◷May-Oct) From May to October the winds along the south-facing sheer limestone cliffs near Nusa Dua are good for paragliding. You can go for a tandem ride with an instructor that lasts up to 30 minutes before settling down onto the reef-protected sandy beaches at the base of the cliffs. Licensed fliers can hire gear and lessons are available.

Bali National Golf Resort GOLF
(☏771 791; www.baligolfandcountryclub.com) This golf club has an 18-hole course which is closed until sometime in 2013 for a major reconstruction. Already upscale, it is set to become more of a duffer's paradise and offer more rewards to the ever-growing number of condos and resorts lining its links.

Gegar Beach BEACH
The once gemlike Gegar Beach has been all but obliterated by a 700-room resort. There's a few water-sports vendors, but it is no longer worth the trek, despite its old legend living on.

🛏 Sleeping

The Nusa Dua hotels are similar in several ways: they are all big (some are huge) and almost every major internatiopnal brand is represented. Each has several restaurants and bars, as well as various pools and other resort amenities (some are right on the

Nusa Dua

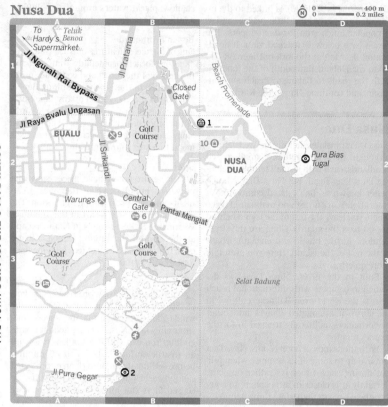

Nusa Dua

◉ Sights
1 Pasifika Museum.....................................C2
2 Pura Gegar...B4

◈ Activities, Courses & Tours
3 Bali National Golf Resort B3
4 Gegar Beach...B4

▣ Sleeping
5 Amanusa..A3

6 Novotel Nusa Dua..................................B3
7 St Regis Bali Resort...............................B3

⊗ Eating
8 Nusa Dua Beach Grill.............................B4
9 Warung Dobiel..B2

⬚ Shopping
10 Bali Collection.......................................C2

placid beach). But what's most important is the detail, as that's where the real differences lie. Some hotels, such as the Westin and Grand Hyatt, have invested heavily in property, adding loads of amenities (such as elaborate pools and day camps for kids) demanded by travellers today. Other hotels seem little changed from when they were built during the heyday of the Suharto era in the 1970s.

If you're considering a stay at Nusa Dua, prowl the internet looking for deals. During the low season you can get excellent deals that bring nightly rates down by up to half.

Amanusa RESORT HOTEL **$$$**
(772 333; www.amanresorts.com; villas from US$850; ✳@☎☂) Overlooking the golf course and across Selat Badung in the distance, the Amanusa is one of Bali's best hotels. The elegant, understated architecture, rich decorations, superb service and brilliant views are the province of just 35 individual villas. Guests enjoy a nearby private beach.

St Regis Bali Resort RESORT **$$$**
(847 8111; www.starwoodhotels.com; ste from US$600; ✳@☎☂) This lavish Nusa Dua resort leaves most of the others in the sand. Every conceivable luxury is provided, from the electronics to the furnishings and the marble to a personal butler. Pools abound and units are huge. The golf course and beach adjoin.

Novotel Nusa Dua HOTEL **$$**
(848 0555; www.novotelnusaduabali.com; r US$100-160; ✳@☎☂) The closest sand to this 188-unit resort is the bunkers on the golf course that surrounds the complex. Large apartments here come with one to three bedrooms and are excellent for families. The beach is a 10-minute walk away.

✗ Eating

Restaurants charging resort prices can be found by the dozen in the huge resorts. For people not staying at the hotels, the best reason to venture in is if you want a bounteous Sunday brunch.

Good warung cluster at the corner of Jl Srikandi and Jl Pantai Mengiat. Also along the latter street, just outside the central gate, there is a string of open-air eateries offering an unpretentious alternative to Nusa Dua dining. None will win any culinary awards, but most will provide transport.

Nusa Dua Beach Grill INTERNATIONAL **$**
(Jl Pura Gegar; meals 50,000-150,000Rp) A hidden gem, this warm-hued cafe is just south of Gegar Beach and the huge Mulia resort on foot, but a circuitous 1.5km by car via the temple. The drinks menu is long, the seafood fresh and the atmosphere heavy with assignations. Lounge your afternoon away in the laid-back bar.

Warung Dobiel BALINESE **$**
(Jl Srikandi; meals from 25,000Rp; ☉10am-3pm) A bit of authentic joy amid the bland streets of Nusa, this warung celebrates pork. And what pork it is! The succulent pork satay is marinated for hours before it's grilled. The pork soup is the perfect taste-bud awakener, while the jackfruit is redolent with spices. Diners perch on stools and share tables.

☆ Entertainment

Most of the hotels offer Balinese dances on one or more nights, usually as part of a buffet deal. Hotel lounges also often have live music, from crooners to mellow rock bands.

🔒 Shopping

Bali Collection MALL
(771 662; www.bali-collection.com) This shopping centre has undergone numerous name changes. Often empty except for the dozens of assistants in the glacially air-conditioned Sogo Department Store, it gamely soldiers on. A few souls try to make merry on their Bali holiday at the deserted Starbucks. Good luck. Although the problems can be traced to Nusa Dua's rigorous security and closed nature, the isolation means that the boom that other local malls are enjoying is a bust here.

ℹ Information

ATMs can be found at the Bali Collection shopping centre, some hotel lobbies and at the huge Hardy's Supermarket on the bypass.

ℹ Getting There & Around

Bus

Bali's new Trans-Sarbagita Bus System serves Nusa Dua on a route that follows Jl Ngurah Rai Bypass up and around past Sanur to Batabulan.

Shuttle

Find out what shuttle-bus services your hotel provides before you start hailing taxis. A free **shuttle bus** (771 662; ☉9am-10pm) connects all Nusa Dua and Tanjung Benoa resort hotels with the Bali Collection shopping centre about every hour. Better: walk the delightful beach promenade.

Taxi

The fixed taxi fare from the airport is 120,000Rp; a metered taxi to the airport will be much less. Taxis to/from Seminyak average 90,000Rp, although traffic can make this a 90-minute trip.

Tanjung Benoa

The peninsula of Tanjung Benoa extends about 4km north from Nusa Dua to Benoa village. It's flat and lined with family-friendly

Tanjung Benoa

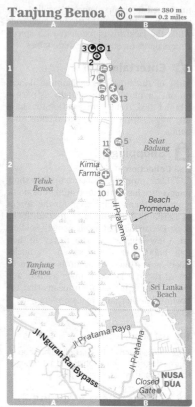

Tanjung Benoa

resort hotels, most of midrange calibre. By day the waters buzz with the roar of dozens of motorised water-sports craft. Group tours arrive by the busload for a day's excitement, straddling a banana boat among other thrills.

Beaches here are protected from waves by an offshore reef, which has allowed a local beach-activities industry to flourish in the placid waters. Overall, Tanjung Benoa is a fairly sedate place and the late-night diversions of Kuta and Seminyak are a bit of a hike.

⊙ Sights

The village of Benoa is a fascinating little fishing settlement that makes for a good stroll. Amble the narrow lanes of the peninsula's tip for a multicultural feast. Within 100m of each other are a brightly coloured **Chinese Buddhist temple**, a domed **mosque** and a **Hindu temple** with a nicely

carved triple entrance. Enjoy views of the busy channel to the port. On the dark side, Benoa's back streets hide Bali's illegal trade in turtles, although regular police raids are helping.

🎓 Courses

Bumbu Bali Cooking School COOKING COURSE
(☏774 502; www.balifoods.com; Jl Pratama; courses US$90; ⊙6am-3pm) Heinz von Holzen runs this much-lauded cooking school at his restaurant that strives to get to the roots of Balinese cooking. Courses start with a 6am visit to Jimbaran's fish and morning markets, continues in the large kitchen and finishes with lunch.

🛏 Sleeping

Tanjung Benoa's east shore is lined with midrange low-key resorts aimed at groups. They are family-friendly, offer kids' programs and enjoy repeat business by holidaymakers who are greeted with banners such as 'Welcome Back Goodhead Family!' There's also a couple of simple guesthouses.

Rumah Bali GUESTHOUSE $$
(☏771 256; www.balifoods.com; r US$85-100, villas from US$320; ⏃@🕸🏊) Rumah Bali is a luxurious interpretation of a Balinese village by Heinz von Holzen of Bumbu Bali fame. Guests have large family rooms or individual villas (some with three bedrooms) with

their own plunge pools. Besides a large communal pool, there's also a tennis court. The beach is a short walk away.

Conrad Bali Resort
RESORT HOTEL $$$

(☎778 788; www.conradhotels.com; Jl Pratama; r from US$260; ✳@🖥✉) Tanjung Benoa's flashiest hotel combines a modern Bali look with a refreshing, casual style. The 298 rooms are large and thoughtfully designed. Some units have patios with steps right down into the 33m pool, easing the morning dip. Bungalows have their own private lagoon and there is a large kids' club.

Pondok Agung
GUESTHOUSE $

(☎771 143; roland@eksadata.com; Jl Pratama; r 250,000-500,000Rp; ✳🖥) The nine airy rooms (most with tubs) in a large, houselike building are spotless. Higher-priced rooms come with small kitchens. The gardens are fairly large and attractive.

Princess Benoa Beach Resort
HOTEL $$

(☎771 604; www.princessbenoaresort.com; Jl Pratama 101; r US$85-120; ✳@✉) Newly constructed on the site of a resort of the same name, the 61-room Princess is across the street from the beach, which means you're that much further away from the howl of the jet skis. The grounds are spacious as is the 25m pool. The service is classically Balinese, relaxed yet caring.

Pondok Hasan Inn
GUESTHOUSE $

(☎772 456; hasanhomestay@yahoo.com; Jl Pratama; r 250,000Rp; ✳🖥) Back off the main road, this family-run homestay has nine immaculate hot-water rooms that include breakfast. The tiles gleam on the outdoor veranda shared by the rooms and there is a small garden.

Bali Khama
RESORT HOTEL $$$

(☎774 912; www.thebalikhama.com; Jl Pratama; villas from US$200; ✳@🖥✉) Set on its own crescent of sand at the northern end of the beach promenade. The mostly individual walled villas are large, tasteful and – obviously – private.

🍴 Eating

Each hotel has several restaurants, with the Conrad Bali Resort having a good and evolving selection. The usual batch of tourist restaurants can be found along Jl Pratama, with their modestly priced – and modestly good – pasta and seafood for the masses.

TOP CHOICE Bumbu Bali
BALINESE $$

(☎774 502; www.balifoods.com; Jl Pratama; mains/ set menus from 90,000/225,000Rp; ⊙noon-9pm) Long-time resident and cookbook author Heinz von Holzen, his wife Puji and an enthusiastic staff serve exquisitely flavoured dishes at this superb restaurant. Many diners opt for one of several lavish set menus. The *rijstaffel* (rice table) shows the range of cooking in the kitchen from satays served on their own little coconut husk grill to the tender *be celeng base manis* (pork in sweet soy sauce) with a dozen more courses in between.

SOUTH BALI & THE ISLANDS TANJUNG BENOA

ROYALTY & EXPATS

Sanur was one of the places favoured by Westerners during their pre-WWII discovery of Bali. Artists Miguel Covarrubias, Adrien Jean Le Mayeur de Merpes and Walter Spies, anthropologist Jane Belo and choreographer Katharane Mershon all spent time here. The first tourist bungalows appeared in Sanur in the 1940s and '50s, and more artists, including Australian Donald Friend (whose antics earned him the nickname Lord Devil Donald), made their homes in Sanur. This early popularity made Sanur a likely locale for Bali's first big tourist hotel, the Sukarno-era Grand Bali Beach Hotel.

During this period, Sanur was ruled by insightful priests and scholars, who recognised both the opportunities and the threats presented by expanding tourism. Properly horrified at the high-rise Grand Bali Beach Hotel, they imposed the famous rule that no building could be higher than a coconut palm. They also established village cooperatives that owned land and ran tourist businesses, ensuring that a good share of the economic benefits remained in the community.

The priestly influence remains strong, and Sanur is one of the few communities still ruled by members of the Brahmana caste. It is known as a home of sorcerers and healers, and a centre for both black and white magic. The black-and-white chequered cloth known as *kain poleng*, which symbolises the balance of good and evil, is emblematic of Sanur.

Another highlight is the amazingly tasty and different *jaja batun bedil* (sticky dumpling rice in palm sugar). Tables are set under the stars and in small pavilions. The sound of frogs can be heard from the fish ponds. There's complimentary transport in the area. It's wise to book.

Bali Cardamon
ASIAN $$

(☏773 745; www.balicardamon.com; Jl Pratama 99; mains from 60,000Rp) A cut above most of the other restaurants on the Jl Pratama strip, this ambitious spot has a creative kitchen that takes influences from across Asia. It has some excellent dishes including pork belly seasoned with star anise. Sit under the frangiapani trees or in the dining room. The staff is especially cheery.

Tao
ASIAN $$

(www.taobali.com; Jl Pratama 96; mains 60,000-100,000Rp) On its own swath of pure-white sand, Tao is one of the few options for a leisurely lunch right by the beach in Tanjung Benoa. Although it is part of the Ramada Resort, the hotel is across the street and Tao avoids the 'sign-for-it' vibe. A large curling pool wends between the tables. The food is an eclectic mix of Asian (but a club sandwich awaits philistines).

ℹ️ Information

Kimia Farma (☏916 6509; Jl Pratama) Reliable chain of pharmacies; gives referrals to doctors.

ℹ️ Getting There & Around

Taxis from the airport cost 120,000Rp. Take a bemo to Bualu, then take one of the infrequent green bemo that shuttle up and down Jl Pratama (5000Rp) – after about 3pm bemo become very scarce on both routes.

A free **shuttle bus** (☏771 662; ⊙9am-10pm) connects all Nusa Dua and Tanjung Benoa resort hotels with the Bali Collection shopping centre about every hour. Or stroll the beach promenade.

SANUR

☏0361

Maybe Sanur is the Bali beachfront version of the youngest of the Three Bears, the one that's not too frantic (like Kuta) or too snoozy (like Nusa Dua). Many do indeed consider Sanur 'just right' (and don't suffer the fate of Goldilocks), as it lacks most of the hassles found to the west while maintain-

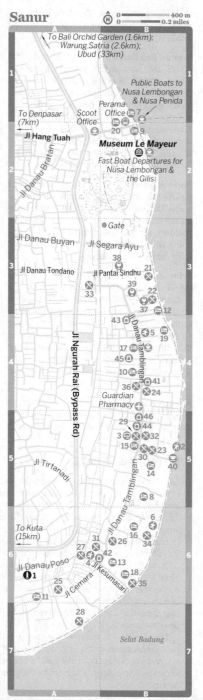

Sanur

Sanur

ing a good mix of restaurants and bars that aren't all owned by resorts.

The beach, while thin, is protected by a reef and breakwaters, so families appreciate the limpid waves. Sanur has a good range of places to stay and it's well placed for day trips around the south, and north to Ubud. Really, it doesn't deserve its local moniker, 'Snore'.

Sanur stretches for about 5km along an east-facing coastline, with the lush and green landscaped grounds of resorts fronting right onto the sandy beach. West of the beachfront hotels is the busy main drag, Jl Danau Tamblingan, with hotel entrances and oodles of tourist shops, restaurants and cafes.

Noxious, traffic-choked Jl Ngurah Rai, commonly called Bypass Rd, skirts the western side of the resort area, and is the main link to Kuta and the airport. You don't want to stay out here.

◎ Sights

Sanur's sights – views to Nusa Penida and of local life amid the tourism – are all readily apparent from its lovely beachfront walk.

TOP
CHOICE **Museum Le Mayeur** MUSEUM
(☎286 201; adult/child 10,000/5000Rp; ☺7.30am-3.30pm) Le Mayeur de Merpes (1880–1958) arrived in Bali in 1932. Three years later, he met and married the beautiful Legong dancer Ni Polok when she was just 15. They lived in this compound, which houses the museum, when Sanur was still a quiet fishing village. The main house must have been delightful – a peaceful and elegant home filled with art and antiques right by the tranquil beach. After the artist's death, Ni Polok lived in the house until she died in 1985. The house is an interesting example of Balinese-style architecture – notice the beautifully

WATER SPORTS

Water-sports centres along Jl Pratama offer daytime diving, cruises, windsurfing and waterskiing. Each morning convoys of buses arrive from all over south Bali bringing day trippers, and by 10am parasailers float over the water.

All feature unctuous salespeople whose job it is to sell the banana-boat ride of your dreams while you sit glassy eyed in a thatched-roof sales centre and cafe. Check equipment and credentials before you sign up, as a few tourists have died in accidents.

Among the established water-sports operators is **Benoa Marine Recreation** (Map p108; ☑0361-77 1757; Jl Pratama). As if by magic, all operators have similar (negotiable) prices. Water sports here include the following (with average prices):

» **Banana-boat rides** Wild rides for two as you try to maintain your grasp on the inflatable fruit moving over the waves (US$20 per 15 minutes).

» **Diving** Around Tanjung Benoa, including equipment hire (US$80/95 for one/two dives).

» **Glass-bottomed boat trips** The nonwet way to see the denizens of the shallows (US$50 per hour).

» **Jet-skiing** Go fast and belch smoke (US$25 per 15 minutes).

» **Parasailing** Iconic; you float above the water while being towed by a speedboat (US$20 per 15-minute trip).

» **Snorkelling** Trips include equipment and a boat ride to a reef (US$25 per hour).

One nice way to use the beach here is at Tao (p110) restaurant, where for the price of a drink, you can enjoy resort-quality loungers and a pool.

carved window shutters that recount the story of Rama and Sita from the Ramayana.

Despite security (some of Le Mayeur paintings have sold for US$150,000) and conservation problems, almost 90 of Le Mayeur's paintings are displayed inside the museum in a naturalistic Balinese interior of woven fibres. Some of Le Mayeur's early works are impressionist paintings from his travels in Africa, India, the Mediterranean and the South Pacific. Paintings from his early period in Bali are romantic depictions of daily life and beautiful Balinese women – often Ni Polok. The works from the 1950s are in much better condition and show fewer signs of wear and tear, displaying the vibrant colours that later became popular with young Balinese artists. Look for the haunting black-and-white photos of Ni Polok.

Stone Pillar
ANCIENT MONUMENT

The pillar, down a narrow lane to the left as you face Pura Belangjong, is Bali's oldest dated artefact and has ancient inscriptions recounting military victories of more than a thousand years ago. These inscriptions are in Sanskrit and are evidence of Hindu influence 300 years before the arrival of the Majapahit court.

Bali Orchid Garden
GARDENS

(☑466 010; www.baliorchidgardens.com; Coast Rd; admission 50,000Rp; ⊙8am-6pm) Given Bali's warm weather and rich volcanic soil, no one should be surprised that orchids thrive in abundance here. At this garden you can see thousands of orchids in a variety of settings. It's 3km north of Sanur along Jl Ngurah Rai, just past the major intersection with the coast road and is an easy stop on the way to Ubud.

🏃 Activities

Sanur's beach curves in a southwesterly direction and stretches for over 5km. It is mostly clean and overall quite serene – much like the town itself. Offshore reefs mean that the surf is reduced to tiny waves lapping the shore. With a couple of unfortunate exceptions, the resorts along the sand are low-key, leaving the beach uncrowded.

Jamu Traditional Spa
SPA

(☑286 595; www.jamutraditionalspa.com; Jl Danau Tamblingan 41; massage from 550,000Rp) The beautifully carved teak and stone entry sets the mood at this gracious spa, which offers a range of treatments including a popular

Earth & Flower Body Mask and a Kemiri Nut Scrub. Can't you just feel the 'ahhhhhhhh'?

Glo Day Spa
SPA
(☏282 826; www.glo-day-spa.com; Jl Danau Poso 57, Gopa Town Centre; sessions from 150,000Rp; ⊙8am-6pm) An insider pick by the many local Sanur expats, Glo eschews a fancy setting for a clean-lined storefront. Services and treatments span the gamut, from skin and nail care to massages and spa therapies.

Surf Breaks
SURFING
Sanur's fickle breaks (tide conditions often don't produce waves) are offshore along the reef. The best area is called **Sanur Reef**, a right break in front of the Inna Grand Bali Beach Hotel. Another good spot is known as the **Hyatt Reef**, in front of, you guessed it, the Bali Hyatt. You can get a fishing boat out to the breaks for 200,000Rp per hour.

Crystal Divers
DIVING
(☏286 737; www.crystal-divers.com; Jl Danau Tamblingan 168; intro dives from US$60) This slick diving operation has its own hotel and a large diving pool right outside the office. Recommended for beginners, the shop offers a long list of courses, including PADI open-water for US$450.

Surya Water Sports
WATER SPORTS
(☏287 956; Jl Duyung 10; ⊙9am-5pm; ⛟) One of several water-sports operations along the beach, Surya is the largest. You can go parasailing (US$20 per ride), snorkelling by boat (US$35, two hours), windsurfing (US$30, one hour) or rent a kayak and paddle the smooth waters (US$5 per hour).

🛏 Sleeping
Usually the best places to stay are right on the beach; however, beware of properties

that have been coasting for decades. Modest budgets will find comfort on the nonbeach side of Jl Danau Tamblingan.

When making your choice of where to stay, keep in mind that you can do better than the high-profile Inna Grand Bali Beach Hotel, which, despite the hype, is not up to the standards of the best places around.

BEACHFRONT
In Sanur you'll find some tasteful smaller beachfront hotels that are surprisingly affordable as well as some plainer beachfront places that are simply very good value.

TOP CHOICE Hotel La Taverna
HOTEL $$$
(☏288 497; www.latavernahotel.com; Jl Danau Tambligan 29; r US$100-200, ste from US$250; ✲@🛜☉) One of Sanur's first hotels, La Taverna has been thoughtfully updated while retaining its artful, simple charms. The pretty grounds and paths linking buildings hum with a creative energy that infuses the 36 vintage bungalow-style units with an understated luxury. It all seems timeless yet with just a hint of sly youth. Art and antiques abound; views beckon.

Tandjung Sari
HOTEL $$$
(☏288 441; www.tandjungsari.com; Jl Danau Tamblingan 29; bungalows from US$180; ✲@🛜☉) The mature trees along the shaded driveway set the gracious tone at this Sanur veteran, which was one of the first Balinese boutique hotels. Like a good tree, it has flourished since its start in 1967 and continues to be lauded for its stylish design. The 26 traditional-style bungalows are superbly decorated with crafts and antiques. At night, lights in the trees above the pool are magical. The gracious staff are a delight. Balinese

---

DON'T MISS

SANUR'S BEACHFRONT WALK

Sanur's **beachfront walk** (Promenade) was the first in Bali and has been delighting locals and visitors alike from day one. Over 4km long, it curves past resorts, beachfront cafes, wooden fishing boats under repair and quite a few elegant old villas built decades ago by the wealthy expats who fell under Bali's spell. While you stroll, look out across the water to Nusa Penida.

A few highlights: just north of the Bali Hyatt are the kinds of lavish villas you wished your friends owned. This was the centre of expat life when Donald Friend ruled the roost. Just south of the Hyatt is a long area where multihued fishing boats are pulled ashore and repaired under the trees. And look for surprises like a cow grazing next to a luxury resort or a bored beach-activities tout tracing beautifully elaborate designs in the sand.

Even if you're not staying in Sanur, the beach walk makes a good day trip or stop on the way to someplace else.

dance classes are taught by one of Bali's best dancers.

Bali Hyatt
RESORT HOTEL $$$

(☎281 234; www.bali.resort.hyatt.com; Jl Danau Tamblingan; r US$150-500; ✸@☀☁) The sprawling Made Wijaya–designed gardens are an attraction in themselves at this 390-room beachfront resort. Hibiscus, wild ginger, lotus and more than 600 species of plants and animals can be found here. Rooms are comfortable; note that balconies shrink on higher floors. Regency Club rooms come with free drinks and food in a serene pavilion. The two pools are oceanic in size, and one has a waterfall-shrouded snogging cave.

Kesumasari
GUESTHOUSE $

(☎287 824; Jl Kesumasari 6; r fan/air-con 300,000/400,000Rp; ✸☀) The only thing between you and the beach is a small shrine. Beyond the lounging porches, the multihued carved Balinese doors don't prepare you for the riot of colour inside the 11 idiosyncratic rooms at this family-run homestay.

Diwangkara Beach Hotel
HOTEL $$

(☎288 577; www.holidayvillahotelbali.com; Jl Hang Tuah 54; r from US$90, villas from US$145; ✸@☀☁) Facing the beach near the end of Jl Hang Tuah, this 38-unit hotel has traditional Balinese architecture. Pool villas have their own plunge pool right off a wooden terrace. Everything here is low-key, from the staff to the regulars snoozing by the small pool.

Hotel Peneeda View
HOTEL $$

(☎288 425; www.peneedaview.com; Jl Danau Tamblingan 89; r 850,000-1,600,000Rp; ✸@☁)

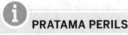

PRATAMA PERILS

Restaurants and hotels are strung out all along Jl Pratama, which runs the length of the peninsula. The southern end may be one of the most perilous streets in south Bali for a stroll. From Nusa Dua north to the Conrad Bali Resort, there are no footpaths and in many places nowhere to walk but on the narrow road, which also has blind curves. Fortunately, the **beach promenade** is a wonderful alternative. It continues from Nusa Dua north to the Bali Khama.

Another basic, small beachfront hotel among the many in Sanur that seem to grow like seaweed, the Peneeda (which is *not* phonetically accurate for Penida) is a good choice for sun, sand and room service at an affordable price. The scope of recent room updates is as narrow as the beach frontage. There's free wi-fi in common areas.

Ananda Beach Hotel
GUESTHOUSE $

(☎288 327; Jl Hang Tuah 51; r 250,000-500,000Rp; ✸☀) Built around a large shrine and right on the busy beach, the veteran Ananda has slightly dark rooms that are a jumble of old furniture. Deluxe room number 7 has a nice balcony with sea views; some of the 20 others are fan-only. Boats to Nusa Lembongan leave nearby.

OFF THE BEACH
The following are near Jl Danau Tamblingan and are short walks from the beach, cafes and shopping. Lacking sand as a feature, they all tend to try a bit harder than their beachfront brethren (besides being more affordable).

⭐ TOP CHOICE Flashbacks
GUESTHOUSE $

(☎281 682; www.flashbacks-chb.com; Jl Danau Tamblingan 110; r with fan/air-con from 250,000/410,000Rp; ✸☀☁) This welcoming retreat has nine rooms that vary greatly in size. The better ones are bungalows or suites while more modest rooms share bathrooms and have cold water. The lovely design takes a lot of cues from traditional Balinese style. Porch Café is out front.

Hotel Palm Garden
HOTEL $$

(Taman Palem; ☎287 041; www.palmgarden-bali.com; Jl Kesumasari 3; r from 450,000Rp; ✸☀☁) Everything is low-key here, from the 17 large rooms (with satellite TVs and fridges) to the relaxed service and pretty grounds. It's one minute to the beach; there is a nice medium-sized pool with a small waterfall. There's wi-fi in common areas.

Gardenia
GUESTHOUSE $$

(☎286 301; www.gardeniaguesthousebali.com; Jl Mertasari 2; r US$50-60; ✸☀☁) Like its many-petalled namesake, the Gardenia has many facets. The seven rooms are visions in white and sit well back from the road. Nice verandas face a small pool in a pretty courtyard. Up front there is a good cafe.

GETTING HIGH OVER SANUR

Travelling through south Bali you can't help but notice scores of kites overhead much of the year. These creations are often huge (10m or more wide, with tails stretching up to an astonishing 160m) and fly at altitudes that worry pilots. Many have noisemakers called *gaganguan* producing eerie humming and buzzing noises that are unique to each kite. Like much in Bali there are spiritual roots: the kites are meant to whisper figuratively into the ears of the gods suggestions that abundant harvests might be nice. But for many Balinese, these high-fliers are simply a really fun hobby (although it has its serious side as when one of these monsters crashes to earth it can kill and injure).

Each July, hundreds of Balinese and international teams descend – as it were – on open spaces north of Sanur for the **Bali Kite Festival**. They compete for an array of honours in such categories as original design and flight endurance. The action is centred around **Padang Galak Beach**, about 2km up the coast from Sanur. You can catch kite-flying Balinese-style here from May to September.

Hotel Segara Agung   HOTEL $
(✉288 446; www.segaraagung.com; Jl Duyung 43; r US$40-60; ❄@🛜🏊) Down a quiet, sandy lane lined with villas, this hotel is only a three-minute walk from the beach. The 18 rooms are clean though spartan; the cheapest have fans and cold water only. The big swimming pool is secluded.

Hotel Rita   HOTEL $
(✉287 969; ritabali2@yahoo.co.id; Jl Danau Tamblingan 152; r 300,000-350,000Rp; ❄) Lovely Rita is tailor-made for those who want a basic room in a nice garden. You've nothing to fear from meter maids at this secluded compound well off busy Jl Danau Tamblingan. The beach is 10 minutes east.

Keke Homestay   GUESTHOUSE $
(✉287 282; Jl Danau Tamblingan 100; r 150,000-250,000Rp; ❄) Set 150m down a gang from the noisy road, Keke welcomes backpackers into its genial family (who are often busy making offerings). The five quiet, clean rooms vary from fan-only to air-con cool.

Watering Hole I   HOTEL $
(✉288 289; www.wateringholesanurbali.com; Jl Hang Tuah 37; r 150,000-300,000Rp; ❄@🛜) In the northern part of Sanur, the Hole is a busy, friendly place close to the Nusa Lembongan boats. It has 20 pleasant, clean rooms; the cheapest have fans and cold water; wi-fi is in common areas. There's a sister Watering Hole at the southern end of Jl Danau Tamblingan.

✖ Eating

Dine on the beach in a traditional open-air pavilion or in a genial bar – the choice is yours in Sanur. Although there are plenty of uninspired places on Jl Danau Tamblingan, there are also some gems.

For groceries and personal items, there's a large **Hardy's Supermarket** (✉285 806; Jl Danau Tamblingan 136). Nearby is the gourmet market of Cafe Batu Jimbar.

On Sundays, there's an **organic market** (Jl Danau Tamblingan; ⊙10am-2pm Sun) in the parking lot next to Cafe Batu Jimbar.

The **Pasar Sindhu night market** (off Jl Danau Tamblingan; ⊙6am-midnight) sells fresh vegetables, dried fish, pungent spices and various household goods.

BEACHFRONT

The beach path offers restaurants, warung and bars where you can catch a meal, a drink or a sea breeze. Sunset drink specials are common (though the beach faces east, so you'll need to enjoy the reflected glow off Nusa Penida). Many beach cafes are part of hotels offering humdrum fare at resort prices.

Bonsai Cafe   PIZZA, SEAFOOD $
(Jl Danau Tamblingan 27; meals 40,000-90,000Rp; 🛜) Although the menu is all beachside standards (and good ones), the real reason to seek this place out is for the proof that the name is not notional: there are hundreds of bonsai trees in sizes from tiny to small.

Sanur Bay   SEAFOOD $$
(✉288 153; Jl Duyung; meals 60,000-160,000Rp) You can hear the surf and see the moonlight reflected on the water at this classic beachside seafood grill, set on the sand amid palm trees and fishing boats.

Donald's Beach Café
INTERNATIONAL **$$**

(📞287 637; Beachfront Walk; meals 50,000-100,000Rp) If this were owned by Donald Trump, the site would no doubt be condoised in a New York minute. And that would be a shame, as the mature trees provide shade over tables with great views out to sea. The timeless (timeworn?) menu comprises Indo standards, pizza and burgers.

Beach Café
GLOBAL **$$**

(📞282 875; Beachfront Walk; meals 50,000-100,000Rp; 🛜) Brings a bit of flashy Med style to the Sanur beach cliché of palm fronds and plastic chairs. Zone out on wicker sofas or hang on a low cushion on the sand. Enjoy salads and seafood.

Stiff Chili
INTERNATIONAL **$$**

(Jl Kesumasari; meals 50,000-150,000Rp) Apart from the evocative name, this beachside cafe has fine views through its near lack of walls. Pizza and pasta head the surprisingly ambitious menu.

JALAN DANAU TAMBLINGAN

TOP CHOICE **Manik Organik**
ORGANIC **$**

(www.manikorganikbali.com; Jl Danau Tamblingan 85; meals from 50,000Rp; 🖉) Actual trees shade the serene terrace at this creative and healthful cafe. Vegetarians are well-cared for but there are also meaty dishes made with free-range chicken and the like. Smoothies include the fortifying 'immune tonic' and there is a range of house-brand products on offer.

Café Smorgås
CAFE **$$**

(📞289 361; Jl Danau Tamblingan; meals 50,000-150,000Rp; 🛜🖉) Set back from the traffic, this popular place has nice wicker chairs on a large terrace outside and cool air-con inside. The menu has a healthy bent of fresh Western fare from breakfasts to sandwiches to soups and salads.

Three Monkeys Cafe
CAFE **$$**

(Jl Danau Tamblingan; meals 60,000-150,000Rp; 🛜) This branch of the splendid Ubud original is no mere knock-off. Spread over two floors, it has cool jazz playing in the background and live performances some nights. Set well back from the road, you can enjoy Sanur's best coffee drinks on sofas or chairs. The menu mixes healthy Western fare with pan-Asian creations.

Char Ming
FUSION **$$**

(📞288 029; www.charming-bali.com; Jl Danau Tamblingan 97; meals 100,000-200,000Rp) Barbecue with a French accent. A daily menu board lists the fresh seafood available for grilling. Other dishes include plenty of pork and beef. The highly stylised location features lush plantings and carved-wood details, and antiques inside and out. Much of the structure was built from wood reclaimed from old boats and buildings.

Porch Cafe
CAFE **$**

(📞281 682; Jl Danau Tamblingan; meals from 40,000Rp; 🛜) Fronting Flashbacks, a charmer of a small hotel, this cafe is housed in a traditional wooden building replete with the namesake porch. Snuggle up to a table out front or shut it all out in the air-con inside. The menu is a tasty mix of comfort food like burgers and freshly baked goods. Popular for breakfast; there's a long list of fresh juices.

Massimo
ITALIAN **$$**

(📞288 942; Jl Danau Tamblingan 206; meals 80,000-200,000Rp) The interior is like an open-air Milan cafe, the outside like a Balinese garden – a combo that goes together like spaghetti and meatballs. Pasta, pizza and more are prepared with authentic Italian flair. No time for a meal? Nab some gelato from the counter up front.

Cafe Batu Jimbar
CAFE, BAKERY **$$**

(📞287 374; Jl Tamblingan 152; snacks from 30,000Rp) Although pricey, this attractive cafe has a shady wooden patio fronting an airy dining room. Succumb to the best banana smoothie in Bali, then let the luscious baked goods work their magic. A gourmet grocery adjoins.

SOUTH SANUR

Gardenia Cafe
INTERNATIONAL **$**

(📞286 301; www.gardeniaguesthousebali.com; Jl Mertasari 2; meals 30,000-80,000Rp; 🛜) The streetside cafe of the attractive guesthouse is shaded by large flowering trees. The menu is a mix of traveller favourites (sandwiches, salads, Asian etc) but has a dash of fresh style. The coffee drinks are the best down here.

Denata Minang
INDONESIAN **$**

(Jl Danau Poso; meals from 15,000Rp) One of the better Padang-style warung, it's located just west of Cafe Billiard, the rollicking expat bar. Like its brethren, it has fab *ayam* (chicken) in myriad spicy forms – only better.

Cat & Fiddle
BRITISH **$$**

(📞282 218; Jl Mertasari 36; meals 30,000-100,000Rp) Look for Brit standards like proper breakfasts and pork pies on the menu at this open-air pub that's – not surprisingly – popular with expats. Surprises include the 'Blarnyschnitzel', which is made with chicken.

Drinking

Many of Sanur's drinking establishments cater to retired expats and are, thankfully for them, air-conditioned. This is not a place where things go late. Note that many places to eat are good for drinks and vice versa.

Less salubriously, Sanur is known as a haven for prostitution. You won't find any at the public bars – except for a couple of dubious ones near Jl Segara Ayu – but along Jl Danau Poso there are numerous huge brothels given away only by the constant traffic.

TOP CHOICE **Warung Pantai Indah** CAFE
(Beachfront Walk) Sit on benches in the sand under a tin roof at this uberauthentic old Sanur beach cafe. Just north of the Hotel Peneeda View and near some of Sanur's most expensive private beach villas, this outpost of good cheer has cheap beer and regular specials on fresh-grilled seafood (100,000Rp). The views and owners are delightful.

Kalimantan BAR
(289 291; Jl Pantai Sindhu 11) Aka Borneo Bob's, this veteran boozer is one of many casual joints on this street. Enjoy cheap drinks under the palms in the large, casual garden or squint at live American football on the satellite TV. The Mexican food features home-grown chilli peppers.

Bali Seaman's Club BAR
(283 992; Jl Danau Tamblingan 27; 9am-midnight;) Hidden away down a small lane, this newly spiffed up bar is where every seaman joke you've ever heard *shouldn't* be repeated. Balinese sailors hang out here between stints on cruise ships. Fascinating stories abound, including one we heard about a vacuum toilet that gives new meaning to 'poop deck'. Simple, gregarious fun.

Street Cafe BAR
(289 259; Jl Danau Tamblingan 21;) A street bar that verges on stylish, with a modern, airy vibe and a choice of loungers, stools or tables. Instead of watching sport on TV, groove to the live piano music here most nights. Sink your teeth into a menu of steaks (average 70,000Rp).

Shopping

Sanur is no Seminyak in the shopping department, although a few designers from there are opening branches here. You can kill an afternoon browsing the length of Jl Danau Tamblingan.

For cheap and tatty souvenirs, try one of the various markets along the beachfront walk.

A-Krea CLOTHES
(Jl Danau Tamblingan 51) A range of items designed and made on Bali are available in this attractive store that takes the colours of the island and gives them a minimalist flair. Clothes, accessories, housewares and more are all handmade.

Ganesha Bookshop BOOKSHOP
(Jl Danau Tamblingan 42) Bali's best bookshop for serious readers has a new shop in the heart of Sanur. Besides excellent choices in new and used fiction, Ganesha has superb selections on local culture and history. There's also a special reading area for kids.

Red Camelia WOMEN'S CLOTHING
(270 046; www.redcamelia.com; Jl Danau Tamblingan 134) Loose, light resort wear you can't find at home.

Nogo FABRIC
(288 765; Jl Danau Tamblingan 100) Look for the wooden loom out front of this classy store, which bills itself as the 'Bali Ikat Centre'. The goods are gorgeous and easy to enjoy in the air-con comfort.

Brothers & Sisters CLOTHING
(Jl Danau Poso 57, Gopa Town Centre) Cute threads for cute kids. The designs are suitably light and airy for tropical holidays. What better way to strut the promenade than in cool new duds? Designed and made on Bali.

Hardy's Supermarket SUPERMARKET
(285 806; Jl Danau Tamblingan 136) Hardy's Supermarket has a range of quality goods on its 2nd floor at very good prices.

Information
Medical Services
Guardian Pharmacy (284 343; Jl Danau Tamblingan 134) The chain pharmacy has a doctor on call.

Money
Moneychangers here have a dubious reputation. There are numerous ATMs along Jl Danau Tamblingan and several banks.

ⓘ Getting There & Away

Bemo

Bemo stop at the southern end of Sanur on Jl Mertasari, and just outside the main entrance to the Inna Grand Bali Beach Hotel on Jl Hang Tuah. You can hail a bemo anywhere along Jl Danau Tamblingan and Jl Danau Poso – although drivers will first try to hail you.

Green bemo go along Jl Hang Tuah to the Kereneng bemo terminal in Denpasar (7000Rp).

Boat

Public boats and the Perama boat to Nusa Lembongan leave from the beach at the end of Jl Hang Tuah.

The fast boat **Scoot** (🕿285 522; Jl Hang Tuah) has an office in Sanur.

Fast boats Depart from a nearby portion of beach. None of these services use a dock – be prepared to wade to the boat.

Gilicat (🕿271 680; www.gilicat.com; Jl Danau Tamblingan 51) has a Sanur office for its Padangbai departures to Lombok.

Tourist Shuttle Bus

The **Perama office** (🕿285 592; Jl Hang Tuah 39; ⏱7am-10pm) is at Warung Pojok at the northern end of town. It runs shuttles to the following destinations, most only once daily.

DESTINATION	FARE (RP)	DURATION (HR)
Candidasa	60,000	2¾
Kuta	25,000	15min
Lovina	125,000	4
Padangbai	60,000	2½
Ubud	40,000	1

ⓘ Getting Around

Official airport taxis cost 100,000Rp.

Bemo go up and down Jl Danau Tamblingan and Jl Danau Poso for 4000Rp, offering a greener way to shuttle about the strip than a taxi.

Metered taxis can be flagged down in the street, or call **Bluebird Taxi** (🕿701 111).

AROUND SANUR

Pulau Serangan

Otherwise known as Turtle Island, Pulau Serangan is an example of all that can go wrong with Bali's environment. Originally it was a small (100-hectare) island offshore of the mangroves to the south of Sanur.

However, in the 1990s it was selected by Suharto's infamous son Tommy as a site for new development. Much of the original island was obliterated while a new landfill area over 300 hectares in size was grafted on. The Asian economic crisis pulled the plug on the scheme until recently, when the heavy equipment began moving again.

Meanwhile, on the original part of the island, the two small and poor fishing villages, **Ponjok** and **Dukuh**, are still there, as is one of Bali's holiest temples, **Pura Sakenan**, just east of the causeway. Architecturally it is insignificant, but major festivals attract huge crowds of devotees, especially during the Kuningan festival.

Benoa Harbour

Bali's main port is at the entrance of Teluk Benoa (Benoa Bay), the wide but shallow body east of the airport runway. Benoa Harbour is on the northern side of the bay – a square of docks and port buildings on reclaimed land, linked to mainland Bali by a 2km causeway. It's referred to as Benoa port or Benoa Harbour to distinguish it from Benoa village, on the southern side of the bay.

Benoa Harbour is the port for tourist daytrip boats to Nusa Lembongan and for Pelni ships to other parts of Indonesia; however, its shallow depth prevents large cruise ships from calling.

DENPASAR

🕿0361

Sprawling, hectic and ever-growing, Bali's capital has been the focus of a lot of the island's growth and wealth over the last five decades. It can seem a daunting and chaotic place but spend a little time on its tree-lined streets in the relatively affluent government and business district of Renon and you'll discover a more genteel side. Southeast of the town centre, Renon is laid out on a grand scale, with wide streets, large car parks and huge tracts of landscaped space. You'll find the government offices here, many of which are impressive structures displaying an ersatz Balinese style.

Denpasar might not be a tropical paradise, but it's as much a part of 'the real Bali' as the rice paddies and clifftop temples. This is the hub of the island for almost 800,000 locals and here you will find their shopping malls and parks. Most enticing, however, is the growing range of fabulous restaurants and cafes aimed at the burgeoning middle class. You'll also want to sample Denpasar's markets, its excellent museum and its purely modern Balinese vibe. Most visitors stay in the tourist towns of the south and visit Denpasar as a day trip (if traffic is kind you can get there in 15 minutes from Sanur and 30 minutes from Seminyak). Others may pass through while changing bemo or catching a bus to Java.

History

Denpasar, which means 'next to the market', was an important trading centre and the seat of local rajahs (lords or princes) before the colonial period. The Dutch gained control of northern Bali in the mid-19th century, but their takeover of the south didn't start until 1906. After the three Balinese princes destroyed their own palaces in Denpasar and made a suicidal last stand – a ritual *puputan* – the Dutch made Denpasar an important colonial centre. And as Bali's tourism industry expanded in the 1930s, most visitors stayed at one or two government hotels in the city of Denpasar.

The northern town of Singaraja remained the Dutch administrative capital until after WWII when it was moved to Denpasar because of the new airport; in 1958, some years after Indonesian independence, the city became the official capital of the province of Bali.

Many of Denpasar's residents are descended from immigrant groups such as Bugis mercenaries (originally from Sulawesi) and Chinese, Arab and Indian traders. Recent immigrants have come from Java and all over Indonesia, attracted by opportunities in schools, business and the enormous tourist economy. Denpasar's edges have merged with Sanur, Kuta and Seminyak.

◎ Sights

Take time for the Museum Negeri Propinsi Bali, but the real appeal of Denpasar is simply exploring everyday Bali life. Roam the traditional markets and even the air-conditioned malls to see how people live today.

TOP
CHOICE **Museum Negeri
Propinsi Bali**   MUSEUM
(✆222 680; adult/child 10,000/5000Rp; ⊙8am-12.30pm Fri, to 4pm Sat-Thu) Think of this as the British Museum or the Smithsonian of Balinese culture. It's all here, but unlike those world-class institutions, you have to work at sorting it out.

This museum was originally established in 1910 by a Dutch resident who was concerned by the export of culturally significant artefacts from the island. Destroyed in a 1917 earthquake, it was rebuilt in the 1920s, but used mainly for storage until 1932. At that time, German artist Walter Spies and some Dutch officials revived the idea of collecting and preserving Balinese antiquities and cultural objects, and creating an ethnographic museum. Today, the museum is well organised and most displays are labelled in English. You can climb one of the towers inside the grounds for a better view of the whole complex.

The museum comprises several buildings and pavilions, including many examples of Balinese architecture. The main building, to the back as you enter, has a collection of prehistoric pieces downstairs, including stone sarcophagi and stone and bronze implements. Upstairs are examples of traditional artefacts, including items still in everyday use. Look for the intricate wood-and-cane carrying cases for transporting fighting cocks, and tiny carrying cases for fighting crickets.

The **northern pavilion**, in the style of a Tabanan palace, houses dance costumes and masks, including a sinister Rangda (widow-witch), a healthy-looking Barong (mythical lion-dog creature) and a towering Barong Landung (tall Barong) figure.

The **central pavilion**, with its spacious veranda, is like the palace pavilions of the Karangasem kingdom (based in Amlapura), where rajahs held audiences. The exhibits are related to Balinese religion, and include ceremonial objects, calendars and priests' clothing.

The **southern pavilion** (Gedung Buleleng) has a varied collection of textiles, including *endek* (a Balinese method of weaving with pre-dyed threads), double ikat, *songket* (silver- and gold-threaded cloth, hand-woven using a floating weft technique) and *prada* (the application of gold leaf or gold or silver thread in traditional Balinese clothes).

Museum staff often play music on a bamboo gamelan to magical effect; visit in the afternoon when it's uncrowded. Ignore 'guides' who offer little except a chance to part with US$5 or US$10.

Denpasar

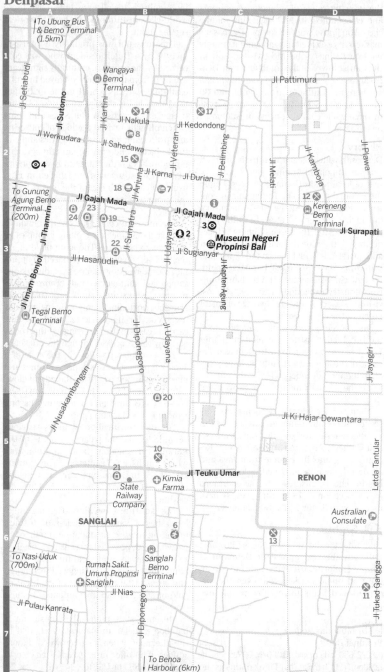

To Ubung Bus & Bemo Terminal (1.5km)

Wangaya Bemo Terminal

Jl Setiabudi

Jl Sutomo

Jl Kartini

Jl Werkudara

⊗14
Jl Nakula

⊗17

Jl Kedondong

Jl Sahedawa

⊗ 8

15 ⊗

Jl Karna

Jl Veteran

Jl Durian

Jl Belimbing

Jl Melati

Jl Pattimura

Jl Kamboja

Jl Plawa

◉4

18 ⊡

⊡ 7

Jl Arjuna

To Gunung Agung Bemo Terminal (200m)

Jl Thamrin

Jl Gajah Mada

23

24 ⊡   ⊡19

Jl Sumatra

Jl Gajah Mada

3 ◉

12 ⊡
Kereneng Bemo Terminal

Jl Surapati

Jl Imam Bonjol

22 ⊡

Jl Hasanudin

Jl Udayana

♣ 2

Jl Sugianyar

🏛 **Museum Negeri Propinsi Bali**

Jl Kapten Agung

⊡ Tegal Bemo Terminal

Jl Diponegoro

Jl Udayana

Jl Nusakambangan

⊡ 20

Jl Ki Hajar Dewantara

10 ⊗

Jl Jayagiri

21 ⊡

State Railway Company

✚ Kimia Farma

Jl Teuku Umar

RENON

Letda Tantular

SANGLAH

6 ✚

13 ⊗

Australian Consulate 🏛

To Nasi Uduk (700m)

Rumah Sakit Umum Propinsi ✚ Sanglah

🏛 Sanglah Bemo Terminal

Jl Nias

11 ⊗

Jl Pulau Kanrata

Jl Diponegoro

Jl Tukad Gangga

To Benoa Harbour (6km)

Pura Jagatnatha TEMPLE

(Jl Surapati) The state temple, built in 1953, is dedicated to the supreme god, Sanghyang Widi. Part of its significance is its statement of monotheism. Although the Balinese recognise many gods, the belief in one supreme god (who can have many manifestations) brings Balinese Hinduism into conformity with the first principle of Pancasila – the 'Belief in One God.'

The *padmasana* (temple shrine) is made of white coral, and consists of an empty throne (symbolic of heaven) on top of the cosmic turtle and two *naga* (mythical snake-like creatures), which symbolise the foundation of the world. The walls are decorated with carvings of scenes from the Ramayana and Mahabharata.

Two major festivals are held here every month, during the full moon and new moon, and feature *wayang kulit* (leather shadow puppet) performances.

Puputan Square PARK

This classic urban park commemorates the heroic but suicidal stand of the rajahs of Badung against the invading Dutch in 1906. A monument depicts a Balinese family in heroic pose, brandishing the weapons that were so ineffective against the Dutch guns. The woman also has jewels in her left hand, as the women of the Badung court reputedly flung their jewellery at the Dutch soldiers to taunt them. The park is popular with locals at lunchtime and with families near sunset.

Pura Maospahit TEMPLE

(off Jl Sutomo) Established in the 14th century, at the time the Majapahit arrived from Java, this temple was damaged in a 1917 earthquake and has been heavily restored since. The oldest structures are at the back of the temple, but the most interesting features are the large statues of Garuda and the giant Batara Bayu.

Bajra Sandhi Monument MONUMENT

(☏264 517; Jl Raya Puputan; adult/child 10,000/5000Rp; ☺8.30am-5pm) Otherwise known as the Monument to the Struggle of the People of Bali, this huge monument is as big as its name and dominates what's already a big park in Renon. Inside this vaguely Borobodur-like structure are dioramas tracing Bali's history. Taking the name as a cue, you won't be surprised that they have a certain jingoistic soap-opera quality. But they're a fun diversion. Note

Denpasar

that in the portrayal of the 1906 battle with the Dutch, the King of Badung is literally a sitting target.

FREE **Taman Wedhi Budaya**   ARTS CENTRE
(☏222 776; ◷8am-3pm Mon-Thu, to 1pm Fri-Sun) This arts centre is a sprawling complex in the eastern part of Denpasar. Established in 1973 as an academy and showplace for Balinese culture, its lavish architecture houses an art gallery with an interesting collection, but few performances or much else most of the year.

From mid-June to mid-July, the centre comes alive for the Bali Arts Festival, right, with dances, music and craft displays from all over Bali. You may need to book tickets at the centre for more popular events.

🏃 Activities

Many Balinese wouldn't think of having a massage from anyone but a blind person. Government-sponsored schools offer lengthy courses to certify blind people in reflexology, shiatsu massage, anatomy and much more. Usually graduates work together in group locations such as **Kube Dharma Bakti** (☏749 9440; Jl Serma Mendara 3; massage per hour 40,000Rp; ◷9am-9pm). In this airy building redolent with liniments, you can choose from a range of therapies and contribute to a very good cause at the same time.

🎉 Festivals & Events

Bali Arts Festival   ARTS
(www.baliartsfestival.com) The annual Bali Arts Festival, based at the Taman Wedhi Budaya arts centre, lasts for about a month starting in mid-June. It's a great time to visit Bali, and the festival is an easy way to see a wide variety of traditional dance, music and crafts from the island. The productions of the *Ramayana* and *Mahabharata* ballets are grand, and the opening ceremony and parade in Denpasar are spectacles. Tickets are usually available before performances, and schedules are available throughout south Bali, in Ubud, at the Denpasar tourist office and online.

The festival is the main event of the year for scores of village dance and musical groups. Competition is fierce with local pride on the line at each performance ('our Kecak is better than your stinkin' Kecak' etc). To do well here sets a village on a good course for the year. Some events are held in a 6000-seat amphitheatre, a venue that allows you to realise the mass appeal of traditional Balinese culture.

🛏 Sleeping

Denpasar has oodles of new midpriced chain hotels, but it's hard to think of a compelling reason to stay here unless you want to revel in the city's bright lights.

TOP CHOICE Nakula Familiar Inn   GUESTHOUSE $

(☑226 446; www.nakulafamiliarinn.com; Jl Nakula 4; r 130,000-200,000Rp; ❀🛜) The eight rooms at this sprightly urban family compound, which has been a traveller favourite since before Seminyak existed, are clean (some with air-con and cold-water showers only) and have small balconies. The traffic noise isn't too bad and there is a nice courtyard and cafe in the middle. Tegal-Kereneng bemo go along Jl Nakula.

Inna Bali   HOTEL $$

(☑225 681; www.innabali.com; Jl Veteran 3; r from 500,000-800,000Rp; ❀🛜🏊) The Inna Bali has simple gardens, a huge banyan tree and a certain nostalgic charm; it dates from 1927 and was once the main tourist hotel on the island. Room interiors are standard and a bit frayed, but many have deeply shaded verandas. The hotel is a good base for the Ngrupuk parades that take place the day before the Nyepi festival, as they pass in front. Get the veteran employees talking – they have many stories. Ask about deals: don't pay rack rates here.

✖ Eating & Drinking

Denpasar has the island's best range of Indonesian and Balinese food. Savvy locals and expats each have their own favourite warung and restaurants. At the **Pasar Malam Kereneng** (Kereneng Night Market; Jl Kamboja; ⊙6pm-5am), dozens of vendors dish up food until dawn.

Also good is Jl Teuku Umar, while in Renon there is a phenomenal strip of eating places on Jl Cok Agung Trisna between Jl Ramayana and Jl Dewi Madri and along Letda Tantular. See what you can discover.

TOP CHOICE Warung Satria   INDONESIAN $

(Jl Kedondong; dishes 8000-15,000Rp; ⊙11am-3pm) This is a long-running warung on a quiet street; try the wonderful seafood satay served with a shallot sambal. Otherwise, choose from the immaculate displays of what's fresh, but don't wait too long after lunch or it will all be gone. There is a **second location** (Jl WR Supratman) near the junction where the main road to Ubud branches off from the bypass, east of the centre of Denpasar.

Warung Beras Bali   ORGANIC $

(☑247 443; Jl Sahedawa 26; mains 8000-15,000Rp) Organic rice underpins organic vegetables and various Chinese dishes at this appropriately green-hued open-front cafe. A long list of fresh juices adds to the healthy patina. Try the unusual – and organic vegetarian – *saté sambal plecina*, which is a tasty skewer of grilled spinach and tomato. Or buy a bag of rice.

Nasi Uduk   INDONESIAN $

(Jl Teuku Umar; meals 8000-15,000Rp) Open to the street, this spotless little stall has a few chairs and serves up Javanese treats such as *nasi uduk* (sweetly scented coconut rice with fresh peanut sauce) and *lalapan* (a simple salad of fresh lemon basil leaves).

Roti Candy   SWEETS $

(☑238 409; Jl Nakula 31; treats 3000Rp) Have a *pia* (a sweet-filled bun) or choose from a variety of other sweets and cakes, plus rolls stuffed with cheesy goodness.

Bhineka Jaya Cafe   COFFEE

(☑224 016; Jl Gajah Mada 80; coffee 4000Rp; ⊙9am-4pm) Home to Bali's Coffee Co, this storefront sells locally grown beans and makes a mean espresso, which you can enjoy at the two tiny tables while watching the bustle of Denpasar's old main drag.

RENON

The slightly gentrified air here temptingly wafts aromas of good cooking.

TOP CHOICE Cak Asm   BALINESE $

(Jl Tukad Gangga; meals from 25,000Rp) Join the government workers and students from the nearby university for superb dishes cooked to order in the bustling kitchen. Order the *cumi cumi* (calamari) with *telor asin* sauce (a heavenly mixture of eggs and garlic). The resulting buttery, crispy goodness could well be the best dish you have while you're in Bali. Fruity ice drinks are a cooling treat. An English-language menu makes ordering a breeze.

Ayam Goreng Kalasan   INDONESIAN $

(Jl Cok Agung Tresna 6; meals from 25,000Rp) The name here says it all: fried chicken *(ayam goreng)* named for a Javanese temple (Kalasan) in a region renowned for its fiery, crispy chicken. The version here falls off the bone on the way to the table; the meat is redolent with lemongrass from a long marinade prior to the plunge into boiling oil. There are several other excellent little warung in this strip.

Warung Lembongan INDONESIAN $

(☑236 885; Jl Cok Agung Trisna 62; meals 10,000-30,000Rp) Silver folding chairs at long tables, shaded by a garish green awning out front. These are details you will quickly forget after you have the house speciality: chicken lightly fried yet delicately crispy like the top of a perfect crème brûlée. The special costs 17,000Rp and includes *ayam* (chicken), rice, soup and a beverage. The KFC in Sanur wants over 200,000Rp for its deeply inferior mass-merchandised version.

Pondok Kuring INDONESIAN $

(Jl Raya Puputan 56; meals from 20,000Rp) The foods of the Sundanese people of west Java are the speciality here. Highly spiced vegetables, meat and seafood draw falavours from an array of herbs. This glossy restaurant has an arty dining room and a lovely and quiet garden out back.

Café Teduh INDONESIAN $

(☑221 631; off Jl Diponegoro; meals 10,000-50,000Rp; 🐾) Amid the big shopping malls, this little oasis is hidden down a tiny lane. Hanging orchids, trees, flowers and ponds with fountains create a bucolic feel. There's a menu of meaty mains such as *ayam bakar rica* (barbecued chicken with ratatouille) but the real treats are just that – treats. Try the *es cakalele,* a refreshing sundae of lychee and coconut milk.

🔒 Shopping

For a complete slice of local life, visit the traditional markets and the large air-con shopping malls.

Markets

Denpasar's largest traditional markets are mostly in a fairly compact area that makes visiting them easy, even if navigating their crowded aisles across multiple floors is not. Like other aspects of Balinese life, the big markets are in flux. Big-box supermarkets are biting into their trade and the evolving middle class say they prefer the likes of Carrefour because it has more imported goods (oh my...) and is cleaner (well...). But the big markets aren't down yet. This is where you come for purely Balinese goods, such as temple offerings, ceremonial clothes and a range of foodstuffs unique to the island, including some types of mangosteen.

TOP CHOICE Pasar Badung MARKET

(Jl Gajah Mada) Bali's largest food market is busy in the morning and evening (although dull and sleepy from 2pm to 4pm); it's a great place to browse and bargain. You'll find produce and food from all over the island, as well as easy-to-assemble temple offerings that are popular with working women. Get lost here as it won't be permanent and revel in the range of fruits and spices on offer. Ignore the services of 'guides'.

Kampung Arab MARKET

(Jl Hasanudin & Jl Sulawesi) Has jewellery and precious-metal stores run by scores of Middle Eastern and Indian merchants.

Pasar Kumbasari MARKET

(Jl Gajah Mada) Handicrafts, a plethora of vibrant fabrics and costumes decorated with gold are just some of the goods at this huge market across the river from Pasar Badung. Note that the malls have taken their toll and there are a lot of empty stalls.

Jalan Sulawesi Fabric Stores

Follow Jl Sulawesi north and, just as the glitter of Kampung Arab fades, the street glows anew as you come upon a strip of fabric stores. The textiles here – batiks, cottons, silks – come in colours that make Barbie look like an old purse. It's immediately east of Pasar Badung.

TOP CHOICE Anis TEXTILES

(Jl Sulawesi 27) Jammed into a string of fabric stores just east of Pasar Badung, this narrow shop stands out for its huge selection of genuine Balinese batik. The colours and patterns are bewildering, while the clearly marked reasonable prices are not.

Shopping Malls

Western-style shopping malls are jammed on Sundays with locals shopping and teens flirting; the brand-name goods are genuine.

Most malls have a food court with stalls serving fresh Asian fare, as well as fast-food joints (which have sated more than one homesick tourist tot).

Bali Mall MALL

(Jl Dipenegoro) Has the top-end Ramayana Department Store, Bali's largest.

Denpasar Junction MALL

(Jl Teuku Umar) Newest, glossiest mall with lots of international chains.

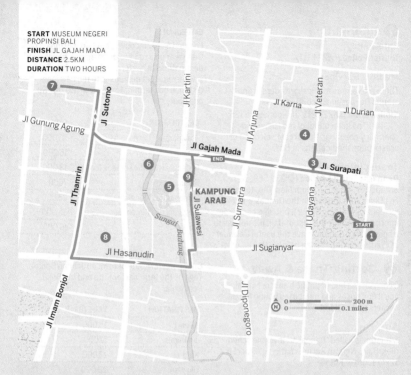

START MUSEUM NEGERI PROPINSI BALI
FINISH JL GAJAH MADA
DISTANCE 2.5KM
DURATION TWO HOURS

Walking Tour
Strolling Denpasar

❯ While Denpasar can seem formidable and traffic choked, it rewards those who explore on foot. This walk includes most attractions in the historic centre of town and a few vestiges of when Denpasar – and Bali – moved at a much slower pace. Allow extra time for visiting the museum or for shopping.

Start the walk at ❶ **Museum Negeri Propinsi Bali**. Opposite is large and green ❷ **Puputan Square**.

Back on the corner of Jl Surapati and Jl Veteran is the towering ❸ **Catur Muka statue**, which represents Batara Guru, Lord of the Four Directions. The four-faced, eight-armed figure keeps a close eye (or is it eight eyes?) on the traffic swirling around him. Head 100m north on Jl Veteran to the ❹ **Inna Bali hotel**. It was a favourite of long-time Indonesian dictator Sukarno – listen for the echoes of his schemes.

Return to the Catur Muka statue and head west on Jl Gajah Mada (named after the 14th-century Majapahit prime minister). Go past banks, shops and a cafe towards the bridge over the grubby Sungai Badung (Badung River). Just before the bridge, on the left, is the renovated ❺ **Pasar Badung**, the main produce market. On the left, just after the bridge, is ❻ **Pasar Kumbasari**, where you will find handicrafts, fabrics and costumes.

At the next main intersection, detour north up Jl Sutomo, and turn left along a small gang (alley) leading to the ❼ **Pura Maospahit temple**.

Turn back, and continue south along Jl Thamrin to the junction of Jl Hasanudin. On this corner is the ❽ **Puri Pemecutan**, a palace destroyed during the 1906 Dutch invasion. It's long since been rebuilt and you can look inside the compound but don't expect anything palatial.

Go east on Jl Hasanudin, then north onto ❾ **Jl Sulawesi**, and its markets. Continue north past Pasar Badung market to return to Jl Gajah Mada. You could save your visit to the Museum Negeri Propinsi Bali for the end, when you'll just want to move slowly.

ⓘ Information

Emergency
Tourist Police (☏224 111)

Medical Services

There are various medical providers in and around Denpasar. See p384 for a list.

Kimia Farma (☏227 811; Jl Diponegoro 125; ⊙24hr) The main outlet of the island-wide pharmacy chain has the largest selection of prescription medications in Bali.

Tourist Information

Denpasar Tourist Office (☏234 569; Jl Surapati 7; ⊙8am-3.30pm Mon-Thu, to 1pm Fri) Deals with tourism in the Denpasar municipality (including Sanur), but also has some information about the rest of Bali. It's not worth a special trip, but may have the useful *Calendar of Events* booklet. Has an official 'tourist toilet'.

ⓘ Getting There & Away

Denpasar is a hub of public transport in Bali – you'll find buses and minibuses bound for all corners of the island.

Air

Sometimes called 'Denpasar' in airline schedules, Bali's Ngurah Rai International Airport is 12km south of Kuta.

Bemo

The city has several bemo terminals – if you're travelling independently around Bali you'll often have to go via Denpasar, and transfer from one terminal to another. The terminals for transport around Bali are Ubung, Batubulan and Tegal, while the Gunung Agung, Kereneng and Sanglah terminals serve destinations in and around Denpasar. Each terminal has regular bemo connections to the other terminals in Denpasar for 7000Rp. Bali has a sputtering bemo network. And note that bemo fares are approximate and at times seem rather subjective. See p377 for details.

UBUNG

Well north of the town, on the road to Gilimanuk, Ubung is the terminal for northern and western Bali. This used to be the long-distance bus terminal, but that has moved 12km northwest to Mengwi.

DESTINATION	FARE (RP)
Gilimanuk (for the ferry to Java)	30,000
Mengwi	12,000
Munduk	27,000
Pancasari (for Danau Bratan)	22,0
Singaraja (via Pupuan or Bedugul)	35,000

BATUBULAN

Located a very inconvenient 6km northeast of Denpasar on a road to Ubud, this terminal is for destinations in eastern and central Bali. This is where you get minibuses to the new long-distance bus terminal in Mengwi (20,000Rp, one hour).

DESTINATION	FARE (RP)
Amlapura	25,000
Gianyar	15,000
Padangbai (for the Lombok ferry)	18,000
Sanur	7000
Semarapura (Klungkung)	23,000
Singaraja (via Kintamani)	35,000
Ubud	13,000

TEGAL

On the western side of town on Jl Iman Bonjol, Tegal is the terminal for Kuta and the Bukit Peninsula.

DESTINATION	FARE (RP)
Airport	15,000
Jimbaran	17,000
Kuta	13,000
Ulu Watu	22,000

GUNUNG AGUNG

This terminal, at the northwestern corner of town (look for orange bemo), is on Jl Gunung Agung, and has bemos to Kerobokan and Canggu (10,000Rp).

KERENENG

East of the town centre, Kereneng has bemo to Sanur (7000Rp).

SANGLAH

On Jl Diponegoro, near the general hospital in the south of the city, Sanglah has bemo to Suwung and Benoa Harbour (10,000Rp).

WANGAYA

Near the centre of town, this small terminal is the departure point for bemo services to northern Denpasar and the outlying Ubung bus terminal (8000Rp).

Bus

Long-distance bus service now uses a new terminal 12km northwest of Denpasar in Mengwi. See p377 for details.

Train

Bali doesn't have trains but the state railway company does have an **office** (☏227 131; Jl Diponegoro 150/B4; 8.30am-6.30pm) in Denpasar. From here, buses leave for eastern Java where they link with trains at Banyuwangi for Surabaya, Yogyakarta and Jakarta among others. Fares and times are comparable to the bus but the air-conditioned trains are more comfortable, even in economy class.

ℹ️ Getting Around

Bemo

Bemo take various circuitous routes from and between Denpasar's many bus/bemo terminals. They line up for various destinations at each terminal, or you can try and hail them from anywhere along the main roads – look for the destination sign above the driver's window. The Tegal–Nusa Dua bemo (dark blue in colour) is handy for Renon; and the Kereneng–Ubung bemo (turquoise) travels along Jl Gajah Mada, past the Museum Negeri Propinsi Bali.

Taxi

Taxis prowl the streets of Denpasar looking for fares. As always, the blue cabs of **Bluebird Taxi** (📞701 111) are the most reliable choice.

NUSA LEMBONGAN & ISLANDS

Look towards the open ocean southeast of Bali and the hazy bulk of Nusa Penida dominates the view. But for many visitors the real focus is Nusa Lembongan, which lurks in the shadow of its vastly larger neighbour. Here, there's great surfing, langorous beaches and the kind of laid-back vibe travellers cherish. It's a popular destination and justly so – it's the one excursion you should make while in Bali.

Nusa Penida is seldom visited, which means that its dramatic vistas and unchanged village life are yours to explore. Tiny Nusa Ceningan huddles between the larger islands. It is an interesting quick jaunt from Lembongan.

The islands have been a poor region for many years. Thin soils and a lack of fresh water do not permit the cultivation of rice, but other crops such as maize, cassava and beans are staples grown here. The main cash crop has been seaweed, although the big harvest on Lembongan now comes on two legs.

Nusa Lembongan

📞0366

It's the Bali many imagine but never find outside of perhaps Balangan Beach: simple rooms on the sand, cheap beers with incredible sunsets, days spent surfing and diving, and nights spent riffling through a favourite book or hanging with new friends.

Nusa Lembongan grows in popularity each year, but even though rooms for travellers proliferate, it remains a mellow place. The new-found wealth is bringing changes though: you'll see boys riding motorbikes 300m to school, temples being expensively renovated, higher-end luxuries being introduced, and time being marked by the arrival of tourist boats rather than the crow of a rooster or the fall of a coconut.

◉ Sights

JUNGUTBATU

The **beach** here, a mostly lovely arc of white sand with clear blue water, has views across to Gunung Agung in Bali. The pleasant seawall walkway is ideal for strolling, especially – as you'd guess – at sunset.

The village itself is mellow, with quiet lanes, no cars and lots of seaweed production. **Pura Segara** and its enormous banyan tree are the site of frequent ceremonies.

The north end of town holds the metal-legged **lighthouse**. To get here, follow the road around east for about 1km to **Pura Sakenan**.

PANTAI SELEGIMPAK

The long, straight **beach** is usually lapped by small waves at this remote-feeling spot with a couple of places to stay (one of which has unfortunately built its seawall *below* the low-tide line). About 200m east along the shoreline path where it goes up and over a knoll is a minute **cove** with a nub of sand and a tiny warung. It's cute.

MUSHROOM BAY

This beautiful bay, unofficially named after the mushroom corals offshore, has a crescent of bright white **beach**. By day, the tranquillity can be disturbed by banana-boat rides or parasailing. At other hours, this is a beach of dreams. Look for the enormous **sacred tree** just east of Waka Nusa Resort.

The most interesting way to get here from Jungutbatu is to walk along the trail that starts from the southern end of the main beach and follows the coastline for a kilometre or so. Alternatively, get a boat from Jungutbatu for about 30,000Rp.

Nusa Lembongan

0   400 m
0   0.2 miles

To Toyapakeh

Selat Badung

To Sanur

Public Boats

Perama Office

JUNGUTBATU

Scoot Office

Medical Clinic

Jungutbatu Beach

Pantai Selegimpak

PURA SEGARA

Mushroom Bay

To Dream Beach & Dream Beach Huts Lembongan(800m)

Nusa Lembongan

DREAM BEACH

Down a track, on the southwestern side of the island, this 150m-deep pocket of white sand has pounding surf and pretty azure waters. It's a good escape although day trippers can crowd in.

A new low-key resort, Dream Beach Huts Lembongan (p132), has a pool that you can use for 50,000Rp plus an OK cafe.

LEMBONGAN

The other main town on the island looks across the seaweed-farm-filled channel to

Nusa Ceningan. It's a beautiful scene of clear water and green hills.

🏃 Activities

Most places hire out gear for aquatic fun.

Surfing

Surfing here is best in the dry season (April to September), when the winds come from the southeast. It's definitely not for beginners, and can be dangerous even for experts. There are three main breaks on the reef, all aptly named. From north to south are **Shipwreck**, **Lacerations** and **Playground**. Depending on where you are staying, you can paddle directly out to whichever of the three is closest; for others it's better to hire a boat. Prices are negotiable – from about 30,000Rp to 50,000Rp for a one-way trip. You tell the owner when to return. A fourth break – **Racecourses** – sometimes emerges south of Shipwreck.

The surf can be crowded here even when the island isn't – charter boats from Bali sometimes bring groups of surfers for day trips from the mainland for a minimum of 800,000Rp.

Monkey Surfing SURFING
(Jungutbatu Beach) Hire surfboards (90,000Rp per two hours) and stand-up paddle boards (120,000Rp per two hours) from this shop on the beach. Surfing lessons are 500,000Rp for 2½ hours.

Diving

Nusa Lembongan is a good base for divers. The number of dive shops is proliferating. Average prices include five-day PADI open-water courses for US$375, and dive trips from US$27 to US$40 per dive to sites around all three islands.

World Diving DIVING
(☑081 2390 0686; www.world-diving.com) World Diving, based at the Pondok Baruna location on Jungutbatu Beach, is well regarded. It offers a complete range of courses plus diving and snorkelling trips to dive sites all around the three islands.

Bali Diving Academy DIVING
(☑0361-270 252; www.scubali.com; Bungalow Number 7) The long-running Bali Diving Academy is a recommended dive operation, which has long experience in the waters around Lembongan and Penida. It has a full range of courses.

Snorkelling

Good snorkelling can be had just off the Mushroom Bay and **Bounty pontoons** off Jungutbatu Beach, as well as in areas off the north coast of the island. You can charter a boat from 150,000Rp per hour, depending on demand, distance and the number of passengers. A trip to the challenging waters of Nusa Penida costs 400,000Rp for three hours; to the nearby mangroves costs about 300,000Rp. Snorkelling gear can be hired for about 30,000Rp per day. World Diving allows snorkellers to join dive trips and charges 230,000Rp for a four-hour trip.

There's good drift snorkelling along the mangrove-filled channel located west of Ceningan Point, between Lembongan and Ceningan.

Cruises

A number of cruise boats offer day trips to Nusa Lembongan from south Bali. Trips include hotel transfer from south Bali, basic water sports, snorkelling, banana-boat rides, island tours and a buffet lunch. Note that with the usually included hotel transfers the following trips can make for a long day.

Bounty Cruise CRUISE
(☑726 666; www.balibountycruises.com; adult/child US$95/47.50) Boats dock at a garish yellow offshore pontoon with water slides and other amusements.

Island Explorer Cruise CRUISE
(☑0366-728 088; www.bali-activities.com; adult/child from 800,000/400,000Rp) Affiliated with Coconuts Beach Resort; uses a large boat that doubles as the base for day-trip aquatic fun. Also has a sailing ship.

🛏 Sleeping & Eating

With notable exceptions, rooms and amenities become increasingly posh as you head south and west along the water to Mushroom Bay. Almost every property has a cafe serving – unless noted – basic Indonesian and Western dishes for about 30,000Rp.

JUNGUTBATU

Many lodgings in Jungutbatu have shed the surfer-shack cliché and are moving upmarket. But you can still find cheapies with cold water and fans.

Indiana Kenanga HOTEL $$$
(www.indiana-kenanga-villas.com; r US$110-460; ❄ 🛜 ⛱) Wow! Jungutbatu will never be the

SEAWEED SUNDAE

The next time you enjoy some creamy ice cream you might want to thank the seaweed growers of Nusa Lembongan and Nusa Penida. Carrageenan is an emulsifying agent that is used to thicken ice cream as well as cheese and many other products. It is also used as a fat substitute in 'diet' foods (just look for it on the endless ingredients label). In nature it turns sea water into a gel that gives seaweed its structure.

On Lembongan, 85% of the population work at farming seaweed for carrageenan (as opposed to 5% in tourism). It's the island's major industry. Although returns are OK, the work is very intensive and time-consuming. Women are the main labourers.

As you walk around the villages, you'll see – and smell – vast areas used for drying seaweed. Looking down into the water, you'll see the patchwork of cultivated seaweed plots. Small pieces of a marine algae (*Eucheuma*) are attached to strings that are stretched between bamboo poles – these underwater fences can be seen off many of the beaches, and especially in the shallows between Lembongan and Ceningan and at low tide. Growth is so fast that new shoots can be harvested every 45 days. This region is especially good for production, as the waters are shallow and rich in nutrients. The dried red and green seaweed is exported around the world for final processing.

same. Six stylish rooms and two posh villas shelter near a pool behind the beach at Lembongan's most-glossy-magazine-ready digs. The French designer-owner has decorated the place with purple armchairs and other whimsical touches. The restaurant has an all-day menu of seafood, sandwiches and various surprises cooked up by the French chef (meals US$10 to US$30). People have been known to swoon over the chocolate fondant.

Pondok Baruna   GUESTHOUSE **$$**
(☑0812 394 0992; www.pondokbaruna.com; r 250,000-700,000Rp; ❈@☎☜) Associated with World Diving, this place offers four very simple rooms with terraces facing the ocean. They are an excellent budget option. Six plusher rooms with air-con surround a dive pool off the beach. Eight more Frangipani rooms have been added back in the palm trees around a large pool. Staff, led by the manager, Putu, are charmers.

Shipwrecks   GUESTHOUSE **$$**
(☑0813 3739 9577; www.nusalembongan.com.au; r from 600,000Rp; ❈☎) This beautiful property is set back from the beach in a coconut-shaded garden, and offers three rooms in a compound constructed in old Balinese style with natural wood. The beds are king-sized and the bathrooms open-air. The open common area is good for lounging or watching movies. Note that there is a two-night minimum and it's adults only.

Two Thousand Cafe & Bungalows   GUESTHOUSE **$**
(☑0812 381 2775; r 200,000-500,000Rp; ❈☎☜) Grassy grounds surround 28 rooms in two-storey blocks; some have hot water and air-con. There's a fun cafe-bar right on the sand, with various sunset drink specials.

Nusa Indah Bungalows   GUESTHOUSE **$$**
(☑081 139 8553; www.lembongansurferbeach cafe.com; r 300,000-500,000Rp; ❈☎☜) Solid cottages on a sizeable beachfront and a popular cafe make this a good choice. Fan-only rooms are a good budget option on the beach. The beach loungers have a fine position.

Lembongan Beach Retreat   GUESTHOUSE **$**
(Map p128; ☑0878 6131 3468; r 150,000-400,000Rp) At the northern end of the beach past the end of the breakwater, this little place lives up to its name. A retreat it is, with nothing stirring by day but the ripple of the surf and the imperceptible sound of seaweed drying in the sun.

TOP CHOICE / Pondok Baruna Warung   INDONESIAN **$**
(Map p128; meals from 40,000Rp) The dining part of the Baruna empire boasts some of the best food on the island. Look for excellent Balinese dishes as well as a range of fine curries. Many order not one but two chocolate brownies.

99 Meals House   INDONESIAN, CHINESE **$**
(meals from 13,000Rp) An absolute bargain. Fried rice, omelettes, Chinese stir-fries and

more prepared by a family at this tiny shop open on two sides. What passes for Lembongan's main drag is right outside. This is a good place for cheap water and snacks.

HILLSIDE

The steep hillside just south of Jungutbatu offers great views and an ever-increasing number of more luxurious rooms. The uppermost rooms at some places have gorgeous views across the water to Bali (on a clear day say hello to Gunung Agung), but such thrills come at a cost: upwards of 120 steep concrete steps. A motorbike-friendly path runs along the top of the hill, good for leg-saving drop-offs.

Playgrounds HOTEL $$

(☑24 524; www.playgroundslembongan.com; r US$70-175; ✳@🛜🏊) On the hillside, Playgrounds' rooms have good views, satellite TV and fridges. The cheaper ones are fan-cooled but do have better views from their long porch. Villas at the top reward climbers with stylish outdoor bathrooms and plenty of space.

Batu Karang HOTEL $$$

(☑559 6376; www.batukaranglembongan.com; r from US$230; ✳@🛜🏊) This upmarket resort has a large infinity pool perched on a ter-

raced hillside with 23 luxury units. Some are villa-style and have multiple rooms and private plunge pools. All have open-air bathrooms and wooden terraces with sweeping views.

Ware-Ware GUESTHOUSE $

(☑0812 397 0572; www.warewaresurfbungalows. com; r 400,000-700,000Rp; ✳🛜🏊) The units at this hillside place are a mix of tradiational square and groovy circular numbers with thatched roofs. The large rooms (some fan-only) have rattan couches and big bathrooms. The cafe scores with a spectacular, breezy location on a cliffside wooden deck. It does well with seafood (meals 30,000–100,000Rp).

Morin Lembongan GUESTHOUSE $

(☑0812 385 8396; wayman40@hotmail.com; r US$30-60; @) More lushly planted than many of the hillside places, Morin has woodsy rooms with views over the water from their verandas. This is a good choice if you want to feel close yet removed from Jungutbatu.

Deck CAFE $$

(Map p128; Batu Kareng; snacks from 20,000Rp; 🛜) Straddling the main hillside walkway, the stylish bar and cafe of the Batu Karang

---

DIVING THE ISLANDS

There are great diving possibilities around the islands, from shallow and sheltered reefs, mainly on the northern side of Lembongan and Penida, to very demanding drift dives in the channel between Penida and the other two islands. Vigilant locals have protected their waters from dynamite bombing by renegade fishing boats, so the reefs are relatively intact. And a side benefit of seaweed farming is that locals no longer rely so much on fishing. The islands were also designated a marine conservation district in 2012.

If you arrange a dive trip from Padangbai or south Bali, stick with the most reputable operators, as conditions here can be tricky and local knowledge is essential. Diving accidents regularly happen and people die diving in the waters around the islands every year.

Using one of the recommended operators on Nusa Lembongan puts you close to the action from the start. A particular attraction are the large marine animals, including turtles, sharks and manta rays. The large (3m fin-to-fin) and unusual *mola mola* (sunfish) is sometimes seen around the islands between mid-July and October, while manta rays are often seen south of Nusa Penida.

The best dive sites include **Blue Corner** and **Jackfish Point** off Nusa Lembongan and **Ceningan Point** at the tip of that island. The channel between Ceningan and Penida is renowned for drift diving, but it is essential you have a good operator who can judge fast-changing currents and other conditions. Upswells can bring cold water from the open ocean to sites such as **Ceningan Wall**. This is one of the world's deepest natural channels and attracts all manner and sizes of fish.

Sites close to Nusa Penida include **Crystal Bay**, **SD**, **Pura Ped**, **Manta Point** and **Batu Aba**. Of these, Crystal Bay, SD and Pura Ped are suitable for novice divers and are good for snorkelling. Note that the open waters around Penida are challenging, even for experienced divers.

HIKING & BIKING LEMBONGAN

You can walk around the entire island in a day, or less on a bike. It's a fascinating journey into remote and rural Balinese life. Start along the hillside trail from Jungutbatu and head past the Mutiara Villa; you'll have to do some freelancing as villa developers have screwed up part of the trail. At Pantai Selegimpak there are more unnecessary manmade obstacles on the beach. Nature provides the challenges to reach Mushroom Bay, but with a little Tarzan spirit, you can stay with the faint trail and be rewarded by refreshments (this is the one segment you can't do by bike: use the roads inland).

From Mushroom Bay, head over to dreamy Dream Beach.

Next go to Lembongan village where you can take the suspension bridge to Nusa Ceningan. Alternatively, from Lembongan village you can take a gentle uphill walk along the sealed road to the killer hill that leads down to Jungutbatu, which cuts the circuit to about half a day.

To explore the rest of the island, stick to the paved road that follows the channel between Nusa Lembongan and Nusa Ceningan and then curves north along the mangroves all the way to the lighthouse. Motorbikes won't be able to navigate the trails.

hotel offers creative drinks, gorgeous views and interesting snacks (it has a good bakery).

MUSHROOM BAY

It's your own treasure island. This shallow bay has a nice beach, plenty of overhanging trees and some of the nicest lodging on Lembongan. Get here from Jungutbatu by road (15,000Rp) or boat (50,000Rp).

Mushroom Beach Bungalows   GUESTHOUSE **$$**
(✍24 515; www.mushroom-lembongan.com; r US$70-125; ✳✉) Perched on a tiny knoll at the eastern end of Mushroom Bay, this family-run place has a great variety of rooms, some fan only. There are good-sized bathtubs and a popular cliffside cafe (meals 40,000–150,000Rp) for viewing sunsets. Packages including direct trasnport from Sanur are avialable.

Bar & Cafe Bali   INTERNATIONAL **$**
(✍24 536, 0828 367 1119; meals 30,000-60,000Rp; ☎) Follow the chicken tracks in the sand to tables under trees above the high-tide mark. Enjoy pizza, pasta, seafood and the Indo usuals. The bar is lively and you can arrange for transport from Jungutbatu.

ELSEWHERE ON LEMBONGAN

Point Resort
Lembongan   BOUTIQUE INN **$$$**
(www.thepointlembongan.com; ste from US$200; ✳☎✉) About 500m west of Mushroom Bay is this eponymously named property with four plush suites. The views are sweeping

and should pirates sail in, you can watch them get dashed on the rocks below the infinity pool. Service is luxe.

Dream Beach Huts
Lembongan   GUESTHOUSE **$$**
(✍0812 398 3772; www.dreambeachlembongan. com; Dream Beach; r from US$75; ✳) Looming over the north side of Dream Beach, this guesthouse has 17 rooms in traditionally styled thatched roof huts as well as a double-tiered swimming pool. The cafe is acceptable and without local competition but if you're looking for a very mellow beach getaway, this is it.

❶ Information

Small markets can be found near the bank, but unless you're on a diet of bottled water and Ritz crackers, the selection is small.

Internet Access

Wi-fi is now common.

Medical Services

Medical Clinic (consultation 150,000Rp) The medical clinic in the village is well versed in minor surfing injuries and ear ailments.

Money

It's vital that you bring sufficient cash in rupiah for your stay, as there is only one ATM (and it was not operating at time of writing).

If the name **money changer** (⏰8am-9pm) conjures images of the usurers being chased from the temple, you'd be right. Cash advances here on credit cards incur an 8% service charge.

ⓘ Getting There & Away

Getting to/from Nusa Lembongan offers numerous choices. In descending order of speed are the fast boats like Scoot, the Perama boat and the public boats. Note: anyone with money for a speedboat is getting into the fast-boat act; be wary of fly-by-night operators with fly-by-night safety.

Boats anchor offshore, so be prepared to get your feet wet. And travel light – wheeled bags are comically inappropriate in the water and on the beach and dirt tracks. Porters will shoulder your steamer trunk for 20,000Rp (and don't be like some low lifes we've seen who have stiffed them for their service).

Public boats leave from the northern end of Sanur beach for Nusa Lembongan at 8am (60,000Rp, 1¾ to two hours). This is the boat used for supplies, so you may have to share space with a chicken.

Perama tourist boat leaves Sanur at 10.30am (return 180,000Rp, 1¾ hours). The **Lembongan office** (www.peramatour.com; Jungutbatu Beach) is near the Mandara Beach Bungalows. It also has boats to Lombok and the Gili Islands.

Scoot (www.scootcruise.com), located on the waterfront in Nusa Lembongan, runs speedboats (return adult/child 550,000/270,000Rp, 30 to 40 minutes) that fly over and through the waves. There are several returns daily; check schedules when you book. It also has Gili services.

Nusa Penida boats take locals between Jungutbatu and Toyapakeh (one hour) between 5.30am and 6am for 30,000Rp. Otherwise, charter a boat for 150,000Rp one way.

ⓘ Getting Around

The island is fairly small and you can easily walk to most places. There are no cars (although pick-up trucks are proliferating); bicycles (25,000Rp per day) and small motorbikes (50,000Rp per hour) are widely available for hire. One-way rides on motorbikes or trucks cost 20,000Rp and up.

Nusa Ceningan

There is a picturesque narrow suspension bridge crossing the lagoon between Nusa Lembongan and Nusa Ceningan, which makes it quite easy to explore the network of tracks on foot or by bicycle. Besides the lagoon filled with frames for seaweed farming you'll see several small agricultural plots and a fishing village. The island is quite hilly and, if you're up for it, you can get glimpses of great scenery while wandering or cycling around the rough tracks.

To really savour Nusa Ceningan, take an overnight tour of the island with **JED** (Village Ecotourism Network; ☑366 9951; www.jed.or.id; per person US$130), the cultural organisation that gives people an in-depth look at village and cultural life. Trips include family accommodation in a village, local meals, a fascinating tour with seaweed workers and transport to/from Bali.

There's a **surf break** at Ceningan reef, but it's very exposed and only surfable when the other breaks are too small.

Nusa Penida

☑0366

Largely overlooked by tourists, Nusa Penida awaits discovery. It's an untrammelled place that answers the question: what would Bali be like if tourists never came? There are not a lot of formal activities or sights; rather, you go to Nusa Penida to explore and relax, to adapt to the slow rhythm of life here, and to learn to enjoy subtle pleasures such as the changing colour of the clouds and the sea. Life is simple; you'll still see topless older women carrying huge loads on their heads.

The island is a limestone plateau with white-sand beaches on its north coast, and views over the water to the volcanoes in Bali. Most beaches are not great for swimming, as most of the shallows are filled with bamboo frames used for seaweed farming. The south coast has 300m-high limestone cliffs dropping straight down to the sea and a row of offshore islets – it's rugged and spectacular scenery. The interior is hilly, with sparse-looking crops and old-fashioned villages. Rainfall is low and parts of the island are arid, although you can see traces of ancient rice terraces.

The population of around 60,000 is predominantly Hindu, although there is a

---

ⓘ BOAT SAFETY

There have been accidents involving boats between Bali and the surrounding islands. These services are unregulated and there is no safety authority should trouble arise. See p378 for information on how to improve your odds for a trouble-free journey.

THE BEST WAY TO VISIT NUSA PENIDA

Stay in a beautiful part of untouristed Nusa Penida, do good work to help restore this island and get a chance to ponder the beautiful and once-thought-extinct Bali starling. **Friends of the National Parks Foundation** (FNPF; ☎0361-977 978; www.fnpf.org) is a non-profit group that does the very work its name implies.

On Nusa Penida, FNPF has a centre in the village of Ped on the island's north coast. Here you can volunteer to do all manner of useful work locally, including aid in the restoration of native bird species. Accommodation is in simple but comfortable rooms with fans and cold water. You can take your meals at warung in the local village.

The cost varies but averages under US$20 per person per night. Transport and food are extra. Volunteers spend the morning working on projects and the afternoon exploring the island.

This is a highly recommended experience and gives you an insight into the very elusive 'real' Bali that so many people seek. For more on volunteering, see p372.

Muslim community in Toyapakeh. The culture is distinct from that of Bali: the language is an old form of Balinese no longer heard on the mainland. It's an unforgiving area: Nusa Penida was once used as a place of banishment for criminals and other undesirables from the kingdom of Klungkung (now Semarapura), and still has a somewhat sinister reputation. Even today there is but one source of water and many hardships.

Services are limited to small shops in the main towns. Bring cash and anything else you'll need.

🏃 Activities

Nusa Penida has world-class **diving**. Make arrangements through a dive shop on Nusa Lembongan. If you plan to go **snorkelling**, bring your own gear.

Between Toyapakeh and Sampalan there is excellent **cycling** on the beautiful, flat coastal road. The hitch is you need to bring a *good* bike with you to Penida. If you really want to explore, bring a mountain bike and camping equipment from the mainland (but remember, Nusa Penida is hilly). Alternatively, plan to do some serious **hiking**, but you will need to come well prepared.

SAMPALAN

Sampalan, the main town on Penida, is quiet and pleasant, with a market, schools and shops strung out along the curving coast road. The market area, where bemo congregate, is in the middle of town. It's a good place to absorb village life.

🛏 Sleeping & Eating

Not many people stay here, although there are plenty of rooms, so just show up. For meals you'll need to try one of the small warung in town – no more than 10 minutes by foot from any of the inns.

Made's Homestay　　　　HOMESTAY **$**
(☎0852 3764 3649; r from 150,000Rp) Four small, clean rooms in a pleasant garden include a small breakfast. A small side road between the market and the harbour leads here.

Nusa Garden Bungalows　　GUESTHOUSE **$**
(☎0813 3812 0660; r from 150,000Rp) Crushed-coral pathways running between animal statuary link the 10 rooms here. Rates include a small breakfast. Turn on Jl Nusa Indah just east of the centre.

TOYAPAKEH

If you come by boat from Nusa Lembongan, you'll probably be dropped at the beach at Toyapakeh, a pretty village with lots of shady trees. The beach has clean white sand, clear blue water, a neat line of boats, and Gunung Agung as a backdrop. Step up from it and you're at the road where bemo can take you to Ped or Sampalan (10,000Rp).

Toyapakeh is ripe for some groovy tourist accommodation, although it's been ripe for a long time. In the meantime, you could be the intrepid traveller and see if rooms have appeared, knowing that you can always go to nearby Sampalan for a simple room.

AROUND THE ISLAND

A trip around the island, following the north and east coasts and crossing the hilly interi-

YOUR OWN PERFECT BEACH

South of Toyapakeh, a 10km road through the village of Sakti leads to idyllic **Crystal Bay Beach**, which fronts the popular dive spot. The sand here is the whitest around Bali and you'll likely have it to yourself. Should you somehow have the gear, this would be a fine place to camp.

or, can be completed in half a day by motorcycle or in a day by bike if you're in shape. You could spend much longer, lingering at the temples and the small villages, and walking to less accessible areas, but there's no accommodation outside the two main towns. The following description goes clockwise from Sampalan.

The coastal road from Sampalan curves and dips past bays with rows of fishing boats and offshore seaweed gardens. After about 6km, just before the village of Karangsari, steps go up on the right side of the road to the narrow entrance of **Goa Karangsari** caves. There are usually people who can provide a lantern and guide you through the cave for a small negotiable fee of around 20,000Rp each. The limestone cave is over 15m tall in some sections. It extends more than 200m through the hill and emerges on the other side to overlook a verdant valley.

Continue south past a naval station and several temples to **Suana**. Here the main road swings inland and climbs up into the hills, while a very rough side track goes southeast, past more interesting temples to **Semaya**, a fishing village with a sheltered beach and one of Bali's best dive sites offshore, **Batu Aba**.

About 9km southwest of Suana, **Tanglad** is a very old-fashioned village and a centre for traditional weaving. Rough roads south and east lead to isolated parts of the coast.

A scenic ridge-top road goes northwest from Tanglad. At Batukandik, a rough road and 1.5km track leads to a spectacular **waterfall** *(air terjun)* that crashes onto a small beach. Get a guide (20,000Rp) in Tanglad.

Limestone cliffs drop hundreds of feet into the sea, surrounded by crashing surf. At their base, underground streams discharge fresh water into the sea – a pipeline was made to bring the water up to the top. Look

for the remains of the rickety old wooden scaffolding women used to clamber down, returning with large pots of water on their heads.

Back on the main road, continue to Batumadeg, past **Bukit Mundi** (the highest point on the island at 529m; on a clear day you can see Lombok), through Klumpu to Sakti, which has traditional stone buildings. Return to the north coast at Toyapakeh, about one hour after Bukit Mundi.

The important temple of **Pura Dalem Penetaran Ped** is near the beach at Ped, a few kilometres east of Toyapakeh. It houses a shrine for the demon Jero Gede Macaling, below. The temple structure is sprawling and you will see many people making offerings for safe sea voyages from Nusa Penida; you may wish to join them.

Across from the temple, the spotless and simple **Depot Anda** (meals 5000-10,000Rp; ⊙6am-9pm) is the eating choice on the island, with tasty local standards. Have a banana juice at **Warung Ibu Nur** (dishes from 3000Rp).

The road between Sampalan and Toyapakeh follows the craggy and lush coast.

ⓘ Getting There & Away

The strait between Nusa Penida and southern Bali is deep and subject to heavy swells – if there is a strong tide, boats often have to wait. You may also have to wait a while for the public boat to fill up with passengers. Boats to/from Kusamba are not recommended.

PENIDA'S DEMON

Nusa Penida is the legendary home of Jero Gede Macaling, the demon who inspired the Barong Landung dance. Many Balinese believe the island is a place of enchantment and *angker* (evil power) – paradoxically, this is an attraction. Although few foreigners visit, thousands of Balinese come every year for religious observances aimed at placating the evil spirits.

The island has a number of interesting temples dedicated to Jero Gede Macaling, including Pura Dalem Penetaran Ped, near Toyapakeh. It houses a shrine that is a source of power for practitioners of black magic, and a place of pilgrimage for those seeking protection from sickness and evil.

SANUR Speedboats leave from the same part of the beach as the public boats to Nusa Lembongan. Maruti Express is the main operator.

PADANGBAI Off the beach just east of the car park in Padangbai, you'll find the twin-engine fibreglass boats that run across the strait to Buyuk, 1km west of Sampalan on Nusa Penida (50,000Rp, 45 minutes, four daily). The boats run between 7am and noon. A large and modern car ferry operates daily (16,000Rp, two hours) from Kusamba.

NUSA LEMBONGAN Boats run between Toyapakeh and Jungutbatu (30,000Rp, one hour) between 5.30am and 6am. Enjoy the mangrove views on the way. Otherwise, charter a boat for 150,000Rp.

🛈 Getting Around

Bemo regularly travel along the sealed road between Toyapakeh and Sampalan, and sometimes on to Suana and up to Klumpu, but beyond these areas the roads are rough and transport is limited. You should be able to charter your own bemo or private vehicle with driver for about 50,000Rp per hour or hire a motorbike for 100,000Rp per day.

You may also be able to negotiate an *ojek* (motorcycle that takes passengers) for about 30,000Rp per hour.

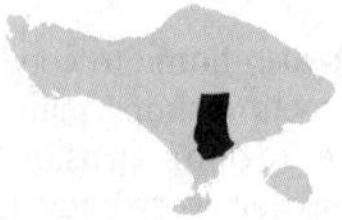

Ubud & Around

Best Places to Eat

» Sopa (p163)

» Mozaic (p164)

» Nasi Ayam Kedewatan (p165)

» Warung Teges (p163)

Best Places to Stay

» Matahari Cottages (p155)

» Swasti Cottage (p157)

» Maya Ubud (p158)

» Warwick Ibah Luxury Villas & Spa (p158)

Why Go?

A dancer moves her hand just so and 200 pairs of entranced eyes follow the exact movement. A gamelan player hits a melodic riff and 200 pairs of feet tap along with it. The Legong goes into its second hour as the bumblebee dance unfolds with its sprightly flair and 200 butts forget they're still stuck in rickety plastic chairs.

So another dance performance works its magic on a crowd in Ubud, the town amid a collection of villages where all that is magical about Bali comes together in one easy-to-love package. From nightly cultural performances to museums showing the works of artists whose creativity flowered here to the unbelievably green rice fields that spill down lush hillsides to rushing rivers below, Ubud is a feast for the soul. Personal pleasures like fine dining, shopping, spas and more only add to the appeal.

When to Go

The weather is slightly cooler but much wetter than in the south; expect it to rain at any time. At night, mountain breezes make air-con unnecessary and let you hear the symphony of frogs, bugs and distant gamelan practices echoing over the rice fields through your screened window. Temperatures during the day average 30°C and at night 20°C, although extremes are possible. Seasonal variation is muted, given the prevalence of precipitation. The real factor in deciding when to come is peak season: July, August and the Christmas holidays mean a large influx of visitors.

Ubud & Around Highlights

❶ Making like the ubiquitous ducks and wandering the rice fields in and around **Ubud** (p138)

❷ Feeling the rhythm of a traditional Balinese **dance performance** (p166), one of Ubud's great night-time pageants

❸ Making new friends and wiling away the hours at a funky **Ubud cafe** (p159)

❹ Discovering your own hidden talents through an **art or cooking course** (p146) as you draw on the knowledge of talented locals

❺ Exploring the green jungle and white water of the **Sungai Ayung valley** (Sayan; p151)

❻ Making like Indiana Jones at the towering ancient wonders at **Gunung Kawi** (p173)

❼ Exploring the myriad villages in the Ubud region, such as **Mas** (p177), for artworks, crafts, ceremonial objects and other treasures

UBUD

☑ 0361

Ubud is culture, yes. It's also home to good restaurants, cafes and streets of shops, many selling goods from the region's artisans. There's somewhere to stay for every budget, and no matter what the price you can enjoy lodgings that reflect the local Zeitgeist: artful, creative and serene.

Ubud's popularity continues to grow. Tour buses with day trippers can choke the main streets and cause traffic chaos. Being named the top city in Asia by *Conde Nast Traveler* only added to the hoopla from bestselling *Eat, Pray, Love*. Fortunately Ubud adapts and a stroll away from the intersection of Jl Raya Ubud and Monkey Forest Rd can quickly restore sanity. There's nothing like a walk through the verdant rice fields to make all right with the world.

Spend a few days in Ubud to appreciate it properly. It's one of those places where days can become weeks and weeks become months, as the noticeable expat community demonstrates.

History

Late in the 19th century, Cokorda Gede Agung Sukawati established a branch of the Sukawati royal family in Ubud and began a series of alliances and confrontations with neighbouring kingdoms. In 1900, with the kingdom of Gianyar, Ubud became (at its own request) a Dutch protectorate and was able to concentrate on its religious and cultural life.

The Cokorda descendants encouraged Western artists and intellectuals to visit the area in the 1930s, most notably Walter Spies, Colin McPhee and Rudolf Bonnet. They provided an enormous stimulus to local art, introduced new ideas and techniques, and began a process of displaying and promoting Balinese culture worldwide. As mass tourism arrived in Bali, Ubud became an attraction not for beaches or bars, but for the arts.

The royal family is still much a part of Ubud life, helping to fund huge cultural and religious displays such as memorable cremation ceremonies.

◉ Sights

Palaces & Temples

Ubud Palace (Map p153; cnr Jl Raya Ubud & Jl Suweta) and **Puri Saren Agung** (Map p153; cnr Jl Raya Ubud & Jl Suweta) share space in the heart of Ubud. The compound has many ornate corners and was mostly built after the 1917 earthquake. The local royal family still live here and you can wander around most of the large compound exploring the many traditional and not excessively ornate buildings. If you really like it, you can stay the night. Take time to appreciate the stone carvings, many by noted local artists like I Gusti Nyoman Lempad.

Just north, **Pura Marajan Agung** (Map p153; Jl Suweta) has one of the finest gates you'll find and is the private temple for the royal family.

Pura Desa Ubud (Map p153; Jl Raya Ubud) is the main temple for the Ubud community. It is often closed. Just a bit west is the very picturesque **Pura Taman Saraswati** (Map p153; Jl Raya Ubud). Waters from the temple at the rear of the site feed the pond in the front, which overflows with pretty lotus blossoms. There are carvings that honour Dewi Saraswati, the goddess of wisdom and the arts, who has clearly given her blessing to Ubud. There are weekly dance performances by night; by day painters set up easels.

Natural Sights

Sacred Monkey Forest
Sanctuary   WILDLIFE RESERVE
(Mandala Wisata Wanara Wana; Map p153; 971304; Monkey Forest Rd; adult/child 20,000/10,000Rp; 8.30am-6pm) This cool and dense swath of jungle, officially called Mandala Wisata Wanara Wana, houses three holy temples. The sanctuary is inhabited by a band of grey-haired and greedy long-tailed Balinese macaques who are nothing like the innocent-looking doe-eyed monkeys on the brochures. The interesting **Pura Dalem Agung** (Map p153) is in the forest and has a real Indiana Jones feel to it. In the temple look for the Rangda figures devouring children at the entrance to the inner temple.

You can enter through one of the three gates: the main one at the southern end of Monkey Forest Rd; 100m further east, near the car park; or from the southern side, on the lane from Nyuhkuning. The forest has recently benefited from an infusion of money. Useful brochures about the forest, macaques and temples are available. Note that the monkeys are ever vigilant for passing tourists who just might have peanuts and ripe bananas available for a quick hand-out. Don't hand food directly to these creatures.

Across from the main entrance, the forest's office accepts donations for a scheme to offset the carbon you created getting to Bali. Get a tree planted for 150,000Rp.

Petulu   NATURAL AREA
Every evening at around 6pm, thousands of big **herons** and **egrets** fly in to Petulu, about 2.5km north of Jl Raya Ubud, squabbling over the prime perching places before settling into the trees beside the road and becoming a tourist attraction.

The herons, mainly the striped Java pond species, started their visits to Petulu in 1965 for no apparent reason. Villagers believe they bring good luck (as well as tourists), despite the smell and the mess. A few warung have been set up in the paddy fields, where you can have a drink while enjoying the spectacle. Walk quickly under the trees if the herons are already roosting.

Petulu is a pleasant walk or bicycle ride on any of several routes north of Ubud, but if you stay for the birds you'll be heading back in the dark.

Museums

TOP CHOICE **Museum Puri Lukisan**   MUSEUM
(Museum of Fine Arts; Map p153; 975 136; www.museumpurilukisan.com; off Jl Raya Ubud; adult/child 20,000Rp/free; 9am-5pm) This museum displays fine examples of all schools of Balinese art. Just look at the lush composition of *Balinese Market* by Anak Agung Gde Sobrat to see the vibrancy of local painting.

The museum's collection is well curated and labelled in English. The museum has a good bookshop and a cafe. The lush, garden-like grounds alone are worth a visit.

It was in Ubud that the modern Balinese art movement started, when artists first began to abandon purely religious themes and court subjects for scenes of everyday life. Rudolf Bonnet was part of the Pita Maha artists' cooperative, and together with Cokorda Gede Agung Sukawati (a prince of Ubud's royal family) and Walter Spies they helped to establish a permanent collection.

Building I, straight ahead as you enter, has a collection of early works from Ubud and the surrounding villages. These include examples of classical *wayang*-style paintings (art influenced by shadow puppetry), fine ink drawings by I Gusti Nyoman Lempad and paintings by Pita Maha artists. Notice the level of detail in Lempad's *The Dream of Dharmawangsa*. Classic works from the 1930s heyday of expats are also here.

Building II, on the left, has some colourful examples of the Young Artist style of

Ubud Area

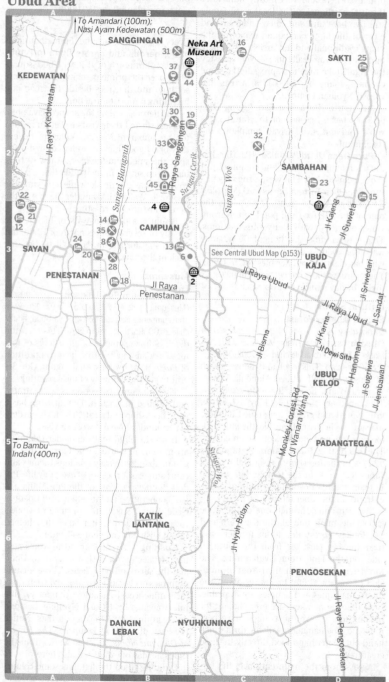

To Amandari (100m);
Nasi Ayam Kedewatan (500m)

KEDEWATAN

SANGGINGAN

Neka Art Museum

SAKTI

SAMBAHAN

CAMPUAN

SAYAN

PENESTANAN

Jl Raya Penestanan

See Central Ubud Map (p153)

UBUD KAJA

Jl Raya Ubud

UBUD KELOD

PADANGTEGAL

To Bambu Indah (400m)

KATIK LANTANG

PENGOSEKAN

DANGIN LEBAK

NYUHKUNING

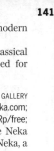

The map shows the area with labels: NAGI, KUTUH, TANAN, Guardian Pharmacy, TEBESAYA, PELIATAN, TEGES, Kimia Pharma, Jl Raya Andong, Jl Sukma, Jl Peliatan, Jl Made Lebah, Jl Raya Goa Gajah, Jl Raya Mas. Scale: 0–500 m, 0–0.25 miles.

painting and a good selection of 'modern traditional' works.

Building III, on the right, has classical and traditional paintings and is used for special exhibitions.

Neka Art Museum — GALLERY

(Map p140; ☑975 074; www.museumneka.com; Jl Raya Sanggingan; adult/child 50,000Rp/free; ⊙9am-5pm Mon-Sat, noon-5pm Sun) The Neka Art Museum is the creation of Suteja Neka, a private collector and dealer in Balinese art. It has an excellent and diverse collection and is a good place to learn about the development of painting in Bali.

You can get an overview of the myriad local painting styles in the **Balinese Painting Hall**. Look for the *wayang* works.

The **Arie Smit Pavilion** features Smit's works on the upper level, and examples of the Young Artist school, which he inspired, on the lower level. Look for the Bruegel-like *The Wedding Ceremony* by I Nyoman Tjarka.

The **Lempad Pavilion** houses Bali's largest collection of works by I Gusti Nyoman Lempad.

The **Contemporary Indonesian Art Hall** has paintings by artists from other parts of Indonesia, many of whom have worked in Bali. The upper floor of the **East-West Art Annexe** is devoted to the work of foreign artists, such as Louise Koke, Miguel Covarrubias, Rudolf Bonnet, Han Snel, Australian Donald Friend, and Antonio Blanco.

The temporary exhibition hall has changing displays, while the **Photography Archive Centre** features black-and-white photography of Bali in the early 1930s and 1940s. Also look for the large collection of ceremonial *keris* (daggers).

The bookshop is noteworthy and there's a cafe.

Agung Rai Museum of Art — GALLERY

(ARMA; Map p153; ☑976 659; www.armamuseum. com; Jl Raya Pengosekan; admission 50,000Rp; ⊙9am-6pm daily, Balinese dancing 3-5pm Mon-Fri, 10.30am-noon Sun) Founded by Agung Rai as a museum, gallery and cultural centre, the impressive ARMA is the only place in Bali to see haunting works by influential German artist Walter Spies and it has many more masterpieces. The museum is housed in several traditional buildings set in gardens with water coursing through channels.

It features work by 19th-century Javanese artist Raden Saleh. It exhibits classical

Ubud Area

Kamasan paintings, Batuan-style work from the 1930s and '40s, and works by Lempad, Affandi, Sadali, Hofker, Bonnet and Le Mayeur. The collection is well labelled in English.

Look for the enigmatic *Portrait of a Javanese Nobleman and His Wife* by Raden Saleh, which predates the similar *American Gothic* by decades.

It's fun to visit ARMA when local children practise **Balinese dancing** and during **gamelan practice**. There are regular Legong and Kecak performances, and myriad cultural courses are offered here.

You can enter the museum grounds from the southern end of Jl Raya Pengosekan or

around the corner on Jl Pengosekan at Kafe Arma, where there's parking.

Museum Rudana   GALLERY
(Map p140; ☏975 779; www.museumrudana.com; admission 50,000Rp; ☉9am-5pm) This imposing museum is the creation of local politician and art-lover Nyoman Rudana and his wife Ni Wayan Olasthini. The three floors contain over 400 traditional paintings, including a calendar dated to the 1840s, some Lempad drawings, and more modern pieces. The museum is beside the Rudana Gallery, which has a large selection of paintings for sale.

Blanco Renaissance Museum   ART MUSEUM
(Map p140; ☏975 502; www.blancomuseum.com; Jl Raya Campuan; admission 50,000Rp; ☉9am-5pm)

The picture of Antonio Blanco mugging with Michael Jackson says it all. His namesake Blanco Renaissance Museum captures the artist's theatrical spirit. Blanco came to Bali from Spain via the Philippines. He specialised in erotic art, illustrated poetry and playing the role of an eccentric artist à la Dalí. He died in Bali in 1999, and his flamboyant home is now this museum. More prosaically: enjoy the waterfall on the way in and good views over the river.

Galleries

Ubud is dotted with galleries – every street and lane seems to have a place exhibiting artwork for sale. They vary enormously in the choice and quality of items on display.

Often you will find local artists in the most unusual places, including your place to stay. A good example is I Wayan Karja, a painter who has a studio in the grounds of his family's Santra Putra guesthouse.

Neka Gallery   GALLERY
(Map p153; ☑975 034; Jl Raya Ubud; ⊙9am-5pm) Operated by Suteja Neka, the low-key Neka Gallery is a separate entity from the Neka Art Museum. It has an extensive selection from all the schools of Balinese art, as well as works by European residents such as the renowned Arie Smit.

Seniwati Gallery of Art by Women   GALLERY
(Map p153; ☑975 485; www.seniwatigallery.com; Jl Sriwedari 2B; ⊙9am-5pm Tue-Sun) This gallery exhibits works by more than 70 Balinese, Indonesian and resident foreign women artists. The information on many of the artists makes for fascinating reading. Works span all media.

Symon Studio   GALLERY
(Map p140; ☑974 721; www.symonstudios.com; Jl Raya Campuan; ⊙9am-6pm) 'Danger! Art!' screams the sign in Campuan. With this you know you've found the gallery/studio of the irrepressible American artist Symon. The gallery is a spacious and airy place full of huge, colourful and exotic portraits. The work ranges from the sublime to the profane. Symon, however, is most often found in his gallery in north Bali.

Komaneka Art Gallery   GALLERY
(Map p153; ☑976 090; Monkey Forest Rd; ⊙8am-8pm) Exhibiting works from established Balinese artists, this gallery is a good place to see high-profile art, in a large and lofty space.

Agung Rai Gallery   GALLERY
(Map p140; ☑975 449; Jl Peliatan; ⊙9am-6pm) This gallery is in a pretty compound and its collection covers the full range of Balinese styles. It functions as a cooperative, with the work priced by the artist and the gallery adding a percentage.

Rio Helmi Gallery   GALLERY
(Map p153; ☑972 304; www.riohelmi.com; Jl Suweta 5; ⊙10am-8pm) Noted photographer and Ubud resident Rio Helmi has a small gallery where you can see examples of journalistic and artistic work. Photos change often and offer beautiful insight into Helmi's travels worldwide and across Bali. His passionate pleas for the preservation of Bali in the face of massive change have appeared on the Huffington Post and elsewhere.

Adi's Gallery   GALLERY
(Map p153; ☑977 104; www.adi-s-gallery.com; Jl Bisma 102; ⊙10am-5pm) Many of the better local artists display their works here. Adi's hosts occasional special events like live music and many popular special exhibits. The gallery is a project of German artist Adi Bachmann.

Pranoto's Art Gallery   GALLERY
(Map p153; ☑970 827; Jl Raya Goa Gajah, Teges) The husband-wife pair of artists Pranoto and Kerry Pendergrast display their works at this gallery/studio/home which backs up to beautiful rice fields southwest of Ubud. Their scenes of Indonesian life are lovely. The studio is about 1km east of Jl Peliatan. Ask them about a lovely path you can take back to central Ubud.

DON'T MISS

THREADS OF LIFE INDONESIAN TEXTILE ARTS CENTER

This small, professional **textile gallery and educational studio** (Map p140; ☑972 187; www.threadsoflife.com; Jl Kajeng 24; ⊙10am-7pm) sponsors the production of naturally dyed, handmade ritual textiles, helping to recover skills in danger of being lost to modern dyeing and weaving methods. Commissioned pieces are displayed in the gallery, which has good explanatory material. It also runs regular textile appreciation courses and has a good shop.

UBUD & AROUND UBUD

> ## UBUD IN...
>
> ### One Day
>
> Stroll the streets of Ubud by starting with the classic loop of Monkey Forest Rd down to the namesake **park** and then coming back up along Jl Hanoman. You can spend hours browsing **shops** and **galleries** and stopping into characterful **cafes**. Wander side streets and gangs, explore Jl Dewi Sita and Jl Goutama and you'll have a great introduction to Ubud. Try to get out on one of the short nearby walks through the verdant rice fields. Go to an evening **dance performance**.
>
> ### Three Days
>
> Take longer walks in the countryside during the mornings, especially the **Campuan Ridge** and **Sayan Valley**. Consider a walking tour. In the afternoons visit the **Museum Puri Lukisan**, **Neka Art Museum** and **Arma**. At night attend **dance performances** not just in Ubud, but also in the nearby villages. Indulge at a local **spa**.
>
> ### A Week or More
>
> Do everything we've listed but take time to simply chill out. Get in tune with Ubud's rhythm. Take naps, read books, wander about. Think about a **course** in Balinese culture. Compare and choose your favourite cafe, get out to craft villages and ancient sites.

Ketut Rudi Gallery   GALLERY
(Map p175; ☎974 122; Pengosekan) These sprawling galleries showcase the works of more than 50 Ubud artists with techniques as varied as primitive and new realism. The gallery's namesake is on display as well; he favours an entertaining style best described as 'comical realism'.

🏃 Activities

Massages, Spas & Salons

Ubud brims with salons and spas where you can heal, pamper, rejuvenate or otherwise focus on your personal needs, physical and mental. Visiting a spa is at the top of many a traveller's itinerary and the business of spas, yoga and other treatments grows each year. Expect the latest trends from any of many practitioners (the bulletin board outside Bali Buddha is bewildering) and prepare to try some new therapies, such as 'pawing'. If you have to ask you don't want to know. You may also wish to seek out a *balian* (traditional healer).

Many spas also offer courses in therapies, treatments and activities like yoga.

TOP CHOICE Bali Botanica Day Spa   SPA
(Map p140; ☎976 739; www.balibotanica.com; Jl Raya Sanggingan; massage from 150,000Rp; ⊗9am-8pm) Set beautifully on a lush hillside past little fields of rice and ducks, this spa offers a range of treatments including Ayurvedic ones. Like a good pesto, the herbal massage is popular. Will provide transport.

Ubud Sari Health Resort   SPA
(Map p140; ☎974 393; www.ubudsari.com; Jl Kajeng; 1hr massage from US$15; ⊗8am-8pm) A spa and hotel in one. It is a serious place with extensive organic treatments bearing such names as 'total tissue cleansing'. Besides a long list of daytime spa and salon services, there are packages that include stays at the hotel. Many treatments focus on cleaning out your colon.

Intuitive Flow   YOGA
(Map p140; ☎977 824; www.intuitiveflow.com; Penestanan; yoga from 100,000Rp) A lovely yoga studio up amid the rice fields – although just climbing the concrete stairs to get here from Campuan may make you too pooped to pop your yoga togs on. Workshops in healing arts.

Taksu Spa   SPA
(Map p153; ☎971 490; www.taksuspa.com; Jl Goutama; massage from 65,000Rp; ⊗9am-10pm; ☎) Somewhat hidden yet still in the heart of Ubud, Taksu has a long and rather lavish menu of treatments as well as a strong focus on yoga. There are private rooms for couples massages, a healthy cafe and a range of classes.

Zen   SPA
(Map p153; ☎970 976; www.zenbalispa.com; Jl Hanoman; 1hr massage from 100,000Rp; ⊗9am-8pm) Down a little lane, this spa has a good

reputation. It offers body scrubs, 90-minute *mandi lulur* (Javanese body scrubs) and a spice bath, among myriad other pleasures.

Nur Salon SPA

(Map p153; ☑975 352; Jl Hanoman 28; 1hr massage 155,000Rp; ⊗9am-8pm) In a traditional Balinese compound filled with labelled medicinal plants; offers a long menu of straightforward spa and salon services, including a Javanese massage that takes two hours.

Eve Spa SPA

(Map p153; ☑973 236; www.evespabali.com; Monkey Forest Rd; 1hr massage 100,000Rp; ⊗9am-9pm) Will cleanse you of toxins. The menu is uncomplicated and affordable, and you can go on something of a spa orgy: an all-day festival of treatments is 510,000Rp.

Milano Salon SALON

(Map p153; ☑973 488; Monkey Forest Rd; 1hr massage 90,000Rp; ⊗10am-9pm) Offers facials and massages in a simple setting, plus haircutting (80,000Rp), styling and colouring.

Cycling

Many shops and hotels in central Ubud display mountain bikes for hire. The price is usually a negotiable 35,000Rp per day. If in doubt where to rent, ask at your hotel and someone with a bike is soon likely to appear.

In general, the land is dissected by rivers running south, so any east–west route will involve a lot of ups and downs as you cross the river valleys. North–south routes run between the rivers, and are much easier going, but can have heavy traffic. Most of the sites in Ubud are reachable by bike.

Riding a bike is an excellent way to visit the many museums and cultural sites located around Ubud, although you'll need to consider your comfort level with traffic south of Ubud.

There are several companies offering cycling tours in or near Ubud; see p148.

Rafting

The **Sungai Ayung** (Ayung River) is the most popular river in Bali for white-water rafting. You start north of Ubud and end near the Amandari hotel in the west. Note that depending on rainfall the run can range from sedate to thrilling. See p39 for a list of operators.

Walking

Walking in and about the Ubud region with its endless beauty, myriad fascinations and delightful discoveries is a great pleasure and a superb reason to visit the area.

There are lots of interesting walks in the area to surrounding villages and through the rice fields. You'll frequently see artists at work in open rooms and on verandas, and the timeless tasks of rice cultivation continue alongside luxury villas. For a list of guided walks, see p148.

A few points worth remembering to enjoy your walk:

» **Bring your own water** In most places there are plenty of warung or small shops

---

ARTISTS' HOMES

The **'Spies house'** (Map p140), home of German artist Walter Spies, is now part of Hotel Tjampuhan. Aficionados can stay if they book well in advance. Spies played an important part in promoting Bali's artistic culture in the 1930s.

Dutch-born artist Han Snel lived in Ubud from the 1950s until his death in 1999, and his family runs his namesake bungalows on Jl Kajeng.

Lempad's House (Map p153; Jl Raya Ubud; admission free; ⊗daylight), the home of I Gusti Nyoman Lempad, is open to the public, but it's mainly used as a gallery for a group of artists that includes Lempad's grandchildren. The Puri Lukisan and Neka museums have more extensive collections of Lempad's drawings.

Music scholar Colin McPhee is well known thanks to his perennial favourite *A House in Bali*. Although the actual 1930s house is long gone, you can visit the riverside site (which shows up in photographs in the book) at the Sayan Terrace hotel (p159). The hotel's Wayan Ruma, whose mother was McPhee's cook, is good for a few stories.

Arie Smit (1916–) is the best-known and longest-surviving Western artist in Ubud. He worked in the Dutch colonial administration in the 1930s, was imprisoned during WWII, and came to Bali in 1956. In the 1960s his influence sparked the Young Artists school of painting in Penestanan, earning him an enduring place in the history of Balinese art. His home is not open to the public.

selling snack foods and drinks but don't risk dehydration between stops.

» **Gear up** Bring a good hat, decent shoes and wet-weather gear for the afternoon showers; long trousers are better for walking through thick vegetation.

» **Start early** Try to begin at daybreak, before it gets too hot. The air also feels crisper and you'll catch birds and other wildlife before they spend the day in shadows. It's also much quieter before the day's buzz begins.

» **Avoid tolls** Some entrepreneurial rice farmers have erected little toll gates across their fields. You can a) simply detour around them, or b) pay a fee (never, ever accede to more than 10,000Rp).

» **Quit while ahead** Should you tire don't worry about reaching some goal – the point is to enjoy your walk. Locals on motorbikes will invariably give you a ride home for around 20,000Rp.

🥢 Courses

Ubud is the perfect place to develop your artistic or language skills, or learn about Balinese culture and cuisine. The range of courses offered could keep you busy for a year.

TOP CHOICE	**Arma**	CULTURAL

(Map p153; ☑976 659; www.armamuseum.com; Jl Raya Pengosekan; ☺9am-6pm) A cultural powerhouse offering classes in painting, woodcarving and batik. Other courses in-

BALI'S VILLAGE ARTISTS

In small villages throughout the Ubud region, from Sebatu to Mas and beyond across Bali, you'll see small signs for artists and craftspeople, often near the local temple. As one local told us, 'we are only as rich of a village as our art,' so the people who create the ceremonial costumes, masks, kris (swords), musical instruments and all the other beautiful aspects of Balinese life and religion are accorded great honour. It's a symbiotic relationship, with the artist never charging the village for the work and the village in turn seeing to the welfare of the artist. Often there are many artists in residence because few events would bring more shame to a village than having to go to another village to procure a needed sacred object.

clude Balinese history, Hinduism and architecture. Classes cost US$25 to US$55.

Threads of Life Indonesian
Textile Arts Center TEXTILE
(Map p140; ☑972 187; www.threadsoflife.com; Jl Kajeng 24) Textile appreciation courses in the gallery and educational studio last from one to eight days. Some classes involve extensive travel around Bali and should be considered graduate level.

Nirvana Batik Course TEXTILE
(Map p153; ☑975 415; www.nirvanaku.com; Jl Goutama 10, Nirvana Pension & Gallery; ☺classes 10am-2pm Mon-Sat) Nyoman Suradnya teaches the highly regarded batik courses. Classes cost about US$45 to US$50 per day depending on duration (one to five days).

Pranoto's Art Gallery PAINTING
(☑970 827; Jl Raya Goa Gajah, Teges; private lessons per 3hr 400,000Rp) Two of Ubud's most accomplished artists offer private classes (materials included) in their lovely studio about 1km southwest of town. They also have model sessions which artists with their own materials can join for 20,000Rp.

IB Anom ART
(☑974 529; Mas) Three generations of some of Bali's best mask-carvers will show you their secrets (from 100,000Rp per day) in a family compound right off the main road; in two weeks you might have something.

Wayan Karja Painting PAINTING
(Map p140; ☑977 810; classes per hr 100,000Rp) Intensive painting and drawing classes are run by abstract artist Karja, whose studio is on the site of his guesthouse, the Santra Putra.

Wayan Pasek Sucipta MUSICAL INSTRUMENTS
(Map p153; ☑970 550; Eka's Homestay, Jl Sriwedari 8) Learn the gamelan and bamboo drums from a master (80,000Rp for one hour).

Pondok Pecak Library &
Learning Centre LANGUAGE COURSE
(Map p153; ☑976 194; Monkey Forest Rd; ☺9am-5pm Mon-Sat, 1-5pm Sun) On the far side of the football field, this centre offers painting, dance, music, language and mask-carving classes; some are geared to kids. One-hour sessions cost from 75,000Rp. Good resource centre for other courses offered locally.

Museum Puri Lukisan ART
(Map p153; www.museumpurilukisan.com; off Jl Raya Ubud; classes from 100,000Rp) One of

BALI'S TRADITIONAL HEALERS

Bali's traditional healers, known as *balian* (*dukun* on Lombok), play an important part in Bali's culture by treating physical and mental illness, removing spells and channelling information from the ancestors. Numbering about 8000, *balian* are the ultimate in community medicine, making a commitment to serve their communities and turning no one away.

Lately, however, this system has come under stress in some areas due to the attention brought by *Eat, Pray, Love* and other media coverage of Bali's healers. Curious tourists are turning up in village compounds, taking *balians'* time and attention from the genuinely ill. However, that doesn't mean you shouldn't visit a *balian* if you're genuinely curious. Just do so in a manner that befits the experience: gently.

Consider the following before a visit:

» Make an appointment before visiting a *balian*.

» Know that English is rarely spoken.

» Dress respectfully (long trousers and a shirt, better yet a sarong and sash).

» Women should not be menstruating.

» Never point your feet at the healer.

» Bring an offering into which you have tucked the consulting fee, which will range from 100,000Rp to 200,000Rp per person.

» Understand what you're getting into: your treatment will be very public and probably painful. It may include deep tissue massage, being poked with sharp sticks or having chewed herbs spat on you.

Finding a *balian* can take some work. Ask at your hotel, which can probably help with making an appointment and providing a suitable offering for stashing your fee. Or consider the following, who do see visitors to Bali:

Ketut Gading (☑970 770)

Man Nyoman (☑0813 3893 5369)

Sirkus (☑739 538)

Made Surya (www.balihealers.com) is an authority on Bali's traditional healers and offers one- and two-day intensive workshops on healing, magic, traditional systems and history, which include visits to authentic *balian*. His website is an excellent resource on visiting healers on Bali.

Some Western medical professionals question whether serious medical issues can be resolved by this type of healing, and suggest patients should see a traditional healer in conjunction with a Western doctor if their ailment is serious.

Ubud's best museums teaches courses in puppet-making, gamelan, offering-making, Balinese dance, mask painting and much more. Classes are taught on demand.

Studio Perak　　　　　　　　　JEWELLERY
(Map p153; ☑081 2365 1809, 974 244; www.studio perak.com; Jl Hanoman; lessons per 3hr 350,000Rp) Specialises in Balinese-style silversmithing courses. In one three-hour lesson you'll make a finished piece.

Taman Harum Cottages　　　　　CULTURAL
(☑975 567; www.tamanharumcottages.com; Mas; lessons per hour from US$20) In the centre of Bali's woodcarving district, this hotel offers a palette of craft, culture, carving and painting

courses. You can learn how to make the temple offerings found just about everywhere.

Cooking

One of the most popular activities for visitors to Ubud. Cooking classes usually start at one of the local markets, where you can learn about the huge range of fruits, vegetables and other foods that are part of the Balinese diet.

TOP **Casa Luna Cooking**
CHOICE **School**　　　　　　　COOKING COURSE
(Map p153; ☑973 282; www.casalunabali.com; Jl Bisma, Honeymoon Guesthouse; classes from 300,000Rp) There are regular cooking courses at Honeymoon Guesthouse and/or Casa Luna. Half-day courses cover ingredients,

ⓘ REFILL YOUR WATER BOTTLE

The number of plastic water bottles emptied in Bali's tropical heat daily and then tossed in the rubbish is appalling. In Ubud there are a few places where you can refill your water bottle (plastic or reusable) for a small fee, usually 3000Rp. The water is the same Aqua brand that is most preferred locally and you'll be helping to save Bali one plastic bottle at a time. A good central location is Pondok Pecak Library & Learning Centre (p146).

cooking techniques and the cultural background of the Balinese kitchen (not all visit the market). Tours are also offered, including a good one to the Gianyar night market.

Amandari   COOKING COURSE
(☎975 333; www.amanresorts.com; classes from US$150) Classes begin early (7am) at the produce market, then move on to a village where you learn how to cook in an actual Balinese home. Instruction is one-on-one.

Bumbu Bali Cooking School   COOKING COURSE
(Map p153; ☎976 698; Monkey Forest Rd) Balinese cooking course (250,000Rp) starts at the produce market (9am) and ends with lunch (2pm). Wide list of dishes prepared.

☞ Tours

Specialised tours in Ubud include thematic walks and cultural adventures. Spending a few hours exploring the area with a local expert is a highlight for many. There are tours of the Ubud area by companies operating across Bali.

Bali Herbal Walk   WALKING TOUR
(☎975 051; www.utamaspicebali.com; walks US$18; ⊙8.30am Mon-Thu) Three-hour walks through lush Bali landscape; medicinal and cooking herbs and plants are identified and explained in their natural environment. Includes herbal drinks. The couple behind the walks also run **Utama Spice** (www.utamaspicebali.com), which makes natural home and spa products.

Banyan Tree Cycling Tours   CYCLING
(☎0813 3879 8516, 805 1620; www.banyantreebiketours.com; tours from 450,000Rp) Enjoy daylong tours of remote villages in the hills above Ubud. It's locally owned by Bagi; the tours (from 450,000Rp) emphasise interaction with villagers. Very popular.

Bali Bird Walks   BIRDWATCHING
(Map p140; ☎975 009; www.balibirdwalk.com; tour US$37; ⊙9am-12.30pm Tue, Fri, Sat & Sun) Started by Victor Mason more than three decades ago, this tour, ideal for keen birders, is still going strong. On a gentle morning's walk (from the former Beggar's Bush Bar) you may see up to 30 of the 100-odd local species.

Dhyana Putri Adventures   CULTURAL TOUR
(☎0812 380 5623; www.balispirit.com/tours/bali_tour_dhyana.html) A bicultural, tri-lingual couple offer custom tours, with emphasis on Balinese performing arts and in-depth cultural experiences.

Bali Nature & Medicine Walk   WALKING TOUR
(☎0818 0539 9228; sangtubud@yahoo.com; price varies depending on walk) Lifelong Ubud resident and herbalist leads walks through the countryside explaining how the Balinese interact with nature.

Ubud Tourist Information   CULTURAL TOUR
(Yaysan Bina Wisata; ☎973 285; Jl Raya Ubud; tours 125,000-200,000Rp; ⊙8am-8pm) Runs interesting and affordable half- and full-day trips to a huge range of places, including Ulu Watu, Mengwi, Alas Kedaton and Tanah Lot, or Goa Gajah, Pejeng, Gunung Kawi and Kintamani.

☆ Festivals & Events

One of the best places to see the many religious and cultural events celebrated in Bali each year is the Ubud area. The tourist office is unmatched for its comprehensive information on events each week.

Bali Spirit Festival   DANCE, MUSIC
(www.balispiritfestival.com) A popular yoga, dance and music festival from the people behind the Yoga Barn. There are over 100 workshops and concerts plus a market and more. It's usually held in early April.

Ubud Writers & Readers Festival   WRITERS FESTIVAL
(www.ubudwritersfestival.com) Brings together scores of writers and readers from around the world in a celebration of writing – especially writing that touches on Bali. It is usually held in October.

🛏 Sleeping

Ubud has the best and most appealing range of places to stay on Bali, including fabled resorts, artful guesthouses and charming, simple homestays. Choices can be bewildering, so give some thought to where you want to stay.

Generally, Ubud offers good value for money at any price level. Simple accommodation within a family home compound is a cultural experience and costs around US$20. Ubud enjoys cool mountain air at night, so air-con isn't necessary, and with your windows open, you'll hear the sym-

---

EAT, PRAY, LOVE & UBUD

'That damn book' is a common reaction by many Ubud residents, who fear the town's popularity is driven in part by *Eat, Pray, Love* fans. *Eat, Pray, Love* is the Elizabeth Gilbert book (and less-than-successful movie) that chronicles the American author's search for self-fulfilment (and fulfilment of a book contract) across Italy, India and, yes, Ubud.

Some criticise Gilbert for not offering a more complete picture of Ubud's locals, dance, art, expats and walks, warts and all. And they decry basic factual errors such as the evocative prose about surf spots on the north coast (there are none), which lead you to suspect things might have been embellished for the plot. Meanwhile, others in Ubud have found myriad ways to profit from *EPL* and are happy to ride the wave (except on the north coast...).

Then there are the genuine fans, those who found a message in *EPL* that resonated, validating and/or challenging aspects of their lives. For some an ultimately magical journey to Ubud wouldn't have happened without *EPL*.

People in the Book

Two characters in the book are easily found in Ubud. Both receive large numbers of *EPL* fans and have lucrative livelihoods because of it.

Ketut Liyer (☏974 092) The genial and inspirational friend of Gilbert is easily found about a 10-minute walk south of Pengosekan (look for the bright new signs). Any driver will happily bring you here. Hours vary and the ageing Ketut has been in ill health, possibly due to the huge demand for an audience from Westerners. Expect to pay about US$25 for a short and public session, during which you will be told a variation on the theme that you're smart, beautiful, sexy and will live to 101 or 105 etc. Or for US$25 you can spend the night in a very simple room in a guesthouse at the rear of the compound (although the nearby chained and caged birds may detract from this experience). The actual Liyer compound is used in the movie, although Ketut is played by a schoolteacher from Java.

Wayan Nuriasih (Map p153; ☏872 9230, 917 5991; balihealer@hotmail.com; Jl Jembawan 5; ⊙9am-5pm) Another star of *Eat, Pray, Love*, Nuriasih is right in the heart of Ubud. Her open-fronted shop has a table where you can discuss your ailments with her and ponder a treatment. During this time, various buff male assistants will silently wander about and soon an elixir may appear at your elbow. The 'vitamin lunch' is a series of extracts and raw foods that is popular with many. Note that it is important to have a very clear understanding of what you're agreeing to, as it's easy to commit to therapies that can cost US$50 or more. For less, you can enjoy a cleansing, during which time several men whack at your body and give you new pains that make you forget the old ones.

Locations in the Movie

Most of the Bali locations for *Eat Pray Love*, the movie, were filmed in and around Ubud. However, don't be surprised if on your walks in the area, you find beautiful rice fields that surpass those shown in the movie.

The beach scenes were shot at Padang Padang, on south Bali's Bukit Peninsula. Oddly, the real beach is more attractive than the sort of grey version seen in the film. But for those hoping to retire to the beach bar where Julia Roberts meets Javier Bardem, there's no point trying, as the bar was created for the movie.

YOGA BARN

The chakra for the yoga revolution in Ubud, the **Yoga Barn** (Map p153; ☑070 992; www.balispirit.com; off Jl Raya Pengosekan; classes from 110,000Rp; ⊘7am-8pm) sits in its own lotus position amid trees back near a river valley. The name exactly describes what you'll find. A huge range of classes in yoga, Pilates, dance and life-affirming offshoots are held through the week. Owner Meghan Pappenheim also organises the popular Bali Spirit Festival.

phony of sounds off the rice fields and river valleys.

Guesthouses may be a bit larger and have amenities like swimming pools but are still likely to be fairly intimate, often nestled amid rice fields and rivers. Hotels generally offer swimming pools and other niceties, and the best are often perched on the edges of deep river valleys, with superb views and service (although even some budget places have amazing views). Some provide shuttle service around the area.

Addresses in Ubud can be imprecise – but signage at the end of a road will often list the names of all the places to stay. Away from the main thoroughfares there are no streetlights and it can be challenging to find your way after dark. If walking, you'll want a torch (flashlight).

CENTRAL UBUD

JALAN RAYA UBUD & AROUND

Nirvana Pension & Gallery　GUESTHOUSE $
(Map p153; ☑975 415; www.nirvanaku.com; Jl Goutama 10; r 250,000-450,000Rp; ☜) There are *alang-alang* (thatched roofs), a plethora of paintings, ornate doorways and six rooms with modern bathrooms in a shady, secluded locale next to a large family temple. Batik courses are also held.

Puri Saren Agung　GUESTHOUSE $$
(Map p153; ☑975 057; Jl Suweta 1; r from US$65; ✳) Part of the Ubud royal family's historic palace. Rooms are tucked behind the courtyard where the dance performances are held. Accommodation is in traditional Balinese pavilions, with big verandas, four-poster beds, antique furnishings and hot water.

Give a royal wave to wandering tourists from your patio.

Puri Saraswati Bungalows　HOTEL $$
(Map p153; ☑975 164; www.purisaraswatiubud.com; Jl Raya Ubud; r US$60-80; ✳☜☒) Very central and pleasant with lovely gardens that open onto the Ubud Water Palace. The 18 bungalow-style rooms are well back from Jl Raya Ubud, so it's quiet. Some rooms are fan-only; interiors are simply furnished but have richly carved details.

Sania's House　GUESTHOUSE $
(Map p153; ☑975 535; sania_house@yahoo.com; Jl Karna 7; r 200,000-600,000Rp; @☜☒) Pets wander about this family-run place, where the large, clear pool, huge terrace and spacious rooms will have you howling at the moon. The 25 rooms are basic but clean; the market is nearly next door.

Agung Cottages　HOMESTAY $
(Map p153; ☑975 414; Jl Goutama; r 300,000-400,000Rp; ✳☜) Follow a short path to reach this slightly rural-feeling family compound. The six huge, spotless rooms (some fan-only) are set in gardens tended by a lovely family. It's well off the already quiet road. Wi-fi is in common areas.

Donald Homestay　HOMESTAY $
(Map p153; ☑977 156; Jl Goutama; r 200,000-250,000Rp; ☜) The four rooms – some with hot water – are in a nice back corner of the family compound. As in many family-compound places, the chickens running around here have a date with a bamboo skewer.

Raka House　GUESTHOUSE $
(Map p153; ☑976 081; www.rakahouse.com; Jl Maruti; r 200,000-350,000Rp; ☜☒) Six bungalow-style rooms cluster at the back of a compact family compound. You can soak your toes in a small trapezoidal plunge pool. More choices nearby.

NORTH OF JALAN RAYA UBUD

Padma Accommodation　GUESTHOUSE $
(Map p153; ☑977 247; aswatama@hotmail.com; Jl Kajeng 13; r 200,000-250,000Rp) There are five very private bungalows in a tropical garden here (three are newish). Rooms are decorated with local crafts and the modern outdoor bathrooms have hot water. Nyoman Sudiarsa, a painter and family member, has a studio here and often shares his knowledge with guests.

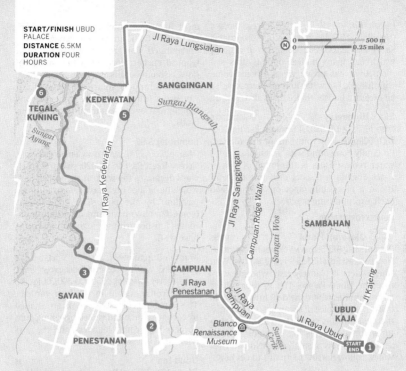

Walking Tour
Penestanan & Sayan

❯ The wonders of Sungai Ayung (Ayung River) are the focus of this outing, where you will walk below the luxury hotels built to take advantage of the lush, tropical river valley.

Begin your walk at ❶ **Ubud Palace** and go west on Jl Raya Ubud. Head over the Campuan bridge (noting the picturesque old bridge just south of the modern one), past the Blanco Renaissance Museum; here a steep uphill road, Jl Raya Penestanan, bends left and winds across the forested gully of Sungai Blangsuh (Blangsuh River) to the art-ists' village of ❷ **Penestanan**. West of Penes-tanan, head north on the small road (it's be-fore the busy main road) that curves around to Sayan. The ❸ **Sayan Terrace** was Colin McPhee's home in the 1930s, as chronicled in his book *A House in Bali*. The views over the valley of the magnificent ❹ **Sungai Ayung** (Ayung River) are superb. The best place to get to the riverside is just north of the Sayan Terrace hotel – look for the downhill path before the gate to the rooms and follow the increasingly narrow tracks down. (This part can be tricky but there are locals who'll show you for a tip of about 5000Rp.)

Following the rough trails north, along the eastern side of the Ayung, you traverse steep slopes, cross paddy fields and pass irrigation canals and tunnels. This is a highlight of the walk for many people, as we're talking about serious tropical jungle here. You don't need to follow any specific trail as you head slowly north along the river; instead just wander and see where your mood takes you. After about 1.5km you'll reach the finishing point for many white-water rafting trips – a good but steep trail goes from there up to the main road at ❺ **Kedewatan**, where you can walk back to Ubud. Alternatively, cross the river on the nearby bridge and climb up to the very untouristy village of ❻ **Tegalkuning** on the other side. There and back through a lot of tropical forest will add about 1km to your walk. Return to Ubud on Jl Raya Sanggingan, with its shops and cafes offering respite.

Lecuk Inn
GUESTHOUSE $

(Map p153; ☑973 445; bahula_lecuk@yahoo.com; Jl Kajeng 15; r 125,000-200,000Rp) On Jl Kajeng, which has many budget options, this six-room treat has ravine views. Rooms come with fridges, hot water and nice terraces. It's an excellent budget choice that's also close in.

Eka's Homestay
HOMESTAY $

(Map p153; ☑970 550; Jl Sriwedari 8; r 150,000-200,000Rp) Follow your ears to this nice little family compound with seven basic hot-| water rooms. Eka's is the home of Wayan Pasek Sucipta, a teacher of Balinese music. It's in a nice sunny spot on a quiet road (well, except during practice).

MONKEY FOREST ROAD

TOP CHOICE Oka Wati Hotel
HOTEL $$

(Map p153; ☑973 386; www.okawatihotel.com; off Monkey Forest Rd; r US$55-95; ❋ 🕸 🛜 🌊) Oki Wati (the owner) is a lovely lady who grew up near the Ubud Palace. The 19 rooms have large verandas where the delightful staff will deliver your choice of breakfast (do not miss the house-made yoghurt). The decor features vintage details like four-poster beds; some rooms view a small rice field and river valley. Follow narrow footpaths to get here.

Sri Bungalows
GUESTHOUSE $$

(Map p153; ☑975 394; www.sribungalowsubud. com; Monkey Forest Rd; r 500,000-800,000Rp; ❋ @ 🛜 🌊) Popular for its iconic views of rice fields (you think you hear it growing but re-ally it's the sound of your soul decompressing). Be sure to get one of the comfy rooms with relaxing loungers that command the views.

Komaneka
HOTEL $$$

(Map p153; ☑976 090; www.komaneka.com; Monkey Forest Rd; r US$150-350; ❋ @ 🛜 🌊) The

FINDING LONG-TERM ACCOMMODATION

There are many houses and flats you can rent or share in the Ubud area. For information about options, check the noticeboards at Pondok Pecak Library (p146), Ubud Tourist Information (p169) and Bali Buddha (p160). Also look in the free *Bali Advertiser* (www.baliadvertiser .biz) newspaper. Prices start at about US$250 a month and climb as you add amenities.

most luxurious hotel close to the centre of Ubud, the Komaneka is gracious yet understated. The grounds hit all the right tropical clichés: coconut palms, a riot of flowers, bamboo this and that. Rooms have marble bathrooms, some with views of private water features. Get one with a balcony looking out over the surrounding verdant lands.

Lumbung Sari
GUESTHOUSE $$

(Map p153; ☑976 396; www.lumbungsari.com; Monkey Forest Rd; r US$65-120; ❋ @ 🛜 🌊) Art-work decorates the walls at the stylish Sari, which has a nice breakfast *bale* (traditional pavilion) by the pool. The eight rooms (some fan-only) have tubs in elegant bath-rooms finished with terrazzo. Not all rooms have wi-fi.

Mandia Bungalows
GUESTHOUSE $

(Map p153; ☑970 965; mandiabungalow@gmail. com; Monkey Forest Rd; r 250,000-300,000Rp; 🛜) It's heliconia heaven in the lush gardens. The four bungalow-style rooms are shaded by coconut palms and cooled by ceiling fans. Porches have comfy loungers, and the guys who run it are sweethearts.

Ubud Inn
HOTEL $$

(Map p153; ☑975 071; www.ubudinn.com; Mon-key Forest Rd; r US$50-135; ❋ 🛜 🌊) Lush loses its meaning in Ubud, but this place takes it to a new level. The 34 rooms are barren compared to the gardens and span several budgets: basic are fan-only; the rest are large and have fridges. The L-shaped pool has a children's area. Not all rooms have wi-fi.

Warsa's Garden Bungalows
GUESTHOUSE $

(Map p153; ☑971 548; warsabungalow@gmail. com; Monkey Forest Rd; r 350,000-450,000Rp; ❋ 🌊) A good-sized pool with fountains enlivens this comfy but simple place in the heart of Monkey Forest action. The 24 rooms are reached through a traditional family-compound entrance. Some have tubs; some are fan-only.

Loka House
GUESTHOUSE $

(Map p153; ☑973 326; off Monkey Forest Rd; r 200,000-250,000Rp; 🛜) The lush entrance sets the mood at this peaceful place, where the two-storey main building overlooks a small carp pond in the garden with rice fields beyond. The four rooms (one with a tub) have hot water and fans.

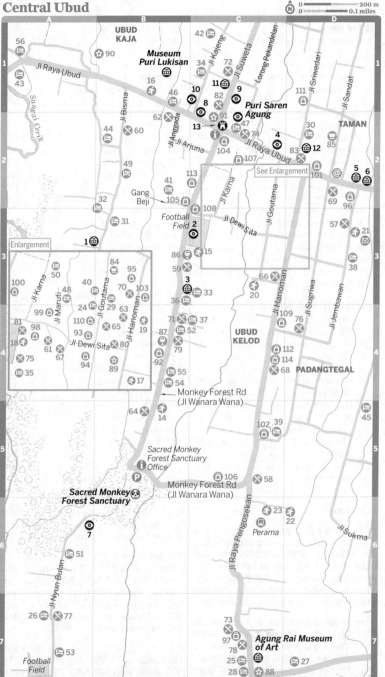

Central Ubud

UBUD KAJA

Museum Puri Lukisan

Puri Saren Agung

TAMAN

Jl Raya Ubud

Jl Bisma

Jl Anggada

Jl Arjuna

Jl Kajeng

Jl Suweta

Lorong Pekandelan

Jl Sriwedari

Jl Sandat

Sungai Cerik

Gang Beji

Football Field

Jl Karna

Jl Dewi Sita

Jl Goutama

See Enlargement

Enlargement

Jl Karna

Jl Maruti

Jl Goutama

Jl Hanoman

Jl Dewi Sita

UBUD KELOD

Jl Hanoman

Jl Sugriwa

Jl Jembawan

PADANGTEGAL

Monkey Forest Rd (Jl Wanara Wana)

Sacred Monkey Forest Sanctuary Office

Sacred Monkey Forest Sanctuary

Monkey Forest Rd (Jl Wanara Wana)

Jl Raya Pengosekan

Perama

Jl Sukma

Jl Nyun Bulan

Football Field

Agung Rai Museum of Art

UBUD & AROUND

Central Ubud

JALAN BISMA

TOP CHOICE Sama's Cottages GUESTHOUSE **$$**
(Map p153; ☏973 481; www.samascottagesubud.
com; Jl Bisma; r 330,000-650,000Rp; ❄❀) Ter-
raced down a hill, the 10 bungalow-style
rooms have lashings of Balinese style layered
on absolute simplicity. The oval pool feels like
a jungle oasis. Ask for low-season discounts.

Honeymoon Guesthouse GUESTHOUSE **$$**
(Map p153; ☏977 409; www.casalunabali.com; Jl
Bisma; r US$50-100; ❄@❀❀) Run by the Casa
Luna clan, the 30 rooms here have terraces
and tubs. There's a play area for kids. Avoid
the dark rooms; some rooms have air-con,
not all have wi-fi. Some of the rooms are in
an annexe and quite spacious, others are in
a second compound across the street.

Pondok Krishna GUESTHOUSE **$**
(Map p153; ☏0815 5821 8103; kriz_tie@yahoo.com; Jl
Bisma; r 250,000-300,000Rp; ❄@❀❀) This light
and airy family compound has four rooms
set among the frog-filled rice fields west of Jl
Bisma. The open common area with its sunny
location is good for nailing that tan.

Ina Inn GUESTHOUSE **$**
(Map p153; ☏971 093; Jl Bisma; r 250,000-
300,000Rp; ❀❀) Stroll the thickly planted
grounds and enjoy views across Ubud and

the rice fields. The 10 fan-cooled rooms are basic but clean and comfy. The pool is ideal after a day of walking. If you want to take the plunge closer to your bed, rooms have tubs.

PADANGTEGAL & TEBESAYA

TOP CHOICE **Matahari Cottages** GUESTHOUSE **$$**
(Map p153; ☑975 459; www.matahariubud.com; Jl Jembawan; r US$50-90; ❋ 🕸 ⚟) This delightful place has six flamboyant, themed rooms, including the 'Batavia Princess' and the 'Indian Pasha'. The library is a vision out of a 1920s fantasy. It also boasts a self-proclaimed 'jungle jacuzzi', an upscale way to replicate the old Bali tradition of river-bathing. There's a multicourse breakfast and high tea elaborately served on silver. And in a nod to the modern day, the hotel recycles.

Ni Nyoman Warini Bungalows HOMESTAY **$**
(Map p153; ☑978 364; Jl Hanoman; r 120,000-150,000Rp; 🕸) There's a whole pod of simple family compounds with rooms for rent back on a little footpath off Jl Hanoman. It's quiet, and without even trying you'll find yourself enjoying the rhythms of family life. The four rooms here have hot water and traditional bamboo furniture.

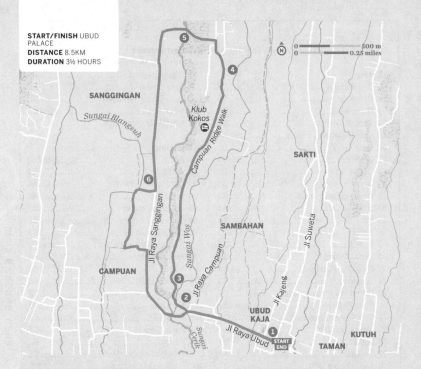

Walking Tour
Campuan Ridge

> This walk passes over the lush river valley of Sungai Wos (Wos River), offering views of Gunung Agung and glimpses of small village communities and rice fields.

Begin your walk at **1** **Ubud Palace** and walk west on Jl Raya Ubud. At the confluence of Sungai Wos (Wos River) and Sungai Cerik (Cerik River) is Campuan, which means 'Where Two Rivers Meet.' This area was among the first to attract Western painters in the 1930s and you'll understand why from the still-lush foliage and the soothing roar of the rivers. The walk leaves Jl Raya Campuan here at the **2** **Ibah Luxury Villas**. Enter the hotel driveway and take the path to the left, where a walkway crosses the river to the small and serene **3** **Pura Gunung Lebah**. From there follow the concrete path north, climbing up onto the ridge between the two rivers. Fields of elephant grass, traditionally used for thatched roofs, slope away on either side. You can see the rice fields above Ubud folding over the hills in all directions. Note the myriad plastic bags and other colourful clutter flapping from long poles. Farmers hope, often in vain, that these will deter rice-hungry birds from having a feast.

Continuing north along Campuan ridge past the Klub Kokos lodging, the road improves as it passes through paddy fields and the village of **4** **Bangkiang Sidem**. On the outskirts of the village, an unsigned road heads west, winding down to Sungai Cerik (the west branch of Sungai Wos), then climbing steeply up to **5** **Payogan**. From here you can walk south to the main road, and continue along Jl Raya Sanggingan, which seems to boast one or two more small boutiques and galleries every week. At the restaurant **6** **Mozaic**, veer to the west onto trails that stay level with the rice fields as the main road drops away. It's a fantasyland of coursing waterways and good views among the rice and villas. If you become entranced with Ubud and decide you can't leave, many of the small bungalows are for rent by the month. When you come to the steep concrete steps, take them down to Campuan and back to Ubud.

Puri Asri 2
GUESTHOUSE $

(Map p153; ☑973 210; Jl Sukma 59; r 150,000-250,000Rp; 🖥🌊) Work your way through a classic family compound and you'll find four bungalow-style rooms with views of a ravine. It's a fabulous deal and rooms come with hot water. Cool off in the nice pool.

Yuliati House
HOMESTAY $

(Map p140; ☑974 044; yuliahouse10@yahoo.com; Jl Sukma 10; r 150,000-200,000Rp) Some of the nine rooms have tubs and some even have river-valley views. The family compound is well back from the already quiet street so this makes it a prime retreat.

Family Guest House
HOMESTAY $$

(Map p140; ☑974 054; familyhouse@telkom.net; Jl Sukma; r 250,000-600,000Rp; ✳🖥🌊) There's a bit of bustle from the busy family at this charming homestay. Healthy breakfasts featuring brown bread from Café Wayan are served. The rooms have all had upgrades and most have air-con and spiffy new decor. Some also include tubs; and at the top, they have a balcony with a valley view.

Biangs
HOMESTAY $

(Map p140; ☑976 520; Jl Sukma 28; r from 150,000Rp) In a little garden, Biangs (meaning 'mama') has six well-maintained rooms, with hot water. The best rooms have views of a small valley.

Aji Lodge
HOMESTAY $

(Map p140; ☑973 255; ajilodge11@yahoo.com; Tebesaya 11; r from 150,000Rp) A group of comfortable family compounds lines a footpath east of Jl Sukma. Get a room down the hill by the river for the full bedtime symphony of birds, bugs and critters.

SAMBAHAN & SAKTI

Waka di Ume
HOTEL $$$

(Map p140; ☑973 178; www.wakadiumeubud.com; Jl Suweta; r/ villas from US$200/350; ✳🖥🌊) Located a gentle 1.5km uphill from the centre, this elegant compound enjoys engrossing verdant views across rice fields. New and old styles mix in the large units; go for a villa with a view. Service is superb yet relaxed. Listening to gamelan practice echoing across the fields at night is quite magical.

Ketut's Place
GUESTHOUSE $$

(Map p140; ☑975 304; www.ketutsplace.com; Jl Suweta 40; r US$35-75; ✳🖥) The nine rooms here range from basic with fans to deluxe versions with air-con and bathtub. All have artful accents and enjoy a dramatic pool shimmering down the hillside and river-valley views. On some nights, an impressive Balinese feast is served by Ketut, a local luminary.

Ubud Sari Health Resort
GUESTHOUSE $$

(Map p140; ☑974 393; www.ubudsari.com; Jl Kajeng; r with fan/air-con US$60/75; ✳🖥🌊) The name for the rooms at this noted health spa says it all: Zen Village. The plants in the gardens are labelled for their medicinal qualities and the cafe serves organic, vegetarian fare. Guests can use the health facilities, including the sauna and whirlpool.

Klub Kokos
GUESTHOUSE $$

(Map p140; ☑978 270; www.klubkokos.com; r US$60-145; ✳@🖥🌊) A beautiful 1.5km walk north along the Campuan ridge, Klub Kokos is a ridge-top hideaway with a big pool and seven spotless bungalow-style rooms. It's reachable by car from the north; call for directions. Rates include breakfast and snacks and there's a cafe.

NYUHKUNING

⭐ TOP CHOICE Swasti Cottage
GUESTHOUSE $$

(Map p153; ☑974 079; www.baliswasti.com; Jl Nyuh Bulan; r 500,000-950,000Rp; @🖥🌊) One of Ubud's most inventive and appealing places to stay is just five minutes' walk from the south entrance to the Monkey Forest. Run by an engaging French-Balinese couple, this guesthouse and bungalow compound has large, manicured grounds that feature a bounteous organic garden (produce is used in the excellent cafe). Some rooms are in simple two-storey blocks; others are in vintage traditional houses brought here from across Bali.

Alam Indah
HOTEL $$

(Map p153; ☑974 629; www.alamindahbali.com; Jl Nyuh Bulan; r US$60-140; ✳🖥🌊) Just south of the Monkey Forest in Nyuhkuning, this isolated and spacious resort has 10 rooms that are beautifully finished in natural materials to traditional designs. The Wos Valley views are entrancing, especially from the multi-level pool area. The walk in at night follows a driveway lined with tea candles.

Saren Indah Hotel
HOTEL $$

(Map p153; ☑971 471; www.sarenhotel.com; Jl Nyuh Bulan; r US$45-95; ✳🖥🌊) South of the Monkey Forest, this 15-room hotel sits in the middle of rice fields – be sure to get a 2nd-floor room to enjoy the views. Rooms are spotless; better ones have sat-TV, fridges and baths with stylish tubs.

PENGOSEKAN

TOP CHOICE **Agung Raka** BOUTIQUE HOTEL $$
(Map p153; ☎975 757; www.agungraka.com; Jl Raya Pengosekan; r/bungalows US$95/120; ❄@☎🏊) This great-value hotel sprawls out across picture-perfect rice fields just south of the centre of Ubud. The rooms are large and suitably Balinese in motif but the real stars are the bungalows set back on a rice terrace amid palm trees. You can live the life of a duck as you hear the night-time symphony of bugs and birds while drinking in the beauty.

Arma Resort HOTEL $$$
(Map p153; ☎976 659; www.armabali.com; Jl Raya Pengosekan; r US$100-175, villas from US$250; ❄@☎🏊) Get full Balinese cultural immersion at the hotel enclave of the Arma compound. The expansive property has a large library and elegant gardens. Villas come with private pools. The fabulous namesake museum is on the grounds.

Casa Ganesha Hotel HOTEL $$
(Map p153; ☎971 488; www.casaganesha.com; Jl Raya Pengosekan; r 600,000-700,000Rp; ❄☎🏊) A solid midrange choice in a great location just south of Ubud's centre, this 24-room hotel has two-storey blocks built around a pool. Rooms are straightforward and have terraces or balconies. There are pretty rice fields nearby.

PELIATAN

TOP CHOICE **Maya Ubud** LUXURY HOTEL $$$
(Map p140; ☎977 888; www.mayaubud.com; Jl Gunung Sari Peliatan; r from US$270; ❄☎🏊) One of the most beautiful large hotels around Ubud, this sprawling property is well integrated into its surrounding river valley and rice fields. The 108 rooms and villas have the sort of open and light feeling combined with traditional materials that defines the concept of 'Bali style'. Renowned chef Kath Townsend ably oversees the delicious eating and drinking options.

CAMPUAN & SANGGINGAN

TOP CHOICE **Warwick Ibah Luxury Villas & Spa** HOTEL $$$
(Map p153; ☎974 466; www.warwickibah.com; off Jl Raya Campuan; ste US$200-300, villas US$400-600; ❄@☎🏊) Overlooking the rushing waters and rice-clad hills of the Wos Valley, the Ibah offers refined luxury in 15 spacious, stylish individual suites and villas that combine ancient and modern details. Each could be a feature in an interior design magazine. The swimming pool is set into the hillside amid gardens and lavish stone carvings.

Hotel Tjampuhan HOTEL $$
(Map p140; ☎975 368; www.tjampuhan-bali.com; Jl Raya Campuan; r US$105-215; ❄@☎🏊) This venerable place overlooks the confluence of Sungai Wos and Campuan. The influential German artist Walter Spies lived here in the 1930s, and his former home, which sleeps four people (US$240), is now part of the hotel. Bungalow-style units spill down the hill and enjoy mesmerising valley views.

Pita Maha HOTEL $$$
(Map p140; ☎974 330; www.pitamaha-bali.com; Jl Raya Sanggingan; villas US$300-600; ❄@☎🏊) Broad, open views across a valley to the rice fields beyond are the highlight of this understated but luxurious hotel. The 24 traditional-style villas are large and built with real attention to detail. More money gets you good views and a private plunge pool – although the main curving infinity pool may seduce you.

Pager Bungalows GUESTHOUSE $$
(Map p153; ☎971 391; Jl Raya Campuan; r US$50-60, villas US$100; ☎) Run by painter Nyoman Pageh and his family, this cute homestay hugs a verdant hillside location that makes you feel like you're lost in the bottom of the spinach bowl on a salad bar. Two large bungalows face the compound; five more rooms are comfortable and have views. The family villa is a fully appointed apartment.

PENESTANAN

TOP CHOICE **Santra Putra** GUESTHOUSE $
(Map p140; ☎977 810; karjabali@yahoo.com; off Jl Raya Campuan; r US$25-35; ☎) Run by internationally exhibited abstract artist I Wayan Karja (whose studio/gallery is also on-site), this place has nine big, open, airy rooms with hot water. Enjoy paddy-field views from all vantage points. Painting and drawing classes are offered by the artist.

Villa Nirvana BOUTIQUE HOTEL $$$
(Map p140; ☎979 419; www.villanirvanabali.com; Penestanan; r US$145-290; ❄☎🏊) You mjay find nirvana just for reaching Villa Nirvana: access is either along a 150m path through a small river valley from the west or along a rice-field path that begins at the top of steep steps from the east. Obviously the compound – designed by local architect

Awan Sukhro Edhi – is a retreat from daily life and you might just take up yoga on the spot.

Indo French Villa GUESTHOUSE **$$**
(Map p140; ☎0813 3866 9028, 790 4518; nengah kuntia@hotmail.com; villa US$35-80; 🔊🌊) Wander a series of lanes through rice fields and you'll find yourself at this very homey two-villa complex. The small one is a steal, with a small pool and two levels plus a kitchen. The second is also great value, with a pool you can train in, plus many more posh details.

Melati Cottages HOTEL **$$**
(Map p140; ☎974 650; www.melati-cottages.com; Jl Raya Penestanan; r US$30-60; 🌸🔊🌊) Set back among the rice fields, the deeply shaded Melati has somewhat spartan rooms in two-storey bungalow-style buildings. All have porches for listening to the sounds of the fields and taking the cool night air.

SAYAN & AYUNG VALLEY

TOP CHOICE Sayan Terrace HOTEL **$$**
(Map p140; ☎974 384; www.sayanterraceresort.com; Jl Raya Sayan; r/ villas from US$130/250; 🌸@🔊🌊) Gaze into the Sayan Valley from this venerable hotel and you'll understand why this was the site of Colin McPhee's *A House in Bali*. Stay here while your neighbours – distant neighbours it should be said – are housed in luxury resorts paying far more. Here the 11 rooms and villas are simply decorated but are large and have *that* view. Rates include afternoon tea.

Bambu Indah GUESTHOUSE **$$$**
(off Map p140; ☎975 124; www.bambuindah.com; house US$100-350; @🔊🌊) Famed expat entrepreneur John Hardy sold his namesake jewellery company in 2007 and became a hotelier. On a ridge near Sayan and his beloved Sungai Ayung, he's assembled a compound of seven 100-year-old royal Javanese houses, each furnished with style and flair. Several outbuildings create a timeless village with underpinnings of luxury. The entire compound is run to a very 'green' standard.

Amandari HOTEL **$$$**
(☎975 333; www.amanresorts.com; ste from US$850; 🌸@🔊🌊) In Kedewatan village, the storied Amandari does everything with charm and grace – sort of like a classical Balinese dancer. Superb views over the jungle and down to the river – the 30m

green-tiled swimming pool seems to drop right over the edge – are just some of the inducements. The 30 private pavilions may prove inescapable.

Four Seasons Resort HOTEL **$$$**
(Map p140; ☎977 577; www.fourseasons.com; ste/ villas from US$450/700; 🌸@🔊🌊) Set below the valley rim, the curved open-air reception area looks like a Cinerama screen of Ubud beauty. Many villas have private pools and all share the same amazing views and striking modern design. At night you hear just the water rushing below. The service wins rave reviews.

Tamen Bebek HOTEL **$$$**
(Map p140; ☎975 385; www.tamanbebekbali.com; Jl Raya Sayan; r US$180-500; 🌸🔊🌊) A spectacular, verdant location overlooking the Sayan Valley may keep you glued to your terrace throughout the day. Eleven rooms and villas here wrap around the Sayan Terrace and enjoy a stylish new common area and entrance. All have understated yet classic Balinese wood-and-thatch architecture as designed by the legendary Made Wijaya.

🍴 Eating

Ubud's cafes and restaurants are some of the best in Bali. Local and expat chefs produce a bounty of authentic Balinese dishes, as well as inventive Asian and other international cuisines.

Many eateries make beautiful use of natural design elements and some offer serene settings with views out over the rice fields. Cafes where you can sip an excellent coffee or juice are common – some people never seem to leave. There are also many inexpensive warung serving fresh and tasty authentic Indonesian dishes. Note: Ubud's nightlife fades fast after the last note of gamelan music; don't wait past 9pm to eat or you won't. Better restaurants will provide transport to and from; call to arrange.

Good organic farmers markets are held each week, at Pizza Bagus (p164) and at the Arma Museum (p141). Bali Buddha (p160) is another good source. And in keeping with the local ethos, organic produce is a feature on many menus.

Delta Mart convenience stores are common but are not recommended (eg they often claim they only have expensive imported water). The ubiquitous Circle Ks are more reliable and sell Bintang around the clock. **Delta Dewata Supermarket** (Map p140; ☎973 049;

WHERE TO STAY IN UBUD

Do you want to be in the centre or the quiet countryside? Have a rice-field view or enjoy a room with stylish design? Choices are myriad. The main areas of accommodation in Ubud are as follows.

Central Ubud

This original heart of Ubud has a vast range of places to rest your weary head and you'll enjoy a location that will cut down on the need for long walks or 'transport'. If you're near Jl Raya Ubud, don't settle for a room with noise from the main drag. Small and quiet streets to the east, including Jl Karna, Jl Maruti and Jl Goutama, have numerous family-style homestays. North of Jl Raya Ubud, streets like Jl Kajeng and Jl Suweta offer a timeless tableau, with kids playing in the streets and women bringing home – balanced on their heads – produce from the market. The same advice goes for the long strip of Monkey Forest Rd, which has the greatest concentration of lodgings. Jl Bisma runs into a plateau of rice fields. New places are popping up all the time and many sit amid the paddies.

Padangtegal & Tebesaya

East of central Ubud, but still conveniently located, Padangtegal has several budget lodgings along Jl Hanoman. A little further east, the quiet village of Tebesaya comprises little more than its main street, Jl Sukma, which runs between two streams. Cute homestays can be found down small footpaths.

Sambahan & Sakti

Going north from Jl Raya Ubud, you are soon in rolling terraces of rice fields. Tucked away here you'll find interesting and often luxurious hotels, yet you can have a beautiful walk to the centre in well under an hour.

Jl Raya Andong) has a huge selection of goods. **Bintang Supermarket** (Map p140; Bintang Centre, Jl Raya Campuan) is well located and has a large range of food and other essentials. The traditional produce market (p167) is a multilevel carnival of tropical foods and worth exploring despite the nearby construction.

CENTRAL UBUD

JALAN RAYA UBUD & AROUND

There are busy and tasty choices on Ubud's main street.

Kué   CAFE $
(Map p153; ✆976 7040; Jl Raya Ubud; meals 30,000-80,000Rp; ✽🖥) A top-end organic bakery and chocolate shop with a couple of stools downstairs; climb the side stairs for a lovely cafe that sits above the road chaos. Good baked items as well as sandwiches, organic wraps and Indo mains make it a great casual stop.

Bali Buddha   CAFE $
(Map p153; Jl Jembawan 1; meals from 30,000Rp; 🖥) This breezy place offers a full range of vegetarian *jamu* (health tonics), salads, tofu curries, savoury crepes, pizzas and gelato. It has a comfy lounging area and is candlelit at

night. On the ground floor a market sells organic fruit and vegetables, wondrous blueberry muffins, breads and cookies. The bulletin board is packed with Ubud notices.

Rendezvousdoux   FRENCH $
(Map p153; ✆747 0163; Jl Raya Ubud 14; meals 30,000-80,000Rp; ✽) How to define it? A fusion of French-accented forms: cafe, library and bookshop, Rendezvousdoux is the most interesting spot on the street. Bonuses include global music (at times live) and historic films about Ubud on loop.

Lada Warung   INDONESIAN $
(Map p153; Jl Hanoman; meals from 30,000Rp; 🖥) You can order off the menu at this neat-as-a-pin open-fronted warung or do what smart diners do and come early for lunch. There is an array of excellent dishes you can choose from warung-style. Those who come early get the best selection.

Casa Luna   INDONESIAN $$
(Map p153; ✆977 409; Jl Raya Ubud; meals from 50,000Rp) Enjoy creative Indonesian-focused dishes like addictive bamboo skewers of minced seafood satay (try to pick out the dozen or so spices). Bread, pastries, cakes

Nyuhkuning

A very popular area just south of the Monkey Forest, Nyuhkuning has some creative guesthouses and hotels, yet is not a long walk to the centre.

Pengosekan

Pengosekan is good for shopping, dining and activities like yoga.

Campuan & Sanggingan

The long sloping road that takes its names from these two communities has a number of posh properties on its east side that overlook a lush river valley.

Penestanan

Just west of the Campuan bridge, steep Jl Raya Penestanan branches off to the left, and climbs up and around to Penestanan, a large plateau of rice fields and lodgings. Simple rooms and bungalows in the rice fields are pitched at those seeking low-priced, longer-term lodgings. Stroll the narrow paths and you will be sure to find options at all prices. You can also get here via a steep climb up a set of concrete stairs off Jl Raya Campuan but the reward – sweeping views and little coursing streams between the fields – is worth it.

Sayan & Ayung Valley

Two kilometres west of Ubud, the fast-flowing Sungai Ayung has carved out a deep valley, its sides sculpted into terraced paddy fields or draped in thick rainforest. Overlooking this verdant valley are some of Bali's best hotels.

UBUD & AROUND UBUD

and more from its well-known bakery are also a must. The owner, Janet de Neefe, is the force behind the lauded Ubud Writers & Readers Festival (p148).

Warung Schnitzel　　　　GERMAN **$$**
(Map p153; Jl Sriwedari 2; mains from 50,000Rp) This multilevel restaurant manages the trick of melding classic schnitzels with Balinese ingredients. The results are delicious and the range of thinly pounded and fried schnitzels is wide. The menu also has seafood specials, fresh and interesting salads and more options for those whose tastes are more local. Get a table on the top floor for breezy views.

Clear　　　　FUSION **$$**
(Map p153; ☑0818 553 015; Jl Hanoman; meals US$4-15) You'll love it or hate it. This high-concept restaurant brings a bit of Hollywood glitz and ditz to Ubud. The dishes are relentlessly healthy but also creative – think soba noodles meets raw food meets curried tofu etc. It's all done rather artfully, which may help you forget the very uncommon BYOB policy. It now has a deli counter out front for picnics and fresh snacks.

NORTH OF JALAN RAYA UBUD

Rumah Roda　　　　BALINESE **$**
(Map p140; ☑975 487; Jl Kajeng 24; meals 15,000-30,000Rp; 🛜) Above Threads of Life, Roda serves astonishingly cheap Balinese dishes with a wonderful overlay of local culture. The extended Roda family live here and prepare dishes handed down for generations. You can order a delectably authentic feast in advance for a mere 35,000Rp per person. (Note: the family is the subject of the cult favourite *A Little Bit One O'clock,* by William Ingram.)

Warung Ibu Oka　　　　BALINESE **$**
(Map p153; Jl Suweta; meals 30,000Rp-50,000Rp; ⊙11am-4pm) Opposite Ubud Palace, you'll see lunchtime crowds waiting for one thing: the Balinese style roast *babi guling* (suckling pig). Line up and find a place under the shelter for one of the most authentic meals you'll have in Ubud. Order a *spesial* to get the best cut. Get there early to avoid the day-tripping bus tours.

Localista　　　　CAFE **$**
(Map p153; Jl Suweta 5; snacks from 20,000Rp) As cute as a cupcake, this tiny cafe is the place to get a cupcake in Ubud. Other baked goods

WALKING FOR ORGANIC TREATS

Looking for a fun walk of an hour or so? In a beautiful location on a plateau overlooking rice terraces and river valleys, **Warung Bodag Maliah** (Map p140; ☎780 1839; meals from 30,000Rp; ☺11am-4pm), a small cafe, is in the middle of a big organic farm belonging to the locally popular Sari Organic brand.

Yes the food's healthy, but more importantly, given that half the fun is getting here, the drinks are cool and refreshing. Look for a little track off Jl Raya Ubud that goes past Abangan Bungalows, then follow the signs along footpaths for another 800m.

Once you are walking through the lush rice fields, you can keep heading north as long as your interest or endurance lasts. Look for little offshoot trails to either side that lead to small rivers.

like brownies are just as good. Coffee drinks, tea and hot chocolate are all suitably excellent. It's run by Soma Helmi, whose father Rio has his gallery next door.

MONKEY FOREST ROAD

TOP CHOICE **Three Monkeys** FUSION $$
(Map p153; Monkey Forest Rd; meals from 80,000Rp) Have a passionfruit-crush cocktail and settle back amid the rice field's frog symphony. Add the glow of tiki torches for a magical effect. By day there are sandwiches, salads and gelato. At night there's a fusion menu of Asian classics (the prawn rolls are a must), pasta and steaks.

Laughing Buddha INDONESIAN $
(Map p153; ☎970 928; Monkey Forest Rd; meals 40,000-70,000Rp; ☎) More stylish than your average warung, this casual cafe serves good Indonesian food aimed at the discriminating Western palate. Get a table at a bench in front and enjoy the passing Monkey Forest parade.

Bumbu Bali INDONESIAN $$
(Map p153; ☎976 698; Monkey Forest Rd; meals 60,000-150,000Rp) A good place for Balinese food in the heart of Ubud. The menu features dishes such as *lawar* (green bean salad), *ayam pelalah* (spicy shredded chicken salad) and *sambal goreng udang* (prawns in a tangy coconut-milk sauce). Like your food? You can also learn to cook it; see p148.

Coffee & Silver CAFE $
(Map p153; ☎975 354; Monkey Forest Rd; snacks from 20,000Rp; ☺10am-midnight) Tapas and more substantial items make up the menu at this comfortable place with seating inside and out. Vintage photos of Ubud line the walls. Have a coffee and watch people strolling down to their fate with the monkeys in the forest.

Sjaki's Warung INTERNATIONAL $
(Map p153; off Monkey Forest Rd; meals 20,000-30,000Rp; ☺9am-6pm Mon-Fri) The best Bintang you'll ever have – in terms of helping others – is right here at this modest cafe with a prize position overlooking the football field. The warung is run by a charity that helps developmentally disadvantaged kids: the staff are all learning the ropes while serving classic Indo fare like *nasi goreng*.

JALAN DEWI SITA & JALAN GOUTAMA

East of Monkey Forest Rd, a short stroll takes you past many fine and diverse options.

Cafe Havana LATIN AMERICAN $$
(Map p153; ☎972 973; Jl Dewi Sita; meals from 60,000Rp) All that's missing is Fidel. Actually, the decrepitude of its namesake city is also missing from this smart and stylish cafe on smart and stylish Dewi Sita. The menu boasts many a dish with Latin flair, such as tasty pork numbers, but expect surprises such as a crème brûlée oatmeal in the morning that simply astounds.

Juice Ja Cafe CAFE $
(Map p153; ☎971 056; Jl Dewi Sita; snacks from 20,000Rp) Glass of spirulina? Dash of wheat grass with your papaya juice? Organic fruits and vegetables go into the food at this funky bakery-cafe. Little brochures explain the provenance of items such as the organic cashew nuts. Enjoy the patio.

Tutmak Cafe CAFE $
(Map p153; Jl Dewi Sita; meals 30,000Rp-90,000Rp; ☎) The breezy multilevel location here, facing both Jl Dewi Sita and the football field,

is a popular place for a refreshing drink or a meal. Locals on the make huddle around their laptops plotting their next move.

Toro Sushi Café
JAPANESE $

(Map p153; Jl Dewi Sita; meals from 35,000Rp) A few stray Japanese lanterns hang over the completely open front of this California-roll-sized sushi joint. But if the decor is a bit lax that's because all the effort is being expended on preparing some of Bali's best sushi. Look for daily specials.

Dewa Warung
INDONESIAN $

(Map p153; Jl Goutama; meals 15,000-20,000Rp) When it rains, the tin roof sounds like a tap-dance convention and the bare lightbulbs sway in the breeze. A little garden surrounds tables a few steps above the road where diners tuck into plates of sizzling fresh Indo fare. Large bottles of Bintang are cheap.

JALAN BISMA

Café des Artistes
BELGIAN $$

(Map p153; ☑972 706; Jl Bisma 9X; meals from 120,000Rp; ⊗noon-11am) In a quiet and cultured perch up off Jl Raya Ubud, the popular (read: book in high season) Café des Artistes serves Belgian-accented food, although the menu strays into France and Indonesia as well. There's also some amazing steaks. Local art is on display and the bar is refreshingly cultured.

PADANGTEGAL & TEBESAYA

TOP CHOICE Sopa
VEGETARIAN $

(Map p153; Jl Sugriwa 36; meals 30,000-60,000Rp; ☎🗐) Open air and oh so groovy, this popular place captures the Ubud vibe with creative and (more importantly) tasty vegetarian fare with a Balinese twist. Look for specials of the day on display; the ever-changing *nasi campur* (rice with side dishes) is a treat.

Kebun
MEDITERRANEAN $$

(Map p153; ☑780 3801; www.kebunbistro.com; 44 Jl Hanoman; mains from 60,000Rp) Napa meets Ubud at this cute little bistro and it's a good match. A long wine list (with specials) can be paired with French- and Italian-accented dishes large and small. There are daily specials including pastas and risottos. Dine inside or out on the appealing terrace.

🖉 Kafe
CAFE $

(Map p153; ☑970 992; www.balispirit.com; Jl Hanoman 44; dishes 15,000-40,000Rp) Kafe has an organic menu great for veggie grazing or just having a coffee, juice or house-made

natural soft drink. Breakfasts are healthy while lunch meals feature excellent salads and burritos, with many raw items. One of *the* places to meet in Ubud, it's always busy.

Mama's Warung
INDONESIAN $

(Map p140; Jl Sukma; dishes 10,000-20,000Rp) A real budget find among the bargain homestays of Tebesaya. Mama herself cooks up Indo classics that are spicy and redolent with garlic (the avocado salad, yum!). The freshly made peanut sauce for the satay is silky smooth.

Bebek Bengil
INDONESIAN $$

(Dirty Duck Diner; Map p153; ☑975 489; Jl Hanoman; dishes 70,000-200,000Rp; ⊗11am-10pm) This pretty, ever-expanding place is hugely popular for one reason: its crispy Balinese duck, which is marinated for 36 hours in spices and then fried up hot. The ducks on the few surviving rice fields outside the open-air dining pavilions look worried.

Down to Earth
VEGETARIAN $

(Map p153; Jl Gotama Selatan, off Jl Hanoman; meals from 30,000Rp; ☎🗐) 'Eliminate Free Radicals' is but one of many healthy drinks at this hard-core outpost for vegetarian dining and drinking. The seemingly endless menu has a plethora of soups, salads and platters that are heavy on Med flavours. The dining area is on the upper floor, putting you above motorbike exhaust. A market is on the main floor.

TEGES

Jl Raya Mas, which runs due south to the namesake village from Peliatan, has two excellent choices for Balinese food.

TOP CHOICE Warung Teges
BALINESE $

(Map p140; Jl Cok Rai Pudak; meals from 20,000Rp) The *nasi campur* is better here than almost anywhere else around Ubud. It gets just about everything right, from the pork sausage to the chicken, the *babi guling* and even the tempeh.

Semar Warung
BALINESE $$

(www.semarwarung.com; Jl Raya Mas 165; meals from 50,000Rp) It doesn't look all that promising from the front, but step through to the breezy dining area and you'll be wrapped up in a green vista of rice fields stretching off to palm trees. It's a beautiful view and the Balinese food lives up to it. The *nasi campur* is excellent and shows off the range of local dishes. This is a good lunch choice or a place for a drink at sunset. It's 1km south of where Jl Raya Mas ends at Jl Raya Pengosekan.

NYUHKUNING

Swasti
INTERNATIONAL $

(Map p153; ☑974 079; Jl Nyuh Bulan; meals 40,000-80,000Rp) This cafe attached to the excellent guesthouse of the same name is reason enough to take a stroll through the Monkey Forest. Indonesian and Western dishes prepared from the large in-house organic garden are fresh and tasty. Have a glass of fresh juice with the beloved chocolate crepes. Watch for children's dance performances.

PENGOSEKAN

Many highly regarded restaurants are found along the curves of Jl Raya Pengosekan. It's always worth seeing what's new.

Pizza Bagus
PIZZERIA $$

(Map p153; ☑978 520; www.pizzabagus.com; Jl Raya Pengosekan; meals 40,000-100,000Rp; ❄☎) First-rate pizza with a crispy thin crust is baked here. Besides the long list of pizza options, there's pasta and sandwiches – all mostly organic. Tables are in and out, there's a play area, and it delivers.

Mama Mia Pizza & Pasta
ITALIAN $$

(Map p153; ☑918 5056; Jl Raya Pengosekan; meals from 50,000Rp) The rustic facade of this roadside eatery doesn't hint at the sophisticated Italian flavours you can find within. The long menu of pastas is fresh and tasty. However, the real action is around the wood-burning oven, which produces some fine thin-crust pizzas. And like its competition just up the street, Mama Mia delivers.

Taco Casa & Grill
MEXICAN $$

(Map p153; www.tacocasabali.com; Jl Raya Pengosekan; meals from 50,000Rp) Sure, Mexico is almost exactly on the opposite side of the globe (get one and check!), but the flavours have found their way to Bali. Surprisingly tasty versions of burritos, tacos and more have the right mix of chiles, cilantro (coriander) and other seasonings.

CAMPUAN & SANGGINGAN

TOP CHOICE Mozaic
FUSION $$$

(Map p140; ☑975 768; www.mozaic-bali.com; Jl Raya Sanggingan; menus from 1,250,000Rp; ☺6-10pm Tue-Sun) Chef Chris Salans oversees this much-lauded top-end restaurant. Fine French fusion cuisine features on a constantly changing seasonal menu that takes its influences from tropical Asia. Dine in an elegant garden or ornate pavilion. Choose from four tastings menus, one of which is simply a surprise. The preparation and service are world-class.

Bridges
FUSION $$$

(Map p140; ☑970 095; www.bridgesbali.com; Jl Raya Campuan; meals US$15-35) The namesake bridges are right outside this multilevel restaurant with sweeping views of the gorgeous river gorge. You'll hear the rush of the water over rocks far below while you indulge in a top-end cocktail over the rocks or choose from the changing and complex menu of fusion fare that mixes Asian with European with a heavy Thai accent. Nightly wine specials at happy hour are popular.

Warung Pulau Kelapa
INDONESIAN $

(Map p140; Jl Raya Sanggingan; dishes 15,000Rp-30,000Rp) A popular place along the road from Campuan to Sanggingan, Kelapa has stylish takes on local classics. The surrounds are stylish as well: plenty of whitewash and antiques. Terrace tables across the wide expanse of grass are best.

Naughty Nuri's
BARBECUE $$

(Map p140; ☑977 547; Jl Raya Sanggingan; meals from 80,000Rp) This legendary expat hangout packs 'em in for grilled steaks, ribs and burgers, even if all the chewing needed gets in the way of chatting. Thursday night grilled-tuna specials are ridiculously popular, making for something of a party scene. Potent martinis are the real draw. Everybody mourns the late Brian Aldinger, the charismatic husband of Nuri.

PENESTANAN

Yellow Flower Cafe
INDONESIAN $

(Map p140; ☑889 9865; meals from 30,000Rp; ☎) New Age Indonesian right up in Penestanan along a little path through the rice fields. Nearby views look out over Ubud but you'll be happier concentrating on organic mains like a good *nasi campur* and rice pancakes. Snackers will delight in the good coffees, cakes and smoothies.

Lala & Lili
INDONESIAN $

(Map p140; ☑0812 398 8037; off Jl Raya Campuan; mains 15,000-50,000Rp; ☎) Fields of rice stretch away like waves of green from this simple cafe set on a path on a plateau. The menu is a familiar mix of Indo and sandwiches. Many local expat artists hang out

UBUD'S HERO OF THE YEAR

Ubud has a long tradition of locals and expats working together for the greater good of Indonesians. Just look at the bulletin boards at Bali Buddha and Kafe and you'll see meetings and all manner of opportunities to get involved. These selfless commitments got high-profile attention in 2011 when CNN named Ubud's Robin Lim as its 'Hero of the Year' from many contenders worldwide. Through her **Bumi Sehat Foundation** (www.bumisehatbali.org), Lim brings healthcare, prenatal services and birthing assistance to thousands of women on Bali and the Aceh province of Sumatra every year. It's an incredible commitment and it brings sorely needed services to women in villages who have no other access to such care.

here while others living in the numerous nearby cheap rentals spring for delivery.

KEDEWATAN

TOP CHOICE **Nasi Ayam Kedewatan**   BALINESE **$**
(off Map p140; 742 7168; Jl Raya Kedewatan; meals 15,000Rp; 9am-6pm) Few locals making the trek up the hill on the main road through Sayan pass this open-air place without stopping. The star is *sate lilit* (minced chicken satay), which here reaches heights that belie the common name. Chicken is minced, combined with an array of spices including lemongrass, then moulded onto bamboo skewers and grilled. Simply amazing, as are the traditional Balinese road snacks: fried chips combined with nuts and spices.

Drinking

Ubud. Bacchanalia. Mutually exclusive. No one comes to Ubud for wild nightlife. A few bars get lively around sunset and later in the night, but the venues certainly don't aspire to the extremes of beer-swilling debauchery and club partying found in Kuta and Seminyak.

Bars close early in Ubud, often by 11pm. Many eating places are also good just for a drink, including Naughty Nuri's and Laughing Buddha. The latter is also good for live music.

TOP CHOICE **Chillout Lounge**   CAFE
(Map p153; Jl Sandat) The name says it all: chill out. Loungers spaced around a large lawn are sheltered from the street thanks to shrubs and a wall. The open-air dining area has long tables with benches. It's the perfect venue for meeting up and planning your night; linger and you can do it under the stars. Best of all the proceeds go to support the **Sacred Childhoods Foundation** (www.sacredchildhoods.org), a nonprofit that

supports programs to help impoverished Indonesian children.

Jazz Café   BAR
(Map p140; Jl Sukma 2; 5pm-midnight) Ubud's most popular nightspot (and that's not faint praise even though competition might be lacking), Jazz Café offers a relaxed atmosphere in a charming garden that features coconut palms and ferns. The menu offers a range of good Asian fusion food and you can listen to live music from Tuesday to Saturday after 7.30pm. The cocktail list is long.

Bar Luna   CAFE
(Map p153; Jl Goutama) Brought to you by the minds behind the Ubud Writers & Readers Festival (p148), this small cafe hosts regular events featuring visiting authors giving readings and talks. The drinks menu is short but good and there are a few Indonesian dishes if you need actual food for thought.

Napi Orti   BAR
(Map p153; Monkey Forest Rd; drinks from 12,000Rp; noon-late) This upstairs place is your best bet for a late-night drink. Get boozy under the hazy gaze of Jim Morrison and Sid Vicious.

Ozigo   BAR
(Map p140; 0812 367 9736; Jl Raya Sanggingan; 9pm-2am) Ubud's late-night action – such as it is – is right here at this small and friendly club up by Naughty Nuri's. DJs are in residence nightly with edgy mixes plus lots of dance competitions and prizes.

Lebong Cafe   BAR
(Map p153; Monkey Forest Rd) Get up, stand up, stand up for your...reggae. This nightlife hub stays open at least until midnight, with live reggae and rock most nights. A few other places good for drinks are nearby.

DANCE TROUPES: GOOD & BAD

Not all dance groups on Ubud's stages are created equal. You've got true artists with international reputations and then you've got some who really shouldn't quit their day jobs. If you're a Balinese dance novice, you shouldn't worry too much about this; just pick a venue and go.

But after a few performances, you'll start to appreciate the differences in talent, and that's part of the enjoyment. Clue: if the costumes are dirty, the orchestra seems particularly uninterested and you find yourself watching a dancer and saying 'I could do that', then the group is B-level.

Excellent troupes who regularly perform in Ubud include the following:

» **Semara Ratih** High-energy, creative Legong interpretations.

» **Gunung Sari** Legong dance; one of Bali's oldest and most respected troupes.

» **Semara Madya** Kekac dance; especially good for the hypnotic monkey chants. A mystical experience for some.

» **Sekaa Gong Wanita Mekar Sari** An all-woman Legong troupe from Peliatan.

» **Tirta Sari** Legong dance.

» **Sadha Budaya** Barong dance.

☆ Entertainment

Few travel experiences can be more magical than attending a Balinese dance performance, especially in Ubud. Cultural entertainment keeps people returning and sets Bali apart from other tropical destinations. Ubud is a good base for the nightly array of performances and for accessing events in surrounding villages.

Dance

Dances performed for visitors are usually adapted and abbreviated to some extent to make them more enjoyable, but usually have appreciative locals in the audience (or peering around the screen!). It's also common to combine the features of more than one traditional dance in a single performance.

In a week in Ubud, you can see Kecak, Legong and Barong dances, *Mahabharata* and *Ramayana* ballets, *wayang kulit* puppets and gamelan orchestras. One of your first stops in town should be the tourist office for the weekly performance schedule.

Venues will usually host a variety of performances by various troupes through the week and aren't tied to a particular group.

Other performances can be found in nearby towns such as Batuan, Mawang and Kutuh.

Ubud Tourist Information (p169) has performance information and sells tickets (usually 80,000Rp). For performances outside Ubud, transport is often included in the price. Tickets are also sold at many hotels, at the venues and by street vendors who hang around outside Ubud Palace – all charge the same price.

Vendors often sell drinks at the performances, which typically last about 1½ hours. Before the show, you might notice the musicians checking out the size of the crowd – ticket sales fund the troupes. Also watch for potential members of the next generation of performers: local children avidly watch from under the screens, behind the stage and from a musician's lap or two.

One note about your mobile phone: nobody wants to hear it; nor do the performers want flash in their eyes. And don't be rude and walk out loudly in the middle (we're shocked at how many boors do this).

Ubud Palace   TRADITIONAL DANCE
(Map p153; Jl Raya Ubud) Performances are held here almost nightly against a beautiful backdrop in the palace compound, with the carvings highlighted by torches. You'll see lots of locals peaking over walls and around corners to see the shows.

Pura Dalem Ubud   TRADITIONAL DANCE
(Map p153; Jl Raya Ubud) At the west end of Jl Raya Ubud, this open-air venue has a flamelit carved-stone backdrop and in many ways is the most evocative place to see a dance performance. Watch for the Semara Ratih troupe.

Pura Taman Saraswati TRADITIONAL DANCE
(Ubud Water Palace; Map p153; Jl Raya Ubud) The beauty of the setting may distract you from the dancers, although at night you can't see the lily pads and lotus flowers that are such an attraction by day.

Arma Open Stage TRADITIONAL DANCE
(Map p153; 976 659; Jl Raya Pengosekan) Has among the best troupes.

Puri Desa Gede TRADITIONAL DANCE
(Map p140; Jl Peliatan) A good, well-lit venue that regularly attracts some of Bali's best troupes.

Padangtegal Kaja TRADITIONAL DANCE
(Map p153; Jl Hanoman) A simple, open venue in a very convenient location. In many ways this location hints at what dance performances have looked like in Ubud for generations.

Puri Agung Peliatan TRADITIONAL DANCE
(Map p140; Jl Peliatan) A simple setting backed by a large carved wall. Has some excellent performances.

Pura Dalem Puri TRADITIONAL DANCE
(Map p140; Jl Raya Ubud) Opposite Ubud's main cremation grounds.

Semara Ratih TRADITIONAL DANCE
(Map p140; Kutuh) Stage with a name that means 'Spirit of Bali'; usually one performance per week.

Ubud Wantilan TRADITIONAL DANCE
(Map p153; Jl Raya Ubud) The unadorned meeting *bale* across from Ubud Palace couldn't be easier to find. It's where your driver shelters from the rain.

Shadow Puppets

You can also find shadow-puppet shows – although these are greatly attenuated from traditional performances, which often last the entire night. Regular performances are held at Oka Kartini (Map p140; 975 193; Jl Raya Ubud; tickets 50,000Rp), which has bungalows and a gallery.

Musician **Nyoman Warsa** (Map p153; 074 807; Pondok Bamboo Music Shop, Monkey Forest Rd) orchestrates highly recommended puppet shows (75,000Rp) on certain evenings.

🔒 Shopping

Ubud has myriad art shops, boutiques and galleries. Many offer clever and unique items made in and around the area. Ubud is the ideal base for exploring the enormous number of craft galleries, studios and workshops in villages north and south.

The large market, Pasar Seni, which once dominated the intersection of Jl Raya Ubud and Monkey Forest Rd has vanished under a cloud of construction. See p168 for details.

Ubud's bountiful **produce market** (Map p153; Jl Raya Ubud; 6am-1pm), which operates to a greater or lesser extent every day, is buried behind the Pasar Seni site. It starts early in the morning and winds up by lunch.

What to Buy

You can spend days in and around Ubud shopping. Jl Raya Ubud, Monkey Forest Rd, Jl Hanoman and Jl Dewi Sita should be your starting points.

You'll find art for sale everywhere. Check the gallery listings for recommendations. Prices range from cheap to collector-level, depending on the artist. Surrounding villages are also hotbeds for arts and crafts – as you'll have noticed on your drive to Ubud.

Ubud has a few clothing designers. Look along Monkey Forest Rd, Jl Dewi Sita and Jl Hanoman. Many will make or alter to order. In these same areas, look for housewares, especially local goods such as weaving and antiques.

Ubud is the best place in Bali for books. Selections are wide and varied, especially for tomes on Balinese art and culture. Many sellers carry titles by small and obscure publishers.

CENTRAL UBUD

JALAN RAYA UBUD & AROUND

Ganesha Bookshop BOOKS
(Map p153; www.ganeshabooksbali.com; Jl Raya Ubud) Ubud's best bookshop has an amazing amount of stock jammed into a small space; an excellent selection of titles on Indonesian studies, travel, arts, music, fiction (including used titles) and maps. Good staff recommendations.

Smile Shop CHARITY
(Map p153; 233 758; www.senyumbali.org; Jl Sriwedari) All manner of creative goods for sale in a shop to benefit the Smile Foundation of Bali.

Threads of Life Indonesian Textile Arts Center FABRIC
(Map p140; www.threadsoflife.com; Jl Kajeng 24) This small store is part of a foundation that

works to preserve traditional textile creation in Balinese villages. There's a small but visually stunning collection of exquisite handmade fabrics in stock.

Moari   MUSICAL INSTRUMENTS
(Map p153; ☑977 367; Jl Raya Ubud) New and restored Balinese musical instruments are sold here. Splurge on a cute little bamboo flute for US$3.

MONKEY FOREST ROAD

Ashitaba   HOMEWARES
(Map p153; ☑464 922; Monkey Forest Rd) Tenganan, the Aga village of East Bali, produces the intricate and beautiful rattan items sold here (and in Seminyak). Containers, bowls, purses and more (from US$5) display the fine and intricate weaving.

Toko   ANTIQUES
(Map p153; Monkey Forest Rd) Amid a string of trashy places selling tourist tat, this elegant store stands out like Audrey Hepburn amid the Spice Girls. Silks, art, antiques and more are beautifully displayed in a lovely shop that will have you pondering your shipping options.

Kou Cuisine   HOMEWARES
(Map p153; ☑972 319; Monkey Forest Rd) Give the gift of exquisite little containers of jams made with Balinese fruit or containers of sea salt made along Bali's shores. Afterwards, clean up with their soap. There are many small and exquisite gifts here.

Pondok Bamboo Music Shop   MUSICAL INSTRUMENTS
(Map p153; ☑974 807; Monkey Forest Rd) Hear the music of a thousand bamboo wind chimes at this store owned by noted gamelan musician Nyoman Warsa, who offers music lessons and stages shadow-puppet shows.

Pusaka   CLOTHING
(Map p153; ☑978 619; Monkey Forest Rd 71) 'Modern ethnic clothing' is the motto here, which translates into cool, comfy yet stylish cottons. Need a gift for somebody small? Adorable house-made plush toys are 50,000Rp.

Periplus   BOOKS
(Map p140; ☑975 178; Monkey Forest Rd) Typically glossy.

JALAN DEWI SITA

TOP CHOICE Sarasari   HANDICRAFTS
(Map p153; Jl Goutama) Wakjaka, a master of Balinese dream-mask carving, works his magic in this tiny shop almost daily. Stop by, watch him work, and learn about Bali's complex and rich traditions around masks.

Kou   BEAUTY
(Map p153; Jl Dewi Sita) Luxurious locally handmade organic soaps perfume your nose as you enter. Put one in your undies drawer and smell fine for weeks. The range is unlike that found in chain stores selling luxe soap.

Kertas Gingsir   PAPER
(Map p153; Jl Dewi Sita) This cute little place specialises in gorgeous and heavily tex-

---

BIG CHANGES IN UBUD

As its popularity has grown Ubud has become traffic-clogged and tourist-choked that in many ways reminds both locals and visitors of – horrors! – Kuta. And day trippers from that very place, having endured 90 minutes or more of traffic, wonder why they bothered coming to Ubud.

In an effort to alleviate the traffic, deal with parked cars and give the wandering masses somewhere to dawdle, the local government announced some big plans in 2012:

Pasar Seni (Art Market; Map p153; Jl Raya Ubud) The large market that has stood at the corner of Jl Raya Ubud and Monkey Forest Rd for generations was demolished. Long the main shopping venue for locals, in recent years it has become little more than a mass market for low-end souvenirs. The new version will have many fewer shops, supposedly higher-quality merchandise and face onto a large open plaza where people can rest and simply hang out.

Football Field (Map p153) A three-level underground parking garage is planned for the land under the iconic Football Field in the centre of Ubud. Other parking lots will be built on the periphery with shuttles bringing visitors into the centre.

Jl Raya Ubud The central part of the main drag will be closed off to through traffic and a new bypass road built to the north of the palace.

tured papers handmade from banana, pineapple and taro plants. If you're into pulp, ask about factory visits as everything is made near Ubud.

Confiture Michèle
FOOD

(Map p153; Jl Goutama) Preserves made from Bali's fruit bounty are the, er, preserve of this cute – and sweet-smelling – shop.

Eco Shop
ACCESSORIES

(Map p153; Jl Dewi Sita) Household items, gifts, T-shirts, bags and much more made from recycled products are sold in this shop which draws a lot of its merchandise from industrious families in Balinese villages.

PADANGTEGAL & PENGOSEKAN

Namaste
NEW AGE

(Map p153; Jl Hanoman 64) Just the place to buy a crystal to get your spiritual house in order, Namaste is a gem of a little store with a top range of New Age supplies. Incense, yoga mats, moody instrumental music – it's all here.

Tegun Galeri
HOMEWARES

(Map p153; 973 361; Jl Hanoman 44) It's everything the souvenir stores are not, with beautiful handmade items from around the island plus ancient art.

Gemala Jewelry
JEWELLERY

(Map p153; 0811 392 058; Jl Raya Pengosekan) One of Ubud's top places for locally designed and produced jewellery.

Goddess on the Go!
WOMEN'S CLOTHING

(Map p153; Jl Raya Pengosekan) Women's clothes for adventure. Supercomfortable, easy to pack and made ecofriendly. There's a lot of selection in this large store.

Yoga Shop
CLOTHING

(Map p153; 970 992; Jl Hanoman 44) Stretchy cottony clothes, mats, yoga gear, music to move by etc.

Galaxyan Atelier
JEWELLERY

(Map p153; 971 430; Jl Hanoman 3) In-house creations in silver and gold, flashy designs.

No 6
CLOTHING

(Map p153; Jl Hanoman 6) The name could be construed as a misnomer as the sizes start at 8 at this shop dedicated to women's clothes that 'love any shape'.

Rainbow Spirit Crystal Shop
NEW AGE

(Map p153; Jl Hanoman) Ubud is a centre for every alternative form of healing you've heard of and many you haven't. This shop delivers just what the name implies.

Arma
BOOKS

(Map p153; 976 659; www.armamuseum.com; Jl Raya Pengosekan; 9am-6pm) Large selection of cultural titles.

ELSEWHERE

Neka Art Museum
BOOKS

(Map p140; 975 074; www.museumneka.com; Jl Raya Sanggingan; 9am-5pm) Good range of art books.

Periplus
BOOKS

(Map p140; 976 149; Bintang Centre, Jl Raya Campuan) Large store with a small cafe.

ℹ️ Information

Visitors will find every service they need and then some along Ubud's main roads. Bulletin boards at Bali Buddha (p160) and Kafe (p163) have info on housing, jobs, classes and much more.

Ubud is home to many nonprofit and volunteer groups.

Internet Access

Many of Ubud's cafes and hotels offer wi-fi.
@Highway (972 107; Jl Raya Ubud; per hr 30,000Rp; 24hr; 🛜) Full-service and very fast.

Libraries

Pondok Pecak Library & Learning Centre (Map p153; 976 194; Monkey Forest Rd; 9am-9pm) On the far side of the football field, this relaxed place is a fitting tribute to its late founder, Laurie Billington. Charges membership fees for library use. Small cafe and a pleasant reading area.

Medical Services

Guardian Pharmacy (Jl Raya Ubud) An outlet of the large international chain.
Kimia Pharma (Jl Peliatan) Large shop of the local and respected pharmacy chain.

Money

Ubud has numerous banks, ATMs and money-changers along Jl Raya Ubud and Monkey Forest Rd.

Post

Main post office (Jl Jembawan; 8am-5pm) Has a sort-it-yourself poste restante system. Address poste restante mail to Kantor Pos, Ubud 80571, Bali, Indonesia.

Tourist Information

Ubud Tourist Information (Yaysan Bina Wisata; 973 285; Jl Raya Ubud; 8am-8pm) The one really useful tourist office in Bali. It has a good range of information and a noticeboard listing current happenings and activities. The staff can answer most regional questions and have up-to-date information on ceremonies and traditional dances held in the area; dance tickets are sold here.

ⓘ Getting There & Away

Bemo

Ubud is situated on two bemo routes. Bemo travel from Gianyar to Ubud (10,000Rp) and larger brown bemo travel from Batubulan terminal in Denpasar to Ubud (13,000Rp), and then head to Kintamani via Payangan. Ubud doesn't have a bemo terminal; there are bemo stops on Jl Suweta near the market in the centre of town.

Tourist Shuttle Bus

Perama (🖉973 316; Jl Hanoman; ⓧ9am-9pm) is the major tourist-shuttle operator, but its terminal is inconveniently located in Padangtegal; to get to your final destination in Ubud will cost another 15,000Rp.

Destination	Fare (Rp)	Duration (hr)
Candidasa	50,000	1¾
Kuta	50,000	1¼
Lovina	125,000	3
Padangbai	50,000	1¼
Sanur	40,000	1

ⓘ Getting Around

Many restaurants and hotels offer free local transport for guests and customers. Ask.

To/From the Airport

Official taxis from the airport to Ubud cost 210,000Rp. A car with driver *to* the airport will cost about the same.

Bemo

Bemo don't directly link Ubud with nearby villages; you'll have to catch one going to Denpasar, Gianyar, Pujung or Kintamani and get off where you need to. Bemo to Gianyar travel along eastern Jl Raya Ubud, down Jl Peliatan and east to Bedulu. To Pujung, bemo head east along Jl Raya Ubud and then north through Andong and past the turn-off to Petulu.

To Payangan, bemo travel west along Jl Raya Ubud, go up past the many places on Jl Raya Campuan and Jl Raya Sanggingan and turn north at the junction after Sanggingan. Larger brown-coloured bemo to Batubulan terminal go east along Jl Raya Ubud and down Jl Hanoman.

The fare for a ride within the Ubud area shouldn't be more than 7000Rp.

Bicycle

Shops hiring out bikes have their cycles on display along the main roads; your accommodation can always arrange bike hire.

Car & Motorcycle

With numerous nearby attractions, many of which are difficult to reach by bemo, hiring a vehicle is sensible. Ask at your accommodation or hire a car and driver.

Taxi

There are no metered taxis based in Ubud – those that honk their horns at you have usually dropped off passengers from southern Bali in Ubud and are hoping for a fare back. Instead, you'll use one of the ubiquitous drivers with private vehicles hanging around on the streets hectoring passersby (the better drivers politely hold up signs that say 'transport').

Most of the drivers are very fair; a few – often from out of the area – not so much. If you find a driver you like, get his number and call him for rides during your stay. From central Ubud to, say, Sanggingan should cost about 40,000Rp – rather steep actually. A ride from the palace to the end of Jl Hanoman should cost about 20,000Rp.

It's easy to get a ride on the back of a motorbike; rates are half those of cars.

AROUND UBUD

🖉0361

The region east and north of Ubud has many of the most ancient monuments and relics in Bali. Some of them predate the Majapahit era and raise as-yet-unanswered questions about Bali's history. Others are more recent, and in other instances, newer structures have been built on and around the ancient remains. They're interesting to history and archaeology buffs, but not that spectacular to look at – with the exception of Bali's own bit of Angkor at Gunung Kawi. Perhaps the best approach is to plan a whole day walking or cycling around the area, stopping at the places that interest you, but not treating any one as a destination in itself.

The area is thick with excursion possibilities. Besides the Elephant Cave, there's the Crazy Buffalo Temple. Heading north you find Bali's most important ancient site at Tampaksiring, and a nearly forgotten shrine, Pura Mengening, nearby that rewards the adventurous.

Bedulu

Bedulu was once the capital of a great kingdom. The legendary Dalem Bedaulu ruled the Pejeng dynasty from here, and was the last Balinese king to withstand the onslaught of the powerful Majapahit from Java. He was defeated by Gajah Mada in 1343. The capital shifted several times after this, to Gelgel and then later to Semarapura (Klungkung). Today Bedulu is absorbed into the greater Ubud sprawl.

◉ Sights

Goa Gajah   CAVE
(Elephant Cave; adult/child 10,000/5000Rp, parking 2000Rp; ◷8am-6pm) There were never any elephants in Bali (until tourist attractions changed that); ancient Goa Gajah probably takes its name from the nearby Sungai Petanu, which at one time was known as Elephant River, or perhaps because the face over the cave entrance might resemble an elephant. It's located some 2km southeast of Ubud on the road to Bedulu.

The origins of the cave are uncertain – one tale relates that it was created by the fingernail of the legendary giant Kebo Iwa. It probably dates to the 11th century, and was certainly in existence during the Majapahit takeover of Bali. The cave was rediscovered by Dutch archaeologists in 1923, but the fountains and pool were not found until 1954.

The cave is carved into a rock face and you enter through the cavernous mouth of a demon. Inside the T-shaped cave you can see fragmentary remains of the lingam, the phallic symbol of the Hindu god Shiva, and its female counterpart the *yoni,* plus a statue of Shiva's son, the elephant-headed god Ganesha. In the courtyard in front of the cave are two square bathing pools with water trickling into them from waterspouts held by six female figures.

From Goa Gajah you can clamber down through the rice paddies to Sungai Petanu (Petanu River), where there are crumbling rock carvings of stupas (domes for housing Buddhist relics) on a cliff face, and a small cave.

Try to get here before 10am, when the big tourist buses begin lumbering into the large souvenir-stall-filled parking lot like, well, elephants. Sarong hire is 3000Rp.

Yeh Pulu   HISTORIC SITE
(adult/child 10,000/5000Rp) A man having his hand munched by a boar is one of the scenes on the 25m-long carved cliff face known as Yeh Pulu, believed to be a hermitage from the late 14th century. Apart from the figure of Ganesha most of the scenes deal with everyday life, although the position and movement of the figures suggests that it could be read from left to right as a story. One theory is that they are events from the life of Krishna, the Hindu god.

You can walk between the sites, following small paths through the paddy fields, but you might need to pay a local to guide you. By car or bicycle, look for the signs to

---

SAVING BALI'S DOGS

Mangy curs. That's the only label you can apply to many of Bali's dogs. As you travel the island – especially by foot – you can't help but notice dogs that are sick, ill-tempered, uncared for and victims to a litany of other maladies.

How can such a seemingly gentle island have Asia's worst dog population (which now has a huge rabies problem)? The answers are complex, but benign neglect has a lot to do with it. Dogs are at the bottom of the social strata: few have owners and local interest in them is nil.

Some nonprofits in Ubud are hoping to change the fortunes of Bali's maligned best friends through rabies vaccinations, spaying and neutering, and public education. Donations are always greatly needed.

Bali Adoption Rehab Centre (BARC; ☏790 4579; www.balidogrefuge.com) Cares for dogs, places strays with sponsors and operates a mobile clinic for sterilisation.

Bali Animal Welfare Association (BAWA; ☏977 217; www.bawabali.com) Runs lauded mobile rabies vaccination teams, organises adoption, promotes population control.

Yudisthira Swarga Foundation (☏742 4048; www.yudisthiraswarga.org) Based in Denpasar, cares for thousands of Bali strays a year and has vaccination and population-control programs.

THE LEGEND OF DALEM BEDAULU

A legend relates how Dalem Bedaulu possessed magical powers that allowed him to have his head chopped off and then replaced. Performing this unique party trick one day, the servant entrusted with lopping off the king's head and then replacing it unfortunately dropped it in a river and, to his horror, watched it float away. Looking around in panic for a replacement, he grabbed a pig, cut off its head and popped it upon the king's shoulders. Thereafter, the king was forced to sit on a high throne and forbade his subjects to look up at him; Bedaulu means 'he who changed heads'.

'Relief Yeh Pulu' or 'Villa Yeh Pulu', east of Goa Gajah.

Even if your interest in carved Hindu art is minor, this site is quite lovely and rarely will you have much company. From the entrance, it's a 300m lush, tropical walk to Yeh Pulu.

Pura Samuan Tiga   TEMPLE
The majestic Pura Samuan Tiga (Temple of the Meeting of the Three) is about 200m east of the Bedulu junction. The name is possibly a reference to the Hindu trinity, or it may refer to meetings held here in the early 11th century. Despite these early associations, all the temple buildings have been rebuilt since the 1917 earthquake.

❶ Getting There & Away

About 3km east of Teges, the road from Ubud reaches a junction where you can turn south to Gianyar or north to Pejeng, Tampaksiring and Penelokan. Ubud–Gianyar bemo will drop you off at this junction, from where you can walk to the sights. The road from Ubud is reasonably flat, so coming by bicycle is a good option.

Pejeng

On the road towards Tampaksiring you come to Pejeng and its famous temples. Like Bedulu, this was once an important seat of power, as it was the capital of the Pejeng kingdom, which fell to the Majapahit invaders in 1343.

◉ Sights

Museum Purbakala   MUSEUM
(📞942 354; Jl Raya Tampaksiring; admission by donation; ⏰8am-3pm Mon-Thu, to 12.30pm Fri) This archaeological museum has a reasonable collection of artefacts from all over Bali, and most displays are in English. The exhibits in several small buildings include some of Bali's first pottery from near Gilimanuk, and sarcophagi dating from as early as 300 BC – some originating from Bangli are carved in the shape of a turtle, which has important cosmic associations in Balinese mythology.

The museum is about 500m north of the Bedulu junction, and is easy to reach by bemo or by bicycle. It's a sleepy place and you'll get the most out of it if you come with a knowledgeable guide.

Pura Kebo Edan   TEMPLE
(Jl Raya Tampaksiring) Who can resist a sight called Crazy Buffalo Temple? Although not an imposing structure, it's famous for its 3m-high statue, known as the **Giant of Pejeng**, thought to be approximately 700 years old. Details are sketchy, but it may represent Bima, a hero of the *Mahabharata,* dancing on a dead body, as in a myth related to the Hindu Shiva cult. There is some conjecture about the giant's giant genitalia – it has what appear to be pins on the side. Some claim this was to give the woman more pleasure.

Pura Pusering Jagat   TEMPLE
(Jl Raya Tampaksiring) So that's what it looks like? The large Pura Pusering Jagat is said to be the centre of the old Pejeng kingdom. Dating from 1329, this temple is visited by young couples who pray at the stone *lingam* and *yoni*. Further back is a large stone urn, with elaborate but worn carvings of gods and demons searching for the elixir of life in a depiction of the *Mahabharata* tale 'Churning the Sea of Milk'. The temple is on a small track running west of the main road.

Pura Penataran Sasih   TEMPLE
(Jl Raya Tampaksiring) This was once the state temple of the Pejeng kingdom. In the inner courtyard, high up in a pavilion and difficult to see, is the huge bronze drum known as the **Fallen Moon of Pejeng**. The hourglass-shaped drum is 186cm long, the largest single-piece cast drum in the world. Estimates of its age vary from 1000 to 2000 years.

It is not certain whether the drum was made locally or imported – the intricate geometric decorations are said to resemble patterns from places as far apart as West Papua and Vietnam.

Balinese legend relates that the drum came to earth as a fallen moon, landing in a tree and shining so brightly that it prevented a band of thieves from going about their unlawful purpose. One of the thieves decided to put the light out by urinating on it, but the moon exploded and fell to earth as a drum, with a crack across its base as a result of the fall.

Although the big noise here is all about the drum, be sure to notice the **statuary** in the temple courtyard that dates from the 10th to the 12th century.

Tampaksiring

Tampaksiring is a small village about 18km northeast of Ubud with a large and important temple, Tirta Empul, and the most impressive ancient site in Bali, Gunung Kawi. It sits in the Pakerisan Valley, and the entire area has been nominated for Unesco recognition.

◉ Sights

TOP
CHOICE **Gunung Kawi**　　　　　MONUMENT
(adult/child 10,000/5000Rp, sarong 3000Rp, parking 2000Rp; ⏱7am-5pm) At the bottom of a lush green river valley is one of Bali's oldest and largest ancient monuments. Gunung Kawi consists of 10 rock-cut *candi* (shrines) – memorials cut out of the rock face in imitation of actual statues. They stand in awe-inspiring 8m-high sheltered niches cut into the sheer cliff face. Be prepared for long climbs, it's over 270 steps.

The strenuous walk is broken up into sections and at times the views as you walk through ancient terraced rice fields are as fine as any on Bali. Each *candi* is believed to be a memorial to a member of the 11th-century Balinese royalty, but little is known for certain.

Legends relate that the whole group of memorials was carved out of the rock face in one hard-working night by the mighty fingernails of Kebo Iwa.

The five monuments on the eastern bank are probably dedicated to King Udayana, Queen Mahendradatta and their sons Airlangga, Anak Wungsu and Marakata. While Airlangga ruled eastern Java, Anak Wungsu ruled Bali. The four monuments on the western side are, by this theory, to Anak Wungsu's chief concubines. Another theory is that the whole complex is dedicated to Anak Wungsu, his wives, concubines and, in the case of the remote 10th *candi,* to a royal minister.

As you wander between monuments, temples, offerings, streams and fountains, you can't help but feel a certain ancient majesty here.

On the northern outskirts of town, a sign points east off the main road to Gunung Kawi and its ancient monuments. From the end of the access road, a steep stone stairway leads down to the river, at one point cutting through an embankment of solid rock.

Tirta Empul　　　　　MONUMENT
(adult/child 10,000/5000Rp, parking 2000Rp; ⏱8am-6pm) A well-signposted fork in the road north of Tampaksiring leads to the popular holy springs at Tirta Empul, discovered in AD 962 and believed to have magical powers. The springs bubble up into a large, crystal-clear pool within the temple and gush out through waterspouts into a bathing pool.

The waters are the main source of Sungai Pakerisan (Pakerisan River), the river that rushes by Gunung Kawi only 1km or so away. Next to the springs, Pura Tirta Empul is one of Bali's most important temples. Come in the early morning or late afternoon to avoid the tourist buses. You can also use the clean, segregated and free public baths here.

Other Sights

There are other groups of *candi* and monks' cells in the area once encompassed by the ancient Pejeng kingdom, notably **Pura Krobokan** and **Goa Garba**, but none so grand as Gunung Kawi. Between Gunung Kawi and Tirta Empul, **Pura Mengening** temple has a freestanding *candi,* similar in design to those at Gunung Kawi and much less visited.

The road running north to Penelokan is lined with dozens of **agritourism attractions**. In reality these are mostly gift shops selling coffee and the usual carvings plus a few plants out back in labelled gardens. They give groups a reason to stop and shop.

Tegallalang

There are lots of shops and stalls in this busy market town you're likely to pass through on your visit to the area's temples. Stop for a stroll and you may be rewarded by hearing the practice of one of the local noted gamelan orchestras. Otherwise, plenty of carvers stand ready to sell you a carved fertility doll or the like.

You can pause at **Cafe Kampung & Cottages** (☎901 201; www.kampungtari.com; dishes 40,000-70,000Rp; ☎), an attractive warung (perfect for lunch) and upmarket guesthouse (rooms from US$150) with jaw-dropping rice-terrace views. The design makes great use of natural rock. Nearby, scores of carvers produce works from albesia wood, which is easily turned into simplistic, cartoonish figures. The wood is also a favourite of wind-chime makers.

Go about 3km west of town on a small, very green road to Keliki, and you'll pass **Alam Sari** (☎240 308; www.alamsari.com; r from US$100; ✳@☎⊞), a small hotel in a wonderfully isolated location where the bamboo grows like grass. There are 12 luxurious yet rustic rooms, a pool and a great view. The hotel treats its own wastewater, among other environmental initiatives.

North of Ubud

Abused and abandoned logging elephants from Sumatra have been given refuge in Bali at the **Elephant Safari Park** (☎721 480; www.baliadventuretours.com; tour with transport adult/child US$66/44; ⊘8am-6pm). Located in the cool, wet highlands of **Taro** (14km north of Ubud), the park is home to almost 30 elephants. Besides seeing a full complement of exhibits about elephants, you can ride an elephant for an extra fee. The park has received praise for its conservation efforts; however, be careful you don't end up at one of the rogue parks, designed to divert the unwary to unsanctioned displays of elephants.

The surrounding region produces ochre-coloured paint pigment. The gentle uphill drive from Ubud is a lush attraction in itself.

The usual road from Ubud to Batur is through Tampaksiring, but there are other lesser roads up the gentle mountain slope. One of the most attractive goes north from Peliatan, past Petulu and its birds, and through the rice terraces between Tegallalang and Ceking, to bring you out on the crater rim between Penelokan and Batur. It's a sealed road all the way and you also pass through **Sebatu**, which has all manner of artisans tucked away in tiny villages.

The one off-note will be **Pujung**, where the rice terraces are beautiful but have attracted a strip of ugly tourist traps overlooking them. A few years ago the farmers got fed up with looking up at others profiting from their labours and installed picture-ruining mirrors until they were cut in on the take.

South of Ubud

The road between south Bali and Ubud is lined with little shops making and selling handicrafts. Many visitors shop along the route as they head to Ubud, sometimes by the busload, but much of the craftwork is actually done in small workshops and family compounds on quiet back roads. You may enjoy these places more after visiting Ubud, where you'll see some of the best Balinese arts and develop some appreciation of the styles and themes.

For serious shopping and real flexibility in exploring these villages, it's worth arranging your own transport, so you can explore the back roads and carry your purchases without any hassles. Note that your driver may receive a commission from any place you spend your money – this can add 10% or more to the cost of purchases (think of it as his tip). Also, a driver may try to steer you to workshops or artisans that he favours, rather than those of most interest to you.

The roads form a real patchwork and you'll be rewarded with surprises if you take some time to wander the lesser routes.

BATUBULAN

The start of the road from south Bali is lined with outlets for stone sculptures – **stone carving** is the main craft of Batubulan (moonstone). Workshops are found right along the road to Tegaltamu, with another batch further north around Silakarang. Batubulan is the source of the stunning temple-gate guardians seen all over Bali. The stone used for these sculptures is a porous grey volcanic rock called *paras,* which resembles pumice; it's soft and surprisingly light. It also ages quickly, so that 'ancient' work may be years rather than centuries old.

The temples around Batubulan are, naturally, noted for their fine stonework. Just 200m to the east of the busy main road, **Pura Puseh Batubulan** (Map p175) is worth a visit for its moat filled with lotus flowers and perfectly balanced overall composition. Statues draw on ancient Hindu and Buddhist iconography and Balinese mythology; however, they are not old – many are copied

South of Ubud

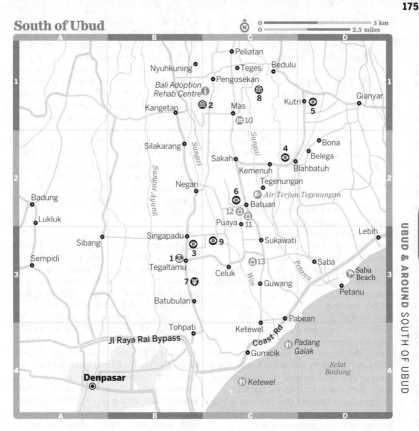

from books on archaeology. An attenuated **Barong dance show** (admission 80,000Rp; ⊘9.30am) about the iconic lion-dog creature is performed in an ugly hall; it's a bus-tour-friendly one-hour-long show. Note that Pura Puseh means 'central temple' – you'll find many around Bali. Some translations have 'Puseh' meaning 'navel', which is apt.

Batubulan is also a centre for making 'antiques', textiles and woodwork, and has numerous craft shops.

BALI BIRD PARK & RIMBA REPTILE PARK

More than 1000 birds from 250 species flit about this **bird park** (Map p175; ☎299 352; www.bali-bird-park.com; both parks adult/child US$25/12.50; ⊘9am-5.30pm), including rare *cendrawasih* (birds of paradise) from West Papua and the all-but-vanished Bali star-lings. Many of these birds are housed in spe-cial walk-through aviaries; in one of them you follow a walk at tree-level, or what some with feathers might say is bird-level. The 2 hectares of landscaped gardens feature a fine collection of tropical plants.

Next door, **Rimba Reptile** (☑299 344) has about 20 species of creatures from Indonesia and Africa, as well as turtles, crocodiles, a python and a solitary Komodo dragon. The parks are popular with kids; allow at least two hours.

Tours stop at the parks, or you can take a Batubulan–Ubud bemo, get off at the junction at Tegaltamu, and follow the signs north for about 600m. There is a large parking lot.

SINGAPADU

The centre of Singapadu is dominated by a huge **banyan tree** (Map p175). In the past, these were community meeting places. Even today the local meeting hall is just across the road. The surrounding village has a traditional appearance, with walled family compounds and shady trees. You can visit the **Nyoman Suaka Home** (Map p175; requested donation 20,000Rp; ⊘9am-5pm), which is 50m off the main road, just south of the big tree. Pass through the old carved entrance to the walled family compound and you'll discover a classic Balinese home. While you snoop about, the family goes about its business. Many pestles are in use in the kitchen producing spices and some of the roofs are still made from thatch on bamboo frames.

Singapadu's dancers now perform mostly at large venues in tourist areas – there are no regular public performances.

ⓘ BEST TIME TO VISIT GUNUNG KAWI

Get to Gunung Kawi as early as possible for the best experience. If you start down the steps by 7.30am, you'll avoid all the vendors and you'll still see residents going about their morning business in the swift-flowing streams such as ablutions and cleaning ceremonial offerings. You can hear the birds, the flowing water and your own voice going 'ooh' and 'aah' without the distractions that come later when large groups arrive. In addition, you'll still have cool air when you start back up the endless steps. Be sure to have a sarong in case there is nobody yet offering them for use. If the ticket office is closed, you can pay on your way out.

CELUK

Celuk is the **silver** and **gold** centre of Bali. The flashier showrooms are on the main road, and have marked prices that are quite high, although you can always bargain.

Hundreds of silversmiths and goldsmiths work in their homes on the backstreets north and east of the main road. Most of these artisans are from *pande* families, members of a subcaste of blacksmiths whose knowledge of fire and metal has traditionally put them outside the usual caste hierarchy. Their small workshops are interesting to visit, and have the lowest prices, but they don't keep a large stock of finished work. They will make something to order if you bring a sample or sketch.

SUKAWATI & PUAYA

Once a royal capital, Sukawati is now known for its specialised artisans, who busily work in small shops along the roads. One group, the *tukang prada,* make temple umbrellas, beautifully decorated with stencilled gold paint, which can be seen in their shops.

In the town centre, the always-bustling **produce market** is a highlight. Vendors with fruit you've likely never seen before are tucked into the corners of the typically grungy main food hall. You'll also see sarongs and temple-ceremony paraphernalia; outside booths sell easy-to-assemble temple-offering kits to time-constrained Balinese faithful. On the surrounding streets you'll find some stalls with high-quality handicrafts mixed in with those peddling 'I Love Bali' handbags. Should you get inspired, there are ATMs at the ready.

About 2km south of town, the much-hyped and very touristy **Pasar Seni** is a two-storey market where every type of knick-knack and trinket is on sale.

Puaya, about 1km northwest of Sukawati, specialises in high-quality **leather shadow puppets** and **masks** for Topeng and Barong dances. On the main street, look for a small sign that reads **Mustika Collection** (Map p175; ☑299 479; Kubu Dauh 62), or ask anyone. Inside the family compound you'll find a workshop for masks and puppets where you can see how cow hide is transformed into these works of art. Nearby, **Baruna Art Shop** (Map p175; ☑299 490; Kubu Duah) has Barongs aplenty. Other workshops nearby are in shadowing rooms behind open doorways; look inside and you might see a fearsome mask staring at you.

BALI'S CHOCOLATE FACTORY

You might think Swiss or Belgian when you think chocolate but soon you could be thinking Bali. **Big Tree Farms** (☏846 3327; www.bigtreefarms.com; Sibang), a local producer of quality foodstuffs that has made a big splash internationally, has built a chocolate factory about 10km southwest of Ubud in the village of Sibang.

And this not just any factory: rather it is a huge and architecturally stunning creation made sustainably from bamboo – an ethos that extends to the company's very philosophy. The chocolate made here comes from cocoa beans grown by over 13,000 farmers across Indonesia. The result is a very high-quality chocolate that you can watch being made on tours.

Just seeing one of the world's largest bamboo structures is an attraction in itself, toss in fabulous chocolate and you've got a great experience.

Reaching the factory is easy as Sibang is on one of the roads linking Ubud to south Bali.

BATUAN

Batuan's recorded history goes back 1000 years, and in the 17th century its royal family controlled most of southern Bali. The decline of its power is attributed to a priest's curse, which scattered the royal family to different parts of the island.

Just west of the centre, the twin temples of **Pura Puseh** (Map p175) and **Pura Dasar** (donation 10,000Rp, includes sarong) are accessible studies in classic Balinese temple architecture. The carvings are elaborate and visitors are given the use of vermilion sarongs, which look good in photos.

MAS

Mas means 'gold' in Bahasa Indonesia, but **woodcarving** is the principal craft in this village. The great Majapahit priest Nirartha once lived here, and **Pura Taman Pule** is said to be built on the site of his home. During the three-day **Kuningan festival**, a performance of *wayang wong* (an older version of the *Ramayana* ballet) is held in the temple's courtyard.

Carving was a traditional art of the priestly Brahmana caste, and the skills are said to have been a gift of the gods. Historically, carving was limited to temple decorations, dance masks and musical instruments, but in the 1930s carvers began to depict people and animals in a naturalistic way. Today it's hard to resist the oodles of winsome creatures produced here.

This is the place to come if you want something custom-made in sandalwood – just be prepared to pay well (and check the wood's authenticity carefully). Mas is also part of Bali's booming furniture industry, producing chairs, tables and antiques

('made to order!'), mainly from teak imported from other Indonesian islands.

Three generations of carvers produce some of Bali's most revered **masks** in the family compound of IB Anom (p146), right off the main road in Mas. There is a small showroom with their works, but mostly the appeal is visiting with the family while they create something out of cedar. You can take lessons (from 100,000Rp per day) and expect to have something half-good in about two weeks.

Along the main road in Mas are the **Taman Harum Cottages** (Map p175; ☏975 567; www.tamanharumcottages.com; Jl Raya Desa Mas; r/villas from US$40/60; ❄@☎). There are 17 rooms and villas – some quite large. By all means get one overlooking the rice fields. They're behind a gallery, which is also a venue for a huge range of art and cultural courses. Ubud shuttles are free.

North of Mas, woodcarving shops make way for the art galleries, cafes, hotels and lights of Ubud.

ALTERNATIVE ROUTES

From Sakah, along the road between Batuan and Ubud, you can continue east for a few kilometres to the turn-off to Blahbatuh and continue to Ubud via Kutri and Bedulu.

In Blahbatuh, **Pura Gaduh** (Map p175) has a 1m-high stone head, believed to be a portrait of Kebo Iwa, the legendary strongman and minister to the last king of the Bedulu kingdom. Gajah Mada – the Majapahit strongman – realised that it wouldn't be possible to conquer Bedulu (Bali's strongest kingdom) while Kebo Iwa was there. So Gajah Mada lured him away to Java (with promises of women and song) and had him

A MAGICAL KINGDOM OF PUPPETS

Setia Darma House of Masks & Puppets (Map p175; ☑977 404; Jl Tegal Bingin; admission by donation; ◷8am-4pm) is both the newest and one of the best museums in the Ubud area. Over 4600 ceremonial masks and puppets from Indonesia and across Asia are beautifully displayed in a series of renovated historic buildings. Among the many treasures, look for the golden **Jero Luh Mask** as well as the faces of royalty, mythical monsters and even the common man. Puppets are unnervingly lifelike. The museum is about 2km northeast of the main Mas crossroads.

murdered. The stone head possibly predates the Javanese influence in Bali, but the temple is simply a reconstruction of an earlier one destroyed in the earthquake of 1917.

See looms busily making ikat and batik fabrics at **Putri Ayu** (☑225 533; Jl Diponegoro). The workshops and showroom are a good complement to the textile shops in Gianyar and are just across from the temple.

West of here, there are A-list views of **rice terraces** off the main road near the village of **Kemenuh**.

About 2km southwest of Blahbatuh, along Sungai Petanu (Petanu River), is **Air Terjun Tegenungan** (Tegenungan Waterfall; aka Srog Srogan). Follow the signs from Kemenuh for the best view of the falls, from the west side of the river.

KUTRI

Heading north from Blahbatuh, Kutri has the interesting **Pura Kedarman** (Map p175) , aka Pura Bukit Dharma. If you climb up Bukit Dharma behind the temple, there's a great panoramic view and a **hilltop shrine**, with a stone statue of the six-armed goddess of death and destruction, Durga, killing a demon-possessed water buffalo.

BONA & BELEGA

On the back road between Blahbatuh and Gianyar, Bona is a **basket-weaving** centre and features many articles made from *lontar* (specially prepared palm leaves). It is also known for fire dances. (Note: most road signs in the area read 'Bone' instead of Bona, so if you get lost, you'll have to ask: 'Do you know the way to Bone?') Nearby, the village of Belega is a centre for bamboo furniture production.

East Bali

Best Places to Eat

» Gianyar Night Market
(p184)

» Cafe Garam (p211)

» Merta Sari (p193)

» Terrace (p197)

Best Places to Stay

» Turtle Bay Hideaway
(p203)

» Meditasi (p210)

» Alam Anda (p213)

» Samanvaya (p189)

Why Go?

Wandering the roads of east Bali is one of the island's great pleasures. Rice terraces spill down hillsides under swaying palms, wild volcanic beaches are washed by pounding surf, and age-old villages soldier on with barely a trace of modernity. Watching over it all is Gunung Agung, the 3142m volcano known as the 'navel of the world' and 'Mother Mountain', which has a perfect conical shape you might glimpse on hikes from lovely Tirta Gangga.

You can find Bali's past amid evocative ruins in the former royal city of Semarapura. Follow the rivers coursing down the slopes on the Sidemen road to find vistas and valleys that could have inspired Shangri-La. Down at the coast, Padangbai and Candidasa cater to the funky and frowsy respectively.

Resorts and hidden beaches dot the seashore and cluster on the Amed Coast. Just north of there, Tulamben is all about external exploration: the entire town is geared for diving.

When to Go

The best time to visit east Bali is during the dry season – April to September – although recent weather patterns have made the dry season wetter and the wet season drier. Hiking and trekking in the lush hills from Gunung Agung over to Tirta Gangga is much easier when it isn't muddy. Along the coast, however, there's little reason to pick one month over another; it's usually just tropical. Top-end resorts may book up in peak season (July, August and Christmas), but it's never jammed like south Bali.

East Bali Highlights

1 Counting the shades of green on the longest and best climb of your life at **Pura Lempuyang** (p205), one of many hikes around Tirta Gangga

2 Marvelling at the combination of the sacred and the sublime and lots of black sand at **Pantai Klotek** (p183)

3 Sensing Bali's violent past and proud traditions of sacrifice at Semarapura's **Kertha Gosa** (p186)

4 Trekking the picture-perfect valley at **Sidemen** (p188)

5 Chilling with new friends at the mellow cafes and laid-back beaches of **Padangbai** (p193)

6 Finding your perfect lotus position at an inn perched along the **Amed Coast** (p207)

7 Plunging into the blue waters at **Tulamben** (p212) to explore the famous shipwreck right off the beach

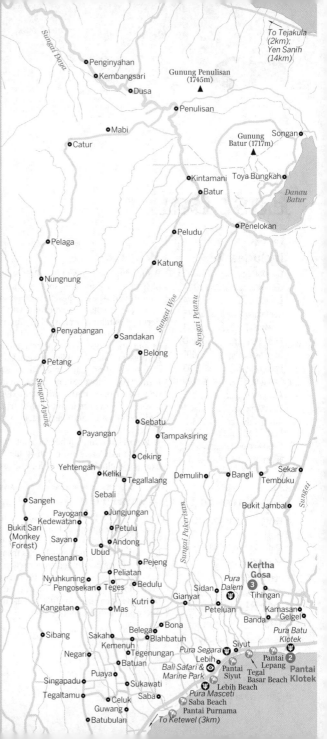

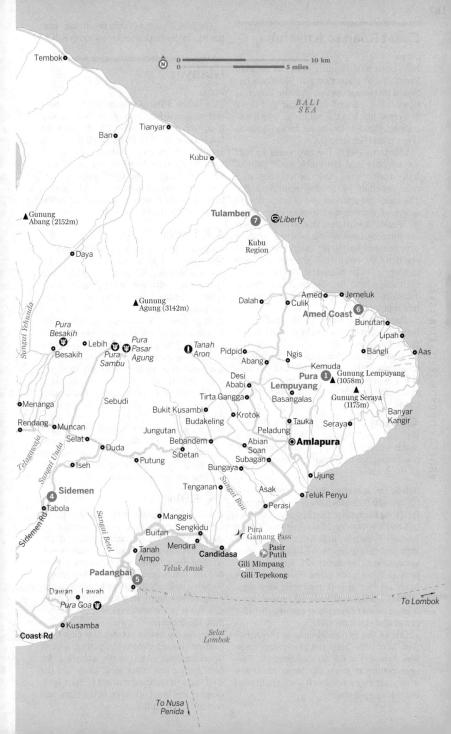

Coast Road to Kusamba

📞0361

Bali's coast road running from just north of Sanur east to a junction past Kusamba has been a hit since it opened in 2006. In fact, at times it gets choked with traffic and slows to a crawl just like the old route, which meandered through towns far inland such as Gianyar and Semarapura.

Efforts to widen the two lanes to four are ongoing and are emblematic both of Bali's traffic woes and the at-times sclerotic schedule of needed improvements. The road has sparked the construction of scores of warung and trucker cafes along its length. And it has opened up numerous formerly inaccessible beaches. Tourism development hasn't yet caught up, but as you drive the road you'll see plenty of new residential villas aimed at foreigners and even more land for sale (signs promising 'beachfront freeholds' are as common as tyre-repair shops).

The coast road (formally the Prof Dr Ida Bagus Mantra Bypass – named for a popular 1980s Balinese governor who did much to promote culture) has brought Padangbai, Candidasa and points east one to two hours closer by road to south Bali. Much of the region is now an easy day trip, depending on traffic.

◉ Sights

You can easily spend a day visiting the beaches that line the coast just south of the coast road. See the boxed text, opposite, for all the details.

Bali Safari & Marine Park   AMUSEMENT PARK
(📞0361-950 000; www.balisafarimarinepark.com; Prof Dr Ida Bagus Mantra Bypass; adult/child from US$49/39; ⊙9am-5pm, Bali Agung show 2.30pm Tue-Sun) Kids love Bali Safari and Marine Park and their parents are happy they love someplace. This big-ticket animal-theme park is filled with critters whose species never set foot in Bali until their cage door opened. Displays are large and naturalistic. A huge menu of extra-cost options includes camel and elephant rides.

One of the latest additions to the attractions here is the huge and glossy stage show **Bali Agung**. For the 60-minute show, Balinese culture is given the Vegas treatment with spectacular results. It's not traditional but it is eye-popping.

The park is north of Lebih Beach; free shuttles run to tourist centres across south Bali.

Gianyar

📞0361

This is the affluent administrative capital and main market town of the Gianyar district, which also includes Ubud. The town has a number of factories producing batik and ikat fabrics, and a compact centre with some excellent food, especially at the famous night market. With so much traffic now diverted to the coast road, the once-busy road through town is now a relaxed and scenic alternative to the newer route.

◉ Sights

Although dating from 1771, **Puri Gianyar** (Jl Ngurah Rai) was destroyed in a conflict with the neighbouring kingdom of Klungkung in the mid-1880s and rebuilt. Under threat from its aggressive neighbours, the Gianyar kingdom requested Dutch protection. A 1900 agreement let the ruling family retain its status and palace, though it lost all political power. The *puri* (palace) was damaged in a 1917 earthquake, but was restored soon after and appears little changed from the time the Dutch arrived. It's a fine example of traditional palace architecture. While tourists are not usually allowed inside, if you report to the guard you may be given a quick look around, which makes for a bit of illicit fun (otherwise the views are good through the wrought-iron gate). The huge banyan tree across from the compound is considered sacred and is a royal symbol.

✗ Eating

People come to Gianyar to sample the market food, like *babi guling* (spit-roast pig stuffed with chilli, turmeric, garlic and ginger – delicious), for which the town is noted. The descriptively named **Gianyar Babi Guleng** (meals from 20,000Rp; ⊙7am-4pm) is favoured by locals (there are lots of cops and bemo drivers here – they know). It's in a tiny side street at the west end of the centre behind the bemo parking area.

Nearby are numerous stands selling fresh food, including delectable *piseng goreng* (fried banana). Also worth sampling for *babi guling* and other local treats are the food stalls in the **food market** (⊙11am-2pm). Good places line both sides of the main section of Jl Ngurah Rai.

COAST ROAD BEACHES

The coast road from Sanur heads east past long stretches of shore that until recently were reached only by long and narrow lanes from roads well inland. Development has yet to catch on here – excepting a few villas – so take advantage of the easy access to enjoy the often-quiet beaches and the many important temples near the sand.

The shoreline the coast road follows is striking, with beaches in volcanic shades of grey and pounding waves. The entire coast has great religious significance and there are oodles of temples. At the many small coastal-village beaches, cremation formalities reach their conclusion when the ashes are consigned to the sea. Ritual purification ceremonies for temple artefacts are also held on these beaches.

Ketewel and **Lebih** are good spots for surfing. Swimming in the often pounding surf is dangerous. You'll need your own transport to reach these beaches. Except where noted, services are few, so bring your own drinking water and towels. On some access roads, locals will charge you a modest fee, say 2000Rp.

From west to east, beaches include the following:

» **Pantai Purnama** is small but has the blackest sand, which the sun studs with billions of reflected sparkles. Religion is big here. The temple, **Pura Erjeruk**, is important for irrigation of rice fields, while some of Bali's most elaborate full-moon purification ceremonies are held here each month.

» **Saba Beach** has a small temple, covered shelters, a shady parking area and a twisting 1.1km, junglelike drive from the coast road; it's about 12km east of Sanur. A few drink vendors recline on the burnt-umber-hued sand.

» **Pura Masceti Beach**, 15km east of Sanur, has a few drink vendors. **Pura Masceti** is one of Bali's nine directional temples. Right on the beach, it is architecturally significant and enlivened with gaudy statuary. There are vendors, which contributes to some litter. A large building back behind the temple is used for cockfights.

» **Lebih Beach** has glittering mica-infused sand. Just off the main road, a strip of shacky warung and cafes leads to the surf. The large Sungai Pakerisan (Pakerisan River), which starts near Tampaksiring, reaches the sea near here. Fishing boats line the shore. North, just across the coast road, impressive Pura Segara (p193) looks across the strait to Nusa Penida, home of Jero Gede Macaling – the temple helps protect Bali from his evil influence.

» **Pantai Siyut**, a mere 300m off the road, and often deserted, is a good place for a parasol: there's no shade otherwise.

» **Tegal Basar Beach** is a turtle sanctuary (don't expect to see any, though) with no shade but offering a good view of Nusa Lembongan. The 600m drive in runs through a dense forest of palms.

» **Pantai Lepang** is worth visiting just for the little slice of rural Bali you pass through on the 600m drive from the main road. Rice and corn grow in profusion. Down at the carbon-coloured sand you'll find small dunes, a few vendors and a lot of reason to snap some pics.

» **Pantai Klotek** offers another lovely drive on an 800m hilly access road and is the most interesting of the beaches. The quiet at **Pura Batu Klotek** belies its great significance: sacred statues are brought here from Pura Besakih for ritual cleansing. Look for a man with a *bakso ayam* (chicken soup) cart. He makes fresh noodles by hand all day.

🛍 Shopping

At the western end of town on the main Ubud road are textile factories, including the large **Tenun Ikat Setia Cili** (☏943 409; Jl Astina Utara; ☺9am-5pm) and **Cap Togog** (☏943 046; Jl Astina Utara 11; ☺8am-5pm). Both are on the main drag west of the centre, about 500m apart. The latter has a fascinating production area below; follow the sounds of dozens of clacking wooden looms.

Connoisseurs of handwoven fabrics will be fit to be tied (dyed?). The factories have showrooms where you can buy material by the metre, or have it tailored. You can at

DON'T MISS

GIANYAR'S TASTY NIGHT MARKET

The sound of hundreds of cooking pots and the glare of bright lights add a frenetic and festive clamour to Gianyar's delicious **Night Market** (Jl Ngurah Rai; ⊙5-11pm), which any local will tell you has some of the best food on Bali.

Scores of stalls set up each night along the main drag in the centre and cook up a mouth-watering and jaw-dropping range of dishes. Much of the fun is just strolling, browsing and choosing. There's everything from *babi guling* (spit-roast pig) to succulent combinations of vegetables that defy description. The average cost of a dish is under 15,000Rp; with a group you can sample a lot, and be the happier for it. Peak time is the two hours after sunset.

Best of all is that the night market is only a 20-minute drive from Ubud: one of the ubiquitous drivers will bring you here for 100,000Rp, including waiting time (be sure to buy him/her something to enjoy as well).

times see weavers at work and observe how the thread is dyed before being woven to produce the vibrantly patterned weft ikat, which is called *endek* in Bali. Prices are 50,000Rp to 100,000Rp per metre for handwoven ikat, depending on how fine the weaving is – costs will rise if it contains silk. You can get a top-quality batik sarong for about 600,000Rp (double that if you include gold accents for your wedding). The industry is struggling from competition with machine-made Javanese fabric, so your arrival will be welcomed.

❶ Getting There & Away

Regular bemo run between Batubulan terminal near Denpasar and Gianyar's main terminal (15,000Rp), which is behind the main market. Bemo from Gianyar's main terminal also serve Semarapura (10,000Rp) and Amlapura (20,000Rp). Bemo to and from Ubud (10,000Rp) use the bemo stop across the road from the main market.

Sidan

When driving east from Gianyar you come to the turn-off to Bangli about 2km out of Peteluan. Follow this road for about 1km until you reach a sharp bend, where you'll find Sidan's **Pura Dalem**. This good example of a temple of the dead has very fine carvings. In particular, note the sculptures of Durga with children by the gate and the separate enclosure in one corner of the temple – this is dedicated to Merajapati, the guardian spirit of the dead.

Bangli

☑0366

Halfway up the slope to Penelokan, Bangli, once the capital of a kingdom, is a humble market town noteworthy for its sprawling temple, Pura Kehen, which is on a beautiful jungle road that runs east past rice terraces and connects at Sekar with roads to Rendang and Sidemen.

History

Bangli dates from the early 13th century. In the Majapahit era it broke away from Gelgel to become a separate kingdom, even though it was landlocked, poor and involved in long-running conflicts with neighbouring states.

In 1849 Bangli made a treaty with the Dutch that gave it control over the defeated north-coast kingdom of Buleleng, but Buleleng then rebelled and the Dutch imposed direct rule there. In 1909 the rajah (lord or prince) of Bangli chose for it to become a Dutch protectorate rather than face suicidal *puputan* (a warrior's fight to the death) or complete conquest by the neighbouring kingdoms or the colonial power.

◎ Sights & Activities

Pura Kehen TEMPLE
(adult/child 10,000/5000Rp; ⊙9am-5pm) The state temple of the Bangli kingdom, Pura Kehen, one of the finest temples in eastern Bali, is a miniature version of Pura Besakih (p190). It is terraced up the hillside, with a flight of steps leading to the beautifully decorated entrance. The first courtyard has a huge banyan tree with a *kulkul* (hollow tree-trunk drum used to sound a warning) entwined in its branches.

Chinese porcelain plates were set into the walls as decoration, but most of the originals have been damaged or lost. The inner courtyard has an 11-roof *meru* (multitiered shrine), and there are other shrines with thrones for the Hindu trinity – Brahma, Shiva and Vishnu. The carvings are particularly intricate. See if you can count all 43 altars.

Pura Dalem Penunggekan   TEMPLE
The exterior wall of this fascinating temple of the dead features vivid relief carvings of wrong-doers getting their just desserts in the afterlife. One panel addresses the lurid fate of adulterers (men in particular may find the viewing uncomfortable). Other panels portray sinners as monkeys, while another is a good representation of evil-doers begging to be spared the fires of hell. It's to the south of the centre.

Bukit Demulih   HILL
Three kilometres west of Bangli is the village of Demulih, and a hill called Bukit Demulih. If you can't find the sign pointing to it, ask local children to direct you. After a short climb to the top, you'll see a small temple and good views over south Bali.

On the way to Bukit Demulih, a steep side road leads down to Tirta Buana, a **public swimming pool** in a lovely location deep in the valley, visible through the trees from the road above. You can take a vehicle most of the way down, but the track peters out and you'll need to walk the last 100m or so.

✕ Eating

A *pasar malam* (night market), on the street beside the bemo terminal, has some good warung, and you'll also find fresh and tasty food stalls in the shambolic market area during the day. Watch where you step.

ℹ Getting There & Away

Bangli is located on the main road between Denpasar's Batubulan terminal (17,000Rp) and Gunung Batur, via Penelokan.

Semarapura (Klungkung)

♪0366
A tidy regional capital, Semarapura should be on your itinerary for its fascinating Kertha Gosa complex, a relic of Bali from the time before the Dutch. Once the centre of Bali's most important kingdom, Semarapura is still commonly called by its old name, Klungkung.

It's a good place to stroll and get a feel for modern Balinese life. The markets are large, the shops many and the streets are almost pleasant now that the coast road has diverted a lot of the traffic away.

History

Successors to the Majapahit conquerors of Bali established themselves at Gelgel (just south of modern Semarapura) around 1400, the Gelgel dynasty strengthening the growing Majapahit presence on the island. During the 17th century the successors of the Gelgel line established separate kingdoms, and the dominance of the Gelgel court was lost. The court moved to Klungkung in 1710, but never regained a pre-eminent position.

In 1849 the rulers of Klungkung and Gianyar defeated a Dutch invasion force at Kusamba. Before the Dutch could launch a counterattack, a force from Tabanan arrived and the trader Mads Lange was able to broker a peace settlement.

For the next 50 years, the south Bali kingdoms squabbled, until the rajah of Gianyar petitioned the Dutch for support. When the Dutch finally invaded the south, the king of Klungkung had a choice between a suicidal *puputan,* like the rajah of Denpasar, or an ignominious surrender, as Tabanan's rajah had done (or cutting a deal like the rajah did up the road in Bangli). He chose the former. In April 1908, as the Dutch surrounded his palace, the Dewa Agung and hundreds of his relatives and followers marched out to certain death from Dutch gunfire or the blades of their own kris (traditional daggers). It was the last Balinese kingdom to succumb and the sacrifice is commemorated in the towering Puputan Monument.

> **WORTH A TRIP**
>
> ## ROAD TO TEMBUKU
>
> Travelling from the flatlands of the east up the slopes for Gunung Batur, Pura Besakih or even as part of a round trip in combination with the Sideman Rd, you have several choices.
>
> One of the best is the road that begins about 5km east of Gianyar on the main road to Semarapura. It runs north for about 12km to the village of Tembuku and is paved for its length. It's narrow, which keeps the truck count down, and passes through a score of tiny, traditional villages. There are **rice-terrace** and **river-valley views** along its length.

Semarapura

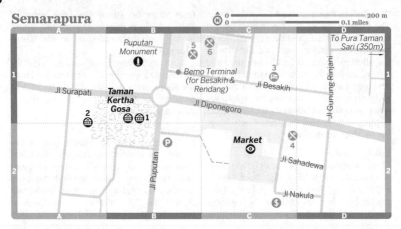

⊙ Sights

TOP CHOICE / Taman Kertha Gosa HISTORIC BUILDING
(adult/child 12,000/6000Rp, parking 2000Rp;
⊙7am-5pm) When the Dewa Agung dynasty
moved here in 1710, the Semara Pura was
established. The palace was laid out as a
large square, believed to be in the form of
a mandala, with courtyards, gardens, pavilions and moats. The complex is sometimes
referred to as Taman Gili (Island Garden).
Most of the original palace and grounds
were destroyed by Dutch attacks in 1908 –
the **Pemedal Agung**, the gateway on the
south side of the square, is all that remains
of the palace itself (but it's worth a close look
to see the carvings).

Two important buildings are preserved in
a restored section of the grounds, and, with
a museum, they comprise the Taman Kertha

Gosa complex. Although vendors are persistent, parking is easy and it's easy to explore
the town from here.

Kertha Gosa

In the northeastern corner of the complex, the **Kertha Gosa** (Hall of Justice) was
effectively the supreme court of the Klungkung kingdom, where disputes and cases
that could not be settled at the village level
were eventually brought. This open-sided
pavilion is a superb example of Klungkung
architecture. The ceiling is completely covered with fine paintings in the Klungkung
style. The paintings, done on asbestos sheet-
ing, were installed in the 1940s, replacing
cloth paintings that had deteriorated.

The rows of ceiling panels depict several
themes. The lowest level illustrates five tales
from Bali's answer to the Arabian Nights,
where a girl called Tantri spins a different
yarn every night. The next two rows are
scenes from Bima's travels in the afterlife,
where he witnesses the torment of evil-
doers. The gruesome tortures are shown
clearly, but there are different interpretations of which punishment goes with what
crime. (There's an authoritative explanation
in *The Epic of Life – A Balinese Journey of
the Soul* by Idanna Pucci, available for reference in the pavilion.) The fourth row of panels depicts the story of Garuda's (mythical
man-bird) search for the elixir of life, while
the fifth row shows events on the Balinese
astrological calendar. The next three rows
return to the story of Bima, this time travelling in heaven, with doves and a lotus flower
at the apex of the ceiling.

Bale Kambang

The ceiling of the beautiful 'Floating Pavilion' is painted in Klungkung style. Again, the different rows of paintings deal with various subjects. The first row is based on the astrological calendar, the second on the folk tale of Pan and Men Brayut and their 18 children, and the upper rows on the adventures of the hero Sutasona.

Museum Semarajaya

This diverting **museum** has an interesting collection of archaeological and other pieces. There are exhibits of songket (silver- or gold-threaded cloth) weaving and palm toddy (palm wine) and palm-sugar extraction. Don't miss the moving display about the 1908 *puputan,* along with some interesting old photos of the royal court. The exhibit on salt-making gives you a good idea of the hard work involved.

Pura Taman Sari   TEMPLE
The quiet lawns and ponds around this temple make it a relaxing stop and live up to the translation of its name: Flower Garden Temple. The towering 11-roofed *meru* indicates that this is a temple built for royalty; today it seems built for the geese who wander the grounds.

🛏 Sleeping & Eating

The best bet for food is browsing the myriad choices in and around the market. There's a small stall selling good coffee at the Taman Kertha Gosa parking lot.

Klungkung Tower Hotel   HOTEL $
(📞25 637; Jl Gunung Rinjani 18; r 225,000-375,000Rp; ✳@) This newish hotel is aimed at local business travellers; its 20 rooms are fairly slick and include satellite TV. Bathrooms have walk-in showers. The restaurant, Puri Ajengan, has a simple menu of Indonesian and Balinese fare. The bar has popular pool tables.

Bali Indah   CHINESE, INDONESIAN $
(📞21 066; Jl Nakula 1; dishes 10,000-20,000Rp) A veteran and affable Chinese sit-down place with simple meals, you'll swear it's 1943. Sumba Rosa almost next door is similar.

Tragia (📞21997; Jl Gunung Batukaru) is a rather tragic supermarket but vital if you need water, while **Pasar Senggol** (🕙5pm-midnight) is a good night market. It's the usual flurry of woks, customers and noise.

ℹ Information

Jl Nakula and the main street, Jl Diponegoro, have several banks with ATMs.

ℹ Getting There & Away

The best way to visit Semarapura is with your own transport and as part of a circuit taking in other sites up the mountains and along the coast.

Bemo from Denpasar (Batubulan terminal) pass through Semarapura (13,000Rp) on the way to points further east. They can be hailed from near the Puputan Monument.

Bemo heading north to Besakih (12,000Rp) leave from the centre of Semarapura, a block northeast of Kertha Gosa. Most of the other bemo leave from the inconvenient Terminal Kelod, about 2km south of the city centre.

Around Semarapura

East of Semarapura, the main road dramatically crosses Sungai Unda (Unda River), then swings south towards Kusamba and the sea. Lava from the 1963 eruption of Gunung Agung destroyed villages here, but the lava flows are now overgrown.

TIHINGAN

Several workshops in Tihingan are dedicated to producing gamelan instruments. Small foundries make the resonating bronze bars and bowl-shaped gongs, which are then carefully filed and polished until they produce the correct tone. Some pieces are on sale, but most of the instruments are produced for musical groups all over Bali.

Workshops with signs out front are good for visits. Look for the welcoming **Tari Gamelan** (📞22339) amid many along the main strip. The often hot work is usually done very early in the morning when it's cool, but at other times you'll still likely see something going on.

From Semarapura, head west along Jl Diponegoro and look for the signs.

◎ Sights

⧉ᵀᴼᴾ CHOICE **Nyoman Gunarsa Museum**   MUSEUM
(📞22 256; Pertigaan Banda, Banda Intersection, Takmung; adult/child 25,000Rp/free; 🕙9am-4pm Mon-Sat) Dedicated to classical and contemporary Balinese painting, this beautiful museum complex was established by Nyoman Gunarsa, one of the most respected and successful modern artists in Indonesia. A vast three-storey building exhibits an impressive

DON'T MISS

SEMARAPURA MARKET

Semarapura's sprawling **market** (Jl Diponegoro) is one of the best in east Bali. It's a vibrant hub of commerce and a meeting place for people of the region. You can easily spend an hour wandering about the warren of stalls on three levels. It's grimy, yes, but also endlessly fascinating. Huge straw baskets of lemons, limes, tomatoes and other produce are islands of colour amid the chaos. A plethora of locally made snacks are offered in profusion; try several.

Glittering jewellery stalls crowd up against shops selling nothing but plastic buckets. On breezeways out back, climb to the top for **views** of multicultural Semarapura, where mosque minarets crowd the sky along with Balinese temples. Mornings are the best time to visit.

The market merges into Jl Diponegoro, where you'll find dusty **curio shops** seemingly as old as the battered goods inside.

variety of well-displayed older pieces, including stone carvings and woodcarvings, architectural antiques, masks, puppets and textiles.

Many of the classical paintings are on bark paper and are some of the oldest surviving examples. Check out the many old puppets, still seemingly animated even in retirement. The top floor is devoted to Gunarsa's own bold, expressionistic depictions of traditional life. Look for *Offering*.

A large space nearby features regular performances; check for times. Enjoy some fine examples of traditional architecture in the compound, a serene place where visitors are always outnumbered by flocks of songbirds.

The museum is about 4km west from Semarapura, near a bend on the Gianyar road; look for the dummy policemen at the base of a large statue nearby.

KAMASAN

This quiet, traditional village is the place where the classical Kamasan painting style originated, and several artists still practise this art. You can see their workshops and small showrooms along the main street. **Suar Gallery** (☎22 064) is a good starting

place; its owner, Gede Wedasmura, is a well-known painter.

The local painting style is often a family affair. Paintings depict traditional stories or Balinese calendars, and although they are sold in souvenir shops all over Bali, the quality is better here. Look for smooth and distinct line-work, evenly applied colours and balance in the overall composition. The village is also home to families of *bokor* (artisans who produce the silver bowls used in traditional ceremonies).

To reach Kamasan, go about 2km south of Semarapura and look for the turn-off to the east.

GELGEL

Situated about 2.5km south of Semarapura on the way to the coast road and 500m south of Kamasan, Gelgel was once the seat of Bali's most powerful dynasty. The town's decline started in 1710, when the court moved to present-day Semarapura, and finished when the Dutch bombarded the place in 1908.

Today the wide streets and the surviving temples are only faintly evocative of past grandeur. **Pura Dasar Bhuana** has huge banyan trees shading grassy grounds where you may feel the urge for a quiet contemplative stroll. The vast courtyards are a clue to its former importance, and festivals here attract large numbers of people from all over Bali.

About 500m to the east, the **Masjid Gelgel** is Bali's oldest mosque. Although modern-looking, it was established in the late 16th century for the benefit of Muslim missionaries from Java, who were unwilling to return home after failing to make any converts.

Sidemen Road

☎0366

Winding through one of Bali's most beautiful river valleys, the Sidemen road offers marvellous paddy-field scenery, a delightful rural character and extraordinary views of Gunung Agung (when the clouds permit). The region is getting more popular every year as a verdant escape, where a walk in any direction is a communion with nature.

German artist Walter Spies lived in Iseh for some time from 1932 in order to escape the perpetual party of his own making in

Ubud. Later the Swiss painter Theo Meier, nearly as famous as Spies for his influence on Balinese art, lived in the same house.

The village of **Sidemen** has a spectacular location and is a centre for culture and arts, particularly *endek* cloth and *songket*. **Pelangi Weaving** (☑23 012; Jl Soka 67; ⊙8am-6pm) has a couple of dozen employees busily creating downstairs, while upstairs you can relax with the Sidemen views from comfy chairs outside the showroom.

There are many **walks** through the rice fields and streams in the multihued green valley. One involves a spectacular 2½-hour climb up to **Pura Bukit Tageh**, a small temple with big views. No matter where you stay, you'll be able to arrange guides for in-depth trekking (about 50,000Rp per hour), or just set out on your own exploration.

🛏 Sleeping & Eating

Views throughout the area are sweeping, from terraced green hills to Gunung Agung. Most inns have restaurants; it can get cool and misty at night.

Near the centre of Sidemen, a small road heads west for 500m to a fork and a signpost with the names of several places to stay. Meals can be arranged at all of these guesthouses, which are spread out.

Samanvaya
TOP CHOICE · INN $$

(☑0821 4710 3884; www.samanvaya-bali.com; r US$70-100; 🕸🏊) Just opened in 2012, this attractive inn has sweeping views over the rice fields all the way south to the ocean. The owners, an energetic couple from the UK, are dedicated to promoting the Sideman area, especially its culture. The individual units have thatched roofs and deep, wooden terraces. The infinity pool is a dream and the cafe has a long list of Asian and Western dishes.

Pondok Wisata Lihat Sawah
GUESTHOUSE $

(☑530 0516; www.lihatsawah.com; r 300,000-1,000,000Rp, 🏊) Take the right fork in the road to this guesthouse with lavish gardens. All 12 rooms have views of the valley and mountain (all have hot water – nice after a morning hike – and the best have lovely wooden verandas); there are also three private bungalows. Water courses through the surrounding rice fields. A cafe offering Thai and Indo menu items shares the views (dishes 13,000Rp to 30,000Rp). It's worth stopping here just for its useful map of the area.

Darmada
GUESTHOUSE $$

(☑0853 3803 2100; www.darmadabali.com; r from 500,000Rp; 🏊) Beautifully set in a small river valley on spacious, lush grounds, this new guesthouse has four stylish rooms set in two villas. There is a large pool amid the palms lined with tiles in gentle shades of green. Rooms are mostly done in shades of white and have hammocks on the patio near the babbling waters. The small cafe has food made with vegetables grown on the grounds.

Subak Tabola
HOTEL $$

(☑0811 386 6197; subak_tebolainn@indo.net.id; r from US$60; 🕸🏊) Set in an impossibly green amphitheatre of rice terraces, 11 rooms here have a bit of style and open-air bathrooms, while two very large bungalows are the real stars. Verandas have mesmerising views down the valley to the ocean. The grounds are spacious and there's a cool pool with frog fountains. It's nearly 2km from the hotel signpost.

Nirarta
GUESTHOUSE $$

(Centre for Living Awareness; ☑530 0636; www.awareness-bali.com; r €25-50) Guests here partake in serious programs for personal and spiritual development, including meditation intensives and yoga. The 11 comfortable rooms are split among six bungalows, some right on the babbling river.

Uma Agung
GUESTHOUSE $$

(☑530 5577; www.umaagungvilla.com; Jl Tebola; r from US$50; 🏊) With impossibly green views, this nine-room inn is a tidy and well-run affair. A good cafe sits among the flower-filled gardens. Deluxe rooms have open-air bathrooms and green-stone tubs for soaking away the healthy glow from your walks.

Kubu Tani
GUESTHOUSE $$

(☑530 0519; www.lihatsawah.com; Jl Tebola; r 500,000-700,000Rp) There are three apartments at this two storey house in a quiet location well away from other buildings. Open-plan living rooms have good views of the rice fields and mountains as well as large porches with loungers. Kitchens allow for cooking; there's no cafe close.

ⓘ Information

There is an excellent website (www.sidemen-bali.com) for the Sideman area that details

EAST BALI SIDEMEN ROAD

accommodation options and the many activities in the area.

ℹ Getting There & Away

The Sidemen road can be a beautiful part of any day trip from south Bali or Ubud. It connects in the north with the Rendang–Amlapura road just west of Duda. Unfortunately the road is in bad shape due to huge trucks hauling rocks for Bali's incessant construction. (Note that all the places to stay listed here are far from the main Sideman road.)

A less-travelled route to Pura Besakih goes northeast from Semarapura, via Sidemen and Iseh, to another scenic treat: the Rendang–Amlapura road.

Pura Besakih

Perched nearly 1000m up the side of Gunung Agung is Bali's most important temple, Pura Besakih. In fact, it is an extensive complex of 23 separate but related temples, with the largest and most important being Pura Penataran Agung. Unfortunately, many people find it a disappointing (and dispiriting) experience due to the avarice of various local characters.

AN UNHOLY EXPERIENCE

So intrusive are the scams and irritations faced by visitors to Besakih that many wish they had skipped the complex altogether. What follows are some of the ploys you should be aware of before a visit.

Near the main parking area at the bottom of the hill is a building where guides hang around looking for visitors. Guides here may emphatically tell you that you need their services and quote a ridiculously high price of US$25 for a short visit. You don't: you may always walk among the temples, and no 'guide' can get you into a closed temple.

Other 'guides' may foist their services on you throughout your visit. There have been reports of people agreeing to a guide's services only to be hit with a huge fee at the end.

Once inside the complex, you may receive offers to 'come pray with me'. Visitors who seize on this chance to get into a forbidden temple can face demands of 100,000Rp or more.

The multitude of hassles aside, the complex comes alive during frequent ceremonies.

History

The precise origins of Pura Besakih are not totally clear, but it almost certainly dates from prehistoric times. The stone bases of Pura Penataran Agung and several other temples resemble megalithic stepped pyramids, and date back at least 2000 years. It was certainly used as a Hindu place of worship from 1284, when the first Javanese conquerors settled in Bali. By the 15th century, Besakih had become a state temple of the Gelgel dynasty.

◎ Sights

The largest and most important temple is **Pura Penataran Agung**. It is built on six levels, terraced up the slope, with the entrance approached from below, up a flight of steps. This entrance is an imposing *candi bentar* (split gateway), and beyond it, the even more impressive *kori agung* is the gateway to the second courtyard. You will find that it's most enjoyable during one of the frequent festivals, when hundreds or even thousands of gorgeously dressed devotees turn up with beautifully arranged offerings. Note that tourists are not allowed inside this temple. For tips on appropriate behaviour when visiting temples, see p324; for a list of recommended temples to visit, see p354.

The other Besakih temples – all with individual significance and often closed to visitors – are markedly less scenic. Just as each village in Bali has a *pura puseh* (temple of origin), *pura desa* (village temple) and *pura dalem* (temple of the dead), Pura Besakih has three temples that fulfil these roles for Bali as a whole – Pura Basukian, Pura Penataran Agung and Pura Dalem Puri, respectively.

When it's mist-free, the view down to the coast is sublime.

ℹ Information

The temple's main entrance is 2km south of the complex on the road from Menanga and the south. Admission is 10,000Rp per person plus 5000Rp per vehicle. The fact that the vehicle fee is charged but not posted, nor a ticket dispensed for it, gives a taste of things to come.

About 200m past the ticket office, there is a fork in the road with a sign indicating Besakih to the right and Kintamani to the left. Go left,

Pura Besakih Complex

To Kintamani
(24km)

To Tourist Fee
Office (2km)

West Ticket
Office

Pura
Peninjoan

Warung &
Souvenir Shops

Pura Dalem
Puri

Pura Ulun
Kulkul

Pura
Merajan
Selonding

Pura
Jenggala

Pura Batu
Madeg

Warung &
Souvenir Stalls

Bemo
Stop

Pura
Manik Mas

Pura
Souvenir
Stalls

Pura Banua
Kawan

Pura
Basukian

Pura
Penataran
Agung

Pura
Pengubengan

Pura
Pesimpangan

Guide
Office

Pura Bangun
Sakti

Pura
Goa

Pura Merajan
Kangnan

Pura
Gelap

To Menanga (6km);
Rendang (8km)

Pura Kiduling
Kreteg

Pura Tirta

0 — 400 m
0 — 0.2 miles

because going to the right puts you in the main parking area at the bottom of a hill some 300m from the complex. Going past the road to Kintamani, where there is another ticket office, puts you in the north parking area only 20m from the complex, and away from scammers at the main entrance.

ⓘ Getting There & Away

The best way to visit is with your own transport, which allows you to explore the many gorgeous drives in the area.

Gunung Agung

Bali's highest and most revered mountain, Gunung Agung is an imposing peak seen from most of south and east Bali, although it's often obscured by cloud and mist. Many sources say it's 3142m high, but some say it lost its summit in the 1963 eruption. The summit is an oval crater, about 700m across, with its highest point on the western edge above Besakih.

As it's the spiritual centre of Bali, traditional houses are laid out on an axis in line with Agung and many locals always know where they are in relation to the peak, which is thought to house ancestral spirits. Climbing the mountain takes you through verdant forest in the clouds and rewards with sweeping (dawn) views.

Climbing Gunung Agung

It's possible to climb Agung from various directions. The two shortest and most popular routes are from Pura Besakih, on the southwest side of the mountain, and from Pura Pasar Agung, on the southern slopes.

It's best to climb during the dry season (April to September); July to September are the most reliable months. At other times the paths can be slippery and dangerous and the views are clouded over (especially true in January and February). Climbing Gunung Agung is not permitted when major religious events are being held at Pura Besakih, which generally includes most of April.

Points to consider for a climb:

» Use a guide.
» Respect your guide's pauses at shrines for prayers on the sacred mountain.
» Get to the top before 8am – the clouds that often obscure the view of Agung also obscure the view *from* Agung.
» Take a strong torch (flashlight), extra batteries, plenty of water (2L per person), snack food, waterproof clothing and a warm jumper (sweater).
» Wear strong shoes or boots and have manicured toes – the descent is especially hard on your feet.

Guides

Trips with guides on either of the routes up Gunung Agung generally include breakfast and other meals as well as a place to stay, but be sure to confirm all details in advance. Guides are also able to arrange transport.

Most of the places to stay in the region, including those at Selat, along the Sidemen road and Tirta Gangga, will recommend guides for Gunung Agung climbs. Expect to pay a negotiable 450,000Rp to 1,000,000Rp for one or two people for your climb.

EAST BALI GUNUNG AGUNG

The following guides are recommended:

Gung Bawa Trekking   GUIDE
(☎0812 387 8168; www.gungbawatrekking.com)
Experienced and reliable.

Ketut Uriada   GUIDE
(☎0812 364 6426; ketut.uriada@gmal.com) This
knowledgeable guide can arrange transport
for an extra fee (look for his small sign on
the road east of Muncan).

Wayan Tegteg   GUIDE
(☎0813 3852 5677; tegtegwayan@yahoo.co.id)
Wins reader plaudits.

From Pura Pasar Agung

This route involves the least walking, because
Pura Pasar Agung (Agung Market Temple) is
high on the southern slopes of the mountain
(around 1500m) and can be reached by a
good road north from Selat. From the temple you can climb to the top in three or four
hours, but be aware it is still very demanding
– as one reader wrote: 'it's a relentless up up
up, followed by down, down, down'.

Start climbing from the temple at around
3am. There are numerous slippery trails
through the pine forest but after an hour
or so you'll climb above the treeline. Then
you're climbing on solidified lava, which can
be loose and broken in places, but a good
guide will keep you on solid ground. At the
top (2900m), you can gawk into the crater,
watch the sun rise over Lombok and see the
shadow of Agung in the morning haze over
southern Bali, but you can't make your way
to the very highest point and you won't be
able to see central Bali.

Allow at least six hours total for this trek.

From Pura Besakih

This climb is much tougher than the already demanding southern approach and
is only for the very physically fit. For the
best chance of a clear view before the clouds
close in, you should start at midnight. Allow
at least six hours for the climb, and four to
six hours for the descent. The starting point
is Pura Pengubengan, northeast of the main
temple complex; attempting this without a
guide would be folly.

Rendang to Amlapura

☎0366

A fascinating road goes around the southern slopes of Gunung Agung from Rendang
almost to Amlapura. It runs through some
superb countryside, descending more or less
gradually as it goes east. Water flows everywhere and there are rice fields, orchards
and carvers of stones for temples most of
the way.

Cyclists enjoy the route and find going
east to be a breezier ride.

You can get to the start of the road in
Rendang from Bangli in the west on a very
pretty road through rice terraces and thick
jungle vegetation. Rendang itself is an attractive mountain village; the crossroads are
dominated by a huge and historic banyan
tree. After going east for about 3km, you'll
come into a beautiful small valley of rice terraces. At the bottom is **Sungai Telagawaja**,
a popular river for white-water rafting.

The old-fashioned village of **Muncan** has
quaint shingle roofs. It's approximately 4km
along the winding road. Note the statues
at the west entrance to town showing two
boys: one a scholar and one showing the na-
ked stupidity of skipping class. Nearby are
scores of open-air factories where the soft
lava rock is carved into temple decorations.

The road then passes through some of
the most attractive rice country in Bali before reaching **Selat**, where you turn north
to get to Pura Pasar Agung, a starting point
for climbing Gunung Agung. **Puri Agung
Inn** (☎530 0887; r 200,000-300,000Rp) has six
clean and comfortable rooms; the inn has
views of rice fields and stone carvers. You
can arrange rice-field walks here or climbs
up Gunung Agung with local guide Yande.

Just before **Duda**, the very scenic Sidemen road branches southwest via Sidemen
to Semarapura. Further east, a side road
(about 800m) leads to **Putung**. This area is
superb for hiking: there's an easy-to-follow
track from Putung to **Manggis**, about 8km
down the hill.

Continuing east, **Sibetan** is famous for
growing *salak*, the delicious fruit with a
curious 'snakeskin' covering, which you can
buy from roadside stalls. This is one of the
villages you can visit on tours and homestays organised by JED (p199), the nonprofit
group that promotes rural tourism.

Northeast of Sibetan, a poorly signposted
road leads north to Jungutan, with its **Tirta
Telaga Tista** – a decorative pool and garden
complex built for the water-loving old rajah
of Karangasem.

The scenic road finishes at **Bebandem**,
which has a cattle market every three days,
and plenty of other stuff for sale as well.
Bebandem and several nearby villages are

Padangbai

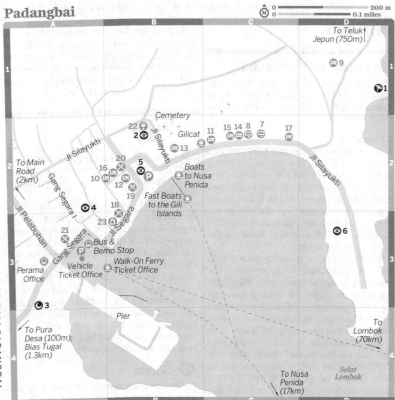

home to members of the traditional metal-worker caste, which includes silversmiths and blacksmiths.

Kusamba to Padangbai

The coast road from Sanur crosses the traditional route to the east at the fishing town of Kusamba before joining the road near Pura Goa Lawah.

KUSAMBA

A side road leaves the main road and goes south to the fishing and salt-making village of Kusamba, where you will see rows of colourful *prahu* (outrigger fishing boats) lined up all along the grey-sand beach. The fishing is usually done at night and the 'eyes' on the front of the boats help navigate through the darkness. The fish market in Kusamba displays the night's catch.

Small local boats travel to Nusa Penida and Nusa Lembongan, which are clearly visible from Kusamba (boats from Padangbai are faster and safer, the modern Kusamba car ferry being the exception). Both east and west of Kusamba, there are small salt-making huts lined up in rows along the beach.

East of Kusamba and 300m west of Pura Goa Lawah, **Merta Sari** (Bingin; meals from 25,000Rp; ◷10am-3pm) is renowned for its *nasi campur* (steamed rice with assorted sides), which includes juicy, pounded fish satay; a slightly sour, fragrant fish broth; fish steamed in banana leaves; snake beans in a fragrant tomato-peanut sauce; and a fire-red sambal. The open-air pavilion is 300m north of the coast road in the village of Bingin. Look for the Merta Sari signs.

Also good is archrival **Sari Baruna** (meals 10,000-15,000Rp; ◷10am-6pm), which also grills fish with attitude and authority. It's in a substantial bamboo hut about 200m west of Pura Goa Lawah.

PURA GOA LAWAH

Three kilometres east of Kusamba is **Pura Goa Lawah** (Bat Cave Temple; adult/child 10,000/5000Rp; car park 2000Rp; ◷8am-6pm), which is one of nine directional temples in Bali. The cave in the cliff face is packed, crammed and jammed full of bats, and the complex is equally overcrowded with tour groups, foreign and local. You might exclaim 'Holy Bat Guano, Batman!' when you get a whiff of the odours emanating from the cave. Superficially, the temple is small and unimpressive, but it is very old and o... significance to the Balinese.

Legend says the cave leads all the w... Pura Besakih, some 19km away, but it'... likely that you'd want to try this route. ... bats provide sustenance for the legend... giant snake, the deity Naga Basuki, whic... also believed to live in the cave.

Padangbai

✆0363

There's a real backpacker vibe about thi... funky little beach town that is also the port for the main public ferry connecting Bali with Lombok.

Padangbai is is an attractive stop: it sits on a small bay and has a nice little curve of beach. A whole compact seaside travellers' scene offers cheap places to stay and some fun cafes. A town beautification drive has cleaned up the beach and added a market area nearby.

The pace is slow, but should ambition strike there's good snorkelling and diving plus some easy walks and a couple of great beaches. Meanwhile you can soak up the languid air punctuated by the occasional arrival and departure of a ferry.

◉ Sights

Padangbai is interesting for a stroll. At the west end of town near the post office there's a small **mosque** and a temple, **Pura Desa**. Towards the middle of town are two more temples, **Pura Dalem** (Gang Segara II) and **Pura Segara**, and the **central market** (Jl Silayukti), which is home to numerous vendors and cafes.

On a headland at the northeast corner of the bay, a path leads uphill to three temples, including **Pura Silayukti**, where Empu Kuturan – who introduced the caste system to Bali in the 11th century – is said to have lived. It is one of the four oldest in Bali.

Beaches

With its protected bay, Padangbai has clear waters and a good beach right in front. Others are nearby; about 500m up and over the headland in the east is the small, light-sand **Blue Lagoon Beach**, an idyllic place with a couple of cafes and gentle, family-friendly surf.

To the southwest, you can drive 1.3km on a curving route past the mosque and

Pura Desa or you can do a shadeless 800m hike up and over a hill past a failed hotel project to the grey sand of **Bias Tugal**, on the exposed coast outside the bay. It rewards the effort with a pretty cove setting and a couple of warung to sate your thirst. Note that the water here is subject to strong currents.

🏃 Activities

Diving

There is good diving on the coral reefs around Padangbai, but the water can be a bit cold and visibility is not always ideal. The most popular local dives are **Blue Lagoon** and **Teluk Jepun** (Jepun Bay), both in Teluk Amuk, the bay just east of Padangbai. There's a good range of soft and hard corals and varied marine life, including sharks, turtles and wrasse, and a 40m wall at Blue Lagoon.

Many local outfits offer diving trips in the area, including to Gili Tepekong and Gili Biaha, and on to Tulamben and Nusa Penida. All dive prices are competitive, costing from US$55 for dives in the area to US$110 for trips out to Nusa Penida.

Recommended operators include the following:

Geko Dive DIVING
(📞41 516; www.gekodive.com; Jl Silayukti) The longest-established operator; has a nice cafe across from the beach.

Water Worx DIVING
(📞41 220; www.waterworxbali.com; Jl Silayukti) Another good dive operator.

Snorkelling

One of the best and most accessible walk-in snorkel sites is off **Blue Lagoon Beach**. Note that it is subject to strong currents when the tide is out. Other sites such as **Teluk Jepun** can be reached by local boat (or check with the dive operators to see if they have any room on their dive boats). Snorkel sets cost about 30,000Rp per day.

Local *jukung* (boats) offer snorkelling trips (bring your own gear) around Padangbai (50,000Rp per person per hour) and as far away as Nusa Lembongan (400,000Rp for two passengers).

🛏 Sleeping

Accommodation in Padangbai – like the town itself – is pretty laid-back. Prices are fairly cheap and it's pleasant enough here that there's no need to hurry through to or from Lombok. It's easy to wander the town comparing rooms before choosing one.

VILLAGE

In the village, there are several tiny places in the alleys, some with a choice of small, cheap downstairs rooms or bigger, brighter upstairs rooms.

Pondok Wisata Parta GUESTHOUSE $
(📞41 475, 0817 975 2668; off Gang Segara III; r 1500,000-350,000Rp; ❄🛜) The pick of the nine rooms in this hidden and snoozy spot is the 'honeymoon room', which has a harbour view and good breezes. The most expensive rooms have air-con and have a common terrace and views.

Kembar Inn GUESTHOUSE $
(📞41 364; kembarinn@hotmail.com; near Gang Segara III; r 100,000-250,000Rp; ❄🛜) There are 11 hot-water rooms (some with fans) in this inn linked by a steep and narrow staircase. The best awaits at the top and has a private terrace with views.

Darma Homestay GUESTHOUSE $
(📞41 394; Gang Segara III; r with fan/air-con from 150,000/200,000Rp; ❄@) A classic Balinese family homestay. The more expensive of the 12 rooms have hot showers and air-con; go for the private room on the top floor.

JALAN SILAYUKTI

On this little strip at the east end of the village, places are close together and right across from the sand.

Topi Inn GUESTHOUSE $
(📞41 424; www.topiinn.com; Jl Silayukti; r from 120,000Rp; @🛜) Sitting at the east end of the strip in a serene location, Topi has five pleasant rooms, some of which share bathrooms. The cafe is excellent fro breakfast.

Padangbai Beach Resort HOTEL $$
(📞41 417; www.padang-bai-beach-resort.com; Jl Silayukti; r US$55-85; ❄🛜🏊) The bungalows are attractive, with open-air bathrooms, and located in a classic Balinese garden setting that boasts a large pool across from the beach. All 24 rooms have air-con and the ones in front have nice, easy-going beach views.

Hotel Puri Rai HOTEL $$
(📞41 385; purirai_hotel@yahoo.com; Jl Silayukti 3; r 400,000-500,000Rp; ❄🛜🏊) The Puri Rai has 30 rooms in a two-storey stone building

pleasantly facing the good-sized pool. Other rooms enjoy harbour views or overlook a yucky parking area. Ask to see a couple. The cafe has a good view.

Padangbai Beach Inn
GUESTHOUSE $
(⌨41 439; Jl Silayukti; r 100,000-200,000Rp) The 18 cold-water rooms in cute bungalows are the pick, but try to avoid the rice-barn-style two-storey cottages, which can get hot and stuffy. Breakfast omelettes are a treat.

Made's Homestay
GUESTHOUSE $
(⌨41 441; madespadangbai@hotmail.com; Jl Silayukti; r 80,000-150,000Rp; ✳🖥) Seven basic, clean and good-value rooms are behind the Gilicat office.

BLUE LAGOON BEACH

🏄 **Bloo Lagoon Village**
HOTEL $$$
(⌨41211; www.bloolagoon.com; r from US$140; ✳@🖥🏊) Perched above Blue Lagoon Beach, the 25 cottages and villas here are all designed in traditional thatched style and the compound is dedicated to sustainable practices. Units come with one, two or three bedrooms and are well thought out and stylish.

✕ Eating & Drinking

Beach fare and backpacker staples are what's on offer in Padangbai – lots of fresh seafood, Indonesian classics, pizza and, yes, banana pancakes. Most of the places to stay have a cafe. You can easily laze away a few hours soaking up the scene at the places along Jl Segara and Jl Silayukti, which have harbour views during the day and cool breezes in the evening.

TOP
CHOICE **Topi Inn**
CAFE $
(⌨41 424; Jl Silayukti; mains 20,000-40,000Rp) Juices, shakes and good coffees served up throughout the day. Breakfasts are big, and whatever is landed by the fishing boats outside the front door during the day is grilled by night. The seats right out on the sandy road are conducive to permanent hanging out.

Depot Segara
SEAFOOD $
(⌨41 443; Jl Segara; dishes 10,000-30,000Rp) Fresh seafood such as barracuda, marlin and snapper is prepared in a variety of ways at this slightly stylish cafe. Enjoy harbour views from the elevated terrace. In a town where casual is the byword, this is the slightly nicer option.

Ozone Café
INTERNATIONAL $
(⌨41 501; mains from 20,000Rp) This popular travellers' gathering spot has more character than every other place in east Bali combined. Slogans cover the walls. Ozone has pizza and live music, sometimes by patrons.

Zen Inn
INTERNATIONAL $
(⌨41 418; Gang Segara; dishes 18,000-30,000Rp; 🖥) Burgers and BBQ mains are served in this airy cafe that goes late by local standards – often until 11pm. Lose yourself on the loungers.

Grand Cafe
INTERNATIONAL $
(Jl Segara; mains from 30,000Rp) Large and breezy cafe with a long food and drink menu with a Dutch accent. Good juices and coffees. The same owners have the neighbouring Joe's Bar, which has a good martini list.

Babylon Bar (Jl Silayukti) and **Kinky Reggae Bar** (Jl Silayukti) are tiny adjoining bars in the market area back off the beach. They have a few chairs, tables and pillows scattered about and are perfect places to while away the evening with new friends.

🛍 Shopping

Ryan Shop
MARKET
(⌨41 215; Jl Segara 38) Year after year, Ryan Shop is always the name you can trust for value. It has a fair selection of secondhand paperbacks and sundries.

ℹ Information

There are several ATMs around town.

ℹ Getting There & Away

Bemo
Padangbai is 2km south of the main Semarapura–Amlapura road. Bemo leave from the car park in front of the port; orange bemo go east through Candidasa to Amlapura (10,000Rp); blue or white bemo go to Semarapura (10,000Rp).

Boat
Anyone who carries your luggage on or off the ferries at the piers will expect to be paid, so agree on the price first or carry your own stuff. Also, watch out for scams where the porter may try to sell you a ticket you've already bought.

LOMBOK & GILI ISLANDS There are many ways to travel between Bali and Lombok. However, be sure to consider important safety information (p378).

Public ferries (child/adult/motorbike/car 23,000/36,000/101,000/659,000Rp, five hours) travel nonstop between Padangbai and Lembar on Lombok. Passenger tickets are sold near the pier. Boats supposedly run 24 hours and leave about every 90 minutes, but the service can be unreliable – boats have caught on fire and run aground.

Perama runs boats to Senggigi and the Gilis. Check details at the **Perama office** (☏41 419; Café Dona, Jl Pelabuhan; ⊙7am-8pm).

Gilicat (☏0361-271 680; www.gilicat.com) serves Gili Trawangan with fast boats. Its local agent is at Made's Homestay (opposite). Several other fast boat services also operate from Padangbai and there are often fare wars.

NUSA PENIDA Fast boats to Nusa Penida leave from just off the beach.

Bus

To connect with Denpasar, catch a bemo out to the main road and hail a bus to the Batubulan terminal (18,000Rp).

Tourist Buses

Perama has a stop here for its services around the east coast.

Destination	Fare (Rp)	Duration
Candidasa	25,000	30min
Kuta	60,000	3hr
Lovina	150,000	5hr
Sanur	60,000	2¼hr
Ubud	50,000	1¼hr

Padangbai to Candidasa

☏0363

It's 11km along the main road from the Padangbai turn-off to the tourist town of Candidasa. Between the two towns is an attractive stretch of coast, which has some tourist development, and a large oil-storage depot in Teluk Amuk.

A short distance beyond Padangbai, the new cruise-ship port at Tanah Ampo has proved a flop. Visions of megaships docking and spewing 5000 free-spending tourists into east Bali were fantasies after it was discovered that the new dock had been built in water too shallow for cruise ships. Blame is going around and around (Benoa Harbour is also too shallow for large cruise ships).

MANGGIS

A pretty village inland from the coast, Manggis is the address used by luxury resorts hidden along the water off the main road.

🛏 Sleeping

TOP CHOICE / Amankila   LUXURY RESORT **$$$**
(☏41 333; www.amankila.com; villas from US$800; ❄@☎☀) One of Bali's best resorts, the Amankila is perched along the jutting cliffs. About 5.6km beyond the Padangbai turn-off and 500m past the road to Manggis, a discreetly marked side road leads to the hotel. It features an isolated seaside location with views to Nusa Penida and even Lombok. The renowned architecture boasts three main swimming pools that step down to the sea in matching shades of blue that actually doesn't seem real. Of the restaurants here, the casual yet superb **Terrace** (lunch US$10-25) has a creative and varied menu with global and local influences. Service vies with the view for your plaudits.

Alila Manggis   RESORT **$$$**
(☏41 011; www.alilahotels.com; r from US$200; ❄@☎☀) The Alila Manggis has elegant, white, thatch-roofed buildings in spacious lawn gardens facing a beautiful stretch of secluded beach. The 55 rooms are large with stylish interiors that are heavy on creams with muted wood accents; go for deluxe ones on the upper floor to enjoy the best views. The restaurant, **Seasalt** (lunch US$10-25), features much-lauded organic fusion and Balinese cuisine. Activities include a kids' camp, a spa and cooking courses.

It is about 1km further east from the Amankila.

MENDIRA & SENGKIDU

Coming from the west, there are hotels and guesthouses well off the main road at Mendira and Sengkidu, before you reach Candidasa. Although the beach has all but vanished and unsightly sea walls have been constructed, this area is a good choice for a quiet getaway if you have your own transport. Think views, breezes and a good book.

🛏 Sleeping

All of the following are on small tracks between the main road and the water; none are far from Candidasa but all have a sense of isolation that makes them seem far from everywhere. They are reached via narrow roads from a single turn-off from the main road 1km west of Candidasa. Look for a

MANGGIS TO PUTUNG ROAD

Winding up a lush hillside scented with cloves, the little-used road linking Manggis on the coast with the mountain village of Putung is worth a detour no matter which way you are heading: east or west, up or down. Heading up you'll round curves to see east Bali and the islands unfolding before you. After stopping for photos, you'll feel good until you round another curve and the views are even better. At some scenic points, adorable families will appear offering beautiful handmade baskets for about 30,000Rp. It's hard not to exceed your basket-buying quota.

Coming from Manggis the road is in good shape for the first half but then deteriorates the rest of the way. It remains just OK for cars but you'll want to go slow for the views anyway; give it an hour.

large sign listing places to stay, a school and a huge banyan tree.

TOP CHOICE Amarta Beach Inn Bungalows INN $
(📞41 230; amartabeachcottages@yahoo.com; r 250,000-400,000Rp, villa from 600,000Rp; ❄@🛜🏊) In a panoramic and private seaside setting, the 10 rooms here are right on the water and are good value. The more expensive ones have interesting open-air bathrooms; villas are even more private. At low tide there is a tiny beach; at other times you can sit and enjoy the views out to Nusas Lembongan and Penida. The cafe is a top choice for lunch whether you are staying here or not.

Pondok Pisang GUESTHOUSE $$
(📞41 065; www.pondokpisang.com; r US$50-80; 🛜) The name here means 'Banana Hut', and there's plenty of appeal (and plenty of banana trees). Six spacious two-level bungalows face the sea in a large compound. Each has an artful interior, including mosaic-tiled bathrooms. Yoga intensives are held at various times. In a small workshop local ladies sew textiles.

Anom Beach Inn HOTEL $$
(📞419 024; www.anom-beach.com; r US$40-60; ❄🏊) This older resort from a simpler time has 24 rooms in a variety of configurations.

The cheapest are fan-only – not a problem given the constant offshore breezes. The best are bungalow-style. Many customers have been coming for years and couldn't imagine staying anyplace else.

TENGANAN

Step back several centuries with a visit to Tenganan, home of the Bali Aga people – the descendants of the original Balinese who inhabited Bali before the Majapahit arrival in the 11th century.

The Bali Aga are reputed to be exceptionally conservative and resistant to change. Well, that's only partially true: TVs and other modern conveniences are hidden away in the traditional houses. But it is fair to say that the village has a much more traditional feel than most other villages in Bali. Cars and motorcycles are forbidden from entering. It should also be noted that this a real village, not a creation for tourists.

The most striking feature of Tenganan is its postcardlike beauty, with the hills providing a photogenic backdrop. The village is surrounded by a wall, and consists basically of two rows of identical houses stretching up the gentle slope of a hill. As you enter the village (10,000Rp donation), you'll likely be greeted by a guide who will take you on a tour – and generally lead you back to his family compound to look at textiles and *lontar* (specially prepared palm leaves) strips. Unlike Besakih, however, there's no pressure to buy anything, so you won't need your own armed guards.

A peculiar, old-fashioned version of the gamelan known as the *gamelan selunding* is still played here, and girls dance an equally ancient dance known as the Rejang. There are other Bali Aga villages nearby, including Tenganan Dauh Tenkad, 1.5km west off the Tenganan road, with a charming old-fashioned ambience and several weaving workshops.

🎎 Festivals

Tenganan is full of unusual customs, festivals and practices.

Usaba Sambah Festival FESTIVAL
At the month-long Usaba Sambah Festival, which usually starts in May or June, men fight with sticks wrapped in thorny *pandanus* leaves. At this same festival, small, hand-powered Ferris wheels are brought out and the village girls are ceremonially twirled around.

👉 Tours

JED   CULTURAL TOUR
(Village Ecotourism Network; ☎0361-366 9951;
www.jed.or.id; tours from US$75) To really experi-
ence the ambience and culture of the village,
consider one of the tours offered by JED.
These highly regarded excursions (some
overnight) feature local guides who explain
the culture in detail and show how local
goods are produced. Tours include transport
from south Bali and Ubud.

🛍 Shopping

A magical cloth known as *kamben gring-
sing* is woven here – a person wearing it is
said to be protected against black magic.
Traditionally this is made using the 'double
ikat' technique, in which both the warp and
weft threads are 'resist dyed' before being
woven. MBAs would be thrilled studying the
integrated production of the cloth: everything, from growing the cotton to producing the dyes from local plants to the actual
production, is accomplished here. It's very
time-consuming, and the exquisite pieces of
double ikat available for sale are quite expensive (from 600,000Rp). You'll see cheaper cloth for sale but it usually comes from
elsewhere in Bali.

Many baskets from across the region,
made from *ata* palm, are on sale. Another
local craft is traditional Balinese calligra-
phy, with the script inscribed onto *lontar* in
the same way that the ancient *lontar* books
were created. Most of these books are Balinese calendars or depictions of the *Ramayana*. They cost 150,000Rp to 300,000Rp,
depending on quality.

Tenganan weaving is also sold in Ashitaba
shops in Seminyak and Ubud.

ℹ Getting There & Away

Tenganan is 3.2km up a side road just west of
Candidasa. At the turn-off where bemo stop,
motorcycle riders offer *ojek* (motorcycles that
take passengers) rides to the village for about
10,000Rp. A nice option is to take an *ojek* up to
Tenganan, and enjoy a shady downhill walk back
to the main road, which has a Bali rarity: wide
footpaths.

Candidasa

☎0363
Candidasa is a relaxed spot on the route
east, with hotels and some decent restaurants. However, it also has problems stemming from decisions made three decades
ago that should serve as cautionary notes to
any previously undiscovered place that suddenly finds itself on the map.

Until the 1970s, Candidasa was just a
quiet little fishing village, then beachside
losmen (small Balinese hotels) and restaurants sprang up and suddenly it was *the*
new beach sensation in Bali. As the facilities
developed, the beach eroded – unthinkingly,
offshore barrier-reef corals were harvested
to produce lime for cement in the orgy of
construction that took place – and by the
late 1980s Candidasa was a beach resort
with no beach.

Mining stopped in 1991, and concrete
sea walls and breakwaters have limited the
erosion and now provide some tiny pock-
ets of sand. The relaxed seaside ambience
and sweeping views from the hotels built
right on the water appeal to a more mature
crowd of visitors. Candidasa is a good base
from which to explore the interior of east
Bali; it's also a place to spend some quiet
time – during the day you inevitably see
people wandering around looking for something to do.

◎ Sights

Pura Candidasa   TEMPLE
(admission by donation) Candidasa's temple is
on the hillside across from the lagoon at the
eastern end of the village strip. It has twin
temples devoted to the male-female gods
Shiva and Hariti.

🏃 Activities

Diving and snorkelling (followed by sleeping)
are the most popular activities in Candidasa.
Gili Tepekong, which has a series of coral
heads at the top of a sheer drop-off, is perhaps
the best dive site. It offers the chance to see
lots of fish, including some larger marine life.
Other features include an underwater canyon,
which can be dived in good conditions, but is
always potentially hazardous. The currents
here are strong and unpredictable, the water
is cold and visibility is variable – it's recommended for experienced divers only.

Hotels hire snorkel sets for about
30,000Rp per day. For the best snorkelling,
take a boat to offshore sites or to Gili Mim-
pang (a one-hour boat trip should cost about
100,000Rp for up to three people).

Apart from the Bali Aga village of Tenganan, there are several traditional villages inland from Candidasa and attractive countryside for walking.

Candidasa

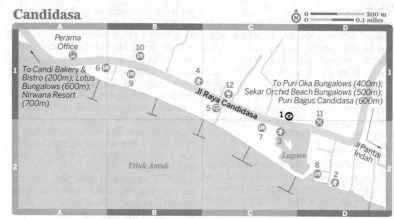

Candidasa

◎ Sights
1 Pura Candidasa.......................................C1

✦ Activities, Courses & Tours
2 Alam Asmara Spa................................. D2
3 Ashram Gandhi Chandi........................C2
4 Dewi Spa B1
5 Dive Lite C1

🛏 Sleeping
6 Ashyana Candidasa.............................. A1

7 Hotel Ida's...C2
8 Rama Shinta Hotel D2
9 Seaside Cottages B1
10 Watergarden.. B1

✕ Eating
Temple Café....................................(see 9)
11 Vincent's...D2

◉ Drinking
12 Crazy Kangaroo C1

Dive Lite   DIVING
(☏41 660; www.divelite.com; Jl Raya Candidasa; dives from US$50) Dive Lite dives the local area plus the rest of the island. An intro to diving course is an excellent deal: US$90 gets you a dive for basic instruction followed by a supervised fun dive. It's a great way to see if diving is for you. Snorkelling trips are US$30.

Dewi Spa   SPA
(☏41 042; Jl Raya Candidasa; massage from 80,000Rp; ◷9am-7pm) On shore, you can catch up on your beauty treatments at the modest Dewi Spa. Waxing, steaming, rubbing, braiding and more are offered.

Alam Asmara Spa   SPA
(☏41 929; ◷9am-9pm) Candidasa's posh option is the Alam Asmara Spa at the hotel of the same name. Organic and natural products are used for a variety of traditional massages (from 150,000Rp) and treatments in a gently restful setting.

Ashram Gandhi Chandi   SPIRITUAL RETREAT
(☏41 108; www.ashramgandhi.com; Jl Raya Candidasa; for 2 overnight about 350,000Rp) Ashram Gandhi Chandi, a lagoon-side Hindu community, follows the pacifist teachings of Mahatma Gandhi. Guests may stay for short or extended periods, but are expected to participate in community life. Simple guest cottages by the ocean are handy after a long day of yoga here.

🛏 Sleeping

Candidasa's busy main drag is well supplied with seaside accommodation, as well as restaurants and other tourist facilities. Another group of places can be found immediately east of the centre along quiet Jl Pantai Indah. These are nicely relaxed and often have a sliver of beach. West of town also offers quiet lodging amid the flaccid lapping of the waves.

WEST OF CANDIDASA
The following pair is a short walk from Candidasa.

Nirwana Resort
HOTEL $$$

(☑41 136; www.thenirwana.com; r US$125-200; ❄@🛜🏊) A dramatic walk across a lotus pond sets the tone at this intimate older resort that has been given a through update. The 18 units are all near the now-standard infinity pool by the ocean. Rates are often discounted; go for one of six units right on the water.

Lotus Bungalows
HOTEL $$

(☑41 104; www.lotusbungalows.com; half-board US$75-150; ❄@🏊) Managed by earnest Europeans, the 20 rooms here (some with aircon, some completely remodelled) are in well-spaced, bungalow-style units. Four are right on the ocean. The decor is bright and airy, and there is a large and inviting pool area. There is free nitrox at the dive centre here.

CENTRAL CANDIDASA

Hotel Ida's
GUESTHOUSE $

(☑41096; jsidas1@aol.com; Jl Raya Candidasa; bungalows 170,000-300,000Rp; 🛜) Set in a dense seaside grove of coconut trees so perfectly realised that it looks like a set for *South Pacific*, Ida's has five thatched bungalows with open-air bathrooms. Rustic balcony furniture, including a daybed, gets you to thinking just what you'd choose for 'Desert Island Discs' – for yet more tropical cliché.

Ashyana Candidasa
HOTEL $$

(☑41 538; www.ashyanacandidasa.com; Jl Raya Candidasa; r US$50-80; 🛜🏊) The staff here are so sharply trained they almost salute – but manage to smile instead. This well-managed waterside hotel has 12 older but immaculate bungalow-style units plus a spa. Most are far enough from the road to escape noise. The waterfront cafe Le-Zat has standard Indonesian fare and fabulous views.

Seaside Cottages
GUESTHOUSE $

(☑41 629; www.balibeachfront-cottages.com; Jl Raya Candidasa; cottages 150,000-470,000Rp; ❄@🛜) The 15 rooms here are scattered in cottages and span the gamut from cold-water basic to restful units with air-con and tropical bathrooms. The seafront has loungers right along the breakwater. The Temple Café is a mellow place.

Watergarden
HOTEL $$

(☑41 540; www.watergardenhotel.com; Jl Raya Candidasa; r US$120-320; ❄🛜🏊) The Watergarden lives up to its name with a swimming pool and fish-filled ponds that wind around the buildings. The gardens are lush and worth exploring. Each of the 13 rooms has a veranda projecting over the lily ponds, which are fresher than the somewhat dated interiors. Wi-fi is limited to the cafe.

Rama Shinta Hotel
HOTEL $$

(☑41 778; www.ramashintahotel.com; r 500,000-700,000Rp; ❄🛜🏊) On a little road near the lagoon and ocean, the 15 rooms are split between a two-storey stone structure and bungalows. Upstairs rooms have views of the lagoon and its birdlife.

EAST OF THE CENTRE

A small road winds through banana trees passing several low-key lodgings that span the budget categories. This is the nicest area for lodging in Candidasa as you are less than 10 minutes by foot from the centre yet there is no traffic noise. And you might find a ripe banana...

Sekar Orchid Beach Bungalows
GUESTHOUSE $

(☑41086; www.sekarorchid.com; Jl Pantai Indah 26; r US$30-40) The grounds here live up to the name with orchids and bromeliads growing in profusion. There's a small beach; the six large rooms are good value with nice views from the 2nd floor. The site feels isolated but is only a short walk from the centre.

Puri Oka Bungalows
GUESTHOUSE $

(☑41 092; www.purioka.com; Jl Pantai Indah; r US$25-90; ❄🛜🏊) Hidden by a banana grove east of town. The cheapest of the 17 rooms here are fan-cooled and small, while the better ones have water views. The beachside pool is small and is next to a cafe, which has wi-fi; at low tide there's a small beach out front. Two roomy bungalows are the pick here.

Puri Bagus Candidasa
HOTEL $$

(☑41 131; www.bagus-discovery.com; Jl Pantai Indah; r US$90-180; ❄🛜🏊) At the eastern end of the shore near an outcropping of outriggers, this mainstream resort is hidden away in the palm trees. Wi-fi is limited to the large pool and restaurant, which have good sea views; the beach is illusory. The 47 rooms have open-air bathrooms; look for deals.

✖ Eating & Drinking

Some of the hotels, such as Lotus Bungalows and Ashyana Candidasa, have seafront restaurants and cafes that are good for views at lunch and water-reflected moonlight at night.

The cafes and restaurants along Jl Raya Candidasa are mostly simple and family-run, but you should beware of traffic noise, although it abates after dark. If you're out of town, some places will provide transport, in which case, call.

TOP CHOICE Vincent's INTERNATIONAL $$
(☑41 368; www.vincentsbali.com; Jl Raya Candidasa; meals 60,000-150,000Rp) Candi's best is a deep and open place with several distinct rooms and a lovely rear garden with rattan lounge furniture. The bar is an oasis of jazz (live the first and third Thursdays each month). The menu combines excellent Balinese, fresh seafood and European dishes.

Candi Bakery & Bistro GERMAN $$
(☑41 883; Jl Tenganan; meals 40,000-150,000Rp) About 100m up from the Tenganan turn-off west of town, this smart cafe is worth the slight detour. The bakery specialises in delicious pastries, cakes and croissants. You can enjoy a menu of local and German meals plus steaks out on the tree-shaded veranda. Or just savour a Bavarian beer.

Temple Café INTERNATIONAL $
(☑41 629; Seaside Cottages, Jl Raya Candidasa; meals 30,000-70,000Rp) Global citizens can get a taste of home at this cafe attached to the Seaside Cottages. It has a few menu items from the owner's native Oz, such as Vegemite. The popular bar has a long drink list.

Crazy Kangaroo BAR
(Map p200; Jl Raya Candidasa) Wild by local standards, this cafe almost qualifies as a roadhouse (mains 40,000Rp–80,000Rp). There's a lively bar and blaring music. On Wednesday nights a bevy of dancers in hot pants perform golden oldies while urging the tourist audience to join in.

ℹ️ Information

Candidasa now has ATMs.

ℹ️ Getting There & Away

Candidasa is on the main road between Amlapura and south Bali, but there's no terminal, so hail bemo as buses probably won't stop. You'll need to change in either Padangbai or Semarapura.

You can hire a ride to Amed in the far east for about 150,000Rp, and Kuta and the airport for 250,000Rp. A driver, **I Nengah Suasih** (☑0819 3310 5020; nengahsuasih@yahoo.com), does day trips to Pasir Putih for 200,000Rp.

Ask at your accommodation about vehicle and bicycle hire.

Perama (☑41114; Jl Raya Candidasa; ⏰7am-7pm) is at the western end of the strip.

Destination	Fare (Rp)	Duration
Kuta	60,000	3½hr
Lovina	150,000	5¼hr
Padangbai	25,000	30min
Sanur	60,000	2¾hr
Ubud	50,000	1¾hr

Candidasa to Amlapura

The main road east of Candidasa curves up to **Pura Gamang Pass** (*gamang* means 'to get dizzy' – an overstatement), from where you'll find fine views down to the coast and lots of greedy-faced monkeys (who have become so prolific that they have stripped crops bare from here up the mountain to Tenganan). If you walk along the coastline from Candidasa towards Amlapura, a trail climbs up over the headland, with fine views over the rocky islets off the coast. Beyond this headland there's a long sweep of wide, exposed black-sand beach.

PASIR PUTIH

No longer a secret, Pasir Putih (aka Dream Beach) is an idyllic white-sand beach whose name indeed means 'White Sand'. When we first visited in 2004, it was empty, save for a long row of fishing boats at one end. Just a few years on, it is sort of an ongoing lab in seaside economic development.

A dozen thatched beach warung and cafes have appeared. You can get *nasi goreng* (fried rice) or grilled fish. Bintang is of course on ice and loungers await bikini-clad bottoms. The beach itself is truly lovely: a long crescent of white sand backed by coconut trees. At one end cliffs provide shade. The surf is often mellow; you can hire **snorkelling** gear to explore the waters.

The one thing saving Pasir Putih from being swamped is the difficult access. Look for crude signs with either 'Virgin Beach Club' or 'Jl Pasir Putih' near the village of Perasi. Turn off the main road (5.6km east of Candidasa) and follow a pretty paved track for about 1.5km to a temple, where locals will collect a fee (per person 2500Rp). You can park here and walk down the gentle hill or drive a further 600m directly to the beach on a road that barely qualifies as such.

As for any qualms you might have about furthering the commercialisation of this beach, here's what the locals told us: 'The money you pay us for a ticket we spend on our school and medicine.' Meanwhile rumours that developers will swoop in are endless.

TELUK PENYU

A little bend in the coast has earned the moniker Teluk Penyu, or Turtle Bay. The shelled critters do indeed come here to nest and there have been some efforts made to protect them. About 5km south of Amlapura, the area has attracted a few expats and villas. It also has one of the most interesting places to stay in this part of Bali.

Turtle Bay Hideaway (☑23 611; www.turtle bayhideaway.com; Jl Raya Pura Mascime; cottages US$135-300; ☜☷) comprises a compound built from old wooden tribal houses brought over from Sulawesi. There are three units, all with ocean views, near a large tiled pool. Interiors combine exotic details and modern comforts – there are fridges and organic food is served. There are enough shady verandas, decks and loungers to keep you busy doing nothing for a week.

Amlapura

☑0363
Amlapura is the capital of Karangasem district, and the main town and transport junction in eastern Bali. The smallest of Bali's district capitals, it's a multicultural place with Chinese shophouses, several mosques, and confusing one-way streets (which are the tidiest in Bali). It's worth a stop to see the royal palaces and is a good part of day trip involving some combination of Candidasa, Amed and/or Tirta Gangga.

◉ Sights

Amlapura's three palaces, on Jl Teuku Umar, are decaying reminders of Karangasem's period as a kingdom at its most important when supported by Dutch colonial power in the late 19th and early 20th centuries.

Outside the orderly **Puri Agung Karangasem** (Jl Teuku Umar; admission 10,000Rp; ☺8am-5pm), there are beautifully sculpted panels and an impressive three-tiered entry gate. After you pass through the entry courtyard (note how all entrances point you towards the rising sun in the east), a left turn takes you to the main building, known as the Maskerdam (Amsterdam), because it was the Karangasem kingdom's acquiescence to Dutch rule that allowed it to hang on long after the demise of the other Balinese kingdoms.

Inside you'll be able to see several rooms, including the royal bedroom and a living room with furniture that was a gift from the Dutch royal family. The Maskerdam faces the ornately decorated Bale Pemandesan, which was used for the royal tooth-filing ceremonies. Beyond this, surrounded by a pond, is the Bale Kambang, still used for family meetings and for dance practice.

Borrow one of the new English-language info sheets and think about what this compound must have been like when the Karangasem dynasty was at its peak in the 19th century, having conquered Lombok.

Across the street, **Puri Gede** (Jl Teuku Umar; donation requested; ☺8am-6pm) is still used by the royal family. Surrounded by long walls, the palace grounds feature many brick buildings dating from the Dutch colonial period. Look for 19th-century stone carving and woodcarvings. The **Rangki**, the main palace building, has been returned to its glory and is surrounded by fish ponds. Catch the stern portrait of the late king AA Gede Putu, while his descendents laughingly play soccer nearby.

The other royal palace building, **Puri Kertasura**, is not open to visitors.

✕ Eating & Shopping

Options are few in Amlapura; there are various warung around the market and the main bus/bemo terminal as well as a good **night market** (☺5pm-midnight). A vast **Hardy's Supermarket** (☑22 363; Jl Diponegoro) has groceries, sundries of all kinds and a row of stalls cooking up good fresh Asian food fast. It has the best range of supplies, like sunscreen, east of Semarapura and south of Singaraja.

❶ Information

The friendly staff at the **tourist office** (☑21 196; Jl Diponegoro; ☺7am-3pm Mon-Thu, to noon Fri) offer the booklet *Agung Info*, which is filled with useful detail.

Bank BRI (Jl Gajah Mada) will change money. Hardy's (above) has ATMs. There is a **pharmacy** (Apotik; Jl Ngurah Rai 47; ☺24hr) and a small hospital across the street.

❶ Getting There & Away

Amlapura is a major transport hub. Buses and bemo regularly ply the main road to Denpasar's Batubulan terminal (25,000Rp, roughly three hours) via Candidasa, Padangbai and Gianyar. Plenty of minibuses also go around the north coast to Singaraja (about 20,000Rp) via Tirta Gangga, Amed and Tulamben.

Around Amlapura

Five kilometres south of Amlapura, **Taman Ujung** is a major complex that may leave you slack-jawed – and not necessarily with wonder. In 1921 the last king of Karangasem completed the construction of a grand water palace here, which was extensively damaged by an earthquake in 1979. A tiny vestige of the old palace is surrounded by vast modern ponds and terraces built for untold billions of rupiah. Today, the windswept grounds are seldom trod by visitors. It's a bit sad really and you can see all that you'd want to from the road. Just a bit further on is the interesting fishing village of **Ujung** (Edge) and the alternative road to Amed (see p208).

Tirta Gangga

📞 0363

Tirta Gangga (Water of the Ganges) is the site of a holy temple, some great water features and some of the best views of rice fields and the sea beyond in east Bali. Capping a sweep of green flowing down to the distant sea, it is a relaxing place to stop for an hour. With more time you can hike the surrounding terraced countryside, which ripples with coursing water and is dotted with temples. A small valley of rice terraces runs up the hill behind the parking area. It is a majestic vision of emerald steps receding into the distance.

◉ Sights

Taman Tirta Gangga   PALACE
(adult/child 10,000/5000Rp, parking 2000Rp; ⊙site 24hr, ticket office 6am-6pm) Amlapura's water-loving rajah, after completing his lost masterpiece at Ujung, had another go at building the water palace of his dreams. He succeeded at Taman Tirta Gangga, which has a stunning crescent of rice-terrace-lined hills for a backdrop. Today, it is an aquatic fantasy with several swimming pools and ornamental ponds filled with huge koi and lotus blossoms, which serve as a fascinating reminder of the old days of the Balinese rajahs.

Originally built in 1948, the water palace was damaged in the 1963 eruption of Gunung Agung and again during the political events that rocked Indonesia two years later. 'Pool A' is good for swimming and is in the top part of the complex. 'Pool B' is pond-like. Look for the 11-tiered fountain and plop down under the huge old banyans.

🏃 Activities

Hiking in the surrounding hills transports you far from your memories of frenetic south Bali. This far east corner of Bali is alive with coursing streams through rice fields and tropical forests that suddenly open to reveal vistas taking in Lombok, Nusa Penida and the lush green surrounding lands stretching down to the sea. The rice terraces around Tirta Gangga are some of the most beautiful in Bali. Back roads and walking paths take you to many picturesque traditional villages.

Sights that make a perfect excuse for day treks are scattered in the surrounding hills. Or for the Full Bali, ascend the side of Gunung Agung. Among the possible treks is a six-hour loop to Tenganan village, plus shorter ones across the local hills, which include visits to remote temples and all the stunning vistas you can handle.

Guides for the more complex hikes are a good idea, as they help you plan routes and see things you simply would never find otherwise. Ask at any of the various accommodation, especially Homestay Rijasa where the owner I Ketut Sarjana is an experienced guide. Another local guide who comes with good marks is **Komang Gede Sutama** (📞 0813 3877 0893). Rates average about 50,000Rp per hour for one or two people.

TOP CHOICE **Bung Bung Adventure Biking**   CYCLING
(📞 21 873, 0813 3840 2132; bungbungbike adventure@gmail.com; Tirta Gangga; tours 250,000-300,000Rp) Ride downhill through the simply gorgeous rice fields, terraces and river valleys around Tirta Gangga with this locally owned tour company. Itineraries last from two to four hours and include use of a mountain bike and helmet plus water. The office is close to Homestay Rijasa, across from the Tirta Gangga entrance. Book in advance.

🛏 Sleeping & Eating

You can overnight in luxury in old royal quarters overlooking the water palace or lodge in humble surrounds in anticipation of an early morning trek. Many places to stay have cafes with mains under 20,000Rp and there's a cluster by the sedate fruit vendors near the shady parking area.

With the exception of Tirta Ayu Hotel and Tirta Gangga Villas, hot water is not a universal option.

Tirta Gangga Villas
VILLA $$$

(☏21 383; www.tirtagangga-villas.com; villas from US$200; ☀) Built on the same terrace as the Tirta Ayu Hotel, the villas are parts of the old royal palace. Thoroughly updated – but still possessing that classic Bali-style motif – the villas look out over the water palace from large shady porches. Private cooks are available and you can arrange to rent the entire complex and preside over your own court under a 500-year-old banyan tree.

Tirta Ayu Hotel
HOTEL $$

(☏22 503; www.hoteltirtagangga.com; villas US$125-175; ✴🛜☀) Right in the palace compound, this has four pleasant villas that are clean and have basic, modern decor in the limited palette of creams and coffees. Flop about like a fish in the hotel's private pool or use the vast palace facilities. The restaurant is a tad upscale (mains from 50,000Rp) and serves creative takes on local classics which you enjoy overlooking the palace.

Homestay Rijasa
GUESTHOUSE $

(☏21 873, 0813 5300 5080; r 150,000-250,000Rp) With elaborately planted grounds, this well-run, nine-room homestay is a recommended choice opposite the water palace entrance. Better rooms have hot water, good for the large soaking tubs. The owner, I Ketut Sarjana, is an experienced trekking guide.

Good Karma
HOMESTAY $

(☏22 445; goodkarma.tirtagangga@gmail.com; r 200,000-250,000Rp; 🛜) A classic homestay, Good Karma has four very clean and simple bungalows and a good vibe derived from the surrounding pastoral rice field. The good cafe's gazebos look towards the parking lot; often you'll see the winsome Nyoman playing bamboo flute music out front.

Puri Sawah Bungalows
GUESTHOUSE $

(☏21 847; www.purisawah.com; r 250,000-350,000Rp) Just up the road from the palace, Puri Sawah has three comfortable and spacious rooms and a family bungalow that sleeps six (with hot water). Besides Indo classics, the restaurant has some interesting sandwiches like 'avocado delight'.

Genta Bali
INDONESIAN $

(☏22 436; meals 15,000-25,000Rp) Across the road from the parking area, you can find a fine yoghurt drink here, as well as pasta and Indonesian food. It has an impressive list of puddings, including ones with banana and jackfruit. Try out the black-rice wine.

Side by Side Organic Farm
BALINESE $

(☏0812 399 5054, 0812 3623 3427; http://sites.google.com/site/sidebysidefarmorg/; Dausa; buffet lunch from 12,500Rp; ✍) Set amid lush rice fields near Tirta Gangga in the tiny village of Dausa, Side by Side Organic Farm is a unique enterprise that works with the local community to raise crops with added value that will increase incomes in what has always been

EAST BALI TIRTA GANGGA

WORTH A TRIP

PURA LEMPUYANG

We swear, you'll thank us for this.

One of Bali's nine directional temples and the one responsible for the east, Pura Lempuyang is perched on a hilltop on the side of 1058m Gunung Lempuyang, a twin of neighbouring 1175m Gunung Seraya. Together, the pair form the distinctive double peaks of basalt that loom over Amlapura to the south and Amed to the north. The Lempuyang temple is part of a compact complex that looks across the mottled green patchwork that is east Bali. Its significance means there are always faithful Balinese in meditative contemplation and you may wish to join them as you recover from the one key detail of reaching the temple: the 1700-step climb up the side of the 768m hill.

Reaching the base of the stairs is about a 30-minute walk from Tirta Gangga. Take the turn south off the Amlapura–Tulamben road to Ngis (2km), a palm-sugar and coffee-growing area, and follow the signs another 2km to Kemuda (ask for directions if the signs confuse you). From Kemuda, climb those steps to Pura Lempuyang, allowing at least two hours, one way. If you want to continue to the peaks of Lempuyang or Seraya, you should take a guide.

one of Bali's poorer areas. Bounteous and delicious buffet lunches are served using the organic foods grown in the village farms. You can also arrange to stay in one of the serene and simple bungalows. Call the day before for directions and to book lunch.

ℹ Getting There & Away

Bemo and minibuses making the east-coast haul between Amlapura and Singaraja stop at Tirta Gangga. The fare to Amlapura should be 7000Rp.

Around Tirta Gangga

The main road running from Amlapura through Tirta Gangga and on to Amed and the coast doesn't do the local attractions justice – although it is an attractive road. To appreciate things, you need to get off the main road or go hiking.

Throughout the area the *rontal* palms all look like new arrivals at army boot camp, as they are shorn of their leaves as fast as they grow them in order to meet the demand for inscribed *lontar* books.

BUKIT KUSAMBI

This small hill has a big view – at sunrise Lombok's Gunung Rinjani throws a shadow on Gunung Agung. Bukit Kusambi is easy to reach from Abian Soan – look for the obvious large hill to the northwest, and follow the tiny canals through the rice fields. On the western side of the hill, a set of steps leads to the top.

BUDAKELING & KROTOK

Budakeling, home to several Buddhist communities, is on the back road to Bebandem, a few kilometres southeast of Tirta Gangga. It's a short drive, or a pleasant three-hour walk through rice fields, via Krotok, home of traditional blacksmiths and silversmiths.

Tanah Aron, an imposing monument to the post-WWII Dutch resistance, is gloriously situated on the southeastern slopes of Gunung Agung. The road is quite good, or you can walk up and back in about six hours from Tirta Gangga.

Amed & the Far East Coast

☎0363

Stretching from Amed to Bali's far eastern tip, this once-remote stretch of semi-arid coast draws visitors to a succession of small, scalloped, black-sand beaches, a relaxed atmosphere and excellent diving and snorkelling.

The coast here is often called simply 'Amed' but this is a misnomer, as the coast is a series of seaside *dusun* (small villages) that starts with the actual Amed in the north and then runs southeast to Aas. If you're looking to get away from crowds, this is the place to come and try some yoga. Everything is spread out, so you never feel like you're in the middle of anything much except maybe one of the small fishing villages.

Traditionally this area has been quite poor, with thin soils, low rainfall and very limited infrastructure. Salt production is still carried out on the beach at Amed. Villages further east rely on fishing, and colourful *jukung* (traditional boats) line up on every available piece of beach. Inland, the steep hillsides are generally too dry for rice – corn, peanuts and vegetables are the main crops.

🏃 Activities

Diving & Snorkelling

Snorkelling is excellent along the coast. Jemeluk is a protected area where you can admire live coral and plentiful fish within 100m of the beach. There's a few bits of wood remaining from a **sunken Japanese fishing boat** at Bayuning – just offshore from Eka Purnama bungalows – and coral gardens and colourful marine life at Selang. Almost every hotel hires snorkelling equipment for about 30,000Rp per day.

Scuba diving is also excellent, with dive sites off Jemeluk, Lipah and Selang featuring coral slopes and drop-offs with soft and hard corals, and abundant fish. Some are accessible from the beach, while others require a short boat ride. The *Liberty* wreck at Tulamben is only a 20-minute drive away.

Three good dive operators have shown a commitment to the communities by organising regular beach clean-ups and educating locals on the need for conservation. All have similar prices for a long list of offerings (eg local dives from about US$75, open-water dive course about US$375).

Eco-Dive   DIVING

(☎23 482; www.ecodivebali.com; Jemeluk Beach; 🛜) Full-service shop with simple, free accommodation for clients. Has led the way on environmental issues.

Euro Dive   DIVING

(☎23 605; www.eurodivebali.com; Lipah) Has a large facility and offers packages with hotels.

Amed & The Far East Coast

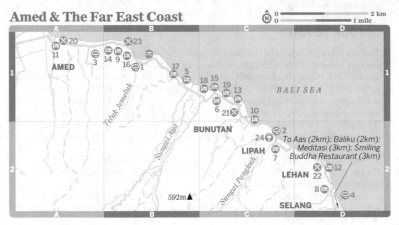

Amed & The Far East Coast

Jukung Dive DIVING
(☏23 469; www.jukungdivebali.com; Amed) Pushes its eco-credentials and has a dive pool. Also has bungalows for dive packages.

Trekking

Quite a few trails go inland from the coast, up the slopes of **Gunung Seraya** (1175m) and to some little-visited villages. The countryside is sparsely vegetated and most trails are well defined, so you won't need a guide for shorter walks; if you get lost, just follow a ridge-top back down to the coast road. Allow a good three hours to get to the top of Seraya, starting from the rocky ridge just east of Jemeluk Bay, near Prem Liong Art Bungalows. To reach the top for sunrise,

you'll need to start in the dark, so a guide is a good idea; ask at your hotel.

⊨ Sleeping

The Amed region is very spread out, so take this into consideration when choosing accommodation. If you want to venture to restaurants beyond your hotel's own, for example, you'll have to walk or find transport.

You will also need to choose between staying in the little beachside villages or on the sunny and dry headlands connecting the inlets. The former puts you right on the sand and offers a small amount of community life while the latter gives you broad, sweeping vistas and isolation.

Accommodation can be found in every price category; there's a crop of new simple

WORTH A TRIP

DETOUR TO AMED

Typically travellers bound for the coast of Amed travel the inland route through Tirta Gangga. However, there is a longer, twistier and more adventurous road much less travelled that runs from Ujung right around the coast to the Amed area. The road climbs up the side of the twin peaks of Seraya and Lempuyang, and the views out to sea are breathtaking. Along the way it passes through numerous small villages where people are carving fishing boats, bathing in streams or simply standing a bit slack-jawed at the appearance of *tamu* (visitors or foreigners). Don't be surprised to see a pig, goat or boulder on the road. After the lush east, it's noticeably drier here and the people's existence thinner; corn replaces rice as the staple.

Near **Seraya** (which has a cute market) look for weavers and cotton-fabric-makers. For lots of the time, you'll just be in the middle of fruit-filled orchards and jungle. About 4km south of Aas there's a lighthouse.

The road is narrow but paved, and covering the 35km to Aas will take about one hour without stops. Combine this with the inland road through Tirta Gangga for a good circular visit to Amed from the west.

budget places right in Amed village. Almost every place has a restaurant or cafe. Places with noteworthy dining are indicated in the listings

EAST OF AMED VILLAGE

TOP CHOICE **Hotel Uyah Amed**　　HOTEL **$$**
(☏23 462; www.hoteluyah.com; r €40-50; ❋ 🛜 🌊) This cute place features four-poster beds set in stylish, conical interiors bathed in light. From all 27 rooms (some with air-con) you can see the saltworks on the beach. The hotel makes the most of this by offering fascinating and free salt-making demonstrations. The tasty Cafe Garam is appropriately named for salt.

JEMELUK

You might say what's now called Amed started here.

Pondok Kebun Wayan　　GUESTHOUSE **$**
(☏23 473; www.amedcafe.com; r €20-50; ❋🌊) This Amed empire features a range of 30 bungalow-style rooms mostly on a hillside across from the beach. The most expensive rooms have views, terraces and amenities like air-con while the cheapest have cold water and showers. The eponymous Amed Cafe has a good grilled seafood menu.

Sama Sama Bungalows　　HOMESTAY **$**
(☏0813 3738 2945; r 150,000-400,000Rp) Choose from a cold-water room with fan or something a scotch more posh (hot water) in a bungalow here (and a good seafood cafe) across from the beach. The family

that runs things is often busy making offerings.

Galang Kangin Bungalows　　GUESTHOUSE **$**
(☏23 480; bali_amed_gk@yahoo.co.jp; r 250,000Rp-550,000Rp; ❋🛜) Set on the hill side of the road amid a nice garden, the 10 rooms here mix and match fans, cold water, hot water and air-con. The beach is right over the pavement, as is the cafe.

BANUTAN BEACH

This is a classic little village with a swath of sand and fishing boats between arid headlands.

TOP CHOICE **Santai**　　HOTEL **$$**
(☏23 487; www.santaibali.com; r US$90-150; ❋🛜🌊) This lovely option is on a slight hill down to the beach. The name means 'relax' and you'll have a hard time not taking the hint. A series of authentic traditional thatched bungalows gathered from around the archipelago hold 10 rooms with four-poster beds, timber floors, open-air bathrooms and big comfy balcony sofas. A swimming pool, fringed by purple bougainvillea, snakes through the property. The cafe is good.

Aiona Garden of Health　　GUESTHOUSE **$$**
(☏0813 3816 1730; www.aionabali.com; r from €30) This characterful place has enough signs outside that it qualifies as a genuine roadside attraction. The simple bungalows are shaded by mango trees and the natural food may be the healthiest of your trip. You can partake of organic potions and lotions,

classes in yoga, meditation, tarot reading etc. If you don't get a natural high, your inner peace might improve with the high-fibre diet, or try the fermented tea, pow! A small **shell museum** (⊙ 2pm to 4pm) boasts that no bivalves died in its creation.

BUNUTAN

These places are on a sun-drenched, arid stretch of highland. Most are on sloping hillsides and spill down to the water.

TOP CHOICE Onlyou Villas
VILLA **$$**

(⌨23 595; www.onlyou-bali.com; villas €50-90; ❄️🛜📶) You could go nuts trying to find the missing y in the name of this hillside villa complex. Happily it is such a good deal that you'll go 'y not!'. Villas are large and have many amenities such as DVD players, multiple beds, luxurious teak furniture and an array of genial pets. Among the services are 'beddye bye candy and cocktails'.

Wawa-Wewe II
HOTEL **$$**

(⌨23 506, 23 522; www.bali-wawawewe.com; ; r 400,000-700,000Rp; ❄️🛜📶) From the headlands, this restful place has 10 bungalow-style rooms on lush grounds that shamble down to the water's edge. The natural-stone infinity pool is shaped like a Buddha and is near the water, as are two rooms with delectable ocean views.

Anda Amed
HOTEL **$$**

(⌨23 498; www.andaamedresort.com; villas €60-110; ❄️🛜📶) This whitewashed hillside hotel feels like it could be on Mykonos. The infinity pool is an ahhh-inducing classic of the genre and has a waterfall and sweeping views of the sea from well above the road. The four villas are a good deal; each has one or two bedrooms and lots of posh details like deep soaking tubs, fridges and other niceties.

Waeni's Sunset View Bungalows
GUESTHOUSE **$$**

(⌨23 515; www.waenis.com; r 400,000-600,000Rp; ❄️🛜) Waeni's is a hillside place with eight unusual rustic stone cottages that have gorgeous views of the mountains behind and the bay below. Some feature hot water and air-con, others are fan-cooled with cold water. The cafe is a good place for a sunset drink.

WORKING IN THE SALT BRINE

For a real day at the beach, try making some salt. You start by carrying, say, 500L of ocean water across the sand to bamboo and wood funnels, which filter the water after it is poured in. Next the water goes into a *palungan* (shallow trough), made of palm-tree trunks split in half and hollowed out, or cement canisters where it evaporates, leaving salt behind. And that's just the start, and just what you might see in Kusamba or on the beach in Amed.

In the volcanic areas around the east coast between Sanur and Yeh Sanih in the north, a range of salt-making methods is used. What is universal is that the work is hard, very hard, but is also an essential source of income for many families.

In some places the first step is drying sand that has been saturated with sea water. It's then taken inside a hut, where more sea water is strained through it to wash out the salt. This very salty water is then poured into a *palungan*. Hundreds of these troughs are lined up in rows along the beaches during the salt-making season (the dry season), and as the hot sun evaporates the water, the almost-dry salt is scraped out and put in baskets. There are good exhibits on this method at the Museum Semarajaya in Semarapura.

Most salt produced on the coast of Bali is used for processing dried fish. And that's where Amed has an advantage: although its method of making salt results in a lower yield than that using sand, its salt is prized for its flavour. In fact there is a fast-growing market for this 'artisan salt' worldwide. The grey and cloudy crystals are finding their way into many top-end kitchens.

Visitors to the Amed area can learn all about this fascinating process at the adjoining Hotel Uyah Amed and Cafe Garam. Many of the staff here also work in salt production. Tours are offered, and you can buy big bags of the precious stuff (10,000Rp per kilogram) for a tiny fraction of what it costs once it's gone through many hands and made its way to your local gourmet market.

❶ DECODING AMED

The entire 10km stretch of far east coast is often called 'Amed' by both tourists and marketing-minded locals. Most development at first was around three bays with fishing villages: **Jemeluk**, which has cafes and a few shops; **Bunutan**, with both a beach and headlands; and **Lipah**, which has warung, shops and a few services. Development has marched onwards through tiny **Lehan**, **Selang**, **Bayuning** and **Aas**, each a minor oasis at the base of the dry, brown hills. To appreciate the narrow band of the coast, stop at the viewpoint at Jemeluk, where you can see fishing boats lined up like a riot of multihued sardines on the beach.

Besides the main road via Tirta Gangga, you can also approach the Amed area from the Aas end in the south.

Puri Wirata   HOTEL $$

(✆23 523; www.puriwirata.com; r US$48-85, villas US$75-260; ❄🛜⛱) The most mainstream Amed choice, this 30-room resort has two pools and rooms ambling down the hill to the rocky ribbon at the waterline. Service is professional and there are many dive packages on offer. Wi-fi is only in the restaurant and pool area.

LIPAH

This village is just large enough for you to go wandering – briefly.

Bayu Cottages   GUESTHOUSE $$

(✆23 495; www.bayucottages.com; r 400,000-750,000Rp; ❄🛜⛱) Bayu has six large, comfortable rooms with balconies overlooking the coast from the hillside above the road. There's a small pool with a grand view and many amenities including open-air marble bathrooms and satellite TV. Wi-fi is just in common areas.

Hidden Paradise Cottages   HOTEL $$

(✆23 514; www.hiddenparadise-bali.com; r US$50-100; ❄🛜⛱) The 16 simply decorated bungalow-style rooms at this older beachside resort are set on manicured grounds and have large patios and open-air bathrooms. The pool is the classic kidney shape in a natural garden setting. Several dive packages are available.

LEHAN

ⓣ Life in Amed   INN $$

(✆23 152, 0813 3850 1555; www.lifebali.com; r US$65-110, villas US$100-170; ❄@🛜⛱) Life here is posh. The six bungalow-style units are in a slightly cramped compound around a sinuous pool; two villas are directly on the beach. Bathrooms are open-air works of art, created from beach stones. The cafe concentrates on seafood and showy local dishes (meals 50,000Rp to 120,000Rp). This is a fave with expats living on Bali.

SELANG

Blue Moon Villas   GUESTHOUSE $$

(✆0817 4738 100; www.bluemoonvilla.com; r from €60-210; ❄🛜⛱) On the hillside across the road from the cliffs, Blue Moon is a small and upmarket place, complete with three pools. The rooms are set in villa-style buildings and have open-air stone bathrooms. Rooms can be combined into larger multibedroom suites. The restaurant serves good Balinese classics and grilled seafood.

BAYUNING

By Bayuning you've left much of Amed's tourist hoopla behind.

Baliku   HOTEL $$

(✆082 8372 2601; www.amedbaliresort.com; r from US$80; ❄❄) Large villa-style units are one of the attractions at this hillside resort that overlooks a pretty bit of Amed coast, where you often see fishing boats flying their brightly coloured sails. King-size beds and separate dressing areas and terraces primed for meals make for good retreats. There are Mediterranean accents throughout including on the menu of the restaurant.

AAS

Once you've reached Aas, hole up for a spell and give your butt a rest.

ⓣ Meditasi   GUESTHOUSE $

(✆082 8372 2738; http://meditasi.8m.com; r 300,000-500,000Rp) Get off the grid and take a respite from the pressures of life at this chilled-out and charming hideaway. Meditation and yoga help you relax, and the eight rooms are close to good swimming and snorkelling. Open-air baths allow you to count the colours of the bougainvillea and frangipani that grow in profusion.

✕ Eating & Drinking

As noted, most places to stay have cafes. Ones worth seeking out are listed here.

Cafe Garam   INDONESIAN **$**
(☎23 462; Hotel Uyah Amed, east of Amed; meals 20,000-50,000Rp) There's a relaxed feel here, with pool tables and Balinese food plus the lyrical and haunting melodies of live *genjek* music at 8pm on Wednesday and Saturday. *Garam* means salt and the cafe honours the local salt-making industry. Try the *salada ayam,* an addictive mix of cabbage, grilled chicken, shallots and tiny peppers.

Smiling Buddha Restaurant   ORGANIC **$**
(☎082 8372 2738; Meditasi, Aas; meals from 30,000Rp; ✍) Newly built, the restaurant at this highly recommended guesthouse has excellent organic fare, much sourced from its own garden. Balinese and Western dishes are excellent and there are good views out to sea. It even manages some full moon fun on the proper nights.

Sama Sama Café   SEAFOOD **$**
(☎0813 3738 2945; meals 30,000-60,000Rp) Superfresh prawns, calamari and whatever else was caught on the nearby boats is grilled however you like at this beachside joint, located right on the sand on this pint-sized bay.

Restaurant Gede   CHINESE **$**
(☎23 517; meals 25,000-50,000Rp) The menu is typical of those found in Chinese restaurants everywhere: long. Views are good from this spot halfway up the hill from the cove. Artwork by the owner decorates the walls.

Sails   FUSION **$$**
(☎22 006; www.restaurantamedbali.com; mains 55,000-110,000Rp) A high-concept restaurant with high standards for food, Sails is one big terrace with 180-degree views from its cliffside perch. Settle back in the chic blonde furniture and enjoy fusion hits like lamb medallions, spare ribs and grilled fillets of fresh fish with Balinese accents.

Wawa-Wewe I   BAR
(☎23 506; meals from 30,000Rp; 🛜) Spend the evening here and you won't know your wawas from your wewes, if you try the local *arak* (fermented spirit) made with palm fronds. This is the coast's most raucous bar – which by local standards means that sometimes it gets sorta loud. Local bands jam on many nights. You can also eat and sleep here (simple air-con rooms from 150,000Rp).

ⓘ Information

You may be charged a tourist tax to enter the area. Enforcement of a 5000Rp per-person fee at a tollbooth on the outskirts of Amed is sporadic. When collected, the funds go in part to develop the infrastructure at the beaches.

There are moneychangers in Lipah but the closest ATMs and banks are in Amlapura. Many places don't take credit cards. Wi-fi is becoming common as the phone lines are extended south.

ⓘ Getting There & Around

Most people drive here via the main highway from Amlapura and Culik. The spectacular road going all the way around the twin peaks from Aas to Ujung makes a good circle.

You can arrange for a driver and car to/from south Bali and the airport for about 400,000Rp.

Public transport is difficult. Minibuses and bemo between Singaraja and Amlapura pass through Culik, the turn-off for the coast. Infrequent bemo go from Culik to Amed (3.5km), and some continue to Seraya until 1pm. Fares average 8000Rp.

You can also charter transport from Culik for a negotiable 50,000Rp (by *ojek* is less than half). Specify which hotel you wish to go to – agree on 'Amed' and you could come up short in Amed village.

Perama (www.perama.com) offers charter tourist-bus services from Candidasa or Padangbai; the cost is 125,000Rp each for a minimum of two people. This is similar to the cost of hiring a car and driver.

Amed Sea Express (www.gili-sea-express. com; Amed; per person 600,000Rp) makes crossings to Gili Trawangan on an 80-person speedboat in under an hour. This makes many interesting itineraries possible.

Many hotels hire bicycles for about 35,000Rp per day.

Kubu Region

Driving along the main road you will pass through vast old lava flows from Gunung Agung down to the sea. The landscape is strewn with a moonscape of boulders, and is nothing like the lush rice paddies elsewhere.

THE WRECK OF THE LIBERTY

In January 1942 the US Navy cargo ship USAT *Liberty* was torpedoed by a Japanese submarine near Lombok. Taken in tow, it was beached at Tulamben so that its cargo of rubber and railway parts could be saved. The Japanese invasion prevented this and the ship sat on the beach until the 1963 eruption of Gunung Agung broke it in two and left it just off the shoreline, much to the delight of scores of divers.

Tulamben

📞0363

The big attraction here sunk over 60 years ago. The wreck of the US cargo ship *Liberty* is among the best and most popular dive sites in Bali and this has given rise to an entire town based on scuba diving. Other great dive sites are nearby and even snorkellers can easily swim out and enjoy the wreck and the coral.

But if you don't plan to explore the briny waves, don't expect to hang out on the beach either. The shore is made up of rather beautiful, large washed stones, the kind that cost a fortune at a DIY store.

For nonaquatic delights, check out the **morning market** in Tulamben village, 1.5km north of the dive site.

🏃 Activities

Diving and **snorkelling** are the reason Tulamben exists.

The **shipwreck** *Liberty* is about 50m directly offshore from Puri Madha Bungalows (where you can park); look for the schools of black snorkels. Swim straight out and you'll see the stern rearing up from the depths, heavily encrusted with coral and swarming with dozens of species of colourful fish – and with scuba divers most of the day. The ship is more than 100m long, but the hull is broken into sections and it's easy for divers to get inside. The bow is in quite good shape, the midships region is badly mangled and the stern is almost intact – the best parts are between 15m and 30m deep. You will want at least two dives to really explore the wreck.

Many divers commute to Tulamben from Candidasa or Lovina, and in busy times it can get quite crowded between 11am and 4pm, with up to 50 divers at a time around the wreck. Stay the night in Tulamben or in nearby Amed and get an early start.

Most hotels have their own diving centre, and some will give a discount on accommodation if you dive with their centre. There are options if you are an inexperienced diver.

Expect to pay from US$40/70 for one/two dives at Tulamben, and a little more for a night dive or dives around Amed. Snorkelling gear is hired everywhere for 30,000Rp.

Note that there is now a privately run parking area behind Tauch Terminal. There are gear-hire stands, vendors, guides and more here ready to get your attention. There are also pay-showers and toilets. You can still park for free by Puri Madha Beach Bungalows.

Tauch Terminal DIVING
(📞774 504, 22 911; www.tauch-terminal.com) Among the many dive operators, Tauch Terminal is one of the longest-established operators in Bali. A four-day PADI open-water certificate course costs from €350.

🛏 Sleeping & Eating

Tulamben is a quiet place, and is essentially built around the wreck – the hotels, all with cafes and many with dive shops, are spread along a 3km stretch either side of the main road. You have your choice of roadside (cheaper) or by the water (nicer). At high tide even the rocky shore vanishes.

TOP CHOICE ► Puri Madha Beach Bungalows HOTEL $
(📞22 921; r 200,000-500,000Rp; ❄🛜🏊) Restyled bungalow-style units are directly opposite the wreck on shore. The best of the 15 rooms have air-con and hot water. The spacious grounds feel like a public park and there is a swish new pool area overlooking the ocean. You can't beat getting out of bed and paddling right out to a famous shipwreck.

Mimpi Resort Tulamben HOTEL $$
(📞21 642; www.mimpi.com; r US$80-180; ❄@🛜🏊) The choice for a traditional resort experience, Mimpi has a lavish spa, room service, loungers by the shore, a refined restaurant and more. The 13 rooms open onto lush gardens as do 12 large cottages. Four more are on the water. The crashing waves should pound the jet lag right out of your head.

Tauch Terminal Resort
HOTEL **$$**

(☎0361 774 504, 22 911; www.tauch-terminal.com; r €65-95; ❄🔊🏊) Down a side road, this sprawling waterfront hotel has 27 rooms in several categories. Many of the rooms are recently built and all are comfortable in a modern, motel-style way. Expect amenities like satellite TV and fridges. Of the two waterfront pools, one is reserved for swimming only. The cafe serves a fine breakfast.

Deep Blue Studio
GUESTHOUSE **$**

(☎22 919; www.subaqua.cz; r US$25-50; 🏊) Owned by Czechs, this dive operation has 10 rooms in two-storey buildings on the hill side of the road. Rooms have fans and balconies. There are variety of packages with the affiliated dive shop.

Ocean Sun
GUESTHOUSE **$**

(☎0813 3757 3434; www.ocean-sun.com; r from 150,000Rp) Ocean Sun has four bungalow-style rooms on the hill side of the road. Units are clean and basic. Feel like some head-bangin'? The beds have thickly cushioned headboards.

ℹ️ Information

You can change cash at a few signposted places at the eastern end of the main road; otherwise services are sparse. For slow internet access, try **Tulamben Wreck Divers Resort** (per min 500Rp).

ℹ️ Getting There & Away

Plenty of buses and bemo travel between Amlapura and Singaraja and will stop anywhere along the Tulamben road, but they're infrequent after 2pm. Expect to pay 12,000Rp to either town.

Perama offers charter tourist-bus services from Candidasa; the cost is 125,000Rp each for a minimum of two people. This is similar to the cost of hiring a car and driver.

If you are driving to Lovina for the night, be sure to leave by about 3pm, so you will still have a little light when you get there. There's a petrol station just south of town.

If you are just going to snorkel the wreck and are day-tripping with a driver, don't let them park at a dive shop away from the wreck where you'll get a sales pitch.

Tulamben to Yeh Sanih

North of Tulamben, the road continues to skirt the slopes of Gunung Agung, with frequent evidence of lava flows from the 1963 eruption. Further around, the outer crater of Gunung Batur slopes steeply down to the sea. The rainfall is low and you can generally count on sunny weather. The scenery is very stark in the dry season and it's thinly populated. The route has public transport, but it's easier to make stops and detours with your own wheels.

There are regular markets in **Kubu**, a roadside village 5km northwest of Tulamben. At **Les**, a road goes inland to lovely **Air Terjun Yeh Mampeh** (Yeh Mampeh Waterfall), at 40m one of Bali's highest. Look for a large sign on the main road and then turn inland for about 1km. Walk the last 2km or so on an obvious path by the stream, shaded by rambutan trees. A 5000Rp donation is requested; there's no need for a guide.

The next main town is **Tejakula**, famous for its stream-fed public bathing area, said to have been built for washing horses and often called the 'horse bath'. The renovated bathing areas (separate for men and women) are behind walls topped by rows of elaborately decorated arches, and are regarded as a sacred area. The baths are 100m inland on a narrow road with lots of small shops – it's a quaint village, with some finely carved *kulkul* (hollow tree-trunk drum used to sound a warning) towers. Take a stroll above the baths, past irrigation channels flowing in all directions.

At Pacung, about 10km before Yeh Sanih, you can turn inland 4km to **Sembiran**, which is a Bali Aga village, although it doesn't promote itself as such. The most striking thing about the place is its hillside location and brilliant coastal views.

🛏️ Sleeping

Bali's remote northeast coast has a growing number of resorts where you can indeed get away from it all. These are places to settle in for a few days and revive your senses. Getting here from the airport or south Bali can take three hours or more via two routes: one up and over the mountains via Kintamani and then down a rustic, scenic road to the sea near Tejakula; the other going right round east Bali on the coast road via Candidasa and Tulamben.

Alam Anda
HOTEL **$$**

(☎0812 465 6485; www.alamanda.de; r €45-110; ❄🏊) The striking tropical architecture at this oceanside resort, near Sambirenteng, is the creation of the German architect-owner. A reef just offshore keeps the dive shop busy.

SAVING BALI'S FORGOTTEN

Long the poorest region of Bali, the arid lands far up the northeast slopes of Gunung Agung were so poor for so long that as recently as the 1990s, government bureaucrats wouldn't even admit that people lived there. Diseases from malnutrition were common, education was nil, incomes were under US$30 a year and so on. It was poverty at its worst on an island that already 20 years ago was experiencing an economic boom from tourism.

Amazingly, this bleak scene no longer exists and although it sounds like a cliché, the tireless efforts of one man, David Booth, are responsible. Irascible, idiosyncratic and relentless, the British-born Booth turned his engineering background on the region (which extends from the tiny village of Ban) starting in the 1990s. A tireless organiser, he rallied the locals, badgered the government, charmed donors and turned his **East Bali Poverty Project** (✆0361-410 071; www.eastbalipovertyproject.org) into a powerful force of change.

There are schools, electricity, clinics and a sense of accomplishment that have liberated the people from their past. Now moving into a sustainable phase of development, the project has built the **Bamboo Centre** in the hamlet of Daya. It shows the possibilities for bamboo as a renewable resource. The now-supportive Balinese government has greatly improved a road running over the mountain from a point near Pura Besakih, all the way down to the coast at Tianyar, 20km northwest of Tulamben. If you're not worried about getting lost, this can make a fascinating day's outing. There may not be anyone at the centre, but if there is, the welcome is warm.

The 28 units come in various sizes, from *losmen* rooms to cottages with views. All are well equipped and have artful thatch and bamboo motifs. The resort is 1km north of Poinciana Resort, roughly between Kubu and Tejakula.

Siddhartha Dive Resort   HOTEL **$$**
(✆0363-23 034; www.siddhartha-bali.de; r €90-200; ❄❅) With 30 separate bungalows that are stylish and modern, this resort which shares owners with the Alam Anda has Euro-style clean lines within a Balinese architectural vibe. Most people staying here plan to join the Tulamben crowd diving. There are two lavish villas.

Spa Village Resort Tembok   HOTEL **$$$**
(✆0362-32033; www.spavillage.com; full board r from US$400; ❄@☎❅) When you arrive at this beachside resort, you realise you're in for

an experience. Guests are asked to choose a path: balance, creativity or vigour (there's no 'leave me alone'). Extensive spa treatments and daily activities are geared to your path. The rooms and seats have a traditional feel with a coffee-and-cream theme accented by carving. Meals are healthful and focus on simple, local ingredients. It is between Kubu and Tejakula, northwest of Tembok.

Bali Sandat Guest House   GUESTHOUSE **$$**
(✆0813 3772 8680; www.bali-sandat.com; Bondalem; r from US$50) You'll feel like you're staying with friends at this low-key guesthouse located deep in a waterfront palm forest in a remote part of east Bali. The four rooms have open-air cold-water bathrooms and deep and shady verandas. Balinese dinners are available. The village of Bondalem is a 1km walk and has a simple morning market and a weaving workshop.

Central Mountains

Best Places to Eat

» Kedisan Floating Hotel (p221)

» Strawberry Stop (p223)

» Puri Lumbung Cottages (p226)

» Sarinbuana Eco-Lodge (p228)

Best Places to Stay

» Puri Lumbung Cottages (p226)

» Sarinbuana Eco-Lodge (p228)

» Bali Mountain Retreat (p229)

» Sanda Bukit Villas & Restaurant (p229)

Why Go?

Bali has a hot soul. The volcanoes stretching along the island's spine are more than just cones of silence; their active spirits are literally just below the surface, eager for expression.

Gunung Batur (1717m) is constantly letting off steam. The other-worldly beauty of the place may overwhelm the attendant hassles of a visit. Danau Bratan has sacred Hindu temples while the village of Candikuning has an engrossing botanic garden.

The old colonial village of Munduk, a hiking centre, has views down the hills to the coast of north Bali that match the beauty of the many nearby waterfalls and plantations. In the shadow of Gunung Batukau (2276m), you'll find one of Bali's most mystic temples. Just south, the Unesco-listed ancient rice terraces in and around Jatiluwih bedazzle.

Amid it all, little roads lead to untouched villages. Start driving north from Antosari for one surprise after another.

When to Go

Bali's central mountains can be cool and misty throughout the year. They also get a lot of rain: this is the starting point for the water that courses through rice terraces and fields all the way to Seminyak. Although you can expect more rain from October to April, it can pour any time. Temperatures show few seasonal variations, although it can get down to 10°C at night at high elevations – it's no wonder locals wander around bundled up. There's no peak tourist season in the hills.

GUNUNG BATUR AREA

📞 0366

The Gunung Batur area is like a giant bowl, with the bottom half covered by water and a set of volcanic cones jutting out of the middle. Sound a bit spectacular? It is. On clear days – vital to appreciating the spectacle – the turquoise waters wrap around the newer volcanoes, which have obvious old lava flows oozing down their sides.

In 2012 Unesco honoured the area by proclaiming the region a part of the Global Geoparks Network, of which there are over 90 worldwide. So far this has meant little on the ground, although some interesting signs detailing the unique geology of the area have started to appear on the road between Kedisan and Toya Bungkah.

The road around the southwestern rim of the Gunung Batur crater is one of Bali's most important north–south routes and has one of Bali's most stunning vistas.

Day trippers should bring some sort of wrap in case the mist closes in and the temperature drops to 16°C.

The villages around the Gunung Batur crater rim have grown together in a continuous untidy strip. The main village is Kintamani, though the whole area is often referred to by that name. Coming from the south, the first village is Penelokan, where tour groups first stop to gasp at the view.

ℹ️ Information

Services are few in the Gunung Batur area. Bring anything you might need, including cash, from the lowlands.

The Gunung Batur area has a reputation as an avaricious place and many visitors leave vowing never to return.

Be wary of touts on motorcycles, who attempt to steer you to a hotel of *their* choice as you descend into the Danau Batur area from the

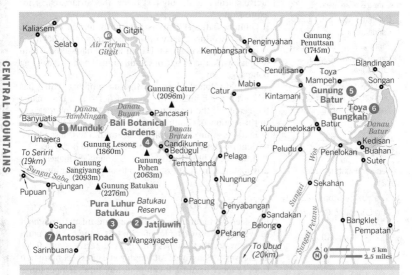

Central Mountains Highlights

❶ Claiming your own waterfall while trekking around **Munduk** (p226)

❷ Identifying each ancient variety of rice grown at the magnificent Unesco-recognised ancient terraces of **Jatiluwih** (p227)

❸ Hearing the chant of priests at one of Bali's holiest temples, **Pura Luhur Batukau** (p228)

❹ Luxuriating among the hundreds of rare plants at Candikuning's **Bali Botanical Gardens** (p223)

❺ Beholding the otherworldly, lava-strewn side of **Gunung Batur** (p216)

❻ Finding your own serenity in the lakeside village of **Toya Bungkah** (p221), in the shadow of steaming Gunung Batur

❼ Exploring the region's maze of back roads, such as the one north from **Antosari** (p229)

village of Penelokan. Vendors in the area can be highly aggressive and irritating.

ℹ️ Getting There & Around

From Batubulan terminal in Denpasar, bemo travel regularly to Kintamani (15,000Rp). Buses on the Denpasar–(Batubulan)–Singaraja route will stop in Penelokan and Kintamani (about 16,000Rp). Alternatively, you can just hire a car or use a driver but be sure to rebuff buffet lunch entreaties.

Bemo shuttle between Penelokan and Kintamani (10,000Rp for tourists). Bemo from Penelokan down to the lakeside villages go in the morning (about 8000Rp to Toya Bungkah). Later in the day, you may have to hire transport (40,000Rp or more).

Arriving by private vehicle, you will be stopped at Penelokan or Kubupenelokan to buy an entry ticket (10,000Rp per person) that's good for the whole Gunung Batur area. You shouldn't be charged again – save your stub.

Gunung Batur

Volcanologists describe Gunung Batur as a 'double caldera', ie one crater inside another. The outer crater is an oval about 14km long, with its western rim about 1500m above sea level. The inner is a classic volcano-shaped peak that reaches 1717m. Activity over the last decade has spawned several smaller cones on its western flank, unimaginatively named Batur I, II, III and IV. More than 20 minor eruptions were recorded between 1824 and 1994, and there were major eruptions in 1917, 1926 and 1963. Geological activity and tremors have continued to occur regularly.

Statistics aside, you really have to see it to believe it. One look at this other-worldly spectacle and you'll understand why people want to go through the many hassles and expenses of taking a trek. Note that the odds of clouds obscuring your reason for coming are greater from July to December, but any time of year you should check conditions with a trekking agency before committing to a trip, or even coming up the mountain.

The **HPPGB** (Mt Batur Tour Guides Association; 📞52 362; ⌚3am-noon) has a monopoly on guided climbs up Gunung Batur. It requires that all trekking agencies that operate on the mountain hire at least one of its guides for trips up the mountain. In addition, the cartel has developed a reputation for tough tactics in requiring climbers to use its guides and during negotiations for its services.

That said, many people use the services of HPPGB guides without incident, and some of the guides win plaudits from visitors for their ideas in customising trips.

The following strategies should help you have a good climb:

Be absolutely clear in your agreement with the HPPGB about the terms you're agreeing to, such as whether fees are per person or group and include breakfast, and exactly where you will go.

Deal with one of the trekking agencies. There will still be an HPPGB guide along, but all arrangements will be done through the agency.

HPPGB rates and times are posted at its office. The **Batur Sunrise** (4 people from 450,000Rp) trek goes from 4am to 8am, the **Gunung Batur Main Crater** (from 550,000Rp) trek from 4am to 10am.

Trekking Agencies

Even reputable and highly competent adventure-tour operators and trekking agencies cannot take their customers up Gunung Batur without paying the HPPGB to have one of their guys tag along. However, they are useful for planning trips off well-trod trails.

Most of the accommodation in the area can match you up with guides and trekking agencies, which will add about 250,000Rp to 450,000Rp to the cost of a trek/climb.

Equipment

If you're climbing before sunrise, take a torch (flashlight) or be absolutely sure that your guide provides you with one. You'll

ℹ️ UNPLANNED EXCITEMENT

The volcanically active area west of the main peak of Gunung Batur can be deadly, with explosions of steam and hot lava, unstable ground and sulphurous gases. To find out about current conditions, ask at the trekking agencies or look at the website of the **Directorate of Volcanology & Geographical Hazard Mitigation** (www.vsi.esdm.go.id); although much of this site is in Bahasa Indonesia you can use Google Language to translate it. Active areas are sometimes closed to visitors for safety reasons.

Gunung Batur Area

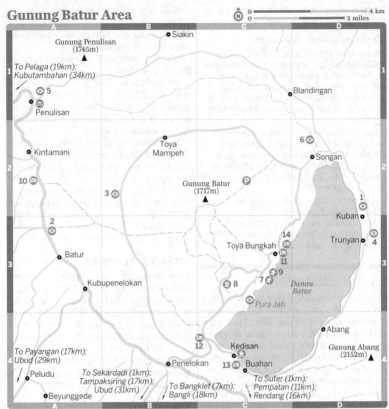

N 0 ——————————— 4 km
  0 ——————————— 2 miles

• Siakin

Gunung Penulisan
(1745m) ▲

To Pelaga (19km);
Kubutambahan (34km)

◎ 5

• Penulisan

• Blandingan

• Kintamani

Toya
Mampeh

6 ◎

• Songan

10 🏛

3 ◎

Gunung Batur
(1717m) ▲

P

1 ◎
Kuban •

14 🏛
Toya Bungkah

11

Trunyan • ◎ 4

2 ◎

• Batur

• Kubupenelokan

🏕 8   7 🍴 9

Danau
Batur

🛕 Pura Jati

• Abang

12 🏛
Kedisan
13 🏛 Buahan

Gunung Abang
(2152m) ▲

To Payangan (17km);
Ubud (29km)

/ • Peludu

• Beyunggede

To Sekardadi (1km);
Tampaksiring (17km);
Ubud (31km)

• Penelokan

To Bangklet (7km);
Bangli (18km)

To Suter (1km);
Pempatan (11km);
Rendang (16km)

need good strong footwear, a hat, a jumper (sweater) and drinking water.

Trekking Routes

The climb to see the sunrise from Gunung Batur is still the most popular trek.

Ideally, trekkers should get to the top for sunrise (about 6am), before mist and cloud obscure the view. It is a magnificent sight, although hardly a wilderness experience – it's not uncommon for there to be 100 people present for the sunrise in the tourist season. It isn't even necessary to be at the top for sunrise – a halfway point is fine. If you start at 5am, you'll avoid the crowds.

Guides will provide breakfast on the summit for a fee (50,000Rp), which often includes the novelty of cooking an egg or banana in the steaming holes at the top of the volcano. There are several pricey refreshment stops along the way.

FROM TOYA BUNGKAH

The basic trek is to start climbing from Toya Bungkah at about 4am, reach the summit for sunrise, and possibly walk right around the main cone, then return to Toya Bungkah. The route is pretty straightforward – walk out of the village towards Kedisan and turn right just after the car park. After about 30 minutes, you'll be on a ridge with a well-defined track; keep going up. It gets pretty steep towards the top and it can be hard walking over the loose volcanic sand. Allow about two hours to reach the top, which is at the northern edge of the inner crater.

Climbers have reported that they've made the journey without a HPPGB guide, though this has risks as a hiker fell to his death at night in 2010. Don't try this when it's dark; by day you can see the paths easily.

You can follow the rim to the western side, where you can view the most recent volcanic activity, continue to the southern

Gunung Batur Area

◉ **Sights**			
1	Cemetery	D2
2	Pura Batur	A3
3	Pura Bukit Mentik	B2
4	Pura Pancering Jagat	D3
5	Pura Puncak Penulisan	A1
6	Pura Ulun Danu Batur	D2

⊕ **Activities, Courses & Tours**		
7	Batur Natural Hot Spring	C3
	C.Bali	(see 12)

8	HPPGB	C3
9	Toya Devasya	C3

⊜ **Sleeping**		
10	Hotel Miranda	A2
11	Hotel Puri Bening Hayato & Restaurant	C3
12	Hotel Segara	C4
13	Kedisan Floating Hotel	C4
14	Under the Volcano III	C3

edge, and then return to Toya Bungkah by the route you climbed up.

Longer trips go around the recent volcanic cones southwest of the summit. This has the most exciting volcanic activity, with smoking craters, bright-yellow sulphur deposits, and steep slopes of fine black sand.

Climbing up Gunung Batur, spending a reasonable time on the top and then strolling back down takes four or five hours; for the longer treks around the newer cones, allow around eight hours.

FROM PURA JATI

A huge parking lot near Pura Jati makes this the main entrance for groups and day trippers. The shortest trek is basically across the lava fields, then straight up (allow about two hours to the top). If you want to see the newer cones west of the peak (assuming the area is safe to visit), go to the summit first – do not go walking around the active area before sunrise. You can also start at the new HPPGB office (p217) and avoid some of the lava-field-trekking.

FROM THE NORTHEAST

The easiest route is from the northeast – but requires transport to the trailhead at 4am. From Toya Bungkah take the road northeast towards Songan, then take the left fork after about 3.5km. Follow this small road for another 1.7km to a badly signposted track on the left – this climbs 1km or so to a parking area. From here, the walking track is easy to follow to the top, and should take less than an hour.

THE OUTER CRATER

A popular place to see the sunrise is on the outer crater rim northeast of Songan. You'll need transport to Pura Ulun Danu Batur, near the northern end of the lake.

From there you can climb to the top of the outer crater rim in under 30 minutes, from where you can see Bali's northeast coast, about 5km away. At sunrise, the silhouette of Lombok looms across the water, and the first rays strike the great volcanoes of Batur and Agung.

Around Gunung Batur Crater

There are several small villages on the ridge around Gunung Batur crater.

PENELOKAN

Appropriately, Penelokan means 'place to look' and you'll be stunned by the view across to Gunung Batur and down to the lake at the bottom of the crater (check out the large lava flow on Gunung Batur).

✕ Eating

Although the huge tourist places on the road from Penelokan to Kintamani disappoint, there are some acceptable choices here, including many humble places where you can sit on a plastic chair and have a simple, freshly cooked meal while enjoying a priceless view. Spotting an *ikan mujair* sign is almost as rewarding as spotting Gunung Agung on a clear day: these vendors sell small sweet fish that are caught in the lake below and then barbecued to a crisp with onion, garlic and bamboo sprouts.

BATUR & KINTAMANI

The villages of Batur and Kintamani now virtually run together. Kintamani is famed for its large and colourful market, which is held every three days. The town is like a string bean: long, with pods of development. Activity starts early, and by 11am everything's all packed up. If you don't want to

CENTRAL MOUNTAINS AROUND GUNUNG BATUR CRATER

TOUR BUS RESTAURANTS

Bring a shovel for the chow served at a lot of the ugly monolithic restaurants lining the crater rim (many have closed, their carcasses littering the view like the forgotten eggrolls inside). Buffet lunches cost 80,000Rp to 100,000Rp or more (your guide usually gets at least 25% of that as a commission) and the food is typically of the bucket-of-slop school of cuisine. Drivers also get in on the action: the most crowded ones often have driver's lounges with gyms, TVs, beds and free food.

go on a trek, the sunrise view from the road here is good.

The original village of Batur was in the crater, but was wiped out by a violent eruption in 1917. It killed thousands of people before the lava flow stopped at the entrance to the village's main temple. Taking this as a good omen, the village was rebuilt, but Gunung Batur erupted again in 1926. This time, the lava flow covered everything except the loftiest temple shrine. Fortunately, few lives were lost.

The village was relocated up onto the crater rim, and the surviving shrine was also moved up there and placed in the current temple, the ever-more-flambouyant **Pura Batur** (admission 6000Rp, sarong & sash hire 3000Rp). Spiritually, Gunung Batur is the second most important mountain in Bali (only Gunung Agung outranks it), so this temple is of considerable importance. It's a great stop for the architectural spectacle. Within the complex is a Taoist shrine.

Sleeping

Hotel Miranda HOTEL $
(☎52 022; Jl Raya Kintamani; r 100,000-200,000Rp) The only accommodation in the area. The six rooms are clean and very basic with squat toilets. It serves meals (20,000Rp) and has a welcome open fire at night. There are simple warung nearby and this is a good place to get trekking info.

PENULISAN

The road gradually climbs along the crater rim beyond Kintamani, and is often shrouded in clouds, mist or rain. Penulisan is where the road bends sharply and heads down towards the north coast and the remote scenic drive to Bedugul. A **viewpoint** about 400m south from here offers an amazing panorama over three mountains: Gunung Batur, Gunung Abang and Gunung Agung.

Near the road junction, several steep flights of steps lead to Bali's highest temple, **Pura Puncak Penulisan** (1745m). Inside the highest courtyard are rows of old statues and fragments of sculptures in the open *bale* (Balinese pavilion). Some of the sculptures date back to the 11th century. The temple views are superb: facing north you can see over the rice terraces clear to the Singaraja coast (weather permitting).

Around Danau Batur

The little villages around Danau Batur have a crisp lakeside setting and views up to the surrounding peaks. There's a lot of fish farming here, and the air is pungent with the smell of onions from the myriad tiny vegetable farms. You'll also see chillies, cabbage and garlic growing, a festival for those who like assertively flavoured food. The lake has ever-more fish farms.

A hairpin road winds its way down from Penelokan to the shore of Danau Batur. At the lakeside you can go left along the road that twists through lava fields to Toya Bungkah. Watch out for huge sand trucks battering the road into dust as they haul materials for construction across Bali.

KEDISAN & BUAHAN

Buahan is a pleasant 15-minute stroll from Kedisan, and has market gardens going right down to the lakeshore.

Activities

C.Bali ADVENTURE TOUR
(☎0813 5342 0541; www.c-bali.com; Hotel Segara; tours from 400,000Rp) Operated by an Australian-Dutch couple, C.Bali offers you bike tours around the craters and canoe tours on the lake. Prices include pick-up across south Bali (significant discounts are available if you're staying locally). Packages also include multiday trips. A very important note: these tours often fill up in advance, so book ahead.

Sleeping & Eating

Beware of the motorcycle touts who will follow you down the hill from Penelokan, trying to nab a hotel commission. Local hotels ask that you call ahead and reserve so that they have your name on record and thus can avoid paying a bounty to the touts.

The restaurants at the following two hotels are good places to sample the garlic-infused local fish.

Hotel Segara GUESTHOUSE $
(☎51 136; www.batur-segarahotel.com; Kedisan; r 200,000-500,000Rp; @⍥) The Segara has bungalows set around a courtyard. The cheapest rooms have cold water, the best rooms hot water and bathtubs – perfect for soaking away the hypothermia.

TOP CHOICE Kedisan Floating Hotel CAFE $$
(☎0813 3775 5411; Kedisan; meals from 35,000Rp) OK, so nothing floats here – except maybe your rubber duck from home in the soaking tubs – but this hotel on the shores of the lake is hugely popular for its daily lunches. On weekends tourists vie with day trippers from Denpasar for tables out on the piers over the lake. The Balinese food, which features fresh lake fish, is excellent. You can also stay (rooms US$30–US$100), the best rooms are cottages at the water's edge.

TRUNYAN & KUBAN
The village of Trunyan is squeezed between the lake and the outer crater rim. It is inhabited by Bali Aga people, but unlike Tenganan in east Bali, it is not a welcoming place.

Trunyan is known for the **Pura Pancering Jagat**, with its 4m-high statue of the village's guardian spirit, but tourists are not allowed to go inside. Touts and guides, however, hang about soliciting exorbitant tips.

A little beyond Trunyan, and accessible only by boat, is the **cemetery** at Kuban. The people of Trunyan do not cremate or bury their dead – they lay them out in bamboo cages to decompose. If you do decide to visit the cemetery you'll be met by characters demanding huge fees (it is a tourist trap). Our advice: don't go.

Lake boats leave from a jetty near Kedisan. The price for a four-hour return trip (Kedisan–Trunyan–Kuban–Toya Bungkah–Kedisan) depends on the number of passengers, with a maximum of seven people (the boat costs 440,000Rp, although extra 'fees' may be added). Our advice? If you'd like to spend time out on the lake, take one of the canoe trips with C.Bali.

TOYA BUNGKAH
The main tourist centre is Toya Bungkah (also known as Tirta), which boasts hot springs (*tirta* and *toya* both mean water). It's a simple village, and travellers stay here so they can climb Gunung Batur early in the morning.

🏃 Activities
Hot springs bubble in a couple of spots, and have long been used for bathing pools.

Batur Natural Hot Spring HOT SPRINGS
(☎0813 3832 5552; admission from 120,000Rp; ⍥8am-6pm) Walk down a cinder path and you'll reach this low-key complex of three pools on the edge of the lake. Different pools have different temps, so you can simmer yourself successively. The overall feel of the hot springs rather nicely matches the slight-

THE ROAD RARELY TRAVELLED

A series of narrow roads links the Danau Bratan area and the Gunung Batur region. Few locals outside of this area even know the roads exist, and if you have a driver, you might need to do some convincing. Over a 30km route you not only step back to a simpler time, but also leave Bali altogether for something resembling less-developed islands such as Timor. The scenery is beautiful and may make you forget you had a destination.

South of Bedugul, you turn east at Temantanda and take a small and winding road down the hillside into some lush ravines cut by rivers. After about 6km you'll come to a T-junction: turn north and travel about 5km to reach the pretty village of **Pelaga**. This area is known for its organic coffee and cinnamon plantations, which you'll both see and smell. Consider a tour and homestay in Pelaga organised by JED (p199), a nonprofit group that offers rural tourism experiences.

From Pelaga, ascend the mountain, following terrain that alternates between jungle and rice fields. Continue north to Catur, then veer east to the junction with the road down to north Bali and drive east again for 1km to Penulisan.

A fun detour on *this* detour is the 2006 **Tukad Bangkung Bridge** at Petang: at 71m it is reputed to be the tallest bridge in Asia. It is a local tourist attraction and the roads here are lined with vendors.

ly shabby feel of the entire region. Lockers and towels are included with admission, and the simple cafe has good views.

Toya Devasya   HOT SPRINGS
(☑51 204; admission 150,000Rp; ☺8am-8pm) This glossy retreat is built around springs. A huge hot pool is 38°C while a comparatively brisk lake-fed pool is 20°C. Admission includes refreshments and the use of loungers.

🛏 Sleeping & Eating

Avoid rooms near the noisy main road through town: opt instead for placid ones with lake views.

Under the Volcano III   GUESTHOUSE $
(☑0813 3860 0081; r 200,000Rp) With a lovely, quiet lakeside location opposite chilli plots, this inn has six clean and pretty rooms; go for room 1 right on the water. There are two other nearby inns in the Volcano empire, all run by the same lovely family.

Hotel Puri Bening Hayato
& Restaurant   HOTEL $
(☑51 234; www.hotelpuribeningbali.com; r from 375,000Rp; ✹) An incongruously modern place for rustic Toya Bungkah. The 21 rooms are motel-like and basically fine. The pool is small, but there's also a hot-spring-fed whirlpool. Free use of mountain bikes is a brilliant amenity.

SONGAN

Two kilometres around the lake from Toya Bungkah, Songan is a large and interesting village with market gardens extending to the lake's edge. At the lakeside road end is **Pura Ulun Danu Batur**, under the edge of the crater rim.

A turn-off in Songan takes you on a rough but passable road around the crater floor. On the northwestern side of the volcano, the village of **Toya Mampeh** (Yeh Mampeh) is surrounded by a vast field of

SUNRISE JOY

For an almost surreal experience, take a quiet paddle across Danau Bratan and see Pura Ulun Danu Bratan at sunrise – arrange it with a boatman the night before. The mobs see it by day, but you'll see something entirely different – and magical – in the mists of dawn.

chunky black lava – a legacy of the 1974 eruption. Further on, **Pura Bukit Mentik** was completely surrounded by molten lava from this eruption, but the temple itself, and its impressive banyan tree, were quite untouched – it's called the 'Lucky Temple'.

DANAU BRATAN AREA

As you approach from the south, you gradually leave the rice terraces behind and ascend into the cool, often misty mountain country around Danau Bratan. Candikuning is the main village in the area, and has the important and picturesque temple, Pura Ulun Danu Bratan. Munduk anchors the region with fine trekking to waterfalls and cloud-cloaked forests.

The choice of accommodation near the lake is limited, as much of the area is geared towards domestic, not foreign, tourists. On Sundays and public holidays, the lakeside can be crowded with courting couples and Toyotas bursting with day-tripping families. Many new inns have opened around Munduk.

Wherever you go, you are likely to see the tasty local strawberries on offer. Note that it is often misty and can get chilly up here.

Bedugul

☑0368

'Bedugul' is sometimes used to refer to the whole lakeside area, but strictly speaking it's just the first place you reach at the top of the hill when coming from south Bali, and even then, you might not pause long as it's small.

🛏 Sleeping & Eating

Hotels on the slope 9km south of Bedugul offer outstanding views to the south, and they're also good choices for a snack or a refreshment if you're just passing by. Beware of a string of rundown places up at the ridge around Bedugul.

Strawberry Hill   GUESTHOUSE $$
(☑21 265; www.strawberryhillbali.com; Bukit Stroberi; r 300,000-650,000Rp; ☎) Five conical little cottages are arrayed on a hill, each with a deep soaking tub and nice views down to south Bali (although some have better views than others, so compare). The cafe has polished floorboards and on a clear day you can see Kuta. The Indo menu includes soul-

healing *soto ayam* (chicken soup) and *gudeg yogya* (jackfruit stew); meals are about 70,000Rp.

Pacung Indah
HOTEL **$$**

(☏21 020; www.pacungbali.com; r 260,000-850,000Rp; ☲) Across the road from the slightly more upscale Saranam Eco-Resort, this hotel has rice-terrace views and the walled rooms have some style – all include a private courtyard. Those at the top end have decks and views. Treks are offered in the green, green, green countryside.

ⓘ Getting There & Away

Any minibus or bemo between south Bali and Singaraja will stop at Bedugul on request.

Candikuning

☏0368

Often misty, Candikuning is home to the fun and attractions of a good botanical garden as well as one of Bali's most photographed temples.

⊙ Sights & Activities

TOP CHOICE Bali Botanical Gardens
GARDENS

(☏21 273; www.balibotanicgarden.org; Kebun Raya Eka Karya Bali; admission walking/driving 7000/12,000Rp, car parking 6000Rp; ⊙7am-6pm) This garden is a showplace. Established in 1959 as a branch of the national botanical gardens at Bogor, near Jakarta, it covers more than 154 hectares on the lower slopes of Gunung Pohen. The garden boasts an extensive collection of trees and flowers.

Some plants are labelled with their botanical names, and a booklet of self-guided walks (20,000Rp) is helpful. The gorgeous orchid area is often locked to foil flower filchers; you can ask for it to be unlocked.

Within the park, you can cavort like an ape or a squirrel at the Bali Treetop Adventure Park (☏0361-852 0680; www.balitreetop.com; Kebun Raya Eka Karya Bali, in Bali Botanical Gardens; adult/child US$21/14; ⊙7am-6pm). Winches, ropes, nets and the like let you explore the forest well above the ground. And it's not passive – you hoist, jump, balance and otherwise circumnavigate the park. Special programs are geared to different ages.

Pura Ulun Danu Bratan
TEMPLE

(adult/child 15,000/10,000Rp, parking 5000Rp; ⊙tickets 7am-5pm, site 24hr) This very impor-

tant Hindu-Buddhist temple was founded in the 17th century. It is dedicated to Dewi Danu, the goddess of the waters, and is actually built on small islands, which means it is completely surrounded by the lake. Pilgrimages and ceremonies are held here to ensure that there is a supply of water for farmers all over Bali.

The tableau includes classical Hindu thatch-roofed *meru* (multitiered shrines) reflected in the water and silhouetted against the often cloudy mountain backdrop. A large banyan tree shades the entrance, and you walk through manicured gardens and past an impressive Buddhist stupa to reach the lakeside.

There's a bit of a sideshow atmosphere, however. Animals in small cages and opportunities to caress a snake or hold a huge bat amuse the punters.

Market
MARKET

(parking 2000Rp) This roadside market is touristy, but among the eager vendors of tat, you'll find locals shopping for fruit, veg, herbs, spices and potted plants.

🛏 Sleeping

Pondok Wisata Dahlia Indah
GUESTHOUSE **$**

(☏21233; Jl Kebun Raya Bedugul; r 100,000-200,000Rp) In the village along a lane near the road to the botanical gardens, this is a decent budget option; its 17 comfortable, clean rooms have hot-water showers set in a garden of mountain flowers.

Bali Botanic Garden
GUESTHOUSE **$$**

(☏22 050; www.kebunrayabali.com; Candikuning; r from US$45) Wake up and smell the roses. The Bali Botanic Garden has 14 comfortable hotel-style rooms in the heart of the gardens. There is hot water and you will be guaranteed to enjoy views of a botanic paradise from the terraces.

✗ Eating

From simple market snacks to meals featuring the region's fresh strawberries, you'll have much to choose from. At the entrance to Pura Ulun Danu Bratan are several Padang warung, and there's a cafe with a view on the grounds.

Strawberry Stop
CAFE **$**

(☏21 060; snacks from 10,000Rp; ⊙8am-7pm) Locally grown strawberries star in milkshakes, juices, pancakes and other treats.

Danau Bratan Area

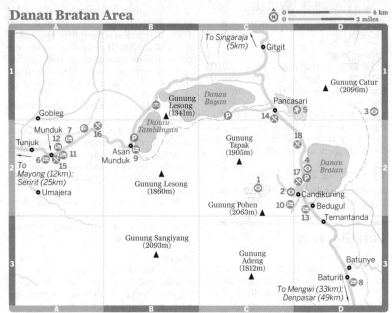

N
0 — 4 km
0 — 2 miles

To Singaraja (5km) ● Gitgit

Danau Bratan Area

You can also get full meals. Bananas are used when berries are out of season, which might drive you to drink the self-proclaimed 'dry' – ha! – strawberry wine (100,000Rp).

Cafe Teras Lempuna   INTERNATIONAL $
(☑0362-29312; meals 25,000-60,000Rp; ❄)
North of the temple, this indoor/outdoor cafe is stylish and modern. The menu ranges from burgers to Japanese, and the coffee, tea and juices refresh no matter what the temperature. When it's sunny, enjoy the inviting covered patio; when it's cool, put on the heat with the hot chilli soup.

Roti Bedugul   BAKERY $
(☑21 838; snacks 5000Rp; ☺8am-4pm) Just north of the market, this growing bakery produces fine versions of its namesake, as well as croissants and other treats all day.

ℹ Getting There & Away

Danau Bratan is along the main north–south road from south Bali or Singaraja.

Although the main terminal is in Pancasari, most minibuses and bemo will stop along the road in Bedugul and Candikuning. There are frequent connections from Denpasar's Ubung terminal (20,000Rp) and Singaraja's Sukasada terminal (20,000Rp).

Pancasari

The broad green valley northwest of Danau Bratan is actually the crater of an extinct volcano. In the middle of the valley, on the main road, Pancasari is a nontourist town with a bustling market and the main terminal for public bemo.

Just south of Pancasari, you will see the entrance to **Bali Handara Kosaido Country Club** (☑0362-22646; www.balihandara kosaido.com; greens fees US$150, club hire from US$25), a well-situated (in that, compared with south Bali courses, there's plenty of water here) 18-hole golf course. It also offers comfortable accommodation (rooms from US$110) in the sterile atmosphere of a 1970s resort, reminiscent of the villain's grand lair in an old James Bond movie.

Danau Buyan & Danau Tamblingan

Northwest of Danau Bratan are two more lakes, Danau Buyan and Danau Tamblingan – neither has been developed for tourism, which is a plus. There are several tiny villages and abandoned temples along the shores of both lakes.

◎ Sights & Activities

Danau Buyan (admission 5000Rp, parking 2000Rp) has parking right at the lake, a pretty 1.5km drive off the main road; when you park, an attendant will find you for the fees. The entire area is home to market gardens growing strawberries and other high value crops, such as the orange and blue flowers used in offerings. The Munduk road on the hill above the lake has some simple cafes and good picnic spots with views.

A 4km hiking trail goes around the southern side of Danau Buyan from the car park, then over the saddle to Danau Tamblingan, and on to Asan Munduk. It combines forest and lake views.

Danau Tamblingan (adult/child 6000/3000Rp, parking 2000Rp) also has parking at the end of the road from the village of Asan Munduk. The lake is a 400m walk from where you park. From here you can catch the trail to Danau Buyan. If you have a driver, walk this path in one direction and be met at the other end.

There are usually a couple of guides (per 6hr 350,000Rp) hanging around the car park (you don't need them for the lake path) who will take you up and around **Gunung Lesong**.

🛏 Sleeping & Eating

Pondok Kesuma Wisata   GUESTHOUSE **$**
(Map p224; ☑0852 3856 7944; r from 300,000Rp) This nice guesthouse features clean rooms with hot water and a pleasant cafe (meals 15,000Rp to 30,000Rp). It's just up from the Danau Tamblingan parking lot. The owners are charmers and have good hiking advice.

Munduk & Around

☑0362
The simple village of Munduk is one of Bali's most appealing mountain retreats. It has a cool misty ambience set among lush hillsides covered with jungle, rice, fruit trees and pretty much anything else that grows on the island. Waterfalls tumble off precipices by the dozen. There are hikes and treks galore and a number of really nice places to stay, from old Dutch summer homes to retreats where you can plunge full-on into local culture. Many people come for a day and stay for a week.

Archaeological evidence suggests there was a developed community in the Munduk region between the 10th and 14th centuries. When the Dutch took control of north Bali in the 1890s, they experimented with commercial crops, establishing plantations for coffee, vanilla, cloves and cocoa. Quite a few Dutch colonial buildings are still intact along the road in Munduk and further west. Look for shrines nestled in the crooks of hills.

◎ Sights & Activities

Heading to Munduk from Pancasari, the main road climbs steeply up the rim of the old volcanic crater. It's worth stopping to enjoy the views back over the valley and lakes – show a banana and the swarms of monkeys here will get so excited they'll go crazy

MUNDUK'S EASIEST WATERFALL

About 2km east of Munduk, look for signs indicating parking for a 15m waterfall near the road; this is the most accessible of many in the immediate area. A very short walk along a decent path brings you to the source of the enticing roar. Clouds of mist from the water add to the already misty air; drips come off every leaf. If you felt wilted in south Bali, you'll feel fully refreshed here.

themselves with joy. Turning right (east) at the top will take you on a scenic descent to the coastal town of Singaraja, via the Gitgit waterfalls. Taking a sharp left turn (west), you follow a ridge-top road with Danau Buyan on one side and a slope to the sea on the other. Coffee is a big crop in the area.

At Asan Munduk, you'll find another T-junction. If you turn left, a trail leads to near Danau Tamblingan, among forest and market gardens. Turning right takes you along beautiful winding roads to the main village of Munduk. Watch for superb panoramas of north Bali and the ocean. Consider a stop at **Ngiring Ngewedang** (☎0828 365 146; snacks 15,000-40,000Rp; ⏲10am-5pm), a coffeehouse 5km east of Munduk that grows its own beans on the surrounding slopes. Staff are happy to show you the process that puts the coffee in your cup.

Wherever you stay, staff will fill you in on **walking** and **hiking** options. Numerous trails are suitable for treks of two hours or much longer to coffee plantations, rice paddies, waterfalls, villages, or around both Danau Tamblingan and Danau Buyan. Most are easy to do on your own, but guides will take you far off the beaten path to waterfalls and other delights that are hard to find. Almost everything in the Munduk area is at an elevation of at least 1000m. You will be able to arrange a guide through your lodgings.

Sleeping & Eating

The hikes around Munduk draw many visitors and consequently there are many places for them to stay. Enjoy simple old Dutch houses in the village or more naturalistic places in the countryside. Most have cafes, usually serving good local fare. There are a couple of cute warung in the village and a few stores with very basic supplies (including bug spray).

TOP CHOICE Puri Lumbung Cottages GUESTHOUSE $$
(☎0812 383 6891, 0812 387 3986; www.purilumbung.com; cottages US$80-160; @📶) Founded by Nyoman Bagiarta to develop sustainable tourism, this lovely hotel has 33 bright two-storey cottages and rooms set among rice fields. Enjoy intoxicating views (units 3, 8, 10, 11, 14A and 14B have the best) down to the coast from the upstairs balconies. Dozens of trekking options and courses, including dance and cooking, are offered. The hotel's restaurant, Warung Kopi Bali, is sponsored by a Swiss cooking school. The menu includes a local dish, *timbungan bi siap* (chicken soup with sliced cassava and fried shallots), as well as a Cobb salad. The hotel is on the right-hand side of the road coming from Bedugul, 700m before Munduk.

Manah Liang Cottages INN $$
(☎700 5211; www.manahliang.com; r US$55-135; 📶) About 800m east of Munduk, this country inn (the name of which means 'feeling good') has traditional cottages overlooking the lush local terrain. The open-air bathrooms (with tubs) are as refreshing as the porches are relaxing. A short trail leads to a small waterfall. There are cooking classes and guided walks.

Meme Surung GUESTHOUSE $
(☎700 5378; www.memesurung.com; r US$35-45; 📶) Two atmospheric old Dutch houses adjoin each other in the village and the compound has a total of 10 rooms. The decor is traditional and simple, which is just as well as the view from the long wooden veranda is both the focus and joy here. The cafe here is good.

Puri Alam Bali GUESTHOUSE $
(☎0812 465 9815; www.purialambali.com; r 250,000-500,000Rp; 📶) Perched on a precipice at the east end of the village, the bungalow-style rooms (all with hot water and balconies) have better views the higher you go. The rooftop cafe is worth a visit for its views. Think of the long concrete stairs down from the road as trekking practice.

Guru Ratna GUESTHOUSE $
(☎0813 3719 4398; r 175,000-300,000Rp; 📶) The cheapest place in the village has seven com-

fortable hot-water rooms in a colonial Dutch house (some share bathrooms). The best rooms have some style, carved wood details and nice porches. Ponder the distant ocean from the cafe.

Don Biyu CAFE $

(www.donbiyu.com; mains 20,000Rp; 🖥) You know Munduk has arrived as a destination when it gets its first travellers cafe. Catch up on your blog, enjoy good coffee, zone out to the sublime views and choose from a mix of Western and Asian fare. It's all served in mellow open-air pavilions.

❶ Getting There & Away

Bemo leave Ubung terminal in Denpasar for Munduk (22,000Rp) frequently. Morning bemo from Candikuning also stop in Munduk (13,000Rp). If you're driving to the north coast, a decent road west of Munduk goes through a number of picturesque villages to Mayong (where you can head south to west Bali). The road then goes down to the sea at Seririt in north Bali.

GUNUNG BATUKAU AREA

📞 0361

Gunung Batukau is Bali's second-highest mountain (2276m), the third of Bali's three major mountains and the holy peak of the island's western end. It's often overlooked, which is probably a good thing given what the vendor hordes have done to Gunung Agung.

You can climb its slippery slopes from one of the island's holiest and most underrated temples, Pura Luhur Batukau, or just revel in the ancient rice-terrace greenery around Jatiluwih, which would be a fantasy if it wasn't real. Extend your stay at lodges far up the slopes of the volcano.

There are two main approaches to the Gunung Batukau area. The easiest is via Tabanan: take the Pura Luhur Batukau road north 9km to a fork in the road, then take the left-hand turn (towards the temple) and go a further 5km to a junction near a school in Wangayagede village. Here you can

DON'T MISS

JATILUWIH RICE FIELDS

At Jatiluwih, which means 'truly marvellous' (or 'real beautiful' depending on the translation), you will be rewarded with vistas of centuries-old rice terraces that exhaust your ability to describe green. Emerald ribbons curve around the hillsides, stepping back as they climb to the blue sky.

The terraces are part of Bali's emblematic ancient rice-growing culture that has achieved Unesco World Heritage status. You'll understand the nomination just viewing the panorama from the narrow, twisting 18km road, but getting out for a rice-field walk is even more rewarding, following the water as it runs through channels and bamboo pipes from one plot to the next. Much of the rice you'll see is traditional, rather than the hybrid versions grown elsewhere on the island. Look for heavy short husks of red rice.

Take some time, leave your driver behind and just find a place to sit and enjoy the views. It sounds like a cliché, but the longer you look the more you'll see. What at first seems like a vast palette of greens reveals itself to be rice at various stages of growth. See how many you can count, from the impossibly iridescent emerald hues of the young shoots to the lazy green-yellows of the rice-laden stalks ready for harvest.

There are cafes for refreshments along the drive. One of the simplest is the best: **Ada Babi Guleng** (lunch 35,000Rp; ⏰10am-4pm) serves an excellent version of Bali's signature dish (roast, marinated suckling pork). It has only four tables but each has lush, emerald views and the fiery sambal is superb.

Because the road is sharply curved, vehicles are forced to drive slowly, which makes the Jatiluwih route a good one for bikes. There is a road toll for visitors (15,000Rp per person, plus 5000Rp per car) which does *not* seem to be going to road maintenance – it's very rough. Still the drive won't take more than an hour – unless you get so caught up in the beauty you can't leave.

You can access the road in the west off the road to Pura Luhur Batukau from Tabanan, and in the east off the main road to Bedugul near Pacung. Drivers all know this road well and locals offer directions.

THE OTHER ROAD TO PUPUAN

You can reach the mountain village of Pupuan on the road from Antosari but there is another route, one that wanders the back roads of deepest mountain Bali. Start at Pulukan, which is on the Denpasar–Gilimanuk road in west Bali. A small road climbs steeply up from the coast providing fine views back down to west Bali and the sea. It runs through spice-growing country – you'll see (and smell) spices laid out to dry on mats by the road. After about 10km and just before Manggissari, the narrow and winding road actually runs right through **Bunut Bolong** – an enormous tree that forms a complete tunnel (the *bunut* is a type of ficus; *bolong* means 'hole').

Further on, the road spirals down to Pupuan through some of Bali's most beautiful rice terraces. It's worth stopping off for a walk to the magnificent **waterfalls** near Pujungan, a few kilometres south of Pupuan. Follow signs down a narrow rough road and then walk 1.5km to the first waterfall; it's nice, but before you say 'is that all there is?' follow your ears to a second that's 50m high.

continue straight to the temple or turn right (east) for the rice fields of Jatiluwih.

The other way is to approach from the east. On the main Denpasar–Singaraja road, look for a small road to the west, just south of the Pacung Indah hotel. Here you follow a series of small paved roads west until you reach the Jatiluwih rice fields. You'll get lost, but locals will quickly set you right and the scenery is superb anyway. Combine the two routes for a nice circle tour.

◉ Sights & Activities

TOP CHOICE **Pura Luhur Batukau**   TEMPLE
(donation 10,000Rp) On the slopes of Gunung Batukau, Pura Luhur Batukau was the state temple when Tabanan was an independent kingdom. It has a seven-roofed *meru* dedicated to Maha Dewa, the mountain's guardian spirit, as well as shrines for Bratan, Buyan and Tamblingan lakes. This is certainly the most spiritual temple you can easily visit in Bali.

The main *meru* in the inner courtyard have little doors shielding small ceremonial items. Outside the compound, the temple is surrounded by forest and the atmosphere is cool and misty; the chants of priests are backed by birds singing.

Facing the temple, take a short walk around to the left to see a small whitewater stream where the air resonates with tumbling water. Note the unusual fertility shrine.

There's a general lack of touts and other characters here – including hordes of tourists. A sign indicates that 'mad ladies/gentlemen' are not allowed to visit. Look sane. Respect traditions and act appropriately

while visiting temples. Sarongs can be borrowed. Get here early for the best chance of seeing the dark and foreboding slopes of the volcano.

Gunung Batukau   VOLCANO
At Pura Luhur Batukau you are fairly well up the side of Gunung Batukau. For the trek to the top of the 2276m peak, you'll need a guide, which can be arranged at the temple ticket booth. Expect to pay 1,000,000Rp for a muddy and arduous journey that will take at least seven hours in one direction.

The rewards are amazing views alternating with thick dripping jungle, and the knowledge that you've taken a trail that is much less travelled than the ones on the eastern peaks. You can get a taste of the adventure on a two-hour mini-jaunt (200,000Rp for two).

🛏 Sleeping

Two remote lodges are hidden away on the slopes of Gunung Batukau. You reach both via a spectacular small and twisting road that makes a long inverted V far up the mountain from Bajera and Pucuk on the main Tabanan–Gilimanuk road in west Bali.

TOP CHOICE **Sarinbuana Eco-Lodge**   LODGE **$$**
(☑743 5198; www.baliecolodge.com; Sarinbuana; bungalows from US$120; 🛜) These beautiful two-level bungalows are built on the side of a hill just a 10-minute walk from a protected rainforest preserve. Notable amenities include fridges, marble bathrooms and handmade soap. It's all rather rustic luxe. There are extensive cultural workshops and trekking opportunities. The lodge has a long list

of green practices and the organic Balinese restaurant is excellent.

Many of the vegetables are grown in the lodge's garden.

Bali Mountain Retreat LODGE $$
(082 8360 2645; www.balimountainretreat.com; r 260,000-850,000Rp;) Luxurious rooms set in refined cottages are arrayed artistically at this hillside location. A pool and gardens mix with mannered architecture that combines new and old influences. Some rooms have large verandas perfect for contemplating the views. Budget options include a bed in a vintage rice-storage barn. There are excellent treks in all directions.

Getting There & Away

The only realistic way to explore the Gunung Batukau area is with your own transport.

THE ANTOSARI ROAD

0361

Although most people cross the mountains via Candikuning or Kintamani, there is a very scenic third alternative that links Bali's south and north coasts. From the Denpasar–Gilimanuk road in west Bali, a road goes north from Antosari through the village of Pupuan and then drops down to Seririt, west of Lovina in north Bali.

Starting through rice paddies, after 8km the road runs alongside a beautiful valley of rice terraces. Another 2km brings you to **Sari Wisata** (0812 398 8773), where a charming family has created what should be the model for roadhouses everywhere. Gorgeous gardens line the bluff and only

enhance the already remarkable vistas. (Did somebody tell the rice farmers to wear red so they pop from the fields of green?) Snacks and drinks are available, and outside you'll find some remarkably healthy and furry bats literally hanging around in the sun.

Once you're deep in the foothills of Gunung Batukau, 20km north of Antosari, you'll smell the fragrant spice-growing village of **Sanda** before you see it. Look for the old wooden elevated rice barns that still feature in every house.

After another 8km north through coffee plantations, you'll reach Pupuan. From here it is 12km or so to Mayong, where you can turn east to Munduk and on to Danau Bratan or go straight on to Seririt.

Sleeping & Eating

TOP CHOICE **Sanda Bukit Villas & Restaurant** LODGE $$
(0828 372 0055; www.sandavillas.com; bungalows from US$90-105;) This boutique hotel offers a serene escape. Its large infinity pool seems to disappear into the rice terraces, while the seven bungalows are really quite luxe. It's well run and the fusion cafe is excellent (dinner from US$5). The engaging owners will recommend walks among the coffee plantations and rice fields. It is just north of the village of Sanda.

Kebun Villas LODGE $$
(780 6068; www.kebunvilla.com; r US$70-95;) Eight antique-filled cottages here are scattered down a hillside and make the most of the sweeping views over rice fields in the valley. The pool area is a hike down to the valley floor but is huge, and once there you may just linger all day. The cafe serves tasty food.

North Bali

Best Places to Eat

» Damai (p240)

» Jasmine Kitchen (p240)

» Seyu (p240)

» Tanjung Alam (p240)

Best Places to Stay

» Taman Sari Bali Cottages (p243)

» Taman Selini Beach Bungalows (p243)

» Pondok Sari (p243)

» Damai (p239)

Why Go?

The land on the other side, that's north Bali. Although one-sixth of the island's population lives here, the vast region is overlooked by many visitors who stay trapped in the south Bali–Ubud axis.

The two big draws are Lovina, the sleepy beach town with cheap hotels and even cheaper sunset beer specials; and Pemuteran. The latter is everything a mellow beach resort should be, with appealing hotels arrayed around a small bay. The major draw is diving and snorkelling at nearby Pulau Menjangan in west Bali.

Getting to north Bali for once lives up to the cliché: it's half the fun. Routes follow the thinly populated coastlines east and west, or you can go up and over the mountains by any number of routes, marvelling at crater lakes and maybe stopping for a misty trek on the way.

When to Go

Most of north Bali doesn't have a high season in terms of visitors. The exception is Pemuteran, which is busy July, August and the weeks around Christmas and New Year. Weather-wise it's always drier in the north as opposed to south Bali. Days of perpetual sun are the norm year-round (most visitors like air-con for sleeping). The only real variation will be found when you venture back into the hills for waterfalls or hikes; mornings will be cool.

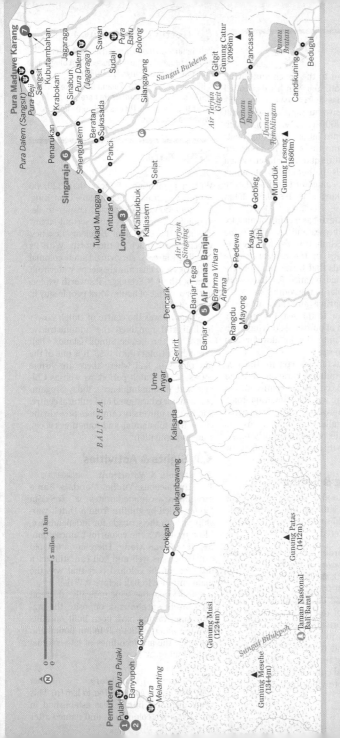

North Bali Highlights

1. Exploring underwater marvels while staying at **Pemuteran** (p242), an idyllic beach town

2. Wandering the beach in front of **Pemuteran's resorts** (p243), trying to choose where to have dinner

3. Losing track of time at **Lovina** (p235), but not of your budget

4. Going for a hike in the lush hills that line north Bali, especially to **hidden waterfalls** (p235) for a swim

5. Getting dirty in the healthy mud of **Air Panas Banjar** (p242)

6. Savouring Buleleng's rich culture at the museums of **Singaraja** (p232), which has a long royal history

7. Marvelling at the carving all around the artful temple **Pura Maduwe Karang** (p235)

Yeh Sanih

☏0362

On the coast road to the beach and diving towns of east Bali, Yeh Sanih (also called Air Sanih) is a hassle-free seaside spot. It's named for its fresh-water springs, **Air Sanih** (adult/child 3000/1000Rp; ☺8am-6pm), which are channelled into large swimming pools before flowing into the sea. The pools are particularly picturesque at sunset, when throngs of locals bathe under blooming frangipani trees – most of the time they're alive with frolicking kids. It's about 15km east of Singaraja.

Pura Ponjok Batu has a commanding location between the sea and the road, some 7km east of Yeh Sanih. It has some very fine limestone carvings in the central temple area. Legend holds that it was built to provide some spiritual balance for Bali, what with all the temples in the south.

Between the springs and the temple, the road is often close to the sea. It's probably Bali's best stretch of pure coast driving, with waves crashing onto the breakwater and great views out to sea.

Completely out of character for the area is a place run by quite a character: **Art Zoo** (www.symonstudios.com; ☺8am-6pm) is 5.7km east of Yeh Sanih on the Singaraja road. Symon, the irrepressible American artist (who also has a gallery in Ubud), owns this gallery and studio, which are fairly bursting with a creativity at times vibrant, exotic and erotic.

🛏 Sleeping & Eating

A few warung (food stalls) hover near the entrance of Yeh Sanih and do a brisk business with the local trade. Otherwise, options are few and scattered.

Cilik's Beach Garden GUESTHOUSE $$
(☏0812 360 1473; www.ciliksbeachgarden.com; r/villas from €60/100; ☻) Coming here is like visiting your rich friends, albeit ones with good taste. These custom-built villas, located 3km east of Yeh Sanih, are large and have extensive private gardens. Other accommodation is in stylish *lumbung* (rice barns with round roofs) set in a delightful garden facing the ocean. There's a real emphasis on local culture; the owners have even more remote villas further south on the coast.

ⓘ Getting There & Away

Yeh Sanih is on the main road along the north coast. Frequent bemo and buses from Singaraja stop outside the springs (10,000Rp).

If heading to Amed or Tulamben, make certain you're on your way south from here by 4pm in order to arrive while there's still some light to avoid road hazards.

Singaraja

☏0362

With a population of more than 120,000 people, Singaraja (which means 'Lion King' and somehow hasn't caused Disney to demand licensing fees) is Bali's second-largest city and the capital of Buleleng Regency, which covers much of the north. With its tree-lined streets, surviving Dutch colonial buildings and charmingly sleepy waterfront area north of Jl Erlangga, it's worth exploring for a couple of hours. Most people stay in nearby Lovina.

Singaraja was the centre of Dutch power in Bali and remained the administrative centre for the Lesser Sunda Islands (Bali through to Timor) until 1953. It is one of the few places in Bali where there are visible traces of the Dutch period, as well as Chinese and Muslim influences. Today, Singaraja is a major educational and cultural centre, and its two university campuses provide the city with a substantial, and sometimes vocal, student population.

⊙ Sights & Activities

Old Harbour & Waterfront NEIGHBOURHOOD
The conspicuous **Yudha Mandala Tama monument** commemorates a freedom fighter killed by gunfire from a Dutch warship early in the struggle for independence. Close by, there's the colourful Chinese temple, **Ling Gwan Kiong**. There are a few old canals here as well and you can still get a little feel of the colonial port that was the main entrance to Bali before WWII.

Check out the cinematically decrepit **old Dutch warehouses** opposite the water. Some warung have been built on stilts over the water. Walk up Jl Imam Bonjol and you'll see the art deco lines of late-colonial Dutch buildings.

FREE **Gedong Kirtya Library** LIBRARY
(☏22 645; ☺8am-4pm Mon-Thu, to 1pm Fri) This small historical library was established in 1928 by Dutch colonialists and named after

Singaraja

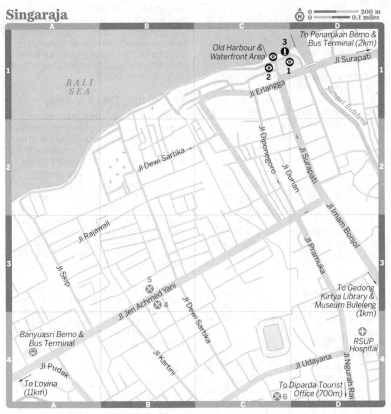

the Sanskrit for 'to try'. It has a collection of *lontar* (dried palm leaves) books, as well as some even older written works in the form of inscribed copper plates called *prasasti*. Dutch publications, dating back to 1901, may interest students of the colonial period.

FREE Museum Buleleng   MUSEUM

(Jl Veteran; 9am-4pm Mon-Fri) Museum Buleleng recalls the life of the last radja (rajah; prince) of Buleleng, Pandji Tisna, who is credited with developing Lovina's tourism. Among the items here is the Royal (brand) typewriter he used during his career as a travel writer (obviously, the rajah was a smart, if poorly remunerated guy) before his death in 1978. It also traces the history of the region back to when there was no history.

🎎 Festivals & Events

Consult with the Diparda tourist office for details on the following festivals.

Singaraja

◎ Sights

1 Ling Gwan Kiong	C1
2 Old Dutch Warehouses	C1
3 Yudha Mandala Tama Monument	C1

✷ Eating

4 Dapur Ibu	B3
5 Istana Bakery	B3
6 Manalagi	C4

Bali Art Festival of Buleng   ART FESTIVAL

Every May or June, the Bali Art Festival of Buleleng is held in Singaraja and surrounding villages. Over one week dancers and musicians from some of the region's most renowned village troupes, such as those of Jagaraga, perform.

LONTAR BOOKS

Lontar is made from the fan-shaped leaves of the *rontal* palm. The leaf is dried, soaked in water, cleaned, steamed, dried again, then flattened, dyed and eventually cut into strips. The strips are inscribed with words and pictures using a very sharp blade or point, then coated with a black stain which is wiped off – the black colour stays in the inscription. A hole in the middle of each *lontar* strip is threaded onto a string, with a carved bamboo 'cover' at each end to protect the 'pages', and the string is secured with a couple of *kepeng* (Chinese coins with a hole in the centre).

The Gedong Kirtya Library in Singaraja has the world's largest collection of *lontar* works.

North Bali Festival   TRADITIONAL ARTS
In August, the North Bali Festival is a celebration of the traditional arts of the regency.

✖️ Eating

Istana Bakery   BAKERY **$**
(☑21 983; Jl Jen Achmed Yani; snacks 3000Rp; ⊙8am-6pm) Fallen in love in Lovina? Get your wedding cake here. For lesser life moments like the munchies, choose from an array of tasty baked goods.

Manalagi   BALINESE **$**
(Jl Sahadewa 8A; meals from 15,000Rp) Down a pretty, tree-shaded street, this Balinese restaurant sits in its own compound and is very popular with locals looking for a special meal that includes fresh fish. The building, with its deep verandas, feels colonial.

Dapur Ibu   INDONESIAN **$**
(☑24 474; Jl Jen Achmed Yani; meals 10,000-20,000Rp) A nice local cafe with a small garden off the street. The *nasi goreng* (fried rice) is fresh and excellent; wash it down with a fresh juice or bubble tea.

ℹ️ Information

Medical Services
RSUP Hospital (☑22 046; Jl Ngurah Rai; ⊙24hr) Singaraja's hospital is the largest in northern Bali.

Tourist Information
Diparda (☑25 141; www.northbalitourism.com; Jl Ngurah Rai 2; ⊙7.30am-3.30pm Mon-Fri) Near the museum, the regional tourist office has some OK maps. Good information if you ask specifically about dance and other cultural events. Useful website.

ℹ️ Getting There & Away

Singaraja is the main transport hub for the northern coast, with three bemo/bus terminals. From the Sukasada terminal, 3km south of town, minibuses go sporadically to Denpasar (Ubung terminal, 35,000Rp) via Bedugul/Pancasari.

The Banyuasri terminal, on the western side of town, has buses heading to Gilimanuk (25,000Rp, two hours) and Java, and plenty of bemo to Lovina (10,000Rp).

The Penarukan terminal, 2km east of town, has bemo to Yeh Sanih (10,000Rp) and Amlapura (about 20,000Rp, three hours) via the coastal road; and also minibuses to Denpasar (Batubulan terminal, 35,000Rp, three hours) via Kintamani.

TO JAVA From Singaraja, several companies have services, which include the ferry trip across the Bali Strait. Buses go as far as Yogyakarta (from 350,000Rp, 16 hours) and Jakarta (from 500,000Rp, 24 hours); book at Banyuasri terminal a day before.

ℹ️ Getting Around

Bemo link the three main bemo/bus terminals and cost about 7000Rp.

Around Singaraja

The interesting sites around Singaraja include some of Bali's most important temples.

SANGSIT
A few kilometres northeast of Singaraja you can see an excellent example of the colourful architectural style of north Bali. Sangsit's **Pura Beji** is a temple for the *subak* (village association of rice-growers), dedicated to the goddess Dewi Sri, who looks after irrigated rice fields. The over-the-top sculptured panels along the front wall set the tone with cartoonlike demons and amazing *naga* (mythical snakelike creatures). The inside also has a variety of sculptures covering every available space. It's 500m off the main road towards the coast.

The **Pura Dalem** (Temple of the Dead) shows scenes of punishment in the afterlife, and other humorous, sometimes erotic, pictures. You'll find it in the rice fields, about 500m northeast of Pura Beji.

Buses and bemo going east from Singaraja's Penarukan terminal will stop at Sangsit.

GITGIT
Around about 11km south of Singaraja, a well-signposted path goes 800m west from the main road to the touristy waterfall, **Air Terjun Gitgit** (adult/child 10,000/5000Rp). The path is lined with souvenir stalls and guides to nowhere. The 40m waterfalls pound away and the mists are more refreshing than any air-con.

About 2km further up the hill, there's a multitiered **waterfall** (donation 5000Rp) about 600m off the western side of the main road. The path crosses a narrow bridge and follows the river up past several small sets of waterfalls, through verdant jungle.

Regular bemo and minibuses between Denpasar and Singaraja stop at Gitgit. Gitgit is also a major stop on organised tours of central and north Bali.

Lovina

📞 0362

'Relaxed' is how people most often describe Lovina and they are correct. This low-key, low-rise beach resort is the polar opposite of Kuta. Days are slow and so are the nights. The waves are calm, the beach is thin and overamped attractions nil.

This is where you catch up on your journal and get plenty of R&R, finish a book or simply let one day disappear into the next.

While not arid, Lovina is also not a tropical jungle. It's sun-drenched, with patches of shade from palm trees. A highlight every afternoon at fishing villages like Anturan is watching *prahu* (traditional outrigger canoes) being prepared for the night's fishing; as sunset reddens the sky, the lights of the fishing boats appear as bright dots across the horizon.

The Lovina tourist area stretches over 8km, and consists of a string of coastal villages – Kaliasem, Kalibukbuk, Anturan, Tukad Mungga – collectively known as Lovina. The main focus is Kalibukbuk, 10.5km west of Singaraja and the heart of Lovina. Daytime traffic on the main road can be loud and constant.

⊙ Sights & Activities

Beaches
The beaches are made up of washed-out grey and black volcanic sand, and while they're mostly clean near the hotel areas, they're not spectacular. Reefs protect the shore, calming the waves and keeping the water clear.

A paved **beach footpath** runs along the sand in Kalibukbuk and extends in a circuitous path along the seashore; it ranges from clean to grubby. Enjoy the postcard view to the east of the mountainous north Bali coast. You'll also enjoy that the sleepy vibe extends to the vendors, who are mostly somnolent.

The best beach areas include the main beach east of the **Dolphin Monument**, as well as the curving stretch a bit west. The cluster of cheap hotels in Anturan also enjoy fun on the sand. While moored near shore, the fishing boats can fascinate with their large, bare engines, menacing-looking props and individual paint schemes.

Dolphin-Watching
Sunrise boat trips to see dolphins are Lovina's much-hyped tourist attraction, so much

---

DON'T MISS

BALI'S FIRST CYCLIST

Pura Maduwe Karang (Temple of the Land Owner) is one of the most intriguing temples in north Bali and is particularly notable for its sculptured panels, including the famous stone-carved **bicycle relief** that depicts a gentleman riding a bicycle with a lotus flower serving as the back wheel. It's on the base of the main plinth in the inner enclosure. The cyclist may be WOJ Nieuwenkamp, a Dutch artist who, in 1904, brought what was probably the first bicycle to Bali.

Like Pura Beji at Sangsit, this temple of dark stone is dedicated to agricultural spirits, but this one looks after nonirrigated land. The temple is easy to find in the village of Kubutambahan – seek the 34 carved figures from the *Ramayana* outside the walls. Kubutambahan is on the road between Singaraja and Amlapura, about 1km east of the turn-off to Kintamani. Regular bemo and buses pass through.

Lovina

so that a large, concrete-crowned monument was erected in their honour.

Some days no dolphins are sighted, but most of the time at least a few surface.

Expect pressure from your hotel and touts selling dolphin trips. The price is fixed at 50,000Rp per person by the boat-owners' cartel. Trips start at a non-holiday-like 6am and last about two hours. Note that the ocean can get pretty crowded with loud, roaring powerboats.

There's great debate about what all this means to the dolphins. Do they like being chased by boats? If not, why do they keep coming back? Maybe it's the fish, of which there are plenty off Lovina.

Diving

Scuba diving on the local reef is better at lower depths and night diving is popular. Many people stay here and dive Pulau Menjangan, a two-hour drive west.

Spice Dive   DIVING
(☑41 512; www.balispicedive.com) Spice Dive is a large operation. It offers snorkelling trips (€25), local intro dives (€45) and popular Menjangan trips (€60). It's based at the west end of the beach path.

Snorkelling

Generally, the water is clear and some parts of the reef are quite good for snorkelling, though the coral has been damaged by bleaching and, in places, by dynamite fishing. The best place is to the west, a few hundred metres offshore from Billibo Beach Cottages. A boat trip will cost about 50,000Rp per person for two people for two hours, including equipment.

Hiking

TOP CHOICE Komang Dodik   HIKING
(☑0877 6291 5128; lovina.tracking@gmail.com) Komang Dodik leads highly recommended

Lovina

hikes in the hills along the north coast. Trips start at 250,000Rp per person and can last from three to seven hours. The highlight of most is a series of waterfalls, over 20m high, in a jungle grotto. Routes can include coffee and vanilla plantations.

Cycling
The roads south of Jl Raya Lovina are excellent for biking, with limited traffic and enjoyable rides amid the rice fields and into the hills for views. Many of the sites beyond Lovina to the west are easily reached by bike.

Most hotels can hire you a bike from 30,000Rp per day.

Other Activities
⊤ᴏᴘ/ **Warung Bambu**
CHOICE/
Pemaron COOKING COURSE
(☑31 455; www.warung-bambu.mahanara.com; Pemaron; 1/2 persons 500,000/660,000Rp; ⊙8am-1pm) Start with a trip to Singaraja's large food market and then in a breezy setting amid rice fields east of Lovina, learn to cook up to eight classic Balinese dishes. The staff are charmers and the fee includes transport within the area. And when you're done you get to feast on your labours.

Araminth Spa SPA
(☑0812 384 4655; www.araminthspa.com; Jl Ketapang; massage from 150,000Rp; ⊙10am-7pm) Araminth Spa offers many types of therapies and massages, including Balinese, Ayurveda and foot massage, in a simple but soothing setting.

🛏 Sleeping

Hotels are spread out along Jl Raya Lovina, and on the side roads going off to the beach. Overall, choices tend to be more budget-focused; don't come here for a luxe experience. Be wary of hotels right on the main road; however, those with rooms down by the water are just fine.

During slow periods in Lovina, all room prices are negotiable but beware of touts who will literally lead you astray and quote prices which include a large kickback to the tout.

ANTURAN
A few tiny side tracks and one proper sealed road, Jl Kubu Gembong, lead to this lively little fishing village, busy with swimming locals and moored fishing boats. It's a real travellers' hang-out. But it's a long way from Lovina's evening delights – expect to pay around 20,000Rp for transport back to Anturan from Kalibukbuk.

Puspa Rama
GUESTHOUSE $

(☎42 070; agungdayu@yahoo.com; Jl Kubu Gembong; r 150,000Rp; ☜) The best budget option on this street, Puspa Rama has grounds a few cuts above the others. The six rooms have hot water. Fruit trees abound – why not pick your own breakfast? Wi-fi is in the common area.

Gede Home Stay Bungalows
HOMESTAY $

(☎41 526; gedehomestay@yahoo.com; Jl Kubu Gembong; r 200,000-300,000Rp; ❋☜) Don't forget to shake the sand off your feet as you enter this beachside eight-room homestay. Cheap rooms have cold water while better ones have hot water and air-con.

ANTURAN TO KALIBUKBUK

Jl Pantai Banyualit has many hotels, although the beach is not very inspiring. There is a little parklike area by the water and the walk along the shore to Kalibukbuk is quick and scenic.

TOP CHOICE Villa Taman Ganesha
GUESTHOUSE $$

(☎41 272; www.taman-ganesha-lovina.com; Jl Kartika 45; r €30-60; ❋☜✉) Down a quiet lane lined with Balinese family compounds is this lovely guesthouse. The grounds are lush and fragrant with frangipani from around the world that have been collected by the owner, a landscape architect from Germany. There's a large pool. The four units are very private and have all the comforts of home. The beach is 400m away and it's a 10-minute walk along the sand to Kalibukbuk.

Hotel Banyualit
HOTEL $$

(☎41 789; www.banyualit.com; Jl Pantai Banyualit; r from 650,000Rp; ❋☜✉) About 100m back from the beach, the Banyualit has a lush garden, statues and a large pool. The 23 rooms offer great choice; best are the good-value villas with whirlpools, fridges and large, shady patios. There's also a small spa.

Suma
GUESTHOUSE $

(☎41 566; www.sumahotel.com; Jl Pantai Banyualit; r 200,000-700,000Rp; ❋@☜✉) In this mannered stone building, you'll find views of the sea from its upstairs rooms; the best of the 13 have air-con and hot water; newish bungalows are quite nice. The pool is large and naturalistic; there's also a pleasant cafe. A much-renovated temple is nearby.

KALIBUKBUK

A little over 10km from Singaraja, the 'centre' of Lovina is the village of Kalibukbuk. Mellow Jl Mawar is quieter and more pleasant than Jl Binaria. Small gang (alleys) lined with cheap places to stay lead off both streets.

Rambutan Hotel
HOTEL $$

(☎41 388; www.rambutan.org; Jl Mawar; r US$25-80, villas US$95-190; ❋@☜✉) The hotel, on one hectare of lush gardens, features two pools, a playground and games for all ages. The 28 rooms are tasteful and decorated with Balinese style. The very cheapest have fans and cold water. Villas are good deals and have a sense of style. The largest are good for families and have kitchens. Wi-fi is best near the restaurant.

Sea Breeze Cabins
GUESTHOUSE $

(☎41 138; Jl Bina Ria; r 350,000-400,000Rp; ❋✉) One of the best choices in the heart of Kalibukbuk and situated right off Jl Binaria, the Sea Breeze has five appealing bungalows by the pool and beach, some with sensational views from their verandas. Two economy rooms have fans and hot water.

Harris Homestay
HOMESTAY $

(☎41 152; Gang Binaria; r 120,000-150,000Rp) Sprightly and white, Harris avoids the weary look of some neighbouring cheapies. The charming family live in back; guests enjoy bright, modern rooms up front.

Nirwana Seaside Cottages
HOTEL $

(☎41 288; www.nirwanaseaside.com; r 200,000-600,000Rp; ❋☜✉) On large and deeply shaded beachfront grounds, the 30-unit Nirwana offers a wide range of rooms. The bungalows are a bit fusty but have hot water. A modern two-storey wing has hotel-style air-con rooms with satellite TV. The pool areas are made from natural stone and have a dash of tropical style. Wi-fi is only in the cafe.

Puri Bali Hotel
HOTEL $

(☎41 485; www.puribalilovina.com; Jl Mawar; r 180,000-800,000Rp; ❋✉) The pool area is set deep in a lush garden – you could easily hang out here all day and let any cares wander off to the ether. The better of the 24 rooms, with hot water and air-con, are simple but comfortable. The cheapest, with fans and cold water, are simply simple.

Padang Lovina
GUESTHOUSE $

(☎41 302; padanglovina@yahoo.com; Gang Binaria; r 150,000-350,000Rp; ✻ ⓢ ⌗) Down a narrow lane in the very heart of Kalibukbuk. There's no pretension at all around the 14 comfortable bungalow-style rooms set around spacious grounds teeming with flowers. The nicest rooms have air-con and bathtubs. There's wi-fi at the pool.

Rini Hotel
HOTEL $

(☎41 386; www.rinihotel.com; Jl Mawar; r 200,000-400,000Rp; ✻ ⓢ ⌗) This tidy 30-room place has a large pool. Cheaper rooms have fans and cold water but the more expensive ones are huge, with air-con and hot water. In fact, should you come across a keg, you could have a party. A big one.

WEST OF KALIBUKBUK

Lovina Beach Hotel
HOTEL $

(☎41 005; www.lovinabeachhotel.com; Jl Raya Lovina; r 250,000-400,000Rp; ✻ ⓢ ⌗) This older, well-run beach hotel hasn't changed in years and neither have its prices. The 24 rooms, in a two-storey block, are clean if a bit frayed. Bungalows feature carving and Balinese details, the ones on the beach are a bargain. The grounds feel like a park.

Aditya Beach Resort
HOTEL $$

(☎41 059; www.adityalovina.com; r US$50-105; ✻ ⓢ ⌗) There are 64 rooms at this big hotel on a sandy beach. The best have views of the ocean and all have a good range of amenities and attractive bathrooms. Swim in the large pool, or in the ocean? Sit on your patio while you're deciding.

Hotel Purnama
HOMESTAY $

(☎41 043; Jl Raya Lovina; r from 80,000Rp) One of the best deals on this stretch, Hotel Purnama has seven clean cold-water rooms, and the beach is only a two-minute walk away. This is a family compound, and a friendly one at that.

AROUND LOVINA

TOP CHOICE Damai
HOTEL $$$

(☎41 008; www.damai.com; villas US$210-450; ✻ ⓢ ⌗) Set on a hillside behind Lovina, Damai has the kind of sweeping views you'd expect. Its 14 luxury villas mix antiques and a modern style accented by beautiful Balinese fabrics. The infinity pool seemingly spills onto a landscape of peanut fields, rice paddies and coconut palms.

Larger villas have private pools and multiple rooms that flow from one to another.

WORTH A TRIP

BACK ROADS DISCOVERIES

The back roads around Singaraja offer interesting, seldom-visited discoveries.

» **Jagaraga** The village's Pura Dalem is a small, interesting temple with delightful sculptured panels along its front wall. On the outer wall, look for a vintage car driving sedately past, a steamer at sea and even an aerial dogfight between early aircraft.

» **Sawan** A centre for the manufacturing of gamelan gongs and instruments. You can see the gongs being cast and the intricately carved gamelan frames being fashioned.

The restaurant is lauded for its organic fusion cuisine. Call for transport or, at the main junction in Kalibukbuk, go south on Jl Damai and follow the road for about 3km.

✕ Eating

Just about every hotel has a cafe or restaurant. Walk along the beach footpath to choose from a selection of basic places with cold beer, standard food and sunsets.

ANTURAN

Warung Rasta
SEAFOOD $

(meals 15,000-50,000Rp) Right on a strip of beach, a growing number of tables, chairs and picnic benches mix with fishing boats. The menu not surprisingly leans towards simply grilled fresh seafood; given the name, the endless loop of music shouldn't surprise either. It's run by dudes who have clearly realised that lounging around here all day beats fishing.

Babi Guling
BALINESE $

(Jl Raya Lovina; meals 20,000Rp; ⓢ11am-4pm) Generically named for the dish it offers, this simple stand is 1km east of Anturan beside the main road to Singaraja. Highly spiced roasted baby pig is served on platters with rice.

ANTURAN TO KALIBUKBUK

Bakery Lovina
CAFE

(Jl Raya Lovina; ✻) Enjoy Lovina's best cup of coffee amid groceries at this upmarket deli that is a short walk from the centre. The croissants and German breads are baked fresh daily and there's a short selection of fresh specials.

Warung Dolphin   SEAFOOD $

(☑0813 5327 6985; Jl Pantai Banyualit; meals 25,000-70,000Rp) Near the beach, this cheery hang-out for dolphin-tour skippers serves a fine grilled seafood platter (which was probably caught by the guy next to you). There's live acoustic music many nights; a few other warung serving tasty food are nearby.

Spunky's   INDONESIAN $

(☑41 134; Jl Pantai Banyualit; meals 20,000-70,000Rp) A real comer in the sunset drinks department, sprightly Spunky's serves Indonesian classics right on the beach. Like Lovina, it's a snoozy place day and night; walk here from anywhere along the sand.

KALIBUKBUK

This is ground zero for nightlife. There's a good range of restaurants, beachside cafes, bars where you can get a pizza and maybe hear some music, or fun places that defy description.

TOP CHOICE **Jasmine Kitchen**   THAI $$

(☑41 565; Gang Binaria; meals 40,000-100,000Rp) The Thai fare at this elegant two-level restaurant lives up to the promise of the trays of chillies drying out front: it's excellent. The menu is long and authentic and the staff gracious. While soft jazz plays, try the homemade ice cream for dessert. You can refill water bottles here for 2000Rp.

TOP CHOICE **Seyu**   JAPANESE $$

(www.seyulovina.com; Jl Binaria; dishes from 40,000Rp; ☎) A great addition to Lovina, this truly authentic Japanese place has a skilled sushi chef and a solid list of fresh nigiri and sashimi choices. The dining room is suitably spare and uncomplicated.

Akar   VEGETARIAN $

(☑0817 972 4717; Jl Binaria; meals 30,000-50,000Rp; ☑) The many shades of green at this cute-as-a-baby-frog cafe aren't just for show. They reflect the earth-friendly ethics of the owners. Refill your water containers here and then enjoy organic smoothies and fresh and tasty noodle dishes that include Asian sesame, beetroot and cheese lasagne and chilli garlic spaghetti. A tiny back porch overlooks the river.

Khi Khi Restaurant   CHINESE $

(☑41 548; meals 10,000-100,000Rp) Well off Jl Raya Lovina and behind the night market, this barn of a place specialises in Chinese food and grilled seafood, including lobster. It's always popular in a rub-elbows-with-your-neighbour kind of way.

Sea Breeze Café   INDONESIAN $

(☑41 138; meals 25,000-60,000Rp) Right by the beach off Jl Binaria, this breezy cafe is the better of the beachside choices. It has Indonesian and Western dishes and excellent breakfasts, all served by an excellent, hard-working staff.

Le Madre   ITALIAN $

(☑0817 554 399; Jl Mawar; meals 40,000-70,000Rp) Two married chefs who worked at some of south Bali's best Italian restaurants run this cute little cafe that looks like somebody's home (actually it is). Enjoy fresh pasta and seafood with crusty Italian bread that's baked daily.

Pappagallo   INTERNATIONAL $

(☑41 163; Jl Binaria; meals 40,000-60,000Rp) A three-level travellers' cafe in the heart of town – the views from the top are good at sunset. Wood-fired ovens on the ground floor produce pizzas and fresh baguettes for sandwiches. There's also pasta and Indo classics.

Night Market   BALINESE

(Jl Raya Lovina; meals from 15,000Rp; ☺5-11pm) Lovina's night market is a good choice for fresh and cheap local food. Each year it adds a few more interesting stands.

AROUND LOVINA

TOP CHOICE **Damai**   FUSION $$$

(☑41 008; www.damai.com; lunch US$5-15, 5-course dinner from US$50) Enjoy the renowned organic restaurant at the boutique hotel in the hills behind Lovina. Tables enjoy views across the north coast. The changing menu draws its fresh ingredients from the hotel's organic farm and the local fishing fleet. Dishes are artful and the wine list one of the best in Bali. Sunday brunch is popular. Call for pick-up.

TOP CHOICE **Tanjung Alam**   SEAFOOD $$

(Jl Raya Lovina; meals 30,000-80,000Rp) You'll see the fragrant column of smoke rising through the palms before you find this entirely open-air waterfront restaurant where grilled seafood is king. Settle back at one of the shady tables, let the gentle lapping of the nearby waves soothe you and enjoy an affordable feast. It's 1.2km west of the centre.

Drinking

Plenty of places to eat are also good for just a drink, especially those on the beach. Happy hours abound. The following are some of the top picks in Kalibukbuk.

Kantin 21 BAR
(☏0812 460 7791; Jl Raya Lovina; ⊙11am-1am) Funky open-air place where you can watch traffic by day and groove to acoustic guitar or garage-band rock by night. There's a long drinks list (jugs of Long Island iced tea for 80,000Rp), fresh juices and a few local snacks. The old VW bus out front completes the groovy tableau.

Poco Lounge BAR
(☏41 535; Jl Binaria; ⊙11am-1am) Movies are shown at various times, and cover bands perform at this popular bar-cafe. Classic travellers' fare is served at tables open to street life in front and the river in back.

☆ Entertainment

Some of the joints on Jl Binaria have live music, follow your ears.

Pashaa CLUB
(www.pashaabalinightclub.com; Jl Raya Lovina; ⊙8pm-late Tue-Sat) A small but high-concept club near the centre; DJs from around the island mix it up and bikini-clad dancers seem utterly tireless.

❶ Information

If you're planning a reading holiday in Lovina, come prepared as there are just a couple of used-book stalls.

Internet Access
Fast internet access is common.
Spice Cyber (☏41 305; Jl Binaria; per min 200Rp; ⊙8am-midnight; ☎) Printing and burning services.

Medical Services
Guardian (Jl Raya Lovina) Local outlet of the international pharmacy chain.

Money
There are many ATMs along Jl Raya Lovina in Kalibukbuk.

❶ Getting There & Away
Bus & Bemo
To reach Lovina from south Bali by public transport, you'll need to change in Singaraja. Regular blue bemo go from Singaraja's Banyuasri termi-

nal to Kalibukbuk (about 10,000Rp); you can flag them down anywhere on the main road.

If you're coming by long-distance bus from the west you can ask to be dropped off anywhere along the main road.

Tourist Shuttle Bus
Perama buses stop at its **office** (☏41 161), in front of Hotel Perama on Jl Raya Lovina in Anturan. Passengers are then ferried to other points on the Lovina strip (10,000Rp).

Destination	Fare (Rp)	Duration (hr)
Candidasa	150,000	5½
Kuta	100,000	4
Padangbai	150,000	4¾
Sanur	100,000	3¾
Ubud	100,000	2¾

❶ Getting Around
The Lovina strip is *very* spread out, but you can easily travel back and forth on bemo (5000Rp).

West of Lovina

The main road west of Lovina passes temples, farms and towns while it follows the thinly developed coast. You'll see many vineyards, where the grapes work overtime producing the sugar used in Bali's very sweet local vintages. The road continues to Taman Nasional Bali Barat (West Bali National Park) and the port of Gilimanuk.

AIR TERJUN SINGSING
About 5km west of Lovina, a sign points to Air Terjun Singsing (Daybreak Waterfall), and 1km from the main road, there's a warung on the left and a car park on the right. Walk past the warung and along the path for about 200m to the lower falls. The waterfall isn't huge, but the pool underneath is ideal for swimming, though not crystal clear. The water, cooler than the sea, is very refreshing.

Clamber further up the hill to another, slightly bigger fall, Singsing Dua. It has a mud bath that is supposedly good for the skin (we'll let you decide about this). These falls also cascade into a deep swimming pool.

The area is thick with tropical forest and makes a nice day trip from Lovina. The falls are more spectacular in the wet season (October to March), and may be just a trickle other times.

AIR PANAS BANJAR

These **hot springs** (adult/child 10,000/5000Rp; ⊙8am-6pm) percolate amid lush tropical plants. You can relax here for a few hours and have lunch at the restaurant, or even stay the night.

Eight fierce-faced carved stone *naga* pour water from a natural hot spring into the first bath, which then overflows (via the mouths of five more *naga*), into a second, larger pool. In a third pool, water pours from 3m-high spouts to give you a pummelling massage. The water is slightly sulphurous and pleasantly steamy (about 38°C). You must wear a swimsuit and you shouldn't use soap in the pools, but you can use an adjacent outdoor shower.

Overlooking the baths, there's a simple cafe.

From the bemo stop on the main road to the hot springs you can take an *ojek* (motorcycle that takes passengers); going back is a 2.4km downhill stroll.

SERIRIT

☑0362

This town is a junction for roads that run south through the central mountains to Munduk or to Papuan and west Bali via the beautiful Antosari road or an equally scenic road to Pulukan.

🛏 Sleeping

Zen Resort Bali   INN $$

(☑93 578; www.zenresortbali.com; r €80-120; ☒)
The name says it all, albeit very calmly, at Zen Resort Bali, a seaside resort devoted to your internal and mental well-being. Rooms in traditional bungalows have a minimalist look designed to not tax the synapses, gardens are dotted with water features and the beach is 200m away. Activities start with yoga and end with a good Ayurvedic cleansing. It's just west of Seririt in the seaside village of Ume Anyar.

PULAKI

Pulaki is famous for its grape vines, watermelons and for **Pura Pulaki**, a coastal temple that was completely rebuilt in the early 1980s, and is home to a large troop of monkeys, as well as troops at a nearby army base.

Pemuteran

☑0362

This oasis in the far northwest corner of Bali has a number of artful resorts set on a little dogbone-shaped bay that's alive with local life such as kids playing soccer until dark. Pemuteran is the place to come for a real beach getaway. Most people dive or snorkel the underwater wonders at nearby Pulau Menjangan while here.

WANT A NEW REEF? CHARGE IT!

Pemuteran is set among a fairly arid part of Bali where people have always had a hard-scrabble existence. In the early 1990s tourism began to take advantage of the excellent diving in the area. Locals who'd previously been scrambling to grow or catch something to eat began getting language and other training to welcome people to what would become a collection of resorts.

But there was one big problem: dynamite and cyanide fishing plus El Niño warming had bleached and damaged large parts of the reef.

A group of local hotels, dive-shop owners and community leaders hit upon a novel solution: grow a new reef using electricity. The idea had already been floated by scientists internationally, but Pemuteran was the first place to implement it on a wide – and hugely successful – scale.

Using local materials, the community built dozens of large metal cages that were placed out along the threatened reef. These were then hooked to *very* low-wattage generators on land (you can see the cables running ashore near the Taman Sari Bali Cottages). What had been a theory became a reality. The low current stimulated limestone formation on the cages which in turn quickly grew new coral. All told, Pemuteran's small bay is getting new coral at five to six times the rate it would take to grow naturally.

The results are win-win all around. Locals and visitors are happy and so are the reefs; the efforts have gained international attention and awards. The local group, **Reef Gardeners of Pemuteran** (www.pemuteranfoundation.com), has an info booth with a sign reading 'Bio Rocks' on the beach by Pondok Sari. Info on their work is in most local resort lobbies.

◉ Sights

Strolling the beach is popular, especially at sunset, as you'd expect. The little fishing village is interesting, and if you walk around to the eastern end of the dogbone, you escape a lot of the development – although new projects are appearing.

Pemuteran is home to the nonprofit Reef Seen Turtle Project, run by **Reef Seen Aquatics** (☑93 001; www.reefseen.com). Turtle eggs and small turtles purchased from locals are looked after here until they're ready for ocean release. More than 8000 turtles have been released since 1994. You can visit the small hatchery and make a donation to sponsor and release a tiny turtle. It's just off the main road, along the beach just east of Taman Selini Beach Bungalows.

🏃 Activities

The extensive coral reefs are about 3km offshore. Coral that's closer in is being restored as part of a unique project. Diving and snorkelling are universally popular. Local dives cost from US$60; snorkelling gear hires from 40,000Rp.

TOP CHOICE **Reef Seen**　　　　　　　DIVING
(☑93 001; www.reefseen.com) Right on the beach in a large compound, Reef Seen is active in local preservation efforts. It is a PADI dive centre and has a full complement of classes. It also offers sunset and sunrise cruises aboard glass-bottomed boats (per person from 250,000Rp), and pony rides on the beach for kids (from 200,000Rp for 30 minutes).

Easy Divers　　　　　　　　　　DIVING
(☑94 736; www.easy-divers.eu) The founder, Dusan Repic, has befriended many a diver new to Bali and this shop is well recommended. It is on the main road near the Taman Sari Bali Cottages and Pondok Sari hotel.

K&K Dive Centre　　　　　　　DIVING
(☑0812 467 9462; www.pemuterandive.com) In the Rare Angon homestay, this diver operation has a loyal following of annual regulars.

🛏 Sleeping & Eating

Pemuteran has one of the nicest selections of beachside hotels in Bali. Many have a sense of style and all are low-key and relaxed, with easy access to the beach, which has nice sand and is good for swimming. There are small warung along the main drag, otherwise all the hotels have good midrange restaurants. You can wander between them along the beach debating which one to choose.

Some of the hotels are accessed directly off the main road, others are off of a small road that follows the west side of the bay.

TOP CHOICE **Taman Sari Bali Cottages**　HOTEL $$
(☑93 264; www.balitamansari.com; bungalows US$50-200; ❄@🛜🏊) Thirty-one rooms are set in gorgeous bungalows that feature intricate carvings and traditional artwork inside and out. The open-air bathrooms inspire extended ablutions. Most rooms are under US$100 – those over are quite palatial. It's located on a long stretch of quiet beach on the bay, and is part of the reef restoration project.

TOP CHOICE **Taman Selini Beach Bungalows**　　　　　BOUTIQUE HOTEL $$
(☑94 746; www.tamanselini.com; r US$100-250; ❄🛜🏊) The 11 bungalows recall an older, refined Bali, from the quaint thatched roofs down to the antique carved doors and detailed stonework. Rooms, which open onto a large garden running to the beach, have four-poster beds and large outdoor bathrooms. The outdoor daybeds can be addictive. It's immediately east of Pondok Sari, on the beach and right off the main road.

Pondok Sari　　　　　　　　　HOTEL $$
(☑94 738; www.pondoksari.com; r €40-170; ❄🏊) There are 36 rooms here set in densely planted gardens that assure privacy. The pool is down by the beach; the cafe has sweet water views through the trees (and serves breakfast until 3pm!). Traditional Balinese details abound; bathrooms are open-air and

---

WORTH A TRIP

THE TEMPLE FOR BUSINESS

About 600m east of Pura Pulaki, a well-signposted 1.7km paved road leads to **Pura Melanting**. This temple has a dramatic setting with steps leading up into the foothills. It's dedicated to good fortune in business. A donation is expected as entry to the complex, although you're not permitted in the main worship area. Look for the dragon statue with the lotus blossom on its back near the entrance as well as villa owners hoping for rentals.

DIVING & SNORKELLING PULAU MENJANGAN

Besides having the best selection of lodgings, Pemuteran is also well placed for diving and snorkelling Menjangan. A dock for boats out to the island is just 7km west of town, so you have only a short ride before you're on a boat for the relaxing and pretty 45-minute journey to Menjangan. The dive shops and all the local hotels run snorkelling trips that cost US$35 to US$50, and dive trips from US$90.

a calling card for the stone-carvers. Deluxe units have elaborate stone tubs among other details. The resort is just off the main road.

Puri Ganesha Villas　　BOUTIQUE HOTEL $$$
(☑94 766; www.puriganeshabali.com; villas US$500-800; ❃@❃) Four two-storey villas on sweeping grounds at the west end of the bay are the basics at Puri Ganesha. Ahh, but the details: each has a unique style that mixes antiques with silks and relaxed comfort. Outside the air-con bedrooms, life is in the open air, including time in your private pool. Dine in the small restaurant or in your villa; the spa is lavish. It is located on the western point of the bay, near Taman Sari.

Amertha Bali Villas　　HOTEL $$
(☑94 831; www.amerthabalivillas.com; r US$80-125, villas US$195-450; ❃❃❃) A slightly older resort with spacious grounds, the Amertha benefits from having large mature trees that give it that timeless tropical cliché. The 14 units are large, with a lot of natural wood and spacious covered patios. Showers are open-air.

Adi Assri　　HOTEL $$
(☑94 838; www.adiassri.com; r US$50-120; ❃❃❃) Amid the village just east of the other hotels, the 60 bungalow-style units here have huge beds, nice porches and views to the beach. A large double pool goes right to the sand. The garden is growing at a tropical pace.

Reef Seen　　GUESTHOUSE $
(☑93 001; www.reefseen.com; r 430,000-610,000Rp; ❃❃) Five simple Balinese-style brick bungalows have open-air bathrooms with showers. This is a well-regarded dive centre and there are room discounts for clients.

Rare Angon Homestay　　HOMESTAY $
(☑94 747, 0812 467 9462; www.pemuterandive.com; r 250,000-500,000Rp; ❃) Good basic rooms in a homestay located on the south side of the main road. K&K Dive Centre is here.

❶ Getting There & Away

Pemuteran is served by any of the buses and bemo on the Gilimanuk–Lovina run. Labuhan Lalang and Taman Nasional Bali Barat are 12km west. It's a three- to four-hour drive from south Bali, either over the hills or around the west coast.

West Bali

Best Places to Eat

» Pondok Pitaya (p250)

» Bali Wisata Bungalows
(p249)

» Pondok Pisces (p250)

Best Places to Stay

» Mimpi Resort Menjangan
(p257)

» Pondok Pitaya (p250)

» Pondok Pisces (p250)

» Gajah Mina (p250)

» Taman Wana Villas & Spa
(p252)

Why Go?

Few who dive or snorkel the rich and pristine waters around Pulau Menjangan forget the experience. It's part of Taman Nasional Bali Barat (West Bali National Park), the only pro-tected place of its kind on the island.

On the coast, waves pound the rocky shore and surfers hit the breaks at funky beaches like Balian and Medewi. Some of Bali's most sacred sites are also here, from the ever-thronging Pura Tanah Lot to the Pura Taman Ayun and on to the wonderful isolation of Pura Rambut Siwi.

The tidy town of Tabanan is at the apex of Bali's Unesco-listed *subak*, the system of irrigation that ensures everybody gets a fair share of the water. On narrow back roads you can cruise beside rushing streams with bamboo arching over-head and fruit piling up below. Or go for the spectacle of huge beasts and flying mud: a bull race.

When to Go

The best time to visit west Bali is during the dry season in April to September, although recent weather patterns have made the dry season wetter and the wet season drier. Hiking and trekking in Taman Nasional Bali Barat is much easier when it isn't muddy, and the waters of Pulau Menjangan are at their world-class best for diving when clear. Along the coast, however, the west has yet to develop a peak season – although surfing is best in months without an 'r'.

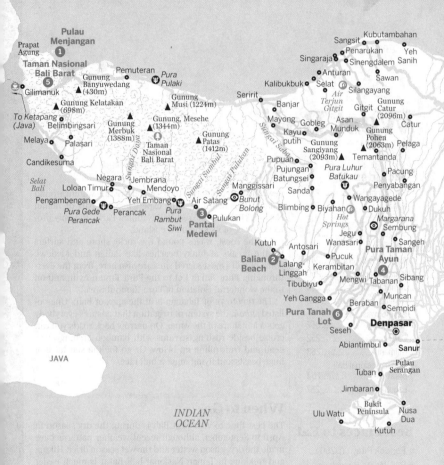

West Bali Highlights

❶ Plunging into the depths
at **Pulau Menjangan** (p256),
Bali's best dive spot, or
enjoying the show while
snorkelling

❷ Revelling in the classic
beach-funk vibe of **Balian
Beach** (p250), where surfer
hangouts and stylish digs rub
shoulders

❸ Nailing the long left break
at **Pantai Medewi** (p251)

❹ Finding your own corner of
serenity at **Pura Taman Ayun**
(p248)

❺ Discovering, by foot or
boat, Bali's national park,
Taman Nasional Bali Barat
(p254), and hoping against
hope to discover Bali's sole

unique species, the possibly
extinct Bali starling

❻ Enjoying the morning
spirituality of **Pura Tanah Lot**
(p247) before it's replaced by
afternoon avarice

❼ Discovering your own
back-road paradise of low-
hanging fruit, arching bamboo
and rushing water

Pura Tanah Lot

♫0361

A popular day trip from south Bali, **Pura Tanah Lot** (adult/child 30,000/15,000Rp, parking 5000Rp) is the most visited and photographed temple in Bali, especially at sunset when crowds and traffic overwhelm the site. However, t has all the authenticity of a stage set – even the tower of rock that the temple sits upon is an artful reconstruction (the entire structure was crumbling) and over one-third of the rock is artificial.

For the Balinese, Pura Tanah Lot is one of the most important and venerated sea temples. Like Pura Luhur Ulu Watu, at the tip of the southern Bukit Peninsula, and Pura Rambut Siwi to the west, it is closely associated with the Majapahit priest Nirartha. It's said that each of the sea temples was intended to be within sight of the next, so they formed a chain along Bali's southwestern coast – from Pura Tanah Lot you can usually see the clifftop site of Pura Ulu Watu far to the south, and the long sweep of sea shore west to Perancak, near Negara.

But at Tanah Lot itself you may just see from one vendor to the next. To reach the temple, a walkway runs through a sideshow of souvenir shops down to the sea. To ease the task of making purchases, there is an ATM.

You can walk onto the temple itself at low tide, but non-Balinese people are not allowed to enter. One other thing: local legend has it that if you bring a partner to Tanah Lot before marriage, you will end up as split as the temple. Let that be a warning – or an inducement.

You won't be able to miss the looming Pan Pacific Nirwana resort with its water-sucking golf course. It's been controversial since the day it was built, as many feel its greater height shows the temple disrespect.

ℹ Getting There & Away

Coming from south Bali take the coastal road west from Kerobokan and follow the signs. From other parts of Bali, turn off the Denpasar–Gilimanuk road near Kediri and follow the signs. During the pre- and post-sunset rush, traffic is awful.

Kapal

About 10km north of Denpasar, Kapal is the garden-feature and temple-doodad centre of Bali. If you need a green tiger or other decorative critter (we saw a pink beaver) rendered in colours not found in nature, then this is your place! (Although shipping might be a pain.) Kapal is on the main road to the west, so it might be worth getting out of the traffic just to walk with the animals.

Marga

Between the walls of traditional family compounds in the village of Marga, there are some beautifully shaded roads – but this town wasn't always so peaceful. On 20 November 1946 a force of 96 independence fighters were surrounded by a much larger and better-armed Dutch force, fighting to regain Bali as a colony after the departure of the Japanese. The outcome was similar to the *puputan* (warrior's fight to the death) of 40 years earlier – Ngurah Rai, who led the resistance against the Dutch (and later had the airport named after him), was killed, along with every one of his men. There was, however, one important difference – this time the Dutch suffered heavy casualties as well, and this may have helped weaken their resolve to hang on to the rebellious colony.

The independence struggle is commemorated at the **Margarana** (admission 5000Rp; ⊙9am-5pm), northwest of Marga village. Tourists seldom visit, but every Balinese schoolchild comes here at least once, and a ceremony is held annually on 20 November. In a large compound stands a 17m-high pillar, and nearby is a **museum** with a few photos, homemade weapons and other artefacts from the conflict (Ngurah Rai's quote-worthy last letter includes the line: 'Freedom or death!'). Behind is a smaller compound with 1372 small stone memorials to those who gave their lives for the cause of independence – they're headstone markers in

---

ENJOYING TANAH LOT

So why shouldn't you skip Tanah Lot? Because it is an important spiritual site and does have an innate beauty. The secret is to arrive before noon: you'll beat the crowds and the vendors will still be asleep. You'll actually hear birds chirping rather than buses idling and people carping. Besides, you can see the sunset from many other places – like a beachfront bar south towards Seminyak.

DON'T MISS

PURA TAMAN AYUN

The huge royal water temple of **Pura Taman Ayun** (adult/child 15,000/7500Rp; ⊙8am-6pm), surrounded by a wide, elegant moat, was the main temple of the Mengwi kingdom, which survived until 1891, when it was conquered by the neighbouring kingdoms of Tabanan and Badung. The large, spacious temple was built in 1634 and extensively renovated in 1937. It's a spacious place to wander around and you can get away from speed-obsessed group-tour mobs ('Back on the bus, pilgrims!'). The first courtyard is a large, open, grassy expanse and the inner courtyard has a multitude of *meru* (multi-tiered shrines). Lotus-blossoms fill the pools. The temple forms part of the *subak* system (village association for rice-growers) of sites recognised by Unesco in 2012 (p249).

Pura Taman Ayun is an easy stop on a drive to/from Bedugal and the Jatiluwih rice terraces. It is also a stop-off on many organised tourist tours.

a military cemetery, though bodies are not actually buried here. Each memorial has a symbol indicating the hero's religion, mostly the Hindu swastika, but also Islamic crescent moons and even a few Christian crosses. Look for the memorials to 11 Japanese who stayed on after WWII and fought with the Balinese against the Dutch.

ℹ Getting There & Away

Even with your own transport it's easy to get lost finding Marga and the memorial, so, as always, ask for directions. You can easily combine this with Pura Taman Ayun and the Jatiluwih rice terraces.

Sangeh

The 14-hectare monkey forest of **Bukit Sari** is strictly for monkey-lovers. There are masses of the creatures here and they will beg food from you and possibly steal something from your bag or head (glasses are a popular item to take). If these sorts of antics don't appeal then you can give this stop a miss.

ℹ Getting There & Away

Most people visit on an organised tour or drive themselves; it's about 20km north of Denpasar.

Tabanan

📞0361

Tabanan, like most regional capitals in Bali, is a large, well-organised place. The verdant surrounding rice fields are emblematic of Bali's rice-growing traditions and are part of its Unesco recognition.

◎ Sights

Mandala Mathika Subak MUSEUM
(Subak Museum; Jl Raya Kediri; adult/child 15,000/7500Rp; ⊙7am-4.30pm) Within a large complex devoted to Tabanan's *subak* organisations, you'll find this museum, which has displays about the irrigation and cultivation of rice and the intricate social systems that govern it. Staff here are very sweet and will show you around; some placards are in English and there is a good model showing the *subak* system in action.

Exhibits are housed in a large building with water streaming by right out front.

🛏 Sleeping & Eating

You can sample village life as part of the **Bali Homestay Program** (📞0817 067 1788; www.bali-homestay.com; r from US$30), an innovative program that places travellers in the homes of residents of the rice-growing village of Jegu, 9km north of Tabanan. Guests (who normally stay at least three nights, packages from US$130) participate in activities like making offerings and go on cultural tours with locals. All meals are included.

There are plenty of warung in the town centre and at the bustling regional market; a tasty **night market** (⊙5pm-midnight) sets up on the south side. Out on the main road, a **babi guling stall** (Jl Bypass; dishes 5000-15,000Rp; ⊙7am-7pm) has batches of fresh-roasted seasoned suckling pork throughout the day.

ℹ Getting There & Away

All bemo and buses between Denpasar (Ubung terminal) and Gilimanuk stop at the terminal at the western end of Tabanan (10,000Rp).

The road to Pura Luhur Batukau and the beautiful rice terraces of Jatiluwih heads north from the centre of town.

South of Tabanan

Driving in the southern part of Tabanan district takes you through many charming villages and past a lot of vigorously growing rice. The fields are revered by many as the most productive in Bali.

Just south of Tabanan, **Kediri** has Pasar Hewan, one of Bali's busiest cattle markets. About 10km south of Tabanan is **Pejaten**, a centre for the production of traditional pottery, including elaborate ornamental roof tiles. Porcelain clay objects, which are made purely for decorative use, can be seen in a few workshops in the village. Check out the small showroom of **CV Keramik Pejaten** (⌨0361-831997), one of several local producers. The trademark pale-green pieces are lovely, and when you see the prices, you'll at least buy a toad.

A little west of Tabanan, a road runs 8km south via Gubug to the secluded coast at **Yeh Gangga**, where there are some good accommodation choices, beach cafes and **Island Horse** (⌨0361-731407; www.baliislandhorse.com; rides adult/child from US$60/55), which offers horse rides along the long flat beach and surrounding countryside.

The next road west from Tabanan turns down to the coast via **Kerambitan**, a village noted for its dance troupe and musicians who perform across the south and in Ubud. Banyan trees shade beautiful old buildings, including two 17th-century palaces. **Puri Anyar Kerambitan** accepts guests and is an attraction in itself with a vast shambolic compound filled with antiques and populated by genial characters. The other palace, **Puri Agung Kerambitan**, is tidy and dull.

About 4km from southern Kerambitan is **Tibubiyu**. For a lovely drive through huge bamboo, fruit trees, rice paddies and more,

take the scenic road northwest from Kerambitan to the main Tabanan–Gilimanuk road.

🛏 Sleeping & Eating

Bali Wisata Bungalows GUESTHOUSE $
(⌨0361-7443561; www.baliwisatabungalows.com; Yeh Gangga; bungalows 260,000-550,000Rp; @☎) Nine kilometres southwest of Tabanan and on the coast at Yeh Gangga, this attractive accommodation has excellent views in a superb setting on 15km of rock and black-sand beach. The cheapest of the 12 rooms have cold water; the best have dramatic oceanfront vistas. The cafe here serves good Balinese food and has splendid views from its open pavilion. It is 9km southwest of Tabanan.

Puri Anyar Kerambitan HOMESTAY $
(⌨0361-812668; giribali@yahoo.co.id; r from 400,000Rp; ❄) Join Anak Agung, the leader of the royal family that lives sitcom style in this intriguing compound. Anak will teach you about kite culture while his son the prince will offer to paint you or do a figure study. Children wandering about provide cute punchlines. The four rooms are filled with royal antiques and vary in tidiness.

North of Tabanan

The area north of Tabanan is good to travel around with your own transport. There are some strictly B-grade attractions; the real appeal here is just driving the fecund back roads where the bamboo arches temple-like over the road.

Antosari & Bajera

At Antosari, the main road takes a sharp turn south to the welcoming breezes of the

WEST BALI SOUTH OF TABANAN

BALI'S UNESCO-RECOGNISED SUBAK

Playing a critical role in rural Bali life, the *subak* is a village association that deals with water, water rights and irrigation. With water passing through many, many scores of rice fields before it drains away for good, there was always the chance that growers near the source would be water-rich while those at the bottom would be selling carved wooden critters at Tanah Lot. Regulating a system that apportions a fair share to everyone is a model of mutual cooperation and an insight into the Balinese character. (One of the strategies used is to put the last person on the water channel in control.)

This complex and vital social system was recognised by Unesco in 2012 and added to the World Heritage List. Specific sites singled out include much of the rice growing region around Tabanan, Pura Taman Ayun and the Jatiluwih rice terraces.

ocean. Turn north and you'll enjoy a scenic drive to north Bali (p229).

Balian Beach

♫0361

One of Bali's new hotspots, Balian Beach has the slight pioneer charm of a place that's still on the brink of discovery. A rolling area of dunes and knolls overlooks the pounding surf here which attracts ever-more people for the surfing. You can easily rent a surfboard on the beach.

A critical mass of villas and beach accommodation has appeared and you can wander between cafes and join other travellers for a beer, to watch the sunset and to talk of surf. Nonsurfers will simply enjoy the wild waves and good cafes.

Black-sand Balian Beach is right at the mouth of the wide Sungai Balian (Balian River). It is 800m south of the town of Lalang-Linggah, which is on the main road 10km west of Antosari.

🛏 Sleeping & Eating

All of the accommodation listed below are fairly close together near the beach. Warung and simple cafes mean a bottle of Bintang is never more than a one-minute walk away.

TOP CHOICE Pondok Pitaya GUESTHOUSE $
(♫0819 9984 9054; www.baliansurf.com; r 200,000-800,000Rp; 🔊🏊) A lodge as memorable as its spray-scented location right on wave-tossed Balian Beach, the complex combines vintage Indonesian buildings (including a 1950 Javanese house and an 1860 Balinese alligator hunter's shack) with more modest accommodation. Room choices are like the surf: variable. Couples have a choice of rather lavish king-bed rooms, and a tribe can occupy a vast house that sleeps eight in one room. The cafe has surfer fare.

Pondok Pisces GUESTHOUSE $$
(♫780 1735, 0813 3879 7722; www.pondokpisces bali.com; r 520,000-1,000,000Rp; 🔊) You can certainly hear the sea at this tropical fantasy of thatched cottages and flower-filled gardens. Of the 10 rooms, those on the upper floor have large terraces with surf views. In-house **Tom's Garden Cafe** has grilled seafood and surf views. Down by the river and slightly upstream, there are three large villas and bungalows in **Balian Riverside Sanctuary**, lushly set in a teak forest.

Gajah Mina INN $$
(♫081 2381 1630; www.gajahminaresort.com; villas from US$110; ✳🏊) Designed by the French architect-owner, this eight-unit boutique hotel is close to the ocean. The private walled bungalows march out to a dramatic outcrop of stone surrounded by surf. The grounds are vast and there are little trails for wandering and pavilions for relaxing. The on-site restaurant overlooks its own little bowl of rice terraces.

Surya Homestay GUESTHOUSE $
(♫0813 3868 5643; wayan.suratni@gmail.com; r 100,000-150,000Rp) There are five rooms here in new bungalow-style units at this sweet little family-run place. It's spotless and rooms have cold water and fans. Ask about long-term rates.

Balian Segara Villas GUESTHOUSE $
(♫081 2385 4879; adusbalian@gmail.com; r 100,000-300,000Rp) Set close to other places to stay and close to the beach, the seven rooms here are clean, basic and have cold water and fans. The little cafe is a fine place to while away an afternoon.

Warung Ayu HOMESTAY $
(♫0812 399 353; r 150,000-200,000Rp) Like some vast surfer shack, the 12 rooms in this two-storey cold-water block look down the road to the surf.

Made's Homestay HOMESTAY $
(♫0812 396 3335; r 150,000Rp) Four basic bungalow-style units are surrounded by banana trees back from the beach. The rooms are basic, clean, large enough to hold numerous surfboards, and have cold-water showers.

❶ Getting There & Away

Because the main west Bali road is usually jammed with traffic, Balian Beach is often at least a two-hour drive from Seminyak. A car and driver will cost about 450,000Rp for a day trip. You can also catch a bus going to Gilimanuk and be dropped off at the road entrance, which is 700m from the places to stay.

Jembrana Coast

About 34km west of Tabanan you'll cross into Bali's most sparsely populated district, Jembrana. The main road follows the south coast most of the way to Negara. There's some beautiful scenery, but little tourist development, with the exception of the surfing

WORTH A TRIP

PURA RAMBUT SIWI

Picturesquely situated on a clifftop overlooking a long, wide stretch of black-sand beach, this superb temple shaded by flowering frangipani trees is one of the important sea temples of west Bali. Like Pura Tanah Lot and Pura Ulu Watu, it was established in the 16th century by the priest Nirartha, who had a good eye for ocean scenery. Unlike Tanah Lot, it remains a peaceful and little-visited place.

Legend has it that when Nirartha first came here, he donated some of his hair to the local villagers. The hair is now kept in a box buried in a three-tiered *meru* (multi-tiered shrine), the name of which means 'Worship of the Hair.' Although the main *meru* is inaccessible, you can view it easily through the gate.

The caretaker rents sarongs for 2000Rp and is happy to show you around the temple and down to the beach. He then opens the guestbook and requests a donation – a suitable sum is about 10,000Rp (regardless of the much higher amounts attributed to previous visitors). A path along the cliff leads to a staircase down to a small and even older temple, **Pura Penataran**.

The temple is located between Air Satang and Yeh Embang, at the end of a 500m side road. You'll find it's well signposted, but look for the turn-off near a cluster of warung on the main road.

action at Medewi. At Pulukan you can turn north and enjoy a remote and scenic drive to north Bali.

MEDEWI

📞0365

On the main road, a large sign points down the short paved road (200m) to the surfing mecca of **Pantai Medewi** and its *long* left-hand wave. The 'beach' is a stretch of huge, smooth grey rocks interspersed among round black pebbles. Think of it as free reflexology. Cattle graze by the shore, paying no heed to the spectators watching the action out on the water. There are a couple of guesthouses aimed at surfers plus board rental/repair shops.

Medewi proper is a classic market town with shops selling all the essentials of west Bali life.

🛏 Sleeping & Eating

You'll find accommodation along the main lane to the surf break and down other lanes about 2km east of the main surf break. For a casual meal, some of the finest fare is freshly stir-fried and served up at a cart right by the beach/rocks.

Puri Dajuma Cottages　　HOTEL $$
(📞43 955; www.dajuma.com; cottages from US$120; ✱@🛜🌊) Coming from the east, you won't be able to miss this seaside resort, thanks to its prolific signage. Happily, the 18 cottages actually live up to the billing. Each has a private garden, an ocean view and a

walled outdoor bathroom. The Medewi surf break is 2km west.

Hotel CSB　　GUESTHOUSE $
(📞0813 3866 7288; r 150,000-300,000Rp; ✱) Located some 900m east of the Medewi surf break at Pulukan; look for signs along the main road. Venture 300m down a track and you'll find a great family-run guesthouse. The best of their simply furnished rooms have air-con, hot water and balconies with views that put anything in south Bali to shame. The coast and churning surf curve to the east, backed by jade-green rice fields and rows of palm trees. It's rather idyllic.

Medewi Beach Cottages　　HOTEL $$
(📞0361-852 8521; www.medewibeachcottages. com; r from 750,000Rp; ✱🌊) A large pool anchors modern, comfortable rooms (with satellite TV) scattered about nice gardens right down by the surf break. The one off-note: security measures obstruct what should be a good view.

Negara

📞0365

Set amid the broad and fertile flatlands between the mountains and ocean, Negara is a prosperous little town and a useful pit stop. Although it's a district capital, there's not much to see. The town springs to life, however, for the region's famous **bull races**. On the main commercial road (south of the Taba-nan–Gilimanuk road), Jl Ngurah Rai, you will find ATMs, warung and a useful **Hardy's Supermarket** (☑40 709; Jl Ngurah Rai).

Around Negara

At the southern fringe of Negara, **Loloan Timur** is a largely Bugis community (originally from Sulawesi) that retains 300-year-old traditions. Look for a few distinctive houses on stilts, some decorated with wooden fretwork.

You can see bull-race practices Sunday mornings at a football field near Delod Berawan. To reach the area, turn off the main Gilimanuk–Denpasar road at Mendoyo and go south to the coast, which has a black-sand beach and irregular surf. You can see bull-race practices Sunday mornings at the nearby football field.

Perancak is the site of Nirartha's arrival in Bali in 1546, commemorated by a limestone temple, **Pura Gede Perancak**. Nearby, ignore the sad little zoo and go for a walk along the fishing harbour.

Once capital of the region, **Jembrana** is the centre of the *gamelan jegog,* a gamelan using huge bamboo instruments that produce a low-pitched, resonant sound. Performances often feature gamelan groups engaging in musical contest. Your best bet to hear this music is at a local festival. Have your driver or other local ask around to see if one is on while you're there.

Belimbingsari & Palasari

Two fascinating religious towns north of the main road are reason enough for a detour.

Christian evangelism in Bali was discouraged by the secular Dutch, but sporadic missionary activity resulted in a number of converts, many of whom were rejected by their own communities. In 1939 they were encouraged to resettle in Christian communities in the wilds of west Bali.

Palasari is home to a Catholic community, which boasts a huge church largely made from white stone and set on a large town square. It is really rather peaceful, and with the gently waving palms it feels like old missionary Hawaii rather than Hindu Bali. The church does show Balinese touches in the spires, which resemble the *meru* in a Hindu temple, and features a facade with the same design as a temple gate.

Nearby Belimbingsari was established as a Protestant community, and now has the largest Protestant church in Bali, although it doesn't reach for the heavens the way the church in Palasari does. Still, it's an amazing structure, with features rendered in a distinctly Balinese style – in place of a church bell there's a *kulkul* (hollow tree-trunk drum used to sound a warning) like those in a Hindu temple. The entrance is through an *aling aling*–style (guard wall) gate, and the attractive carved angels look very Balinese. Go on Sunday to see inside.

🛏 Sleeping

TOP CHOICE Taman Wana
Villas & Spa BOUTIQUE HOTEL **$$$**
(☑0365-470 2208; www.bali-tamanwana-villas. com; Palasari; r US$150-350; ❊☒) For a near-religious experience you might consider staying at this remote resort, a striking 2km drive through a jungle past the Palasari church. This architecturally stunning boutique resort has 27 rooms in unusual round structures. Posh only starts to describe the luxuries at this cloistered refuge. Views are panoramic; get a room with a view of the rice fields.

ℹ Getting There & Away

The two villages are north of the main road, and the best way to see them is on a loop with your own transport. On the main road about 17km west from Negara, look for signs for the Taman Wana Villas. Follow these for 6.1km to Palasari. From the west, look for a turn for Belimbingsari, some 20km southeast of Cekik. A good road leads to the village. Between the two towns, only divine intervention will allow you to tackle the thicket of narrow but passable lanes unaided. Fortunately directional help is readily at hand.

Cekik

At the Cekik junction one road continues west to Gilimanuk and another heads northeast towards north Bali. All buses and bemo to and from Gilimanuk pass through Cekik.

Archaeological excavations here during the 1960s yielded the oldest evidence of human life in Bali. Finds included burial mounds with funerary offerings, bronze jewellery, axes, adzes and earthenware vessels from around 1000 BC, give or take a few centuries. Look for some of these items at the Museum Situs Purbakala Gilimanuk in Gilimanuk.

On the southern side of the junction, the pagoda-like structure with a spiral stairway around the outside is a **war memorial**. It commemorates the landing of independence forces in Bali to oppose the Dutch, who were trying to reassert control of Indonesia after WWII.

Cekik is home to the **park headquarters** (☑61060; ☺7am-5pm) of the Taman Nasional Bali Barat.

Gilimanuk

☑0365

Gilimanuk is the terminus for ferries that shuttle back and forth across the narrow strait to Java. Most travellers to or from Java can get an onward ferry or bus straight away, and won't hang around. The museum is the only attraction – the town is really a place one passes through quickly. It does have the closest accommodation to Taman Nasional Bali Barat, however, if you want to start a trek early.

◉ Sights

This part of Bali has been occupied for thousands of years. The **Museum Situs Purbakala Gilimanuk** (Prehistoric Man Museum; ☑61 328; suggested donation 10,000Rp; ☺8am-4pm Mon-Fri) is centred on a family of skeletons, thought to be 4000 years old, which were found locally in 2004. The very quiet

museum is 500m east of the ferry port and staff will be thrilled to see you.

Stop anywhere along the north shore of town to see the huge clash of waves and currents in the strait. It's dramatic and a good reason *not* to have that dodgy curry dish if you're about to board a ferry.

🛏 Sleeping & Eating

Good sleeping choices are thin on the ground. With one exception, there's nothing worthwhile here. However, there are choices aplenty in Pemuteran (p243). The freshest food sizzles up at the bus station warung. Yikes.

Hotel Lestari　　　　　　GUESTHOUSE $
(☑61 504; r 100,000-400,000Rp; ❄) From fan-cooled singles to air-con suites, you'll have your choice of basic accommodation at this 21-room hotel, which feels strangely 1950s suburban. It has a cafe.

Asli Mentempeh　　　　　　BALINESE $
(Terminal Lama; meals from 15,000Rp) Gilimanuk is known for a local dish and popular delicacy: betutu chicken, a spicy form of steamed chicken that is redolent with herbs. The owners of this small cafe are descendents of the original creators of the dish. They are located in the former bus terminal, about 5km east of the ferry port with several other vendors.

❶ Getting There & Around

Frequent buses hurtle along the main road between Gilimanuk's huge bus depot and Denpasar's Ubung terminal (30,000Rp, two to three

---

BULL RACES

The Negara region is famous for bull races, known as *mekepung,* which culminate in the **Bupati Cup** in Negara in early August. The racing animals are actually the normally docile water buffalo, which charge down a 2km stretch of road or beach pulling tiny chariots. Gaily clad riders stand or kneel on top of the chariots forcing the bullocks on, sometimes by twisting their tails to make them follow the curve of the makeshift racetrack. The winner, however, is not necessarily first past the post. Style also plays a part and points are awarded for the most elegant runner. Gambling is not legal in Bali, but locals do sometimes indulge.

Important races are held during the dry season, from July to October. Races are staged for tourists, including regular and more occasional ones at more traditional venues, such as at Perancak on the coast. Minor races and practices are held at several sites around Perancak and elsewhere on Sunday mornings, including Delod Berawan and Yeh Embang. However, actually finding these events can be somewhat like seeking the Holy Grail. If you're in Negara on a bull-race Sunday, people will gladly direct you, but trying to obtain info remotely is often a quest best not started. Check the **Jembrana Government Tourist Office** (☑ext 224 0365-41210) for details, or show up in Negara on a Sunday morning from July to October and hope to get lucky by asking around.

THE BALI STARLING SAGA

Also known as the Bali myna, Rothschild's mynah, or locally as *jalak putih*, the Bali starling is perhaps Bali's only endemic bird (opinions differ – as other places are so close, who can tell?). It is strikingly white in colour, with black tips to the wings and tail, and a distinctive bright-blue mask. These natural good looks have caused the bird to be poached into virtual extinction. On the black market, Bali starlings command US$7000 or more.

The wild population (maybe in the park) has been estimated at a dozen or none. In captivity, however, there are hundreds if not thousands.

Near Ubud, the Bali Bird Park (p175) has large aviaries where you can see Bali starlings. The park was one of the major supporters of efforts to reintroduce the birds into the wild. Ironically, the most successful efforts to reintroduce the species into the wild have been on Nusa Penida.

hours), or along the north-coast road to Singaraja (25,000Rp).

Car ferries to and from Ketapang on Java (30 minutes, adult/child 6000/5000Rp, car 114,000Rp) run around the clock.

If you have wheels, watch out for police checkpoints around the ferry terminal where commas are counted and the number of dots on i's checked on vehicle documents. Freelance 'fines' are common.

Taman Nasional Bali Barat

☏0365

Call it nature's symphony. Most visitors to Bali's only national park, Taman Nasional Bali Barat (West Bali National Park), are struck by the mellifluous sounds from myriad birds with a nice riff from the various rustling trees.

The park covers 19,000 hectares of the western tip of Bali. An additional 55,000 hectares is protected in the national park extension, as well as almost 7000 hectares of coral reef and coastal waters. Together this represents a significant commitment to conservation on an island as densely populated as Bali.

It's a place where you can hike through forests, enjoy Bali's best diving at Pulau Menjangan and explore coastal mangroves.

Although you may imagine dense jungle, most of the natural vegetation in the park is not tropical rainforest, which requires year-round rain, but rather coastal savannah, with deciduous trees that become bare in the dry season. The southern slopes receive more regular rainfall, and so have more tropical vegetation, while the coastal lowlands have extensive mangroves.

There are more than 200 species of plants growing in the park. Local fauna includes black monkeys, leaf monkeys and macaques (seen in the afternoon along the main road near Sumber Kelompok); rusa, barking, sambar, Java and *muncak* (mouse deer); and some wild pigs, squirrels, buffalo, iguanas, pythons and green snakes. There were once tigers, but the last confirmed sighting was in 1937 – and that one was shot. The bird life is prolific, with many of Bali's 300 species found here, including the possibly extinct Bali starling.

Just getting off the road a bit on one of the many trails transports you into the heart of nature. One discordant note: hikes in fuel prices have seen lots of vendors along the road selling firewood snatched from the forest.

🏃 Activities

By land, by boat or underwater, the park awaits exploration.

Boat Trips

The best way to explore the mangroves of Teluk Gilimanuk (Gilimanuk Bay) or the west side of Prapat Agung is by chartering a boat (maximum of five people) for about 300,000Rp per boat per hour, including a guide and entrance fees. You can arrange this at either of the park offices in Cekik or Labuhan Lalang. This is the ideal way to see bird life, including kingfishers, Javanese herons and more.

Trekking

All trekkers must be accompanied by an authorised guide. It's best to arrive the day before you want to trek, and make enquiries at the park offices in Cekik or Labuhan Lalang.

The set rates for guides in the park depend on the size of the group and the length of the trek – with one or two people it's 350,000Rp for one or two hours, with rates steadily increasing from there. Food (a small lunchbox) is included but transport is extra and all the prices are *very* negotiable. Early morning, say 6am, is the best time to start – it's cooler and you're more likely to see some wildlife.

If, once you're out, you have a good rapport with your guide, you might consider getting creative. Although you can try to customise your hike, the guides are most familiar with the three options listed here:

» **Gunung Kelatakan (Mt Kelatakan)** From Sumber Kelompok, go up the mountain (698m), then down to the main road near Kelatakan village (six to seven hours). You may be able to get permission from park headquarters to stay overnight in the forest – if you don't have a tent, your guide can make a shelter from branches and leaves, which will be an adventure in itself. Clear streams abound in the dense woods.

» **Kelatakan** Starting at the village, climb to the microwave tower, go down to Ambyasari and get transport back to Cekik (four hours). This takes you through the forested southern sector of the park. From the tower you get a feel for what much of Bali looked like centuries ago.

» **Teluk Terima (Terima Bay)** From a trail west of Labuhan Lalang, hike around the mangroves here. Then partially follow Sungai Terima (Terima River) into the hills and walk back down to the road along the steps at Makam Jayaprana. You might see grey macaques, deer and black monkeys. The most popular hike, it takes three to four hours.

🛏 Sleeping

Park visitors will want to spend the night close to the park to get an early start. Gilimanuk is closest and has basic choices. Much nicer are the many options spreading east to Pemuteran (p243), 12km east of Labuhan Lalang.

ℹ Information

The park headquarters (p253) at Cekik displays a topographic model of the park area, and has a little information about plants and wildlife. The **Labuhan Lalang Visitors Centre** (⊙7.30am-5pm) is in a hut located on the northern coast, where boats leave for Pulau Menjangan. Park guides on hand usually include **Nyoman Kawit** (☑0852 3850 5291), who is very knowledgeable.

You can arrange trekking guides and permits at either office; however, there are always a few characters hanging around, and determining who is an actual park official can be like spotting a Bali starling: difficult.

The main roads to Gilimanuk go through the national park, but you don't have to pay an

Taman Nasional Bali Barat

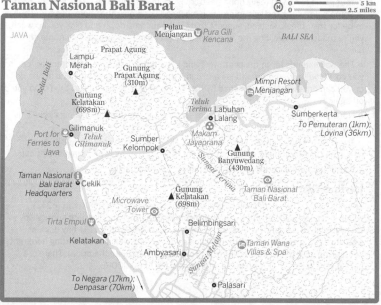

DIVING & SNORKELLING PULAU MENJANGAN

Bali's best-known underwater attraction, Pulau Menjangan has a dozen superb dive sites. The experience is excellent – iconic tropical fish, soft corals, great visibility (usually), caves and a spectacular drop-off.

Lacy sea fans and various sponges provide both texture and myriad hiding spots for small fish that together form a colour chart for the sea. Few can resist the silly charms of parrotfish and clownfish. Among larger creatures, you may well see whales, whale sharks and manta rays swimming gracefully past.

Of the dozen or so named sites here, most are close to shore and suitable for snorkellers or diving novices. Some decent snorkelling spots are not far from the jetty – ask the boatman where to go. Venture a bit out, however, and the depths turn inky black as the shallows drop off in dramatic cliffs, a magnet for experienced divers looking for wall dives. The **Anker Wreck**, a mysterious sunken ship, challenges even experts.

This uninhabited island boasts what is thought to be Bali's oldest temple, **Pura Gili Kencana**, dating from the 14th century and about 300m from the pier. You can walk around the island in about an hour and most people who take to the waters here take a break on the unfortunately not-entirely-unblemished beaches.

Practicalities

Divers have more scope to customise their experience, although it inevitably begins – as it should – at the extraordinary 30m wall. Snorkellers, however, may find themselves conveyed along the underwater beauty by guides who do this day-in and day-out and are just as happy to go home. This can happen with both top-end hotel-sponsored tours and the boats from Labuhan Lalang. Keep the following in mind to maximise what will likely be a highlight of your Bali trip.

» Boats usually tie up to the pier at Pualau Menjangan. The wall, which is where you'll find all the action (even while just floating on the surface), is directly out from the shore. Currents tend to flow gently southwest (the shore is on your right) so you can just literally go with the flow and enjoy the underwater spectacle.

» Your guide (who you really don't need) may try to get you to swim back to the boat at some point along the less-interesting bleached coral near the shore, this turns out to be for their break. Instead, suggest that the boat come down and pick you up when you're ready, thus avoiding the swim against the current followed by downtime at the pier.

» The wall extends far to the southwest and gets more pristine and spectacular as you go. If you're overcome with joy and can't stop, you could get to the end in one go or you can break up the experience by having the boat pick you up and then drop you off again.

» North of the pier, you can snorkel from shore and cover the wall in a big circle. This lets your boat crew take their lunch.

» Try to hover over some divers along the wall. Watching their bubbles sinuously rise in all their multihued silvery glory from the inky depths is just plain spectacular.

» If your guide really adds to your experience, tip accordingly.

Getting There & Away

The closest and most convenient dive operators are found at Pemuteran (p242), where the hotels also arrange diving and snorkelling trips. Independent snorkellers can arrange for a boat (three-hour trip for two, 350,000Rp) from the tiny dock at **Labuhan Lalang** just across the turquoise water from Menjangan. Warung here rent snorkelling gear (a pricey 50,000Rp for four hours; negotiate the price). There is a park diver's fee of 75,000Rp and a snorkeller's fee of 60,000Rp.

entrance fee just to drive through. If you want to stop and visit any of the sites within the park, you must buy a ticket (20,000Rp).

ℹ️ Getting There & Away

The national park is too far for a comfortable day trip from Ubud or south Bali, though many dive operators do it.

If you don't have transport, any Gilimanuk-bound bus or bemo from north or west Bali can drop you at the park headquarters at Cekik (those from north Bali can also drop you at the Labuhan Lalang Visitors Centre). Better to consider the options outlined under Sleeping.

Labuhan Lalang

To catch a boat to visit or snorkel Pulau Menjangan, head to the jetty at this small harbour in the national park. There's also a useful park **visitors centre** (☺7.30am-5pm)

in a hut at the main parking lot. There are warung and a pleasant beach 200m to the east.

🛏️ Sleeping

The closest choice is quite luxurious, with many more in nearby Pemuteran in north Bali.

[TOP CHOICE] **Mimpi Resort Menjangan**   RESORT **$$**
(☏0362-94497, 0361-701070; www.mimpi.com; r US$100-130, villas US$180-400; ✳@☲) At isolated Banyuwedang, this 54-unit resort extends down to a small, mangrove-fringed, white-sand beach. The rooms have an unadorned monochromatic motif with open-air bathrooms. Hot springs feed communal pools and private tubs in the villas. The grand villas with a private pool and a view of the lagoon are one of the best tropical fantasy escapes on Bali.

Lombok

Best Places to Eat

» Astari (p281)

» Warung Bule (p282)

» Ikan Bakar 99 (p262)

» Square (p270)

Best Places to Stay

» Pearl Beach (p265)

» Qunci Villas (p270)

» Rinjani Beach Eco Resort (p272)

» Tugu Lombok (p272)

» Heaven on the Planet (p285)

Why Go?

Long overshadowed by its superstar neighbour across the water, there's a steady hum about Lombok that's beginning to turn into a distinct buzz. Blessed with exquisite white-sand beaches, epic surf, a lush forested interior, and hiking trails through tobacco and rice fields, Lombok is fully loaded with tropical allure. Oh, and you'll probably notice mighty Gunung Rinjani, Indonesia's second-highest volcano, its summit complete with hot springs and a dazzling crater lake.

And there's much more. Lombok's southern coastline is nature on a very grand scale: breathtaking turquoise bays, world-class surf breaks and massive headlands.

For years Lombok has been touted as Indonesia's next hot destination. Finally, the reality seems to have caught up with the hype, and with a new international airport and renewed interest from around the globe, Lombok's time is now.

When to Go

Lombok is hot, sticky and tropical throughout the year, with a marked rainy season (roughly between late October and April). The driest months coincide with the peak period in July and August. The rainy season offers an excellent time to catch a local festival, such as the spectacular rice-throwing event called Perang Topat (held at Pura Lingsar in November or December), Peresean stick-fighting competitions (in December) or the Narmada buffalo races (in April).

WEST LOMBOK

0370

Though the region's biggest city, Mataram, must now cope with the loss of the island's air traffic, the rest of West Lombok appears to be progressing. Senggigi especially looks ready to emerge from its comfortable 1990s time warp thanks to a happening new phase of resort development. Lombok's western hemisphere is at its best south of the Lembar port, where the peninsula bends forward and back, the seas are placid, and bucolic offshore islands beckon.

Mataram

Lombok's capital is a blending sprawl of several (once separate) towns with fuzzy borders: Ampenan (the port); Mataram (the administrative centre); Cakranegara (the business centre, often called simply 'Cakra') and Bertais and Sweta to the east, where you'll find the bus terminal. Stretching for 12km from east to west it's home to half a million people. There aren't many tourist attractions, Senggigi is close by, and the airport has moved too, so unless you're booking plane tickets (easily done elsewhere) or need a hospital there isn't any reason to visit, much less stay the night. Yet Mataram's broad tree lined avenues buzz with bemo, thrum with motorbike traffic and are teeming with classic markets. If you're hungry for a blast of Indo realism, you'll find it here.

◉ Sights

Pura Meru   HINDU

(Jl Selaparang; admission by donation; ⊙8am-5pm) Pura Meru is the largest and second most important Hindu temple on Lombok. Built in 1720, it's dedicated to the Hindu trinity of Brahma, Vishnu and Shiva. The inner court has 33 small shrines and three thatched, teak-wood *meru* (multi-tiered shrines). The central *meru*, with 11 tiers, is Shiva's house; the *meru* to the north, with nine tiers, is Vishnu's; and the seven-tiered *meru* to the south is Brahma's. The *meru* also represent three sacred mountains, Rinjani, Agung and Bromo, and the mythical Mount Meru. The caretaker will lend you a sash and sarong if you need one.

Mayura Water Palace   HINDU

(Jl Selaparang; admission by donation; ⊙7am-7.30pm) Built in 1744, this palace includes the former king's family temple, a pilgrimage site for Lombok's Hindus on 24 December. In 1894 it was the site of bloody battles between the Dutch and Balinese. Unfortunately, it has become a neglected public park with a polluted artificial lake.

🛏 Sleeping

Most folks nest among Cakranegara's quiet streets off Jl Pejanggik/Selaparang, east of Mataram Mall.

Lombok Plaza   BOUTIQUE HOTEL $$

(☎629 718; www.lombokplazahotel.com; Jl Pejanggik 8; r 450,000-785,000Rp; ❋⬛⬛) Mataram's newest and shiniest hotel has welcome flash and class. Rooms are sizeable with stylish wood desks and end tables, wall-mounted flat-screen TVs, high ceilings, a breakfast buffet and 20m lap pool on the second-floor mezzanine. The Chinese restaurant serves excellent dim sum and a wonderful *soto ayam* (chicken soup) at reasonable prices (dishes 30,000-60,000Rp).

Ratu Guesthouse   HOMESTAY $

(☎0852 8100 8284, 0819 1590 4275; Jl AA Gede Ngurah 45; s/d 60,000/80,000Rp; ⬛) A great value place in the heart of Cakranegara, a block from the market. Rooms are spacious and have spring beds, mosquito nets, shared baths and wi-fi.

Hotel Melati Viktor 1   GUESTHOUSE $

(☎633 830; Jl Abimanyu 1; d with fan/air-con 100,000/150,000Rp; ❋) The high ceilings, clean rooms and Balinese-style courtyard, complete with Hindu statues, make this one of the best values in town. If they're full, head to Viktor II across the street, where everything is a bit newer and fresher.

Hotel Lombok Raya   HOTEL $$

(☎632 305; www.lombokrayahotel.com; Jl Panca Usaha 11; d 470,000-510,000Rp; ❋⬛⬛) Still a favorite with old school business travellers, this well-located hotel has spacious, comfortable rooms with balconies and all the mod-cons, including a terrific spa. The local Silk Air airline office lives here.

🍴 Eating

The **Mataram Mall** (Jl Selaparang; ⊙7am-7pm), and the streets around it, are loaded with

Lombok Highlights

1 Surfing (or learning to surf) the ride of your life in **Gerupak** (p280)

2 Scaling **Gunung Rinjani** (p276), Lombok's incomparable sacred peak

3 Setting eyes on idyllic **Mawun beach** (p284) for the very first time

4 Picking your own deserted-cove beach **north of Senggigi** (p267)

5 Catching a **Sasak festival** (p265), such as Peresean near Mataram

6 Lounging in pure island bliss on **Gili Asahan** (p264)

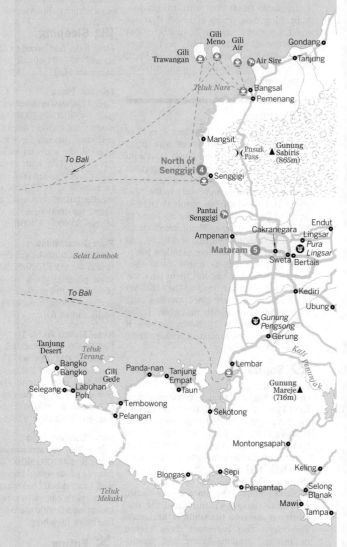

BALI SEA

0 — 10 km
0 — 5 miles

Gili Meno   Gili Air   Gondang
Gili Trawangan   Air Sire   Tanjung
Teluk Nare   Bangsal
Pemenang

Mangsit   Pusuk Pass   Gunung Sabiris (865m)

To Bali

North of Senggigi **4**   Senggigi

Pantai Senggigi

Endut
Ampenan   Cakranegara   Lingsar
Pura Lingsar
Mataram 5   Sweta   Bertais

Selat Lombok

Kediri
Ubung

To Bali

Gunung Pengsong
Gerung

Tanjung Desert   Teluk Terang
Bangko Bangko   Gili Gede   Panda-nan   Tanjung Empat   Lembar
Selegang   Labuhan Poh   Taun   Gunung Mareje (716m)
Tembowong   Kali Pengok
Pelangan   Sekotong

Montongsapah

Keling
Blongas   Sepi
Teluk Mekaki   Pengantap   Selong Blanak
Mawi   Tampa

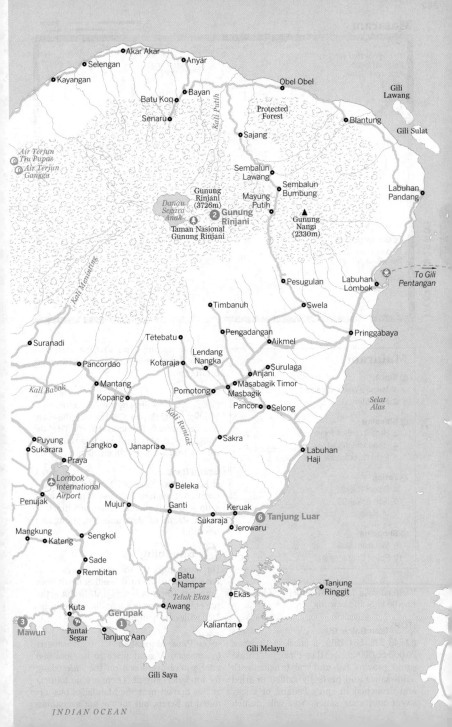

Mataram

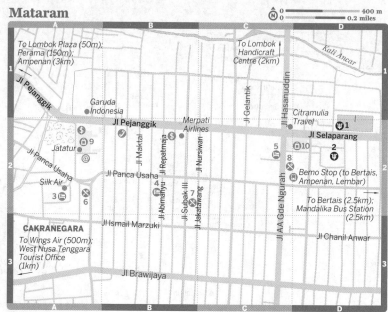

Mataram

◎ Sights

1 Mayura Water Palace	D2
2 Pura Meru	D2

🛌 Sleeping

3 Hotel Lombok Raya	A2
4 Hotel Melati Viktor 1	B2
5 Ratu Guesthouse	C2

✕ Eating

6 Bakmi Raos	A2
7 Ikan Bakar 99	B2
8 Mi Rasa	C2

🛍 Shopping

9 Mataram Mall	A2
10 Pasar Cakranegara	D2

Western-style fast-food outlets, Indonesian noodle bars and warung.

TOP CHOICE Ikan Bakar 99   SEAFOOD $

(☑643 335, 664 2819; Jl Subak III 10; mains 20,000-55,000Rp; ☺11am-10pm) Think: squid, prawns, fish and crab brushed with chilli sauce and perfectly grilled or fried and drenched in spicy Padang or sticky sweet and sour sauce. You will munch

and dine among Mataram families who fill the long tables in the arched, tiled dining room.

Mi Rasa   BAKERY $

(☑633 096; Jl AA Gede Ngurah 88; pastries from 5000Rp; ☺6am-10pm) Cakra's middle-class families adore this modern bakery. They do doughnuts, cookies and cakes as well as local wontons stuffed with chicken.

Bakmi Raos   NOODLES $

(Jl Panca Usaha; dishes 9000-20,000Rp) An authentic yet modern Indonesian noodle-and-soup joint behind the mall that attracts a steady stream of Mataram's hip, young and beautiful.

🛍 Shopping

For handicrafts try the many stores on Jl Raya Senggigi, the road heading north from Ampenan towards Senggigi. Jl Usaha is the pre-eminent upscale shopping street sprinkled with cute boutiques.

TOP CHOICE Pasar Mandalika   MARKET

(☺7am-5pm) A great place to get localised after you've overdosed on the *bule* (slang for foreigner) circuit. There are no tourists at this market near the Mandalika bus terminal in Berais, but they've got everything else: fruit and veggies, fish (fresh and dried), baskets full of colourful, aromatic spices and grains, freshly butchered beef, palm sugar, pungent bricks of shrimp paste and cheaper handicrafts than you will find anywhere else in West Lombok.

Lombok Handicraft Centre   HANDICRAFTS
(Jl Hasanuddin) At Sayang Sayang (2km north of Cakra), there's a wide range of crafts, including masks, textiles and ceramics from across Nusa Tenggara.

Pasar Cakranegara   MARKET
(cnr AA Gede Ngurah & Jl Selaparang) Collection of quirky stalls, some of which sell good-quality ikat, as well as an interesting food market.

❶ Information

Emergency
Police Station (☑631 225; Jl Langko) In an emergency, dial 110.
Rumah Sakit Harapan Keluarga (☑670 000, 617 7000; www.harapankeluarga.co.id/rshk; Jl Ahmad Yani 9) The newest and best private hospital on Lombok is just east of downtown Mataram and has English-speaking doctors and modern facilities.

Internet Access
Yahoo Internet (Mataram Mall, Jl Panca Usaha A11; per hr 5000Rp; ⊘9am-10pm)

Money
You'll find plenty of banks with ATMs scattered along Cakra's main drag. Moneychangers in Mataram Mall and on Jl Pejanggik often provide the best rates for cash.

Post
Post Office (Jl Langko; ⊘8am-4.30pm Mon-Thu, 8-11am Fri, 8am-1pm Sat)

Telephone
Wartel (public telephone offices) are on Jl Pejanggik and at the airport.
Telkom (☑633 333; Jl Pendidikan 23; ⊘24hr) Offers phone and fax services.

Tourist Information
West Lombok Tourist Office (☑621 658; Jl Suprato 20; ⊘7.30am-2pm Mon-Thu, to 11am Fri, 8am-1pm Sat) Stocks a few maps and leaflets, though not much in the way of practical information.
West Nusa Tenggara Tourist Office (☑634 800; Jl Singosari 2; ⊘8am-2pm Mon-Thu, to 11am Fri, to 12.30pm Sat) Offers limited information about Lombok and Sumbawa.

❶ Getting There & Away

Air
Lombok's new airport near Praya opened in 2011, rendering Mataram even more meaningless to most international travellers. However, major airlines retain ticket offices in Mataram, and there are also two excellent travel agencies here, making it a good place to arrange domestic travel. See p375 for a list of airlines.
Citramulia Travel (☑633 469; www.citramulia travel.com; Jl Pejanggik 198; ⊘8am-8pm Mon-Sat, to 7pm Sun) Conscientious English-speaking staff handle domestic and international flights and offer visa services.
Jatatur (☑632 888; www.jatatursurabaya.com; Mataram Mall, Jl Panca Usaha A11) Dependable, long-running travel chain that offers fair pricing on airline tickets and English-speaking service.

Bus
The sprawling Mandalika bus station in Bertais is the main bus and bemo terminal for the entire island, and also for long-distance buses to Sumbawa, Bali and Java . It's a chaotic, badly organised place, so be sure to keep a level head to avoid the 'help' of the commission-happy touts. Long-distance buses leave from behind the main terminal building, while bemo and smaller buses leave from one of two car parks on either side.

Some distances and fares for buses and bemo departing hourly from the Mandalika terminal include the following:

DESTINATION	DISTANCE	FARE (RP)	DURATION
Kuta (via Praya & Sengkol)	54km	13,000	90min
Labuhan Lombok	69km	15,000	2hr
Lembar	22km	5000	30min
Pemenang (for Bangsal)	30km	12,000	40min
Praya (airport)	27km	15,000	1hr

Kebon Roek bemo terminal in Ampenan has bemo to Bertais (2500Rp) and Senggigi (4000Rp).

❶ Getting Around

To/From the Airport
Lombok's (old) Selaparang Airport has been phased out, and a new airport near Praya is up and running. By taxi, it is only about 30 minutes from Mataram. Buses leave from the Mandalika

terminal for the airport (15,000Rp, one hour) on the hour.

Bemo

Mataram is *very* spread out. Yellow bemo shuttle between the Kebon Roek bemo terminal in Ampenan and the Mandalika terminal in Bertais (10km away) along the two main thoroughfares. Outside the Pasar Cakranegara there is a handy bemo stop for services to Bertais, Ampenan, Sweta and Lembar. Fares cost between 2000Rp and 3000Rp.

Taxi

For a reliable metered taxi, call **Lombok Taksi** (☑627 000). Cars with drivers are easily arranged in Mataram and cost about 400,000Rp to 500,000Rp per day.

Around Mataram

There are gorgeous villages, temples and scenery east of Mataram. It's worth a half-day's drive.

⊙ Sights

Pura Lingsar   HINDU
(admission by donation; ⊙7am-6pm) This large temple compound is the holiest in Lombok. Built in 1714 by King Anak Agung Ngurah, and nestled beautifully in the lush rice fields, it's multi-denominational, with a temple for Balinese Hindus (Pura Gaduh) and one for followers of Lombok's mystical take on Islam, the Wektu Telu religion.

Pura Gaduh has four shrines: one orientated to Gunung Rinjani (seat of the gods on Lombok), one to Gunung Agung (seat of the gods in Bali) and a double shrine representing the union between the two islands.

The Wektu Telu temple is noted for its enclosed pond devoted to Lord Vishnu, and the holy eels, which can be enticed from their lair with hard-boiled eggs (available at stalls outside). It's considered good luck to feed them. You will be expected to rent a sash and/or sarong (or bring your own) to enter the temple.

Pura Lingsar is 9km northeast of Mandalika. Take a bemo from the Mandalika terminal to Narmada, and another to Lingsar. Ask to be dropped off near the entrance to the temple complex.

Lembar

Lembar is Lombok's main port for ferries, tankers and Pelni liners coming in from Bali and beyond. Though the ferry port itself is scruffy, the setting – think azure inlets ringed by soaring green hills – is stunning. However, there's no reason to linger, with good transport connections to Mataram and Senggigi. If you need cash, stop by the BNI bank, 100m from the harbour's entrance.

Bemo shuttle regularly between Lembar and the Mandalika terminal in Bertais (15,000Rp). From there switch to an Ampenan bound bemo (3000Rp), where you can get another to Senggigi (2500Rp). There are also regular shuttles (per person 45,000Rp) connecting Senggigi and Lembar. A taxi from Mataram is 70,000Rp.

Ferries run hourly, day and night, to Benoa on Bali (child/adult/motorbike/car 23,000/36,000/101,000/659,000Rp, five hours).

Southwestern Peninsula

The sweeping coastline that stretches west of Lembar is blessed with boutique sleeps on deserted beaches and tranquil offshore islands set in azure waters. Pearl Beach (opposite), Dive Zone's new resort on **Gili Asahan**, and Cocotino's (opposite) both offer diving, which is certainly fun if not spectacular. And whether you are a diver or not, you can waste weeks here among the pearl farms, salty old mosques, friendly locals and relatively pristine islands – three of which have accommodation. Our favorites are Gili Gede, and the wonderful Gili Asahan, where soothing winds gust, birds flutter and gather in the grass just before sunset, muted calls to prayer rumble, stars and moon beams bathe the night in sweet tenderness, and silence is deep and nourishing.

The only blot on the landscape is the gold-rush town of **Sekotong**. The hills above Sekotong are rich in the precious metal, and up to 6000 locals mined illegally here in huge open-cast pits (using mercury) until a crackdown in December 2009. The unofficial and not so clandestine mining still continues despite government opposition and severe environmental damage.

You'll see some of those crude goldmines riddle the rugged hills as you follow the narrow (but paved) coastal road, along the contours of the peninsula, skirting white-sand beach after white-sand beach on your way to Bangko Bangko and Tanjung Desert

SASAK FESTIVALS & CEREMONIES

As more Sasaks have adopted orthodox Islam, many ancient cultural rituals and celebrations based on animist and Hindu traditions have dwindled in practice, but some have endured.

Lebaran Topat Held during the seven days after the end of the fasting month (Idul Fitri; Ramadan) in the Islamic calendar, Lebaran Topat is a Sasak ceremony thought to be unique to west Lombok. Relatives gather in cemeteries to pour water over family graves, and add offerings of flowers, betel leaves and lime powder. Visitors can observe ceremonies at the **Bintaro cemetery** on the outskirts of Ampenan.

Malean Sampi Meaning 'cow chase' in Sasak, Malean Sampi are highly competitive buffalo races held over a 100m waterlogged field in Narmada, just east of Mataram. Two buffalo are yoked together and then driven along the course by a driver brandishing a whip. The event takes place in early April, and commemorates the beginning of the planting season.

Gendang Beleq These 'big drum' performances were originally performed before battles. Today, many villages in central Lombok have a *gendang* battery, some with up to 40 drummers, who perform at festivals and ceremonies. The drums themselves are colossal, up to a metre in length and not unlike an oil drum in shape or size. The drummers support the drums using a sash around their necks.

Peresean Martial-art 'stick fighting' performances by two young men stripped to the waist, armed with rattan sticks and square shields made of cowhide. The Sasak believe that the more blood shed on the earth the better the rainfall will be in the forthcoming wet season. In late July, demonstrations can be seen in Senggigi, and in late December there's a championship in Mataram.

(Desert Point) one of Asia's legendary surf breaks.

🛏 Sleeping & Eating

There are a few hotels and resorts sprinkled along the southwest coast, though the best beaches and lodging are on the sweet offshore islands. You'll eat where you sleep.

MAINLAND

Bola Bola Paradis   INN **$**
(☏0817 578 7355; www.bolabolaparadis.com; Jl Raya Palangan Sekotong, Pelangan; r 300,000-465,000Rp; ; ✻) Just west of Pelangan, this nice midranger has superclean octagonal bungalows on grassy palm-shaded grounds that bleed into the sand, and comfortable air-con rooms with tiled floors and private patios in the main lodge building. They also have an aromatic kitchen reccommended for spicy Indonesian food (mains 39,000-82,000Rp).

Cocotino's   RESORT **$$$**
(☏0819 0797 2401; www.cocotinos-sekotong.com; Jl Raya Palangan Sekotong, Tanjung Empat; r/villas from 1,300,000/2,700,000Rp; ✻@🛜🏊) The newest place on this coast (islands not included), this resort has an oceanfront location, private beach and high-quality bungalows (some with lovely outdoor bathrooms), though not all have sea views. There's a professional dive shop, and a full spa here, too. Significant discounts for walk-in guests.

ISLANDS

🏆 Pearl Beach   BUNGALOW **$$**
(☏0813 3954 4998, 0819 0724 7696; www.divezone-lombok.com; Gili Asahan; cottages/bungalows incl breakfast 370,000/570,000Rp; 🛜) A new private island resort with a wonderful sweep of white sand leading to a turquoise sea. The cottages are simple, bamboo affairs with outdoor baths and a hammock on the porch. The bungalows are quite chic, with polished concrete floors, soaring ceilings, sliding glass doors, a gorgeous outdoor bath, and a fabulous day-bed swing on the wood porch.

It's owned by the folks behind Dive Zone, mainland Lombok's best dive shop. So, yes, there is diving. Electricity from 6pm to 6am only. They will organise your transport to Gili Asahan from the mainland if you book in advance.

HAZARD PAY?

So this actually happened. Took a wrong turn on the way to Tanjung Desert (aka Desert Point) for a spot of research. Ended up on a virgin beach, but the wrong virgin beach. A happy accident, say. It looked like ideal kite surf country. The kinda place our readers might dig. You know, wide turquoise striped bay, sugar white sand, thumping waves, heavy metal wind. Made some notes. Place was called Pantai Mukaki (Mukaki Beach), according to the local we met, a reasonably friendly guy. Or was he?

Fixer's face changed and he became anxious to get into the car. I was on the beach taking snapshots. He whistled, I hustled over, and was still jotting notes as we rolled down the road. Then, suddenly, the car was surrounded by an onrushing mob. Fifty villagers with crude yet presumably sharp bamboo spears and glinting sickles. They mistook me, a career renter, for the swindling investor who hath bilked them. Point is, apparently said land was in dispute. And, well, wouldn't be a bad place for a resort, but you know, bad idea jeans.

'Better you go, we kill you,' said the Mouthpiece. A woman. 'We kill you! More people coming!' She barked ominously. They searched the car, painfully slowly and suspiciously for the local landbroker we'd never met and they were sure we knew.

Nobody move, nobody get hurt.

Mouthpiece glanced at my dog-eared research copy of Lonely Planet on the seat beside me and realised that I was indeed just a tourist. Or was I? Mouthpiece let us off with a warning of certain death by dismemberment upon return. Ya, 'bu, don't wait up.

The moral of our tale: ever since the Suharto days, large developers or holding companies (usually based in Jakarta) have attempted to purchase and develop East Indonesian paradise, often by making shady deals with people unfamiliar with the true financial value of their ancestral land. When deals go bad, and some do, tensions flare on the ground. South Lombok (including and especially the Kuta region) has been ground zero for this kind of activity for years, and there are similar land sovereignty issues on Gili Trawangan as well. Although it is incredibly rare to get caught in the middle of the fight.

Madak Belo
BUNGALOW $

(☑ 0878 6471 2981, 0818 0554 9637; www.madak-belo.com; Gili Gede; r/bungalows 125,000/250,000Rp) Here's a sensational French hippie chic paradise with three rooms upstairs in the main wooden and bamboo lodge. They share a bath with wash basins crusted with shells and a magnificent bamboo lounge area strung with hammocks, and blessed with a perfect white sand, turquoise sea view. They also have two spacious private bungalows with queen beds and private baths decorated with stones and shells. Meals (20,000-65,000Rp) are delicious. Electricity only runs for about eight hours each day.

Via Vacare
BUNGALOW $

(☑ 0819 1590 4275; www.viavacare.com; Gili Gede; including meals bungalows 750,000Rp, r 250,000Rp) A secret yoga retreat with four spacious, simple and stylish octagonal bungalows. Backpacker digs are a comfy mattress on the floor and a mosquito net, in a large open-sided longhouse. There's no beach to speak of, but you can go swimming at high tide. There's an open-air yoga pagoda, and fine home-cooked fresh food in the restaurant. Management will arrange free shuttle to the island from nearby Tebowong.

TANJUNG DESERT

Less a working community and more an informal surf camp, only one of the three sleeping options on this beach even have a phone. When the swell comes, it's first come first surf. If these spots are all booked up – and it does happen – you'll have to nest in nearby Labuan Poh where there are a handful of decent choices.

Desert Point Bungalow
BUNGALOW $

(Tanjung Desert; r 250,000Rp) One of the two more formal choices, they have seven clean woven bamboo and thatched bungalows with bamboo beds, hammocks on the porch and private baths attached. They even have one attractive, three-sided shelter stilted above the beach.

Desert Point Lodge
LODGE $

(📞0878 610 4439; Tanjung Desert; d 250,000Rp) Thatched, fan-cooled bungalows with tiled outdoor baths, four-poster beds and private wooden decks set on a lawn in a blooming garden.

Hendra Surf Camp
LODGE $

(Tanjung Desert; r 80,000Rp) Simply a wooden house where you can crash on a mattress on the floor of a cell-like room with thin walls. Simple meals (20,000-30,000Rp) get rave reviews.

Grower Warung
INDONESIAN

(Tanjung Desert; mains 25,000-45,000Rp) Offers simple, basic meals on the cheap.

🛈 Getting There & Away

BEMO Bemo run between Lembar and Pelangan (5000Rp, 1½ hours) via Sekotong and Tembowong every 30 minutes until 5pm. West of Pelangan transport is less regular, but the route is still served by infrequent bemo until Selegang.

TAXI BOATS Taxi boats (per person 10,000Rp) are always willing and able to shuttle you from Tembowong on the mainland to Gili Gede. You'll see them bobbing in the sea near the Pertamina gas station. Chartered boats also connect Tembowong with the islands of Gili Gede and Gili Asahan (300,000Rp return).

Senggigi

Lombok's only bona fide tourist resort, Senggigi enjoys a spectacular location along a series of sweeping bays, with white-sand beaches sitting pretty below a backdrop of jungle-clad mountains and coconut palms. In the late afternoon a setting blood-red sun sinks into the surf next to the giant triangular cone of Bali's Gunung Agung.

Tourist numbers are relatively modest here, except in high season, and you'll find some excellent-value hotels and restaurants. Still, the tacky main strip could look more appealing, the influx of bar girls is an issue, and the resident beach hawkers can be over-persistent. The Senggigi area spans 10km of coastal road; the upscale neighbourhood of Mangsit is 3km north of central Senggigi.

👁 Sights

Pura Batu Bolong
HINDU

(admission by donation; ⊙7am-7pm) It's not the grandest, but Pura Batu Bolong is Lombok's sweetest Hindu temple, and particularly lovely at sunset. Join an ever-welcoming Balinese community as they leave offerings at the 14 altars and pagodas that tumble down a rocky volcanic outcropping into the foaming sea about 2km south of central Senggigi. The rock underneath the temple has a natural hole, hence the name (*batu bolong* literally means 'rock with hole').

🏃 Activities

Snorkelling, Diving & Surfing

There's reasonable snorkelling off the point in Senggigi and in front of Windy Cottages, 3km north of the town. You can rent snorkelling gear (per day 25,000Rp) from several spots on the beach. Diving trips from Senggigi usually visit the Gili Islands.

Blue Coral Diving
DIVING

(📞693 441; www.bluecoraldive.com; Jl Raya Senggigi; two tanks 700,000Rp, Open Water Certificate 3,600,000Rp) Senggigi's newest and biggest dive shop hits the same sites as the shops in the Gilis.

Blue Marlin
DIVING

(📞693 719; www.bluemarlindive.com; Holiday Resort Lombok, Jl Raya Senggigi; per dive 400,000Rp) The Senggigi shingle of Gili T's original.

Dream Divers
DIVING

(📞693 738, 692 047; www.dreamdivers.com; Jl Raya Senggigi; per dive 400,000Rp) The Senggigi depot of the Gili original.

Adventure Lombok
SURFING

(📞665 0238; www.adventurelombok.com; Pasar Seni; short-/longboards per day 100,000/200,000Rp, surf lessons US$40, bike rental per day 50,000Rp) Rents surfboards and offers surf lessons that include a helmet and transport to and from the break. They also organise Gunung Rinjani treks and won't give you the hard sell.

Hiking

Rinjani Trekking Club
ADVENTURE TOUR

(📞693 202; rtc.senggigi@gmail.com; Jl Raya Senggigi Km 8; trips incl transport from 1,750,000Rp) Well informed about routes and trail conditions on Gunung Rinjani and has a wide choice of guided hikes.

Massages, Spas & Salons

Very determined local masseurs armed with mats, oils and attitude hunt for business on Senggigi's beaches. Expect to pay about 60,000Rp for one hour after

Senggigi

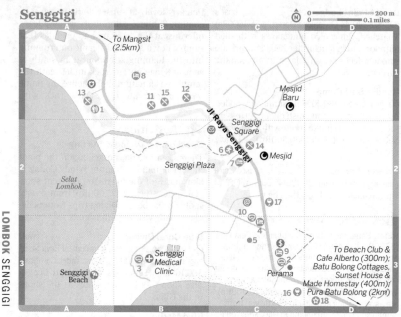

bargaining. Most hotels can arrange a masseur to visit your room; rates start at about 75,000Rp.

Senggigi has a burgeoning spa scene, with everything from simple set-ups to Zen-like wellness centres. The top hotels all have full service spas as well. Be warned, many of the streetside 'salons' you'll find are often fronts for a different sort of touchy-feely.

Qambodja Spa SPA
(☑693 800; Qunci Villas, Mangsit; massage from US$30; ☺10am-10pm) Gorgeous spa where you select your choice of oil (uplifting, harmony) depending on the effect and mood you require from your massage, which includes Thai, Balinese and shiatsu.

Royal Spa SPA
(☑660 8777; Jl Raya Senggigi; treatments from 85,000Rp; ☺10am-9pm) A professional yet inexpensive spa with a tempting range of scrubs, massages and treatments. The *lulur* massage is a real treat and includes a body mask.

🛏 Sleeping

Senggigi's accommodation is very spread out. But even if you're located a few kilometres away (say, in Mangsit) you're not iso-

lated as many restaurants offer free rides to diners and taxis are very inexpensive.

Heavy discounts of up to 50% are common in midrange and top-end places outside the July–August peak season.

SENGGIGI

TOP CHOICE Beach Club BUNGALOW $$
(☑693 637, 0818 0520 8807; www.thebeachclublombok.com; Jl Raya Senggigi; r with fan US$24, bungalows US$70; ❋🛜❄) There are few 3-star bamboo bungalow properties in Indo as comfy and homey as this boutique gem. Bungalows are crafted from wood and bamboo, and outfitted with flat-screens, DVD, queen beds and wired with wi-fi. The outdoor baths are leafy and tasteful, and they all surround a pool shaded by lush foliage and within steps of the rolling sea.

They also have two less expensive rooms, if you're on a budget. The restaurant-bar serves Aussie comfort food, shows the ball games of the moment and can attract a fun crowd. What's not to love?

Wira GUESTHOUSE $
(☑692 153; www.thewira.com; Jl Raya Senggigi Km 8; d 200,000-300,000Rp; ❋) This boutique *losmen* is a nice new addition to the main

Senggigi

Senggigi strip. They have simple, tasteful, sizeable rooms with bamboo furnishings, flat-screens, DVD player, and private porches out back. Cheaper fan rooms can be musty.

Sendok Guesthouse INN $
(www.sendokbali.com; Jl Raya Senggigi; r 200,000-380,000Rp; ❄🖧📶) A kitschy new inn with kitted-out guestrooms behind a friendly pub. Rooms pair lovely Javanese antiques with garrish tile, but they have high ceilings, flat-screens, rain showerheads, wi-fi and security boxes; all are bright and airy with their own private front porch. Superior rooms have hot water.

Batu Bolong Cottages HOTEL $$
(☏693 198, 693 065; Jl Raya Senggigi; d inland 350,000Rp, beachside 500,000-600,000Rp; ❄🖧📶) Bamboo is the operative term at this charming bungalow-style hotel set on both sides of the road south of the centre. Beachfront rooms have quaint touches like carved doors, and there's a lovely pool area off the beach. Some rooms have smelled musty in the past so sniff around.

Sunset House HOTEL $$
(☏667 7196, 692 020; www.sunsethouse-lombok. com; Jl Raya Senggigi 66; r 450,000Rp; ❄🖧) Now with 20 rooms, including six in the new wing and all with the same tasteful, well-equipped simplicity on this quiet stretch of shoreline near Pura Batu Bolong. Rooms on the upper floors have sweeping ocean views towards Bali.

Made Homestay HOMESTAY $
(☏0819 1704 1332; Jl Raya Senggigi; r with fan 100,000-150,000Rp, r with air-con 170,000-200,000Rp ; ❄🖧) A terrific new cheapie. Tiled rooms have big bamboo beds, a private front porch and free wi-fi. The air-con rooms cost a bit more, but remain tremendous value into high season. Cold water showers only.

Central Inn HOTEL $
(☏692 006; Jl Raya Senggigi; d 250,000Rp; ❄🖧) A brand new block hotel set in the center of town. Rooms have high ceilings and crown mouldings, bowl sinks, hot water and wi-fi, fresh tile, and a bamboo seating area out front with views of the surrounding hills.

Santosa Villas RESORT $$$
(Map p268; ☏693 090; www.santosavillasresort. com; Jl Raya Senggigi; d from US$160; ❄🖧📶) The recently renovated and rebranded Santosa resort offers luxurious accommodation ranging from 4-star hotel rooms to high-end luxury villas located on a nice beach and smack in the centre of the Senggigi strip.

Chandi BOUTIQUE RESORT $$$
(☏692 198; www.the-chandi.com; Batu Balong; r from US$150; ❄🖧📶) Another of Senggigi's new mod offerings, this one is about 1km south of the Pura Batu Balong. Each room has an outdoor living room and stylish modern interior with high ceilings, flat-screen TV and groovy outdoor baths. The ample oceanfront perch is pretty damn sweet.

Bale Kampung Homestay
GUESTHOUSE $

(☑ 660 0001, 0818 0360 0001; r with fan 100,000-150,000Rp, r with air-con 200,000Rp; ❄☞) Set 300m south of Pura Batu Bolong, this thatched brick compound is rather cramped, but there's a range of good value new rooms, the most expensive of which have hot water and air-con. It's a little out of the way, but they offer free transport to and from Senggigi town.

MANGSIT

TOP CHOICE Qunci Villas
RESORT $$$

(☑693 800; www.quncivillas.com; Jl Raya Mangsit, Mangsit; r from US$115, plus 21% tax) A spectacular, lovingly imagined property that comes close to a 5-star experience at a fraction of the price. Everything from the food to the pool area (straight jaw-dropping) to the spa, and especially the sea views (160m of beachfront), are magical.

Despite ourselves, we even loved the traditional dance performances preformed poolside at dinner time. It would be hard to find an equivalent hotel on Bali's coast and it's impossible to find one elsewhere on Lombok. This hotel is a destination in itself.

Jeeva Klui
RESORT $$$

(☑693 035; www.jeevaklui.com; Jl Raya Klui Beach; ocean view/beachfront r US$197/263, pool villas US$362 ; ❄☞☰) One of the area's finest offerings, with a shimmering infinity pool and a lovely, almost private, beach sheltered by a rocky out crop. Rooms are stylishly thatched with bamboo columns and private porches. Villas are 5-star luxe. A fine choice if you've got the dosh.

Windy Beach
COTTAGE $$

(☑693 191; www.windybeach.com; Jl Raya Mangsit; cottages 500,000-550,000Rp; ❄☞☰) This is a deservedly popular place situated on a fine sandy beach. Attractive traditional-style thatched cottages (with bamboo walls and mosquito nets) are scattered around a wonderful garden, and there's a bar-restaurant and decent snorkelling offshore.

🍴 Eating

Senggigi's dining scene ranges from fine dining to simple warung. Many places offer free transport for evening diners – phone for a ride.

SENGGIGI

TOP CHOICE Warung Cicak
NOODLES $

(Jl Raya Senggigi; mains 12,000-17,000Rp; ◷3-10pm) Because everybody loves an Asian noodle joint, and these upstart, roadside gourmets use only homemade noodles in their chicken, beef, mushroom or shrimp stir-frys and soups, served in a cute, open air warung sheltered rather tastefully by a tiered tin roof.

Square
INTERNATIONAL $$

(☑693 688; Senggigi Square; mains 40,000-150,000Rp; ☞) Destination restaurant with beautifully crafted seating, and a menu that features Western and Indonesian fusion such as wok-fried king prawns with Worcestershire sauce. The atmosphere is perhaps a little too formal, though the cooking is certainly very accomplished. Steaks get rave reviews from long-time expats.

Office
THAI, INTERNATIONAL $

(☑693 162; Jl Raya Senggigi, Pasar Seni; mains 25,000-65,000Rp; ◷9am-10pm) This art market pub offers the typical Indonesian and Western choices along with the pool tables, ball games and bar flies. But they also have a popular Thai menu thanks to the Bangkok-born manager. Think: authentic *prik king*, pad thai, *phat plaa meuk yat sai* (fried baby squid stuffed with chicken and mushrooms), *som tom* (papaya salad) and a tasty Thai grilled beef salad.

Kayu Manis
INTERNATIONAL $

(☑693 561; Jl Raya Senggigi; mains 25,000-35,000Rp) This exciting new restaurant has a casual vibe (think polished-wood bench seating) and an East-meets-West menu that reflects the life of chef-patron Berri, an Indonesian who lived in Australia for years. Dishes such as beer-battered calamari and snapper fillet topped with green veggies are superb.

Asmara
INTERNATIONAL $$

(☑693 619; www.asmara-group.com; Jl Raya Senggigi; mains 18,000-75,000Rp; 🍴) An ideal family choice, this place spans the culinary globe from tuna carpaccio to Wiener schnitzel to Lombok's own *sate pusut* (minced-meat or fish sate). It also has a playground and kids' menu.

Cafe Alberto
ITALIAN $$

(☑693 039; www.cafealbertolombok.com; Jl Raya Senggigi; mains from 45,000Rp; ◷8am-midnight)

A long-standing and well-loved beachside Italian kitchen. They do three types of ravioli, and six flavours of spaghetti, tagliatelle and penne, but they're known for their pizza. They offer free transport to and from your hotel.

Warung Manega SEAFOOD $$
(Jl Raya Senggigi; meals 75,000-250,000Rp; ☺11am-11pm) If you fled Bali before experiencing the Jimbaran fish grills, you can make up for it at this sister restaurant to one of Jimbaran's finest. Choose from a fresh daily catch of barracuda, squid, snapper, grouper, lobster, tuna and prawns – all of which are grilled over smouldering coconut husks and served on candlelit tables in the sand.

NORTH OF SENGGIGI

Coco Beach INDONESIAN $
(☑0817 578 0055; Pantai Kerandangan; mains from 25,000Rp; ☺noon-10pm; ☑) About 2km north of central Senggigi, this wonderful beachside restaurant features a healthy menu that includes lots of salads and choices for vegetarians (and uses organic produce wherever possible), and their nasi goreng is famous among Senggigi expats. They have a full bar, blend authentic jamu tonics and tastefully secluded seating.

☕ Drinking & Entertainment

Not long ago, Senggigi's bar scene was pretty vanilla. Enter the bar girls. Like something out of a Pattaya fever-dream, cinderblock malls were, um, erected on vacant lots and filled with 'karaoke' joints and massage parlors. One of these bar girl complexes is literally on the doorstep of the local mosque. If that sort of irony isn't your thing, find one of the restaurants or bars that feature live bands playing rock and pop covers, or hunker down over a cocktail by the pool at Qunci (opposite). They host an inviting happy hour.

Hotel Lina BAR
(Map p268; ☑693 237; Jl Raya Senggigi) Lina's seafront deck is another great spot for a sundowner. Happy hour starts at 4pm and ends an hour after dusk.

Papaya Café BAR
(Map p268; ☑693 136; Jl Raya Senggigi) The decor is slick, with exposed stonewalls, rattan furniture and evocative Asmat art from Papua. There's a nice selection of liquor, and they have a tight house band.

ⓘ LOMBOK DURING RAMADAN

Ramadan, the month of fasting, is the ninth month of the Muslim calendar. During daylight hours, many restaurants are closed in the capital and in conservative east and south Lombok. Foreigners eating, drinking (especially alcohol) and smoking in public may attract a negative reaction in these areas. In Senggigi, resort areas and most of north Lombok, cultural attitudes are far less strict.

Paragon CLUB
(☑693 750; Jl Raya Senggigi Km 12; ☺noon-2am; ☑) Part cafe, part nightclub, part karaoke bar, they have a nice perch on the beach, but that thumping music isn't always so magical. It does draw a crowd though, as well as the occasional live act from Jakarta. Look for the cheap louvered facade.

🛍 Shopping

Asmara Collection HANDICRAFTS
(☑693 619; Jl Raya Senggigi; ☺8am-11pm) A cut above the rest, this store has well-selected tribal art, including wonderful carvings and textiles from Sumba and Flores.

ⓘ Information

The nearest hospitals are in Mataram.
BCA (Jl Raya Senggigi) Bank with ATM.
Millennium Internet (☑693 860; Jl Raya Senggigi; per hour 24,000Rp; ☺24hr)
Police Station (☑110)
Post Office (Jl Raya Senggigi; ☺8am-6pm)
Senggigi Medical Clinic (☑693 856; Jl Raya Senggigi; ☺8am-7pm) At the Senggigi Beach Hotel.
Tourist Police (☑632 733)

ⓘ Getting There & Away

Boat

Perama (☑693 007; www.peramatour.com; Jl Raya Senggigi) operates daily fast boats to Padangbai in Bali (400,000Rp, two to three hours) at 1.30pm and shuttles to the Gili Islands (200,000Rp, 75 minutes) at 10am.

Bus, Bemo & Taxi

Regular bemo travel between Senggigi and Ampenan's Kebon Roek terminal (2500Rp).

LOMBOK SENGGIGI

Wave them down on the main drag. Heading to the Gilis? There are also two tourist shuttles running daily between Senggigi and Lembar (45,000Rp). A taxi to Lembar is 70,000Rp. Taxis to the airport in Praya cost a standard 150,000Rp.

Strangely, there's no public bemo service north to Bangsal harbour. Charter one for 75,000Rp.

Perama has tourist shuttle bus/boat services between Senggigi and Bali.

DESTINATION	FARE (RP)
Candidasa by public ferry/Perama fast boat	125,000/425,000
Kuta Bali, Sanur or Ubud by public ferry/Perama fast boat	200,000/500,000
Lovina	600,000

ℹ Getting Around

The central area is easy to negotiate on foot. If you're staying further away remember that many restaurants offer a free lift for diners.

MOTORBIKES Are readily available for hire in Senggigi, starting from 60,000Rp per day.

CAR HIRE There are many places on the main drag with rates starting at 150,000Rp for an ageing Suzuki Jimny to around 350,000Rp for a newish Kijang. Car rental per day with driver costs 400,000-500,000Rp.

NORTH & CENTRAL LOMBOK

📞 0370

Lush and fertile, Lombok's scenic interior is stitched together with rice terraces, lush forest, undulating tobacco fields and fruit and nut orchards, and is crowned by sacred Gunung Rinjani. Entwined in all this big nature are traditional Sasak settlements, some of which are known for their handicrafts. Public transport is not frequent or consistent enough to rely on, but the main roads are in good condition. With your own wheels you can explore black-sand fishing beaches, inland villages and waterfalls.

Bangsal to Bayan

Bangsa is a hassle (see p287), and public transport north from here is infrequent. Several minibuses a day go from Mandalika

terminal in Bertais (Mataram) to Bayan, but you'll have to get connections in Pemenang and/or Anyar, which can be difficult to navigate. Simplify things and get your own wheels.

SIRE

Fast becoming Lombok's most upmarket enclave, the jutting Sire (or Sira) peninsula is blessed with gorgeous, broad white-sand beaches and good snorkelling offshore. Three opulent resorts are now established here, alongside a couple of fishing villages and some amazing private villas. There's one wonderful boutique midrange property in the mix, too. Look out for the small **Hindu temple**, just beyond the Oberoi resort, which has shrines built into the coastal rocks and sublime ocean views.

🛏 Sleeping & Eating

TOP CHOICE Rinjani Beach

Eco Resort BOUTIQUE HOTEL $$

(📞0878 6450 9148, 0813 3993 0773; www.lombok -adventure.com; Karang Atas; bungalows 350,000-900,000Rp; ❄☀) A midrange gem in an exclusive zip code where the sun rises over Rinjani and sets over Agung, they offer five jumbo bamboo bungalows, each with its own colour scheme and theme, a queen bed, upcycled wood floors, and a sofa that can be converted into a twin. They have hammocks on private porches, and a pool on the black-sand beach.

They also have their own dive shop and restaurant, and sea kayaks and mountain bikes for guests. It's got beauty, grace and warmth. And they have cheaper, smaller bungalows for backpackers, too.

Tugu Lombok RESORT $$$

(📞620 111; www.tuguhotels.com; bungalows US$220, villas from US$270, plus 21% tax; ❄@☎☀) An astonishing fantasy of a hotel that's like no other on Lombok. This larger-than-life amalgamation of luxury accommodation, wacky design and spiritual Indonesian heritage sits on a wonderful white-sand beach. Room decor reflects Indonesian tradition, the exquisite spa is modelled on Java's Buddhist Borobudur temple and the main restaurant is like a rice barn on steroids. Service is spot on. Drop by for a meal or drink even if you're not staying here.

Oberoi Lombok RESORT $$$

(📞638 444; www.oberoihotels.com; r from US$260, villas from US$425, plus 21% tax ; ❄@☎☀) For sheer get-away-from-it-all bliss the Oberoi simply excels. The hotel's core is a triple-level pool, which leads the eye to a lovely private beach. Indonesian rajah-style luxury is the look: sunken marble bathtubs, teak floors, antique entertainment armoires and oriental rugs. Service is flawless, facilities are superb, and service, divine.

GONDANG & AROUND

Just northeast of Gondang village, a 6km trail heads inland to **Air Terjun Tiu Pupas**, a 30m waterfall (per person 30,000Rp) that's only worth seeing in the wet season. Trails continue from here to other wet-season waterfalls, including **Air Terjun Gangga**, the most beautiful of all. A guide (about 50,000Rp) is useful to navigate the confusing trails in these parts. Don't worry, they'll find you.

BAYAN

Wektu Telu, Lombok's animist-tinted form of Islam, was born in humble thatched mosques nestled in these Rinjani foothills. The best example is **Masjid Kuno Bayan Beleq**, next to the village of Baleq. Its low-slung roof, dirt floors and bamboo walls reportedly date from 1634, making this mosque the oldest on Lombok. Inside is a huge old drum which served as the call to prayer before PA systems. Ah, the good old days.

Senaru & Batu Koq

These scenic villages merge into one along a steep road with sweeping Rinjani and sea views. Most visitors here are volcano-bound but beautiful walking trails and spectacular waterfalls beckon to those who aren't.

⊙ Sights & Activities

Air Terjun Sindang Gila (5000Rp) is a spectacular set of falls 20 minutes' walk from Senaru via a lovely forest and hillside trail. The hearty and the foolish (guilty!) make for the creek, edge close and then get pounded by the hard, foaming cascade that explodes over black volcanic stone 40m above.

A further 50 minutes or so uphill is **Air Terjun Tiu Kelep**, another waterfall with a swimming hole. The track is steep and guides are compulsory (60,000Rp). Long-tailed macaques (locals call them *kera*) and the much rarer silvered leaf monkey sometimes appear.

In the traditional Sasak village of **Dusun Senaru**, at the top of the road, locals will in-

vite you to chew betel nut (or tobacco) and show you around for a donation.

Guided walks and community tourism activities can be arranged at most guesthouses – they include a **rice-terrace and waterfalls walk** (per person 150,000Rp), which takes in Sindang Gila, rice paddies and an old bamboo mosque, and the **Senaru Panorama Walk** (per person 150,000Rp), which incorporates stunning views and insights into local traditions. Guides are easy to find in town, but a dependable place to start is Transit Cafe (p273).

🛏 Sleeping & Eating

Most of the dozen or so places here are simple mountain lodges, and since the climate's cooler, you won't need fans. All of the following are dotted along the road from Bayan to Senaru and listed in order from the top of the road down.

Gunung Baru Senaru   COTTAGE **$**
(☑0819 0741 1211; d 80,000Rp) A small family-run property with just five simple, tiled cottages with western toilets and *mandi* (bath) in a blooming garden.

Pondok Senaru & Restaurant   LODGE **$**
(☑622 868, 0818 0362 4129; r 250,000-600,000Rp) A class act, this place has lovely little cottages with terracotta-tiled roofs, and some well-equipped superior rooms with TV, four-poster beds and hot water. The restaurant, with tables perched on the edge of a rice-terraced valley, is a sublime place for a bite (dishes 12,000-40,000Rp).

Transit Cafe   INDONESIAN **$**
(☑0818 0365 2874; www.rudytrekker.com; Jl Raya Pariwisata; mains 20,000-40,000Rp; 🛜) Part cafe, part Rinjani launch pad, they serve pastas, sandwiches and assorted Indo classics along with wi-fi, do all the waterfall and panorama hikes, and offer Rinjani trekking packages.

Horizon   LODGE **$**
(☑0817 576 0936; www.horizonsenaru.com; d 300,000Rp) Decent value contemporary rooms (in one, you can gaze over the Senaru valley from your bed), pebble-floored bathrooms and high standards of cleanliness. It's also home to a small restaurant.

Sinar Rinjani   LODGE **$**
(☑081 854 0673; d with cold/hot water 100,000/150,000Rp) Rooms are huge with rain

WEKTU TELU

Wektu Telu is a complex mixture of Hindu, Islamic and animist beliefs, though it's now officially classified as a sect of Islam. At its forefront is a physical concept of the Holy Trinity. The sun, moon and stars represent heaven, earth and water, while the head, body and limbs represent creativity, sensitivity and control.

As recently as 1965, the vast majority of Sasaks in northern Lombok were Wektu Telu, but under Suharto's 'New Order' government, indigenous religious beliefs were discouraged, and enormous pressure was placed on Wektu Telu to become Wektu Lima (Muslims who pray five times a day). But in the Wektu Telu heartland around Bayan, locals have been able to maintain their unique beliefs by differentiating their cultural traditions (Wektu Telu) from religion (Islam). Most do not fast for the full month of Ramadan, only attend the mosque for special occasions, and there's widespread consumption of *brem* (alcoholic rice wine).

showers, crown mouldings and king-sized beds, and the rooftop restaurant has outstanding views.

ℹ Information

Rinjani Trek Centre (RTC; ☑0878 6432 3094, 0817 5724 863; www.info2lombok.com), at the top of the hill, is the local guiding and mountain authority. All Rinjani trips are packaged with their guides and approval.

ℹ Getting There & Away

From Mandalika terminal in Bertais (Mataram), catch a bus to Anyar (25,000-30,000Rp, 2½ hours). Bemo no longer run from Anyar for Senaru, so you'll have to charter an *ojek* (motorcycle that takes passengers; per person 15,000-20,000Rp).

Sembalun Valley

☑0376

High on the eastern side of Gunung Rinjani is the beautiful Sembalun Valley, a rich farming region where the golden foothills turn vivid green in the wet season. When the high clouds part, Rinjani goes full frontal from all angles. The valley has two main settlements, Sembalun Lawang and Sembalun Bumbung, tranquil bread baskets primarily concerned with growing cabbage, potatoes, strawberries and, above all, garlic – though trekking tourism brings in a little income, too. This is the best access point for an attempt at Rinjani's summit.

🏃 Activities

Rinjani Information Centre   HIKING
(☑0878 6334 4119; ☉6am-6pm) The Rinjani Information Centre is the place to enquire about Rinjani treks. They have well-in-

formed English-speaking staff and lots of fascinating information panels about the area's flora, fauna, geology and history. They also offer a four-hour **Village Walk** (per person 150,000Rp, minimum two people) and a two-day rambling **Wildflower Walk** (per person including guide, porters, meals and camping gear 550,000Rp) past flowery grasslands.

They have camping and trekking gear for hire.

🛏 Sleeping

Sembalun Lawang village is rustic and most guesthouses will heat *mandi* water for a fee.

Lembah Rinjani   LODGE $
(☑0852 3954 3279, 0818 0365 2511; d 300,000-400,000Rp) The property has been spruced up lately and is in great shape. Basic but clean tiled rooms have queen beds, wood funishings, private porches and breathtaking mountain and sunrise views.

Rinjani Information Center   LODGE $
(RIC; ☑0878 6334 4119; r 200,000Rp) The rangers at RIC now offer six simple and tiled guest rooms with double beds, cable TV, private baths and tiny decks behind their office.

Maria Guesthouse   GUESTHOUSE $
(☑0852 3956 1340; r 250,000Rp) A new place with large tin-roofed bungalows at the rear of a family compound. Digs are bright with garrish tiled floors and some can smell musty, but the family vibe is fun and the garden location sweet.

ℹ Getting There & Away

From Mandalika bus terminal in Bertais (Mataram), take a bus to Aikmel (20,000Rp) and change there for a bemo to Sembalun Lawang

(15,000Rp). Regular pick-ups connect Lawang and Bumbung.

There's no public transport between Sembalun Lawang and Senaru, so you'll have to charter an *ojek*, for around 150,000Rp.

Gunung Rinjani

Lording over the northern half of Lombok, Gunung Rinjani (3726m) is Indonesia's second-tallest volcano. It's an astonishing peak, and sacred to Hindus and Sasaks who make pilgrimages to the summit and lake to leave offerings for the gods and spirits. To the Balinese, Rinjani is one of three sacred mountains, along with Bali's Agung and Java's Bromo. Sasaks ascend throughout the year around the full moon.

The mountain also has climatic significance. Its peak attracts a steady stream of swirling rain clouds, while its ash emissions bring fertility to the island's rice fields and tobacco crops, feeding a tapestry of paddies, fields, and cashew and mango orchards.

Inside the immense caldera, sitting 600m below the rim, is a stunning, 6km-wide, cobalt-blue crescent lake, **Danau Segara Anak** (Child of the Sea). The Balinese toss gold and jewellery into the lake in a ceremony called *pekelan*, before they slog their way towards the sacred summit.

The mountain's newest cone, the minor peak of Gunung Baru, only emerged a couple of hundred years ago, its scarred, smouldering profile rising above the lake as an ominous reminder of the apocalyptic power of nature. This peak has been erupting fitfully for the last decade, periodically belching plumes of smoke and ash over the entire Rinjani caldera. Also in the crater are natural hot springs known as **Aiq Kalak**. Locals suffering from skin diseases trek here with a satchel of medicinal herbs to bathe and scrub in the bubbling mineral water.

ORGANISED TREKS

Treks to the rim, lake and peak should not be taken lightly, and guides are mandatory. Climbing Rinjani during the wet season (November to March) is usually completely forbidden due to the risk of landslide. June to August is the only time you are (almost) guaranteed minimal rain or clouds. Be prepared with layers and a fleece because it can get cold at the rim (and near-freezing at the summit) at any time of year.

The easiest way to organise a trip is to head to the Rinjani Trek Centre (p274) in Senaru or the **Rinjani Information Centre** (RIC; ☎0878 6334 4119; ☺6am-6pm) in Sembalun Lawang. These centres use a rotation system, and all local guides get a slice of the trekking purse.

Gunung Rinjani

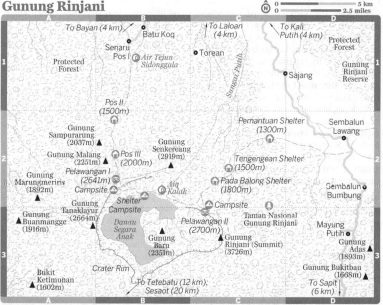

CLIMBING GUNUNG RINJANI

The most popular way to climb Gunung Rinjani is the five-day trek that starts at Senaru and finishes at Sembalun Lawang. Other possibilities include a summit attempt from Sembulan, which sits higher on the slope and can be done as a gruelling two-day return hike. No matter which way you walk, a guide is mandatory, and it's usually forbidden to climb Rinjani during the wet season (November to March) due to the threat of landslides.

Day One: Senaru Pos I to Pos III (Five to Six Hours)

At the southern end of Senaru is the **Rinjani Trek Centre** (Pos I, 601m), where you register, organise your guide and porters and pay the park fee. Just beyond the post, head right when the trail forks. The trail climbs steadily through scrubby farmland for about half an hour to the entrance of **Taman Nasional Gunung Rinjani** (Gunung Rinjani National Park). The wide trail climbs for another 2½ hours until you reach Pos II (1500m), where there's a shelter. Another 1½ hours' steady walk uphill brings you to Pos III (2000m), where there are two shelters in disrepair. Pos III is usually the place to camp at the end of the first day.

Day Two: Pos III to Danau Segara Anak & Aiq Kalak (Four Hours)

From Pos III, it takes about 1½ hours to reach the rim, **Pelawangan I** (2641m). Set off very early for the stunning sunrise. It's possible to camp at Pelawangan I, but level sites are limited, there's no water and it can be very blustery.

It takes about two hours to descend to **Danau Segara Anak** and over to the hot springs, **Aiq Kalak**. The first hour is a very steep descent and involves a bit of bouldering. From the bottom of the crater wall it's an easy 30-minute walk across undulating terrain around the lake's edge. There are several places to camp, but most locals prefer to be near the hot springs to soak their weary bodies.

Day Three: Aiq Kalak to Pelawangan II (Three to Four Hours)

The trail starts beside the last shelter at the hot springs and heads away from the lake for about 100m before veering right. It then traverses the northern slope of the crater,

Roughly the same trek packages and prices are offered by all operators (base guide and porter prices are set by RTC and RIC), though some outfitters have a 'luxury' option. Treks from Senaru to Sembalun Lawang via the lake summit are very popular, and the return hike from Sembalun Lawang to the summit is another well-trodden trail.

Trek prices get cheaper the larger the party. A three-day hike (including food, equipment, guide, porters, park fee and transport back to Senaru) to the summit and lake costs from US$185 per person based on a group of two to four. An overnight trek to the crater rim costs from US$135.

OPERATORS

Agencies in Mataram, Senggigi and the Gili Islands can organise Rinjani treks too, with return transport from the point of origin.

John's Adventures TREKKING
(☏0817 578 8018; www.rinjanimaster.com; per person 3-day, 2-night from 1,750,000Rp) John's Adventures is a very experienced outfitter, which has toilet tents, thick sleeping mats

and itineraries that start from either Senaru or Sembalun.

Transit Cafe TREKKING
(☏0818 0365 2874; www.rudytrekker.com; Jl Raya Pariwisata; 3-day, 2-night trek 1,500,000Rp, private group 1,750,000Rp) Transit Cafe is a conscientious outfitter based in Senaru. They have a variety of itineraries, though most prefer the three-day, two-night package starting from Sembalun.

GUIDES & PORTERS

Hiking independently is simply not allowed, and deeply unwise. If you did manage to bring all of your own gear from home, packed enough provisions, and wish to create your own itinerary on the mountain, you can book your own guide and porters at either the RIC in Sembalun or RTC in Senaru, though indies endure considerably less hassle at the RIC. Senaru-based guides get a standard 200,000Rp per day and porters 150,000Rp per day; tips of 20,000Rp to 50,000Rp per day are sufficient. In Sem-

and it's an easy one-hour walk along the grassy slopes before you hit a steep, unforgiving rise; from the lake it takes about three hours to reach the crater rim (2639m). At the rim, a sign points the way back to Danau Segara Anak. The trail forks here – go straight on to Lawang or continue along the rim to the campsite of Pelawangan II (2700m).

Day Four: Pelawangan II to Rinjani Summit (Five to Six Hours Return)

Gunung Rinjani's summit arcs above the campsite and looks deceptively close. Start the climb around 3am to reach it by sunrise. Depending on wind conditions, it may not be possible to attempt the summit at all, as the trail is along an exposed ridge.

It takes about 45 minutes to clamber up a steep, slippery and indistinct trail to the ridge that leads to Rinjani. Once on the ridge it's a relatively steady walk uphill. After about an hour heading towards a false peak, the real summit of Rinjani (3726m) looms. The trail then gets increasingly steeper. About 350m before the summit, the scree is composed of loose, fist-sized rocks. This section can take about an hour. The views from the top are truly magnificent. In total it takes around three hours to reach the summit, and two to return.

Day Four/Five: Pelawangan II to Sembalun Lawang (Six to Seven Hours)

After negotiating the peak, it's possible to reach Lawang the same day. From the campsite, it's a steep descent to the village; you'll feel it in your knees. From the campsite, head back along the crater rim. Shortly after the turn-off to Danau Segara Anak, there's a signposted right turn down to Pada Balong (also called Pos 3, 1800m). The trail is easy to follow; it takes around two hours to reach Pada Balong shelter.

The trail then undulates toward the Sembalun Lawang savannah, via Tengengean (or Pos 2, 1500m) shelter, beautifully situated in a river valley. It's another 30 minutes through long grass to lonely Pemantuan (or Pos 1, 1300m), and two more hours along a dirt track to Sembalun Lawang.

LOMBOK TETEBATU

balun, guides charge 150,000 per day and porters 125,000Rp per day. You must use guides and porters directly from the centres in Senaru or Sembalun Lawang, as they are licensed for your security. Guides are knowledgeable and informative, but will usually only carry a light day pack for you, so you'll need to take at least one porter. Obviously, ample food and water is vital.

ENTRANCE FEE & EQUIPMENT

Entrance to Taman Nasional Gunung Rinjani is a hefty 150,000Rp – you register and pay at the RTC in Senaru or the RIC in Sembalun Lawang before your trek.

Sleeping bags and tents are essential and can be hired at either RTC or RIC. Decent footwear, warm clothing, wet-weather gear, gloves, cooking equipment and a torch are important (all can be hired if necessary). Expect to pay upwards of 100,000Rp a head per day for all your hired gear. Muscle balm (to ease aching legs) and a swimming costume (for the lake and hot springs) could also be packed.

Poaching firewood at high altitude is an environmental no-no, so take a stove. And bring home your rubbish, including toilet tissue. Sadly several Rinjani camps are litter-strewn.

FOOD & SUPPLIES

Trek organisers at RTC and RIC will arrange trekking food. Mataram is cheapest for supplies but many provisions are available in Senaru and Sembalun Lawang. Take more water than seems reasonable (dehydration can spur altitude sickness), extra batteries (as altitude can wreak havoc on those, as well) and a back-up lighter.

Tetebatu

📕0376

Laced with Rinjani spring-fed streams and blessed with rich volcanic soil, Tetebatu is a Sasak breadbasket. The surrounding countryside is quilted with tobacco and rice fields, fruit orchards and cow pastures that fade into remnant monkey forest gushing with waterfalls. Tetebatu's sweet climate is ideal for long country walks (at 400m it's high enough to mute that hot, sticky coastal mercury). Dark nights come saturated with sound courtesy of a frog orchestra accompanied by countless gurgling brooks. Even insomniacs snore here.

The town is spread out, with facilities on roads north and east (nicknamed 'waterfall road') of the central *ojek* stop, which happens to be the town's main intersection. The internet has yet to colonise tiny Tetebatu. The closest connection is in Kotaraja, 5km away.

◉ Sights & Activities

A shady 4km track leading from the main road, just north of the mosque, heads into the **Taman Wisata Tetebatu** (Monkey Forest) with black monkeys and waterfalls – you'll need a guide.

Waterfalls   WATERFALL
On the southern slopes of Rinjani, there are two waterfalls. Both are accessible by private transport or a spectacular two-hour walk (one way) through rice fields from Tetebatu. If walking, hire a guide (125,000Rp) through your hotel.

A steep 2km hike from the car park at the end of the access road to Taman Nasional Gunung Rinjani leads to beautiful **Air Terjun Jukut**, an impressive 20m drop to a deep pool surrounded by lush forest.

🛏 Sleeping & Eating

TOP CHOICE Tetebatu Mountain Resort   LODGE **$**
(�0819 1771 6440, 081 2372 4040; d/tr 400,000/500,000Rp) These two-story Sasak bungalows are the best digs in town. There are separate bedrooms on both floors – perfect for travelling buddies – and a top-floor balcony with magical rice field views.

Cendrawasih Cottages   COTTAGE **$**
(⊠0878 6418 7063; r 175,000Rp) Sweet little *lumbung* (rice barn)–style brick cottages with bamboo beds and private porches nestled in the rice fields. You'll sit on floor cushions in their stunning stilted restaurant (mains 18,000-40,000Rp), which has Sasak, Indonesian or Western grub and 360-degree paddy views. It's about 500m east of the intersection. Low season discounts are common.

Hakiki Inn   BUNGALOW **$**
(⊠0819 1836 0477; bungalow 150,000-250,000Rp) A collection of sweet if slightly worn Sasak

bungalows in a blooming garden at the edge of the rice fields. The largest of the bunch sleep three. You'll find it perched over the family rice plot about 600m from the intersection.

Pondok Tetebatu   LODGE **$**
(⊠0818 0576 7153, 632 572; d 100,000-150,000Rp) Five hundred metres north of the intersection, these detached, ranch-style rooms set around a flower garden are basic and reasonably clean, but the staff are fantastic, the restaurant, which specialises in Sasak cooking, is a good bet, and they offer guided walks through farming villages to the falls.

ℹ Getting There & Around

Public transport to Tetebatu is infrequent. All cross-island buses pass Pomotong (15,000Rp from Mandalika terminal) on the main east–west highway. Get off here and you can hop an *ojek* (15,000Rp) to Tetebatu.

Private cars (with drivers) can be arranged at Pondok Tetebatu (p278) to all Lombok destinations (300,000Rp to 600,000Rp) including the airport (350,000Rp); bicycles (per day 50,000Rp) and motorbikes (per day 50,000Rp) can be rented here too.

SOUTH LOMBOK

☎0370
Beaches just don't get much better: the water is warm, striped turquoise and curls into barrels, and the sand is silky and snow-white, framed by massive headlands and sheer cliffs that recall Bali's Bukit Peninsula 30 years ago. Village life is still vibrant in south Lombok as well, with unique festivals and an economy based on seaweed and tobacco harvests. The south is noticeably drier than the rest of Lombok and more sparsely populated, with limited roads and public transport. But, with Lombok's new state-of-the-art international airport now operating, flights have already increased and change will surely come. Soon.

Praya

Sprawling Praya is the main town in the south, with tree-lined streets and the odd crumbling Dutch colonial relic. But the real (and only) reason you're here is to fly in or out of Lombok's **new airport**, which is around 5km south of the centre. The bemo terminal is on the northwest side of town.

Although it looks far on the map, a massive four-lane, high-speed bypass shrinks the distance between the airport and Mataram, which is less than 45 minutes away. Taxi rates to and from Mataram (100,000Rp, 45 minutes), Kuta (60,000Rp, 25 minutes), Senggigi (150,000Rp, one hour), Bangsal (200,000Rp, 90 minutes), where you can access the Gili islands, and to the Labuhan Lombok ferry port (230,000Rp, two hours) have been standardised. There is also a Senggigi-bound shuttle (25,000Rp), but they don't leave until they're close to full.

Around Praya

SUKARARA

The main street here is the domain of textile shops, where you can watch weavers work their old looms. **Dharma Setya** (☑660 5204; ⊗8am-5pm) has an incredible array of handwoven Sasak textiles, including ikat and *songket* (handwoven silver or gold-threaded cloth). To reach Sukarara from Praya, take a bemo to Puyung along the main road. From there, hire a *cidomo* (horse cart) or walk the 2km to Sukarara.

PENUJAK

Penujak is well-known for its traditional *gerabah* pottery. Made from chocolatey terracotta-tinted local clay, it's hand-burnished and topped with braided bamboo. Huge floor vases cost US$6 or so, and there are also plates and cups on offer from the potters' humble home studios, most of which huddle around the eerie village cemetery. Any bemo from Praya to Kuta will drop you off here.

REMBITAN & SADE

The area from Sengkol down to Kuta is a centre for Sasak culture – traditional villages full of towering *lumbung* (rice barn) and *bale tani* (family house) homes made from bamboo, mud, and cow and buffalo dung. Regular bemo cover this route.

Sade's **Sasak Village** has been extensively renovated and has some fascinating *bale tani*. Further south, **Rembitan** has more of an authentic feel to it, boasts an authentic cluster of houses and *lumbung* and the 100-year-old **Masjid Kuno**, an ancient thatched-roof mosque that is a pilgrimage destination for Lombok's Muslims.

Both villages are worth a look but it's not possible to look around sans guide (around 30,000Rp).

Kuta

Imagine a crescent bay, turquoise in the shallows and deep blue further out. It licks a huge, white-sand beach, as wide as a football pitch and framed by headlands. It's deserted, save for a few fishermen, seaweed farmers and their children. Now imagine a coastline of nearly a dozen such bays, all backed by a rugged range of coastal hills spotted with lush patches of banana trees and tobacco fields, and you'll have a vague idea of Kuta's majesty.

Southern Lombok's incredible coastline of giant bite-shaped bays is startling, its beauty immediate, undeniable and arresting. Yet this region has historically been the island's poorest, its sun-blasted soil parched and unproductive. These days those hills are also pocked with illegal, undocumented gold mines, which you'll see and hear grinding away as you head west to the surf beaches.

Kuta proper consists of no more than a few hundred houses, a likeable but scruffy-around-the-edges place with a ramshackle market area, and a seafront lined with simple seafood shacks and barefoot bars (and some very persistent, if sweet, child hawkers). Its original attraction was the limitless world-class breaks within a short ride of town. For now everyone seems to be sitting on their land, but with the new airport a 30-minute ride away, the town's real-estate agents – who

NYALE FESTIVAL

On the 19th day of the 10th month in the Sasak calendar (generally February or March), hundreds of Sasaks gather on the beach at Kuta, Lombok. When night falls, fires are built and teens sit around competing in a Sasak poetry slam, where they spit rhyming couplets called *pantun* back and forth. At dawn the next day, the first of millions of *nyale* (worm-like fish that appear here annually) are caught, then teenage girls and boys take to the sea separately in decorated boats, and chase one another with lots of noise and laughter. The *nyale* are eaten raw or grilled, and are considered to be an aphrodisiac. A good catch is a sign that a bumper crop of rice is coming.

Kuta

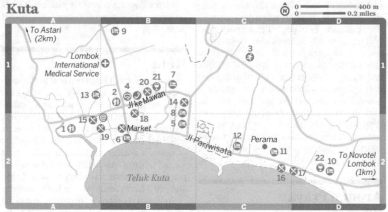

are already spearheading increasing villa development – are betting on change real soon.

🏃 Activities

Surfing

Waves break on the reefs, including lefts and rights, in Teluk Kuta (Kuta Bay), and more on the reefs east of Tanjung Aan. If you're after a reef break, get local boatmen to tow you out for around 100,000Rp. About 7km east of Kuta, **Gerupak** also has good surf shops and no fewer than five breaks. West of Kuta, gorgeous **Mawi** offers consistent world-class surf.

Kimen Surf   SURFING
(☑655 064; www.kuta-lombok.net; board rental per day 50,000Rp, lessons per person 360,000Rp) Swell forecasts, tips, guided surf trips, board rental, repairs and lessons.

Gloro   SURFING
(☑0818 0576 5690; board per day 50,000Rp, lessons for one/two people 300,000/500,000Rp; ⊙10am-6pm) A solid, rootsy local shop. They're on the road to Kuta Indah.

Diving

Scuba Froggy   DIVING
(☑0819 0795 2965, 0878 6426 5958; www.scubafroggy.com; per dive 375,000Rp; ⊙9am-7pm) Scuba Froggy is the only dive shop in town. They run local trips to 12 sites, most above 18m and one site as deep as 26m. From June to November they also run trips to the spectacular ocean pinnacles in Belongas Bay (two dives 1,000,000Rp), famous for schooling hammerheads and mobula rays. Cur-

rents and conditions can be very challenging in Blongas.

Horse Riding

Kuta Horses   HORSE RIDING
(☑0819 1754 2679; 1hr ride 400,000Rp; ⊙rides 8am & 4pm) Kuta Horses offers horseback riding, through Sasak villages, on Kuta's country lanes, and on the beach at sunrise and sunset.

🛏 Sleeping

Prices increase markedly in the short July–August high season.

TOP CHOICE **Yuli's Homestay**   HOMESTAY $
(☑0819 1710 0983; www.yulishomestay.com; r 350,000Rp; ❀🕸🛜🏊) A wonderful new place, their eight rooms are immaculately clean, extremely spacious and nicely furnished with huge beds and wardrobes (and have big front terraces, though cold-water bathrooms). There's a guest kitchen and a huge garden and pool to enjoy.

Hey Hey Homestay   HOMESTAY $
(☑0818 0522 8822; r 100,000Rp) An outstanding homestay with clean, spacious rooms and sea views from private patios. If you get lucky, score the bamboo room on the top floor where the view is epic. Take the dirt road south from the intersection.

Kuta Baru   HOMESTAY $
(☑081 854 8357; Jl Pariswata Kuta; r 125,000Rp; 🛜) One of Kuta's best homestays. There's a cute patio strung with the obligatory hammock, daily coffee service, free wi-fi,

Kuta

sparkling tiles and an all-around good vibe. It's 110m east of the intersection.

GR Homestay GUESTHOUSE $
(0819 0727 9797; s/d 160,000/180,000Rp;) A solid new Balinese-owned spot with 10 simple tiled rooms with crown mouldings, pastel paint jobs, and rain showerheads in otherwise simple baths. There's a nice pool out front.

Lamancha Homestay HOMESTAY $
(615 5186, 0819 3313 0156; s 80,000-100,000Rp, d 100,000-150,000Rp) A super charming homestay offering somewhat frayed bamboo rooms with concrete floors, and charming new fan-cooled rooms, draped with colourful tapestries and canopied beds. Rooms are clean and management is endearing.

Sekar Kuning INN $
(654 856; Jl Pariwisata; r 150,000-180,000Rp;) A charming beach-road inn. Tiled rooms have ceiling fans, high ceilings, pastel paint jobs and bamboo furniture on the patio. Top-floor rooms have ocean views and are more expensive.

Novotel Lombok RESORT $$$
(615 3333; www.novotel.com; r from US$94, villas from US$244, plus 21% tax;) This appealing, Sasak-themed 4-star resort spills onto a superb beach less than 3km east of the junction. Rooms have high sloping roofs and modern interiors. There are two pools, a wonderful spa, good restaurants, a swanky bar and a plethora of activities on offer including catamaran sailing, fishing and scuba diving.

Surfers Inn INN $
(655 582; www.lombok-surfersinn.com; r 180,000-400,000Rp;) A very smart, stylish and orderly place with five classes of modern rooms, each with huge windows and large beds, and some with sofas. Book ahead as it's very popular.

Mimpi Manis B&B $
(0818 369 950; www.mimpimanis.com; r 120,000-220,000Rp;) An inviting English-Balinese-owned B&B with two spotless rooms in a two-storey house, all with ensuite shower and TV/DVD player. There's home-cooked food, plenty of good books to browse and DVDs to borrow. It's 2km inland from the beach, but the owners offer a free drop-off service to the beach and town and arrange bike and motorbike rental.

Seger Reef Homestay INN $
(655 528; Jl Pariwisata; r 130,000-150,000Rp) Seven bright, spotless, family-owned bungalows across the street from the beach. Newest rooms are kitted out with wardrobes, and bizzaro headboards.

Eating & Drinking

Kuta's dining scene has improved with growth, but at most local joints the Indo nosh or fresh seafood are always the smart choices. The market fires up on Sunday and Wednesday.

Astari VEGETARIAN $
(dishes 18,000-30,000Rp; 8am-6pm Tue-Sun) Perched on a mountaintop 2km west of town on the road to Mawan, this breezy, Moroccan-themed vegetarian lounge-restaurant

has spectacular vistas of pristine bays and rocky peninsulas that take turns spilling further out to sea. And its delicious, health-conscious menu lives up to the setting. The blackboard always has a daily dish and drink of the day, but the mainstays are the focaccia sandwiches, salads and superb shakes. You will not eat and run.

Warung Bule
SEAFOOD $$

(☑0819 1799 6256; mains 37,000-135,000Rp; ☉8am-10pm) A recent revelation in Kuta dining, founded by the long-time executive chef at the Novotel who delivers tropical seafood tastes at an affordable price. We like the tempura starter and his Tahitian take on ceviche. The grilled mahi is good, and so is the lobster Tom yam soup. He has other creative concoctions like a Sasak chicken wrap and an angel hair pasta with chilli crab. You'll find something tasty.

Warung Jawa 1
INDONESIAN $

(Jl ke Mawan; meals 10,000Rp; ☉11am-10pm) On the Mawan road about 120m east of the intersection, this little bamboo shack has a cheap and mean *nasi campur*. Munch and watch buffalo graze with an ocean backdrop.

Solah Cafe
CAFE $

(mains 22,000-46,000Rp; ☉9am-10pm; ☜☝) A lovely new addition to the beach strip, they serve up an array of Western and Indonesian breakfasts in the morning (try the *bubur*, a sweet rice porridge with palm sugar). At lunch and dinner the menu diverges into nicoise salads, a pumpkin and coconut milk soup, four flavours of spaghetti and an array of Indonesian and Sasak flavors including a dynamite coconut milk curry that is served vegetarian or with chicken or seafood. They also offer daily yoga (50,000Rp) every morning at 8am and a lovely swatch of beach outfitted with bamboo lounges facing Kuta Bay.

Dwiki's
PIZZERIA $$

(☑0859 3503 4489; mains 35,000-65,000Rp; ☉8am-11pm; ☜☝) The choice spot for wood-fired thin-crust pizza in tiki bar environs. And they deliver!

Spot
INTERNATIONAL $$

(☑702 2100; www.thespotbungalows.com; Jl Pariwisata Kuta 1; mains 30,000-60,000Rp; ☉7am-10pm; ☜) Their collection of nine bamboo bungalows set around a grassy plot is worth checking into but their restaurant is the real find. They do fish and chips,

burgers, and even some Korean BBQ. All is served in a tasteful diningroom wired with wi-fi. Their bar is popular at happy hour and for football matches of international import.

Bong's
INDONESIAN $

(meals 18,000-40,000Rp) *Lumbung*-style restaurant that scores highly for Sasak food, including *olah olah* (vegetables cooked in coconut milk), seared fish and lemon chicken.

Rumah Makan Hidayah
INDONESIAN $

(mains from 12,000Rp) Honest, inexpensive local food including Sasak specials and *kangkung pelecing* (sautéd water spinach) in a family-run beachside shack. The sandy courtyard at the rear has direct ocean views.

Shore Beach Bar
BAR

(Jl Pariwisata; ☉10am-late, live band on Sat night) Owned by Kimen, Kuta's original surf entrepreneur, the open dance-hall interior has been recently renovated, the sound system is fantastic, there's breezy patio seating, cushy red booths, an expansive bar, a projection screen and a new beachside annex. If you're in town on a Saturday night, you'll probably wind up here.

Cafe 7
BAR

(Jl Pariswata Kuta; ☉11am-1pm) The style is lounge bar, there's frequent live music and the vibe is friendly. It's a little pricey, but the cocktails are worth a splurge.

ⓘ Information

Danger & Annoyances

If you decide to rent a bicycle or motorbike, take care whom you deal with – arrangements are informal and no rental contracts are exchanged. We have received occasional reports of some visitors having motorbikes stolen, and then having to pay substantial sums of money as compensation to the owner (who may or may not have arranged the 'theft' himself). Renting a motorbike from your guesthouse is safest.

As you drive up the coastal road west and east of Kuta, watch your back – especially after dark. There have been reports of muggings in the area.

Internet Access

Dehril Cell (internet per hour 10,000Rp; ☉8am-9pm) Has speedy internet access with a hotspot for laptop and smartphone addicts. They rent bicycles (per day 30,000Rp), too.

Medical Services
Lombok International Medical Service
(☎655 155; ☉4-9pm) Doctor and pharmacy.

Telephone
There's a wartel (public telephone office) close to the junction.

Travel Agency
Perama (☎654 846; Jl Pariwisata) Shuttle buses all over Lombok.

❶ Getting There & Away

Kuta is tricky to reach by public transport – from Mataram you'll have to go via Praya (5000Rp), then to Sengkol (3000Rp) and finally to Kuta (2000Rp), usually changing buses at all these places. Perama run shuttle buses to/from Mataram (110,000Rp, two hours), Senggigi (120,000Rp, 2½ hours), the Gilis (180,000Rp, 3½ hours) and Senaru 260,000Rp. Several agents around town can book a seat on an airport shuttle (50,000-65,000Rp) or arrange a private car (80,000-100,000Rp) to pick you up from your hotel.

❶ Getting Around

Irregular bemo go east of Kuta to Awang and Tanjung Aan (5000Rp), and west to Selong Blanak (10,000Rp), or can be chartered to nearby beaches. Guesthouses rent motorbikes for about 50,000Rp per day. *Ojek* congregate around the main junction as you enter Kuta.

East of Kuta

A decent paved road snakes along the coast to the east, passing a seemingly endless series of beautiful bays punctuated by headlands. It's a terrific motorbike ride.

Pantai Segar, a lovely beach about 2km east around the first headland, has unbelievably turquoise water, decent swimming (though no shade) and a break 200m offshore. Continuing 3km east, **Tanjung Aan** is a spectacular sight: a giant horseshoe bay with two sweeping arcs of fine sand. Swimming is good here and there's a little shade under trees and shelters, plus safe parking (for a small charge). The huge international resort project planned here is *habis* (no more).

Gerupak is a fascinating little ramshackle coastal village where the thousand or so local souls earn their keep from fishing, seaweed harvesting and lobster exports. Oh, and guiding and ferrying surfers to the five exceptional surf breaks in its huge bay.

There are a couple of hotels and warung popular with surfers.

Edo Homestay (☎0818 0371 0521; r 120,000Rp) have clean, simple rooms with colourful drapes and double beds. They have a decent restaurant and a surf shop too (boards per day 50,000Rp), and staying here gets you to the break quicker than those who commute from Kuta. But the nicest Gerupak digs are at **Spear Villa** (☎0818 0371 0521; www.s-pear.com; r 300,000Rp; ❃☀), where you'll find clean, modern rooms with air-con and satelite TV that open onto a common plunge pool. **Bumbangku** (☎620 833, 0852 3717 6168; www.bumbangkulombok.com; bamboo/superior r 400,000/650,000Rp; ❃) is set across the bay from Geupuk and is wonderfully remote – almost island-like. They have simple bamboo huts on stilts with outdoor baths – a bit overpriced but you are paying for location, and much nicer and newer concrete rooms with queen beds, outdoor baths, plush linens, satelite TV and flat-screen. Book on Agoda.com for steep discounts. Transfer from Gerupak costs 150,000Rp. You and your gear will get wet. Plan accordingly.

Wherever you stay in Gerupak (Bumbangku prices include surf shuttle), you'll need to hire a boat to ferry you from the fishing harbour, skirting the netted lobster farms, to the break (100,000Rp). The boatman will help you find the right wave and wait patiently. There are four waves inside and a left break outside on the point. All can get head high or bigger when the swell hits.

Unfortunately, even Gerupak can get crowded, so consider moving further on to **Ekas**, where there are more breaks and soaring cliffs that recall Ulu Watu (but an almost deserted Ulu Watu). You can get a boat to Ekas (per person 150,000Rp, private charter 1,000,000Rp) from the fishing village of **Awang**, accessed by a side road that branches off from the east-bound coastal road just before Tanjung Aan. Boats only leave when full.

West of Kuta

West of Kuta is yet another series of awesome beaches and sick surf breaks. Developers are nosing around here, and land has changed hands, but for now it remains almost pristine and the region has a raw

A BLOODY MESS

Every day between one and three fishing boats, crewed by five men each, sail in and out of Tanjung Luar, a long running fish market in southeast Lombok. On new moon nights, crews pull 40 sharks per day, and if more than one boat comes into port around then, as many as 100 sharks and mantas will get finned and gilled. Once in market, the meat is sold locally, but the shark fins and manta gills are auctioned to just four buyers who ship their bounty to Hong Kong via their exporter in Surabaya.

Each buyer represents the same Surabaya exporter and does about 1 billion rupiah in annual business or US$100,000. Multiply that by four and you have US$400,000 worth of shark fins moving through this backwater port each year. After speaking at length with two of the buyers in Tanjung Luar, we learned that this same exporter has similar shark finning operations in Ambon, Sorong (gateway to the Raja Ampats) and in Bau Bau. The buyers confessed that few sharks remain in the sea around Lombok. In the 1990s, fishermen didn't have to go far to hunt their take. These days they travel all the way to the Sumba strait between Australia and Indonesia, an important shark migration channel. Obviously, if things continue this way the future does not bode well for Indonesia's sharks or for these fishermen.

beauty. The road is badly rutted and potholed (and very steep in places, especially around Astari), detouring inland and skirting tobacco, sweet potato and rice fields in between turn-offs to the sand.

The first left after Astari leads to Mawun (or Mawan), truly a vision of paradise. This half-moon cove is framed by soaring headlands with azure water and a swath of empty sand (save a fishing village of a dozen thatched homes). There's safe parking (motorbike/car 1000/5000Rp), and a woman who sells fresh coconuts and instant noodles. It's a terrific swimming beach.

The very next left – although it's quite a bit further down the road – leads through a gate (admission 5000Rp) down a horribly rutted track to Mawi, 16km from Kuta, where there is safe parking. This is a surf paradise, a stunning scene, with legendary barrels and several beaches scattered around the great bay. Watch out for the strong riptide.

Further west from Mawi, and just when you think you've seen the most beautiful beaches Kuta has to offer, you reach Selong Blanak. Park and cross the rickety pedestrian bridge to a wide, sugar-white beach with water streaked a thousand shades of blue, ideal for swimming. There is a fabulous boutique villa property and cafe tucked away on the cliffs and inland from the beach. Sempiak Villas (☑0852 5321 3172; www.sempiakvillas.com; Solong Blanak; d1,500,000Rp; ✳☲) is one of Kuta's upscale properties. The octaganol villas, built

into the hillside above the beach, sleep up to four guests each and share an infinity pool. At sea level, Laut Biru Cafe (Solong Blanak; mains 24,000-54,000Rp, plus 20% tax and service) is open to all comers. They keep it simple here with muesli and yoghurt, eggs and toast for breakfast and Indo classics for lunch and dinner, along with a few departures like a fresh daily soup, and a gluten-free pad thai. It's an exquisite Swiss-Indo-owned, thatched-roof construction, with remixed world music tracks floating through the room and patio.

From Pengantap, the road climbs across a headland then descends to a superb bay; follow this around for 1km then look out for the turn-off west to Blongas – a steep, rough and winding road with breathtaking scenery. Blongas is set on its secluded namesake bay that is positively breathtaking. Lodge at Blongas Bay (☑645 974; www.thelodge-lombok.com; bungalows 850,000-950,000Rp) offers spacious wooden bungalows with tiled roofs in a coconut grove. Dive Zone (☑0813 3954 4998; www.divezone-lombok.com; 2/3 dives 950,000/1,250,000Rp), once based in Kuta, has moved here, because given the wind and sea conditions around the famed dive site, Magnet, it's best to leave Blongas for Magnet-bound dive trips before 7am – and that is simply not possible if you start from Kuta. Magnet is at its best in mid-September when you may see schooling mobula rays in addition to hammerheads, which school around the pinnacle from June to November. It's not an easy dive, so you must be experienced and prepared for heavy current.

EAST LOMBOK

♪0376

All that most travellers see of the east coast of Lombok is Labuhan Lombok, the port for ferries to Sumbawa. But the road around the northeast coast is pretty good, and can be traversed if you're hoping to complete a circumnavigation. The real highlight here is the remote southeastern peninsula. If you've ever wondered what Bali's Bukit looked like before all the villas and surf rats, here's your chance to find out.

Labuhan Lombok

Labuhan Lombok (also known as Labuhan Kayangan or Tanjung Kayangan) is the port for ferries and boats to Sumbawa. The town centre of Labuhan Lombok, 3km west of the ferry terminal, is a scruffy place but it does have great views of Gunung Rinjani. There's only one decent place to stay here, **Losmen Lima Tiga** (Jl Raya Kayangan; r 100,000Rp), 2.5km inland from the port, with small rooms and shared bathrooms.

ℹ Getting There & Away

Bus & Bemo

Very regular buses and bemo buzz between Mandalika terminal in Mataram and Labuhan Lombok (also known as Labuhan Kayangan or Tanjung Kayangan); the journey takes two hours (20,000Rp). Some buses will only drop you off at the port entrance road from where you can catch another bemo to the ferry terminal. Don't walk – it's too far.

Ferry

There are ferry connections between Lombok and Sumbawa and bus connections between Mataram and Sumbawa.

South of Labuhan Lombok

Selong, the capital of the east Lombok administrative district, has some dusty Dutch colonial buildings. The transport junction for the region is just to the west of Selong at

Pancor, where you can catch bemo to most points south.

Tanjung Luar is one of Lombok's main fishing ports (and home to one of Indonesia's most egregious shark finning operations) and has lots of Bugis-style houses on stilts. From here, the road swings west to **Keruak**, where wooden boats are built, and continues past the turn to **Sukaraja**, a traditional Sasak village where you can buy woodcarvings. Just west of Keruak a road leads south to **Jerowaru** and the spectacular southeastern peninsula. You'll need your own transport; be warned that it's easy to lose your way around here and that the roads go from bad to worse.

A sealed road branches west past Jerowaru to **Ekas**, where you'll find a huge bay framed by stunning sheer cliffs on both sides. There are two sensational surf breaks (Inside and Outside) at Ekas and boat charters to **Awang** across the bay. Or just head on to the aptly named, Kiwi-owned **Heaven on the Planet** (📞812 3797 4846, 081 2375 1103; www.heavenontheplanet.co.nz; per person all-inclusive US$150; ▣). Chalets, huts and villas (some with three bedrooms and marble flooring) are scattered along the cliff's edge, from where you'll have mind-blowing bird's-eye views of the sea and swell lines. Discounts are available for longer stays. Heaven is primarily a surf resort (you can even surf at night here thanks to ocean spotlights) but kitesurfing, scuba diving (fun dives and courses) and snorkelling is possible. Southern Lombok's first artificial reef has been installed in Ekas bay. They even have a half-pipe. Yes, this is ocean adrenalin junkie mad scientist heaven (on the planet).

A second resort, **Ocean Heaven** (📞0812 3797 4846; www.oceanheaven.co.nz; r all-inclusive per person AU$170), with chalets right on Ekas beach, is under the same ownership. Both resorts have tasty food, a full bar and friendly staff, and guests receive free airport or ferry transfers and massages (every second day). Rates in both resorts also include free shuttle to and from the outside break.

The road to Heaven is rough and rocky(!); if you're already in Kuta it's easiest to head to Awang and charter a boat from there rather than looping overland.

Gili Islands

Best Places to Eat

» Blu da Mare (p295)

» Kokomo (p295)

» Adeng Adeng (p300)

» Scallywags (p296)

Best Places to Stay

» Shacks 58 & 59 (p299)

» Kai's Beachouse (p301)

» Adeng Adeng (p298)

» Woodstock (p292)

» Karma Kayak (p294)

Why Go?

Picture three miniscule desert islands, fringed by white-sand beaches and coconut palms, sitting in a turquoise sea: the Gilis are a vision of paradise. These islets have exploded in popularity, and are booming like nowhere else in Indonesia – speedboats zip visitors direct from Bali and a new hip hotel opens every month.

It's not hard to understand the Gilis' unique appeal, for a serenity endures (no motorbikes or dogs!) and a green consciousness is growing. Most development is incredibly tasteful and there are few concrete eyesores.

Each island has its own special character. Trawangan is by far the most cosmopolitan, its bar and party scene vibrant, its accommodation and restaurants close to definitive tropical chic. Gili Air has the strongest local character, a mellow atmosphere and lovely views from Rinjani. Meno is simply tranquility on earth. But all have one thing in common: they are incredibly hard to leave.

When to Go

The wet season is approximately late October until late March. But even in the height of the rainy season, when it's lashing it down in Mataram or Bali, the Gilis can be dry and sunny. High season is between June and late August, when rooms are very hard to find and prices can double (though great weather is almost guaranteed). The perfect months to visit are May and September. There's no cyclone season to worry about.

❶ Getting There & Away

From Bali

Several fast boats offer swift connections (about two hours) between Bali and Gili Trawangan. They leave from several departure points in Bali, most dock at Teluk Nare on Lombok before continuing onto Air and Trawangan (you'll have to disembark for Meno). Two helpful websites, **Gili Bookings** (www.gilibookings.com) and **Gili Fastboat** (www.gili-fastboat.com), present a range of fast-boat operations. Gili Bookings is the most discerning, vetting companies for safety and reliability. Be warned that the sea between Bali and Lombok can get very rough (particularly during rainy season). Book ahead in July and August.

Gili Getaway (☑Bali reservations 0813 3707 4147, Gili reservations 0878 6432 2515; www.giligetaway.com; child/adult 490,000/660,000Rp) From Serangan at 9am, returning at 11.30am. We enjoy its impeccable service and race-car seating.

Kuda Hitam Express (☑0363-23482; www.kudahitamexpress.com; child/adult 450,000/650,000Rp) Departs from Amed at 9am daily. Returning from Trawangan at 10.15am.

Amed Sea Express (☑80 852, 0819 3617 6914; www.gili-sea-express.com; per person 600,000Rp) Makes 75-minute crossings to Amed on a 80-person speedboat. This makes many interesting itineraries possible.

Blue Water Express (☑614 4460; www.bluewater-express.com; child/adult US$55/67) From Serangan, Bali direct at 8am and 10am. Returning at 11am and 1.30pm.

Gili Cat (☑0361-271 680; www.gilicat.com; child/adult 475,000/660,000Rp) Departs daily from Padangbai at 9.15 am, returning from Trawangan at 11.20am.

Scoot Cruise (☑612 3433; www.scootcruise.com; adult/child 675,000/550,000Rp) High-speed catamaran service between Sanur and the Gilis, via Nusa Lembongan. Departures from Sanur at 9.30am, returning from Gili at 1.25pm.

Semaya One (☑087 8088 8771; www.semayacruise.com; child/adult 550,000/650,000Rp)

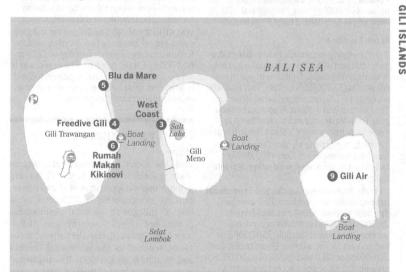

Gili Islands Highlights

❶ Snorkelling with hawksbill and green sea **turtles** (p289)

❷ Raving all night at one of Trawangan's **(in)famous parties** (p296)

❸ Finding serenity on **Gili Meno's west coast** (p297)

❹ Learning to **freedive** (p292) in paradise

❺ Savouring carpaccio and pasta at **Blu da Mare** (p295)

❻ Munching authentic Indonesian food with the dive proletariat at **Rumah Makan Kikinovi** (p295)

❼ **Cycling** (p292) around Gili Trawangan, then climbing the hill for unbeatable sunset views

❽ Diving with reef sharks at **Shark Point** (p293)

❾ Enjoying the sheer thrill of eye-dazzling white sand and striped turquoise sea on **Gili Air** (p301)

GILI ISLANDS

DANGERS & ANNOYANCES

There are seldom police on any of the Gilis (though this is changing). Report thefts to the island *kepala desa* (village head) immediately, who will deal with the issue; staff at the dive schools will direct you to him. On Gili Trawangan, contact **Satgas**, the community organisation that runs island affairs, via your hotel or dive centre. Satgas is usually able to resolve problems and track down stolen property.

Although it's rare, some foreign women have experienced sexual harassment and even assault while on the Gilis – it's best to walk home in pairs to the quieter parts of the islands.

As tranquil as these seas do appear, currents are extremely heavy in the channels between the islands. Do not try to swim between Gili islands unless you fancy a 24-hour swim to Lombok.

The drug trade remains endemic to Trawangan. Weed and mushrooms are the mainstays, but these days crystal meth is on the menu. And it does get annoying after about the 100th cold call.

It runs Gili-bound fast boats from Sanur at 9.15am via Lembongan. They return from Gili T at 1.15pm.

Perama (☑613 8514; www.peramatour.com; per person 400,000Rp) From Padangbai at 1.30pm, returning at 8am daily; it takes three hours.

From Lombok

If you're already on Lombok, head to **Bangsal**, a dirty little port with a big rep for hassle and public boats on the cheap. Boats leave for all three Gili islands (10,000Rp) from 7am. They typically wait until full (26 passengers) before departure. The last boat is at 4.30pm. Keep an eye on your gear. From Mataram, catch a bus or bemo to Pemenang, from where it's about 1km to Bangsal.

From Senggigi there's a daily Perama shuttle bus–boat connection at 10am (200,000Rp), but all things considered, we'd rather deal with Bangsal.

Finally, there are various chartered **speedboat** options available to and from Gili Trawangan. The Beach House (p296) and **Juku** (mains 25,000-45,000Rp) both have dependable services to mainland Lombok (350,000Rp for two people). Or hop a Dream Divers (p289, 4pm, 50,000Rp) or Gili Divers (p290, 5pm, 50,000Rp) crew boat, both of which accept passengers aboard for daily Lombok crossings.

ℹ Getting Around

There's no motorised transport on the Gilis. In fact, the only motorbike in Trawangan is on the Bio-rock reef, 5m deep in front of Gili Cafe.

CIDOMO *Cidomo* (horse cart) operate as taxis and prices have soared in recent years. Even a short ride can cost 50,000Rp. For an hour-long clip-clop around an island expect to pay at least 100,000Rp.

ISLAND-HOPPING There's a twice-daily island-hopping boat service that loops between all three islands (20,000Rp to 23,000Rp), so you can hit the ATM on Trawangan if you're based on Meno, or snorkel another island's reefs for the day. Check the latest timetable at the islands' docks. You can always charter boats between the islands (220,000Rp to 250,000Rp).

WALKING & BIKING The Gilis are flat and easy enough to get around by foot. Bicycles, available for hire on all three islands (per day 40,000Rp; 60,000Rp on Trawangan) are an excellent way to get around. You can circumnavigate each island in an hour or so on a bike, though you may have to push through sand occasionally.

Gili Trawangan

☑0370

Well, the secret is definitely out. Long an obscure speck in the big blue, Gili Trawangan has become a paradise of global repute, ranking alongside Bali and Borobudur as one of Indonesia's essential destinations. Settled just 50 years ago (by Bugis fishermen from Sulawesi), travellers arrived in the 1980s, seduced by the white-sand beaches and coral reefs. By the 1990s Trawangan had mutated into a kind of tropical Ibiza, a stoney idyll where you could rave away from the eyes of the Indonesian police. And then the island began to grow up – resident Western hedonists morphed into entrepreneurs and diving became more important to the island economy than partying.

Today Trawangan's main drag boasts a glittering roster of lounge bars, hip hotels and cosmopolitan restaurants, mini-marts and dive schools. And yet behind this glitzy facade, a bohemian character endures, with rickety warung and reggae joints surviving between the cocktail tables. But even as massive 200+ room hotels begin to colonise the wild and ragged west coast, you can head just inland to a village laced with sandy lanes roamed by free-range roosters, kibbitzing *ibu* (mothers) and wild-haired kids playing hopscotch. Here the call of the *muezzin*, not happy hour, defines the time of day.

◉ Sights & Activities

Other than a few mosques and the turtle hatchery right on the main beach, there are no real sights. Parents, take note: at the time of writing Lutwala (p290) was in the midst of building a mini-golf course and remote control car track.

🎣 Turtle Hatchery   AQUARIUM
Thanks to this glass aquarium hatchery, several hundred green and hawksbill turtle hatchlings are released into local waters annually. It's especially necessary now as unchecked development has all but wiped out natural hatcheries on the island. Donations appreciated.

Diving & Snorkelling
Trawangan is a diving mecca, with 22 professional scuba schools and one of Asia's only freediving schools. Following is a partial list of GIDA-associated dive schools (see also p293). All have accommodation at a high standard unless otherwise noted.

There's fun snorkelling off the beach north of the boat landing – the coral isn't in the best shape here, but there are tons of fish. The reef is in much better shape off the northwest coast accessible from the beach at Lutwala Dive (p290), but at low tide you'll have to scramble over some low coral to access it (take some rubber footwear). Lutwala rents high-end snorkel gear for 50,000Rp.

Big Bubble   DIVING
(☏612 5020; www.bigbubblediving.com) The original engine behind the Gili Eco Trust, and a long-running dive school.

Blue Marlin Dive Centre   DIVING
(☏613 2424, 0813 3993 0190; www.bluemarlindive.com) Gili T's original dive shop, and one of the best tech diving schools in the world.

Dream Divers   DIVING
(☏613 4496; www.dreamdivers.com) One of the longest tenured shops.

GREEN GILI

So you've paid your hotel bill, settled up with the scuba school and cleared that painful bar tab – why should you have to pay a tax on your stay? Well, you don't *have* to. Gili Trawangan's EcoTax (50,000Rp per person) is a voluntary donation, set up by the pioneering **Gili Eco Trust** (www.facebook.com/giliecotrust) to improve the island's environment.

Though Gili T looks like paradise, there's been severe pressure on the island (intensive development and rubbish) and offshore reefs (fishermen using cyanide and dynamite to harvest fish) for years. More recently Trawangan's once-wide-white-sand beaches have eroded. In some places they've been swallowed whole, but several initiatives have tried to reclaim the reef and stem the rising tide.

Biorock, a coral regeneration project, has been staggeringly successful, mitigating beach erosion and nurturing marine life. Loose pieces of living coral (perhaps damaged by an anchor or a clumsy diving fin) are gathered and transplanted onto frames in the sea. Electrodes supplied with low-voltage currents cause electrolytic reactions, accelerating coral growth and ultimately creating an artificial reef. There are now 42 Biorock installations around the Gilis. You'll see them as you snorkel or dive; their shapes look quite startling in the water – flowers, an aeroplane, turtle, star, manta and even a heart – covered in fledgling coral and sponges.

Since 2009 the Gili Eco Trust has also started to tackle rubbish. An education program implemented in schools has raised awareness, and in May 2010 over 1000 recycling bins were introduced to the Gilis. Plastic bags are the main culprit, so strong reusable bags (you can purchase them for 20,000Rp) have been introduced and it's hoped a complete ban will be agreed on in the future. Straws are evil too. Two thousand of them are picked up on Trawangan beaches monthly. If you want to get involved you can join the island clean-up (first Friday of every month) and collect land or sea garbage; kids are very welcome to help out. Or you can simply pay your EcoTax.

Gili Trawangan

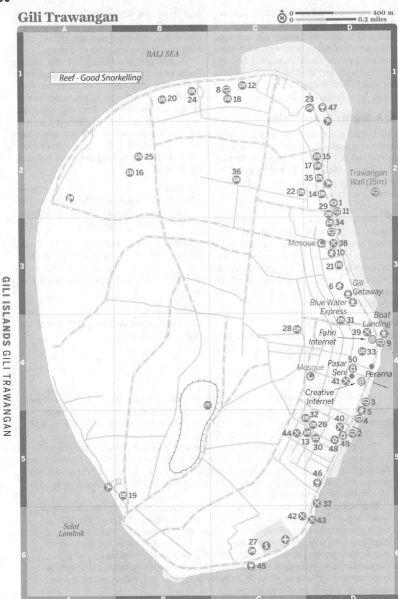

GILI ISLANDS GILI TRAWANGAN

Gili Divers DIVING
(📱0821 4789 0017; www.gilidivers.com; liveaboard per person incl gear rental 14,300,000Rp) A gorgeous new dive centre with terrific-value rooms. It's most noteworthy for its intimate day trips (max four to a group), and its week-long live-aboard to Komodo National Park.

Lutwala Dive DIVING
(📱689 3609; www.lutwala.com) A Nitrox and five-star PADI centre owned by the wom-

Gili Trawangan

en's world-record holder for deepest open-circuit dive (190m). It no longer offers accommodation.

Manta Dive　　　　　　　　　　　DIVING
(☏614 3649; www.manta-dive.com) The biggest and still one of the best dive schools on the island. It also seems to have the most fun.

Trawangan Diving　　　　　　　DIVING
(☏614 9220, 0813 3770 2332; www.trawangandive.com) Another top, long-running dive shop with a fun pool-party vibe.

Boat Trips
A top option is Gili Divers' (left) eight-day live aboard to Komodo National Park.

South Sea Nomads　　　　　　　CRUISE
(☏821 4580 4522; www.southseanomads.com; sunset cruise incl dinner & snorkel gear per person 200,000Rp, Moyo safari 4,000,000; ☺3pm-midnight Mon, Wed & Fri) Book a sunset passage with South Sea Nomads, Gili T's only party boat. In addition to its well-lubricated sunset cruises, it takes this schooner on dive safari to Pulau Moyo in Sumbawa. It's based at Gili Hostel.

Surfing
Trawangan has a fast right reef break that can be surfed year-round (though it is temperamental) and at times swells overhead. The Surf Bar (p297) rents boards (per hour/day 30,000/100,000Rp) on the beach opposite the break.

FREEDIVING THE GILIS

Freediving is an advanced breath-hold technique that allows you to explore much deeper depths than snorkelling (to 30m and beyond!). Trawangan's professional school, **Freedive Gili** (☑614 0503, 0871 5718 7170; www.freedivegili.com; beginner/advanced course 2,150,000/3,150,000Rp), owned by an expert diver who has touched 90m on a single breath, offers two-day beginner and three-day advanced courses that include theory sessions, breathing techniques and depth-training. After a two-day course many students are able to get down to 20m on a single breath of air.

Walking & Cycling

Trawangan is perfect for exploring on foot or by bike. You can walk around the whole island in a couple of hours – if you finish at the hill on the southwestern corner (which has the remains of an old Japanese gun placement c WWII), you'll have terrific sunset views of Bali's Gunung Agung.

Bikes (per day from 60,000Rp) are a great way to get around. You'll find loads of rental outlets on the main strip.

Yoga & Wellness

Gili Yoga   YOGA
(☑0878 6579 4884; www.giliyoga.com; per person 100,000Rp; ☺5.30pm daily, 7.30-9am Mon, Wed, Fri) A superb new yoga centre that runs daily Vinyasa classes.

Exqisit Spa   SPA
(☑612 9405; www.exqisit.com; treatments 30/60min from 80,000/150,000Rp; ☺10am-10pm) A new day spa on the waterfront with curtained-off treatment rooms. It does Tibetan hot stone massage (180,000Rp), shiatsu, and a hangover recovery massage too. Talk about knowing the marketplace.

🛏 Sleeping

Gili T has 5000 rooms and over 100 places to stay, ranging from thatched huts to sleek, air-conditioned villas with private pools. Yet, at peak season the entire island is often booked. It's wise to reserve your room well ahead and to arrive with a relaxed attitude. Many places are owned by local families with little or no experience of running hotels. Virtually all

dive schools offer really good midrange accommodation, which may come with price breaks on diving packages. The cheapest digs are in the village, where the mosque is everyone's alarm clock. You'll pay more for a beachside address. Head to the north or west coasts to escape the crowds.

All budget and most midrange places have brackish tap water. Pure water is available in some upmarket bungalows. The high-season rates quoted can drop up to 50% off-peak. Breakfast is included unless stated otherwise.

VILLAGE

🔺TOP CHOICE **Woodstock**   BUNGALOW $
(☑081 2396 7744; www.woodstockgili.com; d with fan 350,000Rp, with air-con 450,000-700,000Rp; ❄🔊🏊) The hippest spot on Trawangan. Commune with the spirits of the dead, Baez and Hendrix in 11 superclean rooms with tribal accents, private porches and outdoor baths, surrounding a fabulous pool area.

Gili Hostel   HOSTEL $
(☑0877 6526 7037; www.gilihostel.com; per person 100,000Rp; ❄🔊) The island's only dedicated hostel is an all new, all co-ed dorm complex with a shaggy Torajan styled roof. Rooms sleep seven, have concrete floors, high ceilings and a sleeping loft. There's a rooftop bar, with bean bags, sun lounges and hammocks with views of the treetops and the hills, as well as DVD stations to screen your own films.

Alexyane Paradise   BUNGALOW $
(☑0878 6599 9645; r with fan/air-con 350,000/500,000Rp; ❄) Great-quality darkwood cottages with high ceilings, bamboo beds, and lovely light-flooded outdoor baths sprouting with foliage.

Oceane Paradise   COTTAGE $
(☑0812 3779 3533; s/d 200,000/250,000Rp) A terrific new compound of five wooden cottages with stylish outdoor bathrooms.

Lumbung Cottages 2   BUNGALOW $
(☑0819 3679 6353; www.lumbungcottage.com; bungalows from 400,000Rp; ❄🔊) New *lumbung*-style cottages, set deep in the village, tucked up against the hillside, surrounding a black-bottom pool.

Rumah Hantu   GUESTHOUSE $
(☑0819 1710 2444; d 150,000-250,000Rp) A well-tended if simple collection of woven bamboo rooms with high ceilings and fresh

paint in a rootsy garden plot. Management is warm, welcoming and conscientious.

Koi Gili GUESTHOUSE $
(☎0819 5995 760; s/d 250,000/350,000Rp; ❄) The young and hip gravitate to this groovy guesthouse with a daybed in the garden and a mod colour scheme on the facade.

Pondok Gili Gecko GUESTHOUSE $
(☎0818 0573 2814; r 250,000-350,000Rp) An inviting guesthouse with a charming gecko motif. Rooms are super clean, and have ceiling fans and private tiled patios overlooking the garden.

Gili Joglo VILLA $$$
(☎0813 5678 4741; www.gilijoglo.com; villas from €120) Two fabulous villas. One is crafted out of an antique Joglo with polished concrete floors, two bedrooms and a massive indoor-outdoor great room. Though slightly smaller, we prefer the one built from two 1950s *gladaks* (middle-class home). Rooms come with butler service.

MAIN STRIP

Kokomo LUXURY VILLAS $$$
(☎613 4920; www.kokomogilit.com; villas from 1,400,000Rp; ❄🛜🛁) Offering beautifully finished and lavishly equipped modern accommodation, these mini-villas are set in a small complex at the (quiet) southern end of the main strip. All have private pools, contemporary decor and lovely indoor-outdoor living quarters.

Sama Sama Bungalows BUNGALOW $
(☎612 1106; r with fan 150,000, with air-con 400,000-500,000Rp; ❄) We like the six new, fan-cooled backpacker rooms with high

---

ALL ABOUT SCUBA

The Gili Islands are a superb dive destination as the marine life is plentiful and varied. Turtles and black- and white-tip reef sharks are common, and the macro life (small stuff) is excellent, with sea horses, pipefish and lots of crustaceans. Around the full moon, large schools of bumphead parrotfish appear to feast on coral spawn; at other times of year manta rays cruise past dive sites.

Though years of bomb fishing and an El Niño–induced bleaching damaged corals above 18m, the reefs are now well into a profound recovery and haven't looked this great in years. The Gilis also have their share of virgin coral.

Safety standards are reasonably high on the Gilis, but with the proliferation of new dive schools, 14 of them have formed the Gili Island Dive Association (GIDA), which comes together for monthly meetings on conservation and dive impact issues, and all observe a written list of standards that considers the safety of their divers, a limitation on number of divers per day, and preservation of the sites to be paramount concerns, which is why we strongly suggest diving with GIDA-associated shops (identifiable by a logo). All GIDA shops carry oxygen on their boats and have working radios. They also have a price agreement. Each fun dive costs 370,000Rp for the first four, with a 10% discount from your fifth to ninth dives, and a 15% discount thereafter. A PADI or SSI open-water course costs 3,700,000Rp, the Advanced is 2,950,000Rp, Divemaster training starts at 8,350,000Rp. Nitrox, Tri-mix and re-breather courses are also available in Trawangan. For dive-school information, see individual island entries.

Some of the best dive sites include the following:

Deep Halik A canyon-like site ideally suited to drift diving. Black- and white-tip sharks are often seen at 28m to 30m.

Deep Turbo At around 30m, this site is ideally suited to nitrox diving. It has impressive sea fans and leopard sharks hidden in the crevasses.

Mirko's Reef Named for a beloved dive instructor who passed away, this canyon was never bombed and has vibrant, pristine soft and table coral formations.

Japanese Wreck For experienced divers only (it lies at 45m), this shipwreck of a Japanese patrol boat (c WWII) is another site ideal for tech divers.

Shark Point Perhaps the most exhilarating Gili dive: reef sharks and turtles are very regularly encountered, as well as schools of bumphead parrotfish and mantas.

Sunset (Manta Point) Some impressive table coral; sharks and large pelagics are frequently encountered.

GILI T BY THE NUMBERS

» Visitors (annual): about 100,000

» Divers (annual): 20,000

» Dive shops: 22

» Fast-boat companies: 14

» Guestrooms: 5000

» Swimming pools: 201

» Resident feline population: 3000

» Resident felines with tails intact: 13

» Mojitos sold at the Irish (annual): 24,000

» Bintangs sold at the Irish (annual): 160,000

» Pounds of fake cocaine snorted by drunken tourists: unknown

» Straws recovered on Trawangan beaches (monthly): 2000

» Indonesian residents: 2000

» Resident expats: 150

» Resident horses: 300

» Life expectancy of *cidomo* horses: three years

beamed ceilings, modern baths, and a great price.

BEACHSIDE

Blu da Mare BUNGALOW $$
(☏0858 8866 2490; www.bludamare.it; d 500,000-850,000Rp; ❋) Most notable for its exquisite kitchen, you can bed down in one of four lovely, antique Joglo from 1920s Java, with gorgeous old wood floors, queen beds, and fresh water showers in a sunken bath.

Balé Sampan BOUTIQUE HOTEL $$
(☏0812 3702 4048; www.balesampanbungalows. com; r garden/pool 820,000/880,000Rp; ❋⚡☎) Fine modern-edge rooms served with Yogja stone baths, a freshwater pool, plush duvet covers and a proper English breakfast. Rooms have all been recently refreshed right down to the mattresses.

Tanah Qita BUNGALOW $
(☏613 9159; martinkoch-berlin@hotmail.de; bungalows with fan/air-con 200,000/600,000Rp; ❋) Another excellent set-up. Tanah Qita ('Homeland') has four large, immaculate *lumbung* (with four-poster beds) and smaller fan-cooled versions. Cleanliness is taken

very seriously. The garden is a bucolic delight.

Soundwaves BUNGALOW $
(☏0819 3673 2404; www.soundwavesresort.com; d 300,000-350,000Rp) One of Gili T's newest offerings, rooms are simple but clean with tiled floors. Some are set in wooden A-frames and others in a two-storey concrete building with staggered and recessed patios offering beach views from each room.

Trawangan Dive HOSTEL $
(☏614 9220, 0813 3770 2332; www.trawanga ndive.com; dm per person 50,000Rp, bungalows 800,000Rp; ❋⚡☎) Most notable for their 12 backpacker dorms that sleep two on the cheap. Book the whole room for 100,000Rp.

Moz.art BUNGALOW $$
(☏0819 0743 9820; d 350,000-800,000Rp; ❋) Just three creative concrete tile and wood pods with shaggy thatched roof, air-con, fresh-water showers, and an exceptionally tasteful beachfront with cushy beruga that practically demand a drink.

NORTH, SOUTH & WEST COASTS

TOP CHOICE **Karma Kayak** INN $$
(☏0818 0559 3710; www.karmakayak.com; bungalows from 550,000Rp; ❋⚡☎) Simplicity is the key here at this wonderful retreat where everything seems to exist in harmony with the tranquil location. All the fine rooms adopt a less-is-more uncluttered design, with soothing natural colours, large windows and generous balconies or verandas. The beachside cafe is first-class.

Eden Cottages COTTAGE $$
(☏0819 1799 6151; www.edencottages.com; cottage 550,000Rp; ❋⚡) Six clean, thatched concrete bungalows wrapped around a pool, fringed by a garden, and shaded by a coconut grove. Rooms have tasteful rattan furnishings, stone baths, and TV-DVD and fresh-water showers.

Coconut Garden BUNGALOW $$
(☏0821 4781 8912; www.coconutgardenresort. com; s/d 550,000/600,000Rp; ❋⚡) A simple spot with just four bright and airy glass-box Javanese Joglo with tiled roofs connected to outdoor terrazzo baths. Expect plush linens, queen beds and a rolling lawn dotted with coco palms. It's on its own in the quiet middle of the island and can be hard to find. Call ahead.

Alam Gili   HOTEL **$$**
(☑613 0466; www.alamgili.com; r US$55-95; ☀) A stunning mature garden and a quiet beach location are the main draws here. Rooms and villas boast elegant lashings of old-school Balinese style. There's a small pool.

Island Beach Bungalows   BUNGALOW **$**
(☑0818 0571 2224; bungalow 350,000Rp; ☀) Just three basic, stilted, wooden bungalows with open air baths, queen beds, air-con and a sweet slab of white sand out front dotted with beruga and blessed with a quintessential tiki bar.

Danima   HOTEL **$$**
(☑0878 6087 2506; www.giliresortsdanima.com; d 900,000-950,000Rp) An intimate four-room boutique property. Nests are blessed with floating beds, vaulted ceilings, tasteful lighting, rattan deck seating and rain showers. It has a romantic pool and beach area too.

⬛ Gili Eco Villas   VILLA **$$$**
(☑0361 847 6419; www.gilieco villas.com; villas US$297 plus 21% tax; ☀🛜☀) Classy villas made from recycled teak salvaged from old Javanese colonials are set back from the beach on Trawangan's idyllic north coast. Comfort and style are combined with solid green principles (water is recycled, there's an organic vegetable garden, and solar and wind energy provide most of the power). Low season walk-in rates plummet to 1,000,000Rp.

Kelapa Villas   VILLA **$$$**
(☑613 2424; www.kelapavillas.com; villas US$195-620 plus 21% tax; ☀🛜☀💧) Luxury development in an inland location with a selection of 22 commodious villas, all with private pools, that offer style and space in abundance. There's a tennis court and gym in the complex, and five beachfront villas on the way.

Exile   BUNGALOW **$**
(☑0819 0707 7475; d 350,000-500,000Rp; @) One of our favourite newcomers is an uber-groovy compound of woven bamboo bungalows, with a sweet beach bar and bamboo lounges on the sand. Indonesian owned, they're only 15 to 20 minutes to the main strip on foot, or an easy bike ride.

✗ Eating

In the evenings, several places on the main strip display and grill delicious fresh seafood, and there's a marvelous **Pasar Malam** (night market) at Pasar Seni (art market) with more than a dozen stalls and carts serving everything from Javanese style pick-and-mix *nasi campur* to grilled chicken thighs and grilled fish, to noodle soup, *bakso* and satay. Meals hover around 25,000Rp. At write-up there was talk about moving it onto the village soccer field.

TOP
CHOICE Blu da Mare   ITALIAN **$$**
(☑0858 8866 2490; www.bludamare.it; mains 60,000-110,000Rp; ⊙12.30-3pm & 6.30-10pm Sat-Thu) An authentic and intimate (few tables, limited seatings available) Italian-owned trattoria where the lady of the house bakes the bread, makes her own pasta and grills meat, fish and seafood to perfection. Speaking of seafood, her hubbie and co-owner (who, by the way, used to race yachts) spears fresh catch daily, which is carved into melt-in-your-mouth carpaccio. It's on a lovely stretch of beach well away from the hullabaloo on the main strip. Don't leave without enjoying the chocolate salami for desert. If only there was wine.

Rumah Makan Kikinovi   INDONESIAN **$**
(meals from 15,000Rp) Run by a formidable *ibu*, this is Indonesian pick-and-mix cuisine at its tastiest. It's very inexpensive – a big feed is around 15,000Rp. Dishes usually come out fresh at 11.30am, just before the divemaster lunch crush.

Kokomo   INTERNATIONAL **$$**
(☑613 4920; www.kokomogilit.com; mains 60,000-160,000Rp; ☀🛜) Kokomo is the only genuine fine-dining restaurant in town, using hyper-fresh local seafood and select imported meats. Lots of fresh salads, wonderful steaks and pasta, but for the ultimate treat opt for a seafood or sashimi (with Atlantic salmon and yellowfin tuna) platter. Service can be painfully slow, but you'll leave happy.

Trattoria   ITALIAN **$$**
(www.trattoriaasia.com; mains 55,000-152,000Rp; 🛜) The Gili shingle of the Bali original. The Italian chef crafts homemade pastas, excellent pizzas and mains like grilled tuna with basil emulsion, beef tenderloin sliced on a bed of fresh rocket and Parmesan. All served on a dining deck over the marina.

Karma Kayak   TAPAS **$**
(☑0818 0559 3710; tapas from 15,000Rp) Terrific tapas (including sardines, house-cured olives and tempura), sandwiches and salads

are served up on a blissfully tranquil beach location. Wash it all down with a jug of sangria. It's magical at sunset here, with volcanoes filling the pink horizon.

Warung Indonesia INDONESIAN $

(dishes from 15,000-20,000Rp; ⊘8am-9pm; 🛜) Tucked away at the rear of the village, this warung scores high marks for its tasty pick-and-mix bar, as well as a menu of Indo staples like oxtail soup, *soto ayam* and *ikan goreng*. Its lofted, thatched dining room is lit with vintage lanterns, and wired.

Pesona INDIAN $$

(☑660 7233; www.pesonaresort.com; mains 59,000-80,000Rp; ⊘7am-11pm; ❄🛜) Its refined bungalows and lovely pool area are nice, but we love its Indian kitchen, with an abundance of vegetarian options along with a menu of tandoori chicken and fish, and six flavours of naan. Once sated, lay back on the cushions and fire up a sheesha (90,000Rp).

Scallywags INTERNATIONAL $$

(☑614 5301; www.scallywagsresort.com; meals 40,000-100,000Rp; 🛜) Scallywags is an Aussie-owned restaurant that offers casual yet elegant decor, polished glassware, switched-on service, free wi-fi and superb cocktails. The dinner menu features tasty seafood – fresh lobster, tuna steaks, snapper and swordfish and a great salad bar.

Cafe Gili INTERNATIONAL $

(www.facebook.com/cafegilitrawangan; mains 35,000-58,000Rp; ⊘8am-10pm; 🛜) Think: cushioned beachside seating, candlelight, and a bit too much Jack Johnson (an island-wide sin). The kitchen spills from a shabby chic whitewashed dining room and rambles across the street to the shore. The menu meanders from eggs Florentine and breakfast baguettes, to deli sandwiches and salads to decent pasta, quesadillas and seafood dishes.

Beach House INTERNATIONAL $$

(☑614 2352; www.beachhousegilit.com; mains 45,000-125,000Rp; ⊘11am-10pm; 🛜) Boasts an elegant marina terrace, and wonderful nightly barbecue, salad bar, and fine wine.

🍷 Drinking & Entertainment

The island has more than a dozen great beachside drinking dens, ranging from sleek lounge bars with ubercool seating and decadent cocktail lists to simple shacks with nothing more than cold Bintang beer. Parties are held three nights a week, shifting between Blue Marlin (Monday), Tir na Nog (Wednesday), and Rudy's Pub (Friday).

TOP CHOICE Tir na Nog PUB

(☑613 9463; ⊘7am-2am Thu-Tue, til 4am Wed; 🛜) Known simply as 'The Irish', this barn-like place has a sports-bar interior with big screens ideal for international football matches and tasty pub grub (mains 35,000Rp to 80,000Rp). Its shoreside bar is probably the busiest meeting spot on the island. Jovial mayhem reigns on Wednesday nights when the DJ takes over.

Blue Marlin BAR

Of all the party bars, this upper-level venue has the largest dance floor and the meanest sound system – it pumps out trance and tribal sounds on Monday.

Top End Bar BAR

(⊘10am-midnight) If you wish to chill on a luscious white beach, one with bamboo loung-

---

SNORKELLING THE GILIS

Ringed by coral reefs, the Gilis offer superb snorkelling. Masks, snorkels and fins are widely available and can be hired for as little as 25,000Rp per day. It's important to check your mask fits properly: just press it gently to your face, breathe in through your nose, let go and if it's a good fit the suction should hold it in place.

On Trawangan and Meno turtles very regularly appear on the reefs right off the beach. You'll likely drift with the current, so be prepared to walk back to the starting line. Over on Air, the walls off the east coast are good too.

It's not hard to escape the crowds though. Each island has a less-developed side, usually where access to the water is obstructed by shallow patches of coral. Using rubber shoes it's much easier to get in the water. Try not to stamp all over the coral but ease yourself in, and then swim, keeping your body as horizontal as possible.

Top snorkelling spots include the Meno Wall, the north end of Trawangan's beach near Lutwala Dive, and Gili Air's Air Wall.

es, and reggae music pumping from the tiki bar, then you'll come here, to Tranwangan's best beach bar.

Surf Bar
BAR

(⊙8am-late) Located opposite the break and just south of the Villa Ombak, this tiki bar has a sweet slab of beach, a rack of boards to rent, a pumping stereo and a young crowd. It does full- and dark-moon parties.

Sama Sama
BAR

(⊙8am-close) An overly decorated reggae bar–cum-roadhouse with a top-end sound system, a killer live band (and the same set list) at least six nights a week, and a beer garden on the beach.

Rudy's Pub
BAR

(Rudy's hosts arguably the best party on the island, with a good mix of locals and visitors and legendary drinks specials. The huge dance floor at the rear is verging on meat-market terrain on party nights.

🔒 Shopping

Once the domain of cheap knick-knack stalls and not much else, a stream of refinement has slowly filtered in.

⌃ᴛᴏᴘ Vintage
VINTAGE

(www.vintagedelivery.com; ⊙9am-9pm) The best boutique on Gili T is tucked in the back of Pasar Seni, and it's a treasure trove of vintage fashion sourced internationally, and displayed with grace. Browse chunky earrings, superb leather hand and shoulder bags, baby doll dresses, and John Lennon shades. A round of applause please for the stylish lady from Sweden.

Innuendo
FASHION

(☎0828 3709 648; ⊙10am-1pm & 3-10pm) A new boutique owned by a Bali-based French designer, there's elegance here. All the dresses and shoes are store brand, the handbags and accessories are sourced from other indie designers.

ℹ Information

Emergencies
There's a health **clinic** (⊙9am-5pm) just south of Hotel Vila Ombak. For security issues contact Satgas, a community organisation, via your hotel or dive school.

Internet & Telephone
Wi-fi has proliferated on Trawangan, most midrange hotels have wi-fi connections as do several restaurants and bars including Scallywags, Tir na Nog and Cafe Gili. **Creative Internet** (per hour 18,000Rp; ⊙8am-midnight) and **Fahri Internet** (per hour 24,000Rp; ⊙8am-11pm) both offer speedy connections on the strip.

Money
Gili Trawangan has seven ATMs on the main strip. All accept foreign cards. Stores and hotels change cash and travellers cheques, but rates are poor. Cash advances on credit/debit cards involve a commission of up to 10%.

Travel Agencies
Perama
TRAVEL AGENCY

(☎613 8514; www.peramatour.com) Fast-boat tickets to Bali, and connections to all locations on Lombok by shuttle boat and bus. Komodo crossings can also be arranged here.

Gili Meno
☎0370

Gili Meno is the smallest of the three islands and the perfect setting for your Robinson Crusoe fantasy. Even in high season Meno still feels delightfully tranquil. Most accommodation is strung out along the east coast, near the widest and most picturesque beach. Inland you'll find scattered homesteads, coconut plantations and a salty lake.

◎ Sights

Turtle Sanctuary
TURTLE HATCHERY

(www.gilimenoturtles.com; 🚶) Meno's turtle sanctuary consists of an assortment of little

Gili Meno

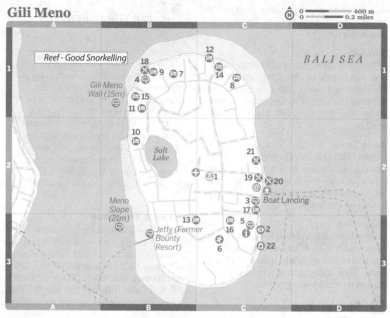

N 0 ——————— 400 m
   0 ——————— 0.2 miles

GILI ISLANDS GILI MENO

pools and bathtubs on the beach, bubbling with filters and teeming with baby turtles, where they're nurtured until they're around eight months old before being released. The impact of the hatchery on the turtle populations have been considerable. A simple snorkel and you're all but guaranteed a sighting. Donations are encouraged.

Taman Burung   WILDLIFE RESERVE
(☑614 2321, 0361 289 032; admission 50,000Rp; ☺9am-5pm) Taman Burung is home to over 200 exotic birds from Asia and Australia, and some Indonesian wildlife.

🏃 Activities
Snorkelling, Diving & Walking
It takes about two hours to circumnavigate Meno on foot. The best beach is the blonde beauty that unfurls south of the main harbour, before the signed turn-off to Tao Kombo.

Snorkelling is good off the northeast coast near Amber House; on the west coast near Good Heart; and also around the former jetty of the (abandoned) Bounty Resort. Gear is available from 25,000Rp per day.

Gili Meno Divers   DIVING
(☑0878 6409 5490; www.giliairdivers.com) French and Indonesian owned and our favourite dive shop on Meno.

Blue Marlin Dive Centre   DIVING
(☑613 9980; www.bluemarlindive.com) The Meno shingle of the Trawangan original. It has rooms here too.

Divine Divers   DIVING
(☑0852 4057 0777; www.divinedivers.com) A new dive shop on the far coast. It also has a restaurant-bar on a sweet slice of beach.

Yoga
Mao Meno   YOGA
(☑0819 9937 8359; www.mao-meno.com; by donation; ☺classes 7am & 10am) Although the property remained under construction at research time, daily Pranayama and Vinyasa classes were already underway.

🛏 Sleeping
Meno has a limited selection of rustic bungalows and it's essential to reserve well ahead in the high season. Prices quoted are high-season rates – reductions of up to 50% are possible the rest of the year. Taman Burung (p298) has backpacker beds on the cheap.

TOP CHOICE **Adeng Adeng**   BUNGALOW $$
(☑0818 0534 1019; www.adeng-adeng.com; bamboo house d 350,000Rp, standard/superior 500,000/650,000Rp) An understated elegant resort set back in the trees from a fine

Gili Meno

stretch of sand. Its simple wooden bungalows have all the creature comforts and stylish outdoor terrazo baths. The rambling property is sprinkled with artisinal accents, and it also manages a two-room bamboo house on the beach for budgeteers.

Shacks 58 & 59   VILLA $$
(📞0813 5357 7045; www.shack58.com; villas €45-70 plus 21% tax; ✳) Tropical slumming as high art. Consider two magnificent one-room villas decorated with a real eye for taste and design using natural materials, antique used furniture and local textiles. Each 'shack' has a lovely private beach gazebo, ideal as a shady retreat from the heat of the day, complete with daybed. Shack 58 is right on the beach, 59 is 150m inland. On-line reservations only.

Ana Bungalow   BUNGALOW $
(📞0819 1595 5234; d 250,000-350,000Rp) Sweet peaked-roof, fan-cooled bungalows with picture windows, and pebbled floors in outdoor baths. There's also an incredibly cute used bookshop on the beach next to its four lovely dining *beruga* lit with paper lanterns.

Paul's Last Resort   BUNGALOW $
(📞0878 6569 2272; r 150,000Rp) Choose from five woven, open-sided bamboo shacks on the beach crafted with care. They have electricity and share a toilet and shower. And while they receive delegations from the insect kingdom and get inundated with

Gili T's thumping bass (they do lack that fourth wall), if you bed down here you will also be privvy to a starry night spectacular and superb Rinjani views when clouds clear.

📷 **Maha Maya**   BOUTIQUE HOTEL $$$
(📞088 8715 5828, 637 616; www.mahamaya.co; d from US$150; ☎✳) A white-washed mod pearl with four star service and plans for 20 rooms. At research just two were complete. Each had natural stone floors, a rough-cut marble patio, white-washed wood furnishings, and free bottled water. Oh, and the kitchen is fabulous.

Rawa Indah   BUNGALOW $
(📞0817 578 6820; bungalows 150,000-350,000Rp) Six spacious A-frame bungalows, simple but super clean, dangling with seashell wind chimes in a garden setting in the village. Bottled water is free.

Balenta Bungalows   BUNGALOW $$
(📞0819 3674 5046; s/d 350,000/500,000Rp; ✳) The half-dozen tin-roof bungalows aren't the most striking from outside but are among the newest and best-maintained on Meno. All have private outdoor baths, patios with bamboo furnishings, queen beds with crisp linens, and fresh-water showers, and the attached cafe specialises in vegetarian dishes.

📷 **Sunset Gecko**   BUNGALOW $
(📞0813 5356 6774; www.thesunsetgecko .com; r 80,000-500,000Rp; ☎) Sometimes

GILI ISLANDS GILI MENO

romantically rickety is just plain rickety, and while we still love this groovy collection of bamboo and wooden houses, it is falling apart in places. However, the 3rd-floor room in the massive African-themed jungle house out back is marvellous and sleeps up to four people.

Villa Nautilus
VILLA $$

(☑642143; www.villanautilus.com; r US$86-99; ❄) A step up in comfort, these well-designed detached villas enjoy a grassy plot just off the beach. They're finished in contemporary style with natural wood, marble and limestone and the hip bathrooms have fresh water.

Tao Kombo
BUNGALOW $

(☑0812 372 2174; www.tao-kombo.com; d 200,000-300,000Rp; ☎) An innovatively designed place with two open-sided backpackers' huts that have bamboo screens for privacy, plus eight *lumbung* cottages with thatched roofs, stone floors and outdoor bathrooms. It's home to the Jungle Bar, located 200m inland from the main strip.

Diana Café
BUNGALOW $

(☑081 3535 6612; bungalow 250,000Rp) Three simple, clean, thatched bungalows by the salt lake, a three-minute walk from the beach. As cheap as 120,000Rp in the low season.

Taman Burung
HOSTEL $

(☑614 2321, 0361 289 032; d per person 30,000Rp) Has a range of rooms from backpacker dorms to more comfortable private digs (150,000Rp to 450,000Rp).

🍴 Eating & Drinking

Virtually all Meno's restaurants have sea views, which is just as well as service can be slow everywhere. Wood-fired pizza ovens are oddly de rigueur on Meno.

Adeng Adeng
THAI

(mains 25,000-70,000Rp) Looking for a splurge? Try the Thai-inspired elegance of Adeng Adeng. Owned by Swedes, it does a few homeland dishes, and has some of the best Thai eats we've had in Indo. Cap the night with a fine cognac or whiskey. Accepts credit cards.

Rust Warung
SEAFOOD $

(☑642 324; mains 15,000-75,000Rp) The only 'proper' restaurant on Meno, and the most visible cog of the 'Rust' empire, this place is renowned for its grilled fish

(with garlic or sweet-and-sour sauce), but has pizza, a grocer, a *wartel* (public telephone office) and bungalows as well. It also serves the only espresso on the island.

Jali Café
INDONESIAN $

(☑613 9800; dishes 10,000-20,000Rp) Friendly owners serve up tasty Indonesian, Sasak and curry dishes. At night they grill fresh fish and strum guitars by the fire.

Balenta Café
INDONESIAN $

(mains from 20,000Rp) A wonderful location for a meal, Balenta has low tables sunk in the sand with turquoise water a metre away. It scores for omelettes, Sasak and Indonesian food like *kelak kuning* (snapper in yellow spice) and staff fire up a seafood barbecue most nights too.

Ya Ya Warung
INDONESIAN $

(dishes 10,000-20,000Rp) Ramshackle warung on the beach that serves up Indonesian faves, curries, pancakes and plenty of pasta.

Diana Café
BAR

(drinks 12,000-30,000Rp; ⊙8am-9pm) If by any remote chance you find the pace of life on Meno too busy, head to this amazing little tiki bar par excellence. Diana couldn't be simpler: a wobbly-looking bamboo-and-thatch bar, a few tables on the sand, a hammock or two, reggae on the stereo and a chill-out zone that certainly makes the most of the zillion-rupiah views.

🛍 Shopping

Art Shop Botol
HANDICRAFTS

(⊙24 hr) Art Shop Botol is a large handicrafts stall just south of Kontiki Meno hotel with masks, Sasak water baskets, wood carvings and gourds. It's run by a 76-year-old shopkeeper with 11 children and 19 grandchildren.

ℹ Information

Minimarkets by the boat landing stock sunscreen and supplies; **internet** (per hour 30,000Rp, 10am to 10pm) and a wartel are available here too. For tours and shuttle-bus/ boat tickets, contact **Perama** (☑632 824; www.peramatour.com) at Kontiki Meno. There's a **medical clinic** (⊙8am-6pm) near the bird park, otherwise head to Mataram for emergencies.

Gili Air

🎵0370

Closest to Lombok, Gili Air falls between Gili T's sophistication and less-is-more Meno. It has both space and life. Air was the first Gili to be settled by Bugis and Sasak fishing families, and there remains a strong, rural community in place. Though tourism does dominate the island's economy today, coconuts and fishing remain vital income streams. The white-sand beaches here are arguably the best of the Gili bunch. Snorkelling is good right from the main strip – a lovely, sandy lane dotted with bamboo bungalows and little restaurants where you can eat virtually on top of a turquoise sea.

🏃 Activities

Snorkelling & Diving

The entire east coast has an offshore reef teeming with colourful fish; there's a drop-off about 100m to 200m out. Snorkelling gear can be hired from Wiwin Cafe and a number of stores from 25,000Rp a day. Watch out for currents. Never try and swim between the islands.

Scuba diving is excellent throughout the Gilis, and no matter where you stay, you'll dive the same sites.

Gili Air Divers   DIVING
(📞0878 6536 7551; www.giliairdivers.com) This new French-Indo–owned dive shop is long on charm and skill.

Blue Marlin Dive Centre   DIVING
(📞634 387; www.bluemarlindive.com) The Meno shingle of the Gili's original dive franchise.

Dream Divers   DIVING
(📞634 547; www.dreamdivers.com) An off-shoot of the Gili T original.

Manta Dive   DIVING
(📞0813 3778 9047; www.manta-dive.com) A long-running dive operation with excellent lodging available.

Oceans 5   DIVING
(📞0813 3877 7144; www.oceans5dive.com) The Gili's leading-edge dive centre has a 25m training pool, and an in-house marine biologist.

7 Seas   DIVING
(📞647 779; www.facebook.com/7seas.international) Can a dive shop become an entire city block on an island with no city? Um, well, yes. It has a range of accommodation and a restaurant.

Cycling

Wiwin Cafe has bikes for hire from 40,000Rp a day. Pedalling on Air is fun but can be annoying, as long slogs of deep sand do swallow the trail at times. You're sure to roll into villagers' backyards if you head inland.

Yoga

H2O Yoga   YOGA
(📞0877 6103 8836; www.h2oyogaandmeditation.com; per class 100,000Rp, massage 125,000-250,000Rp, r with shared bathroom from 150,000Rp; ⊘yoga classes 10-11.30am, 5.30-7pm) H2O Yoga, a wonderful yoga and meditation retreat centre is brand new to Air and set back 500m from the beach on a well-signed path into the village. Top quality classes are held in a lovely circular *beruga*. There's massage available, and a few bungalows, with more on the way.

🛏 Sleeping

Gili Air's 40 or so places to stay are mainly located on the east coast. Steep discounts from listed prices are available off-peak.

TOP CHOICE Kai's Beachouse   VACATION RENTAL $$
(📞0813 3776 4350, 0819 1723 2536; www.kaisbeachhouse.com; d 700,000-1,500,000Rp; ❄🛜🏊) There are just three rooms here, two in the main house and another in a Javanese *gladak* cottage out back. All have sponge-painted walls, four poster beds, outdoor black-rock baths,and tasteful rattan light fixtures. The downstairs room is cushy and groovy with a flat screen, and a massive kitchen. Lounges surround a tiny plunge pool, with a virginal beach just out front. Ideal for a group of friends.

Damai   GUESTHOUSE $$
(📞0878 6142 0416; www.facebook.com/pages/damai-homestay-gili-air; d 500,000-600,000Rp; @) It's worth finding this funky, thatched enclave. Rooms are basic yet tasteful and open onto a garden. The cosy dining patio has cushioned seating, and is elegantly lit with paper lanterns. It's set exquisitely in the coco palms.

Biba   BUNGALOW $$
(📞0819 1727 4648; www.bibabeach.com; bungalows 500,000-700,000Rp; ❄) Biba offers lovely, spacious bungalows with large verandas and zany, grotto-like bathrooms that have walls

Gili Air

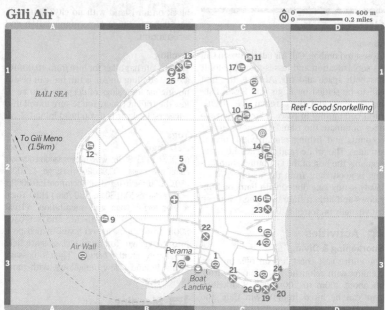

N
0 — 400 m
0 — 0.2 miles

BALI SEA

Reef - Good Snorkelling

To Gili Meno
(1.5km)

Air Wall

Perama

Boat
Landing

Gili Air

inlaid with shells and coral. The gorgeous garden has little chill-out zones. It's also home to a splendid Italian restaurant.

Sejuk Cottages　　　　　BUNGALOW $$
(☏636 461; sejukcottages@hotmail.com; bungalows 500,000-850,000Rp; ❋❄❸) Very well-built, tastefully designed thatched *lumbung* cottages, and pretty two- and three-storey

cottages (some have rooftop living rooms, others satellite TV) scattered around a fine tropical garden.

Youpy Bungalows　　　　BUNGALOW $$
(☏0819 1706 8153; d 600,000Rp; ❋) Among the driftwood-decorated beach cafes strung along the coast north of Blue Marlin, Youpy has some of the best quality bungalows.

Bathrooms have colourful sand walls, the beds are big, and the ceilings high.

Casa Mio BUNGALOW $$
(✆646 160; www.giliair.com; cottages 900,000-1,500,000Rp; ✳︎🛜🏊) Casa Mio is an unusual, quirky, Taiwanese-owned spot with four fine cottages that boast every conceivable mod con, as well as a riot of knick-knacks (from the artistic to the kitsch). It boasts a lovely beach area, fresh-water showers, good Asian food and the fastest wi-fi on the Gilis.

Segar Village BUNGALOW $$
(✆0818 0526 2218; bungalows 800,000-900,000Rp; ✳︎) A half-dozen rather cute concrete rock and coral bungalows with quirky touches and more than a little grace. We love the four-post beds, wrap-around patios and soaring thatched ceilings. The outdoor bathrooms are exceptional, and it's set on the edge of a coconut grove just in front of a coral reef with resident sea turtles. Off-peak season discounts dip as low as 250,000Rp.

Villa Bulan Madu BUNGALOW $$
(✆081907330444;www.bulan-madu.com;standard/superior 850,000/1,200,000Rp; ✳︎🛜🏊) The name means honeymoon and these bungalows are worthy of one. Crafted from wood and glass and exceptionally large, there are throw rugs, queen and double beds, a wet bar and mini fridge, outdoor baths, bamboo accents, and breezy front porches overlooking a pretty Balinese garden.

Gusung Indah BUNGALOW $
(✆0878 6434 2852; bungalows fan/air-con 300,000/600,000Rp; ✳︎) Choose among *lumbung*-style bungalows and concrete rooms at this well-looked-after property. Some bungalows are covered in pebbles, others are dark-wood constructions and all have thatched roofs and outdoor baths. The best have air-con and hot water.

Pelangi Cottages BUNGALOW $
(✆0819 3316 8648; r 400,000Rp; ✳︎) Set out on the north end, with a sweet slab of white sand out front, they have spacious but basic concrete and wood bungalows with friendly management and they rent quality mountain bikes to all comers.

🍴 Eating

Most places on Gili Air are locally owned and offer an unbeatable setting for a meal, with tables right over the water facing Lombok's Gunung Rinjani. Standards don't vary that much. A few smart Western-owned alternatives have opened in recent years.

TOP CHOICE **Biba** ITALIAN $
(✆0819 1727 4648; www.bibabeach.com; mains 25,000-70,000Rp; ⊘11.30am-10pm) Book a table on the sand for a memorable, romantic setting. Biba serves the best wood-oven pizza and foccacia on the islands. It also does authentic ravioli, gnocchi and tagliatelle. The oven fires up at 7pm nightly.

TOP CHOICE **Scallywags** INTERNATIONAL $$
(✆645 301; www.scallywagsresort.com; mains 46,000-95,000Rp; 🕿) Set on Gili Air's softest and widest beach, and more a groovy hippie chic beach club than a mere restaurant, you can make any number of excuses to spend the day here (and many do). There's the elegant decor, upscale comfort food (we love the tuna sashimi drizzled with olive oil and sprinkled with rock salt), homemade gelato, superb cocktails and free wi-fi. But the best of them all is that alluring beach dotted with lounges.

Wiwin Café INDONESIAN $
(dishes 25,000-60,000Rp; ⊘7am-10pm) A great choice for grilled fish in one of five homemade sauces. Service is attentive and there's a nice bar area too.

Paradiso 2 INDONESIAN $
(mains 25,000-60,000Rp) Located on a fabulous stretch of sand, it has beachside bamboo lounges and serves Indonesian food.

Harmony Cafe CAFE $
(✆0878 6416 8463; mains 25,000-60,000Rp; ⊘8am-10pm) This white-washed beach shack feels like the classiest dining spot on the island. Not because of the swank or the menu. Rather, the elements and the vibe are what make it special. It also has two basic all-wood, super clean rooms (75,000Rp to 150,000Rp) with insane beach views.

Tami's Neverland CAFE $
(meals from 35,000Rp; ⊘7am-1am) A large bamboo in-holding in the midst of 7 Seas domination, this place serves hearty Western and Indo grub at fair prices.

Warung Gili INDONESIAN $
(mains 15,000-30,000Rp; ⊘7am-10pm) One of a few Indo greasy spoons in the village. This

one has a *palapa* (thatched) roof, bamboo tables and all the Indo nibbles.

Drinking

Gili Air is usually a mellow place, but there are full-moon parties and things can rev up in high season.

TOP CHOICE **Mirage** BAR

(drinks 40,000-55,000Rp) Set on a sublime stretch of beach with technicolour sunsets nightly and live bands on Fridays. There is no better place for a sundowner.

Chill Out Bar BAR

(www.chilloutbubgalows.com) Its recent expansion puts it on par with some of the splashier beach clubs around. We love its sweet perch, opposite Meno. Come for a swim and sip, stay for dinner (mains 25,000Rp to 55,000Rp) or overnight? It does have bungalows.

Zipp Bar BAR

This large bar has tables dotted around a great beach and an excellent booze selection (try the fresh-fruit cocktails). It hosts a beach party every full moon.

Information

The island's lone ATM is on the 7 Seas strip, and it accepts foreign cards. Dive centres typically charge at least 8% for cash advances on credit cards. There's a **clinic** in the village for medical services.

Ozzy Internet & Wartel Hendra (622 179; internet per hr 24,000Rp; international calls per min 13,000Rp; ⊙8am-9pm) A mini-mart, a warnet, a wartel and money exchange all in one place.

Perama (637 816) Reliable travel agency.

Understand
❭ Bali & Lombok

population per sq km

BALI   AUSTRALIA   UK

↑ ≈ 3 people

Bali & Lombok Today

Change Without Change

'This nation of artists is faced with a Western invasion, and I cannot stand idly by and watch its destruction.' Andre Roosevelt wrote this in 1930. Yet somehow the Balinese have always found a way to stay true to themselves, whether in the face of invasions from Java or volcanoes exploding, or while welcoming three million visitors annually. Who can question the ingenuity of people who fly kites so they can have fun and talk to the gods?

Worrisome Developments

Unconstrained development threatens some of the very qualities that make Bali a wonderful place to visit. The coast is especially vulnerable. In 2000, for example, rice fields extended north from Seminyak all the way to Pura Tanah Lot. Today, this landscape is almost lost to villas and tourist developments, yet on an island where farmers working one hectare of land may only earn US$100 a month, who can begrudge them a chance to sell their plot for huge profits?

Yet even as the rice fields of Bali succumb to development by 700 to 1000 hectares a year, Bali has earned international honours from Unesco, which placed the island's ancient rice-growing traditions on the World Heritage List in 2012. Meanwhile what many would consider a long overdue development, major road projects will try to address the ever-worsening traffic problems. Observers are waiting to see what happens with the new elevated toll road linking Sanur, Nusa Dua and the airport, as there are proposals to build more across the rice fields east and west of the south.

Water in the Wrong Places

Warning signs of overcrowding and overdevelopment are everywhere. It's easy to dismiss the failing electrical grid as the expected outcome of

» Population: Bali 3.9 million; Lombok 3.2 million

» Percentage of Bali's land used for rice production: 29%

» Average monthly wage of a tourism worker: US$80-200

» Down payment on motorbike purchase: US$30

» New motorbikes registered each month: 5000

» Area: Bali 5620 sq km; Lombok 5435 sq km

Top Books

» **Bali Daze: Freefall Off the Tourist Trail** Cat Wheeler's accounts of daily life in Ubud ring more true than other recent books.

» **Secrets of Bali: Fresh Light on the Morning of the World** One of the most readable books about Bali, its people, its traditions and more. Authors Jonathan Copeland and Ni Wayan Murni have a winner.

» **Eat, Pray, Love** Hate it or love it, this bestseller by Elizabeth Gilbert lures believers to Bali every year.

Top Downloads

Gamelan music is hypnotic, addictive and thoroughly Bali. The following are top-sellers on iTunes:

» Gamelan Salunding
» Gamelan Suling
» Sekaha Ganda Sari

belief systems
(% of population)

if Bali & Lombok were 100 people

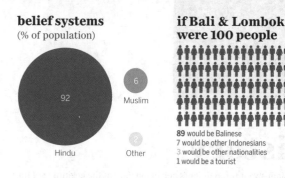

89 would be Balinese
7 would be other Indonesians
3 would be other nationalities
1 would be a tourist

92 Hindu

6 Muslim

2 Other

an old-school power supply unable to meet modern-day demands, but the reality is that electrical consumption is going up faster than anyone predicted.

More ominous are the water shortages. On an island whose self image is based on bounteous, free-flowing water, it doesn't portend well when it's noted that each room in a resort hotel accounts for 1000 litres of water, five times what the average local family requires. Huge demands, from golf courses on the semi-arid Bukit Peninsula to all those villas with plunge pools, have stressed a once-thought-bottomless resource.

And if there is not enough water on shore, there's too much offshore. Each year rising ocean waters cause erosion along another 6km of coast in Bali and Lombok. The once-wide sands of iconic Kuta Beach can get narrow indeed at high tide. A building boom of sand crofts only shoves the problem further down the beach.

Embracing Change

Every time you discover a tiny offering – even just an incense stick still smoking outside your hotel room – you're reminded that the Balinese get it. They never underestimate their power to flourish within the vicissitudes of modern life. That offering would have been in a small shrine amid rice 100 years ago; today, the complex and rich belief system behind it has adapted to the current realities.

Responding to the traffic congestion, local religious leaders decided that outright opposition to 'stacking people' in elevated freeways was wrong, because forcing people to sit in traffic was a greater indignity and the toll road was launched. How Bali will respond to ever-greater indignities is the question of the century.

Visitors to Bali in descending order:

» Australia (27% of arrivals, mate)
» China
» Japan
» Malaysia
» South Korea
» UK
» Russia
» Taiwan
» Singapore
» USA
» France
» Germany
» Netherlands
...and the rest

Top Fruits

» **Mangosteen** It looks like a leathery ball, but inside are luscious sweet segments.

» **Langsat** The bland beige exterior belies a sharp sweet interior.

» **Rambutan** Hairy and scary outside, sweet and juicy inside.

Go Ahead

On Bali you can:

» Accidentally tread on an offering and nobody will take offence.

» Enjoy a beer during a serious dance performance.

» Wear something stupid that would get hoots at home.

» Find inner happiness through the sound of rice growing.

» Buy a souvenir so silly that you'll later claim it was slipped into your bag.

» Discover a culture unlike any you've known.

History

SUTASOMA

When Islam swept through Bali's neighbour Java at the beginning of the 12th century, the kings and courtiers of the embattled Hindu Majapahit kingdom began crossing the straits into Bali, making their final exodus in 1478. The priest Nirartha brought many of the complexities of the Balinese Hindu religion to the island, and established offshore temples, including Rambut Siwi, Tanah Lot and Ulu Watu.

From the early 1700s the Balinese sought to control Lombok with varying success until replaced by the Dutch in 1894.

In the 19th century the Dutch began to form alliances with local princes in north Bali. A dispute over the ransacking of wrecked ships was the pretext for the 1906 Dutch invasion of the south, which climaxed in a suicidal *puputan* (fight to the death). The Denpasar nobility burnt their own palaces and marched straight into the Dutch guns. Other rajahs soon capitulated, and Bali became part of the Dutch East Indies.

In later years Balinese culture was actually encouraged by many Dutch officials. International interest was aroused and the first Western tourists arrived.

After WWII the struggle for national independence was fierce in Bali. Independence was declared on 17 August 1945 (still celebrated as Independence Day), but power wasn't officially handed over until 27 December 1949, when the Dutch finally gave up the fight. The island languished economically in the early years of Indonesian sovereignty, but Bali's greatest national resource, beauty, was subsequently marketed to great effect.

The tourism boom, which started in the early 1970s, has brought many changes, and has helped pay for improvements in roads, telecommunications, education and health. Though tourism has had some marked adverse environmental and social effects, Bali's unique culture has proved to be remarkably resilient.

TIMELINE

50 million BC	2000 BC	AD 7th century
A permanent gap in the Earth's crust forms between Asia and Australia. The Wallace Line keeps Australian species from crossing to Bali until the invention of cheap Bintang specials.	A Balinese gentleman passes away. One of the first known inhabitants of the island, he rests peacefully until his bones are found and placed on display in Gilimanuk.	Indian traders bring Hinduism to Bali. Little is known about what was traded, although some speculate that they left with lots of wooden carvings of penises and bootleg *lontar* books.

The First Balinese

There are few traces of Stone Age people in Bali, although it's certain that the island was populated very early in prehistoric times – fossilised humanoid remains from neighbouring Java have been dated to as early as 250,000 years ago. The earliest human artefacts found in Bali are stone tools and earthenware vessels dug up near Cekik in west Bali, which are estimated to be 3000 years old. Discoveries continue, and you can see exhibits of bones that are estimated to be 4000 years old at the Museum Situs Purbakala Gilimanuk. Artefacts indicate that the Bronze Age began in Bali before 300 BC.

Little is known of Bali during the period when Indian traders brought Hinduism to the Indonesian archipelago, although it is thought it was embraced on the island by the 7th century AD. The earliest written records are inscriptions on a stone pillar near Sanur, dating from around the 9th century; by that time, Bali had already developed many similarities to the island you find today. Rice, for example, was grown with the help of a complex irrigation system, probably very like the one employed now, and the Balinese had already begun to develop their rich cultural and artistic traditions.

If little is known about the earliest inhabitants of Bali, then even less is known about Lombok until about the 17th century. Early inhabitants are thought to have been Sasaks from a region encompassing today's India and Myanmar.

Hindu Influence

Java began to spread its influence into Bali during the reign of King Airlangga (1019–42), or perhaps even earlier. At the age of 16, when his uncle lost the throne, Airlangga fled into the forests of western Java. He gradually gained support, won back the kingdom once ruled by his uncle and went on to become one of Java's greatest kings. Airlangga's mother had moved to Bali and remarried shortly after his birth, so when he gained the throne, there was an immediate link between Java and Bali. It was at this time that the courtly Javanese language known as Kawi came into use among the royalty of Bali, and the rock-cut memorials seen at Gunung Kawi, near Tampaksiring, provide a clear architectural link between Bali and 11th-century Java.

After Airlangga's death, Bali remained semi-independent until Kertanagara became king of the Singasari dynasty in Java two centuries later. Kertanagara conquered Bali in 1284, but the period of his greatest power lasted a mere eight years, until he was murdered and his kingdom collapsed. However, the great Majapahit dynasty was founded by his son, Vijaya (or Wijaya). With Java in turmoil, Bali regained its autonomy, and

Oldest Sites

» Goa Gajah
» Gunung Kawi
» Tirta Empul
» Stone Pillar

9th century	1019	12th century	1292
A stone carver creates an account in Sanskrit of now long-forgotten military victories. Bali's oldest dated artefact proves early Hindu influence and ends up hidden in Sanur.	A future king, Airlangga, is born in Bali. He lives in the jungles of Java until he gains political power and becomes king of the two islands, unifying both cultures.	An incredible series of 10 7m-high statues are carved from stone cliffs at Gunung Kawi north of Ubud.	Bail gains complete independence from Java with the death of Kertanagara, a powerful king who had ruled the two islands for eight years. Power shifts frequently between the islands.

ARTISTS IN CHARGE

The lasting wholesale change to Balinese life because of the mass exodus of Hindu elite from Javanese kingdoms in the 16th century cannot be overstated. It's as if all the subscribers to the opera were put in charge of a town – suddenly there would be a lot more opera. The Balinese had already shown a bent for creativity but once the formerly Javanese intelligentsia exerted control, music, dance, art and more flowered like the lotus blossoms in village ponds. High status was accorded to villages with the most creative talent, a tradition that continues today.

This flair for the liberal arts found a perfect match in the Hinduism that took full hold then. The complex and rich legends of good and evil spirits found ample opportunity to flourish, such as the legend of Jero Gede Macaling, the evil spirit of Nusa Penida.

the Pejeng dynasty rose to great power. Temples and relics of this period can still be found in Pejeng, near Ubud.

Exit Pejeng

In 1343 the legendary Majapahit prime minister, Gajah Mada, defeated the Pejeng king Dalem Bedaulu, and Bali was brought back under Javanese influence.

A Short History of Bali: Indonesia's Hindu Realm, by Robert Pringle, is a thoughtful analysis of Bali's history from the Bronze Age to the present, with excellent sections on the 2002 bombings and ongoing environmental woes caused by tourism and development.

Although Gajah Mada brought much of the Indonesian archipelago under Majapahit control, this was the furthest extent of their power. The 'capital' of the dynasty was moved to Gelgel, in Bali, near modern Semarapura, around the late 14th century, and this was the base for the 'king of Bali', the Dewa Agung, for the next two centuries. The Gelgel dynasty in Bali, under Dalem Batur Enggong, extended its power eastwards to the neighbouring island of Lombok and even westwards across the strait to Java.

The collapse of the Majapahit dynasty into weak, decadent petty kingdoms opened the door for the spread of Islam from the trading states of the north coast into the heartland of Java. As the Hindu states fell, many of the intelligentsia fled to Bali. Notable among these was the priest Nirartha, who is credited with introducing many of the complexities of Balinese religion to the island, as well as establishing the chain of 'sea temples', which includes Pura Luhur Ulu Watu and Pura Tanah Lot. Court-supported artisans, artists, dancers, musicians and actors also fled to Bali at this time and the island experienced an explosion of cultural activity that has not stopped to this day.

Dutch Dealings

In 1597, Dutch seamen were among the first Europeans to appear in Bali. Setting a tradition that has prevailed to the present day, they fell in love

1343	1520	1546	1579
The legendary Majapahit prime minister, Gajah Mada, brings Bali back under Javanese control. For the next two centuries, the royal court is just south of today's Semarapura (Klungkung).	Java fully converts to Islam, leaving Bali in isolation as a Hindu island. Priests and artists move to Bali, concentrating and strengthening the island's culture against conversion.	The Hindu priest Nirartha arrives in Bali. He transforms religion and builds temples by the dozen including Rambut Siwi, Tanah Lot and Luhur Ulu Watu.	Sir Francis Drake, while looking for spice, is thought to be Bali's first European visitor; however, his postcard home is lost permanently so proof is elusive.

with the island and when Cornelius de Houtman, the ship's captain, prepared to set sail from the island, two of his crew refused to come with him. At that time, Balinese prosperity and artistic activity, at least among the royalty, was at a peak, and the king who befriended de Houtman had 200 wives and a chariot pulled by two white buffalo, not to mention a retinue of 50 dwarfs, whose bodies had been bent to resemble the handle of a kris (traditional dagger). By the early 1600s, the Dutch had established trade treaties with Javanese princes and controlled much of the spice trade, but they were interested in profit, not culture, and barely gave Bali a second glance.

In 1710, the 'capital' of the Gelgel kingdom was shifted to nearby Klungkung (now called Semarapura), but local discontent was growing; lesser rulers were breaking away, and the Dutch began to move in, using the old strategy of divide and conquer. In 1846 the Dutch used Balinese salvage claims over shipwrecks as a pretext to land military forces in northern Bali, bringing the kingdoms of Buleleng and Jembrana under their control. Their cause was also aided by the various Balinese princes who had gained ruling interests on Lombok and were distracted from matters at home, and also unaware that the wily Dutch would use Lombok against Bali.

In 1894, the Dutch, the Balinese and the people of Lombok collided in battles that would set the course of history for the next several decades.

With the north of Bali long under Dutch control and the conquest of Lombok successful, the south was never going to last long. Once again, it was disputes over the ransacking of wrecked ships that gave the Dutch an excuse to move in. In 1904, after a Chinese ship was wrecked off Sanur, Dutch demands that the rajah of Badung pay 3000 silver dollars in damages were rejected and in 1906 Dutch warships appeared at Sanur.

Balinese Suicide

The Dutch forces landed despite Balinese opposition and, four days later, had marched 5km to the outskirts of Denpasar. On 20 September 1906, the Dutch mounted a naval bombardment of Denpasar and began their final assault. The three princes of Badung realised that they were completely outnumbered and outgunned, and that defeat was inevitable. Surrender and exile, however, would have been the worst imaginable outcome, so they decided to take the honourable path of a suicidal *puputan*. First the princes burned their palaces, and then, dressed in their finest jewellery and waving ceremonial golden kris, the rajah led the royalty, priests and courtiers out to face the modern weapons of the Dutch.

The Dutch implored the Balinese to surrender rather than make their hopeless stand, but their pleas went unheeded and wave after

Locks of hair from Nirartha, the great priest who shaped Balinese Hinduism in the 16th century, are said to be buried at Pura Rambit Siwi, an evocative seaside temple in west Bali.

Kuta was never a part of mainstream Bali. During royal times, the region was a place of exile for malcontents and troublemakers. It was too arid for rice fields, the fishing was barely sustainable and the shore was covered with kilometres of useless sand...

EXILE

1580

The Portuguese also come looking for spice but in a foreshadowing of today's surfers, they wipe out on rocks at Ulu Watu and give up.

1597

A Dutch expedition arrives off Kuta. A contemporary describes the skipper, Cornelius de Houtman, as a braggart and a scoundrel.

JACK HOLLINGSWORTH/GETTY IMAGES ©

» Cliffs at Ulu Watu (p103)

wave of the Balinese nobility marched forward to their death, or turned their kris on themselves. In all, nearly 4000 Balinese died. The Dutch then marched northwest towards Tabanan and took the rajah of Tabanan prisoner – he also committed suicide rather than face the disgrace of exile.

The kingdoms of Karangasem (the royal family still lives in the palaces of Amlapura) and Gianyar had already capitulated to the Dutch and were allowed to retain some of their powers, but other kingdoms were defeated and their rulers exiled. Finally, in 1908, the rajah of Semarapura followed the lead of Badung, and once more the Dutch faced a *puputan*. As had happened at Cakranegara on Lombok, the beautiful palace at Semarapura, Taman Kertha Gosa, was largely destroyed.

With this last obstacle disposed of, all of Bali was under Dutch control and became part of the Dutch East Indies. There was little development of an exploitative plantation economy in Bali, and the common people noticed little difference between Dutch rule and the rule of the rajahs. On Lombok, conditions were harder, as new Dutch taxes took a toll on the populace.

> For much of the 19th century, the Dutch earned enormous amounts of money from the Balinese opium trade. Most of the colonial administrative budget went to promoting the opium industry, which was legal until the 1930s.

THE BATTLE FOR LOMBOK

In 1894, the Dutch sent an army to back the Sasak people of eastern Lombok in a rebellion against the Balinese rajah who controlled Lombok with the support of the western Sasak. The rajah quickly capitulated, but the Balinese crown prince decided to fight on.

The Dutch camp at the Mayura Water Palace was attacked late at night by a combined force of Balinese and western Sasak, forcing the Dutch to take shelter in a temple compound. The Balinese also attacked another Dutch camp further east at Mataram, and soon, the entire Dutch army on Lombok was forced back to Ampenan where, according to one eyewitness, the soldiers 'were so nervous that they fired madly if so much as a leaf fell off a tree'. These battles resulted in enormous losses of men and arms for the Dutch.

Although the Balinese had won the first battles, they had begun to lose the war. They faced a continuing threat from the eastern Sasak, while the Dutch were soon supported with reinforcements from Java.

The Dutch attacked Mataram a month later, fighting street-to-street against Balinese and western Sasak soldiers and civilians. Rather than surrender, Balinese men, women and children opted for the suicidal *puputan* (a warrior's fight to the death) and were cut down by rifle and artillery fire.

In late November 1894, the Dutch attacked Sasari and, again, a large number of Balinese chose the *puputan*. With the downfall of the dynasty, the local population abandoned its struggle against the Dutch.

1795–1815	1830	1856	1891–1894
European wars mean that control of Indonesia nominally shifts from the Dutch to the French to the British and back to the Dutch. Few on Bali notice.	The Balinese slave trade ends. For over two centuries, squabbling Balinese royal houses helped finance their wars by selling some of their most comely subjects.	Mads Lange, a Danish trader, dies mysteriously in Kuta after earning a fortune selling goods to ships anchored off the beach. His death is blamed on poisoning by jealous rivals.	Years of failed Sasak rebellions in eastern Lombok finally take hold after a palace burning. With Dutch assistance the Balinese rulers are chased from the islands within three years.

WWII

In 1942, the Japanese landed unopposed in Bali at Sanur (most Indonesians saw the Japanese, at first, as anticolonial liberators). The Japanese established headquarters in Denpasar and Singaraja, and their occupation became increasingly harsh for the Balinese. When the Japanese left in August 1945 after their defeat in WWII, the island was suffering from extreme poverty. The occupation had fostered several paramilitary, nationalist and anticolonial groups that were ready to fight the returning Dutch.

Independence

In August 1945, just days after the Japanese surrender, Sukarno, the most prominent member of the coterie of nationalist activists, proclaimed the nation's independence. It took four years to convince the Dutch that they were not going to get their great colony back. In a virtual repeat of the *puputan* nearly 50 years earlier, Balinese freedom fighters led by the charismatic Gusti Ngurah Rai (namesake of the Bali airport) were wiped out by the Dutch in the battle of Marga in western Bali on 20 November 1946. The Dutch finally recognised Indonesia's independence in 1949 – though Indonesians celebrate 17 August 1945 as their Independence Day.

At first, Bali, Lombok and the rest of Indonesia's eastern islands were grouped together in the unwieldy province of Nusa Tenggara. In 1958 the central government recognised this folly and created three new governmental regions from the one, with Bali getting its own and Lombok becoming part of Nusa Tenggara Barat.

Coup & Backlash

Independence was not an easy path for Indonesia to follow. When Sukarno assumed more direct control in 1959 after several violent rebellions, he proved to be as inept as a peacetime administrator as he was inspirational as a revolutionary leader. In the early 1960s, as Sukarno faltered, the army, communists, and other groups struggled for supremacy. On 30 September 1965, an attempted coup – blamed on the Partai Komunis Indonesia (PKI, or Communist Party) – led to Sukarno's downfall. General Suharto emerged as the leading figure in the armed forces, displaying great military and political skill in suppressing the coup. The PKI was outlawed and a wave of anticommunist massacres followed throughout Indonesia.

In Bali, the events had an added local significance as the main national political organisations, the Partai Nasional Indonesia (PNI, Nationalist Party) and the PKI, crystallised existing differences between traditionalists, who wanted to maintain the old caste system, and radicals, who saw the caste system as repressive and were urging land reform. After the

With staff reviews, hard-to-find titles and stellar recommendations, *the* place for books about Bali is Ganesha Books in Ubud. The website (www.ganeshabooks bali.com) offers a vast selection and the shop does mail orders.

A woman of many aliases, K'tut Tantri breezed into Bali from Hollywood in 1932. After the war, she joined the Indonesian Republicans in their postwar struggle against the Dutch. As Surabaya Sue, she broadcast from Surabaya in support of their cause. Her book, *Revolt in Paradise*, was published in 1960.

1908	1912	1925	1936
The Balinese royalty commit suicide. Wearing their best dress and armed with 'show' daggers, they march into Dutch gunfire in a suicidal *puputan* (warrior's fight to the death) in Klungkung.	A German, Gregor Krause, photographs beautiful Balinese women topless. WWI intervenes, but in 1920 an 'art book' of photos appears and Dutch steamers docking in Singaraja now bring tourists.	The greatest modern Balinese dancer, Mario, first performs the Kebyar Duduk, his enduring creation. From a stooped position, he moves as if in a trance to the haunting melody of gamelan.	Americans Robert and Louise Koke build a hotel of thatched bungalows on then-deserted Kuta Beach. Gone is stuffy, starched tourism, replacing it is fun in the sun followed by a drink.

THE TOURIST CLASS

Beginning in the 1920s, the Dutch government realised that Bali's unique culture could be marketed internationally to the growing tourism industry. Relying heavily on images that emphasised the topless habits of Bali's women, Dutch marketing drew wealthy Western adventurers, who landed in the north at today's Singaraja and were whisked about the island on rigid three-day itineraries that featured canned cultural shows at a government-run tourist hotel in Denpasar. Accounts from the time are ripe with imagery of supposedly culture-seeking Europeans who really just wanted to see a boob or two. Such desires were often thwarted by Balinese women who covered up when they heard the Dutch jalopies approaching.

But some intrepid travellers arrived independently, often at the behest of members of the small colony of Western artists, such as Walter Spies in Ubud. Two of these visitors were Robert Koke and Louise Garret, an unmarried American couple who had worked in Hollywood before landing in Bali in 1936 as part of a global adventure. Horrified at the stuffy strictures imposed by the Dutch tourism authorities, the pair (who were later married) built a couple of bungalows out of palm leaves and other local materials on the otherwise deserted beach at Kuta, which at that point was home to only a few impoverished fishing families.

Word soon spread, and the Kokes were booked solid. Guests came for days, stayed for weeks and told their friends. At first, the Dutch dismissed the Kokes' Kuta Beach Hotel as 'dirty native huts', but soon realised that increased numbers of tourists were good for everyone. Other Westerners built their own thatched hotels, complete with the bungalows that were to become a Balinese cliché in the decades ahead.

WWII wiped out both tourism and the hotels (the Kokes barely escaped ahead of the Japanese), but once people began travelling again after the war, Bali's inherent appeal made its popularity a foregone conclusion.

In 1987, Louise Koke's long-forgotten story of the Kuta Beach Hotel was published as *Our Hotel in Bali,* illustrated with her incisive sketches and her husband's photographs.

failed coup, religious traditionalists in Bali led the witch-hunt for the 'godless communists'. Eventually, the military stepped in to control the anticommunist purge, but no one in Bali was untouched by the killings, estimated at between 50,000 and 100,000 out of a population of about two million, a percentage many times higher than on Java. Many tens of thousands more died on Lombok.

The 1963 Eruption

Amid the political turmoil, the most disastrous volcanic eruption in Bali in 100 years occurred in 1963. Gunung Agung blew its top in no uncertain manner, at a time of considerable prophetic and political importance.

1945

Following the Japanese surrender, nationalists, Sukarno among them, proclaim independence from the Netherlands.

1946

Freedom fighter Ngurah Rai dies with the rest of his men at Marga. But this *puputan* slays the Dutch colonial spirit, and soon Indonesia is independent.

BRUNO BARBIER/GETTY IMAGES ©

» Margarana commemorating Ngurah Rai, Marga (p247)

Eka Dasa Rudra, the greatest of all Balinese sacrifices and an event that takes place only every 100 years on the Balinese calendar, was to culminate on 8 March 1963. It had been well over 100 Balinese years since the last Eka Dasa Rudra, but there was dispute among the priests as to the correct and most favourable date.

Naturally, Pura Besakih was a focal point for the festival, but Gunung Agung was acting strangely as final preparations were made in late February. Despite some qualms, political pressures forced the ceremonies forward, even as ominous rumblings continued.

On 17 March, Gunung Agung exploded. The catastrophic eruption killed more than 1000 people (some estimate 2000) and destroyed entire villages – 100,000 people lost their homes. Streams of lava and hot volcanic mud poured right down to the sea at several places, completely covering roads and isolating the eastern end of Bali for some time. Driving the main road near Tulamben you can still see some lava flows.

Suharto Comes & Goes

Following the failed coup in 1965 and its aftermath, Suharto established himself as president and took control of the government. Under his 'New Order' government, Indonesia looked to the West for its foreign and economic policies.

Politically, Suharto ensured that his political party, Golkar, with strong support from the army, became the dominant political force. Other political parties were banned or crippled. Regular elections maintained the appearance of a national democracy, but until 1999, Golkar won every election hands down. This period was also marked by great economic development in Bali, and later on, Lombok as social stability and maintenance of a favourable investment climate took precedence over democracy. Huge resorts – often with investors in government – appeared in Sanur, Kuta and Nusa Dua during this time.

In early 1997, the good times ended as Southeast Asia suffered a severe economic crisis, and within the year, the Indonesian currency (the rupiah) had all but collapsed and the economy was on the brink of bankruptcy.

Unable to cope with the escalating crisis, Suharto resigned in 1998, after 32 years in power. His protégé, Dr Bacharuddin Jusuf Habibie, became president. Though initially dismissed as a Suharto crony, he made the first notable steps towards opening the door to real democracy, such as freeing the press from government supervision.

Peace Shattered

In 1999 Indonesia's parliament met to elect a new president. The front-runner was Megawati Sukarnoputri, who was enormously popular in

---

Bali's airport is named for I Gusti Ngurah Rai, the national hero who died leading the resistance against the Dutch at Marga in 1946. The text of a letter he wrote in response to Dutch demands to surrender ends with 'Freedom or death!'

Hotel Kerobokan is a lurid book detailing conditions inside Bali's notorious Kerobokan jail. Journalist Kathryn Bonella, who has written about noted inmate Schapelle Corby, details the goings on behind the walls. It was nearly destroyed during riots in 2012.

1949	1963	1960s	1965
South Pacific, the musical, opens on Broadway and the song 'Bali Hai' fixes a tropical cliché of Bali in the minds of millions (even though it's based on Fiji).	The sacred volcano Gunung Agung erupts, taking out a fair bit of east Bali, killing a thousand or more and leaving 100,000 homeless.	The lengthening of the airport runway for jets, reasonably affordable tickets and the opening of the Bali Beach Hotel in Sanur mark the start of mass tourism.	Indonesia's long-running rivalry between communists and conservatives erupts after a supposed coup attempt by the former. The latter triumph and in the ensuing purges, tens of thousands are killed in Bali.

THE BALI BOMBINGS

On Saturday, 12 October 2002, two bombs exploded on Kuta's bustling Jl Legian. The first blew out the front of Paddy's Bar. A few seconds later, a far more powerful bomb obliterated the Sari Club.

The number of dead, including those unaccounted for, exceeded 200, although the exact number will probably never be known. Many injured Balinese made their way back to their villages, where, for lack of adequate medical treatment, they died.

Indonesian authorities eventually laid the blame for the blasts on Jemaah Islamiyah, an Islamic terrorist group. Dozens were arrested and many were sentenced to jail, including three who received the death penalty. But most received relatively light terms, including Abu Bakar Bashir, a radical cleric who many thought was behind the explosions. His convictions on charges relating to the bombings were overturned by the Indonesian supreme court in 2006, enraging many in Bali and Australia.

On 1 October 2005, three suicide bombers blew themselves up: one in a restaurant on Kuta Sq and two more at beachfront seafood cafes in Jimbaran. It was again the work of Jemaah Islamiyah, and although documents found later stated that the attacks were targeted at tourists, 15 of the 20 who died were Balinese and Javanese employees of the places bombed.

In 2008 Bashir formed a new group that is suspected of ties to hotel bombings in Jakarta in 2009. In 2011 he was sentenced to 15 years in prison for supporting a jihadi training camp in Aceh.

There was also justice as Umar Patek was convicted in 2012 of helping to assemble the 2002 Bali bombs and sentenced to 20 years in jail. But threats continue: in 2012 police on Bali shot dead five suspected terrorists.

Bali, partly because of family connections (her paternal grandmother was Balinese) and partly because her party was essentially secular (the mostly Hindu Balinese are very concerned about any growth in Muslim fundamentalism). However, Abdurrahman Wahid, the moderate, intellectual head of Indonesia's largest Muslim organisation, emerged as president.

On Lombok, however, religious and political tensions spilled over in early 2000 when a sudden wave of attacks starting in Mataram burned Chinese and Christian businesses and homes across the island. The impact on tourism was immediate and severe, and the island is only now emerging from this shameful episode.

A Balinese Makes Good

After 21 months of growing ethnic, religious and regional conflicts, parliament had enough ammunition to recall Wahid's mandate and hand the presidency to Megawati.

1970

A girl ekes out a living selling candy in Kuta. Surfers offer advice, she posts a menu, then she builds a hut and calls it Made's Warung. She prospers.

1972

Filmmaker Alby Falzon brings a band of Australians to Bali for his surfing documentary *Morning on Earth*, which proves seminal for a generation of Australians who head to Kuta.

AARON BLACK/GETTY IMAGES ©

» Coastline of Kuta, Lombok (p279)

Indonesia's cultural wars continued and certainly played a role in the October 2002 bombings in Kuta. More than 200 tourists and Balinese were killed, and hundreds more were injured. Besides the obvious enormous monetary loss (tourism immediately fell by more than half), the blasts fuelled the ever-present suspicions the Hindu Balinese hold regarding Muslims (that the Muslim Javanese are trying to muscle in on the profitable Bali scene, and the Muslims from Indonesia are, in general, looking to show prejudice against non-Muslim Balinese) and shattered the myth of isolation enjoyed by many locals.

Bali's history is reduced to miniature dramas with stilted dolls at the delightfully unhip Bajra Sandhi Monument in Denpasar. Meaning the 'Struggle of the People,' the museum brings cartoon-like 3-D veracity to important moments in the island's history.

1979	1998	2000	2002
Australian Kim Bradley, impressed by the gnarly surfing style of locals, encourages them to start a club. Sixty do just that (good on an island where people fear the water).	Suharto, who always had close ties to Bali, resigns as president after 32 years. His family retains control of several Bali resorts, including the thirsty Pecatu Indah resort.	Indonesian rioting spreads to Lombok and hundreds of Chinese, Christian and Balinese homes and businesses are looted and burned, particularly after a Muslim-sponsored rally to decry violence turns ugly.	Bombs in Kuta kill more than 200, many at the Sari Club. Bali's economy is crushed as tourists stay away and there is economic devastation across the island.

Local Life & Religion

Bali

Ask any traveller what they love about Bali and, most times, 'culture' – sometimes expressed as 'the people' – will top their list. Since the 1920s, when the Dutch used images of bare-breasted Balinese women to lure tourists, Bali has embodied the mystique and glamour of an exotic paradise.

For all the romanticism, there is a harsher reality. For many Balinese, life remains a near hand-to-mouth existence, even as the island prospers due to tourism and the middle class grows. And the idea of culture can sometimes seem misplaced as overzealous touts test your patience in their efforts to make a living.

But there's also some truth to this idea of paradise. There is no other place in the world like Bali, not even in Indonesia. Being the only surviving Hindu island in the world's largest Muslim country, its distinctive culture is worn like a badge of honour by a fiercely proud people. After all, it's only a 100 years ago that 4000 Balinese royalty, dressed in their finest, walked into the gunfire of the Dutch army rather than surrender and become colonial subjects.

True, development has changed the landscape and prompted endless debate about the displacement of an agricultural society by a tourism-services industry. And the upmarket spas, clubs, boutiques and restaurants in Seminyak and Kerobokan might have you mistaking hedonism, not Hinduism, for the local religion. But scratch the surface and you'll find that Bali's soul remains unchanged.

The island's creative heritage is everywhere you look, and the harmonious dedication to religion permeates every aspect of society, underpinning the strong sense of community. There are temples in every house, office and village, on mountains and beaches, in rice fields, trees, caves, cemeteries, lakes and rivers. Yet religious activity is not limited to places of worship. It can occur anywhere, sometimes smack-bang in the middle of peak-hour traffic.

INTIMACY

Balinese culture keeps intimacy behind doors. Holding hands is not customary for couples in Bali, and is generally reserved for small children; however, linking arms for adults is the norm.

Balinese Tolerance

Luckily, the Balinese are famously tolerant of, and hospitable, towards other cultures, though they rarely travel themselves, such is the importance of their village and family ties, not to mention the financial cost. If anything, they're bemused by all the attention, which reinforces their pride; the general sense is, whatever we're doing, it must be right to entice millions of people to leave their homes for ours.

They're unfailingly friendly, love a chat and can get quite personal. English is widely spoken but they love to hear tourists attempt Bahasa

Indonesia or, better still, throw in a Balinese phrase such as *sing ken ken* (no worries); do this and you'll make a friend for life. They have a fantastic sense of humour and their easygoing nature is hard to ruffle. They generally find displays of temper distasteful and laugh at 'emotional' foreigners who are quick to anger.

Lombok

While Lombok's culture and language is often likened to Bali, this does neither island justice. True, Lombok's language, animist rituals and music and dance are reminiscent of the Hindu and Buddhist kingdoms that once ruled Indonesia, and of its time under Balinese rule in the 18th century. But the majority of Lombok's Sasak tribes are Muslim – they have very distinct traditions, dress, food and architecture, and have fought hard to keep them. While the Sasak peasants in western Lombok lived in relative harmony under Balinese feudal control, the aristocracy in the east remained hostile and led the rebellion with the Dutch that finally ousted their Balinese lords in the late 1800s. To this day, the Sasaks take great joy in competing in heroic trials of strength, such as the stick-fighting matches held every August near Tetebatu.

Lombok remains much poorer and less developed than Bali, and is generally more conservative. Its Sasak culture may not be as prominently displayed as Bali's Hinduism, but that can be its own reward as you peel away the layers.

Family Ties

Through their family temple, Balinese have an intense spiritual connection to their home. As many as five generations share a Balinese home, in-laws and all. Grandparents, cousins, aunties, uncles and various distant relatives all live together. When the sons marry, they don't move out – their wives move in. Similarly, when daughters marry, they live with their in-laws, assuming household and child-bearing duties. Because of this, Balinese consider a son more valuable than a daughter. Not only will his family look after them in their old age, but he will inherit the home and perform the necessary rites after they die to free their souls for reincarnation, so they do not become wandering ghosts.

A Woman's Work Is Work

Men play a big role in village affairs and helping to care for children, and only men plant and tend to the rice fields. But women are the real workhorses in Bali, doing everything from manual labour jobs (you'll see them carrying baskets of wet cement or bricks on their heads) to running

A great resource on Balinese culture and life is www.murnis. com. Find explanations on everything from kids' names to what one wears to a ceremony, to how garments are woven.

SMALL TALK

'Where do you stay?' 'Where do you come from?' 'Where are you going?' You'll hear these questions over and over from your super-friendly Balinese hosts. While Westerners can find it intrusive, it's just Balinese small talk and a reflection of their communal culture; they want to see where you fit in and change your status from stranger to friend.

Saying you're staying 'over there' or in a general area is fine, but expect follow-ups to get increasingly personal. 'Are you married?' Even if you're not, it's easiest to say you are. Next will be: 'Do you have children?' The best answer is affirmative: never say you don't want any. '*Belum*' (not yet) is also an appropriate response, which will likely spark a giggle and an, 'Ah, still trying!'

On Lombok, Sasak language does not have greetings such as 'good morning' or 'good afternoon.' Instead, they often greet each other with 'How's your family?' Don't be surprised if a complete stranger asks about yours!

market stalls and almost every job in tourism. In fact, their traditional role of caring for people and preparing food means that women have established many successful shops and cafes.

In between all of these tasks, women also prepare daily offerings for the family temple and house, and often extra offerings for upcoming ceremonies; their hands are never idle. You can observe all of this and more when you stay at a classic Balinese homestay, where your room is in the family compound and everyday life goes on about you. Ubud has many homestays.

The ancient Hindu swastika seen all over Bali is a symbol of harmony with the universe. The German Nazis used a version where the arms were always bent in a clockwise direction.

Religion

Hinduism

Bali's official religion is Hindu, but it's far too animistic to be considered in the same vein as Indian Hinduism. The Balinese worship the trinity of Brahma, Shiva and Vishnu, three aspects of the one (invisible) god, Sanghyang Widi, as well as the *dewa* (ancestral gods) and village founders. They also worship gods of the earth, fire, water and mountains; gods of fertility, rice, technology and books; and demons who inhabit the world underneath the ocean. They share the Indian belief in karma and reincarnation, but much less emphasis is attached to other Indian customs. There is no 'untouchable caste,' arranged marriages are very rare, and there are no child marriages.

Bali's unusual version of Hinduism was formed after the great Majapahit Hindu kingdom that once ruled Indonesia evacuated to Bali as Islam spread across the archipelago. While the Bali Aga (the 'original' Balinese) retreated to the hills in places such as east Bali's Tenganan to escape this new influence, the rest of the population simply adapted it for themselves, overlaying the Majapahit faith on their animist beliefs, incorporated with Buddhist influences. A Balinese Hindu community can be found in west Lombok, a legacy of Bali's domination of its neighbour in the 19th century.

The most sacred site on the island is Gunung Agung, home to Pura Besakih and frequent ceremonies involving anywhere from hundreds to

---

WHAT'S IN A NAME?

Far from being straightforward, Balinese names are as fluid as the tides. Everyone has a traditional name, but their other names often reflect events in each individual's life. They also help distinguish between people of the same name, which is perhaps nowhere more necessary than in Bali.

Traditional naming customs seem straightforward, with a predictable gender non-specific pattern to names: first-born Wayan, second-born Made, third-born Nyoman, and fourth-born Ketut. Subsequent children reuse the same set, but as many families now settle for just two children, you'll meet many Wayans and Mades. For those from the Sudra caste, these names are preceded by the title 'I' for a boy and 'Ni' for a girl. Upper-caste titles are Ida Bagus for a male and Ida Ayu for a female, followed by Cokorda, Anak Agung, Dewa or Gusti for both males and females.

Traditional names are followed by another given name – this is where parents can get creative. Some names reflect hopes for their child, as in I Nyoman Darma Putra, who's supposed to be 'dutiful' or 'good' (dharma). Others reflect modern influences, such as I Wayan Radio who was born in the 1970s, and Ni Made Atom who said her parents just liked the sound of this scientific term that also had a bomb named after it.

Many are tagged for their appearance. Nyoman Darma is often called Nyoman Kopi (coffee) for the darkness of his skin compared with that of his siblings. I Wayan Rama, named after the *Ramayana* epic, is called Wayan Gemuk (fat) to differentiate his physique from his slighter friend Wayan Kecil (small).

sometimes thousands of people. Smaller ceremonies are held across the island every day to appease the gods, placate the demons and ensure balance between dharma (good) and adharma (evil) forces.

Don't be surprised if on your very first day on Bali you witness or get caught up in a ceremony of some kind.

Islam

Islam is a minority religion in Bali; most followers are Javanese immigrants or descendants of seafaring people from Sulawesi.

The majority of Lombok's Sasak people practise a moderate version of Islam, as in other parts of Indonesia. It was brought to the island by Gujarati merchants via the island of Celebes (now Sulawesi) and Java in the 13th century. The Sasaks follow the Five Pillars of Islam; the pillars decree that there is no god but Allah and Muhammad is His prophet, and that believers should pray five times a day, give alms to the poor, fast during the month of Ramadan and make the pilgrimage to Mecca at least once in their lifetime. However, in contrast to other Islamic countries, Muslim women are not segregated, head coverings are not compulsory, and polygamy is rare. In addition, many Sasaks still practise ancestor and spirit worship. A stricter version of Islam is beginning to emerge in east Lombok.

Wektu Telu

Believed to have originated in Bayan, north Lombok, Wektu Telu is an indigenous religion unique to Lombok (p274). Now followed by a minority of Sasaks, it was the majority religion in northern Lombok until as recently as 1965, when Indonesia's incoming president Suharto decreed that all Indonesians must follow an official religion. Indigenous beliefs such as Wektu Telu were not recognised. Many followers thus state their official religion as Muslim, while practising Wektu traditions and rituals. Bayan remains a stronghold of Wektu Telu; you can spot believers by their *sapu puteq* (white headbands) and white flowing robes.

Wektu means 'result' in Sasak and telu means 'three', and it probably signifies the complex mix of Balinese Hinduism, Islam and animism that the religion is. The tenet is that all important aspects of life are underpinned by a trinity. Like orthodox Muslims, they believe in Allah and that Muhammad is Allah's prophet; however, they pray only three times a day and honour just three days of fasting for Ramadan. Followers of Wektu Telu bury their dead with their heads facing Mecca and all public buildings have a prayer corner facing Mecca, but they do not make pilgrimages there. Similar to Balinese Hinduism, they believe the spiritual world is firmly linked to the natural; Gunung Rinjani is the most revered site.

Ceremonies & Rituals

Between the family temple, village temple and district temple, a Balinese person takes part in dozens of ceremonies every year, on top of their daily rituals. Most employers allow staff to return to their villages for these obligations, which consume a vast chunk of income and time (and although many bosses moan about this, they have little choice unless they wish for a staff revolt). For tourists, this means there are ample opportunities to witness ceremonial traditions.

Ceremonies are the unifying centre of a Balinese person's life and a source of much entertainment, socialisation and festivity. Each ceremony is carried out on an auspicious date determined by a priest and often involves banquets, dance, drama and musical performances to entice the gods to continue their protection against evil forces. The most important ceremonies are Nyepi (p326), which includes a rare day of complete rest,

Black magic is still a potent force and spiritual healers known as *balian* are consulted in times of illness and strife. There are plenty of stories floating around about the power of this magic. Disputes between relatives or neighbours are often blamed on curses, as are tragic deaths.

1. Gunung Rinjani volcano (p275), Lombok 2. Royal cremation procession 3. Terraced rice fields 4. Offering baskets

Top 5 Local Encounters

Sacred Mountain

1 Just as the Balinese have their sacred volcanos, the Sasak people of Lombok have Gunung Rinjani. This volcano, the second-tallest mountain in Indonesia, occupies a vital part of their belief system, which also has elements of Islam. The slopes are the site of many ceremonies.

Cremation

2 Balinese cremations are elaborate ceremonies that are memorable for anyone attending. When someone dies, their body may be temporarily buried while the relatives raise money for a proper – and fiery – send-off in a decorated tower. Visitors are always welcome at these events.

Famous Subak

3 A key to the Balinese psyche is the *subak* system of rice-field irrigation. Through collaborative arrangements, water that starts high in the mountains flows from one farmer's field to the next, with the last plot of land assured it won't be left dry.

Offerings

4 The sizes range from small to XXL. Throughout the day women leave offerings at the over 10,000 temples on Bali, which, like the offerings, also come in many sizes. Offerings may be tiny with a few flower petals on a banana leaf to large and elaborate creations.

Ogoh-Ogoh!

5 Huge monsters appear all over Bali in the weeks before Nyepi, the Day of Silence. Built from papier-mâché, the elaborate figures stand up to 10m tall and may take community organisations weeks to create. On Nyepi these 'evil spirits' are torched in ceremonies in every village on Bali.

SHOWING RESPECT

Bali has a well-deserved reputation for being mellow, which is all the more reason to respect your hosts, who are enormously forgiving of faux pas if you're making a sincere effort. Be aware and respectful of local sensibilities, and dress and act appropriately, especially in rural villages and at religious sites. When in doubt, let the words 'modest' and 'humble' guide you.

Dos & Don'ts

» You'll see shorts and short skirts everywhere on locals but overly revealing clothing is still frowned upon, as is wandering down the street shirtless quaffing a beer.

» Many women go topless on Bali's beaches, although this is offensive as locals are embarrassed by foreigners' gratuitous nudity.

» On Lombok, nude or topless bathing is considered very offensive anywhere.

» Don't touch anyone on the head; it's regarded as the abode of the soul and therefore sacred.

» Pass things with your right hand. Even better, use both hands.

» Beware of talking with hands on hips – a sign of contempt, anger or aggression (as displayed in traditional dance and opera).

» Beckon to someone with the hand extended and a downward waving motion. The Western method of beckoning is considered very rude.

» Don't make promises of gifts, books and photographs that are soon forgotten. Pity the poor Balinese checking their mailbox or email inbox every day.

Religious Etiquette

» Cover shoulders and knees if visiting a temple or mosque; in Bali, a *selandong* (traditional scarf) or sash plus a sarong is usually provided for a small donation.

» Women are asked not to enter temples if they're menstruating, pregnant or have recently given birth. At these times women are thought to be *sebel* (ritually unclean).

» Don't put yourself higher than a priest, particularly at festivals (eg by scaling a wall to take photos).

» Take off your shoes before entering a mosque.

and Galungan, a 10-day reunion with ancestral spirits to celebrate the victory of good over evil.

Under their karmic beliefs, the Balinese hold themselves responsible for any misfortune, which is attributed to an overload of adharma (evil). This calls for a *ngulapin* (cleansing) ritual to seek forgiveness and recover spiritual protection. A *ngulapin* requires an animal sacrifice and often involves a cockfight, satisfying the demons' thirst for blood.

Ceremonies are also held to overcome black magic and to cleanse a *sebel* (ritually unclean) spirit after childbirth or bereavement, or during menstruation or illness.

On top of all these ceremonies, there are 13 major rites of passage throughout every person's life. The most extravagant and expensive is the last – cremation.

> The Balinese tooth-filing ceremony closes with the recipient being given a delicious *jamu* (herbal tonic), made from freshly pressed turmeric, betel-leaf juice, lime juice and honey.

Birth & Childhood

The Balinese believe babies are the reincarnation of ancestors, and they honour them as such. Offerings are made during pregnancy to ensure the mini-deity's well-being, and after birth, the placenta, umbilical cord, blood and afterbirth water – representing the child's four 'spirit' guardian brothers – are buried in the family compound.

Newborns are literally carried everywhere for the first three months, as they're not allowed to touch the 'impure' ground until after a purification ceremony. At 210 days (the first Balinese year), the baby is blessed in the ancestral temple and there is a huge feast. Later in life, birthdays lose their significance and many Balinese couldn't tell you their age.

A rite of passage to adulthood – and a prerequisite to marriage – is the tooth-filing ceremony at around 16 to 18 years. This is when a priest files a small part of the upper canines and upper incisors to flatten the teeth. Pointy fangs are, after all, distinguishing features of dogs and demons. Balinese claim the procedure doesn't hurt, likening the sensation to eating very cold ice: it's slightly uncomfortable, but not painful.

Another important occasion for girls is their first menstrual period, which calls for a purification ceremony.

Marriage

Marriage defines a person's social status in Bali, making men automatic members of the *banjar* (local neighbourhood organisation). Balinese believe that when they come of age, it's their duty to marry and have children, including at least one son. Divorce is rare, as a divorced woman is cut off from her children.

The respectable way to marry, known as *mapadik,* is when the man's family visits the woman's family and proposes. But the Balinese like their fun and some prefer marriage by *ngrorod* (elopement or 'kidnapping'). After the couple returns to their village, the marriage is officially recognised and everybody has a grand celebration.

Death & Cremation

The body is considered little more than a shell for the soul, and upon death it is cremated in an elaborate ceremony befitting the ancestral spirit. It usually involves the whole community, and for important people such as royalty, it can be a spectacular event involving thousands of people.

Because of the burdensome cost of even a modest cremation (estimated at around 5,000,000Rp), as well as the need to wait for an auspicious date, the deceased is often buried, sometimes for years, and disinterred for a mass cremation.

The body is carried in a tall, incredibly artistic, multi-tiered pyre on the shoulders of a group of men. The tower's size depends on the deceased's importance. A rajah's or high priest's funeral may require hundreds of men to tote the 11-tiered structure.

Along the way, the group sets out to confuse the corpse so it cannot find its way back home; the corpse is considered an unclean link to the material world, and the soul must be liberated for its evolution to a higher state. The men shake the tower, run it around in circles, simulate war battles, hurl water at it and generally rough-handle it, making the trip anything but a stately funeral crawl.

At the cremation ground, the body is transferred to a funeral sarcophagus reflecting the deceased's caste. Finally, it all goes up in flames and the ashes are scattered in the ocean. The soul is then free to ascend to heaven and wait for the next incarnation, usually in the form of a grandchild.

In classic Balinese fashion, respectful visitors are welcome at cremations. It's always worth asking around, or at your hotel, to see if anyone knows of one going on. The Ubud tourist office is a good source, too.

Offerings

No matter where you stay, you'll witness women making daily offerings around their family temple and home, and in hotels, shops and other

Traditionally, Balinese men do not cut their hair during their wives' pregnancies. This supposedly gives the baby good hair, while also giving the husband empathy for his wife's discomfort.

The Ubud tourist office is an excellent source for news of cremations and other Balinese ceremonies that occur at erratic intervals.

LOCAL LIFE & RELIGION CEREMONIES & RITUALS

public places. You're also sure to see vibrant ceremonies, where whole villages turn out in ceremonial dress, and police close the roads for a spectacular procession that can stretch for hundreds of metres. Men play the gamelan while women elegantly balance magnificent tall offerings of fruit and cakes on their heads.

There's nothing manufactured about what you see. Dance and musical performances at hotels are among the few events 'staged' for tourists, but they do actually mirror the way Balinese traditionally welcome visitors, whom they refer to as *tamu* (guests). Otherwise, it's just the Balinese going about their daily life as they would without spectators.

Lombok

On Lombok, *adat* (tradition, customs and manners) underpins all aspects of daily life, especially regarding courtship, marriage and circumcision. Friday afternoon is the official time for worship, and government offices and many businesses close. Many, but not all, women wear headscarves, very few wear the veil, and large numbers work in tourism. Middle-class Muslim girls are often able to choose their own partners. Circumcision

BALI PLAYS DEAD

Nyepi

This is Bali's biggest purification festival, designed to clean out all the bad spirits and begin the year anew. It falls around March or April according to the Hindu caka calendar, a lunar cycle similar to the Western calendar in terms of the length of the year. Starting at sunrise, the whole island literally shuts down for 24 hours. No planes may land or take off, no vehicles of any description may be operated, and no power sources may be used. Everyone, including tourists, must stay off the streets. The cultural reasoning behind Nyepi is to fool evil spirits into thinking Bali has been abandoned so they will go elsewhere.

For the Balinese, it's a day for meditation and introspection. For foreigners, the rules are more relaxed, so long as you respect the 'Day of Silence' by not leaving your residence or hotel. If you do sneak out, you will quickly be escorted back to your hotel by a stern *pecalang* (village police officer).

As daunting as it sounds, Nyepi is actually a fantastic time to be in Bali. Firstly, there's the inspired concept of being forced to do nothing. Catch up on some sleep, or if you must, read, sunbathe, write postcards, play board games... just don't do anything to tempt the demons! Secondly, there are colourful festivals the night before Nyepi.

I Go, You Go, Ogoh-Ogoh!

In the weeks prior to Nyepi, huge and elaborate papier-mâché monsters called *ogoh-ogoh* are built in villages across the island. Involving everybody in the community, construction sites buzz with fevered activity around the clock. If you see a site where *ogoh-ogoh* are being constructed, there'll be a sign-up sheet for financial support. Contribute, say, 50,000Rp and you'll be a fully fledged sponsor and receive much street cred.

On Nyepi eve, large ceremonies all over Bali lure out the demons. Their rendezvous point is believed to be the main crossroads of each village, and this is where the priests perform exorcisms. Then the whole island erupts in mock 'anarchy,' with people banging on *kulkuls* (hollow tree-trunk drums), drums and tins, letting off firecrackers and yelling '*megedi megedi!*' (get out!) to expel the demons. The truly grand finale is when the *ogoh-ogoh* all go up in flames. Any demons that survive this wild partying are believed to evacuate the village when confronted with the boring silence on the morrow.

Christians find unique parallels to Easter in all this, especially Ash Wednesday and Shrove Tuesday, with its wild Mardi Gras–like celebrations the world over.

In coming years, dates for Nyepi are 12 March 2013, 31 March 2014 and 21 March 2015.

KEEPING TRACK OF TIME

Wondering what day of the week it is? You may have to consult a priest. The Balinese calendar is such a complex, intricate document that it only became publicly available some 60 years ago. Even today, most Balinese need a priest or *adat* (tradition and customs) leader to interpret it in order to determine the most auspicious day for any undertaking.

The calendar defines daily life. Whether it's building a new house, planting rice, having your teeth filed or getting married or cremated, no event has any chance of success if it does not occur on the proper date.

Three seemingly incompatible systems comprise the calendar (but this being Bali that's a mere quibble): the 365-day Gregorian calendar, the 210-day *wuku* (or Pawukon) calendar, and the 12-month *caka* lunar calendar, which begins with Nyepi every March or April. In addition, certain weeks are dedicated to humans, others to animals and bamboo, and the calendar also lists forbidden activities for each week, such as getting married or cutting wood or bamboo.

Besides the date, each box on a calendar page contains the lunar month, the names of each of the 10 week 'days', attributes of a person born on that day according to Balinese astrology, and a symbol of either a full or new moon. Along the bottom of each month is a list of propitious days for specific activities, as well as the dates of *odalan* temple anniversaries – colourful festivals that visitors are welcome to attend.

In the old days, a priest consulted a *tika* – a piece of painted cloth or carved wood displaying the *wuku* cycle – which shows auspicious days represented by tiny geometric symbols. Today, many people have their own calendars, but it's no wonder the priests are still in business!

of Sasak boys normally occurs between the ages of six and 11 and calls for much celebration following a parade through their village.

The significant Balinese population on Lombok means you can often glimpse a Hindu ceremony while there; the minority Wektu Telu, Chinese and Buginese communities add to the diversity.

Village Life

Village life doesn't just take place in rural villages. Virtually every place on Bali is a village in its own way. Under its neon flash, chaos and otherworldly pleasures, even Kuta is a village; the locals meet, organise, celebrate, plan and make decisions as is done across the island. Central to this is the *banjar* (local neighbourhood organisation).

Local Rule Bali-Style

Within Bali's government, the more than 3500 *banjar* wield enormous power. Comprising the married men of a given area (somewhere between 50 and 500), a *banjar* controls most community activities, whether it's planning for a temple ceremony or making important land-use decisions. Decisions are reached by consensus, and woe to a member who shirks his duties. The penalty can be fines or worse: banishment from the *banjar*. (In Bali's highly socialised society where your community is your life and identity – which is why a standard greeting is 'Where do you come from?' – banishment is the equivalent of the death penalty.)

Although women and even children can belong to the *banjar*, only men attend the meetings where important decisions are made. Women, who often own the businesses in tourist areas, have to communicate through their husbands to exert their influence. One thing that outsiders in a neighbourhood quickly learn is that one does not cross the *banjar*. Entire streets of restaurants and bars have been closed by order of the *banjar* after it was determined that neighbourhood concerns over matters such as noise were not being addressed.

Motorbikes are an invaluable part of daily life. They carry everything from towers of bananas and rice sacks headed to the market, to whole families in full ceremonial dress on their way to the temple, to young hotel clerks riding primly in their uniforms.

Rice Farming

Rice cultivation remains the backbone of rural Bali's strict communal society. Traditionally, each family makes just enough to satisfy their own needs and offerings to the gods, and perhaps a little to sell at market. The island's most popular deity is Dewi Sri, goddess of agriculture, fertility and success, and every stage of cultivation encompasses rituals to express gratitude and to prevent a poor crop, bad weather, pollution or theft by mice and birds. For more on Bali's rice fields, see p359.

Subak: Watering Bali

The complexities of tilling and irrigating terraces in mountainous terrain require that all villagers share the work and responsibility. Under a centuries-old system, the four mountain lakes and criss-crossing rivers irrigate fields via a network of canals, dams, bamboo pipes and tunnels bored through rock. More than 1200 *subak* (village associations) oversee this democratic supply of water, and every farmer must belong to his local *subak*, which in turn is the foundation of each village's powerful *banjar*.

Subak is a fascinating and democratic system; and in 2012 it joined Unesco's World Heritage List. For more on Bali's *subak* system, see p346.

Although Bali's civil make-up has changed with tourism, from a mostly homogenous island of farmers to a heterogeneous population with diverse activities and lifestyles, the collective responsibility rooted in rice farming continues to dictate the moral code behind daily life, even in the urban centres.

Huge decorated *penjor* (bamboo poles) appear in front of homes and line streets for ceremonies such as Galungan. Designs are as diverse as the artists who create them but always feature the signature drooping top – in honour of the Barong's tail and the shape of Gunung Agung. The decorated tips, *sampian*, are exquisite.

Food & Drink

Bali is a splendid destination for food. The local cuisine, whether truly Balinese or drawn from the rest of Indonesia and Asia, draws from the bounty of fresh local foods and is rich with spices and flavours. At bamboo warung (simple local cafes) and top-end restaurants you can savour this fare. And for tastes further afield, you can choose from restaurants offering some of the best dining in the region.

Balinese Cuisine

Food, glorious food. Or should that be food, laborious food? Balinese cooking is a time-consuming activity, but no effort at all is required to enjoy it. That part is easy, and it's one of the best things about travelling around Bali: the sheer variety and quality of the local cuisine will have your taste buds dancing all the way to the next warung.

The fragrant aroma of Balinese cooking will taunt you wherever you go. Even in your average village compound, the finest food is prepared fresh every day. Women go to their local marketplace first thing in the morning to buy whatever produce has been brought from the farms overnight. They cook enough to last all day, diligently roasting the coconut until the smoky sweetness kisses your nose, painstakingly grinding the spices to form the perfect *base* (paste) and perhaps even making fresh fragrant coconut oil for frying. The dishes are covered on a table or stored in a glass cabinet for family members to serve themselves throughout the day.

Six Flavours

Compared with other Indonesian islands, Balinese food is more pungent and lively, with a multitude of layers that make the complete dish. A meal will contain the six flavours (sweet, sour, spicy, salty, bitter and astringent), which promote health and vitality and stimulate the senses.

There's a predominance of ginger, chilli and coconut flavours, as well as the beloved candlenut, often mistaken for the macadamia, native to Australia. The biting combination of fresh galangal and turmeric is matched by the heat of raw chillies, the complex sweetness of palm sugar, tamarind and shrimp paste, and the clean fresh flavours of lemon grass, musk lime, kaffir lime leaves and coriander seeds.

There are shades of South Indian, Malaysian and Chinese flavours, stemming from centuries of migration and trading with seafaring pioneers. Many ingredients have been introduced; the humble chilli was brought by the fearless Portuguese, the ubiquitous snake bean and bok choy by the Chinese, and the rice substitute, cassava, by the Dutch. In true Balinese style, village chefs selected the finest and most durable new ingredients and adapted them to local tastes and cooking styles.

Cooking courses are evermore popular and are great ways to learn about Balinese food and markets. Recommended ones are in Seminyak, Tanjung Benoa and Ubud.

Revered Rice

Rice is the staple dish in Bali and Lombok and is revered as a gift of life from God. It is served generously with every meal – anything not served with rice is considered a *jaja* (snack). It acts as the medium for the various fragrant, spiced foods that accompany it, almost like condiments, with many dishes chopped finely to complement the dry, fluffy grains and for ease of eating with the hand. In Bali, this dish of steamed rice with mixed goodies is known as *nasi campur*. It's the island's undisputed 'signature' dish, eaten for breakfast, lunch and dinner.

There are as many variations of *nasi campur* as there are warung. Just like a sandwich in the West can combine any number of fillings, each warung serves its own version according to budget, taste and whatever ingredients are fresh at the market. There are typically four or five different dishes that make up a single serving, including a small portion of pork or chicken (small because meat is expensive), fish, tofu and/or tempeh (fermented soy-bean cake), egg, various vegetable dishes and crunchy *krupuk* (flavoured rice crackers). Beef seldom features as the Balinese believe cows are sacred. These 'side dishes' are arrayed around the centrepiece of rice and accompanied by the warung's signature sambal (paste made from chillies, garlic or shallots, and salt). The food is not usually served hot, as it has been prepared during the morning.

A Taste of Asia

Bali's multicultural population means many warung serve pan-Indonesian and Asian cuisine, offering a taste of different foods from across the archipelago. Common menu items are often confused with being Balinese, such as *nasi goreng* (fried rice), *mie goreng* (fried noodles), the ever-popular gado gado, which is actually from Java, and *rendang sapi* (beef curry), which is from Sumatra. There are many restaurants serving Padang fare (which originates from Sumatra) in Bali and Lombok, and Chinese food is especially common on Lombok.

Breakfast

Many Balinese save their appetite for lunch. They might kick-start the day with a cup of rich, sweet black coffee and a few sweet *jaja* at the market: colourful temple cakes, glutinous rice cakes, boiled bananas in

---

MARKET LIFE

There's no better place to get acquainted with Balinese cuisine than the local market. But it's not for late sleepers. The best time to go is around 6am to 7am. If you're any later than 10am, the prime selections have been snapped up and what's left has begun to rot in the tropical climate.

Markets offer a glimpse of the variety and freshness of Balinese produce, often brought from the mountains within a day or two of being harvested, sometimes sooner. The atmosphere is lively and colourful with baskets loaded with fresh fruits, vegetables, flowers, spices, and varieties of red, black and white rice. There are trays of live chickens, dead chickens, freshly slaughtered pigs, sardines, eggs, colourful cakes, ready-made offerings and *base*, and stalls selling *es cendol* (colourful iced coconut drink), *bubur* (rice porridge) or *nasi campur* for breakfast. There's no refrigeration, so things come in small packages and what you see is for immediate sale. Bargaining is expected.

Markets ideal for visits include the huge Pasar Badung in Denpasar, the village and fish markets in Jimbaran, the Semarapura market and the produce market in Ubud. Market tours are usually included in cooking courses.

FOOD & DRINK BALINESE CUISINE

SAMBAL JOY

Heinz von Holzen, the chef-owner of Bumbu Bali restaurant and author of numerous books on Balinese cuisine, says many people mistakenly believe Balinese food is spicy. 'The food itself is not normally spicy, the sambal is', Heinz says. That said, the Balinese certainly like some heat, and relish a dollop of fiery sambal with every meal; you may want to taste it to gauge the temperature before ploughing in. If you're averse to spicy food, request *tanpa sambal* (without chilli paste); better for most, though, is *tamba* (more) sambal! One other note on sambal: if your request results in a bottle of the generically sweet commercial gloop, ask for 'Balinese sambal.'

their peels, fried banana fritters and *kelopon* (sweet-centred rice balls). Popular fresh fruits include snake fruit, named after its scaly skin, and jackfruit, which is also delicious stewed with vegetables.

The famous *bubuh injin* (black-rice pudding with palm sugar, grated coconut and coconut milk), which most tourists find on restaurant dessert menus, is actually a breakfast dish and a fine way to start the day. Another variation available at the morning market is the nutty *bubur kacang hijau* (green mung-bean pudding) fragrantly enriched by ginger and *pandanus* leaf and served warm with coconut milk.

Cradle of Flavor is a mouth-watering treatise on Indonesian foods and cooking by James Oseland, the editor of *Saveur* magazine.

Lunch & Dinner

The household or warung cook usually finishes preparing the day's dishes mid-morning, so lunchtime is around 11am when the food is freshest. This is the main meal of the day. Leftovers are eaten for dinner, or by tourists who awake late and do not get around to lunch until well and truly after everyone else has had their fill! Dessert is a rarity; for special occasions, it consists of fresh fruit or gelati-style coconut ice cream.

The secret to a good *nasi campur* is often in the cook's own *base,* which flavours the pork, chicken or fish, and sambal, and which may add just the right amount of heat to the meal at one place, or set your mouth ablaze at another. The range of dishes is endless. Some local favourites include *babi kecap* (pork stewed in sweet soy sauce), *ayam goreng* (fried chicken), *urap* (steamed vegetables with coconut), *lawar* (a dish not for the faint-hearted, which combines vegetables with chopped fried liver, fried entrails, a dollop of congealed pig's blood and coconut milk), fried tofu or tempeh in a sweet soy or chilli sauce, fried peanuts, salty fish or eggs, *perkedel* (fried corn cakes) and various satay made from chunks of goat meat, chicken, pork or even turtle (although there are laws against illegal turtle slaughter).

If you stay at a homestay, like the many in Ubud, you'll see family members busily preparing food throughout the day.

Despite its name, mangosteen is not related to the mango. It is, however, a popular tropical fruit for the peach-like flavour and texture of its white centre, and is often called 'queen of fruit'.

Reason to Celebrate

Food is not just about enjoyment and sustenance. Like everything in Balinese life, it is an intrinsic part of the daily rituals and a major part of ceremonies to honour the gods. The menu varies according to the importance of the occasion. By far the most revered dish is *babi guling* (suckling pig), presented during rites-of-passage ceremonies such as a baby's three-month blessing, an adolescent's tooth filing, or a wedding.

Babi guling is the quintessential Bali experience. The whole pig is stuffed with chilli, turmeric, ginger, galangal, shallots, garlic, coriander seeds and aromatic leaves, basted in turmeric and coconut oil and skewered on a wooden spit over an open fire. Turned for hours, the meat takes

MANGOSTEEN

Top 5 Balinese Treats

Bintang

1 It's a marketers dream: you don't say 'beer' on Bali, you say 'Bintang'. The star of a million branded singlets is a crisp, clean lager that refreshes on a hot day. Whether it's cooling off a fiery feast or making the sunset seem that much rosier, it goes down smooth.

Nasi Campur

2 Bali's equivalent of a national dish, this lunchtime staple defies description. At hundreds of warung (food stalls) across the island you start with a plate and then choose some rice (yellow? white? red?) and then the fun begins. Tempting meat, seafood and veggie dishes are arrayed behind glass; choose what looks best.

Sambal

3 There are as many variations on this staple condiment as there are versions of *nasi campur* and that's only fitting as it's the source of spicy heat in most Balinese foods. Chefs jealously guard their sambal recipes but count on some combination of chillies, garlic, shallots and various herbs and spices.

Night Markets

4 *Pasar malam* (night markets) are popular sources for after-dark eats on Bali and Lombok. The best will have dozens of stalls and stands cooking away like mad on a range of locally favourite dishes. Wander, browse and snack your way to joy. Finish with *piseng goreng* (fried bananas).

Babi Guling

5 What was once a dish reserved for special occasions is now one of Bali's favourite foods: *babi guling*, a suckling pig filled with spices and roasted, is sold at scores of outlets. With incomes rising, average workers can afford a daily plate of this savoury and rich flavoured treat.

1. Cans of local Bintang 2. Plate of Balinese food 3. Chillies (prime ingrediant for sambal) for sale 4. Street food vendor in Denpasar

TOP FIVE WARUNG

The following list scratches the surface. Many more warung are on offer – find your own favourite.

Cak Asm (p123) Spotless place in Denpasar serving truly wonderful fare, especially seafood.

Nasi Ayam Kedewatan (p165) The place for *sate lilit* (minced fish, chicken or pork satay) in a simple open-front dining room on the edge of Ubud.

Warung Kolega (p87) Excellent Balinese dishes by the dozen, in Kerobokan.

Warung Sulawesi (p87) Delicious dishes from across the archipelago, served in a shady family courtyard in Kerobokan.

Warung Teges (p163) Great Balinese fare loved by locals, just south of Ubud.

on the flavour of the spices and the fire-pit, giving a rustic smoky flavour to the crispy crackling.

Short of being invited to a ceremonial feast, you can enjoy *babi guling* at stands, warung and cafes across Bali.

Bebek or *ayam betutu* (smoked duck or chicken) is another ceremonial favourite. The bird is stuffed with spices, wrapped in coconut bark and banana leaves, and cooked all day over smouldering rice husks and coconut husks. Ubud is the best place to enjoy smoked duck – head to Bebek Bengil (it's actually the source for the many restaurants that offer *bebek betutu* if ordered in advance).

Often served at marriage ceremonies, *jukut ares* is a light, fragrant broth made from banana stem and usually containing chopped chicken or pork. The satay for special occasions, *sate lilit*, is a fragrant combination of good-quality minced fish, chicken or pork with lemon grass, galangal, shallots, chilli, palm sugar, kaffir lime and coconut milk. This is wrapped onto skewers and grilled.

The Food of Bali by Heinz von Holzen and Lother Arsana brings to life everything from cram cam *(clear chicken soup with shallots) to* bubuh injin *(black-rice pudding). Von Holzen's books also include a forthcoming one on Balinese markets.*

Warung

The most common place for dining out in Bali and Lombok is a warung, the traditional roadside eatery. There's one every few metres in major towns, and several even in small villages. They are cheap, no-frills hangouts with a relaxed atmosphere; you may find yourself sharing a table with strangers as you watch the world go by. The food is fresh and different at each, and usually displayed in a glass cabinet at the entrance where you can create your own *nasi campur* or just order the house standard.

Both Seminyak and Kerobokan are blessed in particular with numerous warung that are visitor-friendly.

Dining – or Not – Balinese Style

For an exhaustive run-down of eating options in Bali, check out www.balieats.com. The listings are encyclopaedic, continually updated and many have enthusiastic reviews.

Eating is a solitary exercise in Bali and conversation is limited. Families rarely eat together; everyone makes up their own plate whenever they're hungry.

The Balinese eat with their right hand, which is used to give and receive all good things. The left hand deals with unpleasant sinister elements (such as ablutions). It's customary to wash your hands before eating, even if you use a spoon and fork; local restaurants always have a sink outside the restrooms. If you choose to eat the local way, use the bowl of water provided at the table to wash your hands after the meal, as licking your fingers is not appreciated.

The Balinese are formal about behaviour and clothing, and it isn't polite to enter a restaurant or eat a meal half-naked, no matter how many sit-ups you've been doing or new piercings and tattoos you've acquired.

If you wish to eat in front of a Balinese, it's polite to invite them to join you, even if you know they will say 'No', or you don't have anything to offer. If you're invited to a Balinese home for a meal, your hosts will no doubt insist you eat more, but you may always politely pass on second helpings or refuse food you don't find appealing.

Drinks

Beer

Beer drinkers are well catered for in Bali thanks to Indonesia's ubiquitous crisp, clean national lager, Bintang. Locally produced Storm microbrews are excellent. Bali Hai beer sounds promising but isn't.

Wine

Wine connoisseurs had better have a fat wallet. The abundance of high-end eateries and hotels has made fine vino from the world's best regions widely available but it is whacked with hefty taxes. Medium-grade bottles from Australia sell for US$50.

Of the two local producers of wine, the least objectionable is Artisan Estate, which overcomes the import duties by bringing crushed grapes from Western Australia. Hatten Wine, based in north Bali, has gained quite a following among those who like its very sweet pink rosé.

Local Booze

At large social gatherings, Balinese men might indulge in *arak* (fermented wine made from rice or palms or...), but generally they are not big drinkers (watch out for adulterated arak, which can be poisonous; see p386). Lombok's majority Muslim population frowns upon alcohol consumption.

Fresh Juices

Local nonalcoholic refreshments available from markets, street vendors and some warung are colourful, tasty and even a little psychedelic without the hangover! One of Bali's most popular is *cendol*, an interesting mix of palm sugar, fresh coconut milk, crushed ice and various other random flavourings and floaties.

Coffee & Tea

Many Western eateries sell imported coffees and teas alongside local brands, some of which are very good.

The most expensive – and most over-hyped – is Indonesia's peculiar *kopi luwak*, aka 'cat-poo coffee'. Around 200,000Rp a cup, this coffee is named after the catlike civet *(luwak)* indigenous to Sulawesi, Sumatra and Java that feasts on ripe coffee cherries. Entrepreneurs collect the

Admired Local Producers

» Big Tree Farms – chocolate, palm sugar

» FREAK Coffee – coffee

» Kopi Bali – coffee

» Sari Organik – juices, teas

Every town of any size in Bali and Lombok will have a *pasar malam* (night market). You can sample a vast range of fresh offerings from warung and carts after dark. Gianyar has a great one.

FOOD & DRINK DRINKS

NIGHT MARKETS

FAST FOOD BALI STYLE

Usually the most authentic Balinese food is found at street level (although Denpasar has some sit-down places that are excellent). Locals of all stripes gather around simple food stalls in markets and on village streets, wave down *pedagang* (mobile traders) who ferry sweet and savoury snacks around by bicycle or motorcycle, and queue for *sate* or *bakso* (Chinese meatballs in a light soup) at the *kaki-lima* carts. *Kaki-lima* translates as something five-legged and refers to the three legs of the cart and the two of the vendor, who is usually Javanese.

One note on health: food cooked up fresh from carts and stalls is usually fine but that which has been sitting around for awhile can be dodgy at best or riddled with dubious preservatives.

VEGETARIAN DREAMS

Bali is a dream come true for vegetarians. Tofu and tempeh are part of the staple diet, and many tasty local favourites just happen to be vegetarian. Try *nasi saur* (rice flavoured by toasted coconut and accompanied by tofu, tempeh, vegetables and sometimes egg), *urap* (a delightful blend of steamed vegetables mixed with grated coconut and spices), *gado gado* (tofu and tempeh mixed with steamed vegetables, boiled egg and peanut sauce) and *sayur hijau* (leafy green vegetables, usually *kangkung* – water spinach – flavoured with a tomato-chilli sauce).

In addition, the way *nasi campur* is served means it's easy to request no meat, instead enjoying an array of fresh stir-fries, salads and tofu and tempeh. When ordering curries and stir-fries such as *cap cay* in both Bali and Lombok, diners can usually choose meat, seafood or vegetarian.

Western-style vegetarian pasta and salads abound in most restaurants and many purely vegetarian eateries cater for vegans. Seminyak and Ubud are especially good for meat-free fare.

intact beans found in the civet's droppings and process them to produce an extra-bitter, strong brew. Tourist gift shops usually stock it, although this kind of profit means that fakery abounds.

The Arts

Bali's vibrant arts scene makes the island so much more than just a tropical destination. In the paintings, sculpture, dance and music, you will see the natural artistic talent inherent in all Balinese, a legacy of their Majapahit heritage. The artistry displayed here will stay with you long after you've moved on from the island.

But it is telling that there is no Balinese equivalent for the words 'art' or 'artist'. Until the tourist invasion, artistic expression was exclusively for religious and ritual purposes, and almost exclusively done by men. Paintings and carvings were purely to decorate temples and shrines, while music, dance and theatrical performances were put on to entertain the gods who returned to Bali for important ceremonies. Artists did not strive to be different or individual as many do in the West; their work reflected a traditional style or a new idea, but not their own personality.

That changed in the late 1920s when foreign artists began to settle in Ubud; they went to learn from the Balinese and to share their knowledge, and helped to establish art as a commercial enterprise. Today, it's big business. Ubud remains the undisputed artistic centre of the island, and artists still come from near and far to draw on its inspiration, from Japanese glass-blowers to European photographers and Javanese painters.

Galleries and craft shops are all over the island; the paintings, stone-carvings and woodcarvings are stacked up on floors and will trip you up if you're not careful. Much of it is churned out quickly, and some is comically vulgar – put that 3m vision of a penis as Godzilla in your entryway will you? – but you will also find a great deal of extraordinary work.

There are excellent crafts available on Lombok as well, including pottery in villages such as Banyumulek. There are also many good shops and galleries in Mataram and Senggigi.

Dance

Bali

There are more than a dozen different dances in Bali, each with rigid choreography, requiring high levels of discipline. Most performers have learned through painstaking practice with an expert. No visit is complete without enjoying this purely Balinese art form; you will be delighted by the many styles, from the formal artistry of the Legong to crowd-pleasing antics in the Barong.

You can catch a quality dance performance at any place where there's a festival or celebration, and you'll find exceptional performances in and around Ubud. Performances are typically at night and can last several hours. Absorb the hypnotic music and the alluring moves of the performers and the time will, er, dance past. Admission is generally around 70,000Rp. Music, theatre and dance courses are also available in Ubud.

With the short attention spans of tourists in mind, many hotels offer a smorgasbord of dances – a little Kecak, a taste of Barong and some

FESTIVAL

The Bali Arts Festival showcases the work of thousands of Balinese each June and July in Denpasar. It is a major event that draws talent and audiences from across the island.

Legong to round it off. These can be pretty abbreviated, with just a few musicians and a couple of dancers.

One thing Balinese dance is not, is static. The best troupes, like Semara Ratih in Ubud, are continually innovating.

Kecak

Probably the best-known dance for its spellbinding, hair-raising atmosphere, the Kecak features a 'choir' of men and boys who sit in concentric circles and slip into a trance as they chant and sing the 'chak-a-chak-a-chak', imitating a troupe of monkeys. Sometimes called the 'vocal gamelan', this is the only music to accompany the dance re-enactment from the Hindu epic *Ramayana,* the familiar love story about Prince Rama and his Princess Sita.

The tourist version of Kecak was developed in the 1960s. This spectacular performance is easily found in Ubud (look for Krama Desa Ubud Kaja with its 80 shirtless men chanting hypnotically) and also at the Pura Luhur Ulu Watu.

Legong

Characterised by flashing eyes and quivering hands, this most graceful of Balinese dances is performed by young girls. Their talent is so revered that in old age, a classic dancer will be remembered as a 'great Legong'.

Peliatan's famous dance troupe, Gunung Sari, often seen in Ubud, is particularly noted for its Legong Keraton (Legong of the Palace). The very stylised and symbolic story involves two Legong dancing in mirror image. They are elaborately made up and dressed in gold brocade, relating a story about a king who takes a maiden captive and consequently starts a war, in which he dies.

Sanghyang & Kekac Fire Dance

These dances were developed to drive out evil spirits from a village – Sanghyang is a divine spirit who temporarily inhabits an entranced dancer. The Sanghyang Dedari is performed by two young girls who dance a dreamlike version of the Legong in perfect symmetry while their eyes are firmly shut. Male and female choirs provide a background chant until the dancers slump to the ground. A *pemangku* (priest for temple rituals) blesses them with holy water and brings them out of the trance.

In the Sanghyang Jaran, a boy in a trance dances around and through a fire of coconut husks, riding a coconut palm 'hobby horse'. Variations of this are called the Kekak Fire Dance (or Fire and Trance Dance for tourists) and are performed in Ubud almost daily.

Other Dances

The warrior dance, the Baris, is a male equivalent of the Legong – grace and femininity give way to an energetic and warlike spirit. The highly skilled Baris dancer must convey the thoughts and emotions of a warrior first preparing for action, and then meeting the enemy: chivalry, pride, anger, prowess and, finally, regret are illustrated.

In the Topeng, which means 'pressed against the face', as with a mask, the dancers imitate the character represented by the mask. This requires great expertise because the dancer cannot convey thoughts and meanings through facial expressions – the dance must tell all.

Lombok

Lombok also has its own unique dances, but they are not widely marketed. Performances are staged in some top-end hotels and in Lenek village, known for its dance traditions. If you're in Senggigi in July, there are also

---

Women often bring offerings to a temple while dancing the Pendet, their eyes, heads and hands moving in spectacularly controlled and coordinated movements. Every flick of the wrist, hand and fingers is charged with meaning.

Balinese Dance, Drama and Music: A Guide to the Performing Arts of Bali, by I Wayan Dibia and Rucina Ballinger, is a lavishly illustrated and highly recommended in-depth guide to Bali's cultural performances.

A CLASSIC BALINESE DANCER

Besides its cultural importance, Balinese dance just may be a fountain of youth as well. Ask Nyoman Supadmi when she started teaching the art and she says '1970'. A quick mental calculation confirms that she looks at most half her age.

Lithe and lively, Nyoman has taught thousands of women the precise moves and elaborate choreography demanded by classic Balinese dances such as Legong. And the key word is classic, as she has become a major force against the dilution of the island's great dances by what she dismisses as 'modernity'.

And just what is this aberration that brings such a frown to her otherwise serene face? Well, she demonstrates. 'The basic moves of classic dance require enormous discipline,' she says as she slips into the rigid pose with splayed arms and wide eyes that is immediately recognisable to anyone who has seen a performance.

Continuing, she says, 'Modern is like this,' and slumps into a slouch that would do any slacker proud. Still she understands the allure of the modern. 'It's much easier to learn and people have so many distractions that they can't find the time to learn the old ways.'

'My teachers emphasised the basics', says Nyoman – whose dancer mother provided her with a private tutor. 'Your hand went here and your bottom here,' a statement backed up by a seemingly simple shift of position in her chair which leaves no doubt of her meaning. 'Today people just approximate the position.'

In order to preserve classic Balinese dance, Nyoman promotes dance courses in schools for students from age five. She keeps her eye out for promising pupils, who can then be guided for the years needed to master the art. A niece is one of these stars and is now much in demand for temple ceremonies and other occasions where sponsors demand the best.

'But the best is expensive', she admits. There are the fees for large gamelan orchestras, the dancers, actors, transport, food and 'just getting people to commit the time needed to be the best'.

dance and *gendang beleq* (big drum) performances. The *gendang beleq,* a dramatic war dance also called the Oncer, is performed by men and boys who play a variety of unusual musical instruments for *adat* (traditional customs) festivals in central and eastern Lombok.

Music

Bali

Balinese music is based around an ensemble known as a gamelan, also called a *gong*. A *gong gede* (large orchestra) is the traditional form, with 35 to 40 musicians. The more ancient gamelan *selunding* is still occasionally played in Bali Aga villages like Tenganan.

The popular modern form of a *gong gede* is *gong kebyar,* with up to 25 instruments. This melodic, sometimes upbeat and sometimes haunting percussion that often accompanies traditional dance is one of the most lasting impressions for tourists to Bali.

The prevalent voice in Balinese music is from the xylophone-like *gangsa,* which the player hits with a hammer, dampening the sound just after it's struck. The tempo and nature of the music is controlled by two *kendang* (drums) – one male and one female. Other instruments are the deep *trompong* drums, small *kempli* gong and *cengceng* (cymbals) used in faster pieces. Not all instruments require great skill, making music is a common village activity.

Many shops in south Bali and Ubud sell the distinctive gongs, flutes, bamboo xylophones and bamboo chimes; CDs are everywhere.

Colin McPhee's iconic book about Balinese dance and culture, *A House in Bali,* has been made into an opera of the same name. It's the creation of Evan Ziporyn, a composer who spends much time in Ubud.

Lombok

The *genggong,* a performance seen on Lombok, uses a simple set of instruments, including a bamboo flute, a *rebab* (two-stringed bowed lute) and knockers. Seven musicians accompany their music with dance movements and stylised hand gestures.

Theatre

Drama is closely related to music and dance in Bali, with the sound effects and puppets' movements an important part of *wayang kulit* (leather shadow puppet) performances.

Wayang Kulit

Much more than sheer entertainment, *wayang kulit* has been Bali's candle-lit cinema for centuries, embodying the sacred seriousness of classical Greek drama. (The word drama comes from the Greek *dromenon,* a religious ritual.) The performances are long and intense – lasting six hours or more and often not finishing before sun-up.

Originally used to bring ancestors back to this world, the show features painted buffalo-hide puppets believed to have great spiritual power, and the *dalang* (puppet master and storyteller) is an almost mystical figure. A person of considerable skill and even greater endurance, he sits behind a screen and manipulates the puppets while telling the story, often in many dialects.

Stories are chiefly derived from the great Hindu epics, the *Ramayana* and, to a lesser extent, the *Mahabharata.*

An *arja* drama is not unlike *wayang kulit* puppet shows in its melodramatic plots, its offstage sound effects and its cast of easily identifiable goodies (the refined *alus*) and baddies (the unrefined *kras*). It's performed outside and a small house is sometimes built on stage and set on fire at the climax!

MONKEYS & MONSTERS

The Barong and Rangda dance rivals the Kecak as Bali's most popular performance for tourists. Again, it's a battle between good (the Barong) and bad (the Rangda).

The Barong is a good but mischievous and fun-loving shaggy dog-lion, with huge eyes and a mouth that clacks away to much dramatic effect. As the good protector of a village, the actors playing the Barong (who are utterly lost under layers of fur-clad costume) will emote a variety of winsome antics. But as is typical of Balinese dance, it is not all light-hearted as the Barong is a very sacred character indeed and you'll often see one in processions and rituals.

There's nothing sacred about the Barong's buddies, however. One or more monkeys attend to him and these characters often steal the show. Actors are given free rein to range wildly. The best aim a lot of high jinks at the audience, especially members who seem to be taking things a tad too seriously.

Meanwhile, the widow-witch Rangda is bad through and through. The Queen of Black Magic, the character's monstrous persona can include flames shooting out her ears, a tongue dripping fire, a mane of wild hair and large breasts.

The story features a duel between the Rangda and the Barong, whose supporters draw their kris (traditional dagger) and rush in to help. The long-tongued, sharp-fanged Rangda throws them into a trance though, making them stab themselves. It's quite a spectacle. Thankfully, the Barong casts a spell that neutralises the kris power so it cannot harm them.

Playing around with all that powerful magic, good and bad, requires the presence of a pemangku (priest for temple rituals), who must end the dancers' trance and make a blood sacrifice using a chicken to propitiate the evil spirits.

In Ubud, Barong and Rangda dance troupes have many interpretations of the dance, everything from eerie performances that will give you the shivers (until the monkeys appear) to jokey versions that could be a variety show or Brit pantomime.

Barong masks are valued objects; you can find artful examples in the village of Mas, south of Ubud.

You can find performances in Ubud, which are attenuated to a manageable two hours or less.

Painting

Balinese painting is probably the art form most influenced by Western ideas and demand. Traditional paintings, faithfully depicting religious and mythological subjects, were for temple and palace decoration, and the set colours were made from soot, clay and pigs' bones. In the 1930s, Western artists introduced the concept of paintings as artistic creations that could also be sold for money. To target the tourist market, they encouraged deviance to scenes from everyday life and the use of the full palette of modern paints and tools. The range of themes, techniques, styles and materials expanded enormously, and women painters emerged for the first time.

A loose classification of styles is classical, or Kamasan, named for the village of Kamasan near Semarapura; Ubud style, developed in the 1930s under the influence of the Pita Maha; Batuan, which started at the same time in a nearby village; Young Artists, begun post-war in the 1960s, and influenced by Dutch artist Arie Smit; and finally, modern or academic, free in its creative topics, yet strongly and distinctively Balinese.

Where to See & Buy Paintings

There is a relatively small number of creative original painters in Bali, and an enormous number of imitators. Shops, especially in south Bali, are packed full of paintings in whatever style is popular at the time – some are quite good and a few are really excellent (and in many you'll swear you see the numbers used to guide the artists under the paint).

Top museums in Ubud such as the Neka Art Museum, Agung Rai Museum of Art and the Museum Puri Lukisan showcase the best of Balinese art and some of the European influences that have shaped it. Look for the innovative work of women artists at Ubud's Seniwati Gallery.

Commercial galleries like Ubud's Neka Gallery and Agung Rai Gallery offer high-quality works; exploring the dizzying melange of galleries – high and low – makes for a fun afternoon or longer.

Classical Painting

There are three basic types of classical painting – *langse, iders-iders* and calendars. *Langse* are large decorative hangings for palaces or temples that display *wayang* figures (which have an appearance similar to the figures used in shadow puppetry), rich floral designs and flame-and-mountain motifs. *Iders-iders* are scroll paintings hung along temple eaves. Calendars are, much as they were before, used to set dates for rituals and predict the future.

Langse paintings helped impart *adat* (traditional customs) to the ordinary people in the same way that traditional dance and *wayang kulit* puppetry do. The stylised human figures depicted good and evil, with romantic heroes like Ramayana and Arjuna always painted with small, narrow eyes and fine features, while devils and warriors were prescribed round eyes, coarse features and facial hair. The paintings tell a story in a series of panels, rather like a comic strip, and often depict scenes from the *Ramayana* and *Mahabharata*. Other themes are the Kakawins poems, and demonic spirits from indigenous Balinese folklore – see the ceilings of the Kertha Gosa (Hall of Justice) in Semarapura for an example.

A good place to see classical painting in a modern context is at the Nyoman Gunarsa Museum near Semarapura, which was established to preserve and promote classical techniques.

THE ARTS PAINTING

Preserving and performing rare and ancient Balinese dance and gamelan music is the mission of Mekar Bhuana (www.balimusicanddance.com), a Denpasar-based cultural group. It sponsors performances and offer lessons.

Treasures of Bali by Richard Mann is a beautifully illustrated guide to Bali's museums, big and small. It highlights the gems often overlooked by group tours.

MUSEUMS

The Pita Maha

In the 1930s, with few commissions from temples, painting was virtually dying out. European artists Rudolf Bonnet and Walter Spies, with their patron Cokorda Gede Agung Surapati, formed the Pita Maha (literally, Great Vitality) to take painting from a ritual-based activity to a commercial one. The cooperative had more than 100 members at its peak in the 1930s and led to the establishment of Museum Puri Lukisan in Ubud, the first museum dedicated to Balinese art.

The changes Bonnet and Spies inspired were revolutionary. Balinese artists such as the late I Gusti Nyoman Lempad started exploring their own styles. Narrative tales were replaced by single scenes, and romantic legends by daily life: the harvest, markets, cockfights, offerings at a temple or a cremation. These paintings were known as Ubud style.

Meanwhile, painters from Batuan retained many features of classical painting. They depicted daily life, but across many scenes – a market, dance and rice harvest would all appear in a single work. This Batuan style is also noted for its inclusion of some very modern elements, such as sea scenes with the odd windsurfer.

The painting techniques also changed. Modern paint and materials were used and stiff formal poses gave way to realistic 3-D representations. More importantly, pictures were not just painted to fit a space in a palace or a temple.

In one way, however, the style remained unchanged – Balinese paintings are packed with detail. A painted Balinese forest, for example, has branches, leaves and a whole zoo of creatures reaching out to fill every tiny space.

This new artistic enthusiasm was interrupted by WWII and Indonesia's independence struggle, and stayed that way until the development of the young artists' style.

A carefully selected list of books about art, culture and Balinese writers, dancers and musicians can be found at www.ganeshabooks-bali.com, the website for the excellent Ubud bookstore (with branches in Kerobokan and Sanur).

The Young Artists

Arie Smit was in Penestanan, just outside Ubud, in 1956, when he noticed an 11-year-old boy drawing in the dirt and wondered what he could produce if he had the proper equipment. As the legend goes, the boy's father would not allow him to take up painting until Smit offered to pay somebody else to watch the family's ducks.

Other 'young artists' soon joined that first pupil, I Nyoman Cakra, but Smit did not actively teach them. He simply provided the equipment and encouragement, unleashing what was clearly a strong natural talent. Today, this style of rural scenes painted in brilliant Technicolor is a staple of Balinese tourist art.

I Nyoman Cakra still lives in Penestanan, still paints, and cheerfully admits that he owes it all to Smit. Other 'young artists' include I Ketut Tagen, I Nyoman Tjarka and I Nyoman Mujung.

The magazine/comic Bog Bog, by Balinese cartoonists, is a satirical and humorous insight into the contrast between modern and traditional worlds in Bali. It's available in bookshops and supermarkets or online at www.facebook.com/bogbogcartoon.

Other Styles

There are some other variants to the main Ubud and young artists' painting styles. The depiction of forests, flowers, butterflies, birds and other naturalistic themes, for example, sometimes called Pengosekan style, became popular in the 1960s. It can probably be traced back to Henri Rousseau, who was a significant influence on Walter Spies. An interesting development in this particular style is the depiction of underwater scenes, with colourful fish, coral gardens and sea creatures. Somewhere between the Pengosekan and Ubud styles sit the miniature landscape paintings that are popular commercially.

The new techniques also resulted in radically new versions of Rangda, Barong, Hanuman and other figures from Balinese and Hindu mythol-

INFLUENTIAL WESTERN ARTISTS

Besides Arie Smit, several other Western artists had a profound effect on Balinese art in the early and middle parts of the 20th century. In addition to honouring Balinese art, they provided a critical boost to its vitality at a time when it might have died out.

Walter Spies (1895–1942) A German artist, Spies first visited Bali in 1925 and moved to Ubud in 1927, establishing the image of Bali for Westerners that prevails today.

Rudolf Bonnet (1895–1978) Bonnet was a Dutch artist whose work concentrated on the human form and everyday Balinese life. Many classical Balinese paintings with themes of markets and cockfights are indebted to Bonnet.

Miguel Covarrubias (1904–57) *Island of Bali,* written by this Mexican artist, is still the classic introduction to the island and its culture.

Colin McPhee (1900–65) A Canadian musician, McPhee wrote *A House in Bali*. It remains one of the best written accounts of Bali, and his tales of music and house building are often highly amusing. His patronage of traditional dance and music cannot be overstated.

Adrien Jean Le Mayeur de Merpes (1880–1958) This Belgian artist arrived on Bali in 1932 and did much to establish the notions of sensual Balinese beauty, often based on his wife, the dancer Ni Polok. Their home is now an under-appreciated museum in Sanur.

ogy. Scenes from folk tales and stories appeared, featuring dancers, nymphs and love stories, with an understated erotic appeal.

Crafts

Bali is a showroom for crafts from around Indonesia. A nicer tourist shop will sell puppets and batiks from Java, ikat garments from Sumba, Sumbawa and Flores, and textiles and woodcarvings from Bali, Lombok and Kalimantan. The kris, so important to a Balinese family, will often have been made in Java.

On Lombok, where there's never been much money, traditional handicrafts are practical items, but they are still skilfully made and beautifully finished. The finer examples of Lombok weaving, basketware and pottery are highly valued by collectors.

Offerings & Ephemera

Traditionally, many of Bali's most elaborate crafts have been ceremonial offerings not intended to last: *baten tegeh* (decorated pyramids of fruit, rice cakes and flowers); rice-flour cookies modelled into entire scenes with a deep symbolic significance and tiny sculptures; *lamak* (long, woven palm-leaf strips used as decorations in festivals and celebrations); stylised female figures known as *cili,* which are representations of Dewi Sri (the rice goddess); or intricately carved coconut-shell wall hangings. Marvel at the care and energy that goes into constructing huge funeral towers and exotic sarcophagi, all of which will go up in flames.

Textiles & Weaving

Bali

Textiles in Bali and Lombok are woven by women for daily wear and ceremonies, as well as for gifts. They are often part of marriage dowries and cremations, where they join the deceased's soul as it passes to the afterlife.

The most common thread in Bali is the sarong, which can be used as an article of clothing, a sheet or a towel, among other things. The cheap

1. Traditional ikat weaving 2. Legong dancers preparing 3. Kecak dance performance 4. Mask of Rangda for the Barong dance

Top 5 Arts Experiences

Ikat

1 At an ikat factory you may find the frenetic clacking of dozens of ancient wooden looms hypnotic or cacophonous, but you'll likely find the results beautiful. Traditionally dyed threads are woven together to form beautiful and distinctly handmade patterns. Ikat sarongs are greatly prized.

Legong Dancing

2 The movements of the best Legong dancers seem impossibly robotic and rigidly controlled. Young girls and women dressed in tight-embroidered and gold-highlighted finery perform rigorous dances with precise movements of their eyes and virtually every muscle. Watch their hands as they create the flights of butterflies.

Kecak Chanting

3 You'll be haunted for hours after you see a Kecak performance. The sounds of dozens of men chanting and singing for more than an hour is bewitching and you may find you're slipping into a trance not unlike the performers. The sounds are rhythmic, the effect mesmerising.

Barong & Rangda

4 With a brightly coloured carved wooden mask, Barongs are hard to miss in performance – and that's before you take in the rest of their huge shaggy costume. Representing good, Barongs clack their wooden mouths and generally do their best to steal the spotlight from their evil counter-part, Rangda.

Stone Carving

5 If Indiana Jones hired an artist it would be a Balinese carver. Using the island's soft volcanic stone, these craftspeople create elaborate designs that seem to bring the rock alive. Even more evocative is that the stone quickly ages so that a new temple can look like an ancient wonder.

OFFERINGS: FLEETING BEAUTY

Tourists in Bali may be welcomed as honoured guests, but the real VIPs are the gods, ancestors, spirits and demons. They are presented with offerings throughout each day to show respect and gratitude, or perhaps to bribe a demon into being less mischievous.

A gift to a higher being must look attractive, so each offering is a work of art. The most common offering is a palm-leaf tray little bigger than a saucer, artfully topped with flowers, food (especially rice, and modern touches such as Ritz crackers or individually wrapped lollies) and small change, crowned with a *saiban* (temple or shrine offering). More important shrines and occasions call for more elaborate offerings, which can include the colourful towers of fruits and cakes called *baten tegeh*, and even entire animals cooked and ready to eat, as in Bali's famous *babi guling* (suckling pig).

Once presented to the gods an offering cannot be used again, so new ones are made again and again, each day, usually by women. You'll see easy-to-assemble offerings for sale in markets, much as you'd find quick dinner items in Western supermarkets.

Offerings to the gods are placed on high levels and to the demons on the ground. Don't worry about stepping on these; given their ubiquity, it's almost impossible not to (just don't try to). In fact, at Bemo Corner in Kuta offerings are left at the shrine in the middle of the road and are quickly flattened by cars. Across the island, dogs with a taste for crackers hover around fresh offerings. Given the belief that gods or demons instantly derive the essence of an offering, the critters are really just getting leftovers.

cottons, either plain or printed, are for everyday use, and are popular with tourists for beachwear.

For special occasions such as a temple ceremony, Balinese men and women use a *kamben* (a length of *songket* wrapped around the chest). The *songket* is silver- or gold-threaded cloth, hand woven using a floating weft technique, while another variety is the *endek* (like *songket,* but with pre-dyed weft threads).

The men pair the *kamben* with a shirt and the women pair it with a *kebaya* (long-sleeved lace blouse). A separate strip of cloth known as a *kain* (known as *prada* when decorated with a gold leaf pattern) is wound tightly around the hips and over the sarong like a belt to complete the outfit.

Where to Buy

Any market, especially in Denpasar, will have a good range of textiles, as does Jl Arjuna in Legian. Threads of Life in Ubud is a Fair Trade–certified textiles gallery that preserves traditional Balinese and Indonesian hand-weaving skills. Factories around Gianyar in east Bali have large showrooms.

Batik

Traditional batik sarongs, which fall somewhere between a cotton sarong and *kamben* for formality, are handmade in central Java. The dyeing process has been adapted by the Balinese to produce brightly coloured and patterned fabrics. Watch out for 'batik' that's been screenprinted. The colours will be washed out and the pattern is often only on one side (the dye in proper batik should colour both sides to reflect the belief that the body should feel what the eye sees).

Ikat

Ikat involves dyeing either the warp threads (those stretched on the loom) or weft threads (those woven across the warp) before the material is woven. The resulting pattern is geometric and slightly wavy. The colouring typically follows a similar tone – blues and greens; reds and browns; or yellows, reds and oranges. Gianyar, in east Bali, has a few factories where you can watch ikat sarongs being woven on a hand-and-foot-powered loom. A complete sarong takes about six hours to make.

Lombok

Lombok is renowned for traditional weaving on backstrap looms, the techniques handed down from mother to daughter. Abstract flower and animal motifs such as buffalo, dragons, crocodiles and snakes sometimes decorate this exquisite cloth. Several villages specialise in weaving cloth, while others concentrate on fine baskets and mats woven from rotan (hardy, pliable vine) or grass. You can visit factories around Cakranegara and Mataram that produce weft ikat on old hand-and-foot-operated looms.

Sukarara and Pringgasela are centres for traditional ikat and *songket* weaving. Sarongs, Sasak belts and clothing edged with brightly coloured embroidery are sold in small shops.

The nonprofit Lontar Foundation (www.lontar.org) works to get Indonesian books translated into English so that universities around the world can offer courses in Indonesian literature.

THE ARTS CRAFTS

Woodcarving

Woodcarving in Bali has evolved from its traditional use for doors and columns, religious figures and theatrical masks to modern forms encompassing a wide range of styles. While Tegallalang and Jati, on the road north from Ubud, are noted woodcarving centres, along with the route from Mas through Peliatan, you can find pieces in any souvenir store.

The common style of a slender, elongated figure reportedly first appeared after Walter Spies gave a woodcarver a long piece of wood and commissioned him to carve two sculptures from it. The carver couldn't bring himself to cut it in half, instead making a single figure of a tall, slim dancer.

Other typical works include classical religious figures, animal caricatures, life-sized human skeletons, picture frames, and whole tree trunks carved into ghostly 'totem poles'. In Kuta, there are various objects targeting beer drinkers: penis bottle openers (which are claimed to be Bali's bestselling souvenir) and signs to sit above your bar bearing made-to-order slogans.

Almost all carving is of local woods including *belalu* (quick-growing light wood) and the stronger fruit timbers such as jackfruit wood. Ebony from Sulawesi is also used. Sandalwood, with its delightful fragrance, is expensive and soft and is used for some small, very detailed pieces, but beware of widespread fakery.

KRIS: SACRED BLADES

Usually adorned with an ornate, jewel-studded handle and a sinister-looking wavy blade, the kris is Bali's traditional, ceremonial dagger, dating back to the Majapahit era. A kris is often the most important of family heirlooms, a symbol of prestige and honour and a work of high-end art. Made by a master craftsman, it's believed to have great spiritual power, sending out magical energy waves and thus requiring great care in its handling and use. Many owners will only clean the blade with waters from Sungai Pakerisan (Pakerisan River) in east Bali, because it is thought to be the magical 'River of Kris'.

Balinese men literally will judge each other in a variation of 'show me your kris'. The size of the blade, the number owned, the quality, the artistry of the handles and much more will go into forming a judgement of a man and his kris. Handles are considered separately from a kris (the blade). As a man's fortunes allow, he will upgrade the handles in his collection. But the kris itself remains sacred – often you will see offerings beside ones on display. The undulations in the blade (called *lok*) have many meanings. There's always an odd number – three, for instance, means passion.

The Museum Negeri Propinsi Bali in Denpasar has a rich kris collection.

On Lombok, carving usually decorates functional items such as containers for tobacco and spices, and the handles of betel-nut crushers and knives. Materials include wood, horn and bone, and you'll see these used in the recent trend: primitive-style elongated masks. Cakranegara, Sindu, Labuapi and Senanti are centres for carving on the island.

Wooden articles lose moisture when moved to a drier environment. Avoid possible shrinkage – especially of your penis bottle opener – by placing the carving in a plastic bag at home, and letting some air in for about one week every month for four months.

> The website www.lombok-network.com provides details of customs on Lombok, and the arts and crafts of different regions, including areas far off the beaten track.

Mask Carving

Masks used in theatre and dance performances such as the Topeng require a specialised form of woodcarving. The mask master – always a man – must know the movements each performer uses so the character can be accurately depicted in the mask. These masks are believed to possess magical qualities and can even have the ability to stare down bad spirits.

Other masks, such as the Barong and Rangda, are brightly painted and decorated with real hair, enormous teeth and bulging eyes.

Mas is the centre of mask carving and the Museum Negeri Propinsi Bali in Denpasar has an extensive mask collection so you can get acquainted with different styles before buying.

Stone Carving

Traditionally for temple adornment, stone sculptures now make popular souvenirs ranging from frangipani reliefs to quirky ornaments that display the Balinese sense of humour: a frog clutching a leaf as an umbrella, or a weird demon on the side of a bell clasping his hands over his ears in mock offence.

At temples, you will see stone carving in set places. Door guardians are usually a protective personality such as Arjuna. Kala's monstrous face often peers out above the main entrance, his hands reaching out to catch evil spirits. The side walls of a *pura dalem* (temple of the dead) might feature sculpted panels showing the horrors awaiting evildoers in the afterlife.

> Long before the gorilla appears (!), you know *Road to Bali* is one of the lesser 'road' movies of Bob Hope and Bing Crosby. Few last long enough to see the pair vie for the affections of 'Balinese princess' Dorothy Lamour.

Among Bali's most ancient stone carvings are the scenes of people fleeing a great monster at Goa Gajah, the so-called 'Elephant Cave', believed to date to the 11th century. Inside the cave, a statue of Ganesha, the elephant-like god, gives the rock its name. Along the road through Muncan in east Bali you'll see roadside factories where huge temple decorations are carved in the open.

Much of the local work is made in Batubulan from grey volcanic stone called *paras,* so soft it can be scratched with a fingernail (which, according to legend, is how the giant Kebo Iwa created the Elephant Cave).

Other Crafts

Pejaten, near Tabanan, has a number of pottery workshops producing ceramic figures and glazed ornamental roof tiles. Stunning collections of designer, contemporary glazed ceramics are produced at Jenggala Keramik in Jimbaran, which also hosts exhibitions of various Indonesian art and antiques.

Earthenware pots have been produced on Lombok for centuries. They're shaped by hand, coated with a slurry of clay or ash to enhance the finish, and fired in a simple kiln filled with burning rice stalks. Pots are often finished with a covering of woven cane for decoration and extra strength. Newer designs feature bright colours and elaborate decorations.

Architecture

It brings together the living and the dead, pays homage to the gods and wards off evil spirits, not to mention the torrential rain. As spiritual as it is functional, as mystical as it is beautiful, Balinese architecture has a life force of its own.

On an island bound by deep-rooted religious and cultural rituals, the priority of any design is appeasing the ancestral and village gods. This means reserving the holiest (northeast) location in every land space for the village temple, the same corner in every home for the family temple, and providing a comfortable pleasing atmosphere to entice the gods back to Bali for ceremonies.

So while it exudes beauty, balance, age-old wisdom and functionality, a Balinese home is not a commodity designed with capital appreciation in mind; even while an increasing number of rice farmers sell their ancestral land to foreigners for villa developments, they're keeping the parcel on which their home stands.

'For the Balinese, their house where they have the family temple represents the most prestige in their lives,' says renowned architect Popo Danes. 'It's the house of their roots. Selling it would be like selling their ancestors.'

Preserving the Cosmic Order

A village, a temple, a family compound, an individual structure – and even a single part of the structure – must all conform to the Balinese concept of cosmic order. It consists of three parts that represent the three worlds of the cosmos – *swah* (the world of gods), *bhwah* (world of humans) and *bhur* (world of demons). The concept also represents a three-part division of a person: *utama* (the head), *madia* (the body) and *nista* (the legs). The units of measurement used in traditional buildings are directly based on the anatomical dimensions of the head of the household, ensuring harmony between the dwelling and those who live in it.

The design is traditionally done by an *undagi* (a combination architect-priest); it must maintain harmony between god, man and nature under the concept of *Tri Hita Karana*. If it's not quite right, the universe may fall off balance and no end of misfortune and ill health will visit the community involved.

Building on the Bale

The basic element of Balinese architecture is the *bale*, a rectangular, open-sided pavilion with a steeply pitched roof of thatch. Both a family compound and a temple will comprise a number of separate *bale* for specific functions, all surrounded by a high wall. The size and proportions of the *bale*, the number of columns and the position within the compound are all determined according to tradition and the owner's caste status.

The focus of a community is a large pavilion, called the *bale banjar*, used for meetings, debates and gamelan practice, among many other activities. You'll find that large modern buildings such as restaurants and

The rule that no building shall exceed the height of a coconut palm dates back to the 1960s when the 10-storey Bali Beach Hotel caused much consternation. However, soaring land prices in the south and ineffectual enforcement of building codes mean that this 'rule' is being increasingly challenged.

the lobby areas of resorts are often modelled on the larger *bale,* and they can be airy, spacious and very handsomely proportioned.

Humble Palaces

Visitors may be disappointed by Balinese *puri* (palaces), which prove to be neither large nor imposing. The *puri* are the traditional residences of the Balinese aristocracy, although now they may be used as top-end hotels or as regular family compounds. They're unimposing, as a Balinese palace can never be built more than one-storey high. This is because a Balinese noble could not possibly use a ground-floor room if the feet of people on an upper floor were walking above.

The Family Compound

The various open-air *bale* in family compounds are where visitors are received. Typically, drinks and small cakes will be served and friendly conversations will ensue for possibly an hour or more before the purpose of a visit is discussed.

The Balinese house looks inward – the outside is simply a high wall. Inside there is a garden and a separate small building or *bale* for each activity – one for cooking, one for washing and the toilet, and separate buildings for each 'bedroom'. In Bali's mild tropical climate people live outside, so the 'living room' and 'dining room' will be open veranda areas, looking out into the garden. The whole complex is oriented on the *kaja–kelod* (towards the mountains–towards the sea) axis.

Homes from Head to...

Analogous to the human body, compounds have a head (the family temple with its ancestral shrine), arms (the sleeping and living areas), legs and feet (the kitchen and rice storage building), and even an anus (the garbage pit or pigsty). There may be an area outside the house compound where fruit trees are grown or a pig is kept.

There are several variations on the typical family compound. For example, the entrance is commonly on the *kuah* (sunset side), rather than the *kelod* (away from the mountains and towards the sea) side as shown, but *never* on the *kangin* (sunrise) or *kaja* (in the direction of the mountains) side.

Traditional Balinese homes are found in every region of the island; Ubud remains an excellent place to see them simply because of the concentration of homes there. Many accept guests. South of Ubud, you can enjoy an in-depth tour of the Nyoman Suaka Home in Singapadu.

Temples

By long tradition, Balinese doors are ornately carved and painted, and are typically in two halves that open inwards. Traditional houses will have a few.

Every village in Bali has several temples, and every home has at least a simple house-temple. The Balinese word for temple is *pura,* from a Sanskrit word literally meaning 'a space surrounded by a wall'. Similar to a traditional Balinese home, a temple is walled in – so the shrines you see in rice fields or at 'magical' spots such as old trees are not real temples. Simple shrines or thrones often overlook crossroads, to protect passers-by.

All temples are built on a mountains–sea orientation, not north–south. The direction towards the mountains, *kaja,* is the end of the temple, where the holiest shrines are found. The temple's entrance is at the *kelod. Kangin* is more holy than the *kuah,* so many secondary shrines are on the *kangin* side. *Kaja* may be towards a particular mountain – Pura Besakih in east Bali is pointed directly towards Gunung Agung – or towards the mountains in general, which run east–west along the length of Bali.

DOORS

Temple Types

There are three basic temple types found in most villages. The most important is the *pura puseh* (temple of origin), dedicated to the village founders and at the *kaja* end of the village. In the middle of the village is the *pura desa,* for the many spirits that protect the village community in daily life. At the *kelod* end of the village is the *pura dalem* (temple of the dead). The graveyard is also here, and the temple may include representations of Durga, the terrible side of Shiva's wife Parvati. Both Shiva and Parvati have a creative and destructive side; their destructive powers are honoured in the *pura dalem*.

Other temples include those dedicated to the spirits of irrigated agriculture. Because rice growing is so important in Bali, and the division of water for irrigation is handled with the utmost care, these *pura subak* or *pura ulun suwi* (temple of the rice-growers association) can be of considerable importance. Other temples may also honour dry-field agriculture, as well as the flooded rice paddies.

TYPICAL FAMILY COMPOUND

The following are elements commonly found in family compounds. Although there are variations, the designs are surprisingly similar, especially given they occur thousands of times across Bali.

» **Sanggah or Merajan** Family temple, which is always at the *kaja-kangin* (sunrise in the direction of the mountains) corner of the courtyard. There will be shrines to the Hindu 'trinity' of Brahma, Shiva and Vishnu, and to *taksu,* the divine intermediary.

» **Umah Meten** Sleeping pavilion for the family head.

» **Tugu** Shrine to god of evil spirits in the compound but at the far *kaja-kuah* (sunset in the direction of the mountains) corner; by employing the chief evil spirit as a guard, others will stay away.

» **Pengijeng** Small shrine amid the compound's open space, dedicated to the spirit who is the guardian of the property.

» **Bale Tiang Sanga** Guest pavilion, also known as the *bale duah*. Literally the family room, it's used as a gathering place, offering workplace or temporary quarters of lesser sons and their families before they establish their own home.

» **Natah** Courtyard with frangipani or hibiscus shade trees, with always a few chickens pecking about, plus a fighting cock or two in a basket.

» **Bale Sakenam or Bale Dangin** Working and sleeping pavilion; may be used for important family ceremonies.

» **Fruit trees & coconut palms** Serve both practical and decorative purposes. Fruit trees are often mixed with flowering trees such as hibiscus, and caged song birds hang from the branches.

» **Vegetable garden** Small; usually just for a few spices such as lemongrass not grown on larger plots.

» **Bale Sakepat** Sleeping pavilion for children; highly optional.

» **Paon** Kitchen; always in the south, as that is the direction associated with Brahma, god of fire.

» **Lumbung** Rice barn – the domain of both the precious grain and the Dewi Sri, the rice goddess. It's elevated to discourage rice-eating pests.

» **Rice-threshing area** Important for farmers to prepare rice for cooking or storage.

» **Aling Aling** Screen wall requiring visitors to turn a sharp left or right. This ensures both privacy from passers-by and protection from demons, which the Balinese believe cannot turn corners.

» **Candi Kurung** Gate with a roof, resembling a mountain or tower split in half.

» **Apit Lawang or Pelinggah** Gate shrines, which continually receive offerings to recharge the gate's ability to repel evil spirits.

» **Pigsty or garbage pit** Always in the *kangin-kelod* (sunrise in the direction away from the mountains) corner, the compound's waste ends up here.

In addition to these 'local' temples, there are a lesser number of great temples. Often a kingdom would have three of these temples that sit at the very top of the temple pecking order: a main state temple in the heartland of the state (such as Pura Taman Ayun in Mengwi, western Bali); a mountain temple (such as Pura Besakih, eastern Bali); and a sea temple (such as Pura Luhur Ulu Watu, southern Bali).

Every house in Bali has its house temple, which is at the *kaja-kangin* corner of the courtyard and has at least five shrines.

Temple Decoration

Temples and their decoration are closely linked on Bali. A temple gateway is not just erected; every square centimetre of it is carved in sculptural relief and a diminishing series of demon faces is placed above it as protection. Even then, it's not complete without several stone statues to act as guardians.

The level of decoration inside varies. Sometimes a temple is built with minimal decoration in the hope that sculpture can be added when more funds are available. The sculpture can also deteriorate after a few years because much of the stone used is soft and the tropical climate ages it very rapidly (that centuries-old temple you're looking at may in fact be less than 10 years old!). Sculptures are restored or replaced as resources permit – it's not uncommon to see a temple with old carvings, which are barely discernible, next to newly finished work.

Sculpture often appears in set places in Bali's temples. Door guardians – representations of legendary figures such as Arjuna or other protective personalities – flank the steps to the gateway. Above the main entrance to a temple, Kala's monstrous face often pFeers out, sometimes a number of times, and his hands reach out beside his head to catch any evil spirits foolish enough to try and sneak in.

Elsewhere, other sculptures make regular appearances. The front of a *pura dalem* will often feature images of the witch Rangda, and sculpted relief panels may show the horrors that await evil-doers in the afterlife.

Temple Design

Although overall temple architecture is similar in both northern and southern Bali, there are some important differences. The inner courtyards of southern temples usually house a number of *meru* (multi-tiered shrines), together with other structures, whereas in the north, everything is grouped on a single pedestal. On the pedestal you'll find 'houses' for the deities to use on their earthly visits; they're also used to store religious relics.

While Balinese sculpture and painting were once exclusively used as architectural decoration for temples, you'll soon see that sculpture and painting have developed as separate art forms influencing the look of every aspect of the island. And the art of temple and shrine construction is as vibrant as ever: more than 500 new ones in all sizes are built every month.

Temple design follows a traditional formula. A temple compound contains a number of *gedong* (shrines) of varying sizes, made from solid brick and stone and heavily decorated with carvings.

The Birth of Bali Style

Tourism has given Balinese architecture unprecedented exposure and it seems that every visitor wants to take a slice of this island back home with them.

Shops along Ngurah Rai Bypass (the main road in south Bali, running from the airport around to Sanur) churn out prefabricated, knock-down *bale* for shipment to far-flung destinations: the Caribbean, London, Perth and Hong Kong. Furniture workshops in Denpasar and handicraft

---

The gate to a traditional Balinese house is where the family gives clues as to its wealth. They range from the humble – grass thatch atop a gate of simple stones or clay – to the relatively grand, including bricks heavily ornamented with ornately carved stone and a tile roof.

Hard-wearing terracotta tiles have been the traditional roofing material since the Dutch era. Thatch in various forms or bamboo are now reserved for the most traditional and ceremonial sites.

Scores of open-air carving sheds supplying statues and ornamentation to temples and shrines are a highlight of the road between Muncan and Selat in east Bali.

villages near Ubud are flat out making ornaments for domestic and export markets.

The craze stems back to the early 1970s, when Australian artist Donald Friend formed a partnership with Manado-born Wija Waworuntu, who had built the Tandjung Sari on Sanur beach a decade earlier. With a directive to design traditional, village-style alternatives to the Western multi-storeyed hotels, they brought two architects to Bali: Australian Peter Muller and the late Sri Lankan Geoffrey Bawa who took traditional architecture and adapted it to Western standards of luxury.

TYPICAL TEMPLE ELEMENTS

No two temples on Bali are identical. Variations in style, size, importance, wealth, purpose and much more result in near infinite variety. But there are common themes and elements. Use this as a guide and see how many design elements you can find in each Balinese temple you visit.

» **Candi Bentar** The intricately sculpted temple gateway, like a tower split down the middle and moved apart, symbolising that you are entering a sanctum. It can be quite grand, with auxiliary entrances on either side for daily use.

» **Kulkul Tower** The warning-drum tower, from which a wooden split drum (*kulkul*) is sounded to announce events at the temple or warn of danger.

» **Bale** A pavilion, usually open-sided, for temporary use or storage. It may include a *bale gong* (3A), where the gamelan orchestra plays at festivals; a *paon* (3B), or temporary kitchen, to prepare offerings; or a *wantilan* (3C), a stage for dances or cockfights.

» **Kori Agung or Paduraksa** The gateway to the inner courtyard is an intricately sculpted stone tower. Entry is through a doorway reached by steps in the middle of the tower and left open during festivals.

» **Raksa or Dwarapala** Statues of fierce guardian figures who protect the doorway and deter evil spirits. Above the door will be the equally fierce face of a Bhoma, with hands outstretched against unwanted spirits.

» **Aling Aling** If an evil spirit does get in, this low wall behind the entrance will keep it at bay, as evil spirits find it difficult to make sharp turns. (Also found in family compounds.)

» **Side Gate (Betelan)** Most of the time (except during ceremonies), entry to the inner courtyard is through this side gate, which is always open.

» **Small Shrines (Gedong)** These usually include shrines to Ngrurah Alit and Ngrurah Gede, who organise things and ensure the correct offerings are made.

» **Padma Stone** Throne for the sun god Surya, placed in the most auspicious *kaja-kangin* corner. It rests on the *badawang* (world turtle), which is held by two *naga* (mythical snakelike creatures).

» **Meru** A multiroofed shrine. Usually there is an 11-roofed *meru* (10A) to Sanghyang Widi, the supreme Balinese deity, and a three-roofed *meru* (10B) to the holy mountain Gunung Agung. However, *meru* can take any odd number of steps in between, depending on where the intended god falls in the pecking order. The black thatching is made from sugar palm fronds and is very expensive.

» **Small Shrines (Gedong)** At the *kaja* end of the courtyard, these may include a shrine to the sacred mountain Gunung Batur; a Maospahit shrine to honour Bali's original Hindu settlers (Majapahit); and a shrine to the *taksu*, who acts as an interpreter for the gods. (Trance dancers or mediums may be used to convey the gods' wishes.)

» **Bale Piasan** Open pavilions used to display temple offerings.

» **Gedong Pesimpangan** A stone building dedicated to the village founder or a local deity.

» **Paruman or Pepelik** Open pavilion in the inner courtyard, where the gods are supposed to assemble to watch the ceremonies of a temple festival.

Before long, the design sensation known as 'Bali Style' was born. Then, the term reflected Muller and Bawa's sensitive, low-key approach, giving precedence to culture over style, and respect for traditional principles and craftspeople, local renewable materials and age-old techniques. Today, the development of a mass market has inevitably produced a much looser definition.

Look for carved wooden garudas, the winged bird that bears the god Wisnu, in the most surprising places – high up in pavilion rafters, at the base of columns, pretty much anywhere.

Contemporary Hotel Design

For centuries, foreign interlopers, such as the priest Nirartha, have played an intrinsic part in the island's myths and legends. These days, tourists are making an impact on the serenity of Balinese cosmology and its seamless translation into the island's traditional architecture. And while these visitors with large credit limits aren't changing the island's belief system – much – they are changing its look.

Most hotel designs on Bali and Lombok are purely functional or pastiches of traditional designs, but some of the finest hotels on the islands aspire to something greater. Notable examples in rough order of completion:

TOP TEMPLE VISITS

Over 10,000 temples are found everywhere on Bali – from cliff tops and beaches to volcanoes – and are often beautiful places to experience. Visitors will find the following especially rewarding.

Directional Temples

Some temples are so important they are deemed to belong to the whole island rather than particular communities. There are nine *kahyangan jagat* (directional temples) including the following four:

» **Pura Luhur Batukau** (p228) One of Bali's most important temples is situated magically up the misty slopes of Gunung Batukau.

» **Pura Luhur Ulu Watu** (p103) As important as it is popular, this temple has sweeping Indian Ocean views, sunset dance performances and monkeys.

» **Pura Goa Lawah** (p193) See Bali's own Bat Cave at this cliffside temple filled with the winged critters.

Sea Temples

The legendary 16th-century priest Nirartha founded a chain of temples to honour the sea gods. Each was intended to be within sight of the next, and several have dramatic locations on the south coast. They include the following:

» **Pura Rambut Siwi** (p251) On a wild stretch of the west coast and not far from where Nirartha arrived in the 16th century. Locks of his hair are said to be buried in a shrine.

» **Pura Tanah Lot** (p247) Sacred as the day begins, it becomes a temple of mass tourism at sunset.

Other Important Temples

Some temples have particular importance because of their location, spiritual function or architecture. The following reward visitors:

» **Pura Maduwe Karang** (p235) An agricultural temple on the north coast, this is famous for its spirited bas-reliefs, including one of possibly Bali's first bicycle rider.

» **Pura Pusering Jagat** (p172) One of the famous temples at Pejeng, near Ubud, which dates to the 14th-century empire that flourished here. It has an enormous bronze drum from that era.

» **Pura Taman Ayun** (p248) This vast and imposing state temple was a centrepiece of the Mengwi empire and has been nominated for Unesco recognition.

» **Pura Tirta Empul** (p173) The beautiful temple at Tampaksiring, with holy springs discovered in AD 962 and bathing pools at the source of Sungai Pakerisan.

TOP FIVE ARCHITECTURE & DESIGN BOOKS

» **Architecture of Bali** (Made Wijaya) Contains stunning vintage photographs and illustrations, accompanied by informative personal observations from the Australian-born landscape designer.

» **Bali Style** (Rio Helmi and Barbara Walker) Details the clean and open-plan design ethos that's attracted a worldwide following.

» **Architectural Conservation in Bali** (Edo Budihardjo) Makes the case for preserving Bali's architectural heritage.

» **Architecture Bali: Birth of the Tropical Boutique Resort** (Philip Goad) Explores the origin and direction of contemporary Balinese design.

» **A House on Bali** (Colin McPhee) The classic account of the intricacies of building a traditional family compound.

» **Tandjung Sari** (p113) Located in Sanur, it is Wija Waworuntu's classic prototype for the Balinese boutique beach hotel.

» **Amandari** (p159) The crowning achievement of architect Peter Muller, who also designed the two Oberois. Located near Ubud, the inclusion of traditional Balinese materials, crafts and construction techniques, as well as Balinese design principles, respects the island's approach to the world.

» **Oberoi** (p78) The very first luxury hotel, located in Seminyak, and remains Muller's relaxed vision of a Balinese village. The bale agung (village assembly hall) and *bale banjar* form the basis for common areas.

» **Oberoi Lombok** (p272) Both the most luxurious and the most traditionally styled hotel on Lombok.

» **Amanusa** (p107) Avoids the over-grown, hackneyed approach of nearby resorts in Nusa Dua through the brilliant work of Kerry Hill, who drew on Balinese village design for this human-scaled hotel.

» **Amankila** (p197) In east Bali, Amankila adopts a garden strategy, with a carefully structured landscape of lotus ponds and floating pavilions that steps down an impossibly steep site. Hotel Tugu Bali, in Canggu, exemplifies the notion of instant age, the ability of materials in Bali to weather quickly and provide 'pleasing decay'.

» **Four Seasons Resort** (p159) A striking piece of aerial sculpture near Ubud, with a huge elliptical lotus pond sitting above a base structure that appears like an eroded and romantic ruin set within a spectacular river valley.

» **Alila Villas** (p104) In far south Bali, Alila employs an artful contemporary style that's light and airy, conveying a sense of great luxury. Set amid hotel-tended rice fields, it embodies advanced green building principles.

Objects draped in black-and-white checked cloth (*poleng*) are empowered by the spirits. Such objects can be shrines, as you'd expect, but also statues, planters or seemingly everyday objects.

Lombok Architecture

Traditional laws and practices govern Lombok's architecture. Construction must begin on a propitious day, always with an odd-numbered date, and the building's frame must be completed on that day. It would be bad luck to leave any of the important structural work until the following day.

A traditional Sasak village layout is a walled enclosure. There are three types of buildings: the *beruga* (open-sided pavilion), the *bale tani* (family house) and the *lumbung* (rice barn). The *beruga* and *bale tani* are both rectangular, with low walls and a steeply pitched thatched roof, although, of course, the *beruga* is much larger. A *bale tani* is made of bamboo on a base of compacted mud. It usually has no windows and the arrangement of rooms is very standardised. There is a *serambi* (open veranda) at the front and two rooms on two different levels inside – one for cooking and entertaining guests, the other for sleeping and storage. There are some picturesque traditional Sasak villages in Rembitan and Sade, near Kuta.

Environment

The Landscape

Bali is a small island, midway along the string of islands that makes up the Indonesian archipelago. It's adjacent to the most heavily populated island of Java, and immediately west of the chain of smaller islands comprising Nusa Tenggara, which includes Lombok.

The island is visually dramatic – a mountainous chain with a string of active volcanoes, it includes several peaks around 2000m. The agricultural lands in Bali are south and north of the central mountains. The southern region is a wide, gently sloping area, where most of the country's abundant rice crop is grown. The northern coastal strip is narrower, rising rapidly into the foothills of the central range. It receives less rain, but coffee, copra, rice and cattle are farmed there.

Bali also has some arid, less-populated regions. These include the western mountain region, and the eastern and northeastern slopes of Gunung Agung. The Nusa Penida islands are dry, and cannot support intensive rice agriculture. The Bukit Peninsula is similarly dry, but with the growth of tourism, it's becoming quite populous.

Volcanoes

Bali is volcanically active and extremely fertile. The two go hand-in-hand as eruptions contribute to the land's exceptional fertility, and high mountains provide the dependable rainfall that irrigates Bali's complex and amazingly beautiful patchwork of rice terraces. Of course, the volcanoes are a hazard as well – Bali has endured disastrous eruptions in the past, such as in 1963, and no doubt will again in the future. Gunung Agung, the 'Mother Mountain', is 3142m high and thickly wooded on its south side. You can climb it or its steam-spewing neighbour, the comparatively diminutive 1700m Gunung Batur. The latter is a geographic spectacle: a soaring, active volcano rising from a lake that itself is set in a vast crater.

On Lombok, the 3726m Gunung Rinjani is Indonesia's second-tallest volcano. Within the huge caldera is an aquamarine lake, Danau Segara, which astounds those who spy it for the first – or even second – time.

Beaches

For a complete list of Bali and Lombok's best beaches, see p57.

Animals & Plants

Bali is geologically young, most of its living things have migrated from elsewhere and true native wild animals are rare. This is not hard to imagine in the heavily populated and extravagantly fertile south of Bali, where the orderly rice terraces are so intensively cultivated they look more like a work of sculpture than a natural landscape.

In fact, rice fields cover only about 20% of the island's surface area, and there is a great variety of other environmental zones: the dry scrub

DOGS

The plight of Bali's dogs and the irony of the important role they play in island life is captured by filmakers Lawrence Blair and Dean Allan Tolhurst in *Bali: Island of the Dogs*.

of the northwest, the extreme northeast and the southern peninsula; patches of dense jungle in the river valleys; forests of bamboo; and harsh volcanic regions that are barren rock and volcanic tuff at higher altitudes. Lombok is similar in all these respects.

Animals

Wild Animals

Bali has lots and lots of lizards, and they come in all shapes and sizes. The small ones (onomatopoeically called *cecak*) that hang around light fittings in the evening, waiting for an unwary insect, are a familiar sight. Geckos are fairly large lizards, often heard but less often seen. The loud and regularly repeated two-part cry 'geck-oh' is a nightly background noise that many visitors soon enjoy – it's considered lucky if you hear the lizard call seven times.

RESPONSIBLE TRAVEL

The best way to responsibly visit Bali and Lombok is to try to be as minimally invasive as possible. This is, of course, easier than it sounds, but consider the following tips:

» **Watch your use of water** Travel into the rice-growing regions of Bali and you'll think the island is coursing with water, but demand outstrips supply. Take up your hotel on its offer to save itself big money, er, no, to save lots of water, by not washing your sheets and towels every day. Cynicism aside, this will save water. At the high end you can also forgo your own private plunge pool, or a pool altogether – although this is almost impossible at any price level.

» **Don't hit the bottle** Those bottles of Aqua (the top local brand of bottled water, owned by Danone) are convenient but they add up. The zillions of such bottles tossed away each year are a major blight. Still, you're wise not to refill from the tap, so what to do? Ask your hotel if you can refill from their huge containers of drinking water. And if your hotel doesn't give you in-room drinking water in reusable glass containers, tell them you noticed.

In Ubud, stop by the Pondok Pecak Library & Learning Centre (p169) – staff will refill your water bottle and tell you which other businesses offer this service. Elsewhere, simply ask; the service is slowly spreading. In restaurants, ask for '*air putih*', which will get you a glass of water from the Aqua jug out back, saving yet more plastic bottles.

» **Don't play golf** The resorts will hate this, but tough. Having two golf courses on the arid Bukit Peninsula is environmentally unsustainable.

» **Support environmentally aware businesses** The number of businesses committed to good environmental practices is growing fast in Bali and Lombok. Keep an eye out within this guide for the sustainable icon, which identifies environmentally savvy businesses.

» **Conserve power** Sure you want to save your own energy on a sweltering afternoon, but using air-con strains an already overloaded system. Much of the electricity in Bali comes from Java and the rest is produced at the roaring, smoking plant near Benoa Harbour. Open the windows at night in Ubud for cool mountain breezes and the symphony of sounds off the rice fields.

» **Don't drive yourself crazy** The traffic is already bad – why add another vehicle to it? Can you take a tourist bus instead of a chartered or rental car? Would a walk, trek or hike be more enjoyable than a road journey to an over-visited tourist spot? The beach is a fast and fun way to get around Kuta and Seminyak (often faster than a taxi in traffic). Cycling is more popular than ever, and you can hire a bike for US$3.

» **Bag the bags** Bali's governor is trying to get plastic bags banned. Help him out by refusing them (and say no to plastic straws too). Note that many Circle K convenience stores now ask if you want a bag.

SEA TURTLES

Both green sea and hawksbill turtles inhabit the waters around Bali and Lombok, and both species are supposedly protected by international laws that prohibit trade in anything made from sea turtles.

In Bali, however, green sea turtle meat (penyu) is a traditional and very popular delicacy, particularly for Balinese feasts. Bali is the site of the most intensive slaughter of green sea turtles in the world – no reliable figures are available, although in 1999 it was estimated that more than 30,000 are killed annually. It's easy to find the trade on the backstreets of waterside towns such as Benoa.

Still, some progress is being made. 'People in Kuta used to eat turtles, now they save them,' says Wayan Wiradnyana, head of ProFauna (p372) in Bali, a group that works to protect animals across Indonesia. In Bali, the group has spurred police to enforce a 1999 ban on turtle killing and it has helped release turtles seized from poachers. But its biggest achievement has been in public education. 'In Kuta,' he says, '30 turtles a year lay eggs on the beach. The community now helps us guard them and make certain the babies hatch and get to the water'. ProFauna has erected a turtle information centre at the Tuban end of Kuta Beach.

A broad coalition of divers and journalists supports the SOS Sea Turtles campaign (www.sos-seaturtles.ch), which spotlights turtle abuse in Bali. It has been instrumental in exposing the illegal poaching of turtles at Wakatobi National Park in Sulawesi for sale in Bali. This illegal trade is widespread and, like the drug trade, hard to prevent. Bali's Hindu Dharma, the body overseeing religious practice, has decreed that turtle meat is essential in only very vital ceremonies.

Turtle hatcheries open to the public, such as the sanctuary on – fittingly – Turtle Island, do a good job of educating locals about the need to protect turtles and think of them as living creatures (as opposed to satay), but many environmentalists are still opposed to them because they keep captive turtles.

Bali has more than 300 species of birds, but the one that is truly native to the island, the Bali starling, is mostly extinct in the wild, although thousands can be found in cages. (Efforts to reintroduce them on Nusa Penida are so far successful, see p134.) Much more common are colourful birds such as the orange-banded thrush, numerous species of egrets, kingfishers, parrots, owls and many more.

Bali's only wilderness area, Taman Nasional Bali Barat (West Bali National Park), has a number of wild species, including grey and black monkeys (which you will also see in the mountains, Ubud and east Bali), *muncak* (mouse deer), squirrels, bats and iguanas.

One hawksbill sea turtle that visited Bali was tracked for the following year. His destinations: Java, Kalimantan, Australia (Perth and much of Queensland) and then back to Bali.

Domestic Animals

Bali is thick with domestic animals, including ones that wake you up in the morning and others that bark at night. Chickens and roosters are kept as food and as domestic pets.

» **Cockfighting** A popular male activity – a man's fighting bird is his prized possession. If you see a thicket of cars and motorbikes by the side of the road in rural Bali but don't see any people, they may all be at a cockfight 'hidden' behind a building.

» **Dogs** When not pampered pets, dogs have hard lives – they're far down the social ladder, bedeviled by the rabies epidemic and thought by some to be friendly with evil spirits (thus the constant barking). But some people are trying to improve the lives of feral mutts, see p171.

» **Ducks** Another everyday Balinese domestic animal and a regular dish at feasts. Ducks are kept in the family compound, and are put out to a convenient pond or flooded rice field to feed during the day. They follow a stick with a small flag tied to the end, and the stick is left planted in the field. As sunset approaches, the ducks gather around the stick and wait to be led home again. The morning and evening duck parades are one of Bali's small delights.

Marine Animals

For a full discussion of the myriad aquatic creatures around Bali and Lombok, see p64.

Plants

Trees

Much of the island is cultivated. As with most things in Bali, trees have a spiritual and religious significance, and you'll often see them decorated with scarves and black-and-white chequered cloths (*poleng,* a cloth signifying spiritual energy). The *waringin* (banyan tree) is the holiest Balinese tree and no important temple is complete without a stately one growing within its precincts. The banyan is an extensive, shady tree with an exotic feature: creepers that drop from its branches take root to propagate a new tree. *Jepun* (frangipani or plumeria trees), with their beautiful and sweet-smelling white flowers, are found everywhere.

Bali's forests cover 127,000 hectares, ranging from virgin land to tree farms to densely forested mountain villages. The total is constantly under threat from wood poaching for carved souvenirs and cooking fuel, and from development.

Bali has monsoonal rather than tropical rainforests, so it lacks the valuable rainforest hardwoods that require rain year-round. Nearly all the hardwood used for carving is imported from Sumatra and Kalimantan.

Balinese Flora & Fauna, published by Periplus, is a concise and beautifully illustrated guide to the animals and plants you'll see in your travels. The feature on the ecology of a rice field is excellent.

ENVIRONMENT ANIMALS & PLANTS

GROWING RICE

Rice cultivation has shaped the social landscape in Bali – the intricate organisation necessary for growing rice is a large factor in the strength of community life. Rice cultivation has also changed the environmental landscape – terraced rice fields trip down hillsides like steps for a giant, in shades of gold, brown and green, green and more green. Some date back 1000 years or more.

Subak, the village assocation that deals with water rights and irrigation, makes careful use of all the surface water. The fields are a complete ecological system, home for much more than just rice. In the early morning you'll often see the duck herders leading their flocks out for a day's paddle around a flooded rice field; the ducks eat various pests and leave fertiliser in their wake.

A harvested field with its leftover burnt rice stalks is soaked with water and repeatedly ploughed, often by two bullocks pulling a wooden plough. Once the field is muddy enough, a small corner is walled off and seedling rice is planted there. When it is a reasonable size, it's replanted, shoot by shoot, in the larger field. While the rice matures, there is time to practise the gamelan (instruments used to play traditional Balinese orchestral music), watch the dancers or do a little woodcarving. Finally, the whole village turns out for the harvest – a period of solid hard work. While it's only men who plant the rice, everybody takes part in harvesting it.

In 1969, new high-yield rice varieties were introduced. These can be harvested a month sooner than the traditional variety and are resistant to many diseases. However, the new varieties also require more fertiliser and irrigation water, which strains the imperilled water supplies. More pesticides are also needed, causing the depletion of the frog and eel populations that depend on the insects for survival.

Although everyone agrees that the new rice doesn't taste as good as the traditional rice, the new strains now account for more than 90% of the rice grown in Bali. Small areas of traditional rice are still planted and harvested in traditional ways to placate the rice goddess, Dewi Sri. Temples and offerings to her dot every rice field.

THE WALLACE LINE

The 19th-century naturalist Sir Alfred Wallace (1822–1913) observed great differences in fauna between Bali and Lombok – as great as the differences between Africa and South America. In particular, there were no large mammals (elephants, rhinos, tigers etc) east of Bali, and very few carnivores. He postulated that during the ice ages, when sea levels were lower, animals could have moved by land from what is now mainland Asia all the way to Bali, but the deep Lombok Strait would always have been a barrier. He drew a line between Bali and Lombok, which he believed marked the biological division between Asia and Australia.

Plant life does not display such a sharp division, but there is a gradual transition from predominantly Asian rainforest species to mostly Australian plants, such as eucalypts and acacias, which are better suited to long dry periods. This is associated with the lower rainfall as one moves east of Java. Environmental differences – including those in the natural vegetation – are now thought to provide a better explanation of the distribution of animal species than Wallace's theory about limits to their original migrations.

Modern biologists do recognise a distinction between Asian and Australian fauna, but the boundary between the regions is regarded as much fuzzier than Wallace's line. Nevertheless, this transitional zone between Asia and Australia is still called 'Wallacea'.

A number of plants have great practical and economic significance. *Tiing* (bamboo) is grown in several varieties and is used for everything from satay sticks and string to rafters and gamelan resonators. The various types of palm provide coconuts, sugar, fuel and fibre.

Flowers & Gardens

Balinese gardens are a delight. The soil and climate can support a huge range of plants, and the Balinese love of beauty and the abundance of cheap labour means that every space can be landscaped. The style is generally informal, with curved paths, a rich variety of plants and usually a water feature. Who can't be enchanted by a frangipani tree dropping a carpet of fragrant blossoms?

You can find almost every type of flower in Bali, but some are seasonal and others are restricted to the cooler mountain areas. Many of the flowers will be familiar to visitors – hibiscus, bougainvillea, poinsettia, oleander, jasmine, water lily and aster are commonly seen in the southern tourist areas.

The Indonesian Ecotourism Centre (www.indecon.or.id) is devoted to highlighting responsible tourism; Bali Fokus (http://balifokus.asia) promotes sustainable community programs on Bali for recycling and reuse.

Less-familiar flowers include Javanese *ixora (soka, angsoka)*, with round clusters of red-orange flowers; *champak (cempaka)*, a fragrant member of the magnolia family; flamboyant, the flower of the royal poinciana flame tree; *manori (maduri)*, which has several traditional uses; and water convolvulus *(kangkung)*, whose leaves are commonly used as a green vegetable. There are thousands of species of orchid.

Bali's climate means that gardens planted today look mature – complete with soaring shade trees – in just a couple of years. Good places to see Bali's plant bounty include Bali Botanical Gardens, Bali Orchid Garden and the many plant nurseries (north from Sanur and along the road to Denpasar).

National Parks

The only national park in Bali is Taman Nasional Bali Barat (West Bali National Park). It covers 190 sq km at the western tip of Bali, plus a substantial area of coastal mangrove and the adjacent marine area, including the excellent dive site at Menjangan.

The **Taman Nasional Gunung Rinjani** (Gunung Rinjani National Park) on Lombok covers 413 sq km and is the water collector for most of the island. At 3726m, Gunung Rinjani is the second-highest volcanic peak in Indonesia and is very popular for trekking.

Environmental Issues

Fast-growing populations, limited resources, pressure from the increasing number of visitors and lax and/or nonexistent environmental regulations mean that Bali and Lombok are under great threat.

Bali

Some of Bali's environmental worries are larger than the island: climate change is causing increased water levels that are damaging the coast and beaches.

Meanwhile, a fast-growing population in Bali has put pressure on limited resources. The tourist industry has attracted new residents, and there is a rapid growth in urban areas and of resorts and villas that encroach onto agricultural land. Concerns include:

» **Water** Usage is a major concern. Typical top-end hotels use more than 1000L of water a day per room, and the growing number of golf courses – the ones on the arid Bukit Peninsula in the Pecatu Indah development and at Nusa Dua, for example – put further pressure on an already stressed resource.

» **Water pollution** A major problem, both from deforestation brought on by firewood collecting in the mountains, and lack of proper treatment for the waste produced by the local population. Streams that run into the ocean at popular spots like Double Six Beach in Legian are very polluted, often with waste water from hotels. The vast mangroves along the south coast near Benoa Harbour are losing their ability to filter the water that drains here from much of the island.

» **Air pollution** As anyone stuck behind a smoke-belching truck or bus on one of the main roads knows, south Bali's air is often smoggy. The view of south Bali from a hillside shows a brown blanket hanging in the air that could be LA in the 1960s.

» **Waste** The problem is not just all those plastic bags and water bottles but the sheer volume of waste produced by the growing population – what to do with it? The Balinese look with sadness at the enormous amounts of waste – especially plastic – that have accumulated in their once pristine rivers. 'I used to swim there,' said one driver to us looking at a plastic-bag-choked stream near his boyhood home.

Star surfer Kelly Slater caused a stir when he sent out a series of tweets to his Twitter followers decrying Bali's polluted waters. 'I've never been so alarmed by the pollution situation as [on] this trip to Bali/Indo.' Asked to elaborate he continued: 'If Bali doesn't do something serious about this pollution it'll be impossible to surf here in a few years.'

On the upside, there is a nascent effort to grow rice and other foods organically, reducing the amount of pesticide and fertiliser run-off into water supplies. A sewage treatment program in the south where the mangroves are choking may finally move forward (but it will take years and the money is not there). And even as businesses are offered recycling services, the cost – US$10 a month – is more than a small warung can afford.

In Pemuteran, an artifical reef-growing program has won universal praise (p242).

Lombok

On Lombok, environmental disaster in the gold rush town of Sekotong is ongoing. Gold mining using mercury in huge open-cast pits is causing enormous damage to once-pristine areas such as Kuta (p279).

Coastal erosion is a problem as it is on Bali. The Gilis are naturally concerned. On the plus side, the reefs around the Gilis have been quick to recover as tourism has spurred intense preservation efforts (p289).

WASTE

ENVIRONMENT ENVIRONMENTAL ISSUES

Each day Bali produces 150 tons of waste, at least 30% of which is nonbiodegradable and most of which is generated directly or indirectly by tourism. That is everything from plastic water bottles to your empty container of sunblock.

Survival Guide

Directory A–Z

Accommodation

Bali has a huge range of accommodation: approximately 90,000 rooms. It has great value lodging no matter what your budget. The touristy areas of Lombok and the Gili Islands have the same range of options as Bali; elsewhere on Lombok accommodation is simpler and more limited.

Accommodation attracts a combined tax and service charge (called 'plus plus') of 21%. In budget places, this is generally included in the price, but check first. Many midrange and top-end places will add it on, which can add substantially to your bill.

The rates quoted in this book include tax and are those that travellers are likely to pay during the high season. Nailing down rates is difficult, as some establishments publish the rates they actually plan to charge, while others publish rates that are pure fantasy, fully expecting to discount by 50%.

Rates are almost always negotiable, especially outside the main peak season. In the low season, discounts between 30% and 50% aren't uncommon at midrange and top-end hotels. With Bali enjoying record visitor numbers, prices are climbing sharply.

Hotels

Pretty much every place to stay on Bali and Lombok can arrange tours, car rental and other services. Laundry service is universally available, often cheap and sometimes free. For infomation on the surge of moderately priced chain hotels in south Bali, see p67.

BUDGET HOTELS

The cheapest accommodation on Bali and Lombok is in small places that are simple but clean and comfortable. Names usually include the word 'losmen,' 'homestay,' 'inn' or 'pondok.' Many are built in the style of a traditional Balinese home.

There are budget hotels all over Bali (less so on Lombok), and they vary widely in standards and price. Expect:

» Maybe air-con
» Maybe hot water
» Private bathroom with shower and Western-style toilet
» Often a pool
» Simple breakfast
» Carefree and cheery staff

International budget chains are making a splashy entry into south Bali, but note that a tiny US$9 room quickly hits US$40 when you add various extras such as taxes and fees for items included elsewhere like internet and towels.

MIDRANGE HOTELS

Midrange hotels are often constructed in Balinese bungalow style or in two-storey blocks and are set on spacious grounds with a pool. Many have a sense of style that is beguiling and may help postpone your departure. In addition to what you'll get at a budget hotel, expect:

» Balcony/porch/patio
» Satellite TV
» Small fridge
» Often wi-fi

TOP-END HOTELS

Top-end hotels in Bali are world-class. Service is refined and you can expect decor plucked from the pages of a glossy magazine, along with the following:

» Superb service
» Views – ocean, lush valleys and rice fields or private gardens

---

PRICE RANGES

The following price ranges refer to a double room with a bathroom. Unless otherwise stated taxes are included in the price.

$ less than 450,000Rp (around US$50)
$$ 450,000Rp-1,400,000Rp (US$50 to $150)
$$$ more than 1,400,000Rp

BOOK YOUR STAY ONLINE

For more accommodation reviews by Lonely Planet authors, check out http://hotels.lonelyplanet.com. You'll find independent reviews, as well as recommendations on the best places to stay. Best of all, you can book online.

» Spa
» Maybe a private pool
» Not wanting to leave

HOTEL DEALS
For hotels, especially mid-range and top-end places, you can often find the best accommodation deal online. Some hotels offer internet deals on their websites; many more work with agents and brokers to sell their rooms at discounts far below published rates.

Bali Discovery (www.balidiscovery.com) has discount rates for hundreds of places. The following sites are also good resources:
» www.asiarooms.com
» www.gilibookings.com
» www.agoda.com

Villas

Villas are scattered all around south Bali and they're often built in the middle of rice paddies, seemingly overnight. The villa boom has been quite controversial for environmental, aesthetic and economic reasons. Many skip collecting government taxes from guests, which has raised the ire of their luxury hotel competitors and brought threats of governmental crack-downs.

Large villas can be bacchanal retreats for groups of friends and are typically found in Kerobokan and Canggu. Others are smaller, more intimate and part of larger developments – common in Seminyak – or top-end hotels. Expect the following:
» Private garden
» Private pool

» Kitchen
» Air-con bedroom(s)
» Open-air common space

And will also potentially include:
» Your own staff (cook, driver, cleaner)
» Lush grounds
» Private beachfront
» Isolation (which can be good or bad)

Rates range from under US$200 per night for a modest villa to US$2000 per week and beyond for your own tropical estate. There are often deals, especially in the low season, and several couples sharing can make something grand affordable.

You can sometimes save quite a bit by waiting until the last minute, but during the high season the best villas book up far in advance. Recommended choices include:

VILLA RENTAL QUESTIONS

It's the Wild West out there. There are myriad agents, some excellent, others not. It is essential to be as clear as possible about what you want when arranging a rental. Following are some things to keep in mind and ask about when renting a villa:
» How far is the villa from the beach and stores?
» Is a driver or car service included?
» If there is a cook, is food included?
» Is there an electricity surcharge?
» Are there extra cleaning fees?
» Is laundry included?
» What refunds apply on a standard 50% deposit?
» Is there wi-fi?

Villa Agents

Bali Private Villas (☎0361-316 6455; www.baliprivatevillas.com)

Bali Tropical Villas (☎0361-732 083; www.bali-tropical-villas.com)

Bali Ultimate Villas (☎0361-857 1658; www.baliultimatevillas.com) Also has wedding services.

Long-Term Accommodation

For longer stays, you can find flats for US$300 to US$800 a month. Look in the **Bali Advertiser** (www.baliadvertiser.biz)and on notice boards, such as the one at Café Moka in Seminyak and those in Ubud. If your tastes run simple, you can find basic bungalows among the rice fields in Ubud.

Village Accommodation

A good way to arrange a village stay is through the **JED** (Village Ecotourism Network; ☎0361-366 9951; www.jed.or.id; tours from US$75) Village Ecotourism Network. Another good option is the **Bali Homestay Program** (☎0817 067 1788; www.bali-homestay.com; r from US$30), north of Tabanan.

Climate
Denpasar

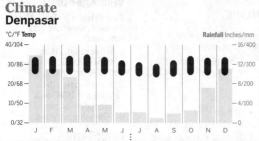

°C/°F Temp

40/104 —

30/86 —

20/68 —

10/50 —

0/32 —

J F M A M J J A S O N D

Rainfall Inches/mm

— 16/400

— 12/300

— 8/200

— 4/100

— 0

Business Hours

Standard hours are as follows:

» **Banks** 8am to 2pm Monday to Thursday, 8am to noon Friday, 8am to 11am Saturday

» **Government offices** 8am to 3pm Monday to Thursday, 8am to noon Friday (although these are not standardised)

» **Post offices** 8am to 2pm Monday to Friday, longer in tourist centres

» **Restaurants and cafes** 8am to 10pm daily

» **Shops and services catering to visitors** 9am to 8pm daily

Customs Regulations

Indonesia's list of prohibited imports includes drugs, weapons, fresh fruit and anything remotely pornographic.

Items allowed include:

» 200 cigarettes (or 50 cigars or 100g of tobacco)

» a 'reasonable amount' of perfume

» 1L of alcohol

Surfers with more than two or three boards may be charged a fee, and this can apply to other items if the officials suspect that you intend to sell them in Indonesia.

There is no restriction on foreign currency, but the import or export of rupiah is limited to 5,000,000Rp. Greater amounts must be declared.

Electricity

120v/60hz

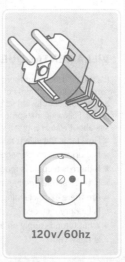

120v/60hz

Embassies & Consulates

Foreign embassies are in Jakarta, the national capital. Most of the foreign representatives in Bali are consular agents (or honorary consuls) who can't offer the same services as a full consulate or embassy. A lost passport may mean a trip to an embassy in Jakarta.

The US, Australia and Japan have formal consulates in Bali (citizens from these countries make up half of all visitors).

Indonesian embassies and consulates abroad are listed on the website of Indonesia's **Department of Foreign Affairs** (www.deplu.go.id).

Australian Consulate (☎0361-241 118; www.bali.indonesia.embassy.gov.au; Jl Tantular 32, Denpasar; ☺8am-4pm Mon-Fri) The Australian consulate has a consular sharing agreement with Canada.

Japanese Consulate (☎0361-227 628; konjpdps@indo.net.id; Jl Raya Puputan 170, Renon, Denpasar; ☺10am-3pm Mon-Fri)

US Consulate (☎0361-233 605; amcobali@indosat.net.id; Jl Hayam Wuruk 310, Renon, Denpasar; ☺9am-3.30pm Mon-Fri)

Food

For complete coverage of the delicious eating and drinking options in Bali and Lombok see p329.

Price Ranges

The following price ranges refer to a typical meal in the establishment reviewed.

CATEGORY	COST
$	less than 60,000Rp (around US$6)
$$	60,000Rp–250,000Rp (US$6 to US$27)
$$$	more than 250,000Rp

STOPPING CHILD-SEX TOURISM

Indonesia has become a destination for foreigners seeking to sexually exploit local children. A range of socio-economic factors make many children and young people vulnerable to such abuse and some individuals prey upon this vulnerability. The sexual abuse and exploitation of children has serious, life-long and even life-threatening consequences for the victims. Strong laws exist in Indonesia to prosecute offenders and many countries also have extraterritorial legislation which allows nationals to be prosecuted in their own country for these crimes.

Travellers can help stop child-sex tourism by reporting suspicious behaviour. Reports can be made to the **Anti Human Trafficking Unit** (☎021 721 8098) of the Indonesian police. If you know the nationality of the individual, you can contact their embassy directly.

For more information, contact the following organisations:

ECPAT (End Child Prostitution & Trafficking; www.ecpat.org) A global network working on these issues, with over 70 affiliate organisations around the world. **Child Wise** (www.childwise.net) is the Australian member of ECPAT.

Humantrafficking.org (www.humantrafficking.org) International group has numerous links to groups working to prevent human exploitation in Indonesia.

PKPA (Center for Study & Child Protection; www.pkpa-indonesia.org) An organisation committed to the protection of Indonesia's children and the prevention of child-sex tourism.

Gay & Lesbian Travellers

Gay travellers in Bali will experience few problems, and many of the island's most influential expat artists have been more-or-less openly gay. Physical contact between same-sex couples is acceptable and friends of the same sex often hold hands, though this does not indicate homosexuality.

There are many venues where gay men congregate, mostly in Seminyak. There's nowhere that's exclusively gay, and nowhere that's even inconspicuously a lesbian scene. Gay men in Indonesia are referred to as *homo* or *gay* and are quite distinct from the female impersonators called *waria*.

Many gays from other parts of the country come to live in Bali, as it is more tolerant, and also because it offers opportunities to meet foreign partners.

On Lombok, gay and lesbian travellers should refrain from public displays of affection (advice that also applies to straight couples). The following are useful organisations:

Gaya Dewata (www.gaya dewata.com) Bali's gay organisation.

Proyekcinta (www.proyekcinta.com) Website for Bali's LGBT community.

Insurance

Unless you are definitely sure that your health coverage at home will cover you in Bali and Lombok, you should take out travel insurance; bring a copy of the policy as evidence that you're covered. It's a good idea to get a policy that pays for medical evacuation if necessary.

Some policies specifically exclude 'dangerous activities,' which can include scuba diving, renting a local motorcycle and even trekking. Be aware that a locally acquired motorcycle licence isn't valid under some policies.

Worldwide travel insurance is available at www.lonelyplanet.com/travel_services. You can buy, extend and claim online anytime – even if you're already on the road.

Internet Access

Internet centres are common anywhere there are tourists in Bali. Expect to pay 300Rp to 500Rp per minute for access. Speeds are usually fine for Skype and the like.

PRACTICALITIES

» Radio in Bali includes Gema Merdeka 97.7FM, the most popular station among locals, plenty of Balinese music; Oz101.2FM, which sounds like a Sydney pop station; and Paradise 100.9FM, which has ABC news from Australia.

» Indonesia uses the PAL broadcasting standard, the same as Australia, New Zealand, the UK and most of Europe.

» Indonesia uses the metric system.

Hotel wi-fi access in rooms is becoming common except in remote areas. Many cafes and restaurants also have free wi-fi.

Indosat (www.indosatm2.com) has a 3G data network across south Bali.

Internet access on Lombok tends to cost 400Rp to 500Rp per minute. Outside of Mataram and Senggigi, access is painfully slow.

Language Courses

Many visitors to Bali like to learn at least the basics of Bahasa Indonesia. Ubud is a good place to learn as there are many private tutors. Formal schools include the following:

Indonesia Australia Language Foundation (IALF; ☑0361-225 243; www.ialf.edu; Jl Raya Sesetan 190, Denpasar) The best place for courses in Bahasa Indonesia.

Seminyak Language School (☑0361-733 342; www.learnindonesianinbali.com; Jl Raya Seminyak 7, Seminyak) Popular with visitors, it is conveniently located down a footpath near the Bintang Supermarket.

Legal Matters

The Indonesian government takes the smuggling, using and selling of drugs very, *very* seriously. If caught with drugs, you may have to wait for up to six months in jail before trial. Gambling is illegal (although it's common, especially at cockfights), as is pornography.

Generally, you are unlikely to have any encounters with the police unless you are driving a rented car or motorcycle.

In both Bali and Lombok, there are police stations in all district capitals. If you have to report a crime or have other business at a police station, expect a lengthy and bureaucratic encounter. You should dress respect-

ably, bring someone to help with translation, arrive early and be polite. You can also call the **Bali Tourist Police** (☑0361-224 111) for advice.

Police officers often expect to receive bribes, either to overlook some crime, misdemeanour or traffic infringement, or to provide a service that they should provide anyway. Generally, it's easiest to pay up – and the sooner this happens, the less it will cost. Travellers may be told there's a 'fine' to pay on the spot, or some travellers offer to pay a 'fine' to clear things up. How much? Generally, 50,000Rp can work wonders and the officers are not proud. If things seem unreasonable, however, ask for the officer's name and write it down.

Maps

Periplus Travel Maps has a decent Bali contour map (1:250,000), with a detailed section on southern Bali, plus maps of the main town areas. However, the labelling and names used for towns are often incomprehensible.

Periplus' Lombok & Sumbawa map is useful. You can find these at most bookshops in Bali.

Money

Indonesia's unit of currency is the rupiah (Rp). There are coins worth 50Rp, 100Rp, 500Rp and 1000Rp. Notes come in denominations of 2000Rp, 5000Rp, 10,000Rp, 20,000Rp, 50,000Rp and 100,000Rp.

Always carry a good supply of rupiah in small denominations. Individuals will struggle to make change for a 50,000Rp note or larger.

ATMs

There are ATMs all over Bali. Most accept nonlocal ATM cards and major credit cards for cash advances. The exchange rates for ATM withdrawals are usually quite good, but check to see if your home bank will hit you with outrageous fees. Most ATMs in Bali allow a maximum withdrawal of one million rupiah. Avoid ones with a sticker saying '100,000Rp' as that's the denomination

THE ART OF BARGAINING

Many everyday purchases in Bali require bargaining. Accommodation has a set price, but this is usually negotiable in the low season, or if you are staying at the hotel for several days.

Bargaining can be an enjoyable part of shopping in Bali, so maintain your sense of humour and keep things in perspective. Try following these steps:

» Have some idea what the item is worth.

» Establish a starting price – ask the seller for their price rather than making an initial offer.

» Your first price can be from one-third to two-thirds of the asking price – assuming that the asking price is not outrageous.

» With offers and counter-offers, move closer to an acceptable price.

» If you don't get to an acceptable price, you're entitled to walk – the vendor may call you back with a lower price.

» When you name a price, you're committed – you must buy if your offer is accepted.

you'll get and you'll struggle to break those bills.

You'll find ATMs in Mataram, Praya and Senggigi on Lombok and also on the Gilis.

Credit Cards

Visa, MasterCard and Amex are accepted by most of the larger businesses that cater to tourists. Be sure to confirm that a business accepts credit cards before you show up cashless.

Moneychangers

US dollars are by far the easiest currency to exchange. Try to have new US$100 bills.

Follow these steps to avoid getting ripped off exchanging money:

» Find out the going exchange rate online. Know that anyone offering a better rate will need to make a profit through other means.

» Stick to banks, airport exchange counters or large and reputable storefront operations.

» Skip any place offering too-good exchange rates and claiming to charge no fees or commissions.

» Avoid exchange stalls down alleys or in otherwise dubious locations (that sounds obvious but scores of tourists are taken in daily).

» Common exchange scams include rigged calculators, sleight of hand schemes, 'mistakes' on the posted rates and demands that you hand over your money before you have counted the money on offer.

» Use an ATM to obtain rupiah.

Tipping

» Tipping a set percentage is not expected in Bali, but if the service is good, it's appropriate to leave 5000Rp or 10% or more.

» Most midrange hotels and restaurants and all top-end hotels and restaurants add 21% to the bill for tax and service (known as 'plus plus'). This service compo-

nent is distributed among hotel staff (one hopes).

» Hand cash directly to individuals if you think they deserve recognition for their service.

» Tip good taxi drivers, guides, people giving you a massage or fetching you a beer on the beach etc; 5000Rp to 10,000Rp is generous.

Travellers Cheques

Travellers cheques are almost impossible to use.

Post

Every substantial town has a *kantor pos* (post office). In tourist centres, there are also postal agencies, which are often open long hours and provide postal services. Sending postcards and normal-sized letters (ie under 20g) by airmail is cheap, but not really fast.

Mail delivery times from Bali:

» **Australia** Two weeks

» **UK & rest of Europe** Three weeks

» **USA** Two weeks

Post offices will properly wrap your parcels over 20g for shipping for a small fee. Although goods usually arrive, don't use the post for anything you'd miss.

International express companies like Fedex and UPS operate on Bali and offer reliable, fast and expensive service.

Public Holidays

The following holidays are celebrated throughout Indonesia. Many of the dates change according to the phase of the moon (not by month) or by religious calendar, so the following are estimates only.

Tahun Baru Masehi (New Year's Day) 1 January

Idul Adha (Muslim Festival of Sacrifice) February

MORE SAFETY INFO

» Warnings specific to the Kuta region, p72.

» Health concerns, p385.

» The many boat services between Bali and the surrounding islands are unregulated and there have been accidents (p378).

Muharram (Islamic New Year) February/March

Nyepi (Hindu New Year) March/April

Hari Paskah (Good Friday) April

Ascension of Christ April/May

Hari Waisak (Buddha's birth, enlightenment and death) April/May

Maulud Nabi Mohammed/Hari Natal (Prophet Mohammed's birthday) May

Hari Proklamasi Kemerdekaan (Indonesian Independence Day) 17 August

Isra Miraj Nabi Mohammed (Ascension of the Prophet Mohammed) September

Hari Natal (Christmas Day) 25 December

The Muslim population in Bali observes Islamic festivals and holidays, including Ramadan. Religious and other holidays on Lombok are as follows:

Anniversary of West Lombok (Government holiday) 17 April

Ramadan Usually October

Idul Fitri (End of Ramadan) November/December

Founding of West Nusa Tenggara (Public holiday) 17 December

Safe Travel

It's important to note that compared with many places in the world Bali is fairly safe. There are some hassles from

SHIPPING LARGE ITEMS

For items that are shipped, you'll pay a 40% or 50% deposit and the balance (plus any taxes or import duties) when you collect the items at home. Arrange for delivery to your door – if you have to pick the items up from the nearest port or freight depot, you may be up for extra port charges.

Most stores selling furniture or heavy artwork can arrange packing, shipping and insurance. Shipping costs for volumes less than a full container load vary greatly according to the company, destination and quantity – think in terms of around US$150-plus per cubic metre. Be aware that packing costs, insurance, fumigation (!) and so on are included in some companies' prices but not others.

Rim Cargo (☎0361-737 670; www.rimcargo.com; Jl Laksmana 32, Seminyak) is a large company adept at dealing with the needs of Bali visitors.

---

the avaricious, but most visitors face many more dangers at home. Petty theft occurs but it is not prevalent.

Annoyances
ALCOHOL POISONING
There are ongoing reports of injuries and deaths among tourists and locals due to *arak* (local booze that should be distilled from palm or cane sugar) being adulterated with methanol, a poisonous form of alcohol. Avoid free cocktails and any offers of *arak*.

DRUGS
Numerous high-profile drug cases on Bali and Lombok should be enough to dissuade anyone from having anything to do with illicit drugs. As little as two ecstasy tabs or a bit of pot have resulted in huge fines and multi-year jail sentences in Bali's notorious jail in Kerobokan. Try smuggling and you may pay with your life. Kuta is filled with cops posing as dealers.

HAWKERS & TOUTS
Many visitors regard hawkers and touts as *the* number one annoyance in Bali (and in tourist areas of Lombok). Visitors are frequently, and often constantly, hassled to buy things. The worst places for this are Jl Legian in Kuta, Kuta Beach, the Gunung Batur area and the over-subscribed temples at Besakih and Tanah Lot. And the cry of 'Transport?!?' – that's everywhere. Many touts employ

fake, irritating Australian accents ('Oi! Mate!').

Use the following tips to deflect attention:

» Completely ignore touts/hawkers.

» Don't make any eye contact.

» A polite *tidak* (no) actually encourages them.

» Never ask the price or comment on the quality of their goods unless you're interested in buying.

Keep in mind, though, that ultimately they're just people trying to make a living, and if you don't want to buy anything, you are wasting their time trying to be polite.

ORPHANAGES
Bali has a number of 'fake' orphanages designed to extract money from well-meaning tourists. If you are considering donating anything to an orphanage, carefully research its reputation online. Orphanages using cab

drivers as hawkers are especially suspect.

SWIMMING
Kuta Beach and those to the north and south are subject to heavy surf and strong currents – always swim between the flags. Trained lifeguards are on duty, but only at Kuta, Legian, Seminyak, Nusa Dua, Sanur and (sometimes) Senggigi. Other beaches can have strong currents, even when protected by reefs.

Water pollution is a problem, especially after rain. Swim far away from any open streams flowing into the surf.

Be careful when swimming over coral, and never walk on it. It can be very sharp and coral cuts are easily infected. In addition, you are damaging a fragile environment.

THEFT
Violent crime is relatively uncommon, but bag-snatching, pickpocketing and theft from rooms and parked cars does occur. A few precautions:

GOVERNMENT TRAVEL ADVICE

Government advisories are often general; however, the following sites have useful tips:

Australia Smart Traveller (www.smarttraveller.gov.au)

New Zealand (www.mfat.govt.nz)

Canada (www.voyage.gc.ca)

UK (www.fco.gov.uk/travel)

US (www.travel.state.gov)

» Secure money before leaving an ATM

» Don't leave valuables on a beach while swimming

» Use front desk/in-room safes

TRAFFIC & FOOTPATHS

Apart from the dangers of driving in Bali, the traffic in most tourist areas is often annoying and frequently dangerous to pedestrians. Footpaths can be rough, even unusable; gaps in the pavement are a top cause of injury. Carry a torch at night.

Telephone

Internet Calling

Most hotel wi-fi service in south Bali and Ubud will allow Skype to work. Internet centres may add a surcharge for the call to your connection time (perhaps 3000Rp per minute).

Mobile Phones

SIM cards for your unlocked GSM mobile phone on Bali cost only 50,000Rp. They come with cheap rates for calling other countries, starting at US$0.20 per minute. You can buy them everywhere, just ask.

Phone Codes

Phone numbers beginning with 08 belong to mobile phones. Useful numbers include the following:

Directory assistance	☑108
Indonesia Country Code	☑62
International Call Prefix	☑001/017
International Operator	☑102

Time

Bali and Lombok are on Waktu Indonesia Tengah or WIT (Central Indonesian Standard Time), which is eight hours ahead of Greenwich Mean Time/Universal Time or two hours behind Australian Eastern Standard Time. Java is another hour behind Bali and Lombok.

Not allowing for daylight-saving time elsewhere, when it's noon in Bali and Lombok, it's 11pm the previous day in New York, 8pm in Los Angeles, 4am in London and 2pm in Sydney and Melbourne.

Toilets

Western-style toilets are almost universally common in tourist areas.

During the day, look for a cafe or hotel and smile (public toilets only exist at some major sights).

Tourist Information

The tourist office in Ubud is an excellent source of information on cultural events. Otherwise, the tourist offices in Bali are not useful.

Some of the best information is found in the many free publications and websites aimed at tourists and expats, which are distributed in south Bali and Ubud. These include the following:

Bali Advertiser (www. baliadvertiser.biz) Local news and a variety of columnists with useful information.

Bali Discovery (www. balidiscovery.com) Has an essential and first-rate Bali news section and a wealth of other island information.

The Beat (www.beatmag. com) Excellent bi-weekly with extensive entertainment and cultural listings.

Yak (www.theyakmag.com) Glossy, cheeky mag celebrating the expat swells of Seminyak and Ubud.

Travellers with Disabilities

Bali is a difficult destination for those with limited mobility. While some of the airlines flying to Bali have a good reputation for accommodating people with disabilities, the airport is not well set up.

Public transport is not accessible; ditto for the minibuses used by shuttle bus and tour companies. Ramps and other disabled facilities at hotels and inns are uncommon. Your best bet are the international chains, but even then you should confirm your needs with the property. Out on the street, the footpaths, where they exist at all, tend to be narrow, uneven, potholed and frequently obstructed.

Visas

The visa situation in Indonesia seems to be constantly in flux. It is essential that you confirm current formalities before you arrive in Bali or Lombok. Failure to meet all the entrance requirements can see you on the first flight out.

WRONG NUMBER?

Bali's landline phone numbers (those with area codes that include ☑0361, across the south and Ubud) are being changed on an ongoing basis through to ☑2014. To accommodate increased demand for lines, a digit is being added to the start of the existing six- or seven-digit phone number. So ☑0361-761 xxxx might become ☑0361-4761 xxxx. The schedule and plans for the new numbers change regularly, but usually you'll hear a recording first in Bahasa Indonesian and then in English telling you what digit to add to the changed number.

No matter what type of visa you are going to use, your passport *must* be valid for at least six months from the date of your arrival.

The main visa options for visitors to Indonesia are as follows:

Visa in Advance Citizens of countries not eligible for Visa Free or Visa on Arrival must apply for a visa before they arrive in Indonesia. Typically this is a visitor's visa, which comes in two flavours: 30 or 60 days. Details vary by country; contact your nearest Indonesian embassy or consulate to determine processing fees and times. Note: this is the only way to obtain a 60-day visitor visa even if you qualify for Visa on Arrival.

Visa on Arrival Citizens of over 60 countries may apply for a visa when they arrive at the airports in Bali and Lombok. The cost is US$25; be sure to have the exact amount in US currency. This visa is good for 30 days; for renewals. Eligible countries include Australia, Canada, much – but not all – of the EU including Germany, Ireland, the Netherlands and the UK, plus New Zealand and the USA.

Visa Free Citizens of Singapore and a smattering of

other countries can receive a nonextendable 30-day visa for free upon arrival.

Whichever type of visa you use to enter Bali or Lombok, you'll be issued with a tourist card that is valid for a 30- or 60-day stay (if you have obtained one of the coveted 60-day visas in advance, be sure the immigration official at the airport gives you a 60-day card). Keep the tourist card with your passport, as you'll have to hand it back when you leave the country. Even staying one day beyond your visa expiration date will likely result in fines and hassles.

Volunteering

There's a plethora of opportunities to lend a hand in Bali and Lombok. Many people have found that they can show their love for these places by helping others.

Bali Spirit (www.balispirit.com/ngos) has information on a number of nonprofit and volunteer groups. There are organisations helping Bali's dogs in Ubud.

Local Organisations

The following organisations need donations, supplies and often volunteers. Check their

websites to see their current status.

East Bali Poverty Project (☎0361-410 071; www.eastbalipovertyproject.org) Works to help children in the impoverished mountain villages of east Bali.

Friends of the National Parks Foundation (☎0361-977 978; www.fnpf.org; Jl Bisma, Ubud) Main office in Bali. Has volunteer programs in and around Tanjung Puting National Park in central Kalimantan as well as programs on Nusa Penida.

IDEP (Indonesian Development of Education & Permaculture; ☎0361-294 993; www.idepfoundation.org) Has projects across Indonesia; works on environmental projects, disaster planning and community improvement.

JED (Village Ecotourism Network; ☎0361-366 9951; www.jed.or.id; tours from US$75) Organises highly regarded tours of small villages, some overnight. Often needs volunteers to improve its services and work with the villagers.

ProFauna (☎081-7970 6066; www.profauna.or.id) A large nonprofit animal-protection organisation operating across Indonesia; the Bali office has been aggressive in protecting sea turtles. Volunteers needed to help with hatchery releases and editing publications.

Sacred Childhoods Foundation (www.sacredchildhoods.org) Reputable nonprofit with a wide range of programs to help children on Bali and Sulawesi.

Smile Foundation of Bali
(Yayasan Senyum; ☎0361-233 758; www.senyumbali.org)
Organises surgery to correct facial deformities; operates the **Smile Shop** (☎233 758; www.senyumbali.org; Jl Sriwedari) in Ubud to raise money.

WISNU (☎0361-735 321; www.wisnu.or.id; Jl Pengubengan Kauh) An environmental group that teaches tourism-related industries how to be more green. It's set up community-based recycling programs with hotels and always needs volunteers.

Yakkum Bali (Yayasan Rama Sesana; ☎0361-247 363; www.yrsbali.org) Dedicated to improving reproductive health for women across Bali.

Yayasan Bumi Sehat (☎0361-970 002; www.bumisehatbali.org) Operates an internationally recognised clinic and gives reproductive services to disadvantaged women in Ubud; accepts donated time from medical professionals.

YKIP (Humanitarian Foundation of Mother Earth; ☎0361-761 208; www.ykip.org) Established after the 2002 bombings, it organises and funds health and education projects for Bali's children.

International Organisations
The following agencies are other possible sources of long-term paid or volunteer work in Bali or Lombok.

Australian Volunteers International (www.australianvolunteers.com) Organises professional contracts for Australians.

Global Volunteers (www.globalvolunteers.org) Arranges professional and paid volunteer work for US citizens.

Voluntary Service Overseas Canada (www.voyage.gc.ca); Netherlands (www.vso.nl); UK (www.vso.org.uk) British overseas volunteer program that accepts qualified volunteers from other countries.

Volunteer Service Abroad (www.vsa.org.nz) Organises professional contracts for New Zealanders.

Women Travellers
Bali
Women travelling solo in Bali will get attention from Balinese men, but these men are, on the whole, fairly benign. Generally, Bali is safer for women than many areas of the world, and with the usual care and common sense, women should feel secure travelling alone. (Although high-profile attacks in south Bali have reminded people of the need for caution.)

Lombok
Traditionally, women on Lombok are treated with respect, but in the touristy areas, harassment of single foreign women may occur. Would-be guides/boyfriends/gigolos are often persistent in their approaches, and can be aggressive when ignored or rejected. Clothes that aren't too revealing are a good idea – beachwear should be reserved for the beach, and the less skin you expose the better. Two or more women together are less likely to experience problems, and women accompanied by a man are unlikely to be harassed. Don't walk alone at night.

Transport

GETTING THERE & AWAY

Most international visitors to Bali will arrive by air, either directly or via Jakarta. For island-hoppers, there are frequent ferries between eastern Java and Bali, and between Bali and Lombok, as well as domestic flights between the islands. Most people visit Lombok via Bali.

Flights, tours and rail tickets can be booked online at www.lonelyplanet.com/travel_services.

Entering the Region

Arrival procedures at Bali's Ngurah Rai International Airport are straightforward, although it can take some time for planeloads of visitors to clear immigration; afternoons are typically worst, although it remains to be seen if the vast new terminal building scheduled to open by 2014 will change this.

At the baggage claim area, porters are keen to help get your luggage to the customs tables and beyond, and they've been known to ask up to US$20 for their services – if you want help with your bags, agree on a price beforehand. The formal price is 5000Rp per piece.

Once through customs, you're out with the tour operators, touts and taxi drivers. The touts will be working hard to convince you to come and stay at some place in the Kuta area. If you go with these guys, you'll pay more than you would if you just show up on your own, as they get large commissions.

Passport

Your passport *must* be valid for six months after your date of arrival in Indonesia.

Air

Although Jakarta, the national capital, is the gateway airport to Indonesia, there are also many international flights to Bali and a few to Lombok.

Airports & Airlines

BALI AIRPORT

The only airport in Bali, **Ngurah Rai Airport** (DPS), is just south of Kuta; it is sometimes referred to internationally as Denpasar or on some internet flight-booking sites as Bali.

Bali is getting a large new airport terminal, parking area and access roads by 2014. Until then the airport is even more chaotic than usual as construction means there are many temporary facilities. It is hoped the new facility will be better able to cope with the surging crowds of international and domestic passengers.

A scheme to lengthen the runway keeps running into hurdles, such as environmental concerns about destroying more of the mangroves (although this didn't stop the toll road from being built). The present runway is too short for planes flying direct to/from Europe, so for these flights passengers need to change planes at places such as Singapore or Jakarta.

CLIMATE CHANGE & TRAVEL

Every form of transport that relies on carbon-based fuel generates CO_2, the main cause of human-induced climate change. Modern travel is dependent on aeroplane, which might use less fuel per kilometre per person than most cars but travel much greater distances. The altitude at which aircraft emit gases (including CO_2) and particles also contributes to their climate change impact. Many websites offer 'carbon calculators' that allow people to estimate the carbon emissions generated by their journey and, for those who wish to do so, to offset the impact of the greenhouse gases emitted with contributions to portfolios of climate-friendly initiatives throughout the world. Lonely Planet offsets the carbon footprint of all staff and author travel.

International airlines flying to and from Bali regularly change. Service is expanding, however, especially to Australia, where a new policy allows almost unlimited flying between Bali and Oz.

Domestic airlines serving Bali from other parts of Indonesia change frequently. All have ticket offices at the domestic terminal, which you may need to use, as internet sales are difficult with some.

Air Asia (www.airasia.com) Serves Jakarta as well as Bangkok, Kuala Lumpur and Singapore, plus Darwin and Perth in Australia.

Cathay Pacific Airways (www.cathaypacific.com) Serves Hong Kong.

China Airlines (www.china -airlines.com) Serves Taipei.

Eva Air (www.evaair.com) Serves Taipei.

Garuda Indonesia (www. garuda-indonesia.com) Serves Australia (Darwin, Melbourne, Perth and Sydney), Japan, Korea and Singapore direct plus cities across Indonesia.

Jetstar (www.jetstar.com) Darwin, Melbourne, Perth, Sydney.

KLM (www.klm.com) Serves Amsterdam via Singapore.

Korean Air (www.koreanair. com) Serves Seoul.

Lion Air (www.lionair.co.id) Serves cities across Indonesia and Singapore.

Malaysia Airlines (www. mas.com.my) Serves Kuala Lumpur.

Merpati Airlines (www. merpati.co.id) Serves many smaller Indonesian cities, in addition to the main ones.

Qatar Airways (www.qatar airways.com) Serves Doha via Singapore.

Singapore Airlines (www. singaporeair.com) Several Singapore flights daily.

Thai Airways International (www.thaiair.com) Serves Bangkok.

Virgin Australia (www. virginaustralia.com) Serves Australia.

LOMBOK AIRPORT

Lombok International Airport (Bandara Internasional Lombok; LOP) is the new airport in the south of the island near Praya. It is linked to the Mataram area by a new highway. Besides domestic flights to a few major Indonesian cities it has limited service.

Silk Air (☎0370-628 254; www.silkair.com; Hotel Lombok Raya, Jl Panca Usaha 11) Serves Singapore direct five times weekly.

Batavia Air (☎021-3899 9888, 0370-648 998; www. batavia-air.com) Daily to Jakarta via Surabaya.

Wings Air (☎0370-629 333; www.lionair.co.id; Hotel Sahid Legi, Jl Sriwijaya) Daily flights to Denpasar, Jakarta and Surabaya.

Merpati Airlines (☎0370-621 111; www.merpati.co.id; Jl Pejanggik 69) Connections to most parts of Indonesia via four daily flights to Denpasar.

Trans Nusa (☎616 2428; www.transnusa.co.id) Flies to Bali and Sumbawa Besar from Lombok daily.

Garuda (☎0804 180 7807; www.garuda-indonesia.com; Jl Pejanggik 42) Three daily flights to Jakarta; one daily flight to Bali.

Tickets

Deregulation in the Asian and Indonesian aviation markets means that there are frequent deals to Bali. Check major web-based travel agents and with the airlines for special promotions.

Asia

Bali is well connected to major Asian hubs such as Hong Kong, Seoul, Singapore and Taipei. Lombok is now linked to Singapore.

Australia

Service to Australia is at record levels as Australia and Indonesia have deregulated flights.

Canada

From Canada, you'll change planes at an Asian hub.

DEPARTURE TAX

The departure tax from Bali and Lombok is 50,000Rp for domestic flights and 150,000Rp for international ones. Have exact cash ready.

Continental Europe

None of the major European carriers can fly to Bali nonstop due to the length of the runway. Singapore is the most likely place to change planes coming from Europe, with Bangkok, Hong Kong and Kuala Lumpur also popular. You can switch to a score of airlines for the final hop to Bali in any of these cities.

New Zealand

You will have to change planes in Australia or Singapore.

Other Indonesian Islands

From Bali, you can get flights to major Indonesian cities, often for under US$50 and definitely for not much more than US$100. One way to shop is to simply compare prices among the ticket counters at the airport as many of Indonesia's smaller airlines lack decent websites. Deals to Jakarta put the price of a plane ticket in the same class as the bus – with a saving of about 22 hours.

From Lombok, you can get some decent deals but direct service is mostly limited to Bali, Surabaya and Jakarta.

UK & Ireland

From London, the most direct service to Bali is via Singapore, Bangkok, Hong Kong and Kuala Lumpur.

USA

The best connections are through any of the major Asian hubs with nonstop service to Bali. No US airline serves Bali.

Land

Bus

The ferry crossing from Bali is included in the services to/from the new long-distance terminal near Mengwi offered by numerous bus companies. It's advisable to buy your ticket at least one day in advance from a travel agent or at the terminal. Note, too, that fierce air competition has put tickets to Jakarta and Surabaya in the range of bus prices.

Fares vary between operators; it's worth paying extra for a decent seat and air-con. Typical fares/travel times from the new terminal include Yogyakarta 250,000Rp/16 hours and Jakarta 350,000Rp/24 hours. You can also get buses from Singaraja in north Bali.

On Lombok, public buses go daily from the Mandalika terminal to major cities on Java. Most buses are comfortable, with air-con and reclining seats.

Train

Bali doesn't have trains but the **State Railway Company** (☎0361-227 131; www.kereta-api.co.id; Jl Diponegoro 150/B4; ⏰8.30am-6.30pm) does have an office in Denpasar. From here buses leave for eastern Java where they link with trains at Banyuwangi for Surabaya, Yogyakarta and Jakarta, among other destinations. Fares and times are comparable to the bus, but the air-conditioned trains are more comfortable, even in economy class. Note: on the website *jadwal* means schedule.

Sea

You can reach Java, just west of Bali, and Sumbawa, just east of Lombok, via ferries. Longer-distance boats serve Indonesia's eastern islands.

Java

When visiting Java from Bali and Lombok, some land travel is necessary.

FERRY

Running constantly, **ferries** (Gilimanuk; adult/child 6000/5000Rp, car & driver 114,000Rp, motorbike 16,000Rp; ⏰24hr) cross the Bali Strait between Gilimanuk in western Bali and Ketapang (Java). The actual crossing takes under 30 minutes, but you'll spend longer than this loading, unloading and waiting around. Car-rental contracts usually prohibit rental vehicles being taken out of Bali.

From Ketapang, bemo travel 4km north to the bus terminal, where buses leave for cities across Java.

Sumbawa

Ferries travel between Labuhan Lombok and Poto Tano on Sumbawa frequently throughout the day.

Other Indonesian Islands

Ferry services to other islands in Indonesia are often in flux, although **Pelni** (www.pelni.co.id), the national shipping line, is reasonably reliable. It schedules large boats on long-distance runs throughout Indonesia.

For Bali, Pelni ships stop at the harbour in Benoa as part of their regular loops throughout Indonesia. Schedules and fares are found on the website. You can inquire and book at the **Pelni ticket office** (☎0361-763 963, 021-7918 0606; www.pelni.co.id; Jl Raya Kuta 299; ⏰8am-noon & 1-4pm Mon-Fri, 8am-1pm Sat) in Tuban.

Pelni ships link Lembar on Lombok with other parts of Indonesia. Check schedules and buy tickets at Mataram's **Pelni office** (☎0370-637 212; Jl Industri 1; ⏰8am-noon & 1-3.30pm Mon-Thu & Sat, 8-11am Fri)

GETTING AROUND

Especially in Bali, the best way to get around is with your own transport, whether you drive, hire a driver or ride a bike. This gives you the flexibility to explore at will and allows you to reach many places that are otherwise inaccessible.

Public transport is cheap but can be cause for very long journeys if you're not sticking to a major route. In addition, some places are just impossible to reach.

There are also tourist shuttle buses, which combine economy with convenience.

Air

Several airlines fly daily between Bali and Lombok. The route is competitive and fares hover at around 600,000Rp.

To/From the Airport

Bali's **Ngurah Rai Airport** is immediately south of Tuban and Kuta. There is fixed price taxi monopoly inside the terminal. You prepay (more than you would a metred taxi) and go. You have to exit the airport to catch a metred

---

BALI'S NEW BUS TERMINAL

Bali's **long-distance bus terminal** (Mengwi) has moved 12km northwest of Denpasar to a large new terminal near Mengwi, just off the main road to west Bali. It even has an airport-style 'control tower,' possibly to guide in the buses arriving from Java.

You can get bemo from here to Denpasar's Batubulan terminal (20,000Rp) and on to Padangbai (50,000Rp) for the Lombok ferry.

Taxis from here to Kerobokan cost 100,000Rp; Kuta is 120,000Rp.

taxi. See the regional listings in this book for the fares.

If you have a surfboard, you'll be charged extra, depending on its size. Ignore any touts that aren't part of the official scheme.

Many hotels will offer to pick you up at the airport; however, there's no need to use these services if they cost more than the official rates.

If you're really travelling light, Kuta Beach is less than a 30-minute walk north.

Any taxi will take you to the airport at a metered rate that should be less than the prepaid monopoly rates from the airport.

Bemo

Bemos are normally a minibus or van with a row of low seats down each side. They usually hold about 12 people in very cramped conditions.

The bemo was once the dominant form of public transport. But widespread motorbike ownership (which can be cheaper than daily bemo use) has caused the system to wither. On Lombok, however, bemos are still important.

Riding bemo can be part of your Bali adventure or a major nightmare, depending on your outlook at that moment in time. You can certainly expect journeys to be lengthy and you'll find that getting to many places is both time-consuming and inconvenient. It's uncommon to see visitors on bemos in Bali.

On Lombok, bemos are minibuses or pick-up trucks and are a major means of transport for visitors.

Fares

Bemo operate on a standard route for a set (but unwritten) fare. The minimum fare is about 5000Rp. If you get into an empty bemo, always make it clear that you do not want to charter it.

Terminals & Routes

Every town has at least one terminal (terminal bis) for all forms of public transport.

BALI'S NEW TOLL ROAD

Due for completion before 2014, Bali's new toll road is meant to avoid the worst of the traffic in and around Kuta. Some 12km in length, it runs from the bypass near Denpasar over the mangroves to a point near Nusa Dua with a branch to Ngurah Rai Airport.

The toll will be 10,000Rp; the time-savings over the current clogged roads is hard to quantify. The road's northern end is at the turn to Benoa off the bypass, already one of the most congested spots in the south.

There are often several terminals in larger towns. Denpasar has four main bus/bemo terminals and three minor ones. Terminals can be confusing, but most bemo and buses have signs, and if you're in doubt, people will usually help you.

To travel from one part of Bali to another, it is often necessary to go via one or more terminals. For example, to get from Sanur to Ubud by bemo, you go to the Kereneng terminal in Denpasar, transfer to the Batubulan terminal, and then take a third bemo to Ubud. This is circuitous and time-consuming, two of the reasons so few visitors take bemo in Bali.

Bicycle

More and more people are touring the island by *sepeda* (bike). Many visitors are using bikes around the towns and for day trips in Bali and on Lombok. Cycling tours are popular, see p38.

Hire

There are plenty of bicycles for rent in the tourist areas, but many are in poor condition. On Lombok, you can find good bikes in Senggigi.

Ask at your accommodation about renting a bike; hotels often have their own. Prices are about 15,000Rp to 35,000Rp per day.

Boat

Taking the boat is more relaxing than the hassle of flying between Bali and Lombok, and fast boats make it competitive time-wise, but there are some important safety considerations that need to be taken into account.

Public ferries travel slowly between Padangbai and Lembar on Lombok. **Perama** (☎613 8514; www.peramatour. com) operates a daily boat service from Padangbai to Senggigi.

There are many fast boats operating between Bali and Lombok's Gilis. Boats from Nusa Lembongan and Amed make for interesting itinerary possibilities.

Bus

Distances in Bali and on Lombok are relatively short, so you won't have cause to ride on many large buses unless you are transferring between islands or going from one side to another.

Public Bus
BALI

Larger minibuses and full-sized buses ply the longer routes, particularly on routes linking Denpasar, Singaraja and Gilimanuk. They operate out of the same terminals as the bemo. However, with everybody riding motorbikes, there are long delays waiting for buses to fill up at terminals before departing.

LOMBOK

Buses and bemo of various sizes are the cheapest and most common way of getting around Lombok. On rough

TRAVELLING SAFELY BY BOAT

Fast boats linking Bali, Nusa Lembongan, Lombok and the Gili Islands have proliferated, especially as the latter places have become more popular. But in many cases these services are accidents waiting to happen as safety regulations are non-existent. Accidents continue to happen.

Crews on these boats may have little or no training: in one accident, the skipper admitted that he panicked and had no recollection of what happened to his passengers. And rescue is far from assured: a volunteer rescue group in east Bali reported that they had no radio.

Conditions are often rough in the waters off Bali. Although the islands are in close proximity and are easily seen from each other, the ocean between can get more turbulent than is safe for the small speedboats zipping across it.

With these facts in mind, it is essential that you take responsibility for your own safety as no one else will. Consider the following points:

» **Bigger is better** It may add 30 minutes or more to your journey, but a larger boat will simply deal with the open ocean better than the over-powered small speedboats. Also, trips on small boats can be unpleasant because of the ceaseless pounding through the waves and the fumes coming from the screaming outboard motors.

» **Check for safety equipment** Ensure your boat has life preservers and that you know how to locate and use them. In an emergency, don't expect a panicked crew to supply them. Also, check for lifeboats. Some promotional materials show boats with automatically inflating lifeboats that have later been removed to make room for more passengers.

» **Avoid overcrowding** Travellers report boats leaving with more people than seats and with aisles jammed with stacked luggage. If this happens, don't use the boat.

» **Look for exits** Cabins may only have one narrow entrance making them death traps in an accident.

» **Avoid fly-by-nighters** Taking a fishing boat and jamming too many engines on the rear in order to cash in on booming tourism is a recipe for disaster. Note that some outfits with safe boats will add unsafe boats to the fleet in order to make a quick profit.

» **Don't ride on the roof** It looks like care-free fun but travellers are regularly bounced off when boats hit swells and crews may be inept at rescue.

» **Use common sense** There are good operators on the waters around Bali but the line-up changes constantly. If a service seems sketchy before you board, go with a different operator. Try to get a refund but don't risk your safety for the cost of a ticket.

---

roads in remote areas, trucks may be used as public transport. Mandalika in Bertais is the main bus terminal for all of Lombok. There are also regional terminals at Praya and Pancor (near Selong). You may have to go via one or more of these transport hubs to get from one part of Lombok to another.

Public transport fares are fixed by the provincial government and displayed on a noticeboard outside the office of the Mandalika terminal. You may have to pay more if you have a large bag or surfboard.

Tourist Bus

Perama (☑0361-751 170; www.peramatour.com) has a near monopoly on this service in Bali (although you may see small-time competitors advertising in Kuta). It has offices or agents in Kuta, Sanur, Ubud, Lovina, Padangbai and Candidasa and at least one bus a day links these Bali tourist centres. Services to Kintamani and along the east coast from Lovina to/from Candidasa via Amed are by demand. Perama also has a very limited service around Senggigi on Lombok.

Consider the following advantages and disadvantages when deciding whether to book your ticket (one day in advance is a good idea).

Advantages:

» Fares are reasonable (eg Kuta to Lovina is 100,000Rp)

» Buses have air-con
» Meet other travellers

Disadvantages:

» Perama stops are often outside the centre, requiring another shuttle/taxi

» Buses may not provide a direct service – stopping, say, at Ubud between Kuta and Padangbai

» Like bemos, the service has ossified, resolutely sticking to the routes it ran years ago and not recognising popular new destinations such as Bingen or Seminyak

» Three or more people can hire a car and also a driver for less

Car & Motorcycle

Renting a car or motorbike can open up Bali and Lombok for exploration – and can also leave you counting the minutes until you return it. It gives you the freedom to explore myriad back roads and lets you set your own schedule. Most people don't rent a car for their entire visit but rather get one for a few days of meandering.

There can be harrowing driving conditions on the islands at certain times.

Driving Licences

CAR LICENCES

If you plan to drive a car, you're supposed to have an International Driving Permit (IDP). You can obtain one from your national motoring organisation if you have a normal driving licence. Bring your home licence as well. Without an IDP, add 50,000Rp to any fine you'll have to pay if stopped by the police (although you'll have to pay this fine several times to exceed the cost and hassle of getting the mostly useless IDP).

MOTORCYCLE LICENCES

If you have a motorcycle licence at home, get your IDP endorsed for motorcycles too; with this you will have no problems. Otherwise you have to get a local licence – something of an adventure.

Officially, there's a 2 million rupiah fine for riding without a proper licence, and your motorcycle can be impounded. Unofficially, you may be hit with a substantial 'on-the-spot' payment (50,000Rp seems average) and allowed to continue on your way. Also, if you have an accident without a licence your insurance company might refuse coverage.

To get a local motorcycle licence in Bali (valid for a year), go independently to the **Poltabes Denpasar** (☏0361-142 7352; Jl Gunung Sanhyang; ☺8am-1pm Mon-Sat), which is northwest of Kerobokan on the way to Denpasar. Bring your passport, a photocopy of your passport (just the page with your photo on it) and a passport-sized photo. Then, follow these steps:

» Ignore the mobbed hall filled with jostling permit seekers.

» Look helpless and ask uniformed officials 'motocycle license?'.

» Be directed to cheery English-speaking officials and pay 250,000Rp.

» Take the written test (in English, with the answers provided on a sample test).

» Get your permit.

Sure it costs more than in the hall of chaos, but who can argue with the service?

Fuel

Bensin (petrol) is sold by the government-owned Pertamina company, and costs about 4500Rp per litre. Bali has scads of petrol stations. On Lombok there are stations in major towns.

Hire

Few agencies in Bali will allow you to take their rental cars or motorcycles to Lombok – the regular vehicle insurance is not valid outside Bali.

CAR

The most popular rental vehicle is a small jeep – they're compact and are well suited to exploring back roads. Automatic transmissions are unheard of.

Rental and travel agencies in tourist centres rent vehicles quite cheaply. A small jeep costs a negotiable 200,000Rp per day, with unlimited kilometres and very limited insurance. Extra days often cost much less than the first day.

There's no reason to book rental cars in advance or with a tour package; doing so will almost certainly cost more than arranging it locally. Any place you stay can set you up with a car, as can the ever-present touts in the street.

MOTORCYCLE

Motorbikes are a popular way of getting around Bali and Lombok – locals ride pillion almost from birth. When you see a family of five all riding cheerfully on one motorbike, it's called a Bali minivan.

Motorbikes are ideal for Lombok's tiny rough roads, which may be difficult or impassable by car. Once you get out of the main centres and off the main roads, there's not much traffic.

Motorbikes are easily rented. Ask at your accommodation or look for the inevitable offers on the street. The engines are modest (a fuel-stingy 125 cc is typical), so your chances of going fast are nil.

Rentals cost 30,000Rp to 50,000Rp a day, less by the week. This should include minimal insurance for the motorcycle (probably with a US$100 excess), but not for any other person or property. Many have racks for surfboards.

Think carefully before renting a motorbike. It is dangerous and every year visitors go home with lasting damage – this is no place to learn to ride. Helmet use is mandatory.

Insurance

Rental agencies and owners usually insist that the vehicle itself is insured, and minimal insurance should be included in the basic rental deal – often with an excess of as much as US$100 for a motorcycle and US$500 for a car (ie the customer pays the first US$100/500 of any claim).

Check to see what your own vehicle, health and travel insurance covers, especially if you are renting a motorbike.

Road Conditions

Bali traffic can be horrendous in the south, up to Ubud, and as far as Padangbai to the east and Tabanan to the west. Finding your way around the main tourist sites can be a challenge, as roads are only sometimes signposted and maps are unreliable. Off the main routes, roads can be rough, but they are usually surfaced.

Roads on Lombok are often very rough but traffic is lighter than on Bali.

Avoid driving at night or at dusk. Many bicycles, carts and vehicles do not have proper lights, and street lighting is limited.

Road Rules

Visiting drivers commonly complain about crazy Balinese drivers, but often it's because the visitors don't understand the local conventions of road use. For instance, the constant use of horns here doesn't mean 'Get the @£*&% out of my way!'; rather it is a very Balinese way of saying 'Hi, I'm here.'

» Watch your front – it's your responsibility to avoid anything that gets in front of your vehicle. In effect, a car, motorcycle or anything else pulling out in front of you has right of way.

» Often drivers won't even look to see what's coming when they turn left at a junction – they listen for the horn.

» Use your horn to warn anything in front that you're there, especially if you're about to overtake.

» Drive on the left side of the road.

Traffic Police

Some police will stop drivers on very slender pretexts. If a cop sees your front wheel half an inch over the faded line at a stop sign, if the chin-strap of your helmet isn't fastened, or if you don't observe one of the ever-changing and poorly signposted one-way traffic restrictions, you may be waved down.

The cop will ask to see your licence and the vehicle's registration papers, and they'll also tell you what a serious offence you've committed. Stay cool and don't argue. Don't offer a bribe. Eventually they'll suggest that you can pay them some amount of money to deal with the matter. If it's a very large amount, tell them politely that you don't have that much. These matters can be settled for something between 10,000Rp and 100,000Rp, although it will be more if you argue.

Hitching

You can hitchhike in Bali and on Lombok, but it's not a very useful option for getting around, as public transport is so cheap and frequent, and private vehicles are often full.

Bear in mind, also, that hitching is never entirely safe in any country. Travellers who decide to hitch should understand that they are taking a small but potentially serious risk.

Local Transport

Dokar & Cidomo

Small *dokar* (pony carts) still provide local transport in some remote areas of Bali, and even in parts of Denpasar and Kuta, but they're uncommon, extremely slow and not particularly cheap.

The horse cart used on Lombok is known as a *cidomo* – a contraction of *cika* (a traditional handcart), *dokar* and *mobil* (because car wheels and tyres are used). A typical *cidomo* has a narrow bench seat on either side. The ponies appear to some visitors to be heavily

---

HIRING A VEHICLE & DRIVER

An excellent way to travel anywhere around Bali is by hired vehicle, allowing you to leave the driving and inherent frustrations to others. If you're part of a group, it can make sound economic sense as well. This is also possible on Lombok but less common.

It's easy to arrange a charter: just listen for one of the frequent offers of 'transport?' in the streets around the tourist centres. Approach a driver yourself; or ask at your hotel, which is often a good method, as it increases accountability. Then consider the following:

» Although great drivers are everywhere, it helps to talk with a few.

» Get recommendations from other travellers.

» You should like the driver and their English should be sufficient for you to communicate your wishes.

» Costs for a full day should average 400,000Rp to 600,000Rp.

» The vehicle, usually a late-model Toyota Kijang seating up to seven, should be clean.

» Agree on a route beforehand.

» Make it clear if you want to avoid tourist-trap restaurants and shops (smart drivers understand that tips depend on following your wishes).

» On the road, buy the driver lunch (they'll want to eat elsewhere, so give them 20,000Rp) and offer snacks and drinks.

» Many drivers find ways to make your day delightful in unexpected ways. Tip accordingly.

BALI ROAD DISTANCES (KM)

	Amed	Bangli	Bedugul	Candidasa	Denpasar	Gilimanuk	Kintamani	Kuta	Lovina	Negara	Nusa Dua	Padangbai	Sanur	Semarapura	Singaraja	Tirtagangga
Bangli	59															
Bedugul	144	97														
Candidasa	32	52	88													
Denpasar	57	47	78	31												
Gilimanuk	197	181	148	165	134											
Kintamani	108	20	89	71	67	135										
Kuta	73	57	57	41	10	144	77									
Lovina	89	86	41	139	89	79	70	99								
Negara	161	135	115	126	95	33	163	104	107							
Nusa Dua	81	81	102	55	24	158	91	14	113	109						
Padangbai	45	39	75	13	18	178	58	28	126	154	42					
Sanur	64	40	85	38	7	141	78	15	96	102	22	37				
Semarapura	37	26	61	27	47	181	46	57	112	124	71	14	52			
Singaraja	78	75	30	128	78	90	59	88	11	118	92	115	85	105		
Tirtagangga	14	65	101	13	84	212	85	112	179	108	26	91	44	142		
Ubud	68	29	35	54	23	157	29	33	40	120	47	41	30	29	95	67

laden and harshly treated, but they are usually looked after reasonably well, if only because the owners depend on them for their livelihood. *Cidomo* are a very popular form of transport in many parts of Lombok, and often go to places that bemo don't, won't or can't.

Fares are not set by the government on either island; prices start at 5000Rp per person for a short trip (3000Rp to 5000Rp on Lombok) but are negotiable.

Ojek

Around towns and along roads, you can always get a lift by *ojek* (a motorcycle or motorbike that takes a paying passenger). Formal *ojek* are less common now that anyone with a motorbike can be a freelance *ojek* (stand by the side of the road, look like you need a ride and people will stop and offer). They're OK on quiet country roads, but a risky option in the big towns. *Ojek* are more common on Lombok.

Fares are negotiable, but about 20,000Rp for 5km is fairly standard.

Taxi
BALI

Metered taxis are common in south Bali and Denpasar (but not Ubud). They are essential for getting around Kuta and Seminyak, where you can easily flag one down. Elsewhere, they're often a lot less hassle than haggling with drivers offering 'transport!'.

The usual rate for a taxi is 5000Rp flag fall and 4000Rp per kilometre, but the rate is higher in the evening. If you phone for a taxi, the minimum charge is 10,000Rp. Avoid any driver who claims meter problems or who won't use the meter.

By far the most reputable taxi company is Bluebird Taxi (☎701 111), which uses blue vehicles with a light on the roof bearing a stylised bluebird. Watch out for fakes – there are many. Look for 'Blue Bird' over the windscreen and the phone number. Drivers speak reasonable English and use the meter at all times. Many expats will use no other firm and the drivers are often fascinating conversationalists.

After Blue Bird Taxi, standards decline. Some other companies are acceptable, although you may have a hassle getting the driver to use the meter after dark. Others may claim that their meter is 'broken' or nonexistent, and negotiated fees can be way over the odds.

LOMBOK

There are plenty of bemo and taxis around Mataram and Senggigi. Drivers for Lombok Taksi (☎627 000), owned by Bali Taxi's Blue Bird Group, always use the meter without you having to ask; this is the best choice. The only place you would need to negotiate a taxi fare is at the harbour at Bangsal

LOMBOK ROAD DISTANCES (KM)

	Bangsal	Bayan	Kuta	Labuhan Lombok	Labuhanhaji	Lembar	Mataram	Pemenang	Praya	Pringgabaya	Sapit	Senaru	Senggigi
Bayan	57												
Kuta	86	143											
Labuhan Lombok	101	66	75										
Labuhanhaji	157	100	57	39									
Lembar	54	121	64	109	77								
Mataram	32	96	54	69	64	27							
Pemenang	1	56	79	109	105	53	26						
Praya	54	121	26	66	39	39	27	53					
Pringgabaya	102	74	83	8	26	102	75	101	62				
Sapit	106	47	101	25	43	120	92	119	80	18			
Senaru	54	102	140	68	106	116	86	63	117	81	54		
Senggigi	18	81	64	79	74	40	10	25	40	88	106	72	
Tetebatu	76	120	50	45	32	98	44	75	29	46	63	130	54

(but not on the main road in Pemenang).

Tours

Standardised organised tours are a convenient way to visit a few places in Bali. There are dozens and dozens of operators who provide a similar product and service. Much more interesting are specialised tour companies that can take you far off the beaten track, offer memorable experiences and otherwise provide you with a different side of Bali and Lombok. You can also easily arrange your own custom tour.

Tours originating on Lombok are based in Senggigi. You can usually book market visits in Mataram, a jaunt out to the Gilis or a trip down the south coast.

Standard Day Tours

Tours are typically in white eight- to 12-seat minibuses with air-con, which pick you up and drop you off at your hotel. Prices range from 50,000Rp to 200,000Rp for what are essentially similar tours, so it pays to shop around. Consider the following:

» Will lunch be at a huge tourist buffet or somewhere more interesting?

» How much time will be spent at tourist shops?

» Will there be a qualified English-speaking guide?

» Are early morning pick-ups for the convenience of the company, which then dumps you at a central point to wait for another bus?

The following are the usual tours sold around Bali. They are available from most hotels and shops selling services to tourists:

» **Bedugul** Includes Sangeh or Alas Kedaton, Mengwi, Jatiluwih, Candikuning and sunset at Tanah Lot.

» **Besakih** Includes craft shops at villages near Ubud, Gianyar, Semarapura (Klungkung), Pura Besakih, and return via Bukit Jambal.

» **Denpasar** Takes in the arts centre, markets, the museum and perhaps a temple or two.

» **East Bali** Includes the usual craft shops, Semarapura (Klungkung), Kusamba, Goa Lawah, Candidasa and Tenganan.

» **Kintamani–Gunung Batur** Takes in the craft shops at Celuk, Mas and Batuan, a dance at Batubulan, Tampaksiring and views of Gunung Batur. Alternatively, the tour may go to Goa Gajah, Pejeng, Tampaksiring and Kintamani.

» **Singaraja–Lovina** Goes to Mengwi, Bedugul, Gitgit, Singaraja, Lovina, Banjar and Pupuan.

» **Sunset Tour** Includes Mengwi, Marga, Alas Kedaton and sunset at Tanah Lot.

Specialist Tours

Many Bali tour operators offer experiences that vary from the norm. These can include cultural experiences hard for the casual visitor to find, such as cremations or trips to remote villages where life has hardly changed in decades. Often you'll avoid the clichéd tourist minibus and travel in unusual vehicles or in high comfort.

See the Bali & Lombok Outdoors chapter for tours involving trekking, cycling and more; there are many tours around Ubud to choose from.

The following operators are recommended. Prices span the gamut but tend to be more expensive than the bog-standard tours:

JED (Village Ecotourism Network; ☑0361-366 9951; www. jed.or.id; tours from US$75) Organises highly regarded tours of small villages, some overnight.

Bali Discovery Tours (☑0361-286 283; www. balidiscovery.com) Personalised and customisable tours across Bali.

Suta Tours (☑0361-788 8865, 0361-741 6665; www. sutatour.com) Standard tours but also arranges trips to cremation ceremonies and special temple festivals, market tours and other custom plans.

Health

emergency evacuation is expensive – bills of more than US$100,000 are not uncommon.

Find out in advance if your insurance plan will make payments directly to providers or reimburse you later for overseas health expenditures. (In many countries doctors expect payment in cash at the time of treatment.) Some policies ask you to call back (reverse charges) to a centre in your home country where an immediate assessment of your problem is made.

Recommended Vaccinations

Specialised travel-medicine clinics are your best source of information; they stock all available vaccines and will be able to give specific recommendations for you and your trip.

Most vaccines don't produce immunity until at least two weeks after they're given. Ask your doctor for an International Certificate of Vaccination (otherwise known as the yellow booklet), which will list all the vaccinations you've received.

The World Health Organization recommendations for Southeast Asia include the following:

» **Hepatitis A** Provides almost 100% protection for up to a year; a booster after 12 months provides at least another 20 years' protection. Mild side effects such as headache and sore arm occur in 5% to 10% of people.

» **Hepatitis B** Now considered routine for most travellers. It's given as three shots over six months. Life-time protection occurs in 95% of people.

» **Measles, mumps & rubella (MMR)** Two doses of MMR required unless you have had the diseases. Many young adults require a booster.

» **Typhoid** Recommended unless your trip is less than a

Treatment for minor injuries and common traveller's health problems is easily accessed in Bali and to a lesser degree on Lombok. However, for serious conditions, you will need to leave the islands.

Travellers tend to worry about contracting infectious diseases when in the tropics, but infections are a rare cause of serious illness or death in travellers. Pre-existing medical conditions, such as heart disease, and accidental injury (especially traffic accidents) account for most life-threatening problems. Becoming ill in some way, however, is relatively common; ailments you may suffer include gastro, overexposure to the sun and other typical traveller woes.

It's important to note certain precautions you should take on Bali and Lombok, especially in regard to rabies, mosquito bites and the tropical sun.

The following advice is a general guide only and does not replace the advice of a doctor trained in travel medicine.

BEFORE YOU GO

Make sure all medications are packed in their original, clearly labelled containers. A signed and dated letter from your physician describing your medical conditions and medications (including generic names) is also a good idea. If you are carrying syringes or needles, be sure to have a physician's letter documenting their medical necessity. If you have a heart condition ensure you bring a copy of your electrocardiogram taken just prior to travelling.

If you take any regular medication bring double your needs in case of loss or theft. You can buy many medications over the counter without a doctor's prescription, but it can be difficult to find some of the newer drugs, particularly the latest antidepressant drugs, blood-pressure medications and contraceptive pills.

Insurance

Even if you are fit and healthy, don't travel without sufficient health insurance – accidents do happen. If you're uninsured,

HEALTH ADVISORIES

It's usually a good idea to consult your government's travel-health website before departure, if one is available:

» **Australia** (www.smarttraveller.gov.au)
» **UK** (www.nhs.uk/nhsengland/healthcareabroad)
» **US** (www.cdc.gov/travel)

week and only to developed cities. The vaccine offers around 70% protection, lasts for two to three years and comes as a single shot.

Required Vaccinations

The only vaccine required by international regulations is yellow fever. Proof of vaccination will only be required if you have visited a country in the yellow-fever zone (primarily some parts of Africa and South America) within the six days prior to entering Southeast Asia.

Medical Checklist

Recommended items for a convenient personal medical kit (more specific items can be easily obtained on Bali if needed):

» antibacterial cream (eg Muciprocin)
» antihistamine – there are many options (eg Cetirizine for daytime and Promethazine for night)
» antiseptic (eg Betadine)
» contraceptives
» DEET-based insect repellent
» first-aid items such as scissors, bandages, digital thermometer (but not a mercury one) and tweezers
» Ibuprofen or another anti-inflammatory
» steroid cream for allergic/itchy rashes (eg 1% to 2% hydrocortisone)
» sunscreen and hat
» throat lozenges
» thrush (vaginal yeast infection) treatment (eg clotrimazole pessaries or diflucan tablet)

Websites

There is a wealth of travel health advice on the internet.

World Health Organization (WHO; www.who.int/ith) Publishes the useful *International Travel & Health*, which is revised annually; has a lot of info online.

MD Travel Health (www.mdtravelhealth.com) Provides travel health recommendations for every country.

Centers for Disease Control & Prevention (CDC; www.cdc.gov) This website also has good travel information.

Further Reading

Lonely Planet's *Asia & India: Healthy Travel* is a handy pocket-sized book that is packed with useful information, including pretrip planning, emergency first aid, immunisation and disease information and what to do if you get sick on the road.

IN BALI & LOMBOK

Availability & Cost of Health Care

In south Bali and Ubud there are clinics catering to tourists and just about any hotel can put you in touch with an English-speaking doctor.

INTERNATIONAL MEDICAL CLINICS

For serious conditions, foreigners would be best served in one of two private clinics that cater mainly to tourists and expats. At both of these places you should confirm that your health and/or travel insurance will cover you. In cases where your medical condition is considered serious you may well be evacuated by air ambulance to top-flight hospitals in Jakarta or Singapore; this is where proper insurance is vital as these flights can cost more than US$10,000.

BIMC (☎0361-761 263; www.bimcbali.com; Jl Ngurah Rai 100X; ◷24hr) On the bypass road just east of Kuta near the Bali Galleria. It's a modern Australian-run clinic that can do tests, hotel visits and arrange medical evacuation. Visits can cost US$100 or more.

International SOS Medical Clinic (☎0361-710 505; www.sos-bali.com; Jl Ngurah Rai 505X; ◷24hr) A clinic aimed at tourists, has English-speaking staff.

HOSPITALS

There are two facilities in Denpasar that offer a good standard of care. Both are more affordable than the international clinics.

BaliMed Hospital (☎0361-484 748; www.balimedhospital.co.id; Jl Mahendradatta 57) On the Kerobokan side of Denpasar, this private hospital has a range of medical services. A basic consultation is 220,000Rp.

Rumah Sakit Umum Propinsi Sanglah (Sanglah Hospital; ☎227 911; ◷24hr) The city's general hospital has English-speaking staff and an ER. It's the best hospital on the island and has a special wing for well-insured foreigners, **Paviliun Amerta Wing International** (☎257 499).

REMOTE CARE

In more remote areas facilities are basic – generally a small public hospital, doctor's surgery or *puskesmas* (community health centre). In government-run clinics and hospitals, services such as meals, washing and clean clothing are normally provided by the patient's family.

The best hospital on Lombok is the new **Rumah Sakit Harapan Keluarga** (📞670 000, 617 7000; www.harapan keluarga.co.id/rshk; Jl Ahmad Yani 9) in Mataram.

PHARMACIES

The **Kimia Farma** chain is good and has many locations. Singapore's **Guardian** chain of pharmacies is also found in tourist areas. Elsewhere you need to be more careful as fake medications and poorly stored or out-of-date drugs are common.

Infectious Diseases

BIRD FLU

Otherwise known as avian influenza, the H5N1 virus has claimed more than 100 victims in Indonesia. Most of the cases have been in Java, west of Bali. Treatment is difficult, although the drug Tamiflu has some effect.

DENGUE FEVER

This mosquito-borne disease is a major problem. As there is no vaccine available it can only be prevented by avoiding mosquito bites. The mosquito that carries dengue bites day and night, so use insect avoidance measures at all times. Symptoms include high fever, severe headache and body ache (dengue was previously known as 'breakbone fever'). Some people develop a rash and experience diarrhoea. There is no specific treatment, just rest and paracetamol as it increases the likelihood of haemor-

rhaging. See a doctor to be diagnosed and monitored.

HEPATITIS A

A problem throughout the region, this food- and water-borne virus infects the liver, causing jaundice (yellow skin and eyes), nausea and lethargy. There is no specific treatment for hepatitis A; you just need to allow time for the liver to heal. All travellers to Southeast Asia should be vaccinated against hepatitis A.

HEPATITIS B

The only sexually transmitted disease that can be prevented by vaccination, hepatitis B is spread by body fluids, including sexual contact. In some parts of Southeast Asia up to 20% of the population are carriers of hepatitis B.

HIV

HIV is a major problem in many Asian countries, and Bali has one of the highest rates of HIV infection in Indonesia. The main risk for most travellers is sexual contact with locals, prostitutes and other travellers.

The risk of sexual transmission of the HIV virus can be dramatically reduced by the use of a *kondom* (condom). These are available from supermarkets, street stalls and drugstores in tourist areas, and from the *apotik* (pharmacy) in almost any town (from about 1500Rp to 3000Rp each – it's worth getting the more expensive brands).

MALARIA

The risk of contracting malaria is greatest in rural areas of Indonesia. Generally malaria is not a concern on Bali or in the main touristed areas of Lombok. Consider precautions if you are going into remote areas or on side trips beyond the two islands.

Two strategies should be combined to prevent malaria: mosquito avoidance and antimalarial medications. Most people who catch ma-

laria are taking inadequate or no antimalarial medication.

Travellers are advised to prevent mosquito bites by taking these steps:

» Use a DEET-containing insect repellent on exposed skin. Wash this off at night, as long as you are sleeping under a mosquito net. Natural repellents such as citronella can be effective, but must be applied more frequently than products containing DEET.

» Sleep under a mosquito net impregnated with permethrin.

» Choose accommodation with screens and fans (if not air-conditioned).

» Impregnate clothing with permethrin in high-risk areas.

» Wear long sleeves and trousers in light colours.

» Use mosquito coils.

» Spray your room with insect repellent before going out for your evening meal.

There are a variety of medications available should you catch malaria:

» **Artesunate** Derivatives of Artesunate are not suitable as a preventive medication.

» **Chloroquine & Paludrine** The effectiveness of this combination is now limited in most of Southeast Asia. Generally not recommended.

» **Doxycycline** This daily tablet is a broad-spectrum antibiotic that has the added benefit of helping to prevent a variety of tropical diseases, including leptospirosis, tick-borne disease, typhus and melioidosis. The potential side effects include a tendency to sunburn, thrush in women, indigestion, heartburn, nausea and interference with the contraceptive pill.

» **Lariam (Mefloquine)** Lariam has received much bad press, some of it justified, some not. This weekly tablet suits many people. Serious side effects are rare but include depression, anxiety, psychosis and having fits.

» **Malarone** This drug is a combination of Atovaquone and Proguanil. Side effects, most commonly nausea and headache, are uncommon and mild. It is the best tablet for scuba divers and for those on short trips to high-risk areas. It must be taken for one week after leaving the risk area.

RABIES
Rabies is a disease spread by the bite or lick of an infected animal, most commonly a dog or monkey. Once you are exposed, it is uniformly fatal if you don't get the vaccine very promptly. Bali has had a major outbreak dating to 2008 and people continue to die each year.

To minimise your risk, consider getting the rabies vaccine, which consists of three injections in all. A booster after one year will then provide 10 years' protection. This may be worth considering given Bali's rabies outbreak. The vaccines are often unavailable on Bali, so get them before you go.

Also, be careful to avoid animal bites. Especially watch children closely.

Having the pre-travel vaccination means the post-bite treatment is greatly simplified. If you are bitten or scratched, gently wash the wound with soap and water, and apply an iodine-based antiseptic. It would be a good idea to also consult a doctor.

Those not vaccinated will need to receive rabies immunoglobulin as soon as possible. Clean the wound immediately and do not delay seeking medical attention. Note that Bali is known to run out of rabies immunoglobulin, so be prepared to go to Singapore immediately for medical treatment.

TYPHOID
This serious bacterial infection is spread via food and water. Its symptoms are a high and slowly progressive fever, headache and possibly a dry cough and stomach pain. It is diagnosed by blood tests and treated with antibiotics.

Traveller's Diarrhoea

Traveller's diarrhoea (aka Bali belly) is by far the most common problem affecting travellers – between 30% and 50% of people will suffer from it within two weeks of starting their trip. In over 80% of cases, traveller's diarrhoea is caused by bacteria (there are numerous potential culprits), and therefore responds promptly to treatment with antibiotics.

Traveller's diarrhoea is defined as the passage of more than three watery bowel actions within 24 hours, plus at least one other symptom such as fever, cramps, nausea, vomiting or feeling generally unwell.

TREATMENT
Loperamide is just a 'stopper' and doesn't get to the cause of the problem. However, it can be helpful, for example, if you have to go on a long bus ride. Don't take Loperamide if you have a fever or blood in your stools. Seek medical attention quickly if you do not respond to an appropriate antibiotic.

» Stay well hydrated; rehydration solutions such as Gastrolyte are the best for this.
» Antibiotics such as Norfloxacin, Ciprofloxacin

or Azithromycin will kill the bacteria quickly.

GIARDIASIS
Giardia lamblia is a parasite that is relatively common in travellers. Symptoms include nausea, bloating, excess gas, fatigue and intermittent diarrhoea. The parasite will eventually go away if left untreated but this can take months. The treatment of choice is Tinidazole, with Metronidazole being a second-line option.

Environmental Hazards

DIVING
Divers and surfers should seek specialised advice before they travel to ensure their medical kit contains treatment for coral cuts and tropical ear infections, as well as the standard problems. Divers should ensure their insurance covers them for decompression illness – get specialised dive insurance through an organisation such as **Divers Alert Network** (DAN; www.danseap.org). Have a dive medical before you leave your home country.

Divers should note that there is a **decompression chamber** in Sanur, which is a fast-boat ride from Nusa Lembongan. Getting here from north Bali can take three to four hours.

HEAT
Most parts of Indonesia are hot and humid throughout the year. For most people it takes at least two weeks to adapt to the hot climate. Swelling of the feet and ankles is common, as are muscle cramps caused by excessive sweating. Prevent these by avoiding dehydration and excessive activity in the heat. Be careful to avoid the following conditions:
» **Heat exhaustion** Symptoms include feeling weak, headache, irritability, nausea or vomiting, sweaty

ALCOHOL POISONING

There are ongoing reports of injuries and deaths among tourists and locals due to *arak* (the local booze that should be distilled from palm or cane sugar) being adulterated with methanol, a poisonous form of alcohol. Avoid free cocktails and any offers of *arak*.

skin, a fast, weak pulse and a normal or slightly elevated body temperature. Treatment involves getting out of the heat and/or sun, fanning the victim and applying cool wet cloths to the skin, laying the victim flat with their legs raised, and rehydrating with water containing one-quarter of a teaspoon of salt per litre. Recovery is usually rapid and it is common to feel weak for some days afterwards.

» **Heatstroke** A serious medical emergency. Symptoms come on suddenly and include weakness, nausea, a hot dry body with a body temperature of over 41°C, dizziness, confusion, loss of coordination, fits and eventually collapse and loss of consciousness. Seek urgent medical help and commence cooling by getting the person out of the heat, removing their clothes, fanning them and applying cool wet cloths or ice to their body, especially to hot spots such as the groin and armpits.

» **Prickly heat** A common skin rash in the tropics, caused by sweat being trapped under the skin. The result is an itchy rash of tiny lumps. Treat by moving out of the heat into an air-conditioned area for a few hours and by having cool showers.

BITES & STINGS

During your time in Indonesia, you may make some unwanted friends.

» **Bedbugs** These don't carry disease but their bites are very itchy. They live in the cracks of furniture and walls and then migrate to the bed at night to feed on you as you sleep. You can treat the itch with an antihistamine.

» **Jellyfish** Most are not dangerous, just irritating. Stings can be extremely painful but

DRINKING WATER

Never drink tap water in Indonesia.

Widely available and cheap, bottled water is generally safe; however, check the seal is intact when purchasing. Look for places that allow you to refill containers, thus cutting down on landfill.

Most ice in restaurants is fine if it is uniform in size and made at a central plant (standard for large cities and tourist areas). Avoid ice that is chipped off larger blocks (more common in rural areas).

Avoid fresh juices outside of tourist restaurants and cafes.

rarely fatal. First aid for jellyfish stings involves pouring vinegar onto the affected area to neutralise the poison. Do not rub sand or water onto the stings. Take painkillers, and anyone who feels ill in any way after being stung should seek medical advice.

» **Ticks** Contracted after walking in rural areas, ticks are commonly found behind the ears, on the belly and in armpits. If you have had a tick bite and experience symptoms such as a rash at the site of the bite or elsewhere, fever or muscle aches, you should see a doctor.

SKIN PROBLEMS

» **Fungal rashes** There are two common fungal rashes that affect travellers. The first occurs in moist areas that get less air such as the groin, armpits and between the toes. It starts as a red patch that slowly spreads and is usually itchy. Treatment involves keeping the skin dry, avoiding chafing and using an antifungal cream such as Clotrimazole or Lamisil. *Tinea versicolor* is also common – this fungus causes small, light-coloured patches, most commonly on the back, chest and shoulders. Consult a doctor.

» **Cuts & scratches** Easily infected in tropical climates, take meticulous care of any cuts and scratches. Immediately wash all wounds in clean water and apply antiseptic. If you develop signs of infection see a doctor. Divers and surfers should be careful with coral cuts as they become easily infected.

SUNBURN

Even on a cloudy day sunburn can occur rapidly, especially near the equator. Don't end up like the dopey tourists you see roasted pink on Kuta Beach. Instead:

» Use a strong sunscreen (at least factor 30).

» Reapply sunscreen after a swim.

» Wear a wide-brimmed hat and sunglasses.

» Avoid baking in the sun during the hottest part of the day (10am to 2pm).

Women's Health

In the tourist areas and large cities, sanitary napkins and tampons are easily found. This becomes more difficult the more rural you go.

Birth-control options may be limited so bring adequate supplies of your own form of contraception.

WANT MORE?

For in-depth language information and handy phrases, check out Lonely Planet's *Indonesian Phrasebook*. You'll find it at **shop.lonelyplanet.com**, or you can buy Lonely Planet's iPhone phrasebooks at the Apple App Store.

Language

Indonesian, or Bahasa Indonesia as it's known to the locals, is the official language of Indonesia. It has approximately 220 million speakers, although it's the mother tongue for only about 20 million. Most people in Bali and on Lombok also speak their own indigenous languages, Balinese and Sasak respectively. The average traveller needn't worry about learning Balinese or Sasak, but it can be fun to learn a few words, which is why we've included a few in this chapter. For practical purposes, it probably makes better sense to concentrate your efforts on learning Bahasa Indonesia.

Indonesian pronunciation is easy to master. Each letter always represents the same sound and most letters are pronounced the same as their English counterparts, with *c* pronounced as the 'ch' in 'chat'. Note also that *kh* is a throaty sound (like the 'ch' in Scottish *loch*), and that the *ng* combination, which is found in English at the end or in the middle of words such as 'ringing', also appears at the beginning of words in Indonesian.

Syllables generally carry equal emphasis – the main exception is the unstressed *e* in words such as *besar* (big) – but the rule of thumb is to stress the second-last syllable.

In written Indonesian there are some inconsistent spellings of place names. Compound names are written as one word or two, eg Airsanih or Air Sanih, Padangbai or Padang Bai. Words starting with 'Ker' sometimes lose the *e*, eg Kerobokan/Krobokan. Some Dutch variant spellings also remain in use, with *tj* instead of the modern *c* (eg Tjampuhan/Campuan), and *oe* instead of *u* (eg Soekarno/Sukarno).

Pronouns, particularly 'you', are rarely used in Indonesian. *Anda* is the egalitarian form used to overcome the plethora of words for 'you'.

BASICS

Hello.	*Salam.*
Goodbye. (if leaving)	*Selamat tinggal.*
Goodbye. (if staying)	*Selamat jalan.*
How are you?	*Apa kabar?*
I'm fine, and you?	*Kabar baik, Anda bagaimana?*
Excuse me.	*Permisi.*
Sorry.	*Maaf.*
Please.	*Silahkan.*
Thank you.	*Terima kasih.*
You're welcome.	*Kembali.*
Yes./No.	*Ya./Tidak.*
Mr/Sir	*Bapak*
Ms/Mrs/Madam	*Ibu*
Miss	*Nona*
What's your name?	*Siapa nama Anda?*
My name is ...	*Nama saya ...*
Do you speak English?	*Bisa berbicara Bahasa Inggris?*
I don't understand.	*Saya tidak mengerti.*

ACCOMMODATION

Do you have any rooms available?	*Ada kamar kosong?*
How much is it per night/person?	*Berapa satu malam/orang?*
Is breakfast included?	*Apakah harganya termasuk makan pagi?*
I'd like to share a dorm.	*Saya mau satu tempat tidur di asrama.*

campsite	*tempat kemah*
guesthouse	*losmen*
hotel	*hotel*
youth hostel	*pemuda*
a ... room	*kamar ...*
single	*untuk satu orang*
double	*untuk dua orang*
air-conditioned	*dengan AC*
bathroom	*kamar mandi*
cot	*velbet*
window	*jendela*

DIRECTIONS

Where is ...?	*Di mana ...?*
What's the address?	*Alamatnya di mana?*
Could you write it down, please?	*Anda bisa tolong tuliskan?*
Can you show me (on the map)?	*Anda bisa tolong tunjukkan pada saya (di peta)?*
at the corner	*di sudut*
at the traffic lights	*di lampu merah*
behind	*di belakang*
in front of	*di depan*
far (from)	*jauh (dari)*
left	*kiri*
near (to)	*dekat (dengan)*
next to	*di samping*
opposite	*di seberang*
right	*kanan*
straight ahead	*lurus*

EATING & DRINKING

What would you recommend?	*Apa yang Anda rekomendasikan?*
What's in that dish?	*Hidangan ituisinya apa?*
That was delicious.	*Ini enak sekali.*
Cheers!	*Bersulang!*
Bring the bill/check, please.	*Tolong bawa kuitansi.*
I don't eat ...	*Saya tidak mau makan ...*
dairy products	*susu dan keju*
fish	*ikan*
(red) meat	*daging (merah)*
peanuts	*kacang tanah*
seafood	*makanan laut*

KEY PATTERNS

To get by in Indonesian, mix and match these simple patterns with words of your choice:

When's (the next bus)?
Jam berapa (bis yang berikutnya)?

Where's (the station)?
Di mana (stasiun)?

How much is it (per night)?
Berapa (satu malam)?

I'm looking for (a hotel).
Saya cari (hotel).

Do you have (a local map)?
Ada (peta daerah)?

Is there (a toilet)?
Ada (kamar kecil)?

Can I (enter)?
Boleh saya (masuk)?

Do I need (a visa)?
Saya harus pakai (visa)?

I have (a reservation).
Saya (sudah punya booking).

I need (assistance).
Saya perlu (dibantu).

I'd like (the menu).
Saya minta (daftar makanan).

I'd like (to hire a car).
Saya mau (sewa mobil).

Could you (help me)?
Bisa Anda (bantu) saya?

a table ...	*meja ...*
at (eight) o'clock	*pada jam (delapan)*
for (two) people	*untuk (dua) orang*

Key Words

baby food (formula)	*susu kaleng*
bar	*bar*
bottle	*botol*
bowl	*mangkuk*
breakfast	*sarapan*
cafe	*kafe*
children's menu	*menu untuk anak-anak*
cold	*dingin*
dinner	*makan malam*
dish	*piring*
drink list	*daftar minuman*
food	*makanan*
food stall	*warung*
fork	*garpu*

Signs

Buka	Open
Dilarang	Prohibited
Kamar Kecil	Toilets
Keluar	Exit
Masuk	Entrance
Pria	Men
Tutup	Closed
Wanitai	Women

glass	gelas
highchair	kursi tinggi
hot (warm)	panas
knife	pisau
lunch	makan siang
menu	daftar makanan
market	pasar
napkin	tisu
plate	piring
restaurant	rumah makan
salad	selada
soup	sop
spicy	pedas
spoon	sendok
vegetarian food	makanan tanpa daging
with	dengan
without	tanpa

Meat & Fish

beef	daging sapi
carp	ikan mas
chicken	ayam
duck	bebek
fish	ikan
lamb	daging anak domba
mackerel	tenggiri
meat	daging
pork	daging babi
shrimp/prawn	udang
tuna	cakalang
turkey	kalkun

Fruit & Vegetables

apple	apel
banana	pisang
beans	kacang
cabbage	kol
carrot	wortel
cauliflower	blumkol
cucumber	timun
dates	kurma
eggplant	terung
fruit	buah
grapes	buah anggur
lemon	jeruk asam
orange	jeruk manis
pineapple	nenas
potato	kentang
raisins	kismis
spinach	bayam
vegetable	sayur-mayur
watermelon	semangka

Other

bread	roti
butter	mentega
cheese	keju
chilli	cabai
chilli sauce	sambal
egg	telur
honey	madu
jam	selai
noodles	mie
oil	minyak
pepper	lada
rice	nasi
salt	garam
soy sauce	kecap
sugar	gula
vinegar	cuka

Drinks

beer	bir
coconut milk	santan
coffee	kopi
juice	jus
milk	susu
palm sap wine	tuak
red wine	anggur merah
soft drink	minuman ringan
tea	teh
water	air
white wine	anggur putih
yogurt	susu masam kental

EMERGENCIES

Help!	*Tolong saya!*
I'm lost.	*Saya tersesat.*
Leave me alone!	*Jangan ganggu saya!*
There's been an accident.	*Ada kecelakaan.*
Can I use your phone?	*Boleh saya pakai telpon genggamnya?*
Call a doctor!	*Panggil dokter!*
Call the police!	*Panggil polisi!*
I'm ill.	*Saya sakit.*
It hurts here.	*Sakitnya di sini.*
I'm allergic to (antibiotics).	*Saya alergi (antibiotik).*

SHOPPING & SERVICES

I'd like to buy ...	*Saya mau beli ...*
I'm just looking.	*Saya lihat-lihat saja.*
May I look at it?	*Boleh saya lihat?*
I don't like it.	*Saya tidak suka.*
How much is it?	*Berapa harganya?*
It's too expensive.	*Itu terlalu mahal.*
Can you lower the price?	*Boleh kurang?*
There's a mistake in the bill.	*Ada kesalahan dalam kuitansi ini.*

credit card	*kartu kredit*
foreign exchange office	*kantor penukaran mata uang asing*
internet cafe	*warnet*
mobile/cell phone	*hanpon*
post office	*kantor pos*
signature	*tanda tangan*
tourist office	*kantor pariwisata*

TIME & DATES

What time is it?	*Jam berapa sekarang?*
It's (10) o'clock.	*Jam (sepuluh).*
It's half past (six).	*Setengah (tujuh).*

Question Words

How?	*Bagaimana?*
What?	*Apa?*
When?	*Kapan?*
Where?	*Di mana?*
Which	*Yang mana?*
Who?	*Siapa?*
Why?	*Kenapa?*

in the morning	*pagi*
in the afternoon	*siang*
in the evening	*malam*
today	*hari ini*
tomorrow	*besok*
yesterday	*kemarin*
Monday	*hari Senin*
Tuesday	*hari Selasa*
Wednesday	*hari Rabu*
Thursday	*hari Kamis*
Friday	*hari Jumat*
Saturday	*hari Sabtu*
Sunday	*hari Minggu*
January	*Januari*
February	*Februari*
March	*Maret*
April	*April*
May	*Mei*
June	*Juni*
July	*Juli*
August	*Agustus*
September	*September*
October	*Oktober*
November	*Nopember*
December	*Desember*

TRANSPORT

Public Transport

bicycle-rickshaw	*becak*
boat (general)	*kapal*
boat (local)	*perahu*
bus	*bis*
minibus	*bemo*
motorcycle-rickshaw	*bajaj*
motorcycle-taxi	*ojek*
plane	*pesawat*
taxi	*taksi*
train	*kereta api*

I want to go to ...	*Saya mau ke ...*
How much to ...?	*Ongkos ke ... berapa?*
At what time does it leave?	*Jam berapa berangkat?*
At what time does it arrive at ...?	*Jam berapa sampai di ...?*

Numbers

1	satu
2	dua
3	tiga
4	empat
5	lima
6	enam
7	tujuh
8	delapan
9	sembilan
10	sepuluh
20	duapuluh
30	tigapuluh
40	empatpuluh
50	limapuluh
60	enampuluh
70	tujuhpuluh
80	delapanpuluh
90	sembilanpuluh
100	seratus
1000	seribu

Does it stop at ...?	Di ... berhenti?
What's the next stop?	Apa nama halte berikutnya?
Please tell me when we get to ...	Tolong, beritahu waktu kita sampai di ...
Please stop here.	Tolong, berhenti di sini.

the first	pertama
the last	terakhir
the next	yang berikutnya

a ... ticket	tiket ...
1st-class	kelas satu
2nd-class	kelas dua
one-way	sekali jalan
return	pulang pergi

aisle seat	tempat duduk dekat gang
cancelled	dibatalkan
delayed	terlambat
platform	peron
ticket office	loket tiket
timetable	jadwal
train station	stasiun kereta api
window seat	tempat duduk dekat jendela

Driving & Cycling

I'd like to hire a ...	Saya mau sewa ...
4WD	gardan ganda
bicycle	sepeda
car	mobil
motorcycle	sepeda motor

child seat	kursi anak untuk di mobil
diesel	solar
helmet	helem
mechanic	montir
petrol/gas	bensin
pump (bicycle)	pompa sepeda
service station	pompa bensin

Is this the road to ...?	Apakah jalan ini ke ...?
(How long) Can I park here?	(Berapa lama) Saya boleh parkir di sini?
The car/motocycle has broken down.	Mobil/Motor mogok.
I have a flat tyre.	Ban saya kempes.
I've run out of petrol.	Saya kehabisan bensin.

LOCAL LANGUAGES

Balinese

How are you?	Kenken kabare?
What's your name?	Sire wastene?
My name is ...	Adan tiange ...
I don't understand.	Tiang sing ngerti.
How much is this?	Ji kude niki?
Thank you.	Matur suksma.
What do you call this in Balinese?	Ne ape adane di Bali?
Which is the way to ...?	Kije jalan lakar kel ...?

Sasak

What's your name?	Saik aranm side?
My name is ...	Arankah aku ...
I don't understand.	Endek ngerti.
How much is this?	Pire ajin sak iyak?
Thank you.	Tampak asih.
What do you call this in Sasak?	Ape aran sak iyak elek bahase Sasek?
Which is the way to ...?	Lamun lek ..., embe eak langantah?

(m) indicates masculine gender, (f) feminine gender and (pl) plural

adat – tradition, customs and manners

adharma – evil

aling aling – gateway backed by a small wall

alus – identifiable 'goodies' in an *arja* drama

anak-anak – children

angker – evil power

angklung – portable form of the *gamelan*

anjing – dogs

apotik – pharmacy

arja – refined operatic form of Balinese theatre; also a dance-drama, comparable to Western opera

Arjuna – a hero of the *Mahabharata* epic and a popular temple gate guardian image

bahasa – language; Bahasa Indonesia is the national language of Indonesia

bale – an open-sided pavilion with a steeply pitched thatched roof

bale banjar – communal meeting place of a *banjar;* a house for meetings and *gamelan* practice

bale tani – family house in Lombok; see also *serambi*

balian – faith healer and herbal doctor

banjar – local division of a village consisting of all the married adult males

banyan – a type of ficus tree, often considered holy; see also *waringin*

bapak – father; also a polite form of address to any older man; also *pak*

Barong – mythical lion-dog creature

Barong Tengkok – portable *gamelan* used for wedding processions and circumcision ceremonies on Lombok

baten tegeh – decorated pyramids of fruit, rice cakes and flowers

batik – process of colouring fabric by coating part of the cloth with wax, dyeing it and melting the wax out; the waxed part is not coloured, and repeated waxing and dyeing builds up a pattern

batu bolong – rock with a hole

belalu – quick-growing, light wood

bemo – popular local transport in Bali and on Lombok; usually a small minibus but can be a small pick-up in rural areas

bensin – petrol (gasoline)

beruga – communal meeting hall in Bali; open-sided pavilion on Lombok

bhur – world of demons

bhwah – world of humans

bioskop – cinema

Brahma – the creator; one of the trinity of Hindu gods

Brahmana – the caste of priests and the highest of the Balinese castes; all priests are Brahmanas, but not all Brahmanas are priests

bu – mother; shortened form of *ibu*

bukit – hill; also the name of Bali's southern peninsula

bulau – month

candi – shrine, originally of Javanese design; also known as *prasada*

candi bentar – entrance gates to a temple

cendrawasih – birds of paradise

cengceng – cymbals

cidomo – pony cart with car wheels (Lombok)

cili – representations of Dewi Sri, the rice goddess

dalang – puppet master and storyteller in a *wayang kulit* performance

Dalem Bedaulu – legendary last ruler of the Pejeng dynasty

danau – lake

dangdut – pop music

desa – village

dewa – deity or supernatural spirit

dewi – goddess

Dewi Sri – goddess of rice

dharma – good

dokar – pony cart; known as a *cidomo* on Lombok

Durga – goddess of death and destruction, and consort of *Shiva*

dusun –small village

endek – elegant fabric, like *songket,* with pre-dyed weft threads

Gajah Mada – famous *Majapahit* prime minister who defeated the last great king of Bali and extended *Majapahit* power over the island

Galungan – great Balinese festival; an annual event in the 210-day Balinese *wuku* calendar

gamelan – traditional Balinese orchestra, with mostly percussion instruments like large xylophones and gongs; may have one to more than two dozen musicians; also used to refer to individual instruments such as drums; also called a *gong*

Ganesha – *Shiva's* elephant-headed son

gang – alley or footpath

Garuda – mythical man-bird creature, vehicle of *Vishnu;* modern symbol of Indonesia and the national airline

gedong – shrine

genggong – musical performance seen in Lombok

gili – small island (Lombok)

goa – cave; also spelt *gua*

gong – see *gamelan*

gong gede – large orchestra; traditional form of the *gamelan* with 35 to 40 musicians

gong kebyar – modern, popular form of a *gong gede,* with up to 25 instruments

gua – cave; also spelt *goa*

gunung – mountain

gunung api – volcano

gusti – polite title for members of the *Wesia* caste

Hanuman – monkey god who plays a major part in the *Ramayana*

harga biasa – standard price

harga turis – inflated price for tourists

homestay – small, family-run accommodation; see also losmen

ibu – mother; also a polite form of address to any older woman

Ida Bagus – honourable title for a male *Brahmana*

ikat – cloth where a pattern is produced by dyeing the individual threads before weaving

Indra – king of the gods

jalak putih – local name for Bali starling

jalan – road or street; abbreviated to *Jl*

jepun – frangipani or plumeria trees

jidur – large cylindrical drums played throughout Lombok

Jl – *jalan;* road or street

kahyangan jagat – directional temples

kain – a length of material wrapped tightly around the hips and waist, over a sarong

kain poleng – black-and-white chequered cloth

kaja – in the direction of the mountains; see also *kelod*

kaja-kangin – corner of the courtyard

kaki lima – food carts

kala – demonic face often seen over temple gateways

Kalendar Cetakan – Balinese calendar used to plan a myriad of activities

kamben – a length of *songket* wrapped around the chest for formal occasions

kampung – village or neighbourhood

kangin – sunrise

kantor – office

kantor imigrasi – immigration office

kantor pos – post office

Kawi – classical Javanese; the language of poetry

kebyar – a type of dance

Kecak – traditional Balinese dance; tells a tale from the *Ramayana* about Prince Rama and Princess Sita

kedais – coffee house

kelod – in the direction away from the mountains and towards the sea; see also *kaja*

kelurahan – local government area

kemben – woman's breast-cloth

kempli – gong

kendang – drums

kepala desa – village head

kori agung – gateway to the second courtyard in a temple

kota – city

kras – identifiable 'baddies' in an *arja* drama

kris – traditional dagger

Ksatriyasa – second Balinese caste

kuah – sunset side

kulkul – hollow tree-trunk drum used to sound a warning or call meetings

labuhan – harbour; also called *pelabuhan*

laki-laki – boy

lamak – long, woven palm-leaf strips used as decorations in festivals and celebrations

lambung – long black sarongs worn by *Sasak* women; see also *sabuk*

langse – rectangular decorative hangings used in palaces or temples

Legong – classic Balinese dance

legong – young girls who perform the *Legong*

leyak – evil spirit that can assume fantastic forms by the use of black magic

lontar – specially prepared palm leaves

losmen – small Balinese hotel, often family-run

lukisan antic – antique paintings

lulur – body mask

lumbung – rice barn with a round roof; an architectural symbol of Lombok

Mahabharata – one of the great Hindu holy books, the epic poem tells of the battle between the Pandavas and the Korawas

Majapahit – last great Hindu dynasty on Java

mata air panas – natural hot springs

meditasi – swimming and sunbathing

mekepung – traditional water buffalo races

meru – multiroofed shrines in temples; the name comes from the Hindu holy mountain Mahameru

mobil – car

moksa – freedom from earthly desires

muncak – mouse deer

naga – mythical snakelike creature

nusa – island; also called *pulau*

Nusa Tenggara Barat (NTB) – West Nusa Tenggara; a province of Indonesia comprising the islands of Lombok and Sumbawa

nyale – wormlike fish caught off Kuta, Lombok

Nyepi – major annual festival in the Hindu *saka* calendar, this is a day of complete stillness after a night of chasing out evil spirits

ogoh-ogoh – huge monster dolls used in the *Nyepi* festival

ojek – motorcycle that carries paying passengers

open – tall red-brick buildings

padi – growing rice plant

padmasana – temple shrine resembling a vacant chair

pak – father; shortened form of *bapak*

palinggihs – temple shrines consisting of a simple, little throne

panca dewata – centre and four cardinal points in a temple

pantai – beach

paras – a soft, grey volcanic stone used in stone carving

pasar – market

pasar malam – night market

pecalang – village or *banjar* police

pedagang – mobile traders

pedanda – high priest

pelabuhan – harbour; also called *labuhan*

pemangku – temple guardians and priests for temple rituals

perempuan – girl

plus plus – a combined tax and service charge of 21% added by midrange and top-end accommodation and restaurants

pondok – simple lodging or hut

prada – cloth highlighted with gold leaf, or gold or silver paint and thread

prahu – traditional Indonesian boat with outriggers

prasada – shrine; see also *candi*

prasasti – inscribed copper plates

pria – man; male

propinsi – province; Indonesia has 27 *propinsi* – Bali is a *propinsi*, Lombok and its neighbouring island of Sumbawa comprise *propinsi Nusa Tenggara Barat* (NTB)

puasa – to fast, or a fast

pulau – island; also called *nusa*

puputan – warrior's fight to the death; an honourable but suicidal option when faced with an unbeatable enemy

pura – temple

pura dalem – temple of the dead

pura desa – village temple for everyday functions

pura puseh – temple of the village founders or fathers, honouring the village's origins

pura subak – temple of the rice growers' association

puri – palace

pusit kota – used on road signs to indicate the centre of town

rajah – lord or prince

Ramadan – Muslim month of fasting

Ramayana – one of the great Hindu holy books; these stories form the keystone of many Balinese dances and tales

Rangda – widow-witch who represents evil in Balinese theatre and dance

raya – main road, eg Jl Raya Ubud means 'the main road of Ubud'

RRI – Radio Republik Indonesia; Indonesia's national radio broadcaster

rumah makan – restaurant; literally 'eating place'

sabuk – Four-metre-long scarf that holds the *lambung* in place

sadkahyangan – 'world sanctuaries'; most sacred temples

saiban – temple or shrine offering

saka – Balinese calendar based on the lunar cycle; see also *wuku*

Sasak – native of Lombok; also the language

sate – satay

sawah – rice field; see also *subak*

selat – strait

sepeda – bicycle

sepeda motor – motorcycle

Shiva – the creator and destroyer; one of the three great Hindu gods

songket – silver- or gold-threaded cloth, handwoven using a floating weft technique

stupas – domes for housing Buddha relics

subak – village association that organises rice terraces and shares out water for irrigation

Sudra – common caste to which the majority of Balinese belong

sungai – river

swah – world of gods

tahun – year

taksu – divine interpreter for the gods

tambulilingan – bumblebees

tanjung – cape or point

teluk – gulf or bay

tika – piece of printed cloth or carved wood displaying the Pawukon cycle

tirta – water

toya – water

trimurti – Hindu trinity

triwangsa – caste divided into three parts (*Brahmana, Ksatriyasa* and *Wesia);* means three people

TU – Telepon Umum; a public telephone

undagi – designer of a building, usually an architect-priest

Vishnu – the preserver; one of the three great Hindu gods

wanita – woman; female

wantilan – large *bale* pavilion used for meetings, performances and cockfights; community hall

waria – female impersonator, transvestite or transgendered; combination of the words *wanita* and *pria*

waringin – large shady tree with drooping branches which root to produce new trees; see *banyan*

warnet – warung with internet access

wartel – public telephone office; contraction of *warung telekomunikasi*

warung – food stall

wayang kulit – leather puppet used in shadow puppet plays; see also *dalang*

Wektu Telu – religion peculiar to Lombok; originated in Bayan and combines many tenets of Islam and aspects of other faiths

Wesia – military caste and most numerous of the Balinese noble castes

wuku – Balinese calendar made up of 10 different weeks, between one and 10 days long, all running concurrently; see also *saka*

yeh – water; also river

yoni – female symbol of the Hindu god *Shiva*

Behind the Scenes

SEND US YOUR FEEDBACK

We love to hear from travellers – your comments keep us on our toes and help make our books better. Our well-travelled team reads every word on what you loved or loathed about this book. Although we cannot reply individually to postal submissions, we always guarantee that your feedback goes straight to the appropriate authors, in time for the next edition. Each person who sends us information is thanked in the next edition – the most useful submissions are rewarded with a selection of digital PDF chapters.

Visit **lonelyplanet.com/contact** to submit your updates and suggestions or to ask for help. Our award-winning website also features inspirational travel stories, news and discussions.

Note: We may edit, reproduce and incorporate your comments in Lonely Planet products such as guidebooks, websites and digital products, so let us know if you don't want your comments reproduced or your name acknowledged. For a copy of our privacy policy visit lonelyplanet.com/privacy.

OUR READERS

Many thanks to the travellers who used the last edition and wrote to us with helpful hints, useful advice and interesting anecdotes:

Erika Baardwijk, Heino Best, Dana Beyer, Nikki Buran, John Burbidge, Samuel Chan, Marilyn Clark-Murphy, Mario Corradi, Alex Curry, Jack Dempsey, Nicole Deussen, Suzy Dior, Ella Kemball Dorey, Sylvia Filter, Marcel & Anouk Flantua, Rachael Foggitt, Franziska Franke, Gauthier Ginisty, Roger Glenfield, Jean-Philippe Goyette, Elizabeth Gray, David Griffin, Linda Madani Grondin, Sussi Hansen, Paul Heisterkamp, Wendy Hoenkamp, Frauke Horstmann, Adrienne Karmouche, Robert Lee, Gavin Leeder, Richard van Leeuweh, Manfred Lenzen, Jens Lichtenberger, Jelle Mollenvanger, Hanafi Nafore, Aneel Nazareth, Olly Niewold, Sonia Osorio, Helen Pearson, Liliana & Raul Pimentel, Simon Pridmore, John Pyle, Cinzia Gloria Redaelli, Angela Reeve, John Richardson, Katrin Riegelnegg, Jeroen Rozeboom, Fredrik Ryderheim, Ronald Sabatini, Ed Schlenk, Samuel Shrosbree, Carina Tanaka, Linda Telleman, Rapheephan Thanduan, Maarten Versluis, Anita Warwick, Diana Weir, George Youn

AUTHOR THANKS

Ryan Ver Berkmoes

This list just seems to grow. Many thanks to friends like Pattycakes Miklautsch, Ibu Cat, Hanafi, Nengah, Eliot Cohen, Jamie James, Kerry and Milton Turner, Pascal and Pika and many more. At Lonely Planet, thanks to my buddy Ilaria Walker and the entire publishing and production teams. My co-author, Adam, rocks. And to Frank Sinatra who night and day picked me a plum and to the golden memories of House 2.

Adam Skolnick

Thanks to Simion Liddiard, Marcus Stevens, Andy Wheatcroft, Fern Perry, Will Goodman, Harriet Chaterley, Astrid and Grace at Karma Kayak, Alina in Senggigi, Barbara at Lombok Guide, Gili Air Divers, Pak Achok on Gili T, Pak Saleh on Gili Air, Anders at Adeng Adeng, George and the Dive Zone family. Thanks as always to Brett and Made in Bali, Ryan Ver Berkmoes, and to sweet and lovely Georgiana Johnson.

THIS BOOK

This is the 14th edition of Lonely Planet's *Bali & Lombok*. We first visited Bali, the island of the gods, way back in the early '70s, when a floral-shirted Tony Wheeler came through while researching the inaugural *Across Asia on the Cheap*. Since then, an army of Lonely Planet authors has returned: following in Tony's sandalled footprints have been (most recently) Ryan Ver Berkmoes and Iain Stewart. For this edition, Ryan Ver Berkmoes returned once again to Bali, while the intrepid, island-hopping Adam Skolnick researched and wrote the Lombok and Gili Islands chapters. This guidebook was commissioned in Lonely Planet's Melbourne office, and produced by the following:

Commissioning Editor Ilaria Walker

Coordinating Editors Gabrielle Innes, Jeanette Wall

Coordinating Cartographer Xavier Di Toro

Coordinating Layout Designer Kerrianne Southway

Managing Editors Brigitte Ellemor, Bruce Evans, Kirsten Rawlings

Senior Editor Catherine Naghten

Managing Cartographers Anita Banh, Mark Griffiths, Anthony Phelan, Diana Von Holdt

Managing Layout Designer Chris Girdler

Assisting Editors Andrea Dobbin, Kate Kiely, Charlotte Orr

Cover Research Naomi Parker

Language Content Branislava Vladisavljevic

Thanks to Laura Crawford, Ryan Evans, Larissa Frost, Jouve India, Kate McDonell, Trent Paton, Dianne Schallmeiner, Amanda Sierp, Gerard Walker

BEHIND THE SCENES

ACKNOWLEDGMENTS

Climate map data adapted from Peel MC, Finlayson BL & McMahon TA (2007) 'Updated World Map of the Köppen-Geiger Climate Classification', Hydrology and Earth System Sciences, 11, 163344.

Cover photograph: Locals on beach with sunrise over Gunung Agung, David Hannah/Getty©.

index

Map Legend

Sights
- Beach
- Buddhist
- Castle
- Christian
- Hindu
- Islamic
- Jewish
- Monument
- Museum/Gallery
- Ruin
- Winery/Vineyard
- Zoo
- Other Sight

Activities, Courses & Tours
- Diving/Snorkelling
- Canoeing/Kayaking
- Skiing
- Surfing
- Swimming/Pool
- Walking
- Windsurfing
- Other Activity/Course/Tour

Sleeping
- Sleeping
- Camping

Eating
- Eating

Drinking
- Drinking
- Cafe

Entertainment
- Entertainment

Shopping
- Shopping

Information
- Bank
- Embassy/Consulate
- Hospital/Medical
- Internet
- Police
- Post Office
- Telephone
- Toilet
- Tourist Information
- Other Information

Transport
- Airport
- Border Crossing
- Bus
- Cable Car/Funicular
- Cycling
- Ferry
- Metro
- Monorail
- Parking
- Petrol Station
- Taxi
- Train/Railway
- Tram
- Other Transport

Routes
- Tollway
- Freeway
- Primary
- Secondary
- Tertiary
- Lane
- Unsealed Road
- Plaza/Mall
- Steps
- Tunnel
- Pedestrian Overpass
- Walking Tour
- Walking Tour Detour
- Path

Geographic
- Hut/Shelter
- Lighthouse
- Lookout
- Mountain/Volcano
- Oasis
- Park
- Pass
- Picnic Area
- Waterfall

Population
- Capital (National)
- Capital (State/Province)
- City/Large Town
- Town/Village

Boundaries
- International
- State/Province
- Disputed
- Regional/Suburb
- Marine Park
- Cliff
- Wall

Hydrography
- River, Creek
- Intermittent River
- Swamp/Mangrove
- Reef
- Canal
- Water
- Dry/Salt/Intermittent Lake
- Glacier

Areas
- Beach/Desert
- Cemetery (Christian)
- Cemetery (Other)
- Park/Forest
- Sportsground
- Sight (Building)
- Top Sight (Building)

OUR STORY

A beat-up old car, a few dollars in the pocket and a sense of adventure. In 1972 that's all Tony and Maureen Wheeler needed for the trip of a lifetime – across Europe and Asia overland to Australia. It took several months, and at the end – broke but inspired – they sat at their kitchen table writing and stapling together their first travel guide, *Across Asia on the Cheap*. Within a week they'd sold 1500 copies. Lonely Planet was born.

Today, Lonely Planet has offices in Melbourne, London and Oakland, with more than 600 staff and writers. We share Tony's belief that 'a great guidebook should do three things: inform, educate and amuse'.

OUR WRITERS

Ryan Ver Berkmoes

Coordinating Author; Kuta & Seminyak, South Bali & the Islands, Ubud & Around, East Bali, Central Mountains, North Bali, West Bali Ryan Ver Berkmoes was first entranced by the echoing beat of a Balinese gamelan in 1993. On his visits since he has explored almost every corner of the island – along with side trips to Nusas Lembongan and Penida, the Gilis and Lombok. Just when he thinks Bali holds no more surprises, he finds, for example, a new seaside temple on nobody's map. Ryan never tires of Bali; sometimes his island social calendar is busier than anywhere else. Away from the gamelans, Ryan writes about travel and more at ryanverberkmoes.com and on Twitter (@ryanvb).

Read more about Ryan at:
lonelyplanet.com/members/ryanverberkmoes

Adam Skolnick

Lombok, Gili Islands Adam Skolnick writes about travel, culture, health and politics for Lonely Planet, *Outside, Men's Health* and *Travel & Leisure*. He has co-authored 18 Lonely Planet guidebooks to destinations in Europe, the US, Central America and Asia. On his recent trip to Lombok his peculiar road karma included several epic dives and the blissful discovery of stunning new beaches, islands, hotels and restaurants. He also encountered runaway horse carts and car crashes, and, well, he was surrounded by a mob of 50 people who wanted to kill him. But he survived! You can read more of his work at adamskolnick.com. Or find him on Twitter (@adamskolnick).

Published by Lonely Planet Publications Pty Ltd
ABN 36 005 607 983
14th edition – Apr 2013
ISBN 978 1 74220 303 4
© Lonely Planet 2013   Photographs © as indicated 2013
10 9 8 7 6 5 4 3 2 1
Printed in China